The Blackwell Companion to Hinduism

Blackwell Companions to Religion

The Blackwell Companions to Religion series presents a collection of the most recent scholarship and knowledge about world religions. Each volume draws together newly-commissioned essays by distinguished authors in the field, and is presented in a style which is accessible to undergraduate students, as well as scholars and the interested general reader. These volumes approach the subject in a creative and forward-thinking style, providing a forum in which leading scholars in the field can make their views and research available to a wider audience.

Published

The Blackwell Companion to Judaism
Edited by Jacob Neusner and Alan J. Avery-Peck

The Blackwell Companion to Sociology of Religion
Edited by Richard K. Fenn

The Blackwell Companion to the Hebrew Bible
Edited by Leo G. Perdue

The Blackwell Companion to Postmodern Theology
Edited by Graham Ward

The Blackwell Companion to Hinduism
Edited by Gavin Flood

The Blackwell Companion to Political Theology
Edited by Peter Scott and William T. Cavanaugh

The Blackwell Companion to Protestantism
Edited by Alister E. McGrath and Darren C. Marks

The Blackwell Companion to Modern Theology
Edited by Gareth Jones

The Blackwell Companion to Christian Ethics
Edited by Stanley Hauerwas and Samuel Wells

The Blackwell Companion to Religious Ethics
Edited by William Schweiker

Forthcoming

The Blackwell Companion to the Study of Religion
Edited by Robert A. Segal

The Blackwell Companion to Eastern Christianity
Edited by Ken Parry

The Blackwell Companion to Christian Spirituality
Edited by Arthur Holder

The Blackwell Companion to the Bible and Culture
Edited by John Sawyer

The Blackwell Companion to the New Testament
Edited by David Aune

The Blackwell Companion to Contemporary Islamic Thought
Edited by Ibrahim Abu-Rabi

The Blackwell Companion to Catholicism
Edited by James Buckley

The Blackwell Companion to Hinduism

Edited by

Gavin Flood

Blackwell Publishing

BLACKWELL PUBLISHING
350 Main Street, Malden, MA 02148-5020, USA
9600 Garsington Road, Oxford OX4 2DQ, UK
550 Swanston Street, Carlton, Victoria 3053, Australia

First published 2003
First published in paperback 2005 by Blackwell Publishing Ltd

2 2005

Library of Congress Cataloging-in-Publication Data

The Blackwell companion to Hinduism / edited by Gavin Flood.
p. cm. – (Blackwell companions to religion)
Includes index.
ISBN 0-631-21535-2 (alk. paper)— ISBN 1-4051-3251-5 (pbk. : alk. paper)
1. Hinduism. I. Flood, Gavin D., 1954- II. Series.

BL1202 .B72 2002
294.5 – dc21

2002071220

ISBN-13: 978-0-631-21535-6 (alk. paper)— ISBN-13: 978-1-4051-3251-0 (pbk. : alk. paper)

A catalogue record for this title is available from the British Library.

Set in 10.5/12.5 pt Photina
by SNP Best-set Typesetter Ltd, Hong Kong

The publisher's policy is to use permanent paper from mills that operate a sustainable forestry policy, and which has been manufactured from pulp processed using acid-free and elementary chlorine-free practices. Furthermore, the publisher ensures that the text paper and cover board used have met acceptable environmental accreditation standards.

For further information on
Blackwell Publishing, visit our website:
www.blackwellpublishing.com

To the memory of Norman Cutler and Wilhelm Halbfass

Contents

Contributors x
Preface and Acknowledgments xii

Introduction: Establishing the Boundaries
Gavin Flood 1

Part I Theoretical Issues 21

1 Colonialism and the Construction of Hinduism
Gauri Viswanathan 23

2 Orientalism and Hinduism
David Smith 45

Part II Text and Tradition 65

The Sanskrit Textual Traditions 67

3 Vedas and Upaniṣads
Michael Witzel 68

4 The Dharmaśāstras
Ludo Rocher 102

5 The Sanskrit Epics
John Brockington 116

6 The Purāṇas
Freda Matchett 129

Textual Traditions in Regional Languages 144

7 Tamil Hindu Literature
Norman Cutler 145

8 The Literature of Hinduism in Malayalam
Rich Freeman 159

9 North Indian Hindi Devotional Literature
Nancy M. Martin 182

Major Historical Developments 199

10 The Śaiva Traditions
Gavin Flood 200

11 History of Vaiṣṇava Traditions: An Esquisse
Gérard Colas 229

12 The Renouncer Tradition
Patrick Olivelle 271

13 The Householder Tradition in Hindu Society
T. N. Madan 288

Regional Traditions 306

14 The Teyyam Tradition of Kerala
Rich Freeman 307

15 The Month of Kārtik and Women's Ritual Devotions to Krishna in Benares
Tracy Pintchman 327

Part III Systematic Thought 343

The Indian Sciences 345

Introduction
Frits Staal 346

16 The Science of Language
Frits Staal 348

17 Indian Mathematics
Takao Hayashi 360

18 Calendar, Astrology, and Astronomy
Michio Yano 376

19   The Science of Medicine
     Dominik Wujastyk   393

Philosophy and Theology   410

20   Hinduism and the Proper Work of Reason
     Jonardon Ganeri   411

21   Restoring "Hindu Theology" as a Category in Indian
     Intellectual Discourse
     Francis Clooney, SJ   447

22   Mantra
     André Padoux   478

Part IV   Society, Politics, and Nation   493

23   On the Relationship between Caste and Hinduism
     Declan Quigley   495

24   Modernity, Reform, and Revival
     Dermot Killingley   509

25   Contemporary Political Hinduism
     C. Ram-Prasad   526

26   The Goddess and the Nation: Subterfuges of Antiquity, the
     Cunning of Modernity
     Sumathi Ramaswamy   551

27   Gender in a Devotional Universe
     Vasudha Narayanan   569

Index   588

GOOD POTTED SADDARŚANA
ф IN RELATION TO
SVATANTRA / ASVATANTRA

GAUDIYA BAKHTI etc.
VISNU AS 'MOHINI'

Contributors

John Brockington is Professor of Sanskrit, Department of Sanskrit, University of Edinburgh, UK.

Francis Clooney, SJ is Professor, Department of Theology, Boston College, Boston, USA.

Gérard Colas is Directeur de recherche, Centre National de la Recherche Scientifique (Centre d'Études de l'Inde et de l'Asie du Sud), Paris, France.

Norman Cutler was Chair, Department of South Asian Languages and Civilizations, University of Chicago, USA.

Gavin Flood is Professor of Religion in the Department of Religious Studies, Stirling University, UK.

Rich Freeman is research associate of the Center for South Asian Studies at the University of Michigan, USA.

Jonardon Ganeri teaches in the Department of Philosophy, University of Liverpool, UK.

Takao Hayashi is Professor of History of Science, Science and Engineering Research Institute, Doshisha University, Kyotanabe, Kyoto, Japan.

Dermot Killingley, now retired, was Reader in Religious Studies, University of Newcastle, UK.

T. N. Madan is Honorary (Emeritus) Professor of Sociology, Institute of Economic Growth (University of Delhi), Delhi, India.

Nancy M. Martin is Associate Professor of Religious Studies, Chapman University, USA.

Freda Matchett is Honorary Research Fellow, Religious Studies Department, University of Lancaster, UK.

Vasudha Narayanan is Professor, Department of Religion, University of Florida, USA and President of the American Academy of Religion.

Patrick Olivelle is Professor of Sanskrit and Indian Religions, University of Texas at Austin, and Chair of the Department of Asian Studies, University of Texas, USA.

C. Ram-Prasad teaches in the Department of Religious Studies, University of Lancaster, UK.

Sumathi Ramaswamy is Associate Professor of History, University of Michigan, Ann Arbor, USA.

Ludo Rocher is Professor of South Asian Studies, University of Pennsylvania, USA.

André Padoux is Directeur de recherche honoraire at the Centre National de la Recherche Scientifique, Paris.

Tracy Pintchman is an associate professor at Loyola University of Chicago, USA.

Declan Quigley has taught at the universities of Cambridge and St. Andrews, and Queen's University Belfast.

David Smith is Reader in Religious Studies in the Department of Religious Studies, University of Lancaster, UK.

Frits Staal is Professor Emeritus, Departments of Philosophy and of South and Southeast Asian Studies, University of California at Berkeley, USA.

Gauri Viswanathan is Class of 1933 Professor of English and Comparative Literature at Columbia University, USA.

Michael Witzel is Professor of Sanskrit, Department of Sanskrit and Indian Studies, Harvard University, USA.

Dominik Wujastyk is Wellcome Senior Research Fellow, Wellcome Centre for the History of Medicine, at University College London.

Michio Yano is Professor, Faculty of Cultural Studies, Kyoto Sangyo University, Japan.

Preface and Acknowledgments

The purpose of this volume is to make available to a wide audience some of the most recent scholarship on the religions of South Asia within the broad category of Hinduism. While many scholars here would wish to place that category under scrutiny, there are nevertheless continuities of tradition and common features that have persisted over very long periods in South Asia. The intention of the book is to cover the major historical trajectories of the traditions that have led to Hinduism and to present accounts of recent developments of Hinduism along with some of the contemporary traditions that comprise it. There are, of course, problems in applying the term "religion" to the history of South Asia, implying as it does in the West a distinction between religion and governance or between religion and science, which have not been universal distinctions. For this reason the book includes an account of historical developments in Indian science along with discussions of philosophy, religion, and politics.

The book contains essays both about the past – stretching back to the time of the composition of the Veda – and about the contemporary situation. Text-historical, anthropological, philosophical, theological, and cultural-critical approaches are therefore represented. This is in line with the broad belief that textual study can contribute to anthropology in South Asia and anthropology can illumine texts. And tools derived from more recent cultural criticism – especially feminism and postcolonial discourse – reveal dimensions to history and the study of texts that would not otherwise be seen. In these pages we also find theological and philosophical engagement with Hindu traditions. There are many ways of studying past cultures and civilizations, but arguably the best means of gaining access to the thoughts and feelings of people in the past and the institutions they inhabited is through the texts they produced. There has been discussion in recent years about the rematerialization of culture and the need to examine material culture in history. While archaeology, epigraphy, and the history of art are undoubtedly important, the emphasis of most scholars in this volume is on text and different readings of text, although some relate text to material history where this is possible and to contemporary practice. Conversely, the essays focusing on anthropological fieldwork often draw on the texts of tradition.

Inevitably, although unfortunately, there are gaps in what could be covered in the present volume. This is due partly to restrictions of space but also due to other contingencies beyond the editor's control. We do not have, for example, specific essays on the Indus Valley civilization, yoga, ritual, the Hindu diaspora, the Goddess and the temple, nor on some major regional traditions. But even so, these essays present systematic accounts of the history of traditions and their texts, examples of important regional traditions, and accounts of the rise of modern Hinduism and its contemporary connections with nationalism and the politics of identity.

The book uses the standard, scholarly transliteration of Indian alphabets, although this is not consistently applied to all place names and some proper names. There is considerable variation in practice, as many names have common anglicized forms.

I would like to thank all the scholars who have participated in the project, particularly Rich Freeman, Patrick Olivelle, and Frits Staal for their encouragement and support, along with the team at Blackwell, particularly Alison Dunnett, Laura Barry, Rebecca Harkin, and Cameron Laux. I would also like to thank Alex Wright who, when at Blackwell, first suggested the project to me. I would like to acknowledge permission from Routledge to publish Jonardon Ganeri's essay "The Motive and Method of Rational Inquiry," first published in *Philosophy in Classical India* (Routledge, 2000). I would also like to acknowledge permission from Routledge to publish Gavin Flood's "The Śaiva Traditions," a version of which is to be published in S. Mittal, ed., *The Hindu World* (Routledge, forthcoming). The book is dedicated to the memory of Wilhem Halbfass who made such a great contribution to the study of the Indian traditions, and to Norman Cutler who sadly passed away before the publication of this book.

Introduction: Establishing the Boundaries

Gavin Flood

That religion is still of central importance in today's world can hardly be doubted in the aftermath of violent events in recent years. In South Asia religion is at the center of controversy and ideological battles and questions about what it is to be a Hindu in the twenty-first century are vibrant. Questions concerning the relation of Hinduism to state and global politics, to the individual, and to the politics of identity are of great relevance to Hindus everywhere. On the one hand we have seen the world shrink through globalization along with the late modern erosion of tradition, while on the other we have seen the reinvigoration of some traditions and the reanimation of traditional forms of knowledge (such as Ayurveda). Secularists in India would wish to see the complete erosion of religion in the public sphere of governance and its relegation to the private realm, while many religious nationalists would wish to see even more growth in the influence of religion in the political and public arena.

It is in the context of such vital issues that scholars in this book examine Hinduism in its widest sense, looking not only at questions of contemporary identity politics but also at historical questions and presenting historical accounts of particular texts and traditions. We certainly understand the present through the past but we also wish to understand the past for the sake of increasing human knowledge. There is therefore great diversity in the following pages that seek both to account for the contemporary situation and to explain the historical trajectories that have led to the modern, global religion we call "Hinduism." From ancient Tamil texts to contemporary politics, all the essays gathered here bear a relation to that nebulous abstraction and raise many questions. Are we dealing with a single religion, an essence manifested in different forms? Or is Hinduism a diversity of distinct traditions sharing certain common features with no single feature being shared by them all? Or are we dealing with a fragmented, cultural reality of widely diverse beliefs and practices, inappropriately classified as a single religion? All of these positions have been adopted in understanding

Hinduism. The answers to these questions will depend upon the historical period in question and the methods employed in their study. Closely connected to the scope of the field are questions about how to study Hinduism, whether anthropology, philology, history of religions, theology, literary studies, archaeology, or art history are appropriate methods, and questions about the different theoretical assumptions and implications of their use. The purpose of this introduction is therefore both to problematize "Hinduism" and to provide a context for the essays that follow.

What is Hinduism?

A simple, if perhaps deceptively simple, response to this question is to say that Hinduism is a term denoting the religion of the majority of people in India and Nepal and of some communities in other continents who refer to themselves as "Hindu." There are approximately 700 million people classed as Hindu by the census in India, which is 83 percent of the population, the remainder being classified as Muslim, Sikh, Christian, Jain, Buddhist, Jew, Parsee, and tibal people (*ādivāsī*). This is in a vast continent with 18 official languages and many dialects. But if we begin to dig deeper, we see that the question is not so straightforward. Because the term denotes such a striking variety of beliefs, practices, and historical trajectories, some would wish to claim that the abstraction "Hinduism" is fairly meaningless and without referent. But others, and this is particularly important in the contemporary politics of Hindu identity, would claim that Hinduism is indeed a unified field of belief, practice, and history, intimately linked to nationhood and the historical struggle of a people against its colonizers. On this view, Hinduism has an essence manifested in multiple forms. Others argue that while Hinduism does not denote a religion with clearly defined boundaries in a way that we might be able to define Christianity or Islam, it nevertheless denotes a group of traditions united by certain common features, such as shared ritual patterns, a shared revelation, a belief in reincarnation (*saṃsāra*), liberation (*mokṣa*), and a particular form of endogamous social organization or caste. This family resemblance approach nevertheless still requires judgments about which forms are prototypical and which are not, judgments which are themselves based on some pre-understanding of the tradition. Many would wish to claim, for example, that caste is not a necessary part of Hinduism whereas some other features are. "What is Hinduism?" is therefore a complex question the response to which ranges from claiming that Hinduism in a unified, coherent field of doctrine and practice to claiming that it is a fiction, a colonial construction based on the miscategorization of indigenous cultural forms.

Defining the parameters of the term is not simply an exercise for scholars but is closely related to the questions, as Brian Smith observes, of "who speaks for Hinduism?" and "who defines Hinduism?" (Smith 2000: 741–2). This debate goes way beyond academic formulations and arguments in the academy into the politics of cultural identity and questions about power. But before we inquire into these questions of value, what of the term itself?

"Hindu" comes from a Persian word *hind*, or in Arabic *al-hind*, for the area of the Indus valley. This word is in turn derived from the Indo-Aryan *sindhu* meaning "ocean" or "river," and from the eighth century, when Muslims settled in the Indus valley, Persian authors distinguished between Muslims and the non-Muslim "Hindus," although it is not strictly true that the term was not used by those non-Muslims themselves. Sanskrit sources, however, are much later. In fifteenth-century Kashmir the term Hindu is employed by the Śaiva historian Śrīvara to distinguish Muslims from non-Muslims (see Sanderson forthcoming) and the term was used in Sanskrit and Bengali Vaiṣṇava sources in the sixteenth century to denote those who were not "Yavanas" or Muslims (O'Connell 1973: 340–4). In these sources it seems to refer to groups united by certain common cultural practices, such as cremation of the dead and veneration of the cow, not practiced by the Muslims (Sanderson: 1). Towards the end of the eighteenth century "Hindu" or "Hindoo" was adopted by the British to refer to the people of "Hindustan," the area of northwest South Asia, who were not Muslim, Sikh, Christian, or Jain, and the "ism" was added to "Hindu" in the early nineteenth century. Indeed, Rammohun Roy was probably the first Hindu to use the term in 1816 (Killingley in this volume: 513). The term became widely adopted during the nineteenth century in the context of establishing a national identity that would become opposed to colonialism and in the creation of a religion that could match Christianity and meet it on a basis of equality (see Killingley and Viswanathan in this volume).

Many scholars have argued that the ascription of "Hinduism" to the multiplicity of South Asian traditions was an exercise in power and that the representation of India in western scholarship in terms of mysticism, caste, and kingship is an expression of the West's desire for domination. On this view India as the West's exotic other became identified with despotism, imagination, superstition, and irrationality in contrast to the democracy, reason, and science of the West arising out of the Enlightenment (Balagangadhara 1994; Inden 1990; King 1999). This postcolonial reading of Western scholarship's engagement with India reveals a complex history, traced by Gauri Viswanathan in the present volume, which shows both positive and negative evaluations are nevertheless based on foundational assumptions about the nature of the West's other. Others have argued not from the perspective of postcolonialism, but on the foundation of Western, philological scholarship itself, that the term "Hinduism" is a misnomer, an attempt to unify into a single religion what in fact is a number of distinct religions (for example, von Stietencron 1997: 32–53). Yet others argue that part of this "error" lies in the inappropriate use of the category "religion" in relation to the diversity of South Asian cultural forms, for that term has particular, Christian theological connotations (Fitzgerald 2000: 134–55; Staal 1989: 388–406). On this view, religion is a category that entails assumptions that belief has primacy over practice, that a person can only belong to one religion, that tradition stems from textual, written revelation, and that a religion is necessarily coherent.

But in spite of these criticisms there are nevertheless Hindu analogues to categories of revelation, tradition, theology, and practice, although these arguably do not point to a unitary referent. We might say, then, that Hinduism contains both uniting and dispersing tendencies that we might, borrowing from Bakhtin, call centripetal and centrifugal forces. On the one hand, there is the Sanskritic tradition of brahmanical orthodoxy, flowing from the ancient revelation of the Veda, concerned with correct ritual procedures, the maintenance of caste boundaries, and the interpretation of scripture. This is a decisive constraint on the traditions that comprise Hinduism. On the other hand, there is a great proliferation of decentered traditions, often founded by a charismatic teacher or guru, and communities expressed in vernacular languages that cannot be defined by a central, brahmanical tradition and which are often set against that tradition. The *teyyam* tradition of Kerala or the Sant devotional tradition of northern India would be examples here (see the essays by Freeman and Martin).

We can trace the history of the fairly recent term "Hindu" and "Hinduism" from its initial coinage by those outside of the Hindu fold to its appropriation as a term of self-description by "Hindus" themselves. Much before the nineteenth century, people of South Asia did not consider themselves to belong to a wider, united religious identity, but would rather be members of a tradition and community whose focus was a particular deity or practice. One would be a Vaiṣṇava whose focus is the deity Viṣṇu, a Śaiva whose focus is Śiva, a follower of particular Tantras (*tāntrika*) and so on (Oberhammer 1997: 19). But there were by the medieval period if not earlier uniting features that cut across these diachronic processes, such as pilgrimage to sacred centers, particularly great regional temples, ritual offerings to deities in concrete form (*mūrti*), devotion (*bhakti*), and the practice of textual exegesis by scholars in centers of learning.

South Asian cultures are highly textualized in the widest sense of the term with many oral traditions, some of which stretch back thousands of years. There are traditions of vedic recitation in several regions of India that function, as Michael Witzel says in this volume, as "three thousand year old tape recordings." This revelation of the Veda, verses believed to have been revealed to and heard by (*śruti*) the ancient sages (*ṛṣi*), as symbol and legitimizing reference if not actual text, is central as a constraining influence on later traditions, providing the authority for tradition (Oberhammer 1997: 21–31). Some would argue that this is a defining feature of Hinduism (Smith 1988: 40). As constraining force the Veda has been used to legitimize different philosophical positions, as the basis of Hindu law and power structures, and has provided a reference point against which some traditions and charismatic teachers have reacted. Whether accepted or rejected, whether traditions are indifferent to its injunctions, it is seldom ignored as symbol. As Heesterman observes, the hold of "Vedism" on Indian thought and imagination has persisted not withstanding the cult of the temple, popular devotion, and tantric texts and practices (Heesterman 1993: 43). Given this reference point, we might say that both centripetal and centrifugal tendencies operate in three interrelated realms, namely discourse (*vāda*), ritual (*yajña*, *pūjā*), and narrative (*itihāsa*).

Discourse

Discourse or reflection and philosophical commentary developed from an early date in the history of Hinduism. The ancient texts of the Veda reflect a symbolic world in which ritual, notably sacrifice performed by a priest for a patron, was central to the thriving of the community. Speculation about the meaning of the sacrifice developed in texts still regarded as revelation, in the theological and ritual commentary of the Brāhmaṇas and Upaniṣads (see Witzel in this volume), and various traditions of textual exegesis and philosophy developed from around the fifth century BCE. These were expressed in the sacred language of Sanskrit in commentaries on sacred scripture and on aphorisms (*sūtra*) formulated within particular schools. The grammatical analysis of the language of revelation, along with the etymological and semantic exploration of language, came to be a prime concern (Kahrs 1998; Staal in this volume). Other sciences also developed such as astronomy and medicine (see Wujastyk and Yano in this volume). The famous six systems of Indian philosophy or "critical worldviews" (*darśaṇa*, namely the three pairs Sāmkhya-Yoga, Mīmāṁsā-Vedānta, and Nyāya-Vaiśeṣika), considered to be "orthodox" because of their acceptance of the revelation of the Veda, follow the pattern of their tenets being articulated in aphorisms and commentaries explaining their meaning. There are other systems outside of this list, with the Śaiva, Buddhist and Jain traditions participating in a shared discourse, along with the extremely important discourse about law (*dharmaśāstra*) that strongly influenced British rule in India (see Rocher in this volume).

By the early centuries CE the textual traditions had defined their boundaries in relation to each other and had developed a shared language, with shared categories, and thinkers in the various traditions were well versed in their opponents' texts and arguments. The authors of these texts were often, although not necessarily, world renouncers who had chosen the fourth estate or stage of life (*āśrama*) (see Olivelle and Madan in this volume). We can note here the highly orthodox Mīmāṁsaka exegetes, whose focus was the interpretation of vedic injunction, the Sāmkhya dualists, and the Vedānta, which developed a number of metaphysical positions in its history from Śaṁkara's nondualism to Madhva's dualist theology. The Śaiva traditions were also important in this picture, regarding their own scriptures, the Tantras, as transcending the lower revelation of the other schools, with the Buddhists and Jains rejecting the very idea of sacred revelation. The tenth-century Śaiva theologian Bhaṭṭa Rāmakaṇṭha, for example, knew the texts of other traditions and placed these at lower levels of understanding and attainment to his own in the hierarchical, Śaiva cosmos (Goodall 1998: 177), a feature common in the tantric traditions. This is a long way from the idea of tolerance that develops with modern Hinduism or the idea of modern, inclusivist interpreters of Hinduism that all paths lead to a common goal. At this period we have rigor of debate and the aggressive defense of the truth of one's tradition against rival philosophical and theological claims.

One response to the question "who speaks for Hinduism?" would therefore be that we should listen to the theologians and religious experts who have discussed questions of the text, of practice, and of metaphysics in a sustained way over centuries. The foremost object of the historian of religion, as some scholars have argued, is its theological articulation, particularly focusing on a tradition's canon and its exegesis (Smith 2000: 744–5; Smith 1982: 43; Olivelle 1993: 7–8). In studying Hinduism we are studying textual traditions with high degrees of reflexivity, traditions, as Alexander Piatigorsky has observed, which have already studied themselves (Piatigorsky 1985). But while there may have been a shared language and terminology, because of the diversity of these philosophical accounts of the world, it is clearly not doctrine that could define Hinduism. The unity provided by textual exegesis in commentary is not a unity of content but a unity of genre, a common reference point in the Veda, and a unity of shared metaphysical concerns.

Ritual

Alongside this shared discourse practiced over the centuries by the high-caste, literate minority, we have popular ritual that has served to provide some coherence to the diversity. Traditionally, ritual has constrained a Hindu's life from birth through marriage to death in the life-cycle rites (*saṃskāra*) and ritual orders social relationships and relationships with divine, embodied beings, the gods of temple and shrine. Ritual is passed through the generations from teacher to student and from mother to child, and while ritual changes, it does so at a much slower rate than other social forms. The relationship between ritual and social history is difficult to assess. All ritual forms have originated at a particular historical period, some have died out, but others have persisted with great tenacity and resistance to change over time. Vedic ritual, such as the elaborate Śrauta transformations of the sacrifice, still persists (Staal 1983). While there has been erosion of tradition with modernity, especially in an urban context, this detraditionalization has also been accompanied by a retradtionalization and traditions reinventing themselves and reconstituting ritual forms. We can see this, for example, with tantric traditions in Kerala and Tamilnadu where a temple priest might perform an old ritual enjoined in the tantric texts in a temple with no previous history of the rite.

The English word "ritual" covers a wide range of human behaviors from elaborate offerings to simple gestures, whereas Sanskrit analogues have more specific reference. In a Hindu context, the central structure of the rite known as *pūjā* is modeled on the gift; the gesture of making an offering to a deity or esteemed person and in return receiving a blessing. There are many social implications of gift giving in Hindu society and gods who receive gifts, as Brahmans who receive gifts from a donor, might also be seen to be absorbing the impurity of the donor (Raheja 1988; Parry 1994; see Quigley in this volume). The god, then, is an honored guest akin to a king who has the power to absolve the person making the offering (Fuller 1992: 107). There are principally two realms where *pūjā* has been enacted, in the public space of the temple and in the domestic sphere of the home. The temple as a home for a god developed around 700 CE and temple ritual became all-pervasive and a marker of social boundaries. Large regional temples developed which housed great deities such as the dancing Śiva at Cidambaram or the form of Viṣṇu, Lord Jagannāth at Puri, and local temples and shrines housed local deities. Different deities and kinds of substance offered, have been closely related to social differentiation, with higher castes being focused on the great deities of the Hindu pantheon and lower castes being focused on local, often ferocious, deities, particularly goddesses (Babb 1975). While high-caste deities and temples generally accept only vegetarian offerings, lower-caste deities at local shrines and temples in order to be appeased often demand offerings of blood and alcohol as well (see Freeman's essay on the *teyyams* of Kerala). Ritual serves to highlight social difference not only through inclusion, but more importantly, through exclusion and high caste *pūjā* in temples has excluded the lower castes who might, in the eyes of the Brahmans, pollute the sacredness of the deity's home.

Along with the shared pattern of making an offering and receiving a blessing, usually in the form of food offered to the deity and received back as blessed food (*prasāda*), there is a common notion that sacred power is embodied in particular, concrete forms (*mūrti, vigraha*). Furthermore, this sacred power is manipulable by specialists, temple or shrine priests, with the authority to do so. A ritual of consecration in which the consciousness or power of the deity is brought into the image awakens the icon in a temple. This consciousness or sacred power can be transferred; thus it can be temporarily placed in the festival icon (*utsava vigraha*) for the purpose of parading the deity for the community to receive the god's vision (*darśaṇa*, see Eck 1981). Or sacred power can also enter or be placed in human beings, who become vessels for the god's presence in the community, perhaps during an annual festival (see, for example, Hiltebeitel 1991; Freeman on *teyyams* in this volume).

Narrative

Closely related but not co-extensive with ritual are the regional narratives in local languages and transregional narratives of the Sanskritic tradition. The close connection between ritual and myth is attested in the Veda, which records some myths and alludes to others, and many of those stories are developed at a later date. There are two important groups of narrative traditions: the epics comprising the *Mahābhārata* and the *Rāmāyaṇa* (see Brockington in this volume) and the vast collections of "ancient stories," the Purāṇas (see Matchett in this volume). The epics reflect the rise of the theistic traditions and devotion (*bhakti*) and are concerned with the restoration of righteousness (*dharma*); a theme expressed in the idea of the incarnations (*avatāra*) of the supreme deity Viṣṇu, so richly elaborated in the Purāṇas. These Sanskrit narrative traditions develop themes present in the Veda, particularly the symbolism of the sacrifice (*yajña*), and have penetrated all levels of society and different regional languages. Thus there are local versions and interpretations of the epic stories, recited in the villages and enacted in rituals (the cult of Draupadī in Tamilnadu, for example; see Hiltebeitel 1988, 1991). The stories also reflect social tensions between Brahman and King. The King cannot be so without the authentication of the Brahmans who are in turn entirely dependent upon the King (Biardeau 1997: 78). The King and the Brahman have been understood as representing a conflict in tradition between the King's order of war and justice, embroiled as he is in the impurity of death, and the Brahman's and world renouncer's realm of transcendence. The King desires to participate in the sacred level of the Brahman, but through performing rituals for the King the Brahman becomes entangled in the world and moves away from the ideal of transcendence (Heesterman 1976: 7–9). The marvelous myths of the Purāṇas can be seen as reflecting attempts by a group of Brahmans called Smārtas, the followers of secondary revelation (*smṛti*), to bring diversity under a single, overarching and controlling system during the Gupta and post-Gupta period (300–700 CE).

But the dominance of the Sanskrit narrative traditions should not occlude the importance of regional narratives in local languages and the great narrative traditions of the South, particularly in Tamil. Here we have Tamil versions of the Sanskrit material along with other accounts of myth and history particular to Tamil culture. Long before the influence of Sanskrit or brahmanical culture, Tamil culture was already rich in narrative traditions and all northern influences were adapted to Tamil sensibilities and ways. Of particular importance are the genres of Tamil poetry of love and war and devotional literature expressing an intense devotion to different forms of Śiva and Viṣṇu (see Cutler in this volume).

Political Essentialism

Because of this narrative and ritual diversity, some scholars have expressed skepticism about the category "Hinduism" and even "Hindu." But nevertheless both terms are here to stay and indeed can be meaningfully used. A last point needs to be made, namely that the term "Hindu" has become charged with cultural and political meaning and arouses strong feelings when its integrity is apparently threatened, as, for example, by the controversial claim that Hindus have been beef eaters at times in their history (Jha 2002). Hinduism is part of the cultural politics of India and the term "Hindu" is now highly politicized as a sign around which to gather the hopes and aspirations of major sections of Indian society (see Ram Prasad in this volume) as are particular religious symbols such as the personification of the Tamil language (see Ramaswamy in this volume). V. D. Savarkar, a president of the Hindu Mahasabha (1937–42), a party that set itself against Congress and the Muslim League in the days before independence, in his highly influential book *Hindutva: Who is a Hindu?* (1923) distinguishes between "Hindu Dharma," the various traditions subsumed under the term "Hinduism," and "Hindutva" or "Hinduness," a sociopolitical force to unite all Hindus against "threatening Others" (Jaffrelot 1996: 25–33). It is *hindutva* that must take precedence as the force to form an exclusivist, national unity. Savarkar defined a Hindu as a person who sees India "as his Fatherland as well as his Holyland, that is, the cradle land of his religion" (quoted in Pandey 1993: 247), and Hinduism as an ideal that rests on the three pillars of geographical unity, common race, and a common culture. In this formulation, Hindus are united by bonds of love for the motherland and bonds of common blood, tracing their descent from the original inhabitants of the land, the vedic Aryans (Pandey 1993: 238; Jaffrelot 1996: 28).

We might call this view "political essentialism" insofar as it sees Hinduism as part of the nation's ideology which is no construct of Western scholarship, but a vibrant, living entity with roots stretching back into an ancient past. On this view, at various times in their long history Hindus have been oppressed by "threatening Others" but can now take a legitimate place in the field of cultural politics and stand for a Hindu nationhood against the secular ideology of Congress. Such sentiments are symbolized, for example, in the martial figure of the god Rāma who comes to express Hindu nationalist aspirations (Kapur 1993: 74–107) and we have seen how forcefully these aspirations were focused in the destruction of the Babri mosque and the further ensuing communal violence in 1992 (Larson 1995). Any ideology to be effective must addresses people's real concerns (Eagleton 1991: 45) and clearly the *hindutva* ideal, looking back to a glorious Hindu past, articulates a Hindu identity that has emerged partly because of its previous occlusion from the political realm (Jaffrelot 1996: 82–3; Larson 1995). The political party, the BJP, expressed nationalist Hindu sentiments and came to power with a complex of alliances in 1996 (see Ram Prasad in this volume). The claim to ideological unity among Hindus is, of course, problematic and dissonant voices such as the Dalit movement and some sections of the women's movement do not recognize themselves in Sanskritic Hinduism let alone in *hindutva* rhetoric (Omvedt 1995; Narayanan in this volume). The ideology of *hindutva* tends to be exclusive, with homogenizing tendencies that move against pluralism and diversity within the Hindu sphere. Some scholars, such as Julius Lipner, would wish to claim back "hinduness" as *hindutā* for a pluralist vision (Lipner 1996: 109–26). On Lipner's account it is perfectly feasible to be both Hindu and Christian, but this kind of hybridity would tend to be excluded by *hindutva* claims.

Philological and Other Methodological Issues

This book does not wish to make assertions about a unified Hinduism stretching into the ancient past; the general thrust of scholarship goes against this. But it does, in its structure, make implicit claims about the centrality and importance of textual traditions and their exegesis that have led to the modern religion, along with the importance of fieldwork. Although some theologians might argue that texts are self-generating and contain their own developmental logic – and it is true that we can trace a meaningful history through texts – they are nevertheless social documents and indices of the communities who produced them. The historian of South Asian religion or Indologist is sometimes able to relate religious texts to other historical documents such as epigraphs, but so often in the Indian context all we have are the texts themselves of uncertain date, although we can often establish a chronology of texts. The study of textual traditions, however, is not straightforward and is inevitably embroiled in a politics of translation.

Comparative philology and its offshoot Indology, the philological study of South Asian languages, notably Sanskrit, developed in the nineteenth century and was strongly advocated as a science akin to the natural sciences by Max Müller. It claims that the philological method discovers an objective order that is not constructed (Inden 1990: 14). In recent years this proclaimed objectivity of philology has come under scrutiny and postcolonial critiques have argued that it is strongly implicated in colonization, as a European colonization of India's languages. Linguistic typologies identified languages with different stages of cultural development and so were able "to inferiorize the languages (and by implication the cultures) of the Other" (Inden 1990: 60). But if we take philology to be the "study of civilization based on its texts" (Witzel 1997: v) then clearly philology is indispensable in any intellectual inquiry into the past. While philology has no doubt been put to different uses, sometimes morally dubious uses, the enterprise itself subject to constant correction, forms the basis of inquiry. In some sense philology is a temporary suspension of subjectivity in highlighting grammar, or perhaps a better way of putting this is to say that subjective (or indeed collective) understandings are constrained by the system of grammar.

There are deeply interesting problems here that go beyond the scope of this introduction, but let us briefly look at a cluster of issues as they relate to the enterprise of this book, as so many of these essays assume the philological method which is used to establish historical sequence (for example, Colas, Olivelle, Witzel) and as the basis of theological inquiry (Clooney). One of the central activities of philology is the establishing of the critical edition through critical emendation and establishing the stemma as the foundation upon which other kinds of investigation can take place. But the establishing of the text inevitably raises questions about authenticity – is the oldest version necessarily the more "authentic"? Is the correction of grammatical forms legitimate, assuming as it does a fixed grammar? And so on.

A text in South Asia does not, of course, necessarily mean a written text. It might well mean an oral one, although an oral text, particularly the Veda, is not necessarily less stable through time than a written text. This compounds the difficulty for the philologist, and the kind of work needed on oral traditions has hardly started, although important work has been done (for example, Blackburn 1988 on Tamil sources; Smith 1991 on the epic of Pabuji; Staal 1961 on vedic recitation). The principle assumed by philology is that we need to establish the text, as Witzel says, to find out what a thinker such as Śaṃkara actually taught (Witzel 1997: vi). If an apparent theological contradiction within a text is really a contradiction, for example, we need to first establish the text and whether contradictory elements are later additions or perhaps have entered from other texts in the intertextuality of oral tradition. Let us look more closely at this problem, taking our examples from the large group of medieval texts called Tantras.

The vast body of tantric material presents us with difficult questions. What is the function of these texts? Who composed them and for whom? What are the procedural difficulties of the outsider in approaching these texts? Is it possible to establish an original text? And so on. Certainly the Tantras were regarded as revelation and treated as words of authority, and certainly they developed in a social context that fostered their dissemination (see Colas's and Flood's essays). But the difficulties of establishing critical editions, along with reading and making informed comment on this material, are considerable. The texts themselves often use forms of Sanskrit at variance with "correct" usage; a form of language known as "divine" or "belonging to Śiva" (*aiśa*), which, Goodall notes, seems to cause commentators some embarrassment (Goodall 1998: lxvi). Reading tantric texts we need to be aware that the context of their reception would have involved oral comment by a teacher, practice, especially supererogatory forms of ritual beyond those required by vedic orthopraxy, as well intellectual speculation about their meaning by commentators and their audiences. The aim of the commentaries is to establish a text within a particular field of interpretation and, presumably, to explicate meanings to an educated, brahmanical audience for whom the text was alive and important. These commentaries are aware of themselves as establishing a particular interpretation over and against other possible readings. Thus Kṣemarāja (ca. 1000–1050 CE) composed his commentary on the *Svacchanda Tantra* to defeat adherence to the dualist interpretation of the rival tradition, the Śaiva Siddhānta (Kahrs 1998: 60). That these texts require commentary is itself an indication of their openness and their non-transparent nature. The "contextualizing practice" (Lemke 1995) of Kṣemarāja certainly relates these texts to the practices of his culture and the texts of his tradition. Indeed, the commentators highlight the texts' intertextuality through quoting other scriptural authorities, sometimes of rival traditions.

Almost from their inception, then, it was not possible to establish originary texts. Even by the time of the commentator on the text, the dualist theologian

Rāmakaṇṭha (ca. 950–1000 CE), sections of the *Kiraṇa Tantra* were probably "corrupt" and he had a number of readings to choose from (Goodall 1998: cxix). That Rāmakaṇṭha could choose from a number of variant readings of the texts upon which he commented, and Goodall quotes his commentary on the *Maṭaṅga Tantra* saying this (Goodall 1998: cxviii–cxix), shows that even at this early date there are a number of textual transmissions. But for Rāmakaṇṭha variant readings (*pāṭhabhedaḥ*) are not original (*na mūlataḥ*) but due to the error of students. For Rāmakaṇṭha there is an original or root text that is the divine revelation of which the concrete texts transmitted through a line of scribes is an imperfect reflection. Indeed, the Tantras themselves maintain that they are imperfect reflections of an original, greater, text conveyed from the mouth of the deity (for example, the *Mālinīvijayottara Tantra* 1.1–4; 14). Rāmakaṇṭha's is an almost idealist understanding of text: an inaccessible, pure originary source, in contrast to its imperfect manifestations or repetitions in human history and its gradual degeneration (a theory perhaps not far removed from the nineteenth-century idea of establishing the oldest, and therefore most authentic, text). On Rāmakaṇṭha's view, the purity of the authorial intention (that is, Śiva's intention) is lost through the generations of the text's transmission; a degeneration due not only to scribal error, but to human ignorance.

This distinction between the authorial (and by implication pure and original) and the scribal (by implication corrupted) text that Rāmakaṇṭha refers to, is echoed in traditional philological practice and theory. But in contrast to Rāmakaṇṭha's position, the general direction of modern philological thinking privileges "the socialized, received, concrete text" (Greetham 1999: 47) over and against some abstract ideal. This position tends towards the view that any edition of a text simply reflects the time and place of its occurrence: as Greetham says, texts "are real enough for our purposes" (p. 35). The concrete, received text is what is presented to us, a repetition of a repetition, and it is this that must be the focus of inquiry rather than a notional, abstract "work."

All textual practice is empowered by theories of the text, even implicit ones, and decisions about a text arrived at – say a critical edition – are not situated beyond cultural consensus. But having said this, any textual interpretation assumes philology and a dialogical reading of texts assumes the work of the philologist in establishing or stabilizing a text within a particular time-frame. If texts are more than systems of grammar then they are constantly in transmission and change, being received through history in different contexts. Rāmakaṇṭha's *Kiraṇa Tantra*, at one level, is the text we read today, but it is also a wholly different text, hedged around with different assumptions by the different communities who read it (a scholarly community or a Śaiva community). It is also questionable whether Rāmakaṇṭha's root text existed as a concrete object and it is quite possible that the text was "corrupted" from its inception; that there was never an "uncorrupted" text in history. While certainly the versions or repetitions of a text are *of a text*, there are theoretical problems in establishing the *same* text. The Tantras' entextualization and contextualization, terms used by Silverstein and Urban for the ways in which texts are recontextualized throughout their history, will affect the understanding conveyed in them (Silverstein and Urban 1996: 1–3).

These methodological considerations about the notion of the text are central to our inquiry into South Asian history and are concerns shared by many contributors to this volume. Both philology and its critique are centered on text and many of the essays here are surveys of South Asian "literatures." While archaeology and art history are important for our understanding of the past and the "materialization" of tradition is important, text remains the primary source of cultural meaning. Along with the emphasis on text there are accounts from contemporary fieldwork (Freeman, Pintchman, Quigley) and readings of tradition through the lens of gender studies (Narayanan), postcolonial studies (Ramaswamy, Viswanathan), and political studies (Ram Prasad). Indeed, implicit in the essays of Viswanathan, Ramaswamy, and Narayanan is the need for a corrective reading of tradition, a corrective reading that can come from the development of critiques in other contexts, such as feminism and Foucaultian studies of power. It is the general contention of the volume that anthropological study and critical reading of tradition in South Asia needs to understand the textual tradition established, however tentatively, through philology, and conversely that the living traditions accessed through anthropology can throw light upon textual history. The meanings of the Kerala tantric manual, the *Tantrasamuccaya* for example, can be made clear with reference to contemporary Nambudri practice, which in turn is based on textual injunction.

An Overview of Contents

The volume is divided into four main parts, theoretical issues, text and tradition, systematic thought, and society, politics, and nation. Each of these either surveys a general area within the wider field, provides a discussion of specific tradition or region, or approaches material from a fresh perspective.

1. *Theoretical issues*

The first part, "Theoretical Issues," contains two very different essays. Gauri Viswanathan opens the inquiry by examining the relation of British colonialism to Hinduism and how the inability to perceive Hinduism in its own terms led to a distortion within comparative religion. She also unravels the limitations within the theory of the construction of Hinduism itself. David Smith, by contrast, in a somewhat controversial essay argues against recent postcolonial critique and defends the study of Indian languages and systems of thought by Western scholars in the last two centuries, critically examining the arguments of Inden and Said. Through these two essays we form a picture of some of the major issues that have dominated discussions about the nature of Hinduism and its study and very different understandings of them.

2. *Text and tradition*

The largest part of the book, "Text and Tradition," systematically provides an overview of the major textual traditions in Sanskrit and provides three examples of traditions in Indian vernacular languages. On the assumption that a textual source cannot be separated from the tradition of which it is a part, this section gives an account of both major texts themselves and the histories of the traditions that revere and preserve them.

Beginning with the foundations of the textual traditions in the Vedas and Upaniṣads, Michael Witzel presents a comprehensive account of the texts and their categorization, the ritual traditions of which they are a part, and the historical developments to the period of the formation of the sūtra literature. We know much more now about this period, about vedic dialects for example, and Witzel brings this recent scholarship to bear. Ludo Rocher takes up some of these developments in his essay on Dharmaśāstras, the treatises on law, giving an account of the texts themselves, problems of dating this material, and the importance and impact of the Dharmaśāstras on the later system of law, especially during the colonial period. The great Indian epics are next accounted for in John Brockington's essay. We see how major themes in the traditions are developed at a narrative level in the texts and their impact on the later traditions. Many themes, deities, and stories from the epics are elaborated and developed in the vast body of "ancient" texts, the Purāṇas. Here Freda Matchett guides us through a complex world of multiple narratives, quasi-history, and sectarian divides and gives us an account of the history of their study. Some of the themes and narratives of the Epics and Purāṇas are also found in the literatures of vernacular languages. The examples provided here are by Norman Cutler, who problematizes the phrase "Tamil Hindu Literature" and goes on to develop a fascinating account of devotion, poetry, ritual, and narrative in court, temple, and village. Rich Freeman charts the development of Kerala's Hindu literature, showing how the Kerala cultural context transforms Tamil themes, and how the texts reflect socioreligious practice. Moving into a very different world, Nancy Martin provides an account of devotional literature in Hindi and the particular form of devotionalism that developed in the north, focused on a transcendent being without qualities or form. The famous poet Kabir is here placed in the context of this devotional movement.

From particular genres, we turn to Gavin Flood's chapter, which presents a historical trajectory of Śaivism. Flood shows how Śaivas considered their religious practices and beliefs to be authorized by the Tantras, a revelation distinct from the Veda, and discusses the relation between the Śaiva and Vaidika traditions. In a similar vein, Gérard Colas gives a detailed account of the history of Vaiṣṇava traditions based on Sanskrit and Tamil sources. He shows how devotion to Viṣṇu articulates with the aristocracy, the yogic and ascetic traditions, and discusses the forms of Vaiṣṇavism in the Pañcrātra and Vaikhānasa traditions, going on to discuss important later developments as well. Vaiṣṇavism (as did Śaivism) expanded beyond the borders of India into southeast Asia where it has left an important legacy. Cutting across historical trajectories, being institutions common to the Śaiva, Vaiṣṇava, and Vaidika traditions, we have the lifestyle options of the householder and the renouncer. T. N. Madan has done very important work on this often neglected aspect of Hinduism. In his essay he looks at what it is to be a householder and examines the idea in the textual sources as both institution and ideal, indicating values set against the value of renunciation and turning one's back on family and society. Closely allied to Madan's essay in that both are examining central institutions and realms of value within Hinduism, Patrick Olivelle discusses the renouncer tradition. Here Olivelle gives an account of the origins and institution of renunciation, showing how the sources reveal a tension between the ascetic values of renunciation and the values of the male householder, discussed by Madan, to marry, father children, and perform ritual enjoined on him by scripture.

Lastly in this part we look at the particularity of contemporary, regional traditions, with two examples taken from different regions and contexts. Rich Freeman describes the fascinating phenomenon of the *teyyam*, the ritualized dance-possession rituals of Kerala performed annually by low-caste specialists. Tracy Pintchman gives an account based on previously unpublished fieldwork, of women's ritual devotions to Krishna in a Benares community, during the month of Kārtik.

3. *Systematic thought*

Moving away from religious traditions and texts as such, part III is concerned with systematic aspects of Indian thought. The part itself is divided into "The Indian Sciences" and "Philosophy and Theology." The section on the Indian sciences is a unique feature of this collection of essays, as these areas are so often neglected in introductory texts and surveys such as this. Rationality is not, of course, the sole possession of the West, and India (as did China) developed very early an empirical investigation of the world, especially an inquiry into language, along with more speculative, philosophical inquiry. The purpose of this section is an examination of some of these developments by scholars who have worked closely together on this project, and to emphasize the importance of systematic, rational thinking that, at some levels, feeds directly into the philosophical discourse of the traditions. Frits Staal, whose work has done so much to highlight the scientific and systematic nature of early Indian thought, begins with a brief account of science in India followed by an essay on the science of language, a precursor to modern linguistics. Takao Hayashi then discusses Indian mathematics and shows how mathematical knowledge developed from practical concerns of calculation, not only in relation to state income, but in relation to the need to make measurements for vedic ritual, particularly the fire altar. More abstract considerations developed and Hayashi discusses, for example, an Indian proof of Pythagorean theorem. While astrology is often acknowledged as an important feature of Indian traditions, the way in which the zodiacal signs relate to mathematics and temporal measurement is not often explicated outside of specialist discussions. In his essay, Michio Yano explains the way in which the science of heavenly bodies (*jyotiḥśāstra*) developed, how the Indians adopted the Greek zodiac, and how this science relates to the measurement of time. Shifting from language, mathematics, and the cosmos to the body, Dominik Wujastyk takes up the inquiry, showing how an early science of medicine developed in India, a science that is still practiced today.

Related to the discussion of the Indian sciences we have the development of logic and rational thought which is often directed to a soteriological end in the Indian context. Jonardon Ganeri's essay takes us through an account of the practice of reason and its application to the goals of life. The various systems of Indian philosophy and theology developed assuming these formal structures of argument. In his essay on "Hindu theology" Francis Clooney critically examines this category and discusses some of the fundamental theological problems as they are dealt with in the Indian sources. These include important questions as to whether there is a transcendent source of being and questions about the problem of evil and suffering, concerns shared by Western theology as well. Clooney discusses responses to these questions through the practice of learning from scripture, meditation, and reasoned reflection. This very rich essay also discusses theological language, the community in which theology takes place, and the style of theological commentary. Related to both Indian linguistics and theology, the essay by André Padoux gives an excellent account of the centrality of mantra in the history of Hindu traditions. He discusses the origin and meaning of the word, of notable importance being Abhinavagupta's definition of mantra as forms of thought leading to liberation. Mantras occur early in the Veda but take on great importance in the Tantras, where mantra is related to the structure of the hierarchical cosmos and to consciousness.

4. *Society, politics, and nation*

The final part of the volume on "Society, Politics, and Nation" examines sociopolitical themes of particular relevance to the contemporary world. Having provided great historical sweeps of the traditions we can now examine the development of Hinduism as an entity in the last two centuries in more detail, the central organizing principle of society, namely caste, the issue of nationhood, and the issue of gender. Declan Quigley's essay on the caste system raises important questions about the nature of social organization in India and asks the central question whether Hinduism can be separated from caste. Quigley thinks it can, but for interesting reasons that take us into problems of ritual and the gift. The forces of modernity linked to European ideas of progress and rationality have set themselves against caste. In his essay on modernity and the rise of the Hindu reform movement, Dermot Killingley traces the nineteenth-century history of Hindu reform with Rammohun Roy, the rise of the Brahmo Samāj and

Ārya Samāj, and the relation of social reform to the British rule of law interfacing with Hindu law. Developing the history into the twentieth century, C. Ram Prasad shows the importance of the idea of Hinduism in contemporary India and the wider Hindu world, discussing the ideology of *hindutva*, the rise of Hindu nationalism, and political developments in the last years of the twentieth century. In parallel to this theme, Sumathi Ramaswamy shows how nationalism functions in relation to the Tamil language and its personification in the Goddess Tamiḻttāy, a deity who performs a similar function to Mother India (Bhārat Mātā). Vasudha Narayanan's essay on gender takes the idea of the social construction of gender and examines this with particular reference to the Śrī Vaiṣṇava tradition (previously contextualized in Colas's essay). The issues raised by Narayanan of the relation of gender to sex, of role play to devotional sensibilities, are centrally important in understanding contemporary gender roles in Hindu society.

All of the essays in the volume are by recognized experts in their field. The reader will appreciate in the range of material covered not only the richness and complexity of Hinduism, but also that Hinduism is a highly contested area of discourse. Yet along with a sense of diversity and the fragmentation of different traditions, historical periods, and problems, it is also hoped that the reader will appreciate some of the links, common threads, and issues that persistently reoccur in the history of this vast and complex entity that "Hinduism" refers to.

References

Babb, L. 1975. *The Divine Hierachy*. New York: Columbia University Press.

Balagangadhara, S. N. 1994. *"The Heathen in his Blindness . . .": Asia, the West, and the Dynamic of Religion*. Leiden: Brill.

Biardeau, M. 1997. "Some Remarks on the Links between the Epics, the Purāṇas and their Vedic Sources," in G. Oberhammer, ed., *Studies in Hinduism: Vedism and Hinduism*. Wien: Österreichischen Akademie der Wissenschaften: 69–173.

Blackburn, Stuart. 1988. *Singing of Birth and Death: Texts in Performance*. Philadelphia: University of Pennsylvania Press.

Eagleton, T. 1991. *Ideology: An Introduction*. London: Verso.

Eck, D. L. 1981. *Darsan, See the Divine Image in India*, 2nd rev. and enl. ed. Chambersburg, PA: Anima Books.

Fitzgerald, T. 2000. *The Ideology of Religious Studies*. Oxford: Oxford University Press.

Frykenberg, R. E. "The Emergence of Modern Hinduism," in Sontehiemer and Kulke 1997: pp. 82–107.

Fuller, C. 1992. *The Camphor Flame: Popular Hinduism and Society in India*. Princeton: Princeton University Press.

Goodall, D. 1998. "Introduction," *Bhaṭṭa Rāmakaṇṭha's Commentary on the Kiraṇatantra*. Pondichéry: Institut Français de Pondichéry.

Greetham, D. C. 1999. *Theories of the Text*. Oxford: Oxford University Press.

Guha, R. and Spivak, Gayatri C., eds. 1988. *Selected Subaltern Studies*. Delhi: Oxford University Press.

Heesterman, J. C. 1976. *The Inner Conflict of Tradition: An Essay in Indian Ritual, Kinship and Society.* Chicago: University of Chicago Press.

——. 1993. *The Broken World of Sacrifice: Essays in Ancient Indian Ritual.* Chicago: University of Chicago Press.

Hiltebeitel, A. 1988, 1991. *The Cult of Draupadi.* Vol. 1, *Mythologies from Gingee to Kuruksetra.* Vol. 2, *On Hindu Ritual and the Goddess.* Chicago: University of Chicago Press.

Inden, R. 1990. *Imagining India.* Oxford: Blackwell.

Jaffrelot, C. 1996. *The Hindu Nationalist Movement and Indian Politics: 1925 to the 1990s: Strategies of Identity-Building, Implantation and Mobilisation (with Special Reference to Central India).* London: Hurst & Co.

Jha, Dwijendra Narayan. 2002. *The Myth of the Holy Cow.* London and New York: Verso.

Kahrs, E. 1998. *Indian Semantic Analysis: The Nirvacana Tradition.* Cambridge: Cambridge University Press.

Kapur, Anuradh. 1993. "Deity to Crusader: The Changing Iconography of Ram," in Pandey, ed., *Hindus and Others: The Question of Identity in India Today.* New Delhi: Viking, pp. 74–107.

King, R. 1999. *Orientalism and Religion: Postcolonial Theory, India and the Mystic East.* London and New York. Routledge.

Larson, G. 1995. *India's Agony Over Religion.* Albany: SUNY Press.

Lemke, Jay. 1995. "Intertextuality and Text Semantics," in M. Gregory and P. Fries, eds., *Discourse in Society: Functional Perspectives.* Norwood, NJ: Ablex.

Lipner, Julius. 1996. "Ancient Banyan: An Inquiry into the Meaning of 'Hinduness,'" *Religious Studies* 32: 109–26.

O'Connell, J. T. 1973. "The Word 'Hindu' in Gaudiya Vaisnava Texts," *Journal of the American Oriental Society* 93 (3): 340–4.

Oberhammer, G. 1997. "Bemerkungen zum phänomen religiöser tradition im Hinduismus," in Oberhammer, ed., *Studies in Hinduism: Vedism and Hinduism.* Vienna: Der Österreichischen Akademie der Wissenschaften: 9–42.

Olivelle, Patrick. 1993. *The Āśrama System: The History and Hermeneutics of a Religious Tradition.* Oxford: Oxford University Press.

Omvedt, Gail. 1995. *Dalit Visions: The Anti-Caste Movement and the Construction of an Indian Identity.* Delhi: Orient Longman.

Pandey, G., ed. 1993. *Hindus and Others: The Question of Identity in India Today.* New Delhi: Viking.

Parry, J. 1994. *Death in Banares.* Cambridge: Cambridge University Press.

Piatigorsky, Alexander. 1985. "Some Phenomenological Observations on the Study of Indian Religions," in Burgardt and Cantille, eds., *Indian Religion.* London: Curzon, pp. 208–24.

Raheja, Gloria G. 1988. *The Poison in the Gift: Ritual, Prestation, and the Dominant Caste in a North Indian Village.* Chicago, London: University of Chicago Press.

Sanderson, A. Forthcoming. "Śaivism: Its Development and Impact" (unpublished paper).

Silverstein, M. and Greg Urban. 1996. *Natural Histories of Discourse.* Chicago and London: University of Chicago Press.

Sontheimer, G.-D. and Kulke, H., eds. 1997. *Hinduism Reconsidered.* Delhi: Manohar.

Smith, B. 2000. "Who Does, Can, and Should Speak for Hinduism?" *Journal of the American Academy of Religion* 68 (4): 741–9.

Smith, B. K. 1988. "Exorcising the Transcendent: Strategies for Redefining Hinduism and Religion," *History of Religions* 27: 32–55.

Smith, J. D. 1991. *The Epic of Pabuji: A Study, Transcription and Translation*. Cambridge: Cambridge University Press.
Smith, J. Z. 1982. *Imagining Religion, from Babylon to Jonestown*. Chicago: University of Chicago Press.
Staal, F. 1961. *Nambudiri Veda Recitation*. Gravenhage: Mouton.
——, ed. 1983. *AGNI: The Vedic Ritual of the Fire Altar*, 2 vols. Berkeley: University of California Press.
——. 1989. *Rules Without Meaning: Ritual, Mantras, and the Human Sciences*. New York: Peter Lang.
Stietencron, H. von. 1997. "Hinduism: On the Proper Use of a Deceptive Term," in Sontheimer and Kulke 1997: 32–53.
Thapar, R. 1993. *Interpreting Early India*. Delhi: Oxford University Press.
Witzel, M., ed. 1997. *Inside the Texts, Beyond the Texts: New Approaches to the Study of the Vedas* (Harvard Oriental Series, Opera Minora 2). Cambridge, MA: Harvard University Press.

PART I

Theoretical Issues

1 Colonialism and the Construction of Hinduism 23
Gauri Viswanathan

2 Orientalism and Hinduism 45
David Smith

CHAPTER 1

Colonialism and the Construction of Hinduism

Gauri Viswanathan

In *The Hill of Devi*, a lyrical collection of essays and letters recounting his travels in India, E. M. Forster describes his visit to a Hindu temple as a tourist's pilgrimage driven by a mixture of curiosity, disinterestedness, loathing, and even fear. Like the Hindu festival scene he paints in *A Passage to India*, the Gokul Ashtami festival he witnesses is characterized as an excess of color, noise, ritual, and devotional fervor. Forcing himself to refrain from passing judgment, Forster finds it impossible to retain his objectivity the closer he approaches the shrine, the cavern encasing the Hindu stone images ("a mess of little objects") which are the object of such frenzied devotion. Encircled by the press of ardent devotees, Forster is increasingly discomfited by their almost unbearable delirium. Surveying the rapt faces around him, he places the raucous scene against the more reassuring memory of the sober, stately, and measured tones of Anglican worship. His revulsion and disgust reach a peak as he advances toward the altar and finds there only mute, gaudy, and grotesque stone where others see transcendent power (Forster 1953: 64).

And then, just as Forster is about to move along in the ritual pilgrims' formation, he turns back and sees the faces of the worshippers, desperate in their faith, hopelessly trusting in a power great enough to raise them from illness, poverty, trouble, and oppression. Transfixed by the scene, Forster sees reflected in their eyes the altered image of the deity before them. As he wends his way through the crowd, he is overwhelmed by the confusion of multiple images of the Hinduism he has just witnessed: of garlanded, ash-smeared, bejeweled stone on one hand, and of the inexpressible power of deepest personal yearnings, desires, and needs on the other. If he is disgusted by the noisy displays of Hindu worship, he is moved beyond words by the eloquent silence of the pain and tribulation from which believers seek deliverance. In their taut, compressed faces he finds a Hinduism to which he can relate, as surely as he is alienated by the other face of Hinduism blazoned by conch shells, camphor, and cymbals. He can conclude that, though "there is no dignity, no taste, no form. . . . I don't think one ought to be irritated with Idolatry because one can see from the faces of the people that it touches something very deep in their hearts" (Forster 1953: 64).

Forster's personal odyssey frames an experience of Hinduism that, in its exquisite detail and ultimate compassion, is far more nuanced than is its portrayal in some of his other better-known works. In *A Passage to India* Hinduism is depicted as a belief system with a "boum" effect, a metaphysically infuriating religion blurring the manichean divisions between good and evil that inform western theology as much as western law, and comprise the dualities that help to define the nature, cause, and agent of crime as well as its punishment. But as Godbole, the novel's comically inscrutable Brahmin character, avers portentously, how can crime be known so categorically when all participate equally in its commission? If everyone is complicit in acts of evil, would not all have to be punished equally too? It is this jumble of incoherent metaphysical murmurings, apparently sanctioned by Hindu belief, that exasperates Fielding, the English character most sympathetic to India. Unlike the colonial officers ruling the country, Fielding develops an emotional affinity with Indians, particularly the effervescent Muslim doctor Aziz. But even the resilient Fielding is overwhelmed by the bewildering course of events culminating in Aziz's trial for rape of an English woman and then his subsequent acquittal. The trial turns Aziz into a fiery nationalist, willing to sacrifice even his friendship with Fielding to act upon his newfound political consciousness. An ecstatic scene of Hindu devotion marks the climax of the novel. As the birth of the god Krishna is celebrated, virtually turning princes and paupers alike into frolicking adolescents, the very imagery of Hinduism as an infantilizing religion fuses into the central image of the infant Krishna. It is no wonder that after the explosive confrontation between colonizer and colonized unleashed by Aziz's wrongful arrest, no one can tell, as the English accuser Adele Quested discovers, whether evil lies in dark, hollow mountain caves or in the cavernous courtrooms of the colonial state. The raucous Hindu festival confirms the indeterminacy of events and their causes. And as the disillusioned Fielding sets sail from India soon after these events, it is only natural that he should feel the return of reassuring order and balance in his life as he passes the stately, proportionate architecture of Venice, described with barely disguised relief as "the civilization that has escaped muddle" (Forster 1970: 275). For Fielding, the decorum and harmony of the Venetian facades restore the principles of perspective and truth that had been entirely lost in the chaos of India, a chaos that is best represented by the metaphysical and aesthetic insufficiency of its religions: "The buildings of Venice, like the mountains of Crete and the fields of Egypt, stood in the right place, whereas in India everything was placed wrong. He had forgotten the beauty of form among idol temples and lumpy hills; indeed, without form, how can there be beauty?" (Forster 1970: 275).

The Modernity of Hinduism

That so sympathetic a figure as Fielding should resort to western aesthetic standards to evaluate Hinduism is a measure of how corrosive was the colonial experience even for those more favorably disposed to India. The western framework was never far from being a point of reference, even when the object was to critique the doctrinaire aspects of Christianity and uphold the east as a spiritual model for the materialistic west. An inability to view Hinduism on its own terms has shaped the study of comparative religion, whether to prove the superiority of Christianity or to show that Hinduism is part of the Christian teleology; to demonstrate, as Antony Copley calls it, a universalist theology that includes Hinduism as much as it does Christianity (Copley 1997: 58). The phase of western scholarly engagement with eastern religions, commonly referred to as the period of Orientalism, is often described as less hostile to Indian culture than the Anglicism that superseded it. Yet colonial perceptions of Hinduism should not be divided along the lines of those who were positively inclined and those who were opposed, since this assumes hostile reactions are produced by the intrusion of a western framework of reference and benevolent ones by its suspension, whereas it is clear the same frame persists regardless of whether the attitude is positive or negative.[1] The comparative perspective reveals that western observers of Hinduism were just as keenly assessing Christianity's place in European world domination as they were looking toward other belief systems to locate the roots of a proto-religion.

The interest in other religions was inevitably sparked by the need to chart the progress of civilization on scientific principles, which included tracing the evolution of religious consciousness. The search for earlier prototypes of the more evolved religions, of which Christianity was the prime example, led scholars to seek out comparable features, such as monotheism, a salvational scheme, and notions of the afterlife, in other religions. While the earliest travelers recorded their accounts of idolatrous worship by the peoples of India (Embree 1971), later scholars found in Vedic, Sanskrit hymns some indication that the object of Hindu worship was not mere stone but an abstract entity bearing some resemblance to the object of monotheistic worship. For such scholars, "Hinduism" was located in this combination of oral and written texts, and this textualized Hinduism was soon privileged as the religion on which subsequent attention was focused. Though Sanskritic Hinduism was far from representative of the worship of diverse peoples, it was made to define a whole range of heterogeneous practices that were then lumped together to constitute a single religious tradition termed "Hinduism" (Hardy 1995).[2]

The new textual discoveries of the eighteenth century led British Orientalists like William Jones, Nathaniel Halhed, and Henry Colebrooke to conclude that the religion practiced by Hindus was highly evolved, confounding the colonial assumption that all cultures outside the Christian pale were primitive, tribalistic, and animistic. As a result, in acknowledgement of the religious authority wielded by Hindu pandits (learned, religious men) who also doubled as native informants and commentators of Sanskrit texts, British authorities scrupulously sought to co-opt them in the colonial enterprise. Rather than alienate them by opposing their practices, administrators found it more strategic to use their knowledge as the basis for codification of Hindu law. Such accommodation of native knowledge and practices was in stark contrast to colonialism's systematic effacement of indigenous practices of religious worship in certain African societies (Hefner 1993).

Whether as rank superstition or sublime philosophy, Hinduism challenged the unimpeded exercise of British rule, especially when it was perceived to be closely associated with the spread of Christianity. Because they feared that the colonial control of India would be regarded entirely as a Christianizing mission, British administrators remained at a distance from Christian missionaries and kept a close eye on their activities to ensure that they did not jeopardize their strategic relations with the comprador classes by provoking conflict with Hindus. To be sure, current scholarship gives much less attention to the colonial engagement with Indian Islam than with Hinduism (although there are notable exceptions: Lelyveld 1978; Metcalf 1982; Gilmartin 1988). The standard rationale is that Islam, like Christianity, was monotheistic, and since Christian missionaries were singularly focused on an anti-idolatry campaign, which Islam also shared, Christianity and Islam would seem to share similar goals, at least with regard to Hinduism. Yet interestingly Christian missionaries never saw themselves in alliance with Muslims in their campaign against Hinduism. In fact, there was a three-way contestation between Hindu pandits, Christian missionaries, and Muslim and Sufi *pirs* whose impact lies in the development of a field of apologetics asserting the claims of the respective religions. In his study of anti-Christian apologetics, Richard Fox Young suggests that "at about the time that Hindu pandits were recovering from their reluctance to counteract the threat posed by an alien and increasingly powerful religion in their midst, scholarly Christian evangelists were engaged in developing specialized terminology in Sanskrit for propagating their message more effectively than had theretofore been possible" (Young 1981: 15; Young's focus is on Hinduism's refutation of Christianity rather than of Islam). In this context Young deems it more appropriate to term the developments in India post-1850 not as renascent but as *resistant* Hinduism.

One of the most striking advances in modern scholarship is the view that there is no such thing as an unbroken tradition of Hinduism, only a set of discrete traditions and practices reorganized into a larger entity called "Hinduism" (Frykenberg 1989; von Stietencron 1989). If there is any disagreement at all in this scholarship, it centers on whether Hinduism is exclusively a construct of western scholars studying India or of anticolonial Hindus looking toward the systematization of disparate practices as a means of recovering a precolonial, national identity. Many will argue that there is in fact a dialectical relation between the two. In this view, as summarized by Richard King in *Orientalism and Religion*, nationalist Hindus appropriated a construct developed by Orientalist scholars and used it for their own purposes, producing the notion of a culturally superior Hinduism. In turn, nationalist adaptations of Orientalist scholarship formed the basis for contemporary (New Age?) representations of India as the eternal land of spirituality. The important point is that Orientalism remains the point of reference for Hinduism's current identification with mysticism and spirituality. Indeed, the work of King among others suggests that it is often impossible to distinguish western understandings of Hinduism from those of Indian nationalists, since "through the colonially established apparatus of the political, economic, and educational institutions of India, contemporary Indian self-awareness remains deeply influenced by Western presuppositions about the nature of Indian culture" (King 1999: 117). In this view, all notions of Hinduism deployed by Indian nationalists to create an overarching cultural unity have little reference to the lived religious experience of the people but, rather, derive from Western readings of a textualized Hinduism reconfigured to correspond to the compulsions of the Judeo-Christian tradition.

To be sure, British colonialism's relation with Hinduism has long been a fraught one, ranging from antagonism to admiration, with a good measure of sheer indifference thrown in between. Some scholars argue there was no such thing as Hinduism in precolonial India, only a set of traditions and practices reorganized by western scholars to constitute a system then arbitrarily named "Hinduism" (Frykenberg 1989). The most radical position states that Hinduism is not a single religion but rather a group of amorphous Indian religions. Heinrich von Stietencron writes that "Hinduism . . . does not meet the fundamental requirements of a historical religion of being a coherent system; but its distinct religious entities do. They are indeed religions, while Hinduism is not" (von Stietencron 1989: 20). In denying Hinduism the status of a religion because it does not constitute a coherent system, this view considers modern Hinduism to be the product of a sociohistorical process distinct from the evolution of a doctrinal system based on successive accretions of philosophical thought. The formation of modern Hinduism involves Christian missionaries and Hindu revivalist organizations alike, which both contribute to the systematization of disparate traditions for their own purposes.

However, the "construction of Hinduism" theory has several limitations. In an effort to recover a more heterogeneous and diachronically diverse religion, some scholars present modern Hinduism as more unified than it actually is. Richard G. Fox's critique of Ronald Inden's anti-Orientalist approach is relevant in this context. Fox's argument that anti-Orientalism preserves the stereotypes it seeks to demolish can be extended to the field of Hinduism studies (Fox 1993: 144–5). The tendency to interpret modern Hinduism as the unification of a loose conglomeration of different belief systems remains trapped within a monotheistic conception of religion, which constitutes the final reference point for judging whether religions are coherent or not. Nineteenth-century Hindu reformers, seeking to rid religion of the features most attacked by Christian missionaries, are believed to have been driven by a similar will to monotheism in their attempts to make the Hindu religion correspond more rigorously to the Judeo-Christian conceptions of a single, all-powerful deity. Only to the extent that the western attribution of unity to Hinduism strategically helped anticolonial Indians create a national identity in religion can it be said that western discourses customized indigenous religions for native consumption. The notion that modern Hinduism represents a false unity imposed on diverse traditions replays a western fascination with – and repulsion from – Indian polytheism. In this enduring perception, the existence of many gods must surely indicate they were the basis of many smaller religions and therefore to describe them under the rubric of "Hinduism" as if they constituted a single religious system must be false, a distortion of heterogeneous religious practices. The reluctance of many scholars to call Hinduism a religion because it incorporates many disparate practices suggests that the Judeo-Christian system remains the main reference point for defining religions. Pointing out that "there is no single, privileged narrative of the modern world," Talal Asad warns against the dangers of writing the history of world religions from the narrow perspective of Judeo-Christian history (Asad 1993: 9).

Moreover, while conceding the need to examine the Orientalist and colonial contributions to Hinduism's modern-day form, one would need to be wary of ascribing total hegemony to western discourses, which are given such power in contemporary scholarship – even in work which purports to be anti-Orientalist – that they appear to rob Indians of any agency in redefining Hinduism for their own purposes. The view that Indians' understanding of Hinduism is primarily drawn from western sources minimizes the significance of local, vernacular traditions for conveying a variety of precepts that are no less "Hindu" than those derived from the neo-Vedānta canon popularized in the west. These often went unnoticed by western commentators, who continued to insist that their "discovery" of Hinduism in such texts as *The Bhagavad Gītā* facilitated Indians' attempt to find a cohesive unity in disparate branches of indigenous worship. Yet *The Bhagavad Gītā*, which exerted a powerful influence on Mohandas K. Gandhi's concept of social action and is said to have reached him primarily through Edwin Arnold's English translation, first affected him through his mother's daily recitation of it in Gujarati (Gandhi 1957: 4–5). Gandhi attributes his self-consciousness as a believing Hindu to his mother's influence, to the oral traditions she made available to him lying outside the formal instruction he received in school and elsewhere. Yet he also contrasts instinctive religious devotionalism, as derived from his mother, with rational critical reflection, which western commentaries on Hinduism helped him to develop.[3]

The presence of vernacular traditions of Hinduism reminds one how difficult it is to locate the precise point at which classical Sanskrit texts became synonymous with Hinduism. It is clearly not sufficient to resort to a "colonial invention of tradition" explanation, with its suggestion that Sanskrit had no prior hegemony in Indian societies before the period of British colonialism. No doubt Sanskrit was a dominant discourse in the precolonial period and acknowledged as such by the Orientalists who undertook its study since the eighteenth century. At the same time, Sanskrit literature contains a heterodox tradition that never gets represented in Western discourse.[4] When its dissenting strains are incorporated into Hinduism, they contribute to that religion's internal tensions. Thus Sanskrit's identification with Hinduism is itself a fraught one. One of the prime difficulties in determining the origins of Hinduism's interchangeability with the Sanskrit literary tradition is how effortlessly that tradition has been naturalized, so much so that it is no longer possible to distinguish between its precolonial authoritative status and its construction by British Orientalism.

At the same time, the new scholarship reveals as much as about the charged political climate of the 1980s and 1990s in which it was produced as it does about the modern history of Hinduism. After all, the absorption of smaller, local cults into a larger entity is not an unfamiliar one, and anthropological theory has long described the process of Hinduization as involving precisely such amalgamations. To scholars like Heinrich von Stietencron, the earlier anthropological approach is unsatisfactory because it is too rigidly structuralist in its orientation and presumes that Hinduism "naturally" evolves from its absorption of smaller cults (von Stietencron 1989: 71). Yet von Stietencron himself shows that Hinduization occurred in pre-Muslim India, when a competitive religious spirit among various sects – Śaivas, Vaiṣṇavas, Jainas, Bauddhas, Smārtas among others – created a tendency to make one religious view prevail over the others.[5] Even without the pressure of a foreign religion, which might have brought competing cults closer together if only to present a concerted front against external threat, the rituals and texts of these various sects prescribed ways of inducting believers into a dominant cult and making it prevail. Somaśambhu's manual, the *Somaśambhupaddhati*, written approximately in the second half of the eleventh century, is the best known example of a text that prepared initiates to enter Śaivism. Its procedural rituals laid the foundation for an enhancement of Śaivism's power through mass conversions, one of the key elements in the expansion of religion and as vital to Hinduization as to Christianization or Islamization for the growth of these religions.

What then distinguishes Hinduization in earlier periods of history from the nineteenth-century construction of Hinduism as a national religion? After all, there is no reason why the pre-Muslim integration of other religious groups within a Hindu framework should not be regarded as a "construction," despite supporting evidence that during this time frame there was a superimposition of ritual structures on already existing rituals (von Stietencron 1989: 71). Von Stietencron's analysis offers a clue, for it suggests that ideological, structural, and institutional differences between the Hinduism of pre-sixteenth-century India and that of the nineteenth century make it impossible to describe the latter formation in terms of Hinduization. One crucial difference is the concept of the nation-state that becomes available to Hindus through the impact of British colonialism. Not only was the Hinduism of the earlier period different, because spiritual leadership was centered in the charismatic authority of individual figures (*gurus*) rather than in all-India, institutional bodies. More importantly, Hinduism was also driven by a missionary zeal to strengthen the claims to salvation of one path rather than many paths. This reflects a pattern consistent with the way conversion works to augment the power of one belief system and gain new adherents by absorbing multiple groups into its fold. After all, early Christianity's growth was precisely through such accretions of smaller cults into a larger institution by means of conversion, and Hinduization in the precolonial period follows a similar pattern of augmentation (Hefner 1993). By contrast, the newly invigorated Hinduism of the nineteenth century is constituted as an exclusive defense against the assault of "foreign" religions, Christianity as much as Islam. This new Hinduism borrows features from European modernity and rational religion; most importantly, it relies on the concept of the nation-state in order to claim a national, all-India character.[6]

The Problem of Historiography

This differential history notwithstanding, the more interesting question to ask concerns the production of knowledge. What developments in history and method have enabled recent scholars to study Hinduism as a relatively modern construction? And to what extent, if at all, are these developments related to studies of the invention of tradition in other disciplines and regions? Since the publication of Eric Hobsbawm and Terence Ranger's influential collection of essays *The Invention of Tradition* in 1983, there has been a proliferation of studies drawing upon the insights of Foucault and Gramsci in order to examine the representation of governmental stratagems as eternal verities. The structure of rituals and ceremonials, diverse schools of thought, academic disciplines, and key canonical texts have all come under the steady gaze of historians, anthropologists, and literary critics, who have turned to examining the conditions reorganizing class interests into unbroken, universal traditions. "Invention of tradition" studies are popular in western scholarship because they have allowed a productive application of both Marxist and poststructuralist theories. They have also opened up a new historiography that claims a skepticism towards all forms of positivism and empiricism, just as it also casts suspicion on concepts of origins as privileged sites of authority.

Yet for all the parallels between the new historiography and contemporary scholarship on the colonial construction of Hinduism, poststructuralism is not the immediate context for studies of Hinduism as a modern construction, though its insights have certainly been important in developing new approaches to the study of Hinduism. Rather, recognition of Hinduism's modernity is possible because of (1) the recent rise of political parties claiming Hindu nationalism as their main election platform (Jaffrelot 1996; Hansen 1999); (2) the important contributions of feminist scholarship to a reexamination of Hinduism and patriarchy (Sangari and Vaid 1998; Mani 1998; Viswanathan 1998); and (3) the growing power of formerly "untouchable" groups in both changing the political equations and challenging the cultural history of India as a history written by the upper castes. These developments in Indian politics, feminism, and caste structures resist any attempts to write off the new scholarship as merely derivative of western academic trends. Indeed, just as much as the subaltern studies collective may be said to have inspired a wave of studies "from below," so too the urgency of the challenges before the Indian electorate has given a new political edge to the study of the "invention of tradition." The point of reference for much of this scholarship is the present struggle for power between so-called secular and religious forces in India. Critical work is motivated by the perception that contemporary electoral politics is caught up in a web of (mis)perceptions of Hinduism that stretch as far back as the first missions to India and the period of British colonialism. One of the key concepts introduced by democracy and the nation-state is numerical representativeness. "Majority" and "minority" are equally legitimate categories organizing the electorate. The need to prove the claims of belonging to a majority group is a powerful one, so powerful that it contributes to a mythology of a coherent religious tradition sanctioned by scripture, confirmed by ritual, and perpetuated by daily practice. "This, indeed, is a case where nationalist politics in a democratic setting succeeded in propagating Hindu religious unity in order to obtain an impressive statistical majority when compared with other religious communities" (von Stietencron 1989: 52).

Likewise, feminist scholarship has had a powerful effect on the deconstruction of Hinduism as a patriarchal religion. Some of the most powerful insights into the colonial construction of Hinduism have come from the perspective of gender studies. Studies of *satī* (Mani 1998), female conversions (Viswanathan 1998), and prepubertal marriages and the age of consent (Chakravarty 1998; Sinha 1995; Chandra 1998) show the extent to which Hindu law was reorganized in British courts to affirm the values and goals of the Hindu elite, the uppercaste Brahmans. Far from applying legal insights based on local practices, as urged by a few exceptional British voices such as James Nelson, British judges relied on the textual interpretations offered by Hindu pandits. Nelson, registering his vehement disapproval of such excessive reliance on elite Hindu interpreters, urged that colonial administrators attend to the nuances of local custom and practice to decide points of law, rather than force Sanskrit-based law upon non-Hindu peoples.[7]

And finally, the political rise of *dalits*, or noncaste groups known also as "untouchables," put a dent into Hinduism as an expression of brahmanism. The writings of dalit leader Bhimrao Ramji Ambedkar punctured the logic of caste hegemony and retold the history of India as a struggle between a power-hungry but stagnant Hinduism and a flourishing Buddhism. In Ambedkar's retelling of Hinduism's conquest of Buddhism, those Buddhists who refused to convert to Hinduism or adopt its non-meat-eating practices were turned into chattel labor. Thus, according to Ambedkar, untouchability was a result of the *refusal* of Buddhists to reconvert to Hinduism, not of their social inferiority. In historicizing untouchability, Ambedkar restored a sense of agency to *dalits*.

As some scholars have noted, one of the pitfalls in challenging the nationalist, exclusivist evocation of an ancient religion, existing uninterruptedly for five thousand years, is that its opposite is asserted more as a matter of counter-argument than historicity. In the attempt to disparage the contemporary Hindu ideologues, Hinduism is also being rewritten as a religion that "originally" had multiple differentiations that have now been lost under the umbrella term "Hinduism." To some extent, this has involved rewriting the very category of religion. If we can assume that most religions have sects, would the presence of Śaivas, Vaiṣṇavas, Jainas, and other groups, though many in number, necessarily invalidate the existence of a loose confederation of religions called Hinduism? After all, the early history of Christianity is no less divided along sectarian lines (some with hairsplitting differences), yet few would deny calling it by the name of Christianity. In the case of Hinduism's history, is the motivation to debunk the claims of Hindu ideologues driving the writing of another history, which involves the separation of "religion" from "sect" and a view of each sect as constituting a separate religion? Indeed, Śaivism is now considered as different from Vaiṣṇavism as it is from, say, Buddhism, yet Śaivism and Vaiṣṇavism have traditionally been described as two competing sects of Hinduism. The important contribution of the new scholarship is that, by questioning whether even rival sects can be regarded as part of one religion, it disaggregates religion from territoriality. After all, if Śaivism and Vaiṣṇavism have different forms of worship, different scriptures, and different concepts of the godhead, one must confront the question whether they are regarded as part of Hinduism solely because they are confined to the specific geography of the subcontinent. Such questions force a critical distance from conventional notions of religion and nationality, and prohibit a discourse of origins based on geography and territory from taking root. History as contested ground is equally evident in what Partha Chatterjee describes as Hindu nationalism's "consciousness of a solidarity that is supposed to act itself out in history," as much as in the secularist attempt to deconstruct that unity as a contrived one (Chatterjee 1993: 110).

Secondly, in seeking to critique Hindu nationalism without rejecting Hinduism *in toto*, some scholars have felt the need to assert a preexisting Hindu–Muslim harmony that had subsequently been disrupted by the policies of a divisive colonial government. Ashis Nandy, for instance, distinguishes Hinduism as a way of life from religious ideology, and argues that as a daily practice Hinduism has traditionally observed religious tolerance, but that subsequent manipulations by state and local political forces disrupted the amity between Muslims and Hindus (Nandy 1993). Drawing upon such data as the 1911 Census, he points out that in some parts of Gujarat individuals identified themselves as "Mohammedan Hindus," and he concludes that these overlapping identities serve to question the arbitrary categories imposed by the British administration for its own bureaucratic purposes. No doubt observations of this kind are occasioned by a strategic necessity to recuperate some aspect of indigenous life not wholly overtaken by colonial power. If Hinduism as a way of life is asked to serve this role, it is offered as an acknowledgement that the social practices of people, as well as their ways of relating and cohabiting with members of other communities, are organized around religion. Religion as social organization and relationality need not necessarily be equivalent to religious ideology, as

Nandy argues, and such distinctions would have to be made to do justice to religion's instrumental value in allowing communities to develop. It is certainly true that on the many occasions when communal violence has broken out in India, activist groups (like Sahmat, for instance) are prone to evoking an earlier spirit of precolonial Hindu–Muslim harmony, tragically marred by the destructive and divisive legacies of the colonial state which persist into the structures of postcolonial India. In fiction Amitav Ghosh evokes memories of a similar fraternal spirit as a counterpoint to the unbearable horror of religious violence between Hindus and Muslims in the aftermath of partition (Ghosh 1992; Viswanathan 1995: 19–34).

The Impetus for Reform in Hinduism

The colonial policy of "divide and rule" has had some of its deepest consequences for Hinduism, its relation to Indian Islam not being the least of them. British colonialism's attitude to Hinduism has long been a fraught one, ranging from antagonism to admiration, but never complete indifference. The existence of a highly evolved religious system practiced by the Hindus confounded the colonial assumption that all cultures outside the Christian pale were primitive, tribalistic, and animistic. Confronting the religious authority wielded by Hindu pandits, British authorities scrupulously sought to win their allegiance rather than alienate them by opposing their practices. This led to strategies of cooptation, which was in stark contrast to colonialism's systematic effacement of indigenous practices of religious worship in other colonized societies, particularly in Africa and the Caribbean. Because of the colonial state's complex negotiation of Hinduism, conversion, as well as colonial governance and educational policy, followed a different course in India than in other colonized societies. The prominence of education in the preoccupations of administrators and missionaries alike can be attributed to the recognition that the exercise of military strength – in the case of administrators – or the practice of itinerating – in the case of missionaries – was not sufficient to securing the consent of the colonized. Subjects had to be persuaded about the intrinsic merits of English culture and Christianity if they were to cooperate willingly in the colonial project (Viswanathan 1989; Copley 1997). The Gramscian theory of hegemony by consent has one of its strongest proofs in the Indian case, as colonial administrators sought to win the consent of Indians. Modifying Indian attitudes to Hinduism was central to the project. One result was the creation of a whole class of Indians alienated from their own culture and religion, even as they were systematically excluded from full participation in the structures of self-governance. It was this class that was later to initiate a series of reforms of Hinduism and establish its modern identity. While some prominent Hindus converted to Christianity, their conversions did not necessarily signify a pro-colonial stance, contrary to what many of their countrymen believed. In fact, many converts were also part of the momentum to reform Hinduism. Pandita Ramabai, Cornelia Sorabjee, Krupabai Satthianadhan, and Narayan Viman Tilak, who all converted to Christianity, were also central figures in the major social reform movements of the nineteenth century. Keshab Chander Sen was one of the founders of the Brahmo Samaj, a reform movement intended to make Hinduism less caste-based and less focused on idol worship and rituals. Tilak turned to vernacular sources to find a meeting point between Hinduism and Christianity, which he wanted to make a national rather than foreign religion. Ramabai, Sorabjee, and Satthianadhan were all involved with women's reform: Ramabai established a home for widows in Pune; Sorabjee was trained as an advocate in England and was keenly involved with issues of property reform, as well as the professional education of women; and Satthianadhan, trained as a medical doctor, took up the cause of education for women (Kosambi 1999; Satthianadhan 1998).

One reason why Indian converts to Christianity were able to maintain a distance from the colonial state was that the history of Christian missions in India was never identical with British colonialism, though this is not to say the missions opposed the colonization of India. Until the passing of the Charter Act of 1813 there were numerous curbs on missionary activity in India because of the apprehension that it jeopardized the Company's relations with a primarily Hindu population. An insurrection at Vellore, near Madras, in 1806 was blamed on missionary proselytization, and the Company feared that Hindu resentment would soon spread and threaten the delicate relationship it had established with Indian merchants. In the name of protecting the Company's commercial interests, a policy of religious neutrality was encouraged, whereby the Company refrained from interfering in indigenous religions. This did not imply that the Company approved of Hinduism, but merely that they considered their own mercantile interests more important. So scrupulous were Company officials in giving no offense that they were even willing to provide funds for religious schools and employ *pandits* and *shastris* as local informants, a practice that appalled Macaulay and James Mill who denounced such funding as a violation of religious neutrality.[8] Missionaries too used this as an opportunity to expose the inconsistencies of the Company, which put restrictions on the work of Christian missionaries but gave grants to Hindu and Muslim schools. Missionaries raised a fierce uproar, organizing the Anti-Idolatry Connexion League in response, and were so vociferous in their protests that in 1833 the government was forced to withdraw its funding and leave the religious endowments in the hands of Hindu religious bodies. Though it was not until 1863 that a law was passed that officially mandated noninterference, Robert Frykenberg argues that by this time a new Hindu public had begun to emerge, which drew upon the "structure of legal precedents for the rise of an entirely new religion" (Frykenberg 1989: 37).

Whether it was perceived negatively or positively, Hinduism posed an effective challenge to the unalloyed exertion of British rule, especially considered interchangeably with the spread of Christianity. The colonial engagement with Indian Islam was never as intense as it was with Hinduism. The conventional explanation is that Islam, like Christianity, was monotheistic, and Christian missionaries were far more focused on an anti-idolatry campaign that Islam, to some extent, also shared. Yet Christian missionaries never saw themselves in alliance with Muslim *pirs*, and there was indeed a three-way contestation between Christianity, Hinduism, and Islam revealing that the tensions between religions have as much to do with historical rivalries between them as with whether they are monotheistic or polytheistic. James Mill regarded Islam more favorably than Hinduism, yet attributed the decline of the Indian polity in the eighteenth century to effete Islamic rule (Mill 1858). The relationship of religion to effective governance, rather than the merits of doctrine, emerges in such accounts as the yardstick for evaluating the quality of religion. A civilizational theory of religion, akin to Hegel's schematization of phases of religious development, gained ground as the post-Enlightenment rationale for religion in culture. Under these conditions, both Hinduism and Islam came under sharp attack for their role in the decline and stagnation of material growth. Christianity's identification with the ascendancy of western civilization was the *sine qua non* of such attacks.

James Mill marked a disruptive moment in the European perception of Hinduism. After a long period of opprobrium, when Hinduism was considered akin to Catholicism in its "paganism" and rank superstition, Hinduism came to be discovered as a highly sophisticated philosophical system. The discovery went in tandem with a progressive, cosmopolitan Enlightenment project that sought out natural reason in religion as the feature that distinguished it from supernaturalism. In India, one consequence of the progressive, cosmopolitan Enlightenment project is to argue that only those elements of native culture that accord with natural reason are authentically Indian and hence that all other native South Asian cultural practices are monstrous and inappropriate for a modern civil society. A Vedāntic concept of Hinduism was already in the making, as an abstract, theistic philosophical system came to represent Hinduism, while all other popular practices were denounced as idolatrous. The splitting of Hinduism into popular and intellectual systems contributed to a parallel splitting of anticolonial responses into those for whom popular beliefs and "superstitions" were an essential part of Hindu identity and those for whom Hinduism was purged of some of its casteist, polytheistic, and ritualistic features. Dipesh Chakrabarty has shown how popular beliefs confounded both colonizers and Indian intellectuals alike and came to be identified with a sinister, subversive underside of subaltern opposition (Chakrabarty 2000: 72–113). Increasingly, there is more interest in these subaltern expressions of Hinduism as the site of an anticolonial, anticasteist resistance that rewrites the very categories of "natural reason" and "supernaturalism." Looking at peasant "superstitions" and animistic beliefs also offers alternative views of Hinduism obscured by the elitist monopoly of theistic religion.

But for Indian intellectuals intent on purifying Hinduism of its popular, idolatrous associations, a newly defined religion could give them an identity compatible with the modernity they craved, while retaining their roots in indigenous traditions. The Hinduism of Vedānta perfectly fit their needs. A rational religion consisting of intellectual systems and critical epistemologies, modern Hinduism made Christianity appear nonrational, intuitive, and idiosyncratic, a religion riddled with inconsistencies and confusing dogmas. To Hindus seeking rational bases in religion, the concept of the Trinity was one of Christianity's most vexing puzzles. The Christian convert Pandita Ramabai's main quarrel with Trinitarianism was that its concepts of God, the Son, and the Holy Spirit dispersed deity in three different figures, and confounded the promise of monotheism that led her to leave Hinduism in the first place. By contrast, Vedāntic Hinduism possessed almost a cold logic that the Hindu elite could proudly display as a sign of their own cultural superiority. Moreover, its severe intellectualism was compatible with the scientific temperament, unlike in the west where religion and science were virtually opposed terms. This was a religion Hindus could be proud of: instead of gaudily decorated stone, theirs was a Hinduism of the mind, that faculty praised by the colonizers as the index of civilization.

On the other hand, the push toward a monotheistic version of Hinduism was intended to contest Christianity on its own ground and win back converts to the Hindu fold by offering the same egalitarian promises as Christianity. The Ārya Samāj, to name one of the most successful of these movements, eliminated many of the cumbersome rituals of Hinduism and loosened caste strictures. It was especially attractive to those who were neither keen on converting to Christianity nor content to remain in a past-oriented Hinduism, out of touch with the compulsions of modernity. Although Hinduism traditionally claimed that, unlike Christianity and Islam, it was not a proselytizing religion and that Hindus were born not made, the Ārya Samāj introduced practices that unsettled those claims. A practice akin to the baptismal rites of conversion, the ritual purificatory act of *śuddhi* initiated non-Hindus to the religion (Seunarine 1977). Though claiming earlier scriptural antecedents, *śuddhi* was intended to help Hindus reclaim converts to Christianity. The ritual is an example of how Hinduism adapted to the new challenges set by colonialism by borrowing some of the very features – such as conversion – that it had earlier repudiated, claiming Hinduism's privileged status on the basis of birth. Reconversion rituals have been a fundamental part of modern Hinduism's attempt to reclaim and sustain its majoritarian status.

Orientalism and reformism thus often went together in the nineteenth-century construction of Hinduism. If the Hinduism approved by Orientalism reflected a European view of natural religion, reform movements were a double reflection of that view. Orientalism and reform enter a dialectic that kept Hinduism bolted within the vise of European perceptions – as if in an interlocking set of infinite mirrors – regardless of whether the intent of Hindu reformers was to break free of them or not. The texts that reformers consulted were often based on translations authorized by western scholars, such as William Jones, Charles Wilkins, Nathaniel Halhed, Henry Colebrooke, and Henry Prinsep. Rarely did reformers turn to oral traditions or local practices for alternative understandings of Hinduism. Rosane Rocher's argument that the privileging of Vedānta by the British and by reform movements within Hinduism was an "accident of intellectual history" fails to account for why reformism was so restricted in its range of textual sources (Rocher 1993). Jadunath Sarkar, a Bengali reformer, reveals how narrow was this range:

> In the nineteenth century we recovered our long lost ancient literatures, Vedic and Buddhistic, as well as the buried architectural monuments of Hindu days. The Vedas and their commentaries had almost totally disappeared from the plains of Aryavarta where none could interpret them; none had even a complete manuscript of the texts. The English printed these ancient scriptures of the Indo-Aryans and brought them to our doors. (Sarkar 1979: 84 in Chakravarty 1998)

The core of Hindu tradition was located in the Vedas and the Upaniṣads, the time of whose composition marked the golden age of India's civilization. The wondrous past unearthed by Orientalist scholars became all the more valuable to the indigenous literati as they faced a present denounced by missionaries and utilitarian reformers alike for its benightedness and social inequalities.

However, drawing upon Orientalist scholarship does not mean that Hindu reformers were passive recipients of knowledge about their glorious past. As Uma Chakravarty points out, the indigenous elite were "active agents in constructing the past and were consciously engaged in choosing particular elements from the embryonic body of knowledge flowing from their own current social and political concerns" (Chakravarty 1998: 32). These concerns interacted with the texts made available by Orientalist scholars through translations and new critical editions, which enabled a reinterpretation of the past as a vital period of Indian history from which a more positive Hinduism could be reconstructed from its now fallen state.

Of particular interest in the return to the golden past was a search for a time when women held a more exalted position than at present or under Muslim rule. Instead of denouncing Hinduism for perpetuating degrading practices like *satī* and infant marriage, as Christian missionaries did, Hindu reformers resolved the problem of seeming to approve a religion they themselves felt some distance from, by claiming that the earlier history of Hinduism showed a much more positive attitude to women. This move consisted of evoking heroic women figures in Hindu narratives, like Savitrī, Gargī, and Maitreyī, whose devotion to their husbands not only earned them the exalted title of *pativrata*, but whose learning, resilience, courage, and assertiveness also made them particularly worthy of general emulation, particularly in a colonial setting where the emasculation of men threatened to rob people of strong role models. Such an exalted view of women in Indian history was in stark contrast to the general portrayal of women as victims, which missionaries were fond of depicting when they alluded to the practices of widow burning, female infanticide, and child marriage. Early Hinduism's capacity to give women a place in society beyond their subordination to men was an underlying refrain in the writings of reformers, who remained dependent on Orientalist presentations of their own texts to them. That these presentations drew upon some of the west's own romantic longings for some essential spiritual unity was not lost on the Hindu elite, whose spiritualization of women, as Partha Chatterjee points out, compensated for their emasculation by colonial control (Chatterjee 1993).

Significantly, the impetus to look for alternative traditions often came from Christian converts who, imbued with a desire to address Hinduism's shortcomings, turned to folk traditions to locate other ways of finding a synthesis of Hinduism and Christianity that could truly be called indigenous. For instance, the Marathi poet Narayan Viman Tilak, who converted to Christianity, was a major Indian nationalist figure who used his conversion as a standpoint from which to offer proposals for a revitalized India. He believed Christianity could help rid Hinduism of its casteist features, yet at the same time he wanted to indigenize Christianity to make it more adaptable to the needs and emotions of the people, as well as to critique the alienating effects of British colonialism. Dissatisfied with Sanskrit texts because they excluded the mass of people, he turned to the older Marathi devotional poetry of Jñāneśvar, Nāmdev, and Tukārām (through whom he claimed he reached Jesus Christ), and sought to adapt the *bhajan* form to Christian hymns (Viswanathan 1998: 40). The result was a unique synthesis of Hindu and Christian cultural forms, largely made possible by mining the folk traditions ignored by Hindu reformers.

Hinduism and Colonial Law

It was in the arena of law that Hinduism received its most definitive colonial reworking. This is one of the most complicated and dense aspects of Britain's involvement with Indian traditions, yet it is also the most far-reaching, as the texts that constituted the basis of legal decisions achieved a canonical power as religious rather than legal texts. This had a great deal to do with the consolidation of patriarchal power over practices involving women, such as *sati*, prepubertal marriage, and conversion to other religions. Each of these had a significant role in the construction of Hinduism. If modern Hinduism's practice is theoretically based on law, it is to that law that one must turn to examine how it was yoked to the interests of both colonizers and the indigenous elite, even as it showed the wide gap between them.

Instead of rehearsing a linear chronology of the laws of India, we would do well to begin with a pivotal act that reveals as much about what preceded it as how it affected (or did not affect) the course of subsequent Indian legal history. The Caste Disabilities Removal Act was passed in 1850, and it was intended to protect converts from disenfranchisement of their rights, including rights to property, maintenance, and guardianship. But its immediate precursor was the Lex Loci Act, which was drafted in 1845 (as the name suggests) to constitute the law of the land, irrespective of individual differences between the various personal, customary, and statutory laws of Hindus and Muslims. The preservation of these laws goes back to Warren Hastings' Judicial Plan of 1772, which provided for the application of different traditional laws for Hindus and Muslims – a decision that, Dieter Conrad argues, was instrumental in introducing a two-nation theory in India: "One has to date from that decision the establishment of personal laws on the plane of state legality in India: laws administered by ordinary courts, yet applying not as the common law of the land on a territorial basis (*lex loci*) but on account of personal status by membership in a social group defined by its religion." Conrad is careful to point out that this was not necessarily a "divide and rule" strategy, but that it was "largely a ratification of existing practices" (Conrad 1995: 306). Even this last statement is only partially correct, as these practices did not have a history that stretched back indefinitely. Indeed, many of them were no more basic to Indian society than the amalgamation of Indian and English law that superseded them. The laws had been carefully developed through translations undertaken by prominent British Orientalist scholars, including William Jones, Nathaniel Halhed, Henry Colebrooke, and William Grady. The application of laws derived from Sanskrit classical texts leveled the community of Hindus to include all those who were not Muslims or Christians, and it absorbed under the category of "Hindu" both outcastes and members of religions as diverse as Buddhism, Jainism, Sikhism, Judaism, and Zorastrianism. Only Islam was considered separate from Hinduism. Christianity suffered a more ambivalent fate. Though there were separate laws for Christians, these depended on what category of Christian one was. British residents, of course, had their own laws; East Indians (Anglo-Indians) too were governed by English law; native Christians claimed English law, but court rulings were inconsistent in this regard, at times deciding that they came under the administration of Hindu law.[9] And finally, from a legal viewpoint, Christian converts were in the most liminal position. One of the paradoxical effects of Christian conversions was a tendency in colonial courts to regard the conversions as not having occurred at all, with the result that Christian converts were still placed as Hindus for purposes of law (Viswanathan 1998: 75–117).

So much has been written about *satī* in recent scholarship that it has come to stand for a pivotal moment in nineteenth-century reform legislation, as well as the culmination of a crisis involving women's subjectivity. Partly because of its sensationalism, and partly because of its romantic representation in both Indian and European texts, *satī* has overshadowed (not always justifiably) other crucial issues involving women, such as education, early marriages, and the effects of conversion. This is not the place to go into the vast literature on *satī*, but several observations are in order for understanding why *satī* has engaged scholarly attention to the extent that it has, and how that attention is now focused on the emergence of Hinduism in its present form. Colonial discourse studies have illuminated the connections between *satī* and the colonial construction of Hinduism in powerful ways. The work of Lata Mani emerges from this approach, though it has been taken to task for attributing too much power to colonial knowledge and not enough to other indigenous sources comprising both textual and oral traditions. Nonetheless, Mani's work is a useful starting point for analyzing the relations of Hinduism and colonial law. Mani's principal argument is that "tradition" is reconstituted under colonial rule and that woman and brahmanic scripture become "interlocking grounds for this rearticulation" (Mani 1998: 90). Drawing from the colonial archive, she shows how women were the ground for defining what constituted authentic cultural tradition. If there was a privileging of brahmanic scripture, and tradition was equated with scripture, Mani suggests that this was the effect of the power of colonial discourse on India, which rewrote woman *as* tradition. Less convincing is Mani's explanation that such representations were forged out of a colonial need for systematic governance. It is more likely that colonial administrators were attempting to find a coherent point in Hindu law on which they could peg certain existing assumptions in British culture about women, tradition, and the domestic sphere, thus achieving a manufactured version of Hinduism suitable for their own purposes.

Considered the bane of Hindu society, child or prepubertal marriages were vehemently opposed by Christian missionaries, who objected on the grounds of both health and morality. Child brides were perceived to be so ill trained in hygiene and well-being that the children they gave birth to were believed to suffer from congenital disorders and not destined to live long. The later a woman married, the longer her children were expected to live. Even Hindu men could not find much to dispute in this argument. However, the issue of morality put them fiercely on the defensive. The right to repudiate an early marriage, especially when there was neither consummation nor formal cohabitation, threatened to destroy the idea of marriage as a sacrament, which none of the male Hindu reformers were willing to do. Nor were they keen to raise the age of consent for females. The infamous Rakhmabai case, involving a woman's right to repudiate a forced marriage, resulted in the woman being returned to her husband. At stake was the sanctity of Hindu marriages: if the verdict had gone in the woman's favor, marriage would been turned from a sacrament to a contract issue, which the Hindu elite resisted fiercely (Chandra 1998).

Finally, colonial conversions reveal the reach of colonial law to fix religious identity, especially in the face of challenges by converts to subvert assigned identities. That the British administration was involved at all was solely due to the fact that missionaries helped in bringing to court the cases of converts denied certain rights upon conversion. Subject to forfeiting their rights to property, conjugality, guardianship and maintenance, converts from Hinduism suffered "civil death," a state of excommunication. Realizing that they could turn their failures in the mission field to good account by becoming legal advocates, Christian missionaries urged the colonial courts to protect the rights of converts on principles dear to English political thought, the right to property being a key one. Of course, the missionaries were primarily interested in removing the obstacles against conversion, since the dreaded prospect of civil death made Hindus more reluctant to convert. But the British judicial decisions reveal a curious feature: while they remained true to form by asserting the right to property by individuals, they did so by denying the subjectivity of converts. That is, the solution to protecting converts' rights was by regarding them as still Hindu under the law. The rationale for this move was the belief that customs and usages (often deferred to in civil suits as a last resort) were slower to change than beliefs. British judges resolved the dilemma of applying English liberal principle that might be offensive to Hindu patriarchy by declaring that converts to Christianity could remain Hindus for purposes of law, especially if their habits and manners remained essentially undifferentiated from so-called Hindu customs. The rationale for this solution was simple: If Christian converts were really Hindus, they could not be treated as civilly dead and their civil rights could not justifiably be revoked under Hindu law. The net result of such judicial rulings was the creation of a homogeneous Hindu community, impervious to the discrepant articulations of individual members claiming fealty to other faiths.

Notes

1 Richard G. Fox's proposal that we distinguish Orientalism between two forms – affirmative and negative – fails to acknowledge that even affirmative Orientalism was deeply embedded in structures of domination. See Fox 1993: 152.

2 Many of the contributors, as well as the editors, of *Representating Hinduism* emphasize Hinduism as a nineteenth-century construct, forged largely as a nationalist response to British colonialism. Of particular interest for this argument are the essays by Friedhelm Hardy and Heinrich von Stietencron.

3 For instance, Gandhi maintained that though he had read *The Bhagavad Gītā* in his native Gujarati, it was only when he read it in an English translation that he was able to make the philosophical connections between such key concepts as *dharma, satyāgraha,* and *ahiṃsā* from which he was then able to develop an activist program of civil resistance (Gandhi 1957: 67–8).

4 It is equally important to note, as Amartya Sen does, that Sanskrit literature has a long history of heterodoxy, yet this tradition of writing does not get as much attention in Western discourses as does a representative "Hindu" text like *The Bhagavad Gītā*. Sen observes that "Sanskrit and Pali have a larger atheistic and agnostic literature than exists in any other classical tradition. . . . Through selective emphases that point up differences with the West, other civilizations can, in this way, be redefined in alien terms, which can be exotic and charming, or else bizarre and terrifying, or simply strange and engaging. When identity is thus defined by contrast, divergence with the West becomes central" (Sen 2000: 36).

5 I use the phrase "pre-Muslim India" with some reservations, even though it is part of von Stietencron's description. As Romila Thapar among other scholars has argued in numerous writings, dividing India into "Hindu India," "Muslim India," "British India" is too neat a formula, since it reintroduces James Mill's language (as present in his *History of British India*) of considering Indian history within this tripartite division. Such a historiography, Thapar argues, has been instrumental in fueling the passions of Hindu nationalists to recover a Hinduism compromised or threatened by Islamic conversions and the destruction of Hindu temples.

6 Von Stietencron observes that Hinduism in pre-Muslim India did not have all-India religious bodies invested with the power to authorize official religious interpretations, and hence heterodox readings could not be banned entirely (von Stietencron 1989: 71).

7 James Nelson, *A View of the Hindu Law as Administered by the High Court of Judicature at Madras* (1877). Nelson noted that the usages and customs of inhabitants of his district in Madurai were altogether different from the practices associated with Hindus and that were "judicially recognized" by the High Court of Judicature at Madras. He concluded from this observation that, far from being Hindu in faith and thought, Tamil people "believe, think, and act in modes entirely opposed to and incompatible with real, modern Hinduism" (p. ii). Lashing out at the "grotesque absurdity" of applying the strictest Sanskrit law to tribals, Nelson argued that no such thing as Hindu law ever existed. The artifact of Sanskritists, Hindu law came into being as a result of the ignorance of the actual history and circumstances of the vast majority of social groups in India, maintained Nelson, one of the few voices in the British judicial administration who dared to take this position.

8 Macaulay's infamous "Minute on Indian Education" is partly inspired by his outrage at the British government's subsidies to indigenous schools, which taught what he described as wildly extravagant fairy tales masquerading as religious truth. His plea for the study of English literature was the culmination of a long argument that originated in an Orientalist policy encouraging indigenous learning. See "Minute on Indian Education," in G. M. Young, ed., *Macaulay: Prose and Poetry* (Cambridge, MA: Harvard University Press, 1957).

9 *Abraham v. Abraham* was one of the most prominent cases involving East Indians. In this case a widow of a native Indian Christian contested her brother-in-law's claim that, as native Christians who were formerly Hindus, even several generations ago, Hindu law was applicable in cases of joint property and coparcenerships. The widow protested that as Christians they were governed by English law. The ruling went in the brother-in-law's favor.

References

Asad, Talal. 1993. *Genealogies of Religion: Discipline and Reasons of Power in Christianity and Islam*. Baltimore: Johns Hopkins University Press.

Chakrabarty, Dipesh. 2000. *Provincializing Europe: Postcolonial Thought and Historical Difference*. Princeton: Princeton University Press.

Chakravarty, Uma. 1998. *Rewriting History: The Life and Times of Pandita Ramabai*. New Delhi: Kali for Women.

Chandra, Sudhir. 1998. *Enslaved Daughters: Colonialism, Law, and Women's Rights*. Delhi: Oxford University Press.

Chatterjee, Partha. 1993. *The Nation and Its Fragments*. Princeton: Princeton University Press.

Conrad, D. 1995: "The Personal Law Question and Hindu Nationalism," in V. Dalmia and H. von Stietencron, eds., *Representing Hinduism: The Construction of Religious Traditions and National Identity*. New Delhi, Thousand Oaks, London: Sage, pp. 306–37.

Copley, Antony. 1997. *Religions in Conflict: Ideology, Cultural Contact and Conversion in Late Colonial India*. Delhi: Oxford University Press.

Embree, Ainslie T., ed. 1971. *Al-Biruni's India*. New York: W. W. Norton.

Forster, E. M. 1953. *The Hill of Devi and Other Indian Writings*. London: Edward Arnold.

——. 1970 (1st ed. 1924). *A Passage to India*. Harmondsworth: Penguin.

Fox, Richard G. 1993 "East of Said," in M. Sprinker, ed., *Edward Said: A Critical Reader*. Oxford: Blackwell.

Frykenberg, Robert E. 1989. "The Emergence of Modern 'Hinduism' as a Concept and as an Institution: A Reappraisal with Special Reference to South India," in Gunther D. Sontheimer and Hermann Kulke, eds., *Hinduism Reconsidered.* Delhi: Manohar.

Gandhi, M. K. 1957 (1st ed. 1929). *My Experiments with Truth: An Autobiography.* Boston: Beacon Press.

Ghosh, Amitav. 1992. *In an Antique Land.* New York: Knopf.

Gilmartin, David. 1988. *Empire and Islam: Punjab and the Making of Pakistan.* Berkeley: University of California Press.

Hansen, Thomas Blom. 1999. *The Saffron Wave: Democracy and Hindu Nationalism in Modern India.* Princeton: Princeton University Press.

Hardy, F. 1995. "A Radical Assessment of the Vedic Heritage – The *Ácaryahrdayam* and Its Wider Implications," in Vasudha Dalmia and Heinrich von Stietencron, eds., *Representing Hinduism: The Construction of Religious Traditions and National Identity.* Delhi: Sage.

Hefner, Robert, ed. 1993. *Conversion to Christianity: Historical and Anthropological Perspectives on a Great Transformation.* Berkeley: University of California Press.

Jaffrelot, C. 1996. *The Hindu Nationalist Movement.* New York: Columbia University Press.

King, Richard. 1999. *Orientalism and Religion: Postcolonial Theory, India, and "The Mystic East."* London: Routledge.

Kosambi, Meera, ed. 1999. *Ramabai in Her Own Words.* Delhi: Oxford University Press.

Lelyveld, David. 1978. *Aligarh's First Generation: Muslim Solidarity in British India.* Princeton: Princeton University Press.

Mani, Lata. 1998. *Contentious Traditions: The Debate on Sati in Colonial India.* Berkeley and Los Angeles: University of California Press.

Metcalf, Barbara D. 1982. *Islamic Revival in British India: Deoband, 1860–1900.* Princeton: Princeton University Press.

Mill, James. 1858. *The History of British India.* London: Piper, Stephinson and Spece.

Nandy, Ashish. 1993. "The Politics of Secularism and the Recovery of Religious Tolerance," in Veena Das, ed., *Mirrors of Violence.* Delhi: Oxford University Press.

Nelson, James. 1877. *A View of the Hindu Law as Administered by the High Court of Judicature at Madras.* Madras: Higginbotham.

Rocher, Rosane. 1993. "British Orientalism in the Eighteenth Century: The Dialectics of Knowledge and Government," in Carol Breckenridge and Peter van der Veer, eds., Orientalism and the Postcolonial Predicament. Philadelphia: University of Pennsylvania Press.

Sangari, Kumkum and Sudesh Vaid, eds. 1998. *Recasting Women: Essays in Colonial History.* Delhi: Kali for Women.

Sarkar, Jadunath. 1979 (1st ed. 1928). *India through the Ages.* Calcutta: Orient Longman.

Satthianadhan, Krupabai. 1998a. *Saguna.* Delhi: Oxford University Press.

——. 1998b. *Kamala: The Story of a Hindu Life.* Delhi: Oxford University Press.

Sen, Amartya. 2000. "Reason in East and West," *New York Review of Books* 47 (12), July 20.

Seunarine, J. F. 1977. *Reconversion to Hinduism through Śuddhi.* Madras: Christian Literature Society.

Sinha, M. 1995. *Colonial Masculinity.* Manchester: Manchester University Press.

Stietencron, Heinrich von. 1989. "Hinduism: On the Proper Use of a Deceptive Term," in Gunther D. Sontheimer and Hermann Kulke, eds., *Hinduism Reconsidered.* Delhi: Manohar.

Viswanathan, Gauri. 1989. *Masks of Conquest: Literary Study and British Rule in India.* New York: Columbia University Press.

——. 1995 "Beyond Orientalism: Syncretism and the Politics of Knowledge," *Stanford Humanities Review* 5 (1): 19–34.

——. 1998. *Outside the Fold: Conversion, Modernity, and Belief.* Princeton: Princeton University Press.

Young, G. M., ed. 1957. "Minute on Indian Education," in *Macaulay: Poetry and Prose.* Cambridge, MA: Harvard University Press.

Young, Richard Fox. 1981. *Resistant Hinduism: Sanskrit Sources on Anti-Christian Apologetics in Early Nineteenth-century India.* Vienna: De Nobili Research Library.

CHAPTER 2

Orientalism and Hinduism

David Smith

"The horror, the horror." These words transposed by Coppola from Conrad's *Heart of Darkness* (1899) sum up in *Apocalypse Now* (1979) both the American war against Vietnam and Oriental religion. In Coppola's film the US soldiers in Cambodia confronted by the ruins of Angkor exclaim at their strangeness, at the giant heads of the Bodhisattva-Śivas entwined with the roots of the all-swallowing jungle. Amid the ruins, the boat rounds a bend in the river to discover a motley array of native soldiers, accompanied by a profusion of hanging corpses. The lost colonel Kurtz – like Conrad's Kurtz – has gone mad and is killing wildly deep in the jungle. He, then, is horrifying to those who are searching for him. But Kurtz has a little shelf of books in his womb-like center of the temple complex, where a statue of the Buddha sits beside him, a shelf that bears the *Golden Bough* and Jessie Weston's *The Quest for the Holy Grail*. The mad colonel, once an "outstanding officer," is not only waging a private war, but is also a solitary student of Religious Studies. He has been overwhelmed by what he sees as the obscenity, the horror of America's war machine, but is driven to rival it, his chamber containing what seems to be a large wall panel of Kālī. The venturing hero of the film slays this wicked colonel with the sacrificial axe from a buffalo sacrifice just about to take place. The film in its released version ends with the wicked American bombers raining destruction on the wickedness of the mad colonel. There is a bizarre diversion here of the American bombing from its perceived exterior foe to Kurtz, its inner self. Perhaps the most startling contrast between the film and Conrad's novel is between the massive fire power of the Americans and the impotence of the French gunboat blindly shelling the jungle shoreline – but the Americans were no less impotent in the end. In Coppola's film we have modernity gone mad, no less mad than the film's version of eastern religion!

A year before Coppola's film a book was published that has proved to be an extraordinarily successful counterblast to the imperialism and colonialism implicit in modernity – Edward Said's *Orientalism*. Once the study of "oriental" or near eastern and Asian languages and literatures, orientalism is now taken to mean the western domination and exploitation of the east, the west viewing the east as alien, as "the other." All study of Hinduism in the west is taken to be an instance of Orientalism in the new sense. It was the literary critic Said, a Palestinian Christian, who brought about this revolution. His first book a study of Joseph Conrad, in *Orientalism* Said introduced and popularized the ideas of Foucault. Although partly inspired by Raymond Schwab's *La Renaissance Orientale* (1950), which makes India the centerpiece of an expected cultural rebirth of Europe through the study of the Orient, Sanskrit performing the role of Greek in the first Renaissance, Said is principally concerned with the Arab world and its treatment by the west. European novels remain his primary area of expertise, and not for a moment does he take on-board Schwab's thesis that the East has influenced the West. Said makes use of Foucault's notion of discourse, of a manner of thinking that is adopted willy-nilly by a generation or more of writers, while at the same time having as his preferred procedure the literary analysis of individual works of literature. The two methods sit ill together: "Said denounces with Foucaultian vitriol what he loves with Auerbachian passion" (Ahmad 1992: 168). Nevertheless, following Foucault, Said suggests that the effect of Orientalist discourse is "to formulate the Orient, to give it shape, identity, definition with full recognition of its place in memory, its importance to imperial strategy, and its 'natural' role as an appendage to Europe" (Said 1978: 86).

A significant and malign maneuver on Said's part is to extend the term Orientalist from students of Oriental languages to all those who deal with the Orient, whether or not they use texts in the original languages. His final option for the meaning of Orientalism of course turns it on its head; as taken up by the sociologist Bryan Turner, Orientalism means ignorance of the Orient: "From the seventeenth century onwards, orientalism had constituted a profound sense of otherness with respect to alien cultures"(Turner 1994: 183). This perverse sleight-of-hand magics away into thin air the editions, translations, and dictionaries of the true and original Orientalists who devoted their lives to understanding the meaning of instances of Oriental culture and civilization. In the words of Gyan Prakash, "The towering . . . images of men like William ('Oriental') Jones have cracked and come tumbling down" (Prakash 1995: 200).

So well established is Said that Joan-Pau Rubies, a young scholar, recently wrote that " 'Orientalism' has traditionally been defined as a western imperialist attitude in which the colonized subjects are perceived according to purely western ideological concerns" (Rubies 2002: 287). Said's brilliant success has swept away all that preceded it, and his redefinition of Orientalism has become "traditional"! The choice of the term Orientalism is unfortunate on several counts. In the first place, why limit it to the west? As Rubies remarks, "If we define orientalism as a manipulative historical gaze based on a crude separation between us and *other*, and which denies the representation of this *other* any intrinsic voice, then there was very little in the Muslim discourse about Hindu

India which was less orientalist than what contemporary Europeans perceived and wrote" (Rubies 2002: 286). Then again, within Hinduism, Brahmans might be said to have an Orientalist attitude to the lower castes. Original Orientalism was precisely the attempt to understand the Oriental Other. This attempt was not completely successful, but it was all the attempt at understanding there was. Orientalism can be faulted for undue concentration on classical texts, but this was only mirroring the crucial role of study of ancient Greek and Latin, the Ancients, in the intellectual life of the west.

First and foremost a literary critic, turning again and again in his *Orientalism* to the modern European novel as his favorite medium and source, Said sweepingly dismisses Orientalists in the strict sense in exactly the same way as he says that the west dismisses the east, as inferior others. Said has not altogether unfairly been dismissed as "a literary critic rummaging through history to find scraps of evidence to support his personal and political purposes" (Kopf 1991: 21) by Kopf, author of a pioneering historical study of British Orientalism in India (Kopf 1969).

Said's work is continued with reference to India by the anthropologist turned historian-Sanskritist, Ronald Inden, in his *Imagining India* (1992), a book whose success has been scarcely less than that of Said's. Indeed, its intellectual basis is perhaps stronger than that of *Orientalism*; Inden's thesis is that Orientalists have deprived Indians of "agency" "by imagining an India kept eternally ancient by various Essences attributed to it, most notably that of caste." Inden contends that Indologists present the texts they study as "distorted portrayals of reality," as "manifestations of an 'alien' mentality" (1992: 1, 39).

Early in the book he gives as an example of some remarks on Vedic ritual by Louis Renou (1896–1966), the great French Sanskritist. These remarks are taken from Renou's masterly survey of the main problems in the study of Indian religion, as he saw them in 1950. Renou says in the quoted passage that Vedic ritual is overburdened with system, that there was "an advancing scholasticism" (1992: 39). Two paragraphs later in Renou's text, the following sentences are quoted by Inden: "Ritual has a strong attraction for the Indian mind, which tends to see everything in terms of the formulae and methods of procedure, even when such adjuncts no longer seem really necessary for its religious experience" (1992: 39). Inden believes that this is to transform "the thoughts and actions of ancient Indians into a distortion of reality." Renou might have shown that the Vedic priests "were part of a coherent and rational whole" based on different presuppositions than his own; but Renou, like many Indologists, holds that there is a single external reality to which Western science has privileged access. Implicit in the text of Renou and other Indologists, is the "metaphor of the Other as a dreamer, as a . . . mad man." Like Freud on dreams, Indologists attribute condensation and displacement to the Indian mind. For Renou, says Inden, "the priestly mind takes up rituals which are not meant to be enacted while the priestly hand performs rituals that have no religious rationale." "Renou, we have seen [!], attributed the same dreaming irrationality to the Indian mind that Hegel did" (1992: 42).

Inden's polemic leads him to distort Renou's statements. When Renou speaks of the Indian mind, he means the Indian mind as expressed in Vedic texts, a continuous and highly specific tradition to which certain general characteristics might fairly be attributed. Renou goes on to say that there is a tendency in the ritual texts to build up complex structures from simpler elements, that they are sometimes intellectual exercises – "we must not regard them as consisting entirely of accounts of actual religious practice" (Renou 1968: 30). Renou's account of Vedism to my mind is sympathetic and luminous. As Renou says, "Of religious feeling and community life in the Vedic period we can know virtually nothing" (Renou 1968: 44). But he gives us a description of a present-day performance of a Vedic sacrifice, ending with the following comment on ancient times: "In those distant days India had a feeling for liturgy comparable to that of the Roman Church" (Renou 1968: 35). We might also note Renou's remark that "the prose-style of the *Śatapatha* [the largest of the sacrificial texts] is a model of skilful articulation, and in its severe purity reminds us of Plato" (Renou 1968: 45). In another essay on Vedic studies Renou notes that "Indian scholars have come relatively late to these studies. It may be that an excess of attachment (very respectable in itself) to the tradition has prevented them from considering the Veda with eyes sufficiently objective, with the same 'indifference' with which a naturalist studies a plant" (Renou 1950: 46).[1]

Not only did Renou devote his life to the objective study of Sanskrit and the Veda, more than most Sanskritists he took the large view, giving an accurate account of the whole scope of classical Indian civilization in the two volumes of *L'Inde Classique* which he edited with Jean Filliozat, writing much of it himself. To say that Renou attributed "dreaming irrationality" to the Indian mind is false. As his pupil Malamoud wrote in the preface to a posthumous collection of Renou's essays, *L'Inde Fondamentale*, Renou described an India that was rigorous and cheerful, animated by a powerful ardor for speculation, directed to the intrepid analysis of language rather than to rumination on the ineffable (Malamoud 1978: 1).

Renou had no conceivable imperial designs on India. Nor did Georg Bühler (1837–98), the Sanskritist's Sanskritist of the second half of the nineteenth century, who worked for the Raj's Bombay Presidency. This Austrian scholar had the reputation of having read everything extant in Sanskrit; and conceived and edited the *Encyclopedia of Indo-Aryan Research*, contributed to by Indologists from all over the world. Renou and Bühler are prime examples of the mastery sought by all scholars, the lordship of understanding that is as complete as possible. British Orientalists had the same ambitions, of understanding through firsthand knowledge. Mill and Hegel, on the other hand, claimed universal dominion for their ideas without any firsthand knowledge of India or Indian languages – this is the difference between scholars and philosophers.

On the other hand, it is certainly true that the understanding of many Sanskritists was limited to their particular texts, and that some had little or no sympathy for modern India. Thus for Garbe, who visited India in 1885/6, the worship of the common Hindu was a worthless fetishism, and he confessed to the anger of a Hebrew prophet, wanting to whip the Hindus, especially the priests, from the stinking lairs that were their temples (Garbe 1925: 56). But it behooves us to remember how far away India was from the west before airplanes – both Garbe and Deussen give a careful account of the ships in which they voyage to India. Very little was known about how Hindus lived and thought. There is nothing to be gained by reduplicating Garbe's moral indignation and heaping it back on him, for he lived on a different planet; and he had a very good understanding of Samkhyan and other texts.

Said's reversal of the meaning of the word Orientalism has been so successful because there was a need for a word for western misunderstanding and mistreatment of the East, but his choice was unfortunate. No one has offered any evidence that Indological Orientalist learning, in the strict old sense of linguistic and textual study, served imperial ends. Those concerned with conquest and exploitation, with practical affairs, had no time and little sympathy for such studies.[2] Warren Hastings was the exception here, but he had a great love of all things Indian. It was he who set Orientalism – in its old and original meaning – in train in India. He found Hinduism scarcely less attractive than Christianity.[3] He spoke of himself as well as others when he told the man he was sending to explore Tibet, "there were 'thousands of men in England' who would listen to the story of an expedition 'in search of knowledge', with 'ten times' the interest they would take in 'victories that slaughtered thousands of the national enemies'" (Feiling 1996: 105). Nor does colonial discourse theory make allowance for the kind of love of learning that led Anquetil-Duperron to enlist as a soldier so that he could get to India and study Old Persian and Sanskrit (Anquetil-Duperron [1771] 1997: 75–7). Indeed, Said speaks of "the madness of Anquetil-Duperron's life" (Said 1984: 252).

Not only does Inden without a shred of justification accuse Renou of attributing "the same dreaming irrationality to the Indian mind that Hegel did," he makes the astonishing claim that the writings of James Mill (*The History of British India*) and Hegel were hegemonic texts for Indology (Inden 1992: 4). As Trautman says, "neither Mill nor Hegel learned an Indian language or set foot in India" and "they used their secondhand knowledge to fashion arguments *against* the authority of the Orientalists and the enthusiasm for India with which it was associated" (Trautman 1997: 23). Numerous writers today claim that Mill was studied at Haileybury, the East India Company's college in England, but a rare published account of life there makes no mention of the *History of British India*. John Beames, an Indian civil servant whose love of learning led him to write a Comparative Grammar of Indo-Aryan languages, describes his time at Haileybury learning languages, but nothing whatever about life in India, not even what Mill has to say.

> [I]t was considered "bad form" to talk about India or to allude to the fact that we were all going there soon. Even the study of Oriental languages, which was the chief feature of the place, and in fact the reason for its existence, was carried on as though we had no personal interest in the countries in which those languages

> were spoken, and no attempt was made to practise talking them or to acquire any practical familiarity with them. If at any time one wanted to know what sort of place India was, or what one's future life or work there was to be like, it was impossible to find anyone who could give the requisite information. (Beames 1996: 64)

The indifference to India on the part of Beames and his fellow students seems to be innocent of any knowledge of the *History* of James Mill.

Oriental Despotism

Coppola transposes the Horror from the African jungle with its cannibals and fences topped with skulls to the jungle of Cambodia, where the giant heads of the divine kings of Angkor loom out of the vegetation. Angkor, "The City," from the Sanskrit *nagara* ("city"), was on the eastern edge of the huge spread of Sanskritic culture. Sanskrit was "the paramount linguistic medium by which ruling elites expressed their power from Purusapura (Peshawar) in Gandhara in the northwest of the subcontinent to as far east as Panduranga in Annam (south Vietnam) and Prambanam in central Java" (Pollock 1996: 198). In describing the formation of what he calls the Sanskrit Cosmopolis, Pollock refers to the "efforts of small groups of traders, adventurers, religious professionals. There is no evidence that large-scale state initiatives were ever at issue, or that anything remotely resembling 'colonization' took place" (Pollock 1996: 241).

Yet, however Sanskritic religious culture spread to southeast Asia, the huge temple-palaces in Cambodia are patent manifestation of royalty's will to power. An important early instance of Said's version of Orientalism is the European notion of Oriental Despotism, a category that allows the west to dismiss eastern political concerns as inherently inferior. The notion goes back to Aristotle: "Asians are more servile by nature . . . hence they endure despotic rule without protest" (Aristotle, *Politics* III, ix, 3 cited in Anderson 1974: 463). Francois Bernier (1620–88), *philosophe* and traveler, is here a key figure, for his account of the despotism of the Mughals was taken up by Montesquieu and Marx, to name only two. In fact, as Murr suggests, Bernier's account of India under Aurangzib and his predecessors reflects his fear that the absolutism of Louis XIV might degenerate into tyranny. He studiously resists using the term despot, and presents Aurangzib as by no means a barbarian, but as a great king worthy of comparison with European kings (Murr 1991). The Mughal emperors differed from European kings in that the most powerful son rather than the first-born became the successor; and in parallel with this lack of regularly rewarded primogeniture there was no landed aristocracy as independent counterweight to the sovereign, since nobles were salaried and liable to dismissal if their performance was not satisfactory. Oriental Despotism becomes a key concept in pro-imperialist interpretations of ancient Indian politics and society. Anquetil-Duperron was the first European to argue against the notion that there was no ownership of land in India, though his motive was primarily antipathy to the British. It is interesting to note a lack of such anti-British animus in the most important Enlightenment work on colonialism, Raynal's *Philosophical and Political History of the Two Indies* (first published 1760), no less a contributory factor to the French Revolution than Rousseau, now scarcely known. For Raynal England is one among four powers in contemporary south India, no more out of place than the Marathas, Tipu Sultan, and the Nizam of Hyderbad (Raynal 1820, vol 3: 187). All four powers were conquering outside their own territories. But the notion of Oriental Despotism is an instance where Said's critique is fully justified. So too the notion of the unchanging Indian village, dealt with by Inden. But in these, and many other cases, the mistaken interpretation arises from ignorance, from lack of sources of information.

Orientalism and Empire

Today the British Empire is widely seen as a blot on the history of the world. Assessment of British rule in India is difficult. Postcolonialism has produced a vast amount of literary criticism predicated on the cruelty and injustice of the Raj; Vinay Lal declares that getting to grips with the products of this industry leaves no time for old-fashioned history – even "the quest for objectivity" in assessing the British Empire is "morally dubious." A balanced judgment relevant in the present context is that of Nirad C. Chaudhuri, even if Lal dismisses him as "an indefatigable Anglophile" (Lal 1997: 100). Describing the 1920s, Chaudhuri's empathy with Englishness – though he disliked the few Englishmen he met while under the Raj – does come out in his not unfavorable summary of early British imperialism as "a mixture of humanitarianism, Evangelism, Utilitarianism, and Liberalism." But Chaudhuri continues:

> That old imperialism had been replaced by the end of the nineteenth century by a wholly shoddy theory, which was nothing better than boastful verbiage. By 1920, even that had been discredited, and the Empire in India survived only as a practical reality supported by vested interests. (Chaudhuri 1988: 775)

Tapan Raychaudhuri in his important assessment of British rule in India remarks that "In post-independence India, serious thinkers and historians who see anything good in the imperial record can probably be counted on the fingers of one hand" (Raychaudhuri 1996: 358); nor is he one of their number.

There can be no doubt that the British, with a few exceptions, had no sympathy for Indian culture or religion, least of all sympathy for Hindus and Hinduism. But that is all the more reason to give due allowance to the exceptions. Kejariwal shows commendable boldness in blaming Indian nationalism for not giving credit to the early British Orientalists: "Indian historians were more than eager to accept the glory of India's past as revealed by British historians, but the historians themselves were rejected as biased and motivated" (Kejariwal 1988: 233).

The British Empire should not be considered in isolation from other empires. Not only is the British Raj to be set beside the Turkish, Persian, Roman, and other Empires, we must also note Chaudhuri's assertion of Hindu imperialism:

> I had better confess that all Hindus are traditionally imperialists, and they condemned imperialism only in so far as British imperialism made them subjects to an empire instead of its masters. This is due to the fact that the strongest political passion of the ancient Hindus was directed towards conquest and domination. All Sanskrit literature and all the historical inscriptions are full of glorification of both. This aspiration to conquer and dominate was suppressed during Muslim and British rule, but today, even if not given practical expression, it conditions the attitude of the present Hindu ruling class towards the neighbours of India. (Chaudhuri 1988: 774)

Har Bilas Sarda's *Hindu Superiority* (1906) invents an account of Hindu colonization of the world (Jaffrelot 1997: 331). R. C. Majumdar's history of India, widely used in schools and colleges in India, sees the spread of Hinduism and Buddhism in southeast Asia as the result of colonization by the Indian master race. Pollock claims that the source of such thinking is European (Pollock 1996: 233). True, but the goal of the traditional Hindu king was universal empire. Pollock concedes that domination did not enter India with European colonialism and that "gross asymmetries of power . . . appear to have characterized India in particular times and places over the last three millennia and have formed the background against which ideological power, intellectual and spiritual resistance, and many forms of physical and psychological violence crystallized" (Pollock 1993: 115) "Sanskrit was the principal discursive instrument of domination in premodern India and . . . it has been continuously reappropriated in modern India by many of the most reactionary and communalist sectors of the population" (Pollock 1993: 116). Inden's *Imagining India* seeks to refute the "Orientalist" account (in Said's sense) of India which Inden says deprives Hindus of agency by defining Hinduism in terms of essence, caste, and spirituality. Yet his refutation of the supposed colonialism and imperialism of his predecessors in the field of Indology proceeds by setting against them the medieval imperialism of Hinduism – universal empire was always the theoretical goal of Hindu kings.

Orientalism and Racial Theories

Various views on the origin and types of mankind were current in seventeenth-century Europe, including the theory of Pre-adamite man, but "racial theory has as its official birthdate 24 April 1664" (Toth 1988: 23), when Bernier published in the *Journal des Scavans* a new division of the earth according to the different races that occupy it. He did not sign his paper because of intense theological opposition to the theory of Pre-adamite man published by his friend La Peyrère nine years earlier. Bernier's conception was biological and based on heredity. Bernier distinguishes four or five "species"; we need only note that he considered Europeans and a good part of Asia (including the States of the Great Mogol, the Kingdom of Golconda, and that of Bijapur) to be of the same race. He made no other mention of India. Amongst the peoples with whom he is well acquainted, Bernier makes no hierarchical distinction.

The worst and most dangerous aspect of the British empire was its racism. As Veer notes, "Racial difference between the British and the colonized and among the colonized themselves became the explanation and legitimation of colonial rule" (Veer 2001: 49). The British thought that they proved their superiority to Indians by conquering and holding India with a remarkably small number of men. They achieved this by convincing themselves of their invincibility and persuading many Indians that they were inferior to the British in respect of ability to rule and wage war; though bribery was often more useful than bravery. The matchless self-confidence of the British produced the inverse effect on those who beheld it. The British rulers kidded themselves and kidded the Indians, but it might well be argued that the confidence trick took its inspiration from India, from the caste system. It was Brahmans who did the trick first, claiming to be the mouth of God, Gods among men, the twice born. The British civil servants took over for themselves the very term "twice born." Brahmans did not eat with non-Brahmans; the British rulers would not eat, drink, or mix with Indians. The Brahmans were essentially different from the other castes, for all castes were essentially different from each other. Well and good, the British rulers would be essentially different from the Indians, just as they were from their own lower classes back in England.

The British caste maintained its mindset all the better by having nothing to do with Hinduism. Their rejigging of the Hindu legal system and their censuses sharpened up notions of caste, but they hid from themselves the caste nature of the imagined essential inner power that enabled them to rule successfully, and they hid this from themselves by having as little as possible to do with Hinduism. In some sense it was their ignorance of Hinduism that enabled the British to rule for so long. When Nietzsche's friend, Paul Deussen, the German Vedānta scholar, traveling by train in India in 1893 rejoiced in friendly relations with Hindus, the cold and unfriendly Englishman in the same compartment remarked, "We have to rule these people" (Deussen [1904] 1995).

Many of the statistics of British imperial presence in India are striking, as for instance that "In one district of Lower Bengal, 20 Britons lived among 2.5 million natives. As late as 1939, about 28 million Punjabis – people not renowned for their docility – were governed by 60 British civil servants." However, the size of the army – "65,000 white soldiers in an area populated by 300 million people that now includes not only India but Pakistan, Bangladesh, and Burma" (Gilmour 1997: 35) – was not puny, given modern weapons and transport. For the civil and military officer cadres English public schools produced "a courage caste with its ambitions turned from gain or learning towards an ideal of rule" (Geddes 1962: 95). The British civil servant, incredible as it seems now, believed that he was infallible and invulnerable in dealing with Indians. The army was there in the background, but many Indians had never seen British soldiers. As Walter Lawrence put it in the 1920s, British power in India was based on "mutual make-believe": "They, the millions, made us believe we had a divine mission. We made them believe that they were right" (Lawrence 1928: 42–3). It rested on mutual collusion, on illusion.

But this dominance came to be explained by race. Risley (1851–1911), Commissioner for the 1901 Census of India, tried to show that caste had its origins in the interactions of the Aryan and Dravidian races: the caste system had its basis in community of race rather than community of function. He takes as starting point in his *People of India* (1915) a carved panel from the Buddhist stupa at Sanchi (100 BC to 100AD) which shows a monkey offering honey to the Buddha.[4] Tutelary spirits, *yakṣas*, look on. The Buddha was not shown in person in this early phase of Buddhist art – his presence is signified by the empty dais beneath a sala tree. Risley bizarrely misreads this compassionate representation of spiritual community as an "expression of the race sentiment of the Aryans towards the Dravidians," showing us "the higher race on friendly terms with the lower, but keenly conscious of the essential difference of type and taking no active part in the ceremony at which they appear as sympathetic but patronizing spectators" (Risley 1915: 5). Through ignorance of the basic conventions of Buddhist art, Risley sees only a primitive ritual devoid of point carried out by a subhuman no better than a monkey. He sees the demi-god *yakṣas* as Aryans, and the monkey as a Dravidian!

In trying to understand caste as race, imperial officials were not setting India aside as a separate ethnographic park, as the Other that is the unavoidable trope of colonial discourse analysis. Such racial analysis was to be applied everywhere. As Susan Bayly has pointed out, their work for them was pathbreaking science (S. Bayly 1997: 167). It was neither oldstyle Orientalism nor new Orientalism. It was for them an application and instance of universal reason, even though today it seems false and absurd.

Cannadine argues that the British Empire was not really concerned with the creation of "otherness": society on the imperial periphery was the same or even superior to society in the imperial metropolis; "for the British, their overseas realms were at least as much about sameness as they were about difference" (Cannadine 2001: 4). British colonialism exacerbated caste, made it a system, but British interest in caste was by no means merely knowledge as power over its object, for it arose from a sense of similarity, of fellow feeling. For many Britons, says Cannadine, "the social arrangements in South Asia seemed easily recognizable and comfortingly familiar" (2001: 16). The rigid hierarchy of the British in British India has often been remarked on. "British India was as much infected by caste as Indian India" (Mason 1978: 80).

Cannadine's revisionism, salutary as it is, must not prevent us from examining the role of racial theory in understanding western and eastern confrontation. The supposition of racial characteristics and stereotypes, beyond the natural tendency of all peoples to believe themselves and their ways the best, has one supremely bad quality. This is ranking, forming a hierarchy, asserting superiority and inferiority. Without going into the question of what is race and what is caste, the clearest model of such ranking of peoples is the caste system, where birth determines value and status. It is striking how the notion of caste comes to permeate English discourse in the nineteenth century, to the point that Marx, for example, worries about his daughters losing caste through not being able to return hospitality (letter to Engels 1867 in Wheen 2000: 298). Doubtless the notion of caste resonated with aspects of the class system in Britain, but the implacable and powerful presence of caste in India, it may be argued, had a profound effect on the British. This effect was much greater once Muslim power was crushed, and the British had ever more consequential dealings with Hindus, whose quite different patterns of hospitality became increasingly significant. It is surely likely that British exclusivity mirrored the pre-existing caste exclusivity of the Brahmans. Cannadine finds similarity between British and Indian society, but the radical change from Georgian to Victorian society marches in parallel with the British discovery of caste. The separation of human levels in the Victorian country house, for instance, where "it was considered undesirable for children, servants and parents to see, smell or hear each other except at certain recognized times and places" (Girouard 1979: 28) parallels the newly discovered social distinctions of the caste system in India.

A term used tirelessly from the appearance of *Orientalism* is "the Other." Its origins go back to Hegel, and Jacques Lacan made much of it. In the context of the Orient, it has been grossly overworked. MacKenzie makes the important point that in the eighteenth and early nineteenth centuries Britain's principal "other" was France; and in the century and a half that followed, France, Russia, Germany and the Soviet Union (MacKenzie 1994: 16). Risley's misinterpretation of the monkey in the Sanchi sculpture referred to above is perhaps less obnoxious when we remember the story that during the Napoleonic wars Hartlepool fishermen hanged a shipwrecked monkey because they took it for a Frenchman. The rudimentary logic of self and other has today led to an exaggerated idea of the importance of the East for nineteenth-century Europe. Bayly points out that "Indological debates were almost always occidental debates as well; Orientalism was as much a representation of the Contested Self as it was of the Other." Many of the offensive characterizations of Hindus made by Englishmen "are indistinguishable from what contemporaries were saying about those addicted to the Demon Drink, the working class, the Irish, Roman Catholics in general, or indeed about women" (C. A. Bayly 1990: 1313).

Orientalism and the Female

It is fascinating to note how the contemporary decline of philology, of the study of foreign literatures in their original languages, has been accompanied by the use of philological terms such as grammar, syntax, and poetics in sociological discourse. Vinay Lal declares that "the trope of effeminacy, the first element of an Orientalist grammar of India, had a particular place in colonial discourse." Lal refers to Robert Orme's essay on "The Effeminacy of the Inhabitants of Hindustan" (1782), summed up in the confident assertion that "very few of the inhabitants" of India were "endowed with the nervous strength, or athletic size, of the robustest nations of Europe" (Lal 1996).

Most frequently cited on this subject are Macaulay's words:

> The physical organisation of the Bengalee is feeble even to effeminacy. He lives in a constant vapour bath. His pursuits are sedentary, his limbs delicate, his movements languid. During many ages he has been trampled upon by men of bolder and more hardy breeds. Courage, independence, veracity, are qualities to which his constitution and his situation are equally unfavourable. (Macaulay [1841] 1895: 611)

Few bother with the context, his characterization of Warren Hastings' implacable foe, the Maharajah Nand Kumar, whose composure and serenity in death Macaulay honors. Nand Kumar "prepared himself to die with that quiet fortitude with which the Bengalee, so effeminately timid in personal conflict, often encounters calamities for which there is no remedy." Of the Bengali in general Macaulay adds,

> Nor does he lack a certain kind of courage which is often wanting to his masters. To inevitable evils he is sometimes found to oppose a passive fortitude, such as the Stoics attributed to their ideal sage.

This is not slight praise from a devoted classicist. But otherwise Macaulay was merely expressing with his incomparable trenchancy the general view of European travelers. For instance, Bernier's compatriot, the jewel merchant Tavernier, noting that for one Muslim there are five or six Hindus, finds it astonishing "to see how this enormous multitude of men has allowed itself to be subjected by so small a number, and has readily submitted to the yoke of the Musalman Princes," but "the Idolators were effeminate people unable to make much resistance." Tavernier finds further explanation for their defeat in their superstition which "has introduced so strange a diversity of opinions and customs that they never agree with one another." He also notes that the second caste is that of warriors and soliders: "These are the only idolators who are brave, and distinguish themselves in the profession of arms" (Tavernier [1676] 1925, vol. 2: 141, 137).

Insofar as there was caste specialization, it is perhaps only reasonable that there should be specialization in bravery. McClintock claims that "imperialism cannot be understood without a theory of gender power . . . gender dynamics were, from the outset, fundamental to the securing and maintenance of the imperial enterprise" (McClintock 1995: 6–7). This is to say that imperialism necessitates feminizing the subjugated, that being colonized makes men effeminate. Kanhayalal Gauba's 1930 study of native princes refers to Bismarck's distinction of male and female European nations. For Bismarck, the Germans and various other peoples including the English and the Turks were essentially male; all Slavonic and Celtic peoples were "female races". Female races were charming but inefficient. Bismarck's view is relevant here in that it shows that the sweeping attribution of femininity to males is not necessarily tied in with prejudices of conquest and colonization. Gauba, not resenting the Raj, credited British India with the "virility of youth," and saw in the India ruled by princes "all the attractiveness of fine clothes, fine living, love and the extravagance associated with the elegant and sensuous female" (Gauba 1930: 13). If one accepted Gauba's analysis, one could well argue that the India of the Princes as he describes it represents a higher level of civilization. Of course, all such talk is really about style and presentation rather than substance.

The British after the Mutiny/War of Independence revised their view of what they saw as the regional differentions between Indians, and General Roberts promulgated a doctrine of martial races. In this doctrine the general problem of the possible unmanning of conquered peoples took on for many Indians, especially Bengalis, a particularly insulting tone. The hypermasculine colonialist claimed to find Indians relatively effeminate. There are many complex issues here, including a degree of homoeroticism in the English public school and in the relationship between British officers and Indian troops, but my concern is to show that this attribution of effeminacy to Hinduism was absent from the work of Orientalists. By and large the British had remarkably little understanding of Hindus and Hinduism. What is at issue is the attitude of those Britons and Europeans who were deeply interested in India and Hinduism, Orientalists in the pre-Saidian sense.

In his chapter on Hinduism in *Imagining India*, Inden tries to show that the west's understanding of Hinduism opposed its own claimed masculine reason to the imputed feminine imagination of India. Inden begins by quoting Spear's likening of Hinduism to a sponge because it absorbs all that enters it. Implicit here, says Inden, is the idea that Hinduism is "a female presence who is able, through her very amorphousness and absorptive powers, to baffle and perhaps even threaten Western rationality." He then quotes Sir Charles Eliot – "Hinduism has often and justly been compared to a jungle" (Inden 1992: 86). Inden quotes several other sentences from Eliot expanding on this, ending, "The average Hindu who cannot live permanently in the altitudes of pantheistic thought, regards his gods as great natural forces akin to mighty rivers which he also worships, irresistible and often beneficent but also capricious and destructive." Inden immediately comments, "There is thus little doubt here that this jungle with its soul, is, like Spear's sponge, also a female, one that can be managed by its male masters and known so long as they don't become entwined in its embraces" (1992: 87). Neither Spear nor Eliot said a word about femininity, nor about managing the forest, though Eliot spoke of Brahmans as "not gardeners but forest officers". Inden unfairly finds a colonial implication in the Brahmans being seen as this way, but Eliot's point is that Hinduism cannot be controlled like a garden.

Far from the jungle of Hinduism being seen as feminine, Eliot in the passage cited by Inden explicitly says that "men and women of all classes . . . and all stages of civilization have contributed to it."

A page later Inden again says that for Western writers, "If Hinduism has a positive essence, it consists of its feminine imaginativeness, its ability to absorb and include, to move from one extreme to the other, and to tolerate inconsistencies" (1992: 88). Again, the femininity is entirely his own addition. It is also interesting that in the final part of his book, an account of what he calls "the imperial formation" in medieval India, Inden happily refers to the traditional idiom wherein the conquered peoples of the universal emperor, the king of kings, are referred to as his wives (1992: 234).

In Inden's next section on Hinduism, "Psychic Origins," we get a long discussion of Mill's *History of British India* (1858), followed by Hegel's India as the sleeper dreaming before he awakes. "What were more or less disconnected examples of Hindu irrationality and superstition for Mill, the empiricist, were, for the German idealists, including Hegel, instances of the core metaphysics of that religion, of its double displacement of the ideal and material, the subjective and objective and of the predominance in it of creative imagination or fantasy over true thought or reason. That becomes the positive inner essence of the female India that a masculine Europe with its inner essence of reason was coming to dominate." . . . "We would not have those later British depictions of India as a feminine sponge or jungle animated by a feminine imagination had the Romantics and Hegel not done their work" (1992: 96).

"When we turn to the historical narratives of this religion, we behold a degenerative psychohistory masterminded by Hegel," says Inden. "Instead of witnessing the triumph of man, reason, and spirit, however, we see the triumph of the effeminate, the sensuous and the parochial . . ." (1992: 129). But no one says this; certainly no one whom Inden cites. Hinduism is indeed a sponge, is a forest, precisely because like Topsy it just growed. There was no overall authority, no Inquisition, no Synod to rule and regulate what men thought; practice was regulated, behavior was governed by caste councils. Social life was, relatively speaking, orderly and stable; intellectual life was a free for all. Inden refers, without any further reference, to the "schizophrenic religion of Shiva and Vishnu" (1992: 129), implying that that attribution of schizophrenia was the view of some or all Indologists. It need hardly be added that a résumé of the history of religion in Europe, careful to note all schisms and sects, would be no less confused and probably more schizophrenic than that of India.

Inden proceeds to expose the Orientalist as claiming a "shift of essences, from a masculine Aryan mentality that had been tropicalized, to a feminine Dravidian or aboriginal mind that had been Aryanized, . . . The change from depicting an Indian mind that was the same in its racial origin as that of the Self to one that was fundamentally different was significant. . . . the imperial jungle officers that took charge after the Mutiny . . . came to imagine themselves as presiding over an India comprised of Dravidian plants that could only be managed" (1992: 120).

Then come the tribals. Inden says it is on to the tribals that the Jungians – Inden's term for scholars interested in Indian mythology and art in themselves, rather than as instrumental in social scientific understanding – "offload the savagery, animal sacrifice, and general fetishism and animism formerly attributed to the Dravidian."

Campbell conjures up this essence: "For the calmly ruthless power of the jungle . . . has supplied the drone base of whatever song has ever been sung in India of man, his destiny and escape from destiny" (122).

Inden performs his customary trick of equating jungle with woman:

> This defining essence consists of nothing more than the female side of the mind, that which threatens to overcome man's consciousness and reason. There has to be sure, been a beneficent side to this femininity: [Inden quotes Campbell again:] "New civilizations, races, philosophies, and great mythologies have poured into India and have been not only assimilated but greatly developed, enriched, and [made?] sophisticated."
>
> [Inden:] But the goddess, Kali, condensation of this jungle essence, is always there:
>
> [Campbell:] "Yet, in the end (and in fact, even secretly throughout), the enduring power in that land has always been the same old dark goddess of the long red dark tongue who turns everything into her own everlasting, awesome, yet finally somewhat tedious, self." (1992: 123).

Inden comments, "Thus have the Jungians pushed the romantic idea of Hinduism as an ambivalent feminine entity to its extreme."

The reader gets from Inden no indication that India contains a great variety of cultures, that there is a real difference in many ways between North India and the Dravidian language speakers of the South, and that the great forests of Central India still contain millions of tribal peoples, who only in the last hundred years or so have given up widescale human sacrifice. These are not figments of the Orientalist imagination but facts. As Felix Padel remarks in his sensitive study of the Konds of Orissa, "tribal India is as different from mainstream India, as that is from Britain, or more so" (1995: 11). The jungle dwelling primitive has been an important factor in Hinduism; Śiva and Pārvatī often dress as tribals. Hinduism, Hindu authors, delight throughout history in running the gamut from the grandeur of metropolitan monarchs to warriors to forest dwelling ascetics to forest dwelling tribals. All part of life's natural hierarchy, just like the caste system.

Inden accuses Campbell of conjuring up an essence, but Inden himself is performing a conjuring trick, conjuring up an ascription of femininity where it does not exist – the Orientalist is the Other over which he seeks hegemony. But the Goddess does play a vital, indeed an essential role, in Hinduism. In his zeal to put words into the mouths of Orientalists, Inden overlooks the realities of Indian texts. The flesh-eating goddess deep in the jungle was a standard theme of Sanskrit and Tamil heroic texts. Inden several times refers to the Emperor Harṣa. Bāṇa, the great prose poet of Harṣa's reign, in his unfinished prose poem

Kādambarī, gives a well known portrayal of a Durgā shrine in the depths of the Vindhya forest, manned by a Dravidian priest. The poem begins with a tribal princess bringing a parrot as present from her father to the King. Her feet marked with leaf patterns in lac resemble Durgā's feet reddened by the buffalo's blood. The leader of the tribal hunters who captured the parrot had his shoulders scarred with making blood offerings to Durgā, his body like Durgā's marked with blood of buffaloes, all this foreshadows the final remaining part of the original, when the prince, having met and fallen in love with the beautiful Kādambarī, is ordered home by his father, and deep in the jungle comes across a shrine of Durgā, described by Bāṇa in great detail; no less detailed is the account of the Dravidian priest who attends this goddess. Quarrelsome, irritable, ill-educated, he is a figure of fun. He is an exponent of all the New Age fads of the day. One eye was destroyed by a fake ointment to make him all-seeing; to the other eye he applied collyrium three times a day; his singing sounded like the buzzing of flies. On and on goes the scornful account of impossible goals – alchemy, levitation, invisibility, and more. The prince laughs aloud when he sees this strange figure, but is then polite to him, restrains his followers from tormenting him, and gives him money when he leaves. The elegant prince, tormented by love in separation, here views an almost complete panorama of southern Hinduism exemplified in the priest, with a distant reserve reminiscent of a colonial administrator.

In fact Bāṇa was playfully referring to what was certainly later a well established theme in Indian literature, namely that of kings visiting a goddess of destruction in the jungle prior to going to battle (as in the *Gauḍavaho* and the *Kaliṅkattupparaṇi*). Goddesses were indeed to be found in jungles, not just in the Orientalist imagination. Bayly remarks on Inden's swingeing critique, "Few authorities escape his blade. If at times he appears in the guise of the many armed goddess Kali strutting through the scholarly carnage sporting a necklace of academic skulls, his goal is still Regeneration" (C. Bayly 1990: 1313). This *jeu d'esprit* by the most authoritative of British historians of India credits Inden with a power he does not in fact achieve; as well as likening him to a Goddess he chooses to ignore. Furthermore the analogy of Inden to Kālī shows a power of imagination that Inden would not approve of, for imagination is the second object of Inden's witch hunt. Imagination unquestionably played a major part in Hinduism, just as it does in every culture.

Britain exploited India and exerted power over India in many ways, but Orientalist Indologists, inevitably contaminated to some extent by the prejudices of their age – how could they not be? – were not "making a career of the East." They sought mastery of a body of knowledge in a way somewhat parallel to a Sanskrit pandit's quest for mastery of a body of knowledge. The procedures were different, but the goal of both was purely intellectual: Orientalists and traditional Indian scholars sought the power and glory of the intellect. The analysis offered by Said and Inden at first had a seductive thrill, an overturning of idols, the laying bare of the dialectic of self and other, seemed to throw a powerful searchlight on the underside of the study of the East. But what this attempted and apparently successful deconstruction overlooks is what is in fact blindingly obvious. In Orientalism in its original meaning was not oppression of the East, but the colonization of the western mind by the East. It is the strength of Indian ideas and Indian texts that overpowers the western scholar, that forces him to spend his life in willing servitude to them.

Notes

1 Salutary is Jamison's acknowledgment of the Vedic scholarship of A. B. Keith, "undervalued, presumably because of the superficial contempt he affects for the texts. (But could he have spent so much care and intelligence without some respect for the texts? And can those who evince more respect for the texts claim as large a contribution to our understanding of them? I cannot.)" (Jamison 1991: xiv).

2 Kejariwal's work establishes that "the world of scholarship and the world of administration . . . were worlds apart" during the period he studies, 1784–1838 (Kejariwal 1988: 226). Trautman notes, "So far from there being a thick institutionalized connection between Orientalism and empire, as readers of Said might be led to imagine, one could say, roughly, that the study of Sanskrit varied *inversely* with imperialism . . . It is as if the British had been persuaded by James Mill's preposterous argument that ignorance of Indian languages was a positive aid to the formation of unclouded views on imperial policy" (Trautman 1997: 189).

3 Hastings quoted the *Bhagavadgītā* in his letters to his wife, finding it a source of inspiration. In his private notebook he asked himself "Is the incarnation of Christ more intelligible than . . . those of Vishnu?" The current European superiority owed nothing to Christianity, but was due to "a free government, cold climate and printing and navigation" (quoted by Trautman 1997: 72).

4 Inner second panel of west pillar of north gate, the Great Stupa, Sanchi. The monkey's story is given in the *Dhammapadatthakattha*; see Sivaramamurti 1977: 190.

References

Ahmad, Aijaz. 1992: *In Theory: Classes, Nations, Literatures*. London: Verso.
Anderson, Perry. 1974: *Lineages of the Absolutist State*. London: New Left Books.
Anquetil-Duperron, A. H. [1771] 1997: *Voyage en Inde 1754–62*, eds. J. Deloche, M. Filliozat, and P. S. Filliozat. Paris: EFEO.
Bayly, C. A. 1990: Review of Inden, *Imagining India*, *TLS* Dec. 7–13.
Bayly, Susan. 1997: "Caste and Race," in Peter Robb, ed., *The Concept of Race in South Asia*, Delhi: Oxford University Press, 165–218.
Beames, John. 1996: *Memoirs of a Bengal Civilian*. London: Eland.
Cannadine, David. 2001: *Ornamentalism: How the British saw their Empire*. London: Allen Lane, Penguin Press.
Chaudhuri, Nirad C. 1988. *Thy Hand, Great Anarch*. London: Chatto and Windus.
Deussen, Paul. [1904] 1995: "My Indian Reminiscences," trans. A. King. New Delhi: Asian Educational Services.
Feiling, Keith. 1996: *Warren Hastings*. London: Macmillan.

Garbe, Richard. 1925: *Indische Reiseskizzen*, 2nd ed. MuenchenNeubiberg: Oskar Schloss.
Gauba, Kanhayalal. 1930: *H. H. Or the Pathology of Princes*. Lahore: The Time Publishing Company.
Geddes, Patrick. 1962: Cited by B. R. Nanda, *The Nehrus: Motilal and Jawaharlal*. London: George Allen & Unwin.
Gilmour, David. 1997: The Ends of Empire. *Wilson Quarterly*, Spring: 32–40.
Girouard, Mark. 1979: *The Victorian Country House*. Yale University Press.
Inden, Ronald. 1992: *Imagining India*. Oxford: Blackwell.
Jaffrelot, C. 1997: "The Ideas of the Human Race in the Writings of Hindu Nationalist Ideologues in the 1920s and 1930s: A Concept between Two Cultures," in Peter Robb, ed., *The Concept of Race in South Asia*. Delhi: Oxford University Press, 327–54.
Jamison, Stephanie W. 1991: *The Ravenous Hyenas and the Wounded Sun: Myth and Ritual in Ancient India*. Ithaca and London: Cornell University Press.
Kejariwal, O. P. 1988: *The Asiatic Society of Bengal and the Discovery of India's Past 1784–1838*. Delhi: Oxford University Press.
Kopf, David. 1969: *British Orientalism and the Bengal Renaissance: The Dynamics of Indian Modernization 1773–1835*. Berkeley and Los Angeles: University of California Press.
——. 1991: "European Enlightenment, Hindu Renaissance and the Enrichment of the Human Spirit: A History of Historical Writings on British Orientalism," in Nancy G. Cassels, ed., *Orientalism, Evangelicalism and the Military Cantonment in Early Nineteenth Century India: A Historiographical Overview*. Lewiston/Queenston/Lampeter: Edwin Mellen Press, 19–53.
Lal, Vinay. 1996: "Masculinity and Femininity in *The Chess Players*: Sexual Moves, Colonial Manoeuvres, and an Indian Game," *Manushi: A Journal of Women and Society* 92/93: 41–50.
——. 1997: "Good Nazis and Just Scholars: Much Ado about the British Empire," review of P. J. Marshall, ed., *Cambridge Illustrated History of the British Empire*. *Race and Class* 38/4: 89–101.
Lawrence, Sir Walter R. 1928: *The India We Served*. London: Cassell.
Macaulay, T. B. [1841] 1895: "On Warren Hastings," *Essays*. London, Longmans Green & Co.
MacKenzie, John M. 1994: "Edward Said and the Historians," *Nineteenth Century Contexts* 18 (1): 9–25.
Malamoud, C. 1978: Preface to Louis Renou, *L'Inde fondamentale*. Paris: Herman.
Mason, Philip. 1978: *Shaft of Sunlight: Memories of a Varied Life*. London: Deutsch.
McClintock, Anne. 1995: *Imperial Leather: Race, Gender and Sexuality in the Imperial Contest*. London: Routledge.
Murr, Sylvia. 1991: "Le politique 'au Mogol' selon Bernier: appareil conceptuel, rhétorique stratégique, philosophie morale," in J. Pouchepadass and H. Stern, eds., *De la royauté à l'état: anthropologie et histoire du politique dans le monde indien*. Paris: EHESS, 239–311.
Padel, Felix. 1995: *The Sacrifice of Human Being: British Rule and the Konds of Orissa*. Delhi: Oxford University Press.
Pollock, Sheldon. 1993: "Deep Orientalism? Notes on Sanskrit and Power Beyond the Raj," in Carol A. Breckridge and Peter van der Veer, eds., *Orientalism and the Postcolonial Predicament*. Philadelphia: University of Pennsylvania Press, 76–133.
——. 1996: "The Sanskrit Cosmopolis, A.D. 300–1300: Transculturation, Vernacularization, and the Question of Ideology, The Ideology and Status of Sanskrit in South

and Southeast Asia," in J. E. M. Houben, ed., *Ideology and Status of Sanskrit: Contributions to the History of the Sanskrit Language*. Leiden: Brill.
——. 2001: "The Death of Sanskrit," *Comparative Studies in Society and History* 43/2: 392–426.
Prakash, Gyan. 1995: *Orientalism* Now: A Review of Reviews. *History and Theory* 34: 199–212.
Raychaudhuri, Tapan. 1996: "British Rule in India: An Assessment," in P. J. Marshall, ed., *Cambridge Illustrated History of the British Empire*. Cambridge: Cambridge University Press.
Raynal, Abbé G. T. 1820: *Histoire Philosophique et Politique des Établissemens, et du Commerce des Européens dans les deux Indes*, 7 vols. Paris: Amable Costes.
Renou, Louis. 1950: *Sanskrit et Culture: L'apport de l'Inde à la civilisation humaine*. Paris: Payot.
——. 1968: *Religions of Ancient India*. New York: Schocken Books.
Risley, Herbert H. 1915: *The People of India*. Calcutta: Thacker, Spink.
Rubies, Joan Pau. 2002: *Travel and Ethnology in the Renaissance: South India through European Eyes, 1250–1625*. Cambridge: Cambridge University Press.
Said, Edward W. 1978: *Orientalism*. London: Routledge & Kegan Paul.
——. 1984: *The World, the Text, and the Critic*. London: Faber and Faber.
Schwab, Raymond. 1950: *La Renaissance Orientale* Paris: Payot.
Sivaramamurti, C. 1977: *Amaravati Sculptures in the Madras Government Museum*. Madras: Government Museum.
Tavernier, Jean Baptiste. [1676] 1925: *Travels in India*, trans. V. Ball, ed. William Crooke. 2nd ed. 2 vols. Oxford: Oxford University Press.
Toth, Lazslo. 1988: "Existe-t-il une doctrine traditionnelle de la race?" *Politica Hermetica* 2: 23.
Trautman, Thomas R. 1997: *Aryans and British India*. Berkeley: University of California Press.
Turner, Bryan S. 1994: *Orientalism, Postmodernism and Globalism*. London: Routledge.
Veer, Peter van der. 2001: *Imperial Encounters*. Princeton: Princeton University Press.
Wheen, Francis. 2000: *Karl Marx*. London: Fourth Estate.

PART II

Text and Tradition

The Sanskrit Textual Traditions 67

3 Vedas and Upaniṣads 68
Michael Witzel

4 The Dharmaśāstras 102
Ludo Rocher

5 The Sanskrit Epics 116
John Brockington

6 The Purāṇas 129
Freda Matchett

Textual Traditions in Regional Languages 144

7 Tamil Hindu Literature 145
Norman Cutler

8 The Literature of Hinduism in Malayalam 159
Rich Freeman

9 North Indian Hindi Devotional Literature 182
Nancy M. Martin

Major Historical Developments 199

10 The Śaiva Traditions 200
Gavin Flood

11 History of Vaiṣṇava Traditions 229
Gérard Colas

12 The Renouncer Tradition 271
Patrick Olivelle

13 The Householder Tradition in Hindu Society 288
T. N. Madan

Regional Traditions 306

14 The Teyyam Tradition of Kerala 307
Rich Freeman

15 The Month of Kārtik and Women's Ritual Devotions to Krishna in Benares 327
Tracy Pintchman

The Sanskrit Textual Traditions

CHAPTER 3

Vedas and Upaniṣads

Michael Witzel

Veda means "(sacred) knowledge" (cf. Greek *(w)oida*, English *wit, witness*, German *wissen*). The Four Vedas are the oldest extant texts of India and contain religious and ritual poetry, ritual formulas and the explanatory prose that interprets these very texts, and additionally, in the late Vedic Upaniṣads, some early philosophy.

According to post-Vedic, medieval Indian tradition, the Four Vedas are called *Śruti*, that is "something (revealed to and) heard" by the "primordial" sages (Ṛṣi). By contrast, the concept of *Smṛti* "something learnt by heart" is restricted to the post-Upaniṣadic texts, such as the Sūtras (see below) or Manu's law book, all of which are believed to have been composed by human beings. However, it is known from internal evidence that the Vedic texts were orally composed in northern India, at first in the Greater Punjab and later on also in more eastern areas, including northern Bihar, between ca. 1500 BCE and ca. 500–400 BCE.

The oldest text, the Ṛgveda, must have been more or less contemporary with the Mitanni texts of northern Syria/Iraq (1450–1350 BCE); these mention certain Vedic gods (Varuṇa, Mitra, Indra, Nāsatya) and some forms of early Sanskrit that slightly predate the Ṛgveda (*mazdā* for Ved. *medhā*, *vašana* for Ved. *vāhana*, etc.). However, there still is no absolute dating of any Ved. text. Pertinent parameters include the first use of iron (in a post-Ṛgvedic text, the Atharvaveda, at ca. 1200/1000 BCE) and the lifetime of the Buddha (at 500 or perhaps rather 400 BCE) who *postdates* almost all Vedic texts. However, all Vedic texts *predate* the grammatical commentary of Patañjali (ca. 150 BCE) and his predecessor Pāṇini, who quote most of them.

The Vedic texts were orally composed and transmitted, without the use of script, in an unbroken line of transmission from teacher to student that was formalized early on. This ensured an impeccable textual transmission superior to the classical texts of other cultures; it is, in fact, something like a *tape-recording* of ca. 1500–500 BCE. Not just the actual words, but even the long-lost musical (tonal) accent (as in old Greek or in Japanese) has been preserved up to the present.

On the other hand, the Vedas have been written down only during the early second millennium CE, while some sections such as a collection of the Upaniṣads were perhaps written down at the middle of the first millennium, while some early, unsuccessful attempts (indicated by certain Smṛti rules *forbidding* to write down the Vedas) may have been made around the end of the first millennium BCE. However, almost all printed editions depend on the late manuscripts that are hardly older than 500 years, not on the still extant and superior oral tradition.

Correct recitation of many texts indeed continues in certain traditional areas, such as Kerala, southern Tamil Nadu, coastal Andhra, Orissa, Kathiawar, at Poona or Benares. In the past few decades there have been attempts by local and foreign scholars to preserve, or at least to record, the oral tradition. However, no complete recording on tape or video of all Vedic recensions (*śākhā*) exists so far, and some texts have been lost even during the past few decades.

According to Indian tradition, the Vedas are divided into four parts (Ṛg-, Sāma-, Yajur-, and Atharva-Veda). This division corresponds to that of the material as used in the post-Ṛgvedic ritual (see below); each Veda again is subdivided into four levels: the Saṃhitā "(Mantra) collections," Brāhmaṇa "(theological/ritual) commentary," Āraṇyaka "wilderness texts," and Upaniṣad "(secret philosophical) texts (of correlations and equivalences learned) sitting at the feet (of the teacher)." One has to add the ritual Sūtra, which are regarded as belonging to the *Smṛti* but are late Vedic in content and language.

These traditional divisions into four kinds of texts, however, actually represent five historical layers (see the Appendix at the end of this chapter, also for abbreviations of texts), as indicated by the development of the Vedic language used: that of Ṛgvedic, of the Mantras, of Yajurveda expository prose, of the Brāhmaṇas (incl. Āraṇyakas, Upaniṣads) and of the Sūtras. These five layers only partially overlap with the traditional divisions.

The Ṛgveda

The oldest Vedic text, the Ṛgveda (RV), is composed in archaic, highly stylized poetical Sanskrit. It contains verses of praise addressed to the Vedic gods and to some early contemporary chieftains; it also includes some speculative hymns and some (probably) nonritual poetry. Most of the hymns, however, were intended to be recited at the yearly Soma ritual, celebrated at the time of New Year.

The RV contains 1,028 hymns arranged in ten books, actually ten "circles" (*maṇḍala*). Book 9 is a separate, fairly late collection containing the texts of Sāman hymns to be sung during the Soma ritual. Book 10 and part of book 1 are even later additions. The RV has been transmitted in one recension (the *śākhā* of Śākalya) while others (such as the Bāṣkala text) have been lost or are only rumored about so far.

The RV text was composed before the introduction and massive use of iron, that is before ca. 1200–1000 BCE. Internal evidence indicates that most hymns were composed over a span of just five generations, under the Pūru and Bharata chieftains, notably the great Bharata king Sudās; they represent the *middle* Ṛgveda period, with such prominent poets as Viśvāmitra and the East Iranian(?) immigrant Vasiṣṭha. A few older hymns apparently come from other tribes, such as the Anu-Druhyu and Yadu-Turvaśa.

They were composed by members of various clans of poets (among which 7 major ones, RV 2–8). The hymns that belonged to them were transmitted as "private property" which often was "copyrighted" by including the names of the individual poets or clans or by typical refrains. Most of the poets belonged to, or were later attributed to, the Aṅgirasa clans and also the Kāṇva. The names attributed to the authors of Ṛgvedic hymns seem to be partially correct, when corroborated by self-reference or indirectly by certain poetic devices; however, many of the names recorded in the clearly post-Ṛgvedic Anukramaṇī ("list" of poets, deities, meters) are artificially derived from some key words in the hymns; these names often do not correspond to those given by the Sāmavedic, Yajurvedic, and Atharvavedic traditions.

Poetic Speech

The most characteristic feature of all Ṛgvedic poetry is the power and prestige of speech (*vāc*) and *verbal behavior* in general, without which the RV itself would not exist. The gods (but also the human listeners, especially the sponsors of the ritual) were most pleased by "the newest hymn," composed with poetic craftsmanship and virtuosity – to which they were entitled as ritual guests; the better the hymn, the greater the reward – to the poet from the patron, to the patron from the god.

Most prized, however, is the putting into words of the much celebrated *Ṛta* (= Avestan *aṣ̌a*) "active realization of truth" or *Wahrheitsverwirklichung* (cf. Lüders 1944, 1951, 1959 "Truth"), is commonly still translated "cosmic order" or "cosmic harmony." The vital force of Ṛta indeed has the power to keep the cosmos and human society functioning correctly. This untranslatable concept thus is similar to the later Hindu *dharma*. The opposite concept of *druh-* (Avest. *druj*) "deceiving, cheating action, (Be)-*Trug*" (cf. Engl. be-*tray*) signifies *active* untruth. Another contrast to *Ṛta* seems to be *nir-ṛti*, the absolute disappearance (*nir-*) of "active, creative truth, law, order," that is absolute destruction, a sort of hell of absolute darkness, with no food, drink, possibility of children, etc. (RV 7.104).

Capturing Ṛta in words is effected by *bráhman*, the "formulation" or capturing in words of a significant and non-self-evident truth (Thieme 1952, cf. Renou and Silburn 1949, Gonda 1950, Schmidt 1968a). The formulator (*brahmán-*) of such truths has special powers, effecting this world and the cosmos. The same power of correctly stated truth is found in the (later) **satyakriyā* or "act of truth"

(Brown 1940, 1968, Lüders 1917, 1944) which has counterparts in other Indo-European (Watkins 1979) and Eurasian cultures (Witzel forthc.). Such formulated speech must be recited correctly, otherwise there is danger of losing one's head (as in the *indraśatru* legend TS 2.4.12.1, ŚB 1.6.3.8). The original author, always a Vedic Ṛṣi, is a *brahmán-* "possessor of *bráhman-*" whose name is remembered and must be uttered to this day.

Contents of the Ṛgveda

Apart from the predominantly ritual contents of the Ṛgveda there are a few hymns of highly poetical value and of early philosophical speculation. Some of these hymns, such as the famous love story of Purūravas and Urvaśī (RV 10.95), have been used by the later Epic and classical poets. All of Ṛgvedic poetry is very complicated and enigmatic: it is based on the poetical norms of the preceding Indo-Iranian and Indo-European periods, it refers to many fragmentarily known myths, uses many archaic formulas and set phrases, and a vocabulary that was already archaic then, and its expression in general is very elliptical.

There also are stanzas that praise the local chieftains, who where sponsors of Ṛgvedic ritual. The area of the Greater Panjab was inhabited by some 30 to 50 tribes and clans in whose service the transient RV poets composed ever "new hymns" in praise of the gods and chieftains.

A number of hymns are in dialogue form; these have hardly been used in later ritual; however, they belong to the most beautiful and poetical pieces of the RV. The hymns dealing with early philosophical speculation have usually been understood as presenting contemporary developments, but many of the topics, such as that of the primordial giant (*Puruṣa*), go back to Indo-European (i.e. the Old Norse *Ymir*) and even to a preceding Eurasian period (i.e. the Chinese/Miao *Pangu*). After the end of the Ṛgveda, this kind of speculative poetry was continued in the AV (Śaunaka AV books 8–12) which still were composed by the *brahmán*, now turned priests, and later, in the Yajurvedic Gāthās and Ślokas, down to the Upaniṣad period.

Ṛgvedic Mythology

Underlying the praise of the gods is a complicated system of mythology that is not stated as such by the text, but must be extracted laboriously, just like all other information about this period. Much of it goes back to the common Indo-Iranian and Indo-European periods.

Many of the deities are transparently "natural" though they have acquired a certain amount of "personality," while others, developed during the Indo-Iranian period, are deified abstractions that belong to the ethical (Varuṇa, Mitra, Aryaman, Bhaga, etc.) and conceptual sphere (Ṛta) as well as to ritual practice

(Soma). However, as Kuiper (1962: 43) has pointed out, "understanding a single mythological figure isolated from the context of the mythological system" is difficult, and a more *structured* arrangement of (semi-)divine beings and their functions in their relevant spheres should be undertaken. They include the heavenly sphere with the deities and their ancestors, other heavenly beings such as the *Gandharvas*, the Ṛṣis, human ancestors (*pitṛ*); further the mundane sphere with human beings and certain spirits, and the nether world with beings such as the *Nāga*, and finally, various demonic beings such as *rakṣas, kimīdin*, and the force of destruction, *Nirṛti*, all of whom are governed by the universal force of "active truth" (*Ṛta*) and its counterpart "deceit, cheating" (*Druh*). These beings and entities are set in juxtaposition or opposition on the various levels of the universe. For example, the promiscuous, extra-societal group of Veda students "on leave," the Vrātyas here on earth, have their counterparts in heaven (*daivya vrātya, Gandharva*, Vasilkov 1991), as well as in the netherworld (*Nāgas*).

The most important (Ṛg)Vedic gods include the following. Agni is deified (ritual) "Fire," one of the few gods that are actually present *and* visible on the offering ground. He receives and transports offerings to the gods.

Indra, originally called *Vṛtrahan* "beating the resistance" (Avest. *Vərəϑragna*, Benveniste and Renou 1934) is the leader of the present generation of the gods and a major actor in the early stages of creation: he pushes up the sky, and prepares the *oikumene* by opening the Vala cave of the Dawns (Schmidt 1968a), by killing the Dragon Vṛtra, and by stealing the Soma (Brown 1968; Lüders 1951: 183ff.; Kuiper 1983; also: Sieg 1926, Schneider 1971, Dandekar 1979). Indra also is the archetypal tricky, voracious, and oversexed leader of the Ārya in the frequent battles among themselves and with the non-Ārya population of the Greater Panjab (E. W. Hopkins 1908, Rau 1957, Dandekar 1997). Many of his characteristics go back to IE (Watkins 1995) and even to the preceding Eurasian mythology. The Maruts, a sort of *Männerbund*, are often associated with Indra. Soma "the one pressed out," is the deified drink, as well as the plant from which it is derived (also called by the Central Asian substrate name *aṁśu*). Without drinking Soma, Indra could not kill Vṛtra (Oberlies 1989, 1991, 1998).

The Ādityas, "the sons of Aditi" are a group of 7/8 (later 12) divinities that were at first interpreted as nature gods (Bergaigne 1878–83, III: 110ff., Keith 1925, 96–104, Hillebrandt (1927–9: 2ff., 41ff.). However, they are personifications of the most important social functions (Meillet 1907, Thieme 1938, 1957a, Dumézil 1934, 1958b, Gonda 1972): Varuṇa is a stern but just king-figure, of unclear etymology (Lüders 1951/1959, Thieme 1957a, Kuiper 1983); Mitra, Varuṇa's constant partner, is a personification of tribal agreements (*mitra*, ntr. "agreement") (Meillet 1907, Brereton 1981); and Aryaman "Arya-hood, hospitality" that of clan relationship and marriage. Further, the popular Bhaga "Luck" (*bhaga* "share"), is god of good luck, and similarly Aṃśa "lot" (*aṃśa* "lot"). The Aśvins (*Nāsatya*) are divine twins who perform miraculous cures and rescues.

Uṣas, "Dawn," is the most prominent goddess, and the often-praised friend of poets. Other deified natural phenomena, who can be traced back to the Indo-

European and even to earlier Eurasian periods, include Sūrya "the male belonging to the sun"; Dyaus "Heaven, Sky" (or Dyaus Pitar "Father Sky") and his consort, Pṛthivī (Mātā) (Mother) "Earth," the Āpas "(flowing) Waters," often called "divine ladies" (Narten 1971); Vāyu or Vāta "Wind," and Parjanya "Thunder." As elsewhere, fire is regarded as masculine and water as a feminine deity, while the "elements" fire and water exist separately as archaic neuters (*athar-/*peh$_2$ur-, udr-/udn-*) – a very old, Indo-European and perhaps pan-Eurasian notion (Witzel 1992). Many rites and customs (offering meat balls to the three closest male ancestors, marriage, fire ritual, horse sacrifice, etc.) are of Indo-European age as well.

Similarly, the notion of an opposition between groups of gods (Deva and Asura), which is later expressed by "The Devas and the Asuras were in contention" (Br. style texts), goes back to the Indo-Iranian and even the IE periods. In the RV, however, *asura* is often used as epithet of the most respected Devas, e.g. Varuṇa and Agni, and in early Iranian religion *ahura* signifies the most prominent god, *Ahura Mazdā* "Lord Wisdom." This difference is one of "the central problems of Vedic religion" (Kuiper 1975: 112, W. E. Hale 1986). It seems (with Kuiper) that the Asuras were the primordial gods, challenged and defeated by the upstart Devas, similar to that of the Titans by the Olympian gods.

The constant contest between the Devas and the Asuras has its mundane counterpart in the Ṛgvedic opposition between the immigrating *Ārya* and their acculturated affiliates on the one hand, and the previous local inhabitants, the *Dasyu* or *Dāsa* on the other; this opposition is replaced in post-RV texts by that of the *Ārya* and *Śūdra*. It is expressed most notably in the New Year ritual (Mahāvrata rite), when the old order breaks down temporarily and carnival-like chaos reigns among the gods and in society. Vedic ritual enforces the social role of *deva/asura* and *ārya/śūdra* precisely at such occasions.

Prajāpati ("Lord of creatures") is a very marginal figure in the late RV, but becomes in the Post-RV prose texts the central creator god embodying the power of the ritual (Gonda 1984, 1986, 1989).

The great Hindu gods Viṣṇu and Śiva are not yet prominent in Vedic. Viṣṇu appears almost only in his role as taking three steps towards heaven and Śiva as a frightening god under his names "Rudra," *ghora* "terrible," or simply as *asau devaμ* "that god." The name *Śiva* "the kindly/auspicious one" occurs only in the late Ved. Kaṭha Āraṇyaka. The process leading to their later prominence is rather controversial. Kuiper (1962) sees Viṣṇu as a central mediating figure between the older Asuras and the younger Devas.

Ṛgvedic Ritual

The important relation between myth and ritual is very evident in the Vedic tradition: Agni and Soma are ritual objects *and* divinities with a developed personal mythology; mythic episodes are recited in liturgical context. Later on, in the

Brāhmaṇa style texts, mythology explains (details of) and refers to ritual activity in mythological narratives. A deep connection was felt by the composers of the texts (K. Hoffmann 1975/6: 516–22, 422–38, Sieg 1902, Schmidt 1968a, Falk 1984, Heesterman 1985, Jamison 1991, Witzel 1986b, 1992, 1998).

Indeed, most of the Ṛgvedic hymns relate to early Vedic ritual. Though the RV does not contain any direct description, various allusions and mentioning of its features in this highly poetical text can be used to establish a fairly consistent description (for its interpretation, see below). However, relatively little systematic work had been done on assembling the details of Ṛgvedic praxis (but, now Proferes 1999, Schmidt 1973, Witzel 1981/2). Except for a brief discussion of the RV Soma ritual (Geldner 1951), scholars had taken the clear descriptions of the Śrauta ritual as their starting points (van Buitenen 1968: Pravargya; Gonda 1980b: Sautrāmaṇī; Hillebrandt 1897: 11–17, Keith 1925: 252–6). However, Schmidt (1973) shows that the sacrificial animal was tied to the offering pole and decapitated, while in the "classical" ritual the animal was still tied to the pole but then suffocated outside the sacrificial ground. Similar developments, also in the assembly of the texts to be recited, are shown by Proferes (1999).

The most important RV ritual is that of the preparation, offering, and consumption of the sacred drink, Soma, dealt with at length in RV 9. It was prepared from an unknown plant (probably Ephedra) growing in the high mountains of the Pamirs (Mt. Muzh, *Mūjavant*), eastern Iran, and the western Himalayas. This plant was soon substituted as the Ṛgvedic civilization expanded eastwards into the Indus and Gangetic plains. Soma seems to be a substitute for the earlier Indo-European sacred drink, made from fermented honey (mead). It most probably was taken over, by both the Indo-Aryans and the Iranians, from the local population of the Bactria/Margiana area who seem to have called it by the non-Indo-Iranian word *aṁśu*. Its antiquity is indeed underlined by the Zoroastrian tradition, where it appears as the important *haoma* ritual.

Other important rituals include the kindling and worship of fire which must be present in all rituals. It is identified with the fire in the sun, as can be seen most clearly in the post-Ṛgvedic Agnihotra ritual and also in the oldest Zoroastrian ritual (Yasna Haptaŋhāiti). Many such features, including some of the names of various (usually seven) priests, such as that of the Hotar (Zaraϑuštra himself was a *Zaotar*), go back to the Indo-Iranian period. Other rituals, such as the Indo-European horse sacrifice (Puhvel 1987) or some equally old domestic rites of passage (death and marriage), are only sparsely attested in the RV.

Several of the Ṛgvedic rituals, just as some of its Śrauta successors, are concerned with the liminal periods in the yearly progression of time (daily, fortnightly, seasonal, and yearly); they are the "rites of passage" of the year. Kuiper stresses that "the oldest nucleus of the Ṛgveda was a textbook for the new year ritual" (1960: 222); Schmidt (1968a) connects the morning pressing of the Soma ritual with the Vala myth and with the New Year/spring season and suggests a connection of the midday pressing with the Vṛtra myth and the rainy reason; H. Falk additionally underlines the spring time "coming of the waters" in an Arachosian context (1997).

Ṛgvedic ritual evolved further during the middle and late Ṛgvedic period (Proferes 1999), especially under the influence of the Viśvāmitra clan, and was rather artificially elaborated, systematized, and codified; it emerged, by the time of the early post-Ṛgvedic/early Mantra period collections (Witzel 1997a,b), as the famous "classical Śrauta ritual" that is prominent in all post-RV texts and still is performed in some traditional areas of India and Nepal.

Collecting and Ordering the Early Vedic Texts

Accordingly, the *first* collection of (most) available RV hymns dealing with ritual was made under the Bharata dynasty of the early Kuru kings, such as the famous Parikṣit; he is first attested in the early post-RV Khila collection (5.22) and later on is a prominent figure in the *Mahābhārata*. His time, one of great political, societal, religious, and linguistic change (Witzel 1989a, 1997a) is praised as a golden age, among other with the telling refrain (RVKh 5.22): "the people thrive in the realm of King Parikṣit." The break-up of the old tribal society of the Ṛgveda and the rise of the intertribal Kuru realm (Witzel 1997a,b) thus saw strikingly new developments in ritual and in the development of Brahmanical pre-scientific science of correlations (see below).

The other Vedic Saṃhitās dealing with the new Śrauta ritual (SV, YV, and AV) were collected during the early Kuru period, too. These are linguistically younger than the RV, younger even than its late appendix book 10. At this time, the traditional jobs of the various Vedic priests were divided into four classes, attributed to the four main Śrauta priests who were to represent and use the Four Vedas. They include (each with three helpers) the Hotar who now only recites Mantras from the RV, the Ugātar who sings the Sāman melodies, the Adhvaryu who is the main offering priest carrying out the actions of the Śrauta ritual while mumbling Yajurveda Mantras, and the Brahmán priest who supervises the whole of the ritual, mostly in silence (Renou 1949, Brereton 1988) and remedies it, in case of mistakes, by reciting a few Mantras from the Atharvaveda (Bodewitz 1983).

When the Saṃhitā texts were collected, they were each ordered in particular but individual ways: The RV is arranged according to strict, mostly numerical principles (Oldenberg 1888): Its first level of order is that of author (family/clan), followed by that of deity and meter, that is, inside each family collection the hymns are arranged according to deities: Agni and Indra come first, then other deities, depending on the number of hymns addressed to them (in *decreasing* order); inside each deity collection the longer hymns come first and the shortest last; in case of equal length, a hymn with a longer meter comes first. This organization is well reflected in the core ("family") books of the RV. All hymns that do not follow this order were added after the initial collection, as is clear by their many late grammatical and other features. The family books of the RV are arranged in *increasing* order, from short books (RV 2) to longer ones (RV

7); this is visible, however, only when the additional hymns are excised. Thus, if one knows – as is still prescribed today before reciting a hymn – its author, deity, and meter, one can pinpoint its location in the RV family books accurately. This "numerical" arrangement was perfect for society without script.

The Other Vedic Saṃhitās

While the RV contains original compositions, the Sāmaveda was extracted, except for 75 verses, from RV 9 and 8. These stanzas are sung, mostly during the Soma ritual, in a very elaborate fashion, including much *coloratura* and the often nonsensical *stobhas* (such as the string *hā o hā o hā hāyi* or *bhā, dada, hup*). They are the earliest preserved music of India. The SV is divided into two main sections, the Arcika containing the actual text used, and the Gāna which containing the melodies themselves. These are designated by the *text* of well known melodies, somewhat in the following fashion: one should sing a certain text according to the melody "God save the Queen," which is also applied to the American song "America it is thee," to the imperial hymn of Germany, and to the royal one of Norway.

In stark contrast to the other Veda texts, the Atharvaveda contains, in its oldest sections, magical poems used for healing and for all sorts of magic, including destructive sorcery (AV 1–7). To these sometimes very old texts (reminiscent of Germanic and Hittite sorcery stanzas), a large number of speculative hymns (AV 8–12), other hymns dealing with the most important life cycle rituals (AV 13–18) as well as two appendixes (AV 19–20) have been added.

The AV is ordered, most clearly in its Paippalāda version, in clear opposition to the arrangement of the Ṛgveda: it starts with a book that is composed entirely of short hymns of just 4 stanzas and increases to one that has 19. To this nucleus of sorcery stanzas (PS 1–15), the speculative (PS 16–17) and Gṛhya type hymns (PS 18) as well as the appendixes (PS 19–20) were added.

The Yajurveda, however, mainly contains prose Mantras (*yajuṣ*) that are used as offering formulas; they must accompany each individual action in ritual (*yajña*) carried out by the Adhvaryu priest who mumbles them as he proceeds, for example "you are heaven, you are earth," "move through the interspace!"

These prose Mantras have not been recorded in the Ṛgveda, though the *yajuṣ* genre is mentioned, and the extant YV Mantras are younger in form and grammar than the RV. Originally, they consisted only of simple, though rhythmical prose; but already in the first collections (MS, KS, TS), verses from the RV have been added in a linguistically later form that is often slightly degraded by perseveration. Once the YV Saṃhitās were collected according to diverse *śākhā* traditions, however, the form of the Mantras did no longer change and they were transmitted faithfully to this very day.

To these Mantras, large sections of *brāhmaṇa* style expository prose have been added during the YV prose period (see below). Both of them combined constitute the texts of the Black Yajurveda, while the explanatory prose (ŚB) is separated from the Mantras (VS) in the White YV whose Saṃhitā (VS) was only secondarily extracted from the late Vedic ŚB.

The YV Mantras have not been arranged numerically as in the RV, SV, and AV but in the order they are used in Śrauta ritual: they form small, individual Mantra collections meant for each ritual. However, the order of these individual Mantra collections inside the two dozen extent YV Saṃhitās followed a fixed order already by the time of the first YV Saṃhitā collection; this order is maintained, with minor variations, down to the Sūtras.

The YV starts with two small collections, that of the vegetarian New and Full Moon offerings (*haviryajña*) and of that of the all important Soma ritual, both of which form the paradigm (*prakṛti*) of (most) other Śrauta rituals; even the animal sacrifices (*paśubandha*) are technically considered as *haviryajñas*.

The Post-Ṛgvedic Reform of the Śrauta Ritual

While the Śrauta ritual (*yajña*) has been central to most post-Ṛgvedic texts, detailed descriptions are only found in the late Vedic period, in the Śrauta Sūtras. Earlier texts, such as the *Mantra* Saṃhitās and the discussion of selected details in the Brāhmaṇa texts allow only to infer the general course of the ritual, while its exact order is not strictly followed. We need a new, detailed survey of Śrauta rituals and their contents (Hillebrandt 1897, Keith 1925, Renou & Filliozat 1947; Gonda 1960, Mylius 1973: 475–98, cf. Renou 1953 with a lexicon of ritual terminology, Dandekar and Kashikar 1958–, with the extensive but still only half-complete Śrautakośa compendium).

A thorough interpretation of the Śrauta ritual that uses the wealth of Vedic descriptions and contemporaneous native interpretation is a desideratum. Though begun a hundred years ago (S. Lévi 1898, Hubert & Mauss 1923–4, Mus 1935: 79–121, cf. Sahlins 1972, Witzel 1992, 1998, Lopez 1997), a comprehensive interpretation still is outstanding – disregarding for the moment recent monolateral theories (agonistic origins: Heesterman 1985, 1993; meaninglessness: Staal 1979a,b; 1990). In addition, the structure(s) of the ritual, the interrelations of particular rituals, and their internal development (Staal 1982, 1990, cf. Witzel 1981/2, 1997a,b, Falk 1986, 1988) still deserve more study. The Śrauta ritual is built up of multiple frames or "boxes" (Heesterman 1957, 1993, Witzel 1984b, 1986b: 172, 1987a, 1992, Minkowski 1992). For example, *avāntaradīkṣā* means "the lower, inner consecration," i.e. the one which has been inserted into the normal consecration rite of the Soma ritual. Smaller and larger sets put together form new (sub)units, and there is a tendency, just as in Paṇinean grammar, to substitute one set by another (Hillebrandt 1897, Heesterman 1957, Witzel 1986b).

For now, the *meaning* of Vedic ritual (*yajña*) may be summarized as follows (Witzel 1992, 1998, Jamison and Witzel, 2002): its most important feature,

'MECHANISM' OF YAJÑA

mostly neglected until recently, is the principle of reciprocal exchange (Witzel 1979, 1998, Weber-Brosamer 1988, Malamoud 1989, Wilden 1992, Lopez 1997; denied by Heesterman, 1985: 83): the classical "*dō ut dēs*" is expressed as "give me, I give you" (*dehi me dadāmi te*, TS 1.8.4.1, VS 3.50, Mylius 1973: 476). The ritual oblations and the hymns of praise are just *one* act in an endless cycle of exchanges of *anna* "food" between the humans and the gods. The term *anna* in fact stands for a variety of substances, so that a whole Upaniṣad chapter (TU 3) surprisingly can deal with "food" (Lopez 1997). The concept survives to this day as "code substance" in *actual* exchange, especially in village society (Marriot 1976). In Vedic ritual and in modern society it is the code substance "food" that is given, altered, consumed and *partially* returned, keeping the path open for future transactions (Sahlins 1972).

In some detail: the fire god (Agni) carries the offerings to the gods. Fire also *transubstantiates* the offerings, not simply (Malamoud 1972) by a conversion from a raw, uncooked state into a palatable, cooked one but also by one from a *mundane* substance into one with divine characteristics; during this process its various consistent parts are split up and take new shapes (Vādh. Br. 4.19a = Caland 1990: 416ff).

As such, "food" travels towards the gods in the form of smoke and aroma (*medha*) and is consumed by them. The remains here on earth are a return gift of the gods who have tasted the food while sitting at the sacred fire, soiled it by their spittle and rendered it consumable only by their socially inferior relations, the human beings: this is the remnant (*ucchiṣṭa*), greatly extolled (AV 11.6) as having enormous potential (Malamoud 1975, Wezler 1978, Lopez 1997). The gods also give other return gifts to men, e.g. rain, sons, food, long life – the standard wishes of a Vedic Indian.

Apart from the gods, the ancestors and the ancient sages and poets, the Ṛṣis, are part of the system of exchange as well. Offering to all of them is regarded as delivering oneself from the innate *ṛṇa* "debt, obligation" (cf. Malamoud 1989: 115–36) that is inherent to all men. It is based on the simple fact that human beings are the somatic descendants of the gods (via the Āditya Vivasvant/ Mārtāṇḍa and his son Manu, the ancestor of mankind). As such, they have to take care of their direct and ultimate ancestors, just as the present gods (*deva*) do of their own ancestors (Aditi myth, MS 1.6.12) by offering food (*śrāddha*, *piṇḍa*) and water to their three direct ancestors and to a vague group of less immediate *pitṛs*.

For the brahmins the Ṛṣis represent both direct somatic and spiritual ancestors; these, the poets of the RV, are a dead poets' society who have actually gained access to heaven. While both Pitṛs and Ṛṣis are fed with actual food offerings, the seers additionally receive their own sort of "code substance" (*anna*), that is speech (*vāc*), through the daily recitation by humans of their Ṛgvedic poetry. Even today, Vedic recitation is preceded by the actual mentioning of the poet's name as to supply him with "spiritual food." The circle is closed by the release of "divine" inspiration (*dhī*) to latter-day poets who want to compose "a new song" (*bráhman*), such as a speculative hymn in the AV, a ritual *gāthā*, or a sorcery spell (*bráhman*) all of which make truth work (*satyakriyā*).

The ritual system, however, does not work without *śraddhā* (lit. "place the heart," Latin *crēdō*), the "confidence" in the efficacy of the ritual, i.e. its ability to motivate counter-gifts and to lead to heaven (Köhler 1948/1973, Lüders 1924, Hara 1964, Hacker 1963.)

The ritual procedure thus represents an eternal cycle which functions within the bounds of *Ṛta*. Various more or less abstract notions take part as well, e.g. *vāc*, *bráhman*, *śraddhā/manas*, *karman* (action), *anna*, *ucchiṣṭa*, many of which are dealt with in the speculative hymns of the RV and AV and are in need of detailed study.

Reciprocity is not confined to sentient beings but also found in the phenomenal world as a system of constant recycling: phenomena originating in heaven (such as rain) come to earth and nourish and are even transformed into other entities (such as plants and other living beings, semen, milk) that ultimately make their way to heaven again (as offering). In this cycle nothing is wasted or lost (Frauwallner 1953: 49, Schneider 1961, Bodewitz 1973: 243ff.), a concept that contributed largely to the middle Vedic system of homologies and correlations.

This mutual exchange is also seen in the social relations between men – e.g. between a sponsor (*yajamāna*) and his priest or his poet. The poet bestows praise on the patron, aids him in praising the gods, and expects material rewards in return, as is clearly and detailedly expressed in the so-called *dānastuti* or "Praise of the gift" of the RV. Similarly, the priests expect their *dakṣiṇā* "priestly gift," whose extent and nature is mandated by the reciprocal system and by the nature of the ritual in question. The *dakṣiṇā* seems to be a "diversion" to the priest of the original gift given to the departing guest (i.e. the gods!). For, the ritual system of exchange is based on the formalized rules of (human) hospitality (Thieme 1957b) and of marriage, where reciprocity is seen in the function of Aryaman as god of marriage who supervises guest friendship and the inherent exchange of brides.

Other major features of the Śrauta ritual include: there is no fixed place of performance, no temple or permanent structure: the Śrauta ritual is "portable," with a new sacrificial ground and with new, simple (archaic) wooden and clay implements in each ritual. The ground is prepared by careful measurement and demarcation (see Śulba Sūtra, Michaels 1978) and the building of fire altars. The central act of almost all Vedic rituals is the offering of various edible or drinkable substances into these 3–5 (and in some rites even more) fires.

The ritual is sponsored by the *yajamāna* or "sacrificer" (lit. "one sacrificing on his own behalf"), who first has to become an *āhitāgni* (one "having established fires"), after studentship and marriage, and belonging to the three "Twice Born" *Ārya* classes, (*Brāhmaṇa*, *Kṣatriya*, *Vaiśya*); only these thus could gain direct access to heaven through Śrauta ritual; the *Śūdra* were then and still are excluded.

Ritual performance involves a number of priests (up to 16 or 17, divided into four groups). These, and the four Vedas they represent, cooperate closely in the performance of a particular Śrauta sacrifice ("as in a violin quartet," Caland 1990).

The *main* participants, however, are the (except for Soma and Agni) invisible deities who are invited to attend as guests in a formal, ceremonial act of hospitality; they are fed and entertained by praise and song (Thieme 1957a,b). Medieval and modern *pūjā* still retain this pattern (Witzel 1980, Bühnemann 1988).

The rituals range from the simplest one, the Agnihotra or "Fire Offering," to the most elaborate of the *Śrauta* rituals, such as the Agnicayana ("piling of the fire [altar]") and the horse sacrifice (Aśvamedha). Their complexity is derived from incorporation of many less complex Śrauta rites (Hillebrandt 1897, 1987; Heesterman 1957, 1985; Staal 1982, 1990; Witzel 1987a, 1992, Minkowski 1992).

The most important rituals include the following. The initial establishment of the fire, the Agnyādheya (Moody 1989, Krick 1982); then, the Haviryajñas, most of which are determined by the rhythm of the year, and of the sun and the moon. The early morning and evening offering of milk (and similar products) into the fires (Agnihotra) ensures the survival of the sun during the night (Dumont 1939, Bodewitz 1976, Witzel 1986a, 1992). Brief as it is (some 15 minutes), it comprises about 100 actions; a number of extraneous rites have been added, such as an offering of milk to the Aśvins, the setting in motion of the heavenly waters of the Milky Way and of semen for men and milk for women (Witzel 1992); in addition we find the usual Vedic wishes: sons, rain, cattle, superiority within clan and tribe, living for the proverbial hundred years, and finding a way to Heaven. Śrauta ritual clearly is multivocal; the original meaning of any Śrauta ritual cannot easily be found; all its actions and the Mantras used *and* their history have to be traced first (Witzel 1981/2).

Other liminal rituals include the "New (and) Full Moon" sacrifice (Dārśapūrṇamāsa), offered twice per lunar month (Hillebrandt 1879, Rustagi 1981), and the seasonal rituals, the "four-monthly" Cāturmāsya, in spring, rainy season, and autumn, and additionally, around New Year (Bhide 1979, Einoo 1985, 1988).

The Paśubandha or "Animal Sacrifice" (Schwab 1886) is also integrated into the Soma ritual, and involves the killing of an animal. The inauspicious effect of killing is undone by involving substitution for the Adhvaryu priests and "bloodless" suffocation outside the actual offering ground; both are major features of the Śrauta mind set, as exemplified by the foundational (charter) myth of the Aśvins as the Adhvaryu priests of the gods (Witzel 1987a,b, 1997b, see below.)

The Soma Sacrifices are based on the *Agniṣṭoma*, a one day ritual (Caland-Henry 1906–7) that involves a special consecration (*dīkṣā*) of the Yajamāna and the pressing and offering of Soma in the early morning, at midday, and in the late afternoon. An important preliminary (and charter type) rite is the Pravargya, a hot milk drink for the Aśvins (van Buitenen 1968, Kashikar 1972). Variants of the Soma ritual last up to a year or even more; in the important 12 (or more) day *Sattra* ("Sitting") variety, the priests themselves undertake the ritual for their joint benefit (Falk 1985).

Other important Śrauta rituals include the *Rājasūya* ("Consecration of the King," Weber 1893, Heesterman 1957), the *Aśvamedha* ("Horse Sacrifice," Dumont 1927, S. Bhawe 1939) which can only be performed by a great king, and also the atypical *Agnicayana* ("Piling of the Fire Altar," Staal 1983, Kolhatkar 1986), a Soma ritual in which an additional raised fire altar of bricks is used. (A film and video tapes of the 1975 performance in Kerala have been used by Staal 1983.)

The Brāhmaṇa Texts

All aspects of the Śrauta ritual have been discussed at length in the so-called *brāhmaṇa* texts. The oldest texts, in a stark expository style, are contained in the YV Saṃhitās of the Black Yajurveda. The linguistically younger ones are independent texts, the Brāhmaṇas proper, which are attached to each of the four Vedas-Saṃhitās (see the Appendix at the end of this chapter). The most important texts are the JB of southern and the ŚB of eastern North India, the early AB of the eastern Panjab (its later sections, AB 6–8, come from the East), and the still largely unused VādhB, which is situated between the JB and ŚB.

Differently from the power entailed in poetic composition (*bráhman*) and its correct recitation, the Brāhmaṇa style text stress correct knowledge ("he who knows thus," *ya evaṃ veda*) of the hidden meanings of the ritual and the correlations (homologies) on which it is based (Witzel 1979, Wezler 1996). This so-called "identification" technique *correlates* certain items in the three spheres of microcosm (humans, society), mesocosm (*yajña*, i.e. ritual), and macrocosm (gods, universe, cf. Klaus 1986). This procedure led to a complex, amorphous (and still not completely described) web of "hidden" cosmic and mundane interrelations that was known only to the ritual specialists who used it to obtain certain desired effects.

The universe thus is a rich and esoteric system of homologies. This "ritual science" (Oldenberg 1919, Schayer 1925, Witzel 1979, B. K. Smith 1989, Wezler 1996) is based on the *strictly logical* application of the rule of cause and effect, even though its *initial* propositions (e.g. "the sun is gold") are something that we would not accept. The power of such esoteric Brahmanical knowledge has led – a fact that is not always recognized – directly to the speculations found in the Upaniṣads. The system was increasingly systematized by whole sets of parallel and interlinking correlations, so that by the time of the Upaniṣads, certain truths about the world and the humans could be expressed by a simple summation such as "*tat tvam asi*" (Brereton 1986).

The Brāhmaṇa style prose texts thus are the oldest explanations, in fact native commentaries, of the literal meaning of the Mantras, of their ritual applications, and of their often hidden secret import; futher, these texts discuss many of the individual actions of the ritual. In addition, they deal with a large variety of topics, from etymology to customs and beliefs; they also include many mythological tales that are meant to bolster the status of individual rites, as well as much incidental ritual speculation.

An all-important point of discussion in this period is how to avoid evil (*agha, enas, pāpa*) and pollution. This wish – and not the avoidance of violence as such (Heesterman 1985), which always remains involved in the classical ritual – is one of the important driving forces behind the Kuru time Śrauta reform. The little studied and less understood myth of Indra cutting off the head of Dadhyañc is the "charter myth" of the main priests acting in ritual, the Adhvaryus, who want to avoid *direct* involvement in the evil and pollution caused by killing necessary in ritual. They delegate these actions to helpers, working outside the sacrificial ground, and killing is not even referred to overtly: the animal is "pacified" (*śam*) (Witzel 1987a: n. 103); similarly, evil and illnesses are sent off in all directions (Witzel 1980).

The *actual reform* of the ritual, and its origins in the early Kuru realm, however, can clearly be attributed to a combination of late/post-RV political, social and religious changes (Witzel 1989b, 1995/1997a,b). The relationship between the development of Vedic ritual and changing social and political structures still is a promising field for further inquiry (Zimmer, 1879: 425–8; W. Rau 1957, Falk 1986, Witzel 1989b, 1997a,b).

The Āraṇyaka Texts

Āraṇyaka (Ār.) should have been translated, for nearly a century (Oldenberg 1915), as "wilderness (texts)," *not* as frequently still met with, as "forest texts." For, these texts are *not* texts meant for ascetics but as regular *brāhmaṇa* style texts which discuss the more secret and dangerous rituals. Therefore, they have been prescribed to be learned and recited outside, "from where one cannot see the roofs of the settlement." The main focus are the Mahāvrata (RV Ār.) and the Pravargya (YV Ār.) rituals. The treatment of the Pravargya in Śatapatha Br. is not only part of the Br. itself (ŚB 14) but even is referred to in ŚB 4 (Witzel, 1987a).

Because of their special position as additional texts the Ār. have become an open category where one could add all sorts of later Vedic texts, such as many Upaniṣads and even one early Sūtra (in ŚĀ). Many extraneous items have added to the nucleus of dangerous Śrauta rituals, including even post-Vedic Upaniṣads (MNU).

The often maintained connection of the Ār. texts with the post-Vedic life stage of the *vānaprastha* is only a medieval fiction. Also, the idea that these texts are spiritually more complex and evolved than the Brāhmaṇas is modern myth. In effect, it is only the Upaniṣads (often part of the Āraṇyakas) that are of philosophical content. In sum, the view that both the Ār. and the Upaniṣads should be aligned with the latter two of the (classical, medieval) four life stages (*vānaprastha, sannyāsin*) is to be rejected as later, post-Vedic interpretation.

The Upaniṣads

The Upaniṣads (Up.) contain the secret teaching, by a variety of late Vedic teachers, of early philosophical speculation about the nature of the world and of humans and their fate after death, as well as the earliest discussion of the workings of rebirth and *karma*. Various small heterogeneous sections have subsequently been added, such as last admonitions of the teacher to his "graduating," departing students (Witzel 1980, Thieme 1989). The texts were often called *Rahasya* "secret," as they were supposed to be learned only by specially selected students, which explains their often less well preserved state of transmission. Tradition, indeed, sees the Up.s as the end of the Veda (*vedānta*), that is of the four "historical" levels of the Saṃhitās, Br.s, Ār.s, and Up.s, while in fact, the late Vedic Sūtras (see below) still are an integral part of the Vedic canon.

It is from the background of the Brāhmaṇa style texts that the thinking of the Upaniṣads emerges. If not radically new, it still involves a thorough rethinking of the existing correlative premises, in part influenced by late Vedic social conditions of the eastern territories of North India (Kosala, Videha). Here, a thorough reorganization of the *brāhmaṇa* style texts (in ŚB) took place, including a rethinking of many of the earlier "theological" positions. Further, the increasing Sanskritization of the area along western (Kuru) models brought about the formation of canonical texts, a general ordering of Śrauta procedure, and new deliberations of its inherent meaning (Witzel 1997a,b).

Thus, the Upaniṣads do not break with tradition but rather continue it, influenced by the current and local religious background (Renou 1953). While they are often treated as the beginning of philosophical tradition in India (or as a precursor to early Buddhist and Jain thought) they are in fact the almost inevitable outcome of the intellectual development of the Brāhmaṇa period, when such questioning was prominent both inside and between the Vedic schools (*śākhā*). However, it was expressed differently, not in Upaniṣadic dialogue form, but by statements such as "some say . . ." or by the frequent quotations of divergent views in the *brāhmaṇa* type texts, especially in ŚB where various "solutions" to a problem are habitually discussed and still presented as authoritative, positive statements of truths. The Up.s, however, contain discussions in the form of real dialogues, involving severe questioning and reluctant admission of innocence or boastful claims of knowledge.

The Up.s deal with the eternal problems of humankind, that is: where do we come from, why we are here, where go? In other words, with the nature of body and soul, their fate after a death, and their position in the Universe. Additionally, following the trend towards larger scale correlations, the ritual itself increasingly becomes the subject of cosmic identifications (e.g. the horse of the Aśvamedha in BĀUK 1.1). But, ritual also is interiorized and can be performed entirely mentally (Bodewitz 1973). Both positions are signs of the intense contemporaneous intellectual activity that apparently included also some Kṣatriyas and women (Oldenberg 1915, Renou 1953, Horsch 1966, Witzel 1989a).

speculative
*

Certain new doctrines emerge: The late Brāhmaṇa opinion on the fate of humans after death (*punarmṛtyu*), and most importantly, *karma* which is now joined to the older concept of automatic rebirth (Kane 1962, Horsch 1971, O'Flaherty 1981, Tull 1989, Göhler 1990). Most studies, however, fail to investigate these concepts in their proper setting, that is by asking: what happens, in the view of Vedic people, at conception, at birth and at death to a human being (Witzel 1984a, 1998, Ikari 1989)?

The older Vedic (and probably Indo-European) idea involved an automatic, continuous cycle of human beings: after death, a stay in the blissful world of the ancestors, limited only by the "amount" of one's ritual actions (*iṣṭāpūrta, sukṛta*), and a subsequent automatic rebirth (MS 1.8.6), preferably within one's own clan and usually after the third of fourth generation. Nobody wanted to escape from this cycle of eternal return, except for the wealthy sponsors of Śrauta ritual who hoped to attain, eternally, the Heaven of the gods. The opposite, getting out of the cycle by becoming a renouncer (*sannyāsin*), developed only during the Up. period. The only other "escapees" are precisely those who have committed some serious actions that undermine the closed Vedic system of exchanges: murderers of embryos, of the brahmins' cow, etc.: that is, destroyers of the all-important "line of progeny" (*prajātantu* TU 1.11, 11, Witzel 2000) and of poetic inspiration (*dhī, dhenā*), the "cow" (*dhenu*) of the Brahmins (Witzel 1991); all these drop forever into "deepest darkness," into the lap of Nirṛti "destruction."

The earlier system of automatic recycling was now replaced by one conditioned by the *moral* value of the actions undertaken during one's lifetime. The new concept has its predecessors, on the one hand, in the fear of a second death (*punarmṛtyu*) occurring after a limited stay in the ancestor's world, and on the other, by the fear of a retribution in the other world, as exemplified by the vision of Bhṛgu (ŚB 11.6.1, JB 1.42): humans are cut up by trees felled by them and they are devoured by animals slaughtered in this world.

The old concept of cause and effect thus was linked with some new anxieties. One was no longer sure of the beneficial effects of ritual that allowed to neutralize all violent, "evil" actions carried out in ritual, to "beat away the second death," and to attain the desired permanent stay in heaven (Schmidt 1997). Now, *all* human actions (*karma*), not just the ritual ones, have their automatic consequence, as expressed by the new and secret *karma* idea. The juncture of the old concept of automatic rebirth with that of the younger one of automatic *karma* set the stage (Schmidt 1968b) for the development of a consistent theory of retribution in one's next life according to the actions (*karma*) undertaken in this one. This is the basis of nearly all of later Indian philosophy and should be studied as such.

Once, ChU 5.3.7 clearly says that the *karma* concept was known only to the Kṣatriyas, and in BĀU 3.2.6 Yājñavalkya takes his fellow brahmin Ārtabhāga apart to talk with him privately about *karma*. Apparently, the idea was not very "popular" at first. It originated with some brahmins in Yājñavalkya's time in northern Bihar (Witzel 1989a), and spread at an uneven pace: even in the last part of ChU, at 8.15, it was still felt necessary to speak about killing in ritual as *not* being evil, in fact, as guiltless (Witzel 1987a,b), and the beginning of the Bhagavadgītā still defends the *dharma* of a Kṣatriya as the norm – that is the duty to fight and kill.

However, the cycle of automatic rebirths has now been broken for the first time. The Upaniṣadic ascetics (such as Yājñavalkya, when he "went forth into homelessness," BĀU 4.5.15) and the contemporaries of the Buddha strive for emancipation that frees them from the *saṃsāra* of rebirth. Formerly, this was only the undesired lot destined for felons who had committed severe offenses. Now, one leaves home forever to strive for the knowledge of *brahman*. Traditional society quite consequently regarded such persons, once they had left, as socially "dead," and it did not allow for their return. Some middle level Upaniṣad texts (Kaṭha-Śruti Up., Mānava Śrautasūtra 8.25, Sprockhoff 1987) have preserved a ritual of taking leave from home and all one's possessions while declaring non-violence (*ahiṃsā*) to all beings.

Several factors thus come together and lead to a qualitative breakthrough, which results in the new karmic rebirth idea and, based on increasing use of higher levels of correlations, in the assertion of the identity of the human soul (*ātman*) with that of *brahman* (neuter) in such famous sentences as *tat tvam asi* (ChU 6.10.3, Brereton 1986).

Many facets of the newly introduced concepts still are in need of detailed study, e.g. that of a scale on which one's deeds are weighed and other Iranian/Zoroastrian/(Śaka?) concepts. However, the often repeated conviction that it was the Kṣatriyas who introduced the *karma* concept is far-fetched (Horsch 1966, Olivelle 1996: xxxiv). The mentioning of the topic by a king, a god (Varuṇa), or Yājñavalkya's secretive conference rather are *literary* devices (Witzel 1997a) which merely underline the *importance* of the theme. Using a woman, Gārgī, in BĀU 3 has similar effect as women usually do not appear in public assemblies of learned disputation and when they do so, they stand out. The other prominent woman in BĀU, Maitreyī, quite untypically *had* learnt Brahmanical lore. It is only to her that Yājñavalkya speaks about eschatology (BĀU 4.5.15). Similarly, the idea that it was the Jainas, the local aboriginal people, etc. who "invented" these ideas is, of course nothing more than an admission of ignorance (O'Flaherty 1981), as there simply are no early records of the Jainas and even less of the aboriginal inhabitants. Rather, later Vedic thought quite naturally led to this stage, and to a whole range of more or less contemporary and quite diverse points of view, as discussed in the Pali canon (Dīghanikāya 2).

Why did these developments take place precisely at this moment, and in this area of Northern India (Kosala, E. Uttar Pradesh, and Videha, N. Bihar)? The breakthrough is similar to the more or less contemporary ones elsewhere – even if Jaspers' idea of an "axial age" suffers from some severe incongruencies in the actual time frame. Indeed, external influence is not likely in Bihar, unless one posits some Iranian influence (see above): after all, Zoroastrianism first stressed individual decision making: one had to chose between "good" and "evil" and had to face a last judgment after death.

The Kosala–Videha area was one of great mixture of peoples due to various movements of tribes and individuals, and consequently also of ideas (Witzel 1989a: 236, 1997a). It also was a part of the spread-zone of the western, Kuru type Vedic orthopraxy. Some late- or post-Vedic immigrants such as the Malla, Vṛji (Vajji), or especially the Śākya, may be Iranian tribes (Witzel 1989a: 239) who may have transmitted (para-)Zoroastrian influence. Further, there was admixture of local Muṇḍa peoples (AB 7.18), of older, eastern Indo-Aryan settlers, and of contemporaneous immigrants including many western Brahmins. A comparison of the late Vedic and early Buddhist texts indicates admixture of the older, para-Vedic Indo-Aryan religion of the East with the orthodoxy and orthopraxy of the "missionary" Kuru-Pañcāla Brahmins of the West, who were invited by such kings as Mahākosala and (Mahā)-Janaka (Witzel 1989a, 1997a) of the emerging large kingdoms of Kosala and Magadha. Finally, there was the social ferment created by the contemporaneously emerging cities (of the so-called second urbanization, after the Indus civilization). The Vedic texts hardly, if ever, speak about towns (Mylius 1969); however, Brahmins never liked their polluting social atmosphere and rather preferred to live in the countryside where they could regulate their life properly. Yet, by the time of the Pali texts, cities are fully established, with rich merchants carrying out a long distance overland trade (of the luxury article, Northern Black Polished Ware), and brahmins living in the formerly off-limits lands of Magadha and Aṅga.

All of these admixtures supplied the ideal breeding ground for the meeting of ideas and the development of new concepts. Just as the break-up of the old Ṛgvedic tribal society caused enormous social and religious change (see above), the new stratified and partly aristocratic, partly oligarchic (not a "republican" one, Rhys-Davies 1911), and partly urban society of the East witnessed the emergence of many of the typically Upaniṣadic ideas described above.

The so-called Middle Up.s (Īśa, Kaṭha, Kena, Praśna, Muṇḍa, Māṇḍūkya, Śvetāśvatara, Mahānārayaṇa, etc.) are no longer composed in prose but in verse and are heavily influenced by the post-Vedic (Epic) language. Many of them show a tendency towards the sectarian worship of a particular deity. The Saṃnyāsa Up.s (Sprockhoff 1976, Olivelle 1992), composed around 300 BCE, discuss the newly introduced life stage of the renouncer. The *Bhagavadgītā* of the *Mahābhārata* is sometimes regarded as an Up. as well. Sectarian Up.s (in Epic/ Classical Sanskrit) have been composed well into the Middle Ages. In the interpretation of the Upaniṣads the eighth century monistic philosopher Śaṅkara has played an important but generally overrated role. We still are in need of a detailed philological edition and discussion of the important older Upaniṣads.

The Śrautasūtras

The Vedic canon concludes with the late Vedic Sūtras ("thread, guideline," or *Kalpasūtra* "ritual guidelines") which form the *true* end of the Vedic period and its texts, though the classical/medieval tradition assigns them to a separate category, the Smṛti texts. Indeed, the older ones among them (BŚS, VādhŚS, etc.) are still composed in late Br. language. The Sūtras are descriptive and prescriptive texts that deal systematically, in the proper order of ritual procedure, with the solemn ritual (Śrauta Sūtra), with the domestic rituals (Gṛhya Sūtra), and with the rules of proper behavior as a Veda student or as householder (Dharma Sūtra). (There also are various later additions to all Vedic texts, *Pariśiṣṭa*.)

The older Sūtras such as BŚS, VādhŚS explain the complicated ritual step-by-step and at great length, in clear prose and by quoting the Mantras *in extenso*. Even if a ritual that is described later in the text is built out of ritual blocks described earlier, these older Sūtras still describe such complex rituals in extenso. Later Sūtras make increasing use of the referring technique which points back to earlier parts of the text by quotation ("as said earlier") and of using just the initial words of a Mantra (*pratīka*). The later texts use shorter and shorter (nominal) clauses, a technique seen in its apogee in Pāṇini's grammatical Sūtras, the Aṣṭādhyāyī.

The most important Sūtras include the early BaudhŚS and VādhŚS, the somewhat later ĀpŚS (with many quotations from other texts), all of the YV; the early KŚS of the RV, the LŚS and JŚS of the SV, and the rather late VaitS of the AV. The ŚS of the White YV, the late KŚS is the one most developed one along the lines described above.

The contents of the Śrautasūtras follow, by and large, the scheme first set out in the Mantra collection of the Yajurveda Saṃhitās, and the individual rules follow those of the Brāhmaṇa style texts (Tsuji 1952).

The Gṛhyasūtras

The Gṛhya Sūtras (GS) often form part of, or actually are, an appendix to the Śrauta Sūtras, and some of them refer back to ritual details described earlier in the same text or even in the Śrauta Sūtra. Their contents, however, often are very old. Some of the rites of passage (*saṃskāra*, Pandey 1957, P. V. Kane 1930–62, Gonda 1980a), such as burial and marriage, have been described already in the RV and AV, and some of the details may in fact go back even to the Indo-European period, for example the offering of three meat balls (later, made of rice) in the anniversary rituals (*śrāddha*) for one's three immediate ancestors (Schrader 1919), or the cult of the fire, or the marriage ceremony; other items, such as the initiation of the student by a girdle, are of Indo-Iranian age (Avest. *aiβiiā̊ŋhana*, Ved. *mekhalā*).

By and large, the GS deal with the rites of passage form birth to death (Stenzler 1864, Hillebrandt 1897, Apte 1939, transl. Oldenberg 1886/1892), or rather, from one's conception to one's dissolution in the vague group of ancestors (*pitṛ*). The GS thus are a cyclical set of rituals variously arranged as starting with marriage, with initiation to Veda study (*upanayana*), or even with pregnancy.

The "original" contents of the Gṛhya texts (Oldenberg 1892), however, have been influenced by the much more predominant ritual form, that of the Śrauta ritual (Gonda 1977, B. K. Smith 1986). Thus, even in the supposedly "simple" domestic ritual, the activity of the *yajamāna* was superseded by the actions of the Brahmin house priest (*purohita*). However, there is only a single fire as compared to the 3–5 of the Śrauta ritual, and many of the simple Gṛhya rituals have counterparts in the solemn Śrauta ones, including the morning and evening offerings (*homa*), the New and Full Moon offerings, etc. Their exact (pre)history is difficult to establish.

This is different, as indicated, for marriage and death as even the RV contains hymns devoted to marriage (10.85, expanded in AV 14, PS 18.1–14) and to funerals (10.14–18, AV 18, PS 18.57–82); in addition, PS 20 even contains some of the actual dialogue of the *upanayana* rituals (cf. ŚB 11, TĀ 2, TU 1.11, KaṭhŚiU), similar to the verbal exchanges at the marriage ceremony (Kajihara 2002). The rather composite RV marriage hymn is a recounting of the mythical origin and prototype of human marriage, that of the goddess Sūryā with Soma. Some marriage features of the GS (Apte 1978, Winternitz 1892, Zachariae 1977, 1989, Tsuji 1960) are clearly present in the RV, others are not yet mentioned (the circumambulation of the fire, the mounting of the stone, the gazing at the pole-star) but already appear in the AV. The funeral hymns clearly describe cremation, though the RV also refers to burial, exposure on trees and "throwing away" of the dead body. *Satī* was not practiced (Witzel 1996); in fact, there is evidence for levirate marriage (Schmidt 1987). Much space is given in the GS to ancestor worship (Caland 1893, 1896, 1914, Winternitz 1892).

The yearly return of the Veda student to his teacher (Heesterman 1985) follows a period of about half a year away from "school" when the young men (*marya*) were members in a Vrātya *Männerbund*, as reflected already in some earlier Vedic texts (cf. AV 15, PS 18; Falk 1986, Bollée 1981, Heesterman, 1981: 251–71). The *vrātyas*, frequently still misunderstood as semi- or non-Ārya, live a roaming, independent and promiscuous life while trying to collect a "starting capital" of cattle, by threatening, from the settled section of society. They are reflected, in the divine sphere by the *daivya vrātya*, the Gandharvas (Vasilkov 1991).

Women are not prominently discussed in these and other Vedic texts (Jamison 1996), though their role in the *saṃskāras* of marriage and child birth is of course prominent. However, the role of women in the Upaniṣads is usually overstated. The only(!) two famous ones, Gārgī and Maitreyī, are inserted – just like Kṣatriyas and kings, or the son of a god, Bhṛgu – at critical, innovative or striking junctures of a dialogue. Yet, there also is clear, though sparse evidence of female learned activity, such as at BĀU 6.4.17 which has a prescription of how to obtain a female Ṛṣi in one's family, as is indeed mentioned for the Atri clan (JB 2.219).

Just as the AV Saṃhitās, the "Gṛhya Sūtra" of the AV (KauśS, Bloomfield 1889, Caland 1900) contains many facets of early Indian life that would otherwise escape us. The text uses the same, magical system of homologies that correlate and control macrocosmic forces by microcosmic manipulation (Henry 1904, Stutley 1980). Earlier, comparable texts are the official Śrauta rituals, the *Kāmyā Iṣṭi* "wish offerings" of the YV (Caland 1908). The KauśS provides many usages for the AV Saṃhitā spells; other sorcery practices are found in the (late) Sāmavidhāna Brāhmaṇa. Many obscure magical terms have been preserved in more recent sorcery (Türstig 1980). The only partially translated Kauś.S. is a virtual handbook of customs and beliefs, of common white and black sorcery, of healing procedures (Filliozat 1975, Zysk 1985), of omina and portenta (Weber 1859). Many such details can be followed up later on in the AV Pariśiṣṭa and in the medieval books on dreams (Stuhrmann 1982, v. Negelein 1912), or in the Jyotiṣa literature (Pingree 1981).

The Dharmasūtras

These Sūtras deal with *dharma* "proper behavior," beginning with that of a Veda student, and moving to that of a married man (*gṛhastha*), his daily and seasonal ritual duties, family life, to the death rituals and ancestor worship and inheritance; some also include the duties of a king and his jurisprudence, the four stages in life, and long sections on atonements for wrong behavior. These rules have provided the basis for medieval and modern Anglo-Indian Hindu law.

Many of these rules overlap with those of the Gṛhya Sūtras, and some may be quite old, such as the incidental rule, found also in Pindar's *Erga*, not to urinate towards the sun. The Up.s, too, contain a Dharma Sūtra in nuce, the final admonition about good behavior in adult life by a Veda teacher to his departing student (TU 1, KaṭhŚiU, Witzel 1980).

Finally, there are a number of appendixes to the Vedic texts, of various periods, such as the Ṛgvedakhila, or the AV-Pariśiṣṭa, some of which are already composed in the style of the Epic and Purāṇas.

Personal and Popular Religion

Personal, popular and non-Brahmanical religion are much less visible in the Vedic texts, which therefore must be compared with the slightly later Pali canon, and the evidence of the (still little defined) older strata of the Mahābhārata.

Religious feelings and experiences are mentioned by very few poets in the RV, such as Vasiṣṭha in RV 7.86–9 (Goto 2000), who speaks, not unlike Zoroaster, of a very personal relationship with Varuṇa, or Bharadvāja Bārhaspatya who describes (RV 6.9.6–7) not, as usual, a vision but also an acoustic experience of God Agni. Other items include the old Indo-Iranian (and Eurasian) topic of flying through the night time sky on a boat, (both in RV and in Avesta, Oettinger 1988). There also is a shaman-like experience of the "(long) haired one" (Keśin,

RV 10.136), cf. also that of the bird Laba (RV 10.119) who touches heaven and earth with his wings. The AV contains much popular sorcery and magic, but in a form that has been influenced by the priests. Later on, we have the infernal visions of Bhṛgu (ŚB, JB) or those of Yājñavalkya of the dream state (BĀU 4.3), or about the way of the emancipated to the "heavenly" palace of Brahman (KU, Thieme 1951/2).

Popular festivals at New Year include horse chariot races and bow shooting, public riddles, sexual banter and public intercourse of two "outcasts" (a prostitute, *mahānagnikā*, and a *Māgadha* man); further, singing and dancing at summer solstice. Such materials have been collected by Zimmer 1879 for the Saṃhitās, and by W. Rau 1957, 1977, Mylius 1971–4, Basu 1969, Gopal 1959 for the later texts.

Some late sections in the GS deal with the worship of particular gods, such as Rudra/Mahādeva/Īśāna, Viṣṇu/Nārāyaṇa, Śrī, Durgā (Baudhāyana Gṛhyaśeṣasūtra, Atharveda Pariśiṣṭa etc., Einoo 1992, 1996). They contain *pūjā*-like rites that cannot be pinpointed in time. *Pūjā* is, however, a clear continuation (Witzel 1980) of the Ṛgvedic guest worship offered to the gods. Other worship, such as that of snake deities (*Nāga*), trees, etc. is even more opaque. The worship of images is first visible in texts in Patañjali's Mahābhāṣya (5.3.99: 429.3), at ca. 150 BCE.

True heterodoxy is attested by ca. 400 BCE when several such systems had developed, including those of wandering teachers such as the Buddha and Mahāvīra (Dīghanikāya 2). Nearly all them stem from eastern North India, where the constantly changing cultural ferment favored dialogue and competition. Yājñavalkya's departure into homelessness (BĀU 4.5.15) takes up the tradition of (long distance) wandering by Veda students and Vrātyas; indeed, the Buddhist *saṅgha* has, unobserved so far, some *vrātya* features as well: a single leader of a larger group of equals who wander about in the countryside and live on extortion (or by begging), stay away from settlements, have special dress and speech, etc.

The east was indeed quite different from the western parts of Northern India, as seen in language (Witzel 1989a), social structure including the oligarchic states, and in burial practices: while the Kurus built small square grave mounds, the "easterners and others(!)" have "demonic" round graves (ŚB 12.8.1.5).

We get only glimpses of what may have been other aberrant (ritual?) sexual behavior at AB 7.13, or in the Gosava ritual, or already in the RV notion of *śiśnadeva, mūradeva.*

Even less can be said about the pre-Vedic religion of the Indus Civilization and of the contemporaneous aboriginal tribes. They were assimilated by Sanskritization, e.g., a leader (*sthapati*, MS 2.2.4) of the Niṣādas, or at AB 7.18, where the Ṛgvedic(!) Ṛṣi Viśvāmitra assists the eastern Ikṣvāku king Hariścandra by symbolically adopting local "barbarian" tribes (*dasyu*), such as the Andhra, Puṇḍra, Śabara "who live in large numbers beyond the borders."

Though some ideas, customs and beliefs of the Harappan civilization seem to have been incorporated into the subsequent Vedic world view (tree worship, etc.), a Vedic connection of the so-called Śiva Paśupati found on some Harappa seals (D. Srinivasan 1984) cannot be established; this mythological concept is due, rather, to common Eurasian ideas of the "Lord of the Animals" who is already worshipped by many Neolithic hunting societies. Similarly, the remnants of the so-called fire rituals at Kalibangan (B. B. Lal 1997) involve clearly non-Vedic offerings of animal bones; they (and the so-called "liṅga steles," actually supports for cooking pots) may represent nothing but a community kitchen of the Indus Civilization (R. S. Sharma 1995: 47).

Bibliography

Apte, V. M. *Social and religious life in the Gṛhyasūtras.* Ahmedabad, 1939.

——. *The sacrament of marriage in Hindu society from Vedic period to Dharmaśāstras.* Delhi, 1978.

Basu, J. *India of the age of the Brāhmaṇa.* Calcutta, 1969.

Benveniste, E. and L. Renou. *Vṛtra et Vṛthragna: Etude de mythologie indo-iranienne.* Paris, 1934.

Bergaigne, A. *La religion védique*, 3 vols. (Bibliothèque de l'école des Hautes études 36, 53–4.) Paris, 1878–83. Engl. trans. V. G. Paranjpe, Poona, 1978.

Bhawe, S. *Die Yajus' des Aśvamedha.* Stuttgart, 1939.

Bhide, V. V. *The Cāturmāsya sacrifices. With special reference to the Hiraṇyakeśi Śrauta Sūtra.* Poona, 1979.

Bloomfield, M. 1889. "The Kauśika Sūtra of the Artharvaveda," *Journal of the American Oriental Society* 14, repr. Delhi, 1972.

Bodewitz, H. W. *Jaiminīya Brāhmaṇa I, 1–65. Translation and commentary with a study of the Agnihotra and Prāṇāgnihotra.* Leiden, 1973.

——. *The daily evening and morning offering (Agnihotra) according to the Brāhmaṇas.* Leiden, 1976.

——. "The fourth Priest (the Brahmán) in Vedic ritual," *Studies in the History of Religions* 45, 1983: 33–68.

Bollée, W. B. "The Indo-European sodalities in Ancient India," *Zeitschrift der Deutschen Morgenländischen Gesellschaft* 131, 1981: 172–91.

Brereton, J. P. *The Ṛgvedic Ādityas.* New Haven, 1981.

——. "Tat tvam asi in Context," *Zeitschrift der Deutschen Morgenländischen Gesellschaft* 136, 1986: 98–109.

——. "Unsounded speech: Problems in the interpretation of BU(M) I.5.10 = BU (K) 1.5.3," *Indo-Iranian Journal* 31, 1988: 1–10.

Brown, W. N. "The Basis for the Hindu Act of Truth," *Review of Religions* 5, 1940: 36–45.

——. "The Metaphysics of the Truth Act (*Satyakriyā)," in *Mélanges d'Indianisme à la mémoire de L. Renou.* Paris, 1968, 171–7.

Bühnemann, G. *Pūjā: A study in Smārta ritual.* Wien, 1988.

Buitenen, J. A. B. van. *The Pravargya.* Poona, 1968.

Caland, W. 1893. *Altindischer Ahnenkult: Das Śrāddha nach den verschiedene Schulen mit Benutzung handschriftlicher Quellen dargestellt.* Leiden, 1893.

——. *Die altindischen Todten- und Bestattungs-gebräuche.* Amsterdam, 1896.

——. *Altindisches Zauberritual. Probe einer Übersetzung der wichtigsten Theile des Kauśika Sūtra.* Amsterdam, 1900.

——. *Altindische Zauberei. Darstellung der altindischen "Wunschopfer."* Amsterdam, 1908.
——. "Die vorchristlichen baltischen Totengebräuche," *Archiv für Religionswissenschaft* 17, 1914: 476–512.
——. *Kleine Schriften*, ed. M. Witzel. Wiesbaden, 1990.
Dandekar, R. N. *Vedic Mythological Tracts*. Delhi, 1979.
——. "Vedic Mythology: A Rethinking," in M. Witzel, ed., *Inside the texts, beyond the texts: New approaches to the study of the Vedas*. Cambridge, MA, 1997, pp. 39–48.
——, and C. G. Kashikar. *Śrautakośa*. [English and Sanskrit Sections.] Poona, 1958–.
Dumézil, G. *Ouranós-Váruṇa*. Paris, 1934.
——. 1958. "Arí, Aryamán à propos de Paul Thieme '*arí*,' 'Fremder,'" *Journal asiatique* 246: 67–84.
Dumont, P.-E. *L'Aśvamedha: Description du sacrifice solonnel du cheval dans le culte védique d'après les textes du Yajurveda blanc*. Paris, 1927.
——. *L'Agnihotra: Description de l'agnihotra dans le rituel védique d'après les Śrautasūtras*. Baltimore, 1939.
Einoo, S. "The Interpretation of the Cāturmāsya Sacrifice according to the Ancient Indian Brāhmaṇa Literature" [in Japanese, with Engl. summary], *Journal of the Nat. Museum for Ethnology* (Kokuritsu Minpaku Hakubutsukan) 10, 1985: 1001–68.
——. *Die Cāturmāsya oder die altindischen Tertialopfer dargestellt nach den Vorschriften der Brāhmaṇas und der Śrautasūtras*. Monumenta Serindica No. 18. Tokyo, 1988.
——. "Some Aspects of the Ritual Development in the Gṛhyasūtras" (in Japanese, Engl. summary). In *Memoirs of the Institute of Oriental Culture* 118, 1992: 43–86.
——. "The Formation of the Pūjā Ceremony," *Studien zur Indologie und Iranistik* 20, 1996: 73–87.
Falk, H. "Die Legende von Śunaḥśepa vor ihrem rituellen Hintergrund," *Zeitschrift der Deutschen Morgenländischen Gesellschaft* 134, 1984: 115–35.
——. "Zum Ursprung der Sattra-Opfer," *Zeitschrift der Deutschen Morgenländischen Gesellschaft, Supplement VI*, 1985: 275–81.
——. *Bruderschaft und Würfelspiel*. Freiburg, 1986.
——. "Vedische Opfer im Pali-Kanon," *Bulletin des Etudes indiennes* 6, 1988: 225–54.
——. "The Purpose of Ṛgvedic Ritual," in M. Witzel, ed., *Inside the texts, beyond the texts: New approaches to the study of the Vedas*. Cambridge, MA, 1997, pp. 67–88.
Filliozat, J. *La doctrine classique de la médecine indienne*. Paris, 1949, repr. 1975 [Engl. trans.: *The classical doctrine of Indian medicine, its origins and its Greek parallels*. Delhi, 1964].
Frauwallner, E. *Geschichte der indischen Philosophie I*. Salzburg, 1953.
Geldner, K. F. *Der Rigveda: Aus dem Sanskrit ins Deutsche übersetzt und mit einem laufenden Kommentar versehen*, 3 vols. (Harvard Oriental Series 33, 34, 35) Cambridge, MA (*Index*, ed. J. Nobel, HOS vol. 36, 1957).
Göhler, L. *Zu philosophisch-methodologischen Grundlagen der Erforschung des vedischen Opferrituals*. Frankfurt, 1990.
Gonda, J. *Notes on Brahman*. Utrecht, 1950.
——. *Die Religionen Indiens. I. Veda und älterer Hinduismus*. Stuttgart, 1960.
——. *The Vedic god Mitra*. Leiden, 1972.
——. *A history of Indian literature*: I.2 *The ritual Sūtras*. Wiesbaden, 1977.
——. *Vedic ritual: The non-solemn rites*. Leiden, 1980a.
——. *The Mantras of the Agnyupasthāna and the Sautrāmaṇī*. Amsterdam, 1980b.
——. *Prajāpati and the year*. Amsterdam, 1984.

——. *Prajāpati's rise to higher rank*. Leiden, 1986.

——. *Prajāpati's relations with Brahman, Bṛhaspati and Brahma*. Amsterdam, 1989.

Gopal, Ram. *India of Vedic Kalpasūtras*. Delhi, 1959.

Goto, T. "Vasiṣṭha und Varuṇa in RV VII 88 – Priesteramt des Vasiṣṭha und Suche nach seinem indoarischen Hintergrund," in *Indoarisch, Iranisch, und die Indogermanistik. Arbeitstagung der Indogermanischen Gesellschaft vom 2. bis 5. Oktober 1997 in Erlangen*; hg. B. Forssman & R. Plath. Wiesbaden, 2000, 147–61.

Hacker, P. "Śraddhā," *Wiener Zeitschrift zur Kunde Südasiens* 3, 1963: 151–89.

Hale, W. E. *Asura in early Vedic religion*. Delhi, 1986.

Hara, M. "Note on Two Sanskrit Religious Terms: *bhakti* and *śraddhā*," *Indo-Iranian Journal* 7, 1964: 124–45.

Heesterman, J. C. *The ancient Indian royal consecration: The Rājasūya described according to the Yajus texts and annoted* [*sic*]. s'Gravenhage, 1957.

——. Householder and wanderer, *Fs. L. Dumont*, ed. T. N. Madan. New Delhi, 1981, 251–71.

——. *The inner conflict of tradition. Essays in Indian ritual, kingship, and society*. Chicago, 1985.

——. *The broken world of sacrifice: An essay in ancient Indian ritual*. Chicago, 1993.

Henry, V. *La magie dans l'Inde antique*. Paris, 1904 [2nd ed. 1909].

Hillebrandt, A. *Das altindische Neu- und Vollmondopfer in seiner einfachsten Form*. Jena, 1879.

——. *Ritualliteratur: Vedische Opfer und Zauber*. Strassburg, 1897.

——. *Kleine Schriften*, ed. R. P. Das. Stuttgart, 1987.

——. *Vedische Mythologie*, 2 vols. Breslau, 1927–9. (English trans. Delhi.)

Hoffmann, K. H. *Aufsätze zur Indoiranistik*, ed. J. Narten, 2 vols., Wiesbaden, 1975, 1976; vol. 3, eds. S. Glauch, R. Plath, and S. Ziegler, Wiesbaden, 1992.

Hopkins, E. W. "Gods and Saints of the Great Brāhmaṇa," *Transactions of the Connecticut Academy of Arts and Sciences* 15, 1908: 19–69.

Horsch, P. *Die vedische Gāthā- und Ślokalitteratur*. Bern, 1966.

——. "Vorstufen der indischen Seelenwanderungslehre," *Asiatische Studien* 25, 1971: 99–157.

Hubert, H. and M. Mauss, *Essai sur la nature et la fonction du sacrifice*. Paris, 1923–4.

Ikari, Y. "Some Aspects of the Idea of Rebirth in Vedic Literature," *Studies in the History of Indian Thought (Indo-Shisōshi-Kenkyū)*, no. 6 [Special issue dedicated to Professor Masaaki Hattori on the occasion of his retirement from Kyoto University, Nov. 1989].

Jamison. S. W. *The ravenous hyenas and the wounded sun: Myth and ritual in ancient India*. Ithaca–London, 1991.

——. *Sacrificed wife/sacrificer's wife: Women, ritual, and hospitality in ancient India*. New York, 1996.

—— and M. Witzel. "Vedic Hinduism," in A. Sharma, ed., *The study of Hinduism*. Columbia, SC, 2002.

Kajihara, M. *The Brahmacārin*. Harvard Ph.D. thesis, 2002.

Kane, P. V. *History of Dharmaśāstra*. Bhandarkar Oriental Research Inst., Poona, 1930–62.

Kashikar, C. G. "Apropos of the Pravargya," *CASS Studies*, 1, 1972: 1–10. Centre of Advanced Studies in Sanskrit, Poona.

Keith, A. B. *The religion and philosophy of the Veda and Upanishads*, 2 vols. (Harvard Oriental Series 31, 32). Cambridge, MA, 1925 [repr. Delhi 1970].

Köhler, H.-W. *Śrad-dhā- in der vedischen und altbuddhistischen Literatur*, ed. K. L. Janert. Wiesbaden, 1973 [diss. 1948].
Krick, H. *Das Ritual der Feuergründung (Agnyādheya)*. Wien, 1982.
Kolhatkar, M. "The Relation between the Agnicayana and the Sautrāmaṇī," *Annals of the Bhandarkar Oriental Research Institute* 67, 1986: 109–15.
Klaus, K. *Die altindische Kosmologie, nach den Brāhmaṇas dargestellt*. Bonn, 1986.
Kuiper, F. B. J. "The Ancient Aryan Verbal Contest," *Indo-Iranian Journal* 4, 1960: 217–81 [repr. in Kuiper 1983: 151–215].
——. "The Three Strides of Viṣṇu," in *Fs. N. Brown*, ed. E. Bender. New Haven, 1962, pp. 137–51 [repr. 1983].
——. "The Basic Concept of Vedic Religion," *History of Religions* 15, 1975: 107–20 [= Kuiper 1983: 9–22].
——. *Ancient Indian cosmogony*, ed. J. Irwin. Delhi, 1983.
Lal, B. B. *The earliest civilization of South Asia (rise, maturity and decline)*. New Delhi, 1997.
Lévi, S. *La doctrine du sacrifice dans les Brāhmaṇas*. Paris, 1898 [repr. Paris, 1966].
Lopez, C. "Food and Immortality in the Veda: A Gastronomic Theology?," *Electronic Journal of Vedic Studies* 3 (3), October 1997. http://nautilus.shore.net/~india/ejvs/ejvs0303/ejvs0303.txt
Lüders, H. "Eine arische Anschauung über den Vertragsbruch," *Sitzungsberichte der Preussischen Akademie der Wissenschaften* 1917: 347–74.
——. "Die Śraddhā und die Wiedergeburt," *Sitzungsberichte der Preussischen Akademie der Wissenschaften* 1924: 228.
——. "Die magische Kraft der Wahrheit im alten Indien," *Zeitschrift der Deutschen Morgenländischen Gesellschaft* 98, 1944: 1–14.
——. *Varuṇa*, 2 vols, ed. L. Alsdorf. Göttingen, 1951, 1959.
Malamoud, C. "Observations sur la notion de 'reste' dans le brahmanisme," *Wiener Zeitschrift zur Kunde Südasiens* 17 (1972): 6–26 [= 1989: 13–33].
——. "Cuire le monde," *Puruṣārtha* 1, 1975: 91–135 [= 1989: 35–70].
——. *Cuire le monde: Rite et pensée dans l'inde ancienne*. Paris, 1989.
Marriot, McKim. "Hindu Transactions: Diversity without Dualism," in B. Kapferer, ed., *Transaction and meaning: Directions in the anthropology of exchange and symbolic behavior*. Philadelphia, 1976: 109–42.
Meillet, A. "Le dieu indo-iranien Mitra," *Journal asiatique* 10, 1907: 143–59.
Michaels, A. *Beweisverfahren in der vedischen Sakralgeometrie: ein Beitrag zur Entstehungsgeschichte von Wissenschaft*. Wiesbaden, 1978.
Minkowski, C. Z. "The Rathakāra's Eligibility to Sacrifice," *Indo-Iranian Journal* 32, 1989: 177–94.
——. *Priesthood in ancient India: A study of the Maitrāvāruṇa priest*. Vienna, 1992.
Moody, T. F. *The Agnyādheya: Establishment of the sacred fires*. Thesis, McMaster Univ., Hamilton, Ont., 1989.
Mus, P. *Barubuḍur: Esquisse d'une histoire du bouddhisme fondée sur la critique archéologique des texts*. Hanoi, 1935, 79–121.
Mylius, K. "Gab es Städte im jungvedischen Indien?," *Ethnologisch-Archäologische Zeitschrift* 10, 1969: 33–9.
——. "Die gesellschaftliche Entwicklung Indiens in jungvedischer Zeit nach den Sanskritquellen," *Ethnologisch-Archäologische Zeitschrift* 12, 1971: 171–97; 13, 1972: 321–65; 14, 1973: 425–99; 15, 1974: 385–432.
Narten, J. "Vedisch *aghnyā-* und die Wasser," *Acta Orientalia Neerlandica*, ed. P. W. Pestman, Leiden, 1971, 120–34.
von Negelein, J. *Der Traumschlüssel des Jagaddeva*. Giessen, 1912.

Oberlies, Th. König Somas Kriegszug. *Studien zur Indologie und Iranistik* 15, 1989, 71–96.
——. *Eine Kompositions-Analyse der Somahymnen des Ṛigveda.* D.Litt., Tübingen, 1991, = *Die Religion des Ṛgveda* [vol. 1. *Das religiöse System des Ṛgveda;* vol. 2, *Kompositionsanalyse der Soma-Hymnen des Ṛgveda*]. Wien, 1998–.
Oettinger, N. "Zu den Mythen von Bhujyu- und von Pāuruua-," *Indo-Iranian Journal* 31, 1988: 299–300.
O'Flaherty, W. D. *The Rig Veda: An anthology.* Harmondsworth, 1981.
Oldenberg, H. *The Gṛihya-Sūtras: Rules of Vedic domestic ceremonies,* 2 vols. Oxford, 1886, 1892 [repr. Delhi, 1964, 1967].
——. *Metrische und textgeschichtliche Prolegomena zu einer kritischen Rigveda-Ausgabe.* Berlin, 1888 [repr. Wiesbaden, 1982].
——. "Āraṇyaka," *Nachrichten von der Gesellschaft der Wissenschaften zu Göttingen* 1915: 382–401 [repr. *Kleine Schriften,* ed. K. Janert, Wiesbaden, 1967, 419–38].
——. *Vorwissenschaftliche Wissenschaft: Die Weltanschauung der Brāhmaṇa-Texte.* Göttingen, 1919.
Olivelle, P. *Saṃyāsa Upaniṣads: Hindu scriptures on asceticism and renunciation, translated with introduction and notes.* New York, 1992.
——. *Upaniṣads: Translated from the Original Sanskrit.* Oxford/New York, 1996.
Pandey, Raj Bali. *Hindu Samskaras.* Varanasi, 1957 [2nd ed. Delhi, 1969].
Pingree, D. *Jyotiḥśāstra: astral and mathematical literature.* [A history of Indian literature, vol. 6, fasc. 4.] Wiesbaden, 1981.
Proferes, Th. *The formation of Vedic liturgies.* Harvard, Ph.D. thesis, 1999.
Puhvel, J. *Comparative mythology.* Baltimore/London, 1987.
Rau, W. *Staat und Gesellschaft im alten Indien nach den Brāhmaṇa-Texten dargestellt.* Wiesbaden, 1957.
——. "Vedische Lebensweisheit," in *Beiträge zur Indienforschung, Ernst Waldschmidt zum 80. Geburtstage gewidmet,* ed. H. Härtel. Berlin, 1977, pp. 346–52.
Renou, L. "La valeur du silence dans le culte védique," *Journal of the American Oriental Society* 69, 1949: 11–18.
——. *Religions of Ancient India.* London, 1953.
—— and J. Filliozat. *L'Inde classique: Manuel des études indiennes.* Paris, 1947, 1953 [repr. Paris, 1985].
—— and L. Silburn. "Sur la notion de bráhman," *Journal Asiatique* 1949: 7–46.
Rustagi, U. *Darśapūrṇamāsa: A comparative ritualistic study.* Delhi, 1981.
Rhys-Davies, T. W. *Buddhist India.* London, 1911.
Sahlins, M. D. *Stone age economics.* Chicago, 1972.
Schayer, S. "Die Struktur der magischen Weltanschauung nach dem Atharvaveda und den Brāhmaṇa-Texten," *Zeitschrift für Buddhismus* 6, 1925: 259–310.
Schmidt, H.-P. *Bṛhaspati und Indra.* Wiesbaden, 1968a.
——. *The origin of ahiṃsā: Mélanges d'indianisme à la mémoire de Louis Renou.* Paris, 1968b, pp. 625–55.
——. "Vedic *Pāthas,*" *Indo-Iranian Journal* 15, 1973: 1–39.
——. *Some women's rites and rights in the Veda.* Poona, 1987.
——. "Ahiṃsā and Rebirth," in *Inside the texts, beyond the texts: new approaches to the study of the Vedas.* Harvard Oriental Series, Opera Minora, vol. 2. Cambridge, MA, 1997, pp. 207–34.
Schneider, U. "Die altindische Lehre vom Kreislauf des Wassers," *Saeculum* 12, 1961: 1–11.
——. *Der Somaraub des Manu: Mythus und Ritual.* Freiburg, 1971.

Schrader, O. *Die Indogermanen*. Leipzig, 1919.
Schwab, J. *Das altindische Thieropfer.* Erlangen, 1886.
Sharma, R. S. *Looking for the Aryans*. Madras, 1995.
Sieg, E. *Die Sagenstoffe des Ṛgveda und die indische Itihāsatradition, 1 (Itihāsas zum Ṛgveda).* Stuttgart, 1902 [= 1991: 89–243].
——. "Indra und der Somaraub nach dem RV," in *Fs. Jacobi*, ed. W. Kirfel, 1926, 228–39.
Smith, B. K. "The Unity of Ritual: The Place of the Domestic Sacrifice in Vedic Ritualism," *Indo-Iranian Journal* 29, 1886: 79–96.
——. *Reflections on resemblance, ritual, and religion*. New York–Oxford, 1989.
Sprockhoff, J. *Saṃnyāsa: Quellenstudien zur Askese im Hinduismus I: Untersuchungen über die Saṃnyāsa-Upaniṣads.* Wiesbaden, 1976.
——. "Kaṭhaśruti und Mānavaśrautasūtra, – eine Nachlese zur Resignation," *Studien zur Indologie und Iranistik* 13/14, 1987: 235–57.
Srinivasan, D. "Unhinging Śiva from the Indus Civilization," *Journal of the Royal Asiactic Society* (1984): 77–89.
Staal, J. F. "The Meaninglessness of Ritual," *Numen* 26, 1979a: 2–22.
——. "Ritual Syntax," in M. Nagatomi et al., eds., *Sanskrit and Indian studies: Essays in honor of D. H. H. Ingalls*. Dordrecht, 1979b.
——. *The science of ritual*. Poona, 1982.
——. *Agni: The Vedic ritual of the fire altar*, 2 vols. Berkeley, 1983.
——. *Jouer avec le feu: Pratique et théorie du ritual védique*. Paris, 1990.
Stenzler, M. A. F. *Indische Hausregeln: Sanskrit und Deutsch*. Leipzig, 1864.
Stuhrmann, R. *Der Traum in der altindischen Literatur im Vergleich mit altiranischen, hethitischen und griechischen Vorstellungen*. Diss., Tübingen, 1982.
Stutley, M. *Ancient Indian magic and folklore: An introduction*. Delhi, 1980.
Thieme, P. *Der Fremdling im Rigveda*. Leipzig, 1938.
——. "Bráhman," *Zeitschrift der Deutschen Morgenländischen Gesellschaft* 102, 1952: 91–129.
——. *Mitra and Aryaman*. New Haven, 1957a.
——. "Vorzarathustrisches bei den Zarathustriern und bei Zarathustra," *Zeitschrift der Deutschen Morgenländischen Gesellschaft* 107, 1957b: 67–104.
——. Unpublished lecture, on receiving the Kyoto Prize, Kyoto 1989.
Tsuji, N. *On the relation between Brāhmaṇas and Śrautasūtras*, [*Burāhumana to shurauta sūtora to no kanken*. Repr. 1982, pp. 1–247, Engl. summary, pp. 181–247]. Tokyo, 1952.
——. *The Marriage-section of the Āgniveśya-Gṛhyasūtra*. (Memoirs of the Research Department of the Toyo Bunko, no. 19.) Tokyo, 1960.
Türstig, H.-G. *Jyotiṣa: das System der indischen Astrologie*. Wiesbaden, 1980.
Tull, H. W. *The Vedic origins of karma: Cosmos and man in ancient Indian myth and ritual.* Albany, 1989.
Vasilkov, Ya. V. "Draupadī in the Assembly-hall: Gandharva-husbands and the origin of the Gaṇikās," *Indologica Taurinensia* 15–16 (1989–90). [*Proceedings of the Seventh World Sanskrit Conference, Leiden, August 23rd–29th, 1987.*] Turin, 1991, 387–98.
Watkins, C. "Is tre fir flathemon: Marginalia to Ardacht Morainn," *Eriu* 30, 1992: 181–98.
——. *How to kill a dragon: aspects of Indo-European poetics*. New York, 1995.
Weber, A. *Adbhutabrahmana: Zwei vedische texte über omina und portenta*. Von A. Weber. 1. *Das Adbhutabrahmana des Samaveda*. 2. *Der Adbhutadhyaya des Kaucikasutra*. Berlin, 1859.

——. *Über die Königsweihe, den Rājasūya*. Berlin, 1893.

Weber-Brosamer, Bernhard. *Annam: Untersuchungen zur Bedeutung des Essens und der Speise im vedischen Ritual*. Religionswissenschaft und Theologien 3, Freiburg, 1988.

Wezler, Albrecht. *Die wahren "Speiserestesser" (Skt. vighāśin)*. [Engl. summary, pp. 121–7.] Akademie der Wissenschaften zu Mainz. Wiesbaden, 1978.

——. "Zu den sogenannten Identifikationen in den Brāhmaṇas," *Studien zur Indologie und Iranistik*, 20, 1996: 485–522.

Wilden, Eva. *Das Opfer als Bindeglied in der Beziehung zwischen Göttern und Menschen gemäss den Brāhmaṇas*. MA thesis, Hamburg, 1992.

Winternitz, M. *Das altindische Hochzeitsritual nach dem Āpastambīya-Gṛihyasūtra und einigen anderen verwandten Werken. Mit Vergleichung der Hochzeitsgebräuche bei den übrigen indogermanischen Völkern*. [Denkschriften der Kaiserlichen Akademie der Wissenschaften, Philosophisch-historische Klasse, 40. Band, 1. Abhandlung.] Wien, 1892.

Witzel, M. *On magical thought in the Veda*. Leiden, 1979.

——. "Die Kaṭha-Śikṣā-Upaniṣad und ihr Verhältnis zur Śīkṣāvallī der Taittirīya-Upaniṣad," *WZKS* 24, 1980: 21–82.

——. *Review of*: J. Gonda, *The Mantras of the Agnyupasthāna and the Sautrāmaṇī*. Amsterdam, 1980: *Kratylos* 26, 1981/2: 80–5.

——. "The Earliest Form of the Concept of Rebirth in India, (Summary)." 31st CISHAAN (Tokyo-Kyoto), *Proceedings*, ed. T. Yamamoto, Tokyo, 1984a, 145–6.

——. "On the Origin of the Literary Device of the 'Frame Story' in Old Indian Literature, (Summary)." 31st CISHAAN (Tokyo-Kyoto), *Proceedings*, ed. T. Yamamoto, Tokyo, 1984b, p. 534.

——. "Agnihotra-Rituale in Nepal," in *Formen kulturellen Wandels und andere Beiträge zur Erforschung des Himālaya*, ed. B. Kölver u. S. Lienhard, St. Augustin, 1986a, 157–87.

——. "JB palpūlanī. The Structure of a Brāhmaṇa Tale," *Felicitation Volume B, ed. R. Sharma*, ed. M. D. Balasubrahmaniam. Tirupati, 1986b, pp. 189–216.

——. "On the Origin of the Literary Device of the 'Frame Story' in Old Indian Literature," in *Hinduismus und Buddhismus, Festschrift für U. Schneider*, ed. H. Falk. Freiburg, 1987a, pp. 380–414.

——. "The Case of the Shattered Head," *Festschrift für W. Rau, Studien zur Indologie und Iranistik* 13/14, 1987b: 363–415.

——. "Tracing the Vedic Dialects," in *Dialectes dans les littératures indo-aryennes*, ed. Colette Caillat. Paris, 1989a, pp. 97–264.

——. "The Realm of the Kurus: Origins and Development of the First State in India," *Nihon Minami Ajia Gakkai Zenkoku Taikai, Hōkoku Yōshi* [Summaries of the Congress of the Japanese Association for South Asian Studies], Kyoto, 1989b, pp. 1–4.

——. "Ushi.wo meguru Indojin.no kagae" (On the Sacredness of the Cow in India; in Japanese). *The Association of Humanities and Sciences*, Kobe Gakuin University, 1991, no. 1, pp. 9–20.

——. "Meaningful ritual. Structure, Development and Interpretation of the Tantric Agnihotra Ritual of Nepal," in *Ritual, State and History in South Asia. Essays in honour of J. C. Heesterman*, eds. A. W. van den Hoek, D. H. A. Kolff, and M. S. Oort. Leiden, 1992, pp. 774–827.

——. "Early Sanskritization," *Electronic Journal of Vedic Studies* 1 (4) (Dec. 1995): www1.shore.net/~india/ejvs

——. "No Satī, Little Dowry: The Lot of Women in the Vedic Period," *Journal of South Asia Women Studies* 2 (4) (Dec. 1996): http://www.asiatica.org/publications/jsaws/

——. "The Development of the Vedic Canon and its Schools: The Social and Political Milieu" (Materials on Vedic Śākhās 8). In *Inside the Texts, Beyond the Texts: New Approaches to the Study of the Vedas*. Harvard Oriental Series, Opera Minora, vol. 2. Cambridge, MA, 1997a, pp. 257–345.

——. "Early Sanskritization. Origins and Development of the Kuru State," in *Recht, Staat und Verwaltung im klassischen Indien. The state, the law, and administration in classical India*, ed. B. Kölver. München, 1997b, pp. 27–52.

——. "Macrocosm, Mesocosm, and Microcosm: The Persistent Nature of 'Hindu' Beliefs and Symbolical Forms," in *IJHS Symposium on Robert Levy's MESOCOSM, International Journal of Hindu Studies*, ed. S. Mittal. Dec. 1–3, 1998, pp. 501–53.

——. "Prajātantu," in *Harānandalaharī: Volume edited in Honour of Professor Minoru Hara on his Seventieth Birthday*, eds. Ryutaro Tsuchiyama and Albrecht Wezler Reinbek, 2000, pp. 457–80.

Zachariae, T. "Zum altindischen Hochzeitsritual," *Wiener Zeitschrift zur Kunde des Morgenlandes* 17, 1903: 135–55, 212–31.

——. *Opera minora zur indischen Wortforschung, zur Geschichte der indischen Literatur und Kultur, zur Geschichte der Sanskritphilologie*, ed. C. Vogel. Wiesbaden, 1977.

——. *Kleine Schriften zur indischen Philologie, zur vergleichenden Literaturgeschichte, zur vergleichenden Volkskunde*. Hildesheim, 1989.

Zimmer, H. *Altindisches Leben*. Berlin, 1879.

Zysk, K. *Religious healing in the Veda*. Philadelphia, 1985.

Appendix: A Synopsis of the Vedic Texts

Ṛgvedic texts		Sāmavedic texts			Linguistic Period
Ṛgveda Saṃhitā (Śākala) RV					**1. Ṛgvedic**
(Bāṣkala, Māṇḍukeya Saṃhitā lost)					
		Sāmaveda Saṃhitā			**2. Mantra language**
RVKh **Ṛgveda Khilāni** (Śākha unclear perhaps Māṇḍ.)		SV(K) = **Kauthuma** Śākha	SV(R) **Rāṇāyanīya** Śākha	SVJ **Jaiminīya** Śākha	(Mantras only not expository prose)
					3. YV Saṃhitā prose (prose only)
AB **Aitareya-Brāhmaṇa** 1–5 old	KB **Kauṣītaki-Br.**	PB **Pañcaviṃśa-Br.** (= Tāṇḍya-Br., Mahā-Br.)		JB **Jaiminīya-Br.** (1.1–65 late; 2–3 earlier)	**4. Brāhmaṇa lang.** (older and later stages)
6–8 late		ṢB **Ṣaḍviṃśa-Br.** (= Tāṇḍya Br.26) **Sāmavidhāna-Br.**			
AĀ **Aitareya -Āraṇyaka** contains:	KĀ **Kauṣītaki-Ār. Ār.** contains:	ChU **Chāndogya-Up.**		JUB **Jaiminīya- Upaniṣad Brāhmaṇa** contains:	
Ait.Up. **Aitareya-Upaniṣad**	Kauṣ.Up. **Kauṣ.Up.**			-------------- **Kena-Up.**	
SŪTRAS:		**Maśaka-Kalpa Sūtra** (Ārṣeyakalpa) **Kṣudra Sūtra**			**5. Sūtra language**
AŚS **Āśvalāyana-Śrautrasūtra**	ŚŚS **Śānkhāyana-Śr.S.**	LŚS **Lāṭyāyana-Śr.S.**	DŚS **Drāhyāyana-Śr.S.**	JŚS **Jaiminīya-Śr.S.**	
AGS **Āśv. Gṛhyasūtra**	KauṣGS **Kauś Śāmbavya GS**	GGS/KauthGS/DGS/KhādGS **Gobhila- Kauthuma- Drāhyāyana- Khādira-GS**		JGS **Jaim.GS**	
VāsDhS **Vāsiṣṭha Dharmasūtra**			GautDhS **Gautama DhS.**		
		(various late, Sūtra-like "Brāhmaṇas": (**Ārṣeya-, Devatādhyāya-, (Upaniṣad- = Mantra-),** (**Saṃhitopaniṣad-, Vaṃśa-Brāhmaṇa;** (further Sūtras: **Kalpanupāda-, Upagrantha-,** (**Anupada-, Nidāna-, Upanidāna-, Pañcavidhā-Sūtra,** (**Ṛktantra, Sāmavedatantra, Mātrālakṣaṇa-S.,** (**Stobhānusaṃhāra, Gāyatrīvidhāna-S., Puṣpa-S.**)			
Various **Pariśiṣṭa**					**6. Post-vedic: Epic**

ʼajurvedic texts					Atharvavedic texts	
ʼlack YV			White YV			
ʌS **ʌai- rā- ʼaṇi ʼaṃh·**	KS/KpS **Kaṭha-/ Kapi- ṣṭhala Saṃh·**	TS **Taitti- rīya S.**	VS(M) **Vājasasa– neyi Mādhy. Saṃhitā** (VS 40 = ĪśāUp, late)	VS(K) **Vāj. Kāṇva S.**	AV,ŚS **Śaunaka S.** (= vulgate)	PS **Paippalāda S.**
- - ɔnly rag.	KaṭhB/KpB – only frag.	TB **Taitt.B** 1–3.9 are old, TB 3.10–12 from KaṭhB **Vādhūla Brāhmaṇa** (Anvākhyāna)	ŚB(M) **ŚatapathaB** (Mādhy.) 1–5 Eastern 6–10 Western add. 11–13	ŚBK **Śat.B.** (Kāṇva) = 1–7 = 7–12 = 13–15	(no text)	*Paipp.Br (text not recovered)
nan- ras n ʌS ł.9	KaṭhĀ **Kaṭha- Ār.** ~ TĀ 4–5	TĀ **Taitt. Āraṇyaka** 1–2 < KaṭhB 3–6 = Ār. proper 7–9 = TU **Taitt. Upaniṣad** --------------------- TĀ 10 = MNU (late) **Mahānārāyaṇa-Up.**	14.1–3 = Āraṇyaka 14.4–9 = Up. BĀUM **Bṛhadāraṇyaka-Upaniṣad**	= 16.1–3 = 16.3– BĀUK	GB (adopted from Paipp.) **Gopatha Br.** mostly adopted from other Br. texts (**Praṇava Up** = GB 1.16–30 post-Pāṇinean, as such later than KauśS)	

Black YV					White YV		
MŚS VārŚS	*KaṭhŚS	BŚS VādhŚS	BhŚS	ĀpŚS HŚS VkhŚS	KŚS	VaitS	*ĀgŚS-
Māna- va-Śr. Sūtra **Vārāha Śr.S**	(almost compl. lost)	**Baudhā- yana Śr.S.** **Vādhūla**	**Bhārad- vāja ŚrS** **Śr.S.**	**Āpa- stamba, Hiraṇyakesi Vaikhānasa ŚrS** (very late)	**Kātyā- yana ŚrS.**	**Vaitāna Sūtra**	***Āgastya ŚrS** (lost)
VārGS **Mān. GS Vār.**	MGS KGS LGS **Kaṭha/ Laugākṣi**	BGS VādhGS ĀgGS **Baudh.Vādh. Āgniveśya**	BhGS HGS **Bhār. Āp. Hir. Vaikh.**	ĀpGS VkhGS	PGS **Pāras- kara Gṛhyasūtra**	KauśS **Kauśika Sūtra**	*PaiṭhGS **Paiṭhī- nasi GS (fragments)**
*Mānava- Dharma Sūtra	*Kaṭh. DhS	Baudh. DhS	Āp. DhS	Vaikh. DhS			
Manu- Smṛti Various Pariśiṣṭa	**Viṣṇu- Smṛti**	**Vādhūla- Smṛti**			**Yājñavalkya- Smṛti**		**Sumantu- DhS** (frag.)
LATER UPANIṢADS:							
MU **Maitr. – Upaniṣad**	KU **Kaṭha- Up.**	MNU **Mahānārāyaṇa- Up.**	IU **ĪśāUp**			various AV-Up.s **Praśna, Māṇḍ. etc. Up.s**	

CHAPTER 4
The Dharmaśāstras

Ludo Rocher

The Concept of Dharma

Śāstras are treatises, usually ancient and authoritative treatises, in Sanskrit, on a variety of topics: Bharata's *Nāṭyaśāstra* on poetics, drama, music, etc.; Kauṭilya's *Arthaśāstra* on politics and statecraft; *jyotḥśāstra* on astrology; even *aśvaśāstra* on horses and *gajaśāstra* on elephants; etc. *Dharmaśāstras* are ancient Sanskrit treatises on the subject of *dharma*, one of the most central and fundamental concepts in Hinduism. Along with *artha* and *kāma*, *dharma is* one of the three goals (*trivarga*) in the life of a Hindu.

There is no equivalent term for *dharma* in Western languages. The noun *dharma* is derived from the verbal root *dhṛ*, which means "uphold, maintain, sustain, keep in balance." Hence *dharma* is the way, the right way, to maintain order and balance in the universe generally. As long as every element in the cosmos – the sun, water (the monsoon), animals, plants, and humans in particular – acts according to its *dharma*, the overall balance is maintained. As soon as any element in the cosmos in some way deviates from its *dharma*, i.e. commits *adharma*, the overall balance is disturbed. At the human level, *dharma* governs every aspect of and every activity in the life of a Hindu. *Dharma* is not synonymous with "law" which has become an often used translation for *dharma* – the *dharmaśāstras* became known in the West as "law books" (see below) – nor with "religion" which is the meaning *dharma* acquired in modern Indian languages. In addition to legal rules (legal procedure, substantive law) and religious rules (birth rituals, marriage rituals, rituals for the dead, etc.), there are in the *dharmaśāstras* a number of injunctions which, in Western terms, would be labeled "dietary" (allowed and forbidden foods), "hygienic" (bathing, brushing the teeth), "moral," etc. These rules, which every Hindu is supposed to live by, are supplemented by other rules, which concern members of certain sections of

Hindus only. An individual's specific *dharma* (his *sva-dhartna*) is primarily determined by two criteria: his social class and his stage of life.

The members of the four social classes (*varṇa*, often translated with the more modern term "caste"), Brahman/Brahmin (*Brāhmaṇa*), *Kṣatriya*, *Vaiśya*, and *Śūdra*, have different *dharmas*. The three higher classes, the *dvijas* "twice-born," have three kinds of *dharma* in common: study the sacred texts (*adhyayana*), patronize sacrifices for their own benefit (*yajana*), and generosity toward others (*dāna*). The Brahman's specific *dharma* includes teaching the Vedic texts (*adhyāpana*, the causative form of *adhyayana*), performing sacrifices for the benefit of others (*yājana*, the causative form of *yajana*), and receiving special gifts to which only Brahmans are entitled (*pratigraha*). The Kṣatriya maintains law and order inside the territory and defends the country against outsiders; the king who, theoretically though not always in practice, is the principal Kṣatriya, has his own *rājadharma*. The Vaiśya earns a living with trade, crafts, and agriculture. The members of the sole class that is not twice-born, the Śūdras, have only one *dharma:* be of service (*śuśrūṣa*) to the members of the three higher classes.

There are also four life stages (*āśrama*), during each of which the *dharma* of the Hindu is different. At an early age (5 or later, depending on his social class) the boy born in one of the three higher classes undergoes a rite of passage (*saṁskāra*, often translated as "sacrament") called *upanayana*. This ritual is conceived as a second birth, as a result of which the boy is invested with the sacred thread (*yqjñopavīta*), and becomes a *brahmacārin*. The main *dharma* of the *brahmacārin is* to move in with and study the sacred texts under the guidance of a teacher (*guru*), to serve his *guru*, and to observe strict celibacy (*brahmacarya*). Unless he decides to spend his entire life as a permanent (*naiṣṭhika*) *brahmacārin*, at the end of the first life stage, the length of which depends on his *varṇa*, another rite of passage, consisting in a ritual bath (*samāvartana*), makes the young man a *snātaka*. This prepares him for marriage and the second stage of life, that of a *gṛhastha* "householder." The *gṛhastha* establishes and sustains a family, including the primary duty of fathering a son who will perform the necessary funeral rites (*śrāddha*) after his father's death. After the second life stage the Hindu may enter the third *āśrama*, retire from active life, and become a *vanaprastha* "forest dweller," eventually to enter the fourth stage, that of a *saṁnyāsin* "renouncer." Note that, for women, there is only one single rite of passage, their wedding.

The treatises on *dharma* recognize but do not elaborate in detail on other *dharmas* that are not applicable to all, but to specific groups of Hindus only. They provide some examples of *dharmas* followed by "the Northerners" or "the Southerners." They also refer to regional *dharmas* (*deśadharma*), "caste" *dharmas* (*jātidharma*), even to family/clan *dharmas* (*kuladharma*), as well as to *dharmas* restricted to members of guilds (*śreṇidharma*) and *dharmas* that are observed in the army. In other words, forms of behavior (*ācāra*) that are recognized as proper for the members of these groups are *dharma*, even if they are not described in or even if they are incompatible with the rules codified in the *dharmaśāstras*.

Another important aspect of the texts on *dharma* is that they recognize special circumstances, emergencies (*āpad*), in which the strict rules they lay down in the texts are suspended. In such cases *āpaddharma* applies: the Brahman is allowed to pursue a military career, the Kṣatriya may practice the life style normally reserved for the Vaiśya, etc.

It cannot be stressed enough that, except for the rules that apply to one and all, in Hinduism *dharma* is different for different individuals and under different circumstances. What is *dharma* for one individual may constitute a breach of *dharma* (*adharma*) for others; what is *adharma* under certain circumstances may be *dharma* in other situations.

The *Dharmasūtras*

The term *dharmaśāstra* is used with two different meanings. It either encompasses both the *dharmaśāstras* and the *dharmasūtras*, i.e. the entire *smṛti*, or it is restricted to the *dharmaśāstras* in a narrower sense (see below). Although occasionally mixed with verse, the *dharmasūtras* are in prose. By definition, a *sūtra* is a brief, aphoristic statement, in which not a single word or syllable is meaningless. *Sūtras* are meant to be learned by heart first, only later to be explained by means of an oral or written commentary. Typical examples of works written in *sūtra* style are Pāṇini's grammatical treatise (the *Aṣṭādhyāyī*), Vātsyāyana's *Kāmasūtra*, the basic texts of the six systems of Hindu philosophy (*darśanas*), etc. Note that the meaning of the Sanskrit term *sūtra* in this context is different from that of the Pāli term *sutta* in the Buddhist texts.

The *dharmasūtras* are only a part of a much vaster literature. They are subsumed under the broader category of *kalpasūtras*, together with three other kinds of *sūtras*. First, the *śrautasūtras*, which describe major rituals requiring an elaborate "altar" (*vedi*), three sacrificial fires, and the participation of several classes of priests; the *dharmasūtras* are often appendages of the *śrautasūtras*. Second, the *gṛhyasūtras*, which deal with minor domestic rituals performed on the perpetual house fire, requiring the service of only a single priest, and the contents of which partly overlap with those of the *dharmasūtras*. Third, the *śulbasūtras* which teach how properly to construct vedic altars by means of bricks of different geometrical forms, and which contain the earliest Indian statements on mathematics.

One important feature of the *kalpasūtras*, and hence of the *dharmasūtras*, is that they are an integral, though relatively late, part of the Veda. The *kalpasūtras* are one of the six *vedāṅgas* "(subsidiary) members of the Vedas." Each of the four Vedas, *Ṛgveda*, *Yajurveda*, *Sāmaveda*, and *Atharvaveda*, more correctly, each of the several "branches" (*śākhā*) of the four Vedas, is supposed to have had a *kalpasūtra* including a *dharmasūtra*, but not all of these texts have been preserved (Renou 1947). In reality, the connection of some *dharmasūtras* with the vedic schools is at best a loose one. Yet, the fact that the *dharmasūtras* are at least theoretically a part of vedic literature entails that they are considered to be revealed texts transmitted to humans by ancient sages (*ṛṣi*). The authority of these texts is only slightly lower than that of the older *saṁhitās* and *brāhmaṇas*: the latter are *śruti* "hearing," the *dharmasūtras* are *smṛti* "recollection." Some of the *dharmasūtras* start with the phrase: "the source of *dharma* is the Veda." The fact that not all rules on *dharma* can be found in the Vedas was accounted for by means of a variety of fictions, resulting in the belief either that the *ṛṣis* who were privileged to "see" the Veda did *not* see it in its entirety, or that parts of the Veda are lost to us. And, even though the *dharmaśāstras* make it clear that in case of conflict between the *śruti* and the *smṛti*, the former prevails, the *smṛti*, occasionally supplemented by the behavior (*ācāra*) agreed on by those who know the Veda, is considered to be a source of *dharma* which is "eternal" (*sanātana*): the *sanātana-dharma* has been revealed once, perfectly, for all time to come.

Few *dharmasūtras* have been preserved. Four of them were translated with extensive introductions and notes, more than a century ago, by Georg Bühler, in volumes II (Āpastamba and Gautama) and XIV (Vasiṣṭha and Baudhāyana) of F. Max Müller's *Sacred Books of the East* series. Recently, Oxford University Press published a new translation of the four *sūtra* texts (Olivelle 1999; the translation of each *dharmasūtra* is preceded by a detailed survey of its contents).

Even though the *ṛṣi* Gautama is traditionally connected with the *Sāmaveda*, the *Gautamadharmasūtra* is not part of any known *kalpasūtra*. It may not have been the first *dharmasūtra* since it refers to earlier *ācāryas* "teachers," but there seems to be general, though not absolute, agreement that the *Gautamadharmasūtra* is older than any of the other preserved *dharmasūtras* to none of which it alludes. Differently from the other *dharmasūtras*, it is entirely in prose, without inserting any verses either as part of the text or in the form of quotations from earlier sources. It is divided into 28 *adhyāyas* ("chapters"), either numbered throughout from 1 to 28, or numbered separately within three *praśnas* ("questions") containing 9, 9, and 10 *adhyāyas* respectively. Hence a reference to a particular Gautama *sūtra* may consist of either two or three digits: 10.1 = 2.1.1; 19.1 = 3.1.1.

Some scholars consider not the *Gautamadharmasūtra* but the *Āpastambadharmasūtra* to be the oldest preserved *dharmasūtra*. In this case the *dharmasūtra* is an integral part (chapters 28–9; chapter 27 contains the *gṛhyasūtra*, chapter 30 the *śulbasūtra*) of the *śrautasūtra* of the Āpastamba school of the *Taittirīya* branch of the Black (*kṛṣṇa*) *Yajurveda*. The text is subdivided into two *praśnas*, each of which contains 11 *paṭalas* ("baskets"); concurrently with the *paṭalas* the first *praśna* comprises 32, and the second *praśna* 29 *khaṇdas* ("sections"). A reference to an Āpastamba *sūtra* contains four digits, e.g. 1 (*praśna*), 11 (*paṭala*), 32 (*khaṇḍa*), 1 (*sūtra*); some omit the reference to the *paṭala*, so that 1.11.32.1 may appear as 1.32.1. As far as the subject matter is concerned, the *Āpastambadharmasūtra* is far better organized than the other *dharmasūtras*. After a brief introduction on the sources of *dharma* and on the four social classes, the first *praśna* deals with the duties of a *brahmacārin*, up to the ritual bath at the conclusion of his studentship. The second *praśna* is primarily devoted to the *gṛhastha*, and, as such, includes passages on marriage, on sons (and inheritance), and on ritual for the dead (*śrāddha*). It ends with a description of the king as the protector of his subjects, the collector of taxes, and the head of the judicial system.

In connection with the *Āpastambadharmasūtra* reference must be made to the *Hiraṇyakeśidharmasūtra*, which can hardly be considered a *dharmasūtra* in its own right. It does belong to the preserved *Hiraṇyakeśikalpasūtra* of the *Taittīryya* branch of the Black *Yajurveda*, but it nearly literally corresponds to, i.e. borrows from, the *Āpastambadharmasūtra*. Bühler has listed a number of variant readings in an appendix to his edition of the *Āpastambadharmasūtra* (3rd ed., 1932: 197–212); for a more general comparison of both texts see Kane (1968: 91–4).

Even as, but far less clearly defined than, the *Āpastamba-dharmasūtra*, the *Baudhāyanadharmasūtra* too, forms the final part of a *kalpasūtra* belonging to the Black *Yajurveda*, which, however, has been the object of additions throughout. In the preserved text of the *Baudhāyanakalpasūtra* the *dharmasūtra* occupies *praśnas* 35 to 38, preceded by the *śrautasūtra* and other ritual texts (*praśnas* I to 29), the *śulbasūtra* (*praśna* 30), and the *gṛhyasūtra* (*praśnas* 31 to 34). There is general agreement that only the first two *praśnas* (35–6), out of four, belong to the original *dharmasūtra*. The first two *praśnas* are divided into concurrent *adhyāyas* and *kaṇḍikās* ("sections"): 11 and 22 in the first, 10 and 18 (17 and 18, on renunciation, seem to have been added from an extraneous source) in the second. The last two *praśnas* are divided into *adhyāyas* only, 10 in the third, 8 in the fourth. References to the *Baudhāyanadharmasūtra* may, therefore, appear confusing: four digits (of which the second is often omitted) for the first two *praśnas*, three only for the third and the fourth.

Even though the name of the Sage Vasiṣṭha (also Vaśiṣṭha) is traditionally associated with the *Ṛgveda*, the *Vasiṣṭha-* (or *Vāsiṣṭhadharmasūtra*, like the *Gautamadharmasūtra*, does not belong to any vedic school. Also like Gautama, it is divided only into *adhyāyas*, here numbered throughout from one to thirty. Paucity of manuscripts (cf. Alois Anton Führer's editions 1883, 1914, and 1930) and absence of written commentary (except for a mid-nineteenth-century one by Kṛṣṇapaṇḍita; an earlier one, by Yajñasvāmin, is lost) have left the text of the *Vasiṣṭhadharmasūtra* highly corrupt.

In addition to the four (or five, including Hiraṇyakeśi) major *dharmasūtras*, a text variously called *Vaikhānasadharmapraśna* or *Vaikhānasasmārtasūtra* (edited and translated by Willem Caland in the *Bibliotheca Indica* series, works 242 and 251, 1927, 1929) qualifies both as a *gṛhyasūtra* (*praśnas* I to 7) and as a *dharmasūtra* (*praśnas* 8 to 10). Even though the name *vaikhānasa* appears in the *dharmasūtras* of Gautama, Baudhāyana, and Vasiṣṭha, and even though the *Manusmṛti* (6.21) seems to allude to a Vaikhānasa treatise, the text in its present form is more recent, with a strong leaning toward Vaiṣṇavism (see Colas in this volume).

Among the many lost *dharmasūtras* from which extracts have been preserved in later texts, the *Hārītadharmasūtra* (Jolly 1928: 505–24, on law only) is one of the more prominent ones. The topics of *dharma* dealt with in these fragments, in prose and in verse, are so varied that Kane (1968: 133) suggested that the *Hārītadharmasūtra* may have been one of the most extensive *dharmasūtras*. Also well represented in quotations is a *dharmasūtra* attributed to Śaṅkha and Likhita, whom the *Mahābhārata* describes as brothers. Kane collected and edited 463 fragments, both in prose and in verse (1926–7, 101–228; 1927–8, 93–132). Karl Scriba edited and translated passages from the *Pītamahadharmasūtra* (Berlin 1902). Fragments of a *Paiṭhīnasidharmasūtra* were collected and edited by T. R. Cintamani (1939). Fragments of several other lost *dharmasūtras* are discussed by Kane (1968: 261–9).

The *Dharmaśāstras*

Differently from the *dharmasūtras*, the *dharmaśāstras* (in the narrow sense of the word, see above) are entirely in verse. They are composed nearly exclusively in the same *anuṣṭubh* or *śloka* meter (4 times 8 syllables to the stanza) that is familiar from the epics (*Mahābhārata* and *Rāmāyana*), from the *Purāṇas*, and from other types of *śāstra* literature. The *dharmaśāstras* deal with the same subject matter as the *dharmasūtras*, and, even though they are held to be more recent and no longer attached to specific vedic schools, they too are part of the revealed and eternally valid *smṛti*. Even as the *dharmasūtras*, the *dharmaśāstras* are attributed to ancient Sages.

Few versified *dharmaśāstras* have been preserved in their entirety; they are attributed to Manu, Yājñavalkya, Nārada, and Parāśara.

Traditionally the *Manusmṛti* or *Mānavadharmaśāstra* is recognized as the oldest and most important of all versified *dharmasūtras*. The theory that it was based on an older and lost *Mānavadharmasūtra* – even Gautama refers to Manu – has no longer any followers. It was the first *dharmaśāstra* to become known in Europe, in William Jones's English translation (London 1794). It has been translated several times since then, most authoritatively, with an elaborate introduction and abundant references to the commentaries, by Bühler, in volume XXV of the *Sacred Books of the East* (1886), and most recently by Wendy Doniger and Brian K. Smith, in the Penguin Books series (1991). The *Manusmṛti* is divided into 12 chapters (*adhyāyas*), ranging from 97 (chapter 6) to 420 (chapter 8) verses. One of the most enduring features of the *Manusmṛti*, throughout the later *dharmaśāstras*, the commentarial literature, into modern times, has been its subdivision of substantive law into 18 – an important number in Hinduism, Buddhism, and Jainism – *vivādapadas* "heads/titles of litigation."

The *Yajñavalkyasmṛti* largely deals with the same subject matter as the *Manusmṛti*, but in a more systematic way. The text is divided into three chapters, on *ācāra* (proper behavior; 367/368 verses), *vyavahāra* (law; 307 verses), and *prāyaścitta* (penance; 334/335 verses). There is no complete translation of the *Yajñavalkyasmṛti* into English, even though Adolf Friedrich Stenzler edited and translated the text into German as early as 1849. There is general agreement that the *Yajñavalkyasmṛti* is more recent than the *Manusmṛti*. More than any other *dharmaśāstra* text, the *Yajñavalkyasmṛti*, through its commentary *Mitākṣarā* by Vijñāneśvara (eleventh century CE) on the subject of inheritance, has become prominent in the administration of justice in India under British rule and in Independent India (see below).

The *Nāradsmṛti* has been preserved in three versions. A shorter text was translated by Jolly from an unpublished Sanskrit source (London, 1876). A longer one was edited, with Asahāya's partly preserved commentary, in the *Bibliotheca Indica* series (work 102) in 1885, and translated in volume XXXIII of the *Sacred Books of the East* in 1889, both by Jolly. A third text was published (1929) under the title *Nāradiyamanusaṁhitā*, the readings of which are largely corroborated by those attested in manuscripts written in Newārī script found in Nepal. Jolly's longer recension has received most scholarly attention and has most often been referred to as *the Nāradasmṛti*. Yet, in a new edition and translation (Philadelphia 1989) Richard Lariviere has shown that many verses included in Jolly's edition and translation are not part of the *Nāradasmṛti*, but of Asahāya's commentary, and that the *Nāradīyamanusaṁhitā* Newārī recension may well represent the original text. Nārada is the only *dharmaśāstra* that is totally and exclusively devoted to one single aspect of *dharma*, "law." After an introductory section (*mātṛkā*) on legal procedure, the text proceeds systematically through the 18 heads of litigation, more or less in the order in which Manu established them. The *Nāradasmṛti* became known for its detailed treatment of ordeals (*divya*) to be used as one of the types of admissible evidence in courts of law. The fact that Manu knows two forms of ordeal, Yājñavalkya five, and Nārada nine, has often been used as an argument to consider the *Nāradasmṛti* more recent than the *Manusmṛti* and the *Yājñavalkyasmṛti*. In view of Lariviere's conclusions some forms of ordeal may, however, have been added by the commentator Asahāya. In that case, Nārada may antedate Yājñavalkya. The *Nāradasmṛti* impressed comparative legal historians, to the point of unnecessarily assuming contact with or influence from Roman law.

Less well known and less widely read than the *dharmaśāstras* attributed to Manu, Yājñavalkya, and Nārada, the *Parāśarasmṛti*, edited, with the extensive gloss (*vyākhyā*) by Mādhavācārya, in the *Bombay Sanskrit Series* (1893–1911) and in the *Bibliotheca Indica* series (work 94, 1890–9), deals with *ācāra* and *prāyaścitta* only. The commentator Mādhava does introduce an important section on *vyavahāra*, but only on the occasion of Parāśara's brief reference to the *dharma* of the *kṣatriyas*. Even though Yājñavalkya (1.4–5) includes Parāśara in a long list of composers of *dharmaśāstras*, the preserved *Parāśarasmṛti* must be far more recent. The text specifically claims to be a *dharmaśāstra* for the *kaliyuga*, the last and worst of the four world ages within the current cycle, in which we live at the present moment. Among the practices for which it is known to deviate from those prescribed in other *dharmaśāstras* is a brief eulogy of *satī*, "widow burning."

Subsequent to the four preserved *dharmaśāstras* reference must be made to a text on *dharma* that has created more problems of categorization and interpretation than most. It is variously called *Viṣṇudharmasūtra*, *Viṣṇudharmaśāstra*, or, with the neutral term, *Viṣṇusmṛti*. The text was edited and translated by Jolly in the *Bibliotheca Indica* series (work 91) in 1881, and in volume VII of the *Sacred*

Books of the East (1880), respectively. The *Viṣṇusmṛtii* is divided into 100 chapters (*adhyāya*) of very uneven length: 5 (chapters 34, 39, 40, 42, 76) with just one *sūtra* and one verse, one with 101 *sūtras* followed by one verse (chapter 98). The body of the text is in prose, but, with one exception (chapter 74), all chapters end in verses, from a single *śloka* to 32 (chapter 20, after 21 *sūtras*). The first and the last two chapters are entirely in verse. The conclusion is that there may have been an early *Viṣṇudharmasūtra*, entirely in prose, which to some degree belonged to the *Kāṭhaka* branch of the Black *Yajurveda*. At a later time verses were added to the core, many of them equivalent to and probably borrowed from Manu (160 verses are identical), Yājñavalkya, Nārada, the *Bhagavadgitā*, and other sources. Finally, the initial and the last two chapters made the text into a Vaiṣṇava work, thereby creating the single *dharmaśāstra* text in which it is Viṣṇu who, in his boar (*varāha*) incarnation, proclaimed *dharma* to the goddess Earth at the time when the world was recreated after one of the recurring cosmic destructions (*pralaya*).

Even as some of the *dharmasūtras* are preserved only in fragments, several *dharmaśāstras* too, are known only from more or less abundant quotations in later works. From the collections of these fragments edited by modern scholars it is obvious that some of these lost *dharmaśāstras* were extensive and important.

This is especially true of the *Bṛhaspatismṛti*, from which Jolly translated a collection of verses on legal procedure and substantive law (*vyavahāra*) in volume XXXIII of the *Sacred Books of the East* (1889). K. V. Rangaswarni Aiyangar (Baroda, 1941) not only edited a far larger collection of fragments on legal issues; he also added extracts dealing with *saṁskāra* (648 verses and two prose passages), *ācāra* (101 verses), *śrāddha* (155 verses), *aśauca* (ritual impurity, 78 verses), *āpaddharma* (53 verses), and *prāyaścitta* (90 verses).

Of the equally important *Kātyāuanasmṛti* we so far have only 973 verses on legal procedure and substantive law that were collected and translated by Kane (Poona, 1933), to which 121 more were added by K. V. Rangaswami Aiyangar (*Festschrift Kane*, Poona, 1941: 7–17).

Further, 268 verses on law and legal procedure, attributed to the Sage Vyāsa, have been collected by B. K. Ghosh (*Indian Culture* 9, 1942, 65–98). Recently, M. L. Wadekar edited 2,475 verses on *ācāra*, *vyavahāra*, and *prāyaścitta* (*plus* 81 verses on *jyotiṣa*) from the lost *Devalasmṛti* (Delhi, 1996–7, 2 vols.).

A collection of 19 *dharmaśāstras*, many of them attributed to Sages mentioned earlier (often preceded by adjectives such as *Bṛhad-* "major," *Laghu-* "minor," *Vṛddha-* "senior") but probably of more recent origin, were published under the title *Dharmaśāstrasaṃgrahaḥ* by Jivananda Vidyasagara (Calcutta, 1876). Twenty-seven similar texts, titled *Smṛtināṃ samuccayaḥ*, were printed in volume 48 of the *Ānandāśrama Sanskrit Series* (Poona, 1905), and 20 were edited and translated under the title *The Dharmaśāstra* by M. N. Dutt (Calcutta, 1906–8). Gustav Herberich (Würzburg, 1893) edited and translated 103 verses ascribed, not always consistently, to Vṛddhamanu or Bṛhanmanu.

At this stage it is necessary also to refer to extensive passages dealing with various topics of *dharma* that are found in numerous passages of the two Indian epics, the *Rāmāyana* and, even more so, the *Mahābhārata* (Kane 1968: 349–408), as well as in several *Purāṇas* (Kane 1968: 408–21 and Rocher 1986: 37–8 and *passim*). In fact, verses from the *Mahābhārata* and entire sections from a number of *Purāṇas* correspond nearly literally with passages from the *dharmaśāstras*. In addition, even though Kautilya's *Arthaśāstra is* primarily devoted to the study of policy and statecraft (*artha*), it too comprises sections dealing with topics related to *dharma* (Kane 1968: 149–256).

Dating

Dating most classical Indian texts remains a difficult task, and the *dharmasūtras* and *dharmaśāstras* are no exception. Dating in absolute terms is possible only to the extent to which there is agreement on the relative dates of the several texts. If the *Manusmṛti* is indeed the oldest versified *dharmaśāstra* and if we accept, with the majority of scholars, that it was composed between 200 BCE and 200 CE (the time when the *Mahābhārata* was about to reach its final form), then all *dharmasūtras* are older than 200 BCE, and all *dharmaśāstras* other than Manu's are more recent than 200 CE. Even repeated and detailed comparison, based on internal criteria, did not always lead to identical conclusions. Yet, it is more or less established that, of the preserved *dharmasūtras*, Gautama or, according to some, Āpastamba is the oldest, followed by Baudhāyana and Vasiṣṭha. How far back these texts go prior to the time of Manu is less certain, at most as far as 500 BCE, and possibly less. Among the *dharmaśāstras* Manu was probably followed by Yājñavalkya, Nārada (unless the original Nārada is earlier than Yājñavalkya), Bṛhaspati, and Kātyāyana. The *Viṣṇudharmasūtra* may be very old, but the text as it has been preserved, both in prose and in verse, may be dated between 400 and 600 CE. The period of the principal *dharmasūtras* and *dhamaśāstras* may, therefore, be tentatively fixed between the limits of 500 BCE and 500 CE.

The *Dharmaśāstras* in the Commentarial Literature

The *dharmasūtras* and *dharmaśāstras* constitute a vast and, even more so, a complex body of literature. First, not only are the *sūtras* brief and aphoristic as mentioned earlier; they are often cryptic and they easily lend themselves to very different interpretations. Even the verses of the more verbose *dharmaśāstras* are not always as clear as one would wish normative texts to be; some of the most crucial *ślokas* can be interpreted in very different ways. Second, it is not surprising that texts composed over a period of about one millennium, in distant parts of the subcontinent, exhibit injunctions that are not only different, but even incompatible.

Such, however, is not the traditional view. For the Hindu the *dharma* as revealed by the Sages is perfect. There are neither uncertainties nor contradictions in the *dharmasūtras* and the *dharmaśāstras*. If texts appear unclear or contradictory, it is because humans fail properly to understand their meanings. Hence arose, probably from around 700 CE, if not earlier, a vast commentarial literature, which continued well into the eighteenth century. For reasons which will become clear later in this essay, a number of the more recent commentaries were composed at the instance of the British rulers, most prominent among them the *Vivādārṇavasetu* "Bridge across the ocean of litigation" (Bombay, 1888), a text composed by a group of 11 pandits in Calcutta, better known, in Nathaniel Brassey Halhed's English rendition of a Persian translation, as *A Code of Gentoo Laws* (London, 1776), and Jagannlātha Tarkapañcānana's as yet unpublished *Vivādabhaṅgārnava* "Ocean of solutions of litigation," which, in Henry Thomas Colebrooke's translation, became known as *A Digest of Hindu Law* (Calcutta, 1797).

The commentaries on the *dharmasūtras* and *dharmaśāstras* are of two kinds. Some are commentaries *stricto sensu* (called *ṭīka*, *bhāṣya*, *vṛtti*, etc.). They comment on one particular *dharmasūtra* or *dharmaśāstra* text from beginning to end, *sūtra* after *sūtra*, or verse after verse. So far we have two commentaries on Gautama, one on Āpastamba, one on Baudhāyana, eight on Manu (the recently discovered commentary by Bhāruci may be one of the earliest texts of this genre), five on Yājñavalkya (one of them, Vijṅāneśvara's *Mitākṣarā* was to play a prominent role under British rule; it has its own two super commentaries), one on each version of Nārada, and one on Viṣṇu.

Few commentators, even on one particular *dharmasūtra* or *dharmaśāstra*, limit themselves to a mere word by word interpretation of the text. To prove their point the more learned among them also introduce into their discussions quotations from other *dharmasūtras* and *dharmaśāstras*, and their works come close to the second type of commentaries, the *nibandhas*. *Nibandhas* "compendia, digests" do not comment on any particular *dharmasūtra* or *dharmaśāstra*. The authors of these texts rather bring together extracts from various *dharmasūtras* and *dharmaśāstras* on one particular aspect of *dharma*, and harmonize the apparent contradictions into one coherent system of their own, most often with very different results. It is from these learned commentaries and *nibandhas* that scholars have been able to gather fragments of *dharmasūtras* and *dharmaśāstra* that are otherwise lost.

Some of the *nibandhas* are voluminous; they are veritable encyclopedias of Hindu *dharma*. Under one general title they comprise several book-length texts, each of them with their own sub-titles, on every imaginable branch of *dharma*. Lakṣmīdhara's *Kṛtyakalpataru* (twelfth century), for example, consists of 14 *kāṇḍas*, Mitramiśra's *Vīramitrodaya* (seventeenth century) contains 10 *prakāśas*, and Raghunandana's *Smṛtitattva* (sixteenth century) is divided into 28 *tattvas*.

Most important in this essay on the *dharmasūtras* and *dharmaśāstra* is the fact that the commentators do not hesitate to impose interpretations of their own on the ancient texts, in order to make all of them fit harmoniously within coherent systems. To achieve that goal the authors have recourse to a vast array of traditionally recognized exegetical principles, which can only be briefly illustrated here. When two *smṛti* texts are contradictory, it is possible to invoke for one of them the concept of *kalivarjya* "a practice to be avoided in the *kaliyuga*." Thus, when Manu first recognizes levirate as a valid form of marriage (9.59) and, immediately thereafter, rejects it as being *dharma* fit for cattle (9.65–6), the commentators avoid the contradiction by arguing that levirate marriage was allowed in earlier world eras, but that it should not be practiced in the wretched *kaliyuga*. The texts often compare *dharma* with a cow, which in the *kṛta-* or *satyayuga* stands on four feet, on three feet in the *tretāyuga*, on two in the *dvāparayuga*, and on one foot in the *kaliyuga*. Or, when a *smṛti* text includes a number of items in a list, the commentator is at liberty to interpret the list either as comprehensive or as merely illustrative. Thus, when Gautama (10.39 = 2.1.39) enumerates five ways of acquiring property (inheritance, purchase, partition, seizure, and discovery), commentators who, for reasons of their own, wish to recognize the fact of being born as a means of acquiring a right of ownership in the joint family property, argue that Gautama's list is illustrative. Others, who claim that the head of the family is the sole owner of the entire joint family property, in their turn argue that Gautama's list ought to be taken literally. The often intricate arguments which the commentators proffer in defense of their interpretation of the *smṛti* texts – not unlike other branches of Sanskrit commentarial literature, the commentaries and *nibandhas* on the *dharmaśāstras* often take the form of dialogues between named or unnamed opponents and the authors – are grounded in their vast knowledge of other scholarly disciplines, including the different systems of Sanskrit grammar, the principles of textual exegesis elaborated in the *Mīmāṃsāsūtras* and their commentaries, the rules of logic (*nyāya*), etc. (For a detailed analysis of the various devices used by the commentators to interpret the *dharmaśāstras*, see Lingat 1973: 143–75.)

The *Dharmaśāstras* in Modern Times

In 1772, in an effort to prevent Indians being subjected to English law, which was totally foreign to them, the Governor (later Governor-General) of Bengal, Warren Hastings, encouraged a decree to the effect that "in matters of inheritance, marriage and other religious matters, the Gentoos shall be governed by the laws of the Shaster, the Muhammadans by the law of the Koran." In other words, from 1772 onward "the Shaster," i.e. the ancient *dharmaśāstras* – rather, the entire, undefined body of Sanskrit *dharmaśāstra* literature – were elevated *en bloc* to the rank of law books to be used by the Anglo-Indian courts of law to decide civil and religious disputes among Hindus.

Many British servants of the East India Company were familiar with Persian or even Arabic, and applying the law of the Koran to Indian Muslims was not expected to present major problems. Sanskrit, on the other hand, was totally unknown. As a result, administering the "law" of the *dharmaśāstras* to Hindus led to interesting developments in the understanding and interpretation of the ancient, revealed Sanskrit texts. This essay cannot go into detail on the early experiments that were resorted to to obviate the problem: attaching to the courts of law one or more pandits, who were able to consult the Sanskrit texts and advise the judges; trying to gain access to the Sanskrit texts in English via the intermediary of translations into Persian (e.g., the *Code of Gentoo Laws* mentioned earlier), etc. These experiments may have made legal proceedings cumbersome and not always reliable, but they had little impact on the *dharmaśāstras* themselves. It must be mentioned, though, that it was the need to understand the legal sections of the *dharmaśāstras* in the original, that became the first and primary incentive for British judges in India to embark on the study of the Sanskrit language. Some of the letters by Sir William Jones, a judge in the Calcutta Supreme Court, make it abundantly clear that his *Institutes of Hindu Law; or the Ordinances of Menu . . . Comprising the Indian System of Duties Religious and Civil* (Calcutta, 1794), was a natural and pragmatic reaction to his distrust in court pandits and second-hand translations.

Other developments did have an impact on the understanding and practical application of the ancient *dharmaśāstras*. First, "law" and "religion," which were inextricably linked in the *smṛti* texts, were artificially separated. Thus, in the *smṛti* texts one of the requirements for an adoption to be valid is a ritual called *dattahoma*. With the "religious" aspect of adoption, as with any other aspect of the Hindu religion, the Courts explicitly refused to interfere: if the *dattahoma* was performed as a part of an adoption, the parties were free to do so. But, the task of the Courts was to administer "law," and they declared adoptions valid without the performance of *dattahomas*. Or, the *dharmaśāstras* prohibit the adoption of an only son, because such an act was bound to deprive the son's natural father of the ideal person to perform the required *śrāddha* rituals after his death. The Anglo-Indian courts of law overlooked this "religious" aspect of adoption, and declared the adoption of an only son valid. Second, as mentioned earlier, one of the characteristic traits of the commentaries and *nibandhas* was that they interpreted the apparently contradictory statements in the ancient texts so as to integrate them into coherent systems. These coherent systems of the commentaries and *nibandhas* were more appealing to the courts than the often unclear and contradictory texts of the *sūtras* and *śāstras*. As a result, the courts decided it was not their duty to investigate the correct meaning of the ancient texts themselves, but to apply them only as they had been interpreted by the commentators. In other words, the meaning of the ancient, revealed texts was made subordinate to the interpretations they received at the hands of human commentators. Thus, the distinction between those who did not recognize birth as a means to acquire a right of ownership in the joint family property and those who did (see above), led to the creation of the two major "Schools of Hindu law," the *Dāyabhāga* school for Bengal and the *Mitākṣarā* school for the rest of India. And the Courts went one step further. While still claiming to base their judgments on the Sanskrit texts, be it the human commentaries rather than the revealed *śāstras*, in reality the courts made even the Sanskrit commentaries subordinate to the British Common Law concept of legal precedent. The *Manusmṛti* and other *dharmaśāstras* were referred to in every judgment, but via the commentaries, and the commentaries were quoted indirectly via earlier decisions. Even when a member of the Court or the attorney for a party convincingly demonstrated that a text from a *dharmaśāstra* or commentary had been wrongly interpreted in earlier cases, the Court invoked Latin maxims such as *stare decisis* or *communis error facit ius* to overrule the proper meaning of the Sanskrit text. Finally, there were aspects of the *dharmaśāstras*, such as their inferior treatment of women and members of lower castes, which the British rulers considered objectionable. Their decisions, based on the principles of justice, equity, and good conscience, as well as a number of Acts, starting with the *Caste Disabilities Removal Act* (1850) and the *Women's Right to Property Act* (1856), slowly but gradually restricted the range of the issues on which Hindus continued to be governed by the law of the "shaster."

The legal system as elaborated in the colonial period was applied unchanged in the courts of law of Independent India. That is, until 1955–6, when the Indian Parliament passed four modern Acts (on marriage, inheritance, minority and guardianship, and adoptions and maintenance), and thereby, in Derrett's words, wrote "the epitaph for the Rishis" (subtitle of *The Death of a Marriage Law*, Delhi, 1978). Yet, even today, in all matters that are not covered by the four Acts, the *dharmaśāstras* and the commentaries and *nibandhas* continue to be quoted and debated in the courts of law throughout India.

Epilogue

I have saved 'till the end a question that has been raised primarily for the *dharmasūtras* and *dharmaśāstra* as law books, but that equally applies to any other aspect of *dharma* dealt with in these texts. The question is whether the composers of the *dharmasūtras* and *dharmaśāstras* actually laid down rules that were and that they expected to be applied in daily life, or whether the texts merely present a picture of how their Brahman composers envisaged *dharma* in an ideal world. Answers to this question by modern scholars, both Indian and non-Indian, vary widely, from absolute trust in to total denial of the applicability of the texts in real life. Hastings and the early British translators of the *dharmaśāstras* were confident enough to build an entire modern legal system on the ancient texts. In F. Max Müller's opinion, even for those not involved in Indian administration "they are of great importance for forming a correct view of the old state of society in India" (1859: 134). P. V. Kane's multi-volume work on the *History of Dharmaśāstra*, Jolly's, Lingat's, and Derrett's general surveys of *dharmaśāstra* literature, and numerous volumes and articles on specific aspects of *smṛti*, are all based on the tacit assumption that the texts provide a true picture of life in ancient India. Yet, others were less convinced, to the point of calling the *dharmaśāstras* nothing more than "a pious wish of its metaphysically-minded, ceremonial ridden priestly promulgators, and but seldom a stern reality" (Das 1914: 8). It is possible, though, to find a middle ground between the two extreme positions. Most, if not all, the injunctions or prohibitions contained in the several *sūtras* and *ślokas* may reflect real situations, real customs and practices. Even when texts appear contradictory, they represent the different kinds of *dharma* that were observed within certain groups of individuals, regional, social, professional, etc. Some of the injunctions and prohibitions contained in the texts were *dharma* for the members of specific groups only, but all these rules needed to be incorporated in the overarching, authoritative, and prescriptive texts on the subject of *dharma*. None of the groups concerned may have known the *dharmaśāstras* as they were eventually written down and transmitted in manuscript form. They may have been ignorant of the *dharma* of other groups, but they perfectly knew the specific rules, transmitted orally from father to son, or from teacher to disciple, which they themselves were supposed to live by (Rocher 1993).

SVA DHARMA
SADHARANA DHARMA
SANATANA DHARMA

References

Das, Govinda. 1914: *The Real Character of Hindu Law*. Banaras: Chowkhamba.

Derrett, J. Duncan M. 1973a: *Dharmaśāstra and Juridical Literature*. Wiesbaden: Harrassowitz.

——. 1973b: *History of Indian Law (Dharmaśāstra)*. Leiden: Brill.

Flood, Gavin. 1996: *An Introduction to Hinduism*. Cambridge: Cambridge University Press, pp. 51–74.

Halbfass, Wilhelm. 1988: "Dharma in Traditional Hinduism," in *India and Europe: An Essay in Understanding*. Albany: State University of New York Press, pp. 310–33.

Jolly, Julius. 1928: *Hindu Law and Custom*. Calcutta: Greater India Society. Translated from the German (*Recht und Sitte, einschliesslich der einheimishen Litteratur*, Strassburg: Trübner, 1896) by Batakrishna Ghosh.

Kane, Pandurang Vaman. 1930–77: *History of Dharmaśāstra* (*Ancient and Medieval Religious and Civil* Law). 5 vols. in 8 parts (some parts in 2nd ed.). Poona: Bhandarkar Oriental Research Institute. [Vol. 1, 2nd ed., in two parts (1968, 1975), contains a historical survey of *dharmaśātra* literature.]

Lingat, Robert. 1973: *The Classical Law of India*. Translated from the French (*Les sources du droit dans le système traditionnel de l'Inde*, The Hague: Mouton, 1967) with additions by J. Duncan M. Derrett. Berkeley: University of California Press.

Müller, F. Max. 1959. *A History of Ancient Sanskrit Literature*. Allahabad.

Olivelle, Patrick. 1999: *The Dharmasūtras: The Law Codes of Ancient India*. Oxford: Oxford University Press.

Renou, Louis. 1947: *Les éoles védiques et la formation du véda*. Paris: Imprimerie Nationale.

Rocher, Ludo. 1986: *The Purāṇas*. History of Indian Literature, vol. 2. Wiesbaden: Harrassowitz.

——. 1993. "Law Books in an Oral Culture," in *Proceedings of the American Philosophical Society* 137: 254–67.

CHAPTER 5

The Sanskrit Epics

John Brockington

"Whatever is here concerning the four aims of mankind may be found elsewhere, but what is absent from here does not exist anywhere." This assertion, which prefaces and concludes the *Mahābhārata* narrative (at 1.56.33 and 18.5.38), illustrates well the encyclopedic nature of the larger of the two Sanskrit epics in its present form. The two epics are indeed among the largest literary works in the world: the *Mahābhārata*, "the great <story/war> of Bharata's descendants," traditionally contains 100,000 verses and even the text established in the Critical Edition has nearly 75,000, while the other epic, the *Rāmāyaṇa*, "the journey/career of Rāma," though less than a third as long, still contains almost 20,000 verses. However, these originally orally transmitted bardic poems have grown to this immense size over an extended period of time, from around the fifth century BCE to the fourth century CE by the usual reckoning, and in the process have gained substantial additions to their narratives and also – particularly in the case of the *Mahābhārata* – didactic elements, while their basically heroic ethos has been transformed into a religious outlook as a major figure in each came to be identified as an *avatāra*, "descent," of Viṣṇu.

Originating in the period following that of the Vedic literature and reflecting the interests and concerns of the *kṣatriya* aristocracy, the epics reveal much about the process by which the more theistic emphases of classical Hinduism emerged from late Vedic ritualism. Their origins may perhaps be traced to some of the ballads about gods and heroes recited within the overall context of Vedic rituals, but their real growth was owed to the bardic tradition which emerged at the courts of *kṣatriya* rulers, where stories about the exploits of heroes were naturally welcomed. The framework stories of both epics present them as oral compositions and show the importance not only of the bard or reciter, but also of the audience in their transmission, while also setting them within the largest possible context. For the *Mahābhārata*, this means that the first 50 or so sections of its first book are concerned with the origins of the world and then the ancestry of the epic's heroes. However, at some point around the middle of their main period of growth (possibly the first century CE), each epic was committed to writing and their transmission passed into the hands of the brāhmans, the main custodians by then of traditional values. These two developments may well be linked and have occurred simultaneously.

The basic plot of the *Mahābhārata*, which is traditionally ascribed to the sage Vyāsa, "the arranger," concerns the struggle for control of the Kuru kingdom between two sets of cousins: the hundred sons of Dhṛtarāṣṭra, usually called the Kauravas, and the five sons of Pāṇḍu, the Pāṇḍavas. Both fathers have ruled in turn, so the line of succession to the throne is by no means clear and the rights of the situation are debatable. This leads eventually to open warfare between the cousins, although this is preceded by various events of which the most significant is the dicing match in which the oldest Pāṇḍava, Yudhiṣṭhira, first loses everything to the Kaurava champion and then the five brothers, along with their wife Draupadī, are exiled to the forest for 12 years, plus a further year to be spent undetected within society. After their return and the continued refusal by the Kauravas to reach an agreement, war becomes inevitable and, as the actual battle is about to begin, the third Pāṇḍava brother, Arjuna, confides to his friend Kṛṣṇa, chief of the Yādavas, his qualms about fighting the opposing side because they are his relatives. This is the setting for Kṛṣṇa's sermon to him, the *Bhagavadgītā*, which has become the best known part of the whole epic. The battle itself, over 18 days, occupies the middle part of the epic (itself comprising 18 books) and is followed by the lamentations of the women, two lengthy books of advice to Yudhiṣṭhira by the dying Bhīṣma (the senior member of the family), and several shorter books narrating various events up to the end of the Pāṇḍavas' lives.

Whereas the *Mahābhārata* has been regarded by several modern scholars as an exploration of the problems involved in establishing the nature of *dharma* and in applying it in particular situations, the *Rāmāyaṇa* is an affirmation of the centrality of *dharma* to all right endeavour. The *Rāmāyaṇa* ascribed to Vālmīki contains the story of prince Rāma and his adventures when exiled to the forest by the machinations of his step-mother; when Kaikeyī abruptly demands his banishment, Rāma accepts his father Daśaratha's reluctant decree with absolute submission and with the calm self-control which regularly characterizes him. The narrative thus ranges from accounts of intrigue at Daśaratha's court in Ayodhyā to wanderings among hermits in the forest, and culminates in the great battle for Laṅkā, when Rāvana, the king of the Rākṣasas, is punished for his abduction of Rāma's wife, Sītā. In his search for Sītā, Rāma is helped by the monkey counselor, Hanumān, who becomes a much-loved figure as the story develops, because of his devotion to Rāma. The *Rāmāyaṇa* thus deals with some of the most basic themes of human existence and constitutes a powerful exploration of the concept of *dharma*.

Deity and Ritual

Within the narratives of both epics the older pattern of deities and of rituals based on sacrifice, leading to heaven (*svarga*), is more prominent, but the newer patterns of worship, usually seen as leading to liberation (*mokṣa*), do also occur from time to time – and are then more predominant in the didactic parts. The deities alluded to or playing any part in the narrative are largely those of the Vedic pantheon. Indra is particularly prominent, both as the leader of the gods and as the performer of various heroic deeds (in particular the slaying of Vṛtra), among the gods mentioned in the *Mahābhārata*. In the story about the five Pāṇḍavas being actually fathered by the gods, Indra fathers Arjuna, the finest warrior among them. In the *Rāmāyaṇa* Rāma is compared most often with Indra and at the climax of the whole story, in his duel with Rāvana, he receives the help of Indra's charioteer, Mātali. Yama appears quite often in similes and in various boastings by the warriors of the *Mahābhārata*, where his role in the older pantheon as the king of the dead makes this natural (a role that is at odds with the later concept of *saṃsāra*), and similarly in the *Rāmāyaṇa* a common formulaic expression refers to leading or sending warriors to Yama's abode. The fire-god, Agni, also plays quite an appreciable role in the narrative of the *Mahābhārata* and, in a development of the basic narrative of the *Rāmāyaṇa*, he returns Sītā to Rāma with her purity vindicated by her passing through the fire. Even Varuṇa still appears as a lingering survival, mainly as the lord of the ocean but also in the notion that heroes are equal to Indra and Varuṇa. In general, the opposition between Devas and Asuras, their contests for supremacy and the myth of the churning of the ocean all show a Vedic or immediately post-Vedic pattern. Even in the allusions or episodes relating to Viṣṇu or Śiva there are still traces of the older pattern, with Viṣṇu, for example, still in some passages subordinate to Indra.

The religious activities mentioned within the main narratives also reveal a pattern which still reflects the Vedic situation to a large extent, while the actual narrative of the *Mahābhārata* is built around the *rājasūya* (in the dicing game and the other events of the second book) and around other rituals at various points; there are even occasional direct references to Vedic ritual officiants or the ritual itself in the narrative books. On the other hand, some late parts of the narrative provide the earliest instances of the practice of pilgrimage to *tīrthas*, which becomes such a feature of later Hinduism, while on occasion more popular beliefs, such as in omens and portents, are included. In the *Rāmāyaṇa*, the commonest rituals mentioned are the morning and evening worship, but sacrifice in general, various individual sacrifices and the sacrificial altar are all mentioned occasionally in the core narrative, although little detail is given. Significantly *saṃnyāsa* and related terms for renunciation do not occur within the *Rāmāyaṇa*, whereas it is found occasionally in the *Mahābhārata*; indeed, the various forest sages who feature in the *Rāmāyaṇa* narrative are clearly hermits (*vānaprastha*), not ascetics (*saṃnyāsin*). Another aspect in which the *Rāmāyaṇa* appears more archaic is that its earliest parts largely ignore the concept of *saṃsāra*, mentioning instead *svarga*, "heaven," while both *saṃsāra* and *karma* do feature in parts of the *Mahābhārata* narrative.

By the middle of the period of growth of the epics, not only are Viṣṇu and Śiva becoming more significant but also the figure of Brahmā becomes important for a time, in the last century or two BCE and the first century or so CE. Basically Brahmā represents a fusion of the Upaniṣadic absolute, *Brahman*, with the concept of a creator deity, and so he is credited with some of the cosmogonic myths told in the later vedic period about Prajāpati. He is often called Pitāmaha, "grandfather," or Svayaṃbhū, "self-born," and he is especially linked with Brāhmans and ascetics (e.g. Mbh. 1.203). His main attribute is to distribute favours and particularly weapons to those who have pleased him by their ascetic penance, as he does in the *Rāmāyaṇa* to both Rāvana and his son, Indrajit, although he does also on occasion utter curses. However, it is Brahmā who leads the gods when they assemble at the end of the main *Rāmāyaṇa* narrative to reveal to Rāma his divinity (Ram. 6.105). There are possible hints of the classical *trimūrti* concept – which links Brahmā, Viṣṇu, and Śiva together rather arbitrarily – a couple of times in the *Mahābhārata* (12.328.17 and 13.14.183), but already in the later parts of the epics Viṣṇu and Śiva have totally eclipsed Brahmā, just as the importance of Indra has significantly declined.

The complementarity of Viṣṇu and Śiva in the *Mahābhārata* is a feature which has been highlighted from a structuralist perspective by several scholars (Biardeau, Hiltebeitel, and others). Since both epics eventually become Vaiṣṇava works, the Vaiṣṇava aspects come to dominate, but this should not obscure the fact that Śiva plays an appreciable role in the *Mahābhārata* narrative: for example, he ordains that Draupadī shall have five husbands (1.157 and 1.189), Arjuna struggles with the Kirāṭa who is Śiva in disguise (3.38–41), Śiva goes before Arjuna in the battle killing those whom Arjuna will strike (7.173), and Aśvatthāman invokes Śiva before the night attack in which he murders the remaining Pāṇḍava forces (10.7). Not all of these fit the pattern of Śiva as the destroyer and Kṛṣṇa as the preserver so often posited (and in broad terms correctly so). Indeed, there are occasional references which link him with birth and fertility: in particular, Gāndhārī gained the boon of a hundred sons from him (1.103.9) and Sagara that of many sons (3.104). Śiva is less often mentioned in the *Rāmāyaṇa* than in the *Mahābhārata*, although he becomes more prominent in the first and last books, which extend the main narrative backwards (to the birth of Rāma and his brothers) and forwards (to Rāma's righteous rule, *rāmarājya*, after the victory over Rāvana – whose previous exploits fill the first part of the last book – up to his final departure from this world).

The *Mahābhārata*

Within the narrative of the *Mahābhārata*, Kṛṣṇa plays a prominent but scarcely central role, one which nonetheless is enhanced as he comes to be seen as divine.

To be exact, he appears in a dual role, as the Yādava chief who sides with the Pāṇḍavas and gives them frequently devious and unscrupulous advice, and as the supreme personal deity who only occasionally reveals his true identity (most notably, of course, to Arjuna in the *Bhagavadgītā*). This less than central position is to some extent modified in the 16th book, the *Mausalaparvan* or "Book of the Clubs," which tells the story of the deaths of Kṛṣṇa and his half-brother Balarāma (also called Baladeva and Saṃkarṣaṇa) and is then more fully remedied in the *Harivaṃśa*, "the dynasty of Hari" (i.e. Viṣṇu = Kṛṣṇa), composed during the second half of the period of growth of the *Mahābhārata* itself as a supplement to it; Kṛṣṇa's centrality in the *Harivaṃśa* is in marked contrast to the *Mahābhārata*, where he stands aside from the central action. In the *Mahābhārata* narrative, Kṛṣṇa is most prominent in the preparations for war, when he acts as a negotiator on the Pāṇḍavas' behalf with the Kauravas (e.g. 5.30 and 5.71) but appears as one of the strongest protagonists of the conflict, urging Yudhiṣṭhira on. So too, in the *Bhagavadgītā* (6.23–40), Kṛṣṇa encourages his friend Arjuna, for whom he has agreed to act as charioteer, to abandon his misgivings and to engage in the battle.

The inclusion of the *Bhagavadgītā* at this crucial point of the *Mahābhārata* narrative sets it firmly in the battle context and it is precisely the ethics of Arjuna's position which is the starting point for Kṛṣṇa's discourse, although as a whole it develops a philosophically and theologically significant message which ranges far beyond its immediate setting; that setting was, however, undoubtedly useful in securing it a much wider popular audience than was enjoyed by the Vedic literature and it seems clear that it was subsequently inserted within the *Mahābhārata* for just that reason. The contrast between Kṛṣṇa's revelation of himself as the supreme deity and Arjuna's casual familiarity with him in the rest of the epic is indeed striking. Kṛṣṇa begins his answer to Arjuna's doubts by stressing the need to fulfil one's role in society and asserting that, since the self (*ātman*) is eternal and indestructible, it does not die with the body and so, since death is not final, there is no need to grieve over the imminent deaths in battle. He then goes on to affirm that all activity is a sacrifice if undertaken correctly, in a spirit of detachment, thus incorporating both sacrifice and renunciation within the context of life in the world; actions as such have no particular effect, provided one acts without interest in the result, and indeed actions are in reality performed by the *guṇas*, the constituents of nature, which are completely separate from the *ātman*. Other themes which Kṛṣṇa explores are *Brahman*, the self-discipline of yoga, the nature of the supreme deity and his attributes, and loyal service (*bhakti*) to the deity; the *Bhagavadgītā* thus synthesizes into an overall theistic framework various strands of thought then current, while drawing most heavily on the Upaniṣads.

The climax of the *Bhagavadgītā* comes in the theophany in the eleventh chapter, where Kṛṣṇa reveals to Arjuna his universal, terrifying form, which produces in Arjuna the response of humble adoration and penitence for his former casual attitude (soon to be resumed). In the remaining chapters, which contain a variety of topics, there is a gradual return to the theme of devotion or *bhakti*, which reaches its climax in Kṛṣṇa's declaration of his attachment (*bhakti*) to Arjuna and the promise that by his grace he can be reached and entered into. This way of devotion is available to all, unlike the way of knowledge, which few can achieve, or the way of action without attachment, and so is superior to either. It is worth noting that Kṛṣṇa presents himself in the *Bhagavadgītā* as the supreme, identical to or more often superior to *Brahman* and that there is no real trace of his identification with Viṣṇu, either directly or as *avatāra*.

The substantial transformation in the view of Kṛṣṇa which we find in the *Harivaṃśa* (which revolves around the figure of Kṛṣṇa) is undoubtedly one of the most pivotal innovations in the history of Hinduism. Here for the first time is presented Kṛṣṇa the child hero of the forests in Vṛndāvana and protector of cows, the figure who over the centuries is to become the adorable infant, the cowherd and the lover of the cowgirls (*gopīs*). Although there may be occasional hints of this facet of his nature in the *Mahābhārata* (but this is debatable), the *Harivaṃśa* provides the first connected account of this and other aspects of his life, such as the taming of the water snake Kāliya (55–6), his lifting of Mount Govardhana in defiance of Indra, whose continuing decline is still more marked in other episodes (60–1), the killing of his evil uncle Kaṃsa (72–76), the attack on Mathurā by Jarāsaṃdha (80–2) and the move from Mathurā to the new city of Dvārakā (84 and 93). Equally, his older brother Balarāma, who appears in only a minor role in the *Mahābhārata*, is now a much more important figure and there is much about the youthful exploits of the two brothers. The other members of their clan are still presented in the *Harivaṃśa* as being generally ignorant of Kṛṣṇa's divine nature, in which it contrasts with later narrations in, for example, the *Viṣṇu* and *Bhāgavata Purāṇas*.

The *Rāmāyaṇa*

In the *Rāmāyaṇa* Rāma is, of course, central and its portrayal of him as the *kṣatriya* ideal or prince and warrior prompts the understanding of Rāma as an *avatāra* of Viṣṇu and eventually as supreme deity himself precisely through *dharma*; an alternative view stresses the theme of the divine king in Indian thought as the key to Rāma's divinity (on this view, present from the earliest phases of the epic). In the core narrative, the second to sixth books, Rāma is presented as the outstanding martial figure (often compared to Indra, the divine warrior) whose adherence to ethical values is equally outstanding (he is frequently called "the best of upholders of *dharma*"), a basically human but exemplary figure. As his moral elevation is emphasized, various episodes of the original story receive a moralistic gloss, in order to eliminate the possibility of moral lapses on his part; so, for example, his killing of the *vānara* chief Vālin while the latter is fighting his brother Sugrīva, with whom Rāma has made a pact, is given an elaborate justification, as are his martial activities to protect the hermits while they go about their religious activities (basically in terms of his duty as a prince to uphold law and order). Similarly, the comparison with Indra gives way to an identification with Viṣṇu, first seen at the conclusion of the sixth book – a later expansion – where various gods, led by Brahmā, gather to reveal his divinity to Rāma (6.105). This recognition is, however, expressed in terms of identity and not yet as incarnation.

The increasing veneration shown to Rāma is then reflected in the first and seventh books, which include not only material presenting Rāma as divine but also narratives enhancing the status of his opponent Rāvana and so indirectly of Rāma, the only person able to defeat him. The purpose of the first book is to narrate Rāma's birth, youthful exploits, and marriage, and generally to provide a framework for the narrative; at the gods' request, Viṣṇu agrees to become incarnate as Daśaratha's four sons as the only means of destroying Rāvana, the evil king of Laṅkā. The last book is set in Ayodhyā after Rāma's victorious return to rule in Ayodhyā but the first half details Rāvana's genealogy and his misdeeds before his encounter with Rāma (making him into an adversary of the gods), while the rest of the book deals with events after Rāma's installation; these include Rāma reluctantly ordering Sītā's exile to Vālmīki's hermitage (placing public opinion above his own feelings for his wife) and the birth of the twins, Kuśa and Lava, at Vālmīki's hermitage. Eventually, after a long and prosperous reign, described in ideal terms, Rāma settles the kingdom on his sons and publicly immolates himself in the river Sarayu (thus returning to his form as Viṣṇu).

Whereas the *Mahābhārata* narrative of Kṛṣṇa was next developed in a supplement to it, the *Harivaṃśa*, the account of Rāma in the *Rāmāyaṇa* is developed in the Purāṇas and in the later Sanskrit *Rāmāyaṇas*. Thus, for example, the *Kūrma Purāṇa* account contains the important theological development of the illusory Sītā created by Agni before she is seized by Rāvaṇa, thus safeguarding the real Sītā's purity; this motif then occurs also in the *Adhyātma Rāmāyaṇa*, Tulsīdās's *Rāmcaritmānas* and elsewhere. The later Sanskrit *Rāmāyaṇas* give a Vedāntin slant to the emerging *bhakti* emphasis; the *Yogāvasiṣṭha*, though claiming to be by Vālmīki, also asserts that it is the twelfth telling of the story and lays considerable stress on Rāma as a liberated being (*jīvanmukta*) in a unique blend of abstract philosophy and vivid narrative, while the *Adhyātma Rāmāyaṇa* teaches a form of Advaita Vedānta combined with belief in Rāma's saving grace and also incorporates the *Rāmagītā*, perhaps the first significant attempt to give Rāma a teaching role analogous to Kṛṣṇa's. Already in the *Adhyātma Rāmāyaṇa* we see a motif which is common in many later retellings, that those killed by Rāma are thereby blessed. The first version of the *Rāmāyaṇa* in a regional language is Kampaṉ's Tamil *Irāmāvatāram*, appearing in the wake of the impassioned *bhakti* poetry of the Āḻvārs; already in this there is something of the emphasis on the name of Rāma which becomes so significant later. In North India, the first major adaptation is that into Bengali by Kṛttibās but the Hindi *Rāmcaritmānas* of Tulsīdās has become much the best known, notable for its vision of Rāma's righteous rule and the saving power of his name, as well as for its use as the base text for the Rāmlīlā, a dramatic enactment of the story staged annually by local communities across much of North India.

Doctrinal Developments

Kṛṣṇa and Rāma are the most widely worshipped of the *avatāras* of Viṣṇu but the *avatāra* concept as such only begins to emerge in the later stages of development of the epics, even though the *Bhagavadgītā is* commonly regarded as proclaiming the basic rationale for Viṣṇu's "descents," when Kṛṣṇa declares that he incarnates himself in age after age to destroy the wicked and to protect the righteous (4.5–8). Indeed, didactic parts of the *Mahābhārata* list just four or six of Viṣṇu's "manifestations" (*prādurbhāva*, the term it uses rather than the later term *avatāra*), while the *Rāmāyaṇa* shows no awareness of the concept. The fish, *matsya*, which saved Manu from a great deluge is identified with Brahmā in the *Mahābhārata* (3.195), just as in the *Rāmāyaṇa* (6.105) the boar which raises the earth from the waters is Brahmā; their identification with Viṣṇu comes later. The exploits of Rāma Jāmadagnya (later known more commonly as Paraśurāma) are given some prominence in the *Mahābhārata* and he also occurs in an episode in the first book of the *Rāmāyaṇa* where he is worsted by the young Rāma Dāśarathi. The *Mahābhārata* also lists Vāmana, the dwarf, and Narasiṃha (12.326 and 337) and predicts the future *avatāra*, Kalkin (3.188–9). In the version of the Vāmana myth found in the *Rāmāyaṇa* (1.28.2–11), Viṣṇu presents the three worlds that he has regained to Indra, who by implication is still superior to him.

The lists of Viṣṇu's manifestations occur within the didactic portions (primarily books 12–13) which also contain a significant amount of material relating to the emergence of Vaiṣṇavism as such, as well as a certain amount of broadly philosophic material. The process of fusion of Nārāyaṇa with Viṣṇu is under way by now; whereas the story of Mārkaṇḍeya entering the mouth of Nārāyaṇa and seeing the whole universe inside his body (3.186) uses only the name Nārāyaṇa and there is no hint of his identity with Viṣṇu or Kṛṣṇa Vāsudeva, in the *Nārāyaṇīya* (12.321–39) from chapter 328 onwards the name Viṣṇu is often used instead of Nārāyaṇa, while elsewhere it is often stated that Arjuna and Kṛṣṇa are Nara and Nārāyaṇa, who are ancient *ṛṣis*, sages, and also divine beings noted for the eternality and perfection of their friendship. The *Nārāyaṇīya* is the main but relatively late passage (probably no earlier than the third century CE) on worship of Nārāyaṇa and is clearly a composite text: the first six chapters form a complex sequence of emboxed narratives, while the remaining chapters contain a series of subsequent expansions. With its doctrine of the fourfold nature of the supreme being, it presents the formative stages of the Pāñcarātra system, which appears to have stood somewhat outside the mainstream of orthodoxy.

The text declares that the supreme deity Nārāyaṇa is gracious to those who are single-mindedly devoted to him and that they attain the highest goal, which is Vāsudeva, thus bringing into relationship with Nārāyaṇa the name Vāsudeva which is elsewhere regarded as a patronymic of Kṛṣṇa. Nārāyaṇa explains to his devotee, the ancient seer Nārada, that Vāsudeva is the supreme *puruṣa*, the inner ruler of everyone, Nārāyaṇa himself being the ordainer of the universe and the creator. Much of the first six chapters of the text presents the doctrine of the inaccessibility of the supreme deity through the story of Nārada's journey to a mysterious white continent, *śvetadvīpa*, inhabited by white beings who worship Nārāyaṇa, who is invisible to all except his exclusive devotees. The worshippers are called by various names, Bhāgavata, Sātvata, Ekāntin, and Pāñcarātra (the variety no doubt indicating the existence of differing groups, the Bhāgavatas no doubt being the worshippers of Kṛṣṇa as *bhagavat*, the lord), and overall the impression is of several originally separate trends that are in the process of merging.

Doctrinally too the *Nārāyaṇīya* shows a blend of Upaniṣadic monism, dualistic elements similar to Sāṃkhya and Yoga, and Brāhmanical ritualism, with the devotional worship of a personal deity – through a synthesis of several separate passages – and assigning a higher value to ritual and asceticism than in the comparable synthesis presented in the slightly earlier *Bhagavadgītā*. Virtually every mention of the term Pāñcarātra occurs within the *Nārāyaṇīya*, which is also the only part of the *Mahābhārata* where the theory of the *vyūhas*, the divine expansions, is presented in detail. This represents an adaptation of the story of Kṛṣṇa and his relatives to a cosmogonic perspective. Beneath Viṣṇu-Nārāyaṇa, the immutable ultimate deity, are the four *vyūhas*, who take charge of creation: Vāsudeva, presented as superior to the other three, gives rise to Saṃkarṣaṇa, from whom emanates Pradyumna (who, however, in the Yādava lineage is Kṛṣṇa's son), who in turn fathers Aniruddha. After this the gross creation commences through the agency of Brahmā, but all activity belongs to the four divine forms, who are also assimilated to the *tattvas*, constituent principles of Sāṃkhya. This theory seems to have evolved around the first to second century CE concurrently with the *avatāra* theory, which in the long run becomes more popular. Although the developed Pāñcarātra system is mainly concerned with ritual practice, there is surprisingly little about this aspect in the *Mahābhārata*.

Sāṃkhya and Yoga

These two long books of the *Mahābhārata* in which Bhīṣma propounds his advice to Yudhiṣṭhira contain a substantial amount of teaching which can broadly be called philosophical, of which the largest part is related to the later Sāṃkhya and Yoga systems, but there are also passages relating to a number of other approaches; these are mostly to be found in the third section of the *Śāntiparvan*, called the *Mokṣadharmaparvan* (12.168–353). In addition, there are similar passages elsewhere in the *Mahābhārata*, most obviously the *Bhagavadgītā*, but also the recapitulation of it which Kṛṣṇa delivers to Arjuna after the battle (the *Anugītā*, 14.16–50), an early such passage attributed to the mythical sage Sanatsujāta (the *Sanatsujātīya*, 5.43–5) and a few others. In contrast, neither Sāṃkhya nor Yoga occur in the *Rāmāyaṇa*. While in the *Mahābhārata* the concept of *karma* as the determinant of human destiny is on the whole the dominant one, the prevalence of other views about this, not uncommonly in the narrative and even occasionally in the didactic parts, is worth noting. In various passages fate (*daiva*, etc.), time, death, nature and one's own nature are each regarded as the supreme principle; ideas were still evidently in flux and indeed we see here the more popular equivalent of the ferment of ideas recorded in the Upaniṣads.

More traditional practices are still advocated and even deliberately contrasted with the philosophical approaches labeled Sāṃkhya and Yoga (which in any case are emerging trends rather than definite systems – the terms may at times mean no more than theory and practice respectively) or with developing Vaiṣṇava theism. For example, in one passage (12.189–93), Bhīṣma declares that *japa*, the murmuring of Vedic verses, constitutes a way of life belonging to the Vedic tradition and distinct from Sāṃkhya and Yoga – which he has treated successively in the two preceding chapters – and he emphasizes that someone practicing *japa* selflessly is equal to a Yogin in achievements; the passage is clearly intended to defend this traditional practice from the challenge of the newer ideas. Again, immediately after the *Nārāyaṇīya* – and so in implicit contrast to it – comes an episode designed to extol the merits of living on the grain gleaned after harvest (12.340–53, cf. 3.245–7). Other passages tackle the emerging ethical and religious issues of nonviolence (*ahiṃsā*), vegetarianism, and veneration of the cow (e.g. 12.253–6, 257, 260–2 and 264, and 13.115–17).

Several teachers are cited in the *Mokṣadharmaparvan* as teaching some form of Sāṃkhya, but the doctrines attributed to them vary and are not necessarily specific to Sāṃkhya; three of these teachers are often referred to later as important precursors of the developed system (Kapila, Āsuri, and Pañcaśikha). However, most epic descriptions of Sāṃkhya are not by Sāṃkhya teachers but report their views. Although consequently these passages are not primary sources for knowledge about the system, they do include ideas then current and may well have been composed during the period when Sāṃkhya schools were emerging. Indeed, Sāṃkhya had not assumed its later distinctive shape even by the end of the epic period; the nearest approach to the classical system is found in the very late *Anugītā*, which also incorporates significant Yoga elements. One early passage (12.187 ≈ 12.239–40) contains a synthesis of ancient cosmological speculations and yogic theories of evolution. Other passages mention three types of Sāṃkhya thinkers – those who accept just 24 categories, those who accept 25, and those who accept 26, the last being the supreme deity – but mostly the versions of Sāṃkhya found in the *Mahābhārata* are nontheistic, unlike Yoga. The clearest theistic version is found in the *Bhagavadgītā*.

Yoga and yogins occur quite widely in the *Mahābhārata* in contexts which suggest a wider and to some extent a different understanding of the terms than that found in classical Yoga. Also, the older practice of *tapas* and that of Yoga are often linked (but are often seen just as effective means to gain worldly ends). However, by the time of the *Nārāyaṇīya*, *tapas* and Yoga are both being subordinated to *bhakti*, with Nārāyaṇa identifying himself as the goal of Yoga proclaimed in Yoga texts (12.326.65), while the juxtaposition of Sāṃkhya and Yoga has become a commonplace in the *Nārāyaṇīya*, whereas they are more distinct and even contrasted in earlier passages. In all the Yoga passages there is a strong emphasis on discipline and control of the senses; the supernatural powers to which they lead should be avoided by the true Yogin, for the proper goal is the attainment of the state of Brahman or union with the one. Yoga practice, as presented in the *Mahābhārata*, comprises four main aspects of general preparations through moral conduct; diet, posture and surroundings; breath-control; and withdrawal of the senses, concentration and meditation. Although Īśvara, the supreme deity, is recognized, he is not active and tends to be equated with the self in its enlightened state. Two striking aspects of Yoga in the *Mahābhārata* are the concern with techniques of dying and the use of the imagery of light. These are sometimes combined as in the death of Drona, where he resorts to Yoga, becomes a light, and ascends to heaven, so that it seems to those below that there are two suns in the sky (7.165.35–40).

In addition to this more obviously philosophical material in its third section, the *Śāntiparvan* also contains in its first two sections much material that, in the context of its broadly practical purpose, also has religious implications. These two sections focus on and take their names from the duties of kings, *rājadharma*, and what is allowable in hard times, *āpaddharma*, both incorporating the term *dharma* with its meanings of morality and tradition. The second in particular has had considerable influence on later Hinduism through its accommodation of theory – for example, that Brāhmans should only teach – with actual practice – that in reality they follow a wider range of occupations in order to earn a living.

Later Influence

The influence of the epics on later Hinduism, and more generally on Indian culture as a whole, is shown not only by the summaries of the stories of Rāma and Kṛṣṇa in the Purāṇas and by the later Sanskrit *Rāmāyaṇas* that have already been briefly mentioned but also in pure literature, art and theatre right up to the present day. Indeed, the impact extends more widely still, since the Jain universal history makes the Kṛṣṇa story a model for much of its structure, while versions of the Rāma story are found in both Buddhist and Jain texts in India and spread throughout Southeast Asia and as far as China and Japan, with the story on occasion being localized in the individual cultures (this is seen most obviously in Thailand, where the Thai kings were frequently called Rāma and the Thai capital was named Ayutthiya after Rāma's Ayodhyā), and many plays on the Rāma and Pāṇḍava stories are performed in the Wayang Kulit puppet theatre of Java. The plots of much of classical Sanskrit literature are drawn from one or other of the epics (and even now modern Indian writers not infrequently draw on them). Sculptural representations are found on temples in North India from perhaps as early as the fifth century CE and one of the most famous examples of

South Indian art is the carving, covering a massive granite outcrop, of Arjuna's Penance or the Descent of the Gaṅgā from the *Mahābhārata* carved at Māmallapuram in the middle of the seventh century. Scenes drawn specifically from the *Mahābhārata* and *Rāmāyaṇa* (not simply of the Rāma and Kṛṣṇa stories) are carved on the outer walls of temples in many regions and at many periods. Miniature painters in the sixteenth to eighteenth centuries frequently illustrated episodes from the epics, under both Mughal and Rājput patronage, with several complete illustrated manuscripts being produced, some on a very lavish scale.

Adaptations of both epics into modern Indian languages were commonly among the first significant works to be produced in each language; in all of these adaptations the religious aspects are given greater prominence and the original heroic emphasis is correspondingly reduced. The earliest examples come from the Dravidian languages of South India but in due course, from about the fifteenth century, adaptations in the languages of North India followed. Their importance to the culture as a whole is clearly demonstrated by the fact that the great Mughal emperor Akbar commissioned translations of both into Persian in the 1580s as part of his strategy for understanding his subjects, just as the guru of the Marāṭhī nationalist leader, Śivājī, used the *Rāmāyaṇa* story in the service of Marāṭhā nationalism against Muslim rule in the seventeenth century. The popularity of the serializations shown on Indian television (the *Rāmāyaṇa* in 1987–8, the *Mahābhārata* in 1989–90) and subsequently made available on video (and so accessible to Hindus abroad as well) has been enormous, but one of the most striking features about them was the extent to which their format was dictated by traditional religious values and thus the viewing of them was treated as a form of worship; much of the style and presentation of the *Rāmāyaṇa* serial was based on that of the Rāmlīlā, that traditional community-based dramatic presentation of the story which is performed annually in so many locations across North India and which has clearly played so major a part in the popularity of the Rāma story and in particular in its broad appeal beyond sectarian boundaries. It is no surprise, therefore, that various political parties have appropriated the Rāma story and in particular the concept of *rāmrāj* (*rāmarājya*, Rāma's righteous rule) for their own purposes, from the Ram Rajya Parishad through to the Bharatiya Janata Party and the Ramjanmabhumi agitation.

As the vital link between the Vedas, commonly regarded as the source of authority within Hinduism, and the popular forms of Hinduism first found in the Purāṇas and still current today, the two Sanskrit epics have played a significant role in shaping that family of religions. The designation of the *Mahābhārata* as the "fifth Veda" makes a claim both to continuity and to the authoritativeness of the Vedas – an authority which also includes a claim to comprehensiveness (as in the assertion quoted at the beginning of this chapter). This continuity is also implicit in the belief that the *Mahābhārata* was first recited by Vyāsa ("arranger"), the sage whom tradition regards as the compiler of the Vedas and often the composer of the Purāṇas. The equivalent for the *Rāmāyaṇa* is the tradition, recorded late in its development at the beginning of the first book, that its author Vālmīki is granted a vision of Brahmā, the creator deity, who commissions him to compose the story of the ideal person, Rāma, just identified as such by the sage Nārada.

This continuity lies not only in the extended period over which both epics were growing to their present dimensions but also in the way that both were taken up by all succeeding periods both culturally and religiously, so that they have become part of the very fabric of the culture. Indeed, they have been used not only in support of traditional orthodoxy, as one might expect, but also by many marginalized groups who have found a special affinity with one of their characters; for example, Sītā's trials have enabled women to air the problem of a husband's neglect, Rāvana's defiance of the establishment has been glorified by some South Indians and some outcaste groups, and Vālmīki has become central to the beliefs of one untouchable group. Such selective appropriation of the epic narratives serves to underline both their richness and their flexibility. Yet the position of the epics within Hindu culture is even more basic than that: A. K. Ramanujan's assertion that no Indian ever hears the *Rāmāyaṇa* story for the first time conveys the very real truth, applicable to both epics, that their stories and their characters are integral to every Hindu's consciousness.

Bibliography

Biardeau, Madeleine. 1976/1978. "Études de mythologie hindoue: Bhakti et avatāra," *Bulletin de l'École Française d'Extrême Orient* 63 (1976): 111–263 and 65 (1978): 87–238.

Brockington, John. 1984. *Righteous Rāma: The Evolution of an Epic*. Delhi: Oxford University Press.

——. 1998. *The Sanskrit Epics (Handbuch der Orientalistik*, 2.12). Leiden: Brill.

Hiltebeitel, Alf. 1976. *The Ritual of Battle: Krishna in the Mahābhārata*. Ithaca: Cornell University Press.

Lipner, Julius, ed. 1997. *The Fruits of our Desiring: An Inquiry into the Ethics of the Bhagavadgītā for Our Times*. Calgary: Bayeux Arts.

The Mahābhārata, critically ed. by V. S. Sukthankar et al., 19 vols. Poona: Bhandarkar Oriental Research Institute, 1933–66.

The Mahābhārata [Books 1–5], trans. J. A. B. van Buitenen, 3 vols. Chicago: University of Chicago Press, 1973–8.

Pollock, Sheldon I. 1984. "The Divine King in the Indian Epic," *Journal of the American Oriental Society* 104: 505–28.

The Rāmāyaṇa of Vālmīki, critically edited, G. H. Bhatt and U. P. Shah, gen. eds., 7 vols. Baroda: Oriental Institute, 1960–75.

The Rāmāyaṇa of Vālmīki, An Epic of Ancient India, trans. Robert P. Goldman et al. Princeton: Princeton University Press, 1984–.

Schreiner, Peter, ed. 1997. *Nārāyaṇīya Studien* (Purāṇa Research Publications, Tübingen, 6). Wiesbaden: Harrassowitz.

CHAPTER 6

The Purāṇas

Freda Matchett

At the end of her introduction to *Purāṇa Perennis* Wendy Doniger, as editor, invites her readers "to sally forth into the living jungle of texts known as Purāṇas" (Doniger 1993: xii). There is a hint of danger in the metaphor, and a suggestion that selection is necessary here if one is to find the path through the jungle. Even without such a metaphor, however, there are several features of the Purāṇas which would instill caution into anyone proposing to study them. It is not only that they are vast in extent and miscellaneous in content. They offer information about themselves which is strangely at odds with their perceived actuality. First of all, their best-known examples announce that the Purāṇas are 18 in number, but in reality there are far more: Ludo Rocher's standard work on them lists 82 by name without making any claim that this number is exhaustive. Moreover, the Purāṇas are not the homogeneous group of texts which a number as small as 18 might lead one to expect. They are not simply a Hindu genre: there are Jaina Purāṇas also. They are not simply a Sanskrit phenomenon either: there are Purāṇas in many Indian vernaculars, some of them translated from Sanskrit originals and others composed from the start in the vernacular.

Secondly, the Purāṇas define themselves as *pañcalakṣaṇa*, having five characteristic topics, yet an eminent Indian scholar has estimated that these topics "occupy less than three percent of the extant Mahāpurāṇas" (Kane 1977: 841). Thirdly, there is a discrepancy between the way in which the Purāṇas classify themselves and their actual contents. A fourth problem arises, not from the Purāṇas' statements about themselves, but from their present existence in printed and bound editions. In this form they give the impression of being books, intended for reading, commentary, and annotation, but originally they would have been more accurately described as performances, intended to be seen, heard, and enjoyed. Unless some appreciation of this is present, today's reader of the Purāṇas fails to understand them.

A closer examination of these four issues will now be made, beginning with the last one, then dealing with the other three in the order in which they have just been mentioned. In some cases this may uncover more problems rather than offering solutions, but it should convey to the reader that the study of the Purāṇas is a challenging and rewarding field.

Books or Performances?

The difference between the Purāṇas' oral origins and their current existence as books is one which continues to create misunderstandings as to their nature and purpose. It is hard to remember that the text which the reader sees is not a fixed entity deliberately intended by a writer or group of writers (although it is possible that the *Bhāgavata* is an exception here; cf. Hardy 1990: 76; Doniger 1993: 127), but something fluid, a snapshot of a river of tradition, made up of many tributaries, which might look very different if the shot had been taken further up or downstream.

Like the *Mahābhārata*, the Purāṇas are generally thought by scholars to have been first recited by *sūtas*, bards who attended *kṣatriya* leaders and provided them with inspiration and entertainment in the form of stories of their ancestors. According to *Vāyu* 1.31–2:

> *svadharma eṣa sūtasya sadbhir dṛṣṭaḥ purātanaiḥ / devātānām ṛṣīnāṃ ca rājñāṃ cāmitatejasām // vaṃśānāṃ dhāraṇaṃ kāryaṃ śrutānāṃ ca mahātmanām / itihāsapurāṇeṣu diṣṭā ye brahmavādibhiḥ //* (The *sūta*'s special duty as perceived by good men of old was to preserve the genealogies of gods, rishis and most glorious kings, the traditions of great men, which are displayed by those who declare sacred lore in the Itihāsas and Purāṇas. (Pargiter's translation, Pargiter 1972: 15; cf. *Padma* 5.1.27–8)

A good deal of the material which is known today as making up the Purāṇas must have circulated orally for centuries in the repertoires of such men as these, no doubt in the form of short pieces which they would combine together in longer sequences, adapting their material to suit their audiences.

Almost all the Purāṇas are said to have the Sūta (either Lomaharṣaṇa or his son Ugraśravas) as their overall narrator, even though his chief task is sometimes – as in, for example, the *Bhāgavata* – to introduce a previous narrator from whom he has heard the story. But the Sūta is not seen as the composer of the Purāṇa, which has a more exalted origin. According to *Matsya* 53.3–4, it was Brahmā who first proclaimed the one Purāṇa of a billion *ślokas*. This was mediated to the human world by Viṣṇu in the form of Vyāsa, who condensed the divine text into a shorter version and divided it into 18.

This theory of divine origin shows that the Purāṇas regard themselves as religious texts with an importance equal to that of the Vedas; they are *vedasammita* (*Vāyu* 1.11, 4.12). At some point in their transmission they became carriers of

Vedic values, used by brahmans for three main purposes: to make the brāhmaṇic ideology accessible to a wider public, to draw popular myths, rituals and practices into the framework of this ideology, and to create a synthesis between the *varṇāśramadharma* which gave society its norms and the *śramaṇa*-derived values of the renouncer. Although they were still performed to entertain their audiences, there was now a stronger didactic purpose behind their recitation. Like the week-end newspapers of the West at the end of the twentieth century, they were telling their hearers not only how to live but also how to see the world.

In spite of this strong didactic character, the Purāṇas are not the monologues one might expect. They have a dialogic structure which conveys something of the interaction between narrator and audience which took place in the days when they were performances rather than books. All the Purāṇas have a respondent as well as a narrator – or perhaps he should be given the more active title of questioner, since he requests information, changes the direction of the narrative, determines the amount of detail which the narrator provides, and generally helps to shape the course of the Purāṇa (cf. Bailey 1995: 75–7). Moreover, there are hierarchies of interlocutors, and other pairs besides the chief narrator and respondent are employed to introduce the stories and other types of material which are embedded in the main narratives or major didactic passages.

The Purāṇic narratives are of various kinds. Some are creation myths found also in the *Mahābhārata*, such as the churning of the Ocean of Milk (*Mbh.* 1.15.4–17.30; *Viṣṇu* 1.9) or the raising of the earth from beneath the cosmic waters (*Mbh.* 3.100.19; *Mārkaṇḍeya* 47.2–14; *Padma* 1.3.25b–52a; 5.3.20b–52a; *Varāha* 2.21–6; *Viṣṇu* 4.1–52). Others are stories of kings and princes which augment the Purāṇic genealogies. Others again are stories of gods or goddesses: Kṛṣṇa has a full-scale biography in *Bhāgavata* 10–11, *Brahmavaivarta* 4 (*Śrīkṛṣṇajanmakhaṇḍa*), *Padma* (*Pātālakhaṇḍa* 69–99), and *Viṣṇu* 5, while much "biographical" information about Śiva and his family is given in various parts of the *Śiva* and the *Skanda*. There are also stories celebrating the power of *bhakti*, e.g. Viṣṇu's deliverance of Ambariṣa from the wrath of Durvāsas (*Bhāgavata* 9.4.15–5.27), as well as others which present violations of *dharma* which are not to be followed, e.g. *Viṣṇu* 3.18.52–94, which tells of King Śatadhanu, who has to suffer a number of animal rebirths as a consequence of talking with a heretic (*pāṣaṇḍa*), and is only reborn eventually as a man through the loyalty of his virtuous wife.

In spite of their awareness of their own religious significance, there is no indication that the Purāṇas were ever like the Vedas in being memorized as exactly as possible for word-perfect transmission from one generation to the next. On the contrary, their nature as performances and the audience participation which is symbolized by the respondent/questioner meant that they preserved the core of their message by continually changing, perhaps incorporating the praises of a newly-built temple (e.g. the celebration of the Sūrya temple at Koṇārka in *Brahma* 28), referring to some important event in the life of the society around them (as *Viṣṇu* 3.17 may refer to the expulsion of Buddhists from the region of the Narmadā), or showing changes in the religious affiliation of the group which was transmitting the text (e.g. the *Kūrma* appears to be a Pāśupata reworking of what was originally a Pāñcarātra text). To quote Giorgio Bonazzoli, "the purāṇa-s grow like trees: old branches are pruned, things are transformed or removed, new blossoms appear, things are added and the result is a continuously changing living reality, always equal to itself although always different" (Bonazzoli 1983: 101).

Yet however much one may stress their oral origins or the fluidity of their transmission, the Purāṇas in their present form undoubtedly exist as books. Some of them contain passages (e.g. *Matsya* 53) which praise such activities as making copies of them in whole or in part, or giving away such copies to others, so it is obvious that this transition from oral to written transmission met with no suspicion or disapproval. There is no information as to when it took place. Indeed the whole question of dating the Purāṇas in their earliest oral or written forms, is attended by daunting uncertainties. It is not a question which interests the Purāṇas themselves: as far as they are concerned, they all come into being at the same time as a result of Vyāsa's work in each *dvāparayuga* as it rolls round (*Viṣṇu* 3.3.5–21). If one looks to texts other than the Purāṇas, the earliest known appearance of the word *purāṇa*, as a name for a literary genre, is in *Atharvaveda* 11.7.24, and it occurs several times, both in the singular and the plural, in the *Mahābhārata*, but there is little to indicate the nature of these *purāṇas* or to link them with those which exist today.

Rocher's examples of attempts to date the Purāṇas show how twentieth-century scholars have tried to put specific dates upon texts in spite of appreciating the difficulties involved. He himself concludes: "I submit that it is not possible to set a specific date for any purāṇa as a whole" (Rocher 1986: 103). Maybe one need not be totally agnostic. It would be hard to disagree, for instance, with Hardy's view that "the most reasonable date" for the *Bhāgavata* is "the ninth or early tenth century" (Hardy 1983: 488). Yet Hardy shares Rocher's general view in that he declares "On the whole it is meaningless to speak of 'the date' of a Sanskrit *purāṇa*, because many generations of bards, etc., have been involved in the accumulation of material which at some stage has been given a name . . ." (1983: 486).

The Great Eighteen

Several of the essays in *Purāṇa Perennis* spell out the diversity of purāṇic literature. John Cort gives "An Overview of the Jaina Purāṇas" (Doniger 1993: 185–206), saying that "a list of all the known Jaina Purāṇas would total about several hundred" (1993: 185). A. K. Ramanujan discusses what he calls the "folk Purāṇas," of which he says the best known are the Tamil *sthalapurāṇas* studied by David Shulman (Doniger 1993: 101). Shulman himself draws attention to vernacular Purāṇas by comparing an episode from the Sanskrit *Bhāgavatapurāṇa* with the same episode as told in the fifteenth-century Telugu

Mahābhāgavatamu (Doniger 1993: 121–57). Friedhelm Hardy also draws upon *sthalapurāṇas* ("local Purāṇas," as he calls them elsewhere, Hardy 1990: 77), both Sanskrit and vernacular, in order to illustrate "the Purāṇic process" (1990: 159–82). The only type of Purāṇa which is not discussed at some point in *Purāṇa Perennis* is the caste-*purāṇa* (e.g. the *Malla* and the *Kālikā* which are the subject of Das 1968).

The point that I wish to make by referring to these studies of purāṇic diversity is that concentration on the 18 texts which have a special place in the brāhmaṇical Sanskrit tradition involves a considerable limitation of one's horizons as far as the whole purāṇic field is concerned. Because I am writing just one short chapter, rather than a whole book, most of what I say will be concerned with this more limited field. Yet it is important to remember the wider horizon – not least because it demonstrates the audacity of the claim made by the brāhmaṇical *paurāṇikas* to have produced the "great," i.e. normative and authoritative, examples of purāṇic literature.

Before discussing the nature of this claim it would be as well to look at the names of the Eighteen. The following list is given in *Viṣṇu* 3.6.20–4:

Brahma	*Brahmavaivarta*
Padma	*Liṅga*
Viṣṇu	*Varāha*
Śiva	*Skanda*
Bhāgavata	*Vāmana*
Nārada	*Kūrma*
Mārkaṇḍeya	*Matsya*
Agni	*Garuḍa*
Bhaviṣya	*Brahmāṇḍa*

This list coincides exactly with that which the Muslim scholar al-Bīrūnī (973–1048 CE) says was read to him from the *Viṣṇu*. It is almost identical with that given in *Matsya* 53.13–53, the only difference being that *Vāyu* appears in the latter instead of *Śiva*. There are other lists also, with slight variations, and even a completely different list which al-Bīrūnī claims to have heard in addition to the one from the *Viṣṇu* (Rocher 1986: 32–3), but on the whole the list is generally agreed. The discrepancy between *Śiva* and *Vāyu* is explained in *Skanda* 5.3.1.33–4 by saying that these are two names for the same Purāṇa (Rocher 1986: 33). Another possible explanation is that there was some confusion between the two because one of the sections of the *Śiva* is called the *Vāyavīyasaṃhitā*. Besides these 19 Purāṇas, there is another text which is sometimes ranked with them. This is the *Harivaṃśa*, a supplement (*khila*) of the *Mahābhārata* which is purāṇic rather than epic in its content and tone, and contains much material which has close parallels in some Purāṇas. Nevertheless, I shall continue to refer to this group of Purāṇas as 18 in number, because they see themselves as 18.

Occasionally these 18 Purāṇas are styled *mahāpurāṇas* (*Bhāgavata* 12.7.10,22; *Viṣṇu* 3.6.24), as though singling them out from a general corpus and conferring a special status upon them. Sometimes the 18 "major Purāṇas" are contrasted with 18 "minor Purāṇas" (*upapurāṇas*; cf. *Brahmavaivarta* 4.132. 10,22), but there is far less agreement as to the names of the latter than there is for the *mahāpurāṇas*. Rocher discusses the two categories, and concludes that the distinction between them is purely artificial, because "there is no basic difference between the mahāpurāṇas on the one hand and the upapurāṇas on the other" (Rocher 1986: 69).

However, it may be that the number 18 was not intended originally to single out a particularly weighty group of Purāṇas from the rest. Originally it may have been a statement about the Purāṇas generally. There were 18 Purāṇas, just as there were 18 *parvans* in the *Mahābhārata*, 18 chapters in the *Bhagavadgītā*, 18 days of the *Mahābhārata* battle, and 18 armies fighting in it. In other words, the "18-ness" of the Purāṇas may be a symbol of their close connection with the *Mahābhārata*. There are other signs of such a connection: almost all the brāhmaṇical Sanskrit Purāṇas begin, as the *Mahābhārata* does, with a conversation between the Bard (Sūta) and the *ṛṣis* of the Naimiṣa forest. Without exception, their standard meter is that of the *Mahābhārata*, the *śloka*. This, of course, is not peculiar to the *Mahābhārata* – indeed the *Rāmāyaṇa* claims that its composer Vālmīki invented the *śloka* (*Rām* 1.2). But while the *Rāmāyaṇa* introduces its speeches with metrical formulas which are part of its essential structure, the Purāṇas follow the *Mahābhāārata* in using "prose formulae . . . of the type *arjuna uvāca* and *ṛṣaya ūcuḥ*. . . and so on" (Goldman 1984: 17). Their reputed author, Vyāsa, is held to be the composer of the *Mahābhārata* also. They almost all employ the *Mahābhārata*'s introductory verse, applying to themselves the title *Java* that it uses for the *Mahābhārata*.

The exact meaning of this claim is not certain. Do the Purāṇas regard themselves as some kind of extension to the *Mahābhārata*? Perhaps: they extend and systematize its mythic chronology, and retell many of its myths. But the human beings who appear in purāṇic stories do not struggle to understand and follow *dharma* in the manner of the *Mahābhārata*'s protagonists. They are for the most part exemplars or opponents of *bhakti* who play stereotyped roles in relation to the Supreme God whom they adore or defy. Perhaps what the Purāṇas are claiming is that they complement the *Mahābhārata* in some way, making up together the *itihāsapurāṇa* which is necessary to augment the Veda (*Mbh* 1.1.204; 1.2.235/*Vāyu* 1.200–1).

The "Five Characteristic Topics"

In the preface to his *Viṣṇupurāṇa* (the first translation of a Purāṇa into English, originally published in 1840), H. H. Wilson said that "that which has five characteristic topics" (his translation of *pañcalakṣaṇa*) meant that the contents of a Purāṇa were:

> 1. Primary creation, or cosmogony; 2. Secondary creation, or the destruction and renovation of worlds, including chronology; 3. Genealogy of gods and patriarchs; 4. Reigns of the Manus, or periods called Manvantaras; and 5. History, or such particulars as have been preserved of the princes of the solar and lunar races, and of their descendants to modern times. (Wilson 1961: iv)

This translation puts an explanatory gloss on the lines which are found in several Purāṇas:

> *sargaś ca pratisargaś ca vaṃśo manvantarāṇi ca / vaṃśānucaritaṃ ceti purāṇaṃ pañcalakṣaṇam //* (*Vāyu* 4.10b–11a; cf. *Matsya* 53.65bc; *Viṣṇu* 3.6.25,27).

Most scholars since Wilson's time have more or less followed his translation. Yet there are difficulties in it. *Sarga* is undoubtedly "creation" and *manvantarāṇi* "periods called Manvantaras," but the other three items are more problematic. One might expect *pratisarga* to mean "counter-creation," i.e. "destruction," rather than "secondary creation." Indeed, Willibald Kirfel, whose attempt to constitute a text which represented the earliest form of the *pañcalakṣaṇa* material was as influential in 1927 as Wilson's work had been almost a century earlier, stated that this was the most obvious meaning of the word (Kirfel 1979: xxxvii; he draws upon the *Prapañcahṛdaya* and Vācaspatimiśra's *Sāṃkhyatattvakaumudī*). But he found it difficult to accept this meaning, because it did not occur in any of the texts which made up his reconstituted *purāṇaṃ pañcalakṣaṇam*. Instead, he relied upon two verses found in the *Matsya* and its parallels in the *Padma* (*Matsya* 8.1, *Padma* 1.7.68, 5.7.68; *Matsya* 9.6, *Padma* 1.7.85, 5.7.85) and deduced from these that, in this context, *pratisarga* meant "further creation" (*Weiterschöpfung*), in line with the translation offered by Wilson.

Nevertheless, *pratisarga* is found in at least four Purāṇic passages with the meaning "destruction." In *Viṣṇu* 6.1.1–2, the respondent/questioner Maitreya says that the narrator Parāśara has told him about *sarga*, *vaṃśa*, the duration of the *manvantaras* (*manvantarasthiti*), and *vaṃśānucarita*, and that now he wants to hear about the dissolution of the universe. Only when Parāśara has given him this information does Maitreya declare that he has been told about *sarga*, *pratisarga*, *vaṃśa*, *manvantarāṇi*, and *vaṃśānucarita*. In *Brahmāṇḍa* 4.1.239–40, *Vāyu* 100.133, and 102.132,5, *pratisarga* also occurs with the meaning "destruction."

One reason for Kirfel's preferring the meaning "further creation" was that he thought of *pañcalakṣaṇa* as indicating five successive blocks of material, so that it functioned as a kind of table of contents, in which *pratisarga* ought to stand for something that could come between *sarga* and *vaṃśa*. This seems to have been the thinking behind Wilson's translation of the *pañcalakṣaṇa* components also (and presumably the thinking of the pandits who had assisted Colebrooke with the translation which Wilson adopted), since he regarded *vaṃśa* as "genealogy of gods and patriarchs," which would fit in well with its position between "secondary creation" and "reigns of the Manus," while *vaṃśānucarita* was referred to "the princes of the solar and lunar races" whom one would expect to come later. Yet the plain meaning of *vaṃśa* is "genealogy" in general rather than of any particular group, and *vaṃśānucarita* is equally general in its reference: "stories about those included in the genealogies." Moreover, some of the passages in Kirfel's *vaṃśa* section include stories (e.g. *Vāyu* 65.144–59), while his *vaṃśānucarita* section has passages in it which are purely genealogical (e.g. *Vāyu* 88.62–77). From the way in which these *vaṃśa* and *vaṃśānucarita lakṣaṇas* are mixed together, it would appear that they were never intended to be taken as "sections" which could be neatly carved out and distinguished from each other, but rather they were seen as "strands," interwoven with each other into patterns which could vary from one Purāṇa to another.

Today more flexible interpretations of *pañcalakṣaṇa* are available alongside those of Kirfel and Wilson. Greg Bailey sees the *pañcalakṣaṇa* scheme as marking the Purāṇic genre as a whole, and controlling the contents of individual Purāṇas only "in varying degrees of completeness or fragmentation according to the empirical and ideological conditions determining their composition and recitation" (Bailey 1995: 13 n. 7). Velcheru Narayana Rao sees *pañcalakṣaṇa* as "the ideological frame that transforms whatever content is incorporated into that frame" (Doniger 1993: 87). It does not refer to contents of the Purāṇas but to the world-view which is imposed upon whatever contents any given Purāṇa may have, Seen thus, it is of no importance that it occupies so little space in the Purāṇas overall:

> Since the ideas of *pañcalakṣaṇa* are tacitly assumed in the Brahminic worldview, they do not even appear in every Purāṇa and do not constitute a sizeable length of the text even when they appear. (Doniger 1993: 87–8)

Before leaving the subject of *lakṣaṇas* it is necessary to mention briefly the claim of the *Bhāgavata* to be *daśalakṣaṇa* (*Bhāgavata* 2.10.1, 12.7.9). This expanded list is more likely to represent a conscious self-aggrandizement on the part of the *Bhāgavata* than a new stage in the development of the Purāṇas generally. Again, its components may be taken to indicate an overall perspective, rather than to function as a table of contents. In the introduction to his translation of the *Bhāgavata*, Tagare lists the commentators who have assigned one of the *daśalakṣaṇa* to each of *skandhas* 3–12, but says that this "traditional application" is no more than "broadly justifiable," since "there is so much overlapping and repetition of these topics beyond the Skandhas which are supposed to represent them" (Tagare 1976: xxiii–xxxiii).

Classification Versus Contents

Wilson was so convinced that all Purāṇas ought to contain five blocks of *pañcalakṣaṇa* material that he produced a theory to account for their failure to include the "five topics" in sufficient abundance. They were, he decided, "the partial and adulterated representatives of an earlier class of Purāṇas" (Wilson 1961: vi), embellished and altered in the interests of sectarianism so that they promoted the worship of one particular god, usually Viṣṇu or Śiva.

The idea of sectarianism is one which has been imposed upon the Hindu tradition by Western scholars. They saw Vedic religion as the equivalent of the Western Catholic church, from which various "sects" had broken away, becoming "cut off" (the literal meaning of the Latin "sectum") from the central core of their ancient tradition. But this model of an ancient rock from which segments can be separated, is not an appropriate one for Hinduism. Julius Lipner's metaphor of "an ancient banyan . . . an interconnected collection of trees and branches in which the same life-sap flows" is much more appropriate (Lipner 1994: 5), opening up a perspective in which different branches of the Hindu tradition can be linked together without declaring one to be a later development or breakaway from another. In other words, the *bhakti* element found in the Purāṇas is as ancient a rooting of this banyan as the Vedic one, even though it may have taken longer to bear fruit in terms of texts and historically discernible movements.

Whether or not sectarianism is an appropriate word to use in this context, the Purāṇas classify themselves as belonging to three groups, each connected with one of the *guṇas* of Sāṃkhya psychocosmology and thus with one of the divinities of the *trimūrti*. *Viṣṇu*, *Nārada*, *Bhāgavata*, *Garuḍa*, *Padma*, and *Varāha* are sāttvic and therefore associated with Viṣṇu; *Matsya*, *Kūrma*, *Liṅga*, *Śiva*, *Skanda*, and *Agni* are tāmasic (Śiva); *Brahmāṇḍa*, *Brahmavaivarta*, *Mārkaṇḍeya*, *Bhaviṣya*, *Vāmana*, and *Brahmā* are rājasic (Brahmā). This division is found in *Padma* 5.263.81–4, and the connection with the *trimūrti* is given by *Matsya* 53.68–9 (although these verses say that Agni, as well as Śiva, is praised in the tāmasic Purāṇas, and acknowledges the existence of mixed Purāṇas also, linked with Sarasvatī). It might appear to strengthen Wilson's theory that the earlier *pañcalakṣaṇa* material had been displaced by later sectarian texts, but in fact this neat threefold grouping, assigning exactly one-third of the Eighteen to each *guṇa*, is entirely artificial.

To begin with, this is not the only self-classification given by the Purāṇas, although it is by far the best-known: Rocher quotes "an alternative, fivefold subdivision, with purāṇas dedicated to five different gods" (Brahmā, Sūrya, Agni, Śiva, and Viṣṇu), found in the *Skanda* (Rocher 1986: 21). Furthermore, there are no Purāṇas which proclaim Brahmā as the Supreme God, since Brahmā does not appear to have been regarded in this light on any significant scale (cf. Biardeau 1981: 175–8). Even Wilson was not convinced that the Purāṇas listed in the rājasic division ought to be connected with Brahmā, and pointed out that there is a Śākta tendency in some of those included in this list (e.g. *Mārkaṇḍeya*, *Brahmavaivarta*; Wilson 1961: xii). But even if this traditional division of the Purāṇas is seen as Vaiṣṇava, Śaiva, and Śākta, it is still misleading, since there are comparatively few Purāṇas which are devoted exclusively to the worship of one deity. There are some which can be described unambiguously as Vaiṣṇava (e.g. *Viṣṇu*, *Bhāgavata*) or Śaiva (e.g. *Śiva*), but these are in the minority. The *Matsya* has passages of Vaiṣṇava and Śaiva tendency in roughly equal proportions; the *Vāmana* has different portions centered upon Viṣṇu, Śiva, and Devī; the *Kūrma*, as has already been noted, shows traces of both Pāñcarātra and Pāśupata shaping; the *Brahma* may be centered upon the worship of Kṛṣṇa in Orissa as Jagannātha, but there are also passages which praise Sūrya and his temple at Koṇarka, and Śiva, worshipped at Ekāmra; the inclusion of the *Devīmāhātmya* in the *Mārkaṇḍeya* suggests a Śākta tendency, but apart from this there is little to connect this Purāṇa with any divinity.

It may be that the classification of the Purāṇas under the heading of the three *guṇas* was never meant to affiliate them with the Great Gods of *bhakti*. Just as the number 18 may have been intended to connect them with the *Mahābhārata*, so the division into three may have been a way of suggesting that the Purāṇas are part of the basic fabric of the cosmos, just as the *guṇas* are, and just as much linked as the *guṇas* are with its basic processes (*rajas*: creation; *sattva*: maintenance; *tamas*: destruction). Each one embodies its own version of the brāhmaṇic world-view to which they all subscribe.

The Religious World-view of the Purāṇas

When used as an adjective, the word *purāṇa* means "old." As a noun it can mean a past event, or a story of past events. Therefore the Purāṇas have sometimes been regarded as traditional Indian history, compiled and transmitted in order to preserve a record of the past. Nevertheless, the general consensus of scholarly opinion has always been that the motives behind the Purāṇas' composition were religious and ideological rather than antiquarian or historical. They are interested in the past, not for its own sake but as a repository of values for the present and future. They are purveyors of a comprehensive religious world-view rather than of historical information, a world-view which reflects both the brāhmaṇic ideology which shaped their development and the popular elements which they incorporated (cf. Brockington 1987). The features of this world-view are not identical in all the Purāṇas, even if "all" is restricted only to the Eighteen. But there is enough consistency of viewpoint among them to allow one to sketch out a coherent picture, provided that one remembers that this is a simplified outline.

The Purāṇic cosmos has been aptly described by Madeleine Biardeau as "the universe of *bhakti*" (*l'univers de la* bhakti, Biardeau 1981: 149, 172). By this she means a cosmos in which the elements of the Vedic world-view have been rearranged so as to be transformed into a universe where one supreme God is the overarching Reality, the ultimate object of all worship. This God's name may be Viṣṇu, Śiva, or Devī, but the role and status are the same whatever the name: this is the God who is both the all-containing, all-pervading Reality in which time and space exist, and the accessible and gracious Lord whom worshippers may encounter in a loving relationship.

It would thus be possible to speak of Purāṇic religion as monotheistic. Yet the Purāṇas bring together a great many mythical themes, and in doing so provide several frameworks into which various divine figures can be fitted at different levels. There is the "triple form" (*trimūrti*) in which the cosmic functions of creation, maintenance, and destruction are personified by the forms of Brahmā, Viṣṇu, and Śiva respectively. There are the *avatāras*, the "descents" which the Supreme God makes into the human context. These were originally associated with Viṣṇu alone, and perhaps started from a nucleus of four found in the *Nārāyaṇīyaparvan*, a late section of the *Mahābhārata* (boar, man-lion, dwarf, human being, *Mbh.* 12.337.35). Within the Purāṇas lists of different length are found (e.g. *Matsya* 47.237–48/*Vāyu* 98.71–104/*Brahmāṇḍa* 2.3.73.72–105a: 3 divine and 7 human forms; *Bhāgavata* 1.3.6–26: 22 forms: *Garuḍa* 1.202: 19), only occasionally (e.g. *Agni* 2.1–16.27) coinciding with the eventual standard list of 10: fish, tortoise, boar, man-lion, dwarf, Paraśurāma, Rāma Dāśarathi, Kṛṣṇa (or Balarāma), Buddha, and Kalki. These figures open up different seams of Vaiṣṇava mythology, making room within it for another supreme figure besides Viṣṇu himself. This is Kṛṣṇa, already the Supreme God of the *Bhagavadgītā*, and supplied by the Purāṇas (e.g. *Viṣṇu* 5; *Bhāgavata* 10) with a biography which gave him a universal appeal in human terms as well as divine. Although the Purāṇas also present Śiva as having *avatāras* (e.g. *Śiva*: *Śatarudrasaṃhitā*), these appear to be modeled on their Vaiṣṇava counterparts. The network of divinities which seems to be more authentically Śaiva appears to be that provided by Śiva's family: his wife Umā/Pārvatī (herself a form of the Supreme Godhead seen as feminine) and their sons Gaṇeśa and Skanda/Kārttikeya.

In whatever form the Supreme God may be envisaged, the Purāṇas are in general agreement as to the temporal and spatial dimensions of the cosmos over which he/she is supreme. Time is projected on two scales, human and divine. A day and night of the gods is the equivalent of a human year, so that a divine year is 360 human years. As in the *Mahābhārata*, human "history" is divided into four ages (*yugas*), the *kṛta*, *tretā*, *dvāpara*, and *kali*, joined together by "twilight" periods. Each *yuga* lasts for thousands of divine years, but their duration becomes progressively shorter and their religious and moral characteristics deteriorate from one age to the next, until they are renewed as the next *kṛtayuga* comes round. A thousand of these *caturyuga* periods constitute a day of Brahmā, which is called a *kalpa*. (Although Brahmā is never regarded as supreme in the Purāṇas his status, as creator of the *trailokya*, the triple world of gods, mortals, and demons, is much higher than that of the other *devas*, and he therefore has much longer days than theirs.)

A significant feature of the *yuga* scheme, in both the *Mahābhārata* and the Purāṇas, is that the time of narration is somewhere in the *kaliyuga*, usually regarded as having begun with the death of Kṛṣṇa (cf. *Bh* 1.18.6; *Viṣṇu* 5.38.8/*Brahma* 212.8). This cannot really be said to be a pessimistic view of life.

Not only is the *kṛtayuga* somewhere in the future, but there are purāṇic passages which say that *mokṣa* is easier to attain in the *kaliyuga* than in any other age (e.g. *Viṣṇu* 6.2.15–18). Yet it does suggest that perfection belongs to the past – perhaps one reason why the Purāṇas want to associate themselves with it.

Another timescale used in the Purāṇas is that of *manvantaras*, periods ruled over by a primal king and his descendants. There are 14 of these in all, 6 in the past, the present one (that of Vaivasvata Manu), and 7 more to come. These are regarded as making up a *kalpa*, and thus being equal to a thousand *caturyuga* periods (although the division of 1,000 by 14 produces so many decimal pionts that it is hard to believe that *manvantaras*, *caturyugas*, and *kalpas* were originally part of the same system). Again, the present time is seen as coming near the center of the *kalpa* system, since the present *kalpa*, the *varāha* (the era of the Boar), is the beginning of the second half of Brahmā's lifetime. At the end of each *kalpa* the dissolution (*pralaya*) of the *trailokya* takes place, to be followed by its recreation by Brahmā at the beginning of the next. At the end of Brahmā's lifetime a more radical *pralaya* occurs, however, when all being is destroyed, except that of the Supreme Being itself.

The Purāṇic world-view is anthropocentric in that it gives human beings the central place in its systems of *manvantaras* and *kalpas*. But it also places them within a vast time-span, so that they could easily be dwarfed into insignificance by it. In a similar way, it places human beings at the center of a vast expanse of space. Bhāratavarṣa, the territory which they inhabit, is one of 9 regions (in an earlier scheme it may have been 4) in an island-continent (*dvīpa*) named Jāmbūdvīpa. Around this island-continent spreads the Ocean of Milk, and around this spreads another *dvīpa*. In all there are 7 *dvīpas*, with 7 oceans surrounding them, extending to the Lokāloka mountains, the boundary between the world (*loka*) and what is not the world (*aloka*).

This is the horizontally extended cosmos, but the Purāṇas also have a view of the cosmos as extended vertically, through different upper *lokas* inhabited by gods, divine seers, and other celestial beings, and through lower levels (*talas*) inhabited by serpents (*nāgas*) and demons (*asuras*). It is these upper and lower regions which make up the *trailokya*, together with the earth, the home of human beings and other animals. The lower levels are not hells, although hells (*narakas*) also exist. Through all these regions beings may transmigrate in *saṃsāra*, the cycle of rebirths which is regulated by *karma*, and from which *mokṣa* brings release. In all this expanse, only Bhārata is the home of human beings as we know them. It is the only place where the *caturyuga* system operates, where the religious exercises of sacrifice, asceticism, and giving are practiced, the only place from which *mokṣa* can be attained (*Viṣṇu* 2.3.19–26).

However, in this universe of *bhakti* neither sacrifice, asceticism, nor giving is absolutely central. The chief quality required in each human life is devotion to the Supreme God, either in his/her own transcendent form or in some manifestation. Whether expressed in terms of reflective, thoughtful piety (e.g. by Bharata in *Viṣṇu* 2.13.9–11), or in displays of extreme emotion (e.g. by Prahlāda in *Bhāgavata* 7.4.38–41) the important factor in *bhakti* is its power to bind together the human and the divine, not in bonds of duty or domination, but in a relationship of loving protection on the divine side and loving service on the human.

Thus the religion of *bhakti* consists of honoring all aspects in which the Supreme God makes his/her presence manifest in the *trailokya*. Holy cities are lovingly described in the Purāṇas (e.g. *Skanda; Kāśīkhaṇḍa*; *Nārada; Uttarabhāga* 48–61); holy rivers are enumerated (e.g. *Śiva*: *Vidyeśvarasaṃhitā* 12; *Garuḍa* 1.81); instructions are given for the construction and worship of images (e.g. *Viṣṇudharmottara* 3.44–85), for making pilgrimages (e.g. *Vāyu* 110–11); *Nārada*: *Uttarabhāga* 62–3; *Skanda* 3.51), and for the carrying out of special *pūjās* (*Nārada*: *Uttarabhāga* 43; *Śiva*: *Koṭirudrasaṃhitā* 38–9) and *vratas* (*Nārada* 4.110–24; *Matsya* 54–82; *Garuḍa* 1.116–37). *Bhakti* gives rise to a highly sacramental form of worship which nourishes itself upon all the traces of the divine encounter with humanity. Even sinners who do not worship are saved by the God of *bhakti*, for instance, the dying Ajāmila who cries "Nārāyaṇa" because it is the name of his youngest son (*Bhāgavata* 6.1–2), or Devarāja who is saved by accidentally hearing the *Śiva* recited (*Śiva* 1.2.15–40). It may appear the *karma* is set aside and any idea of *dharma* overthrown. Yet this is not the case. The Purāṇas contain many passages in which the rules of *varṇāśramadharma* are set out firmly and clearly, sometimes introduced by the idea that this is what God wants (cf. *Viṣṇu* 3.8.1–19). *Dharma* and the four *puruṣārthas* (*dharma*, *artha*, *kāma*, and *mokṣa*) are still in place, but they are now transformed and transcended by *bhakti*.

The Purāṇas Today

Although present-day Hindus may refer to the Vedas as the foundation of their tradition, it is the Purāṇas which give the myths and rituals by which their religious life is sustained. Even among the diaspora in Britain there are some Purāṇas which have been recited in their entirety from time to time. (Lipner 1994: 153, 339–40). The *Bhāgavata* has not only become the foundation text of several Kṛṣṇaite *sampradāyas* in India, but in the second half of the twentieth century has become familiar to Kṛṣṇa-worshippers throughout the world, thanks to the activities of the International Society for Krishna Consciousness, an American organization derived directly, through its founder A. C. Bhaktivedanta Swami Prabhupada, from the Kṛṣṇaite tradition started by Caitanya in sixteenth-century Bengal.

At the level of scholarly study, the Purāṇas have received plentiful attention in the last quarter of the twentieth century. Rocher's comprehensive survey, published by Harrassowitz in 1986 as part of their *History of Indian Literature*, has already been mentioned, and is a work to which all subsequent Purāṇa scholars are deeply indebted (cf. Doniger 1993: viii). Anthologies of Purāṇic myths, translated into English, compiled and introduced by Wendy O'Flaherty (1975) and by Cornelia Dimmitt and J. A. B. van Buitenen (1978), have enabled a wider range of readers to discover the Purāṇas for themselves, while in *The Origins of Evil in*

Hindu Mythology (1976), O'Flaherty has shown how the analysis of Purāṇic myths can yield profounder and more sophisticated answers to some religious questions than any philosophical approach.

In 1982 the University of Tübingen's Purāṇa Research Project started, which has produced valuable tools for purāṇic study: the work done by Peter Schreiner and Renate Söhnen, (1987, 1989) on the *Brahmāpurāṇa*, the two-volume *Epic and Purāṇic Bibliography* (Stietencron et al. 1992) which includes a wide range of editions of the Purāṇas, as well as all works written about them up to 1985. Its latest publication, Greg Bailey's introduction to and translation of the first part of the *Gaṇeśapurāṇa* (1995) is much more comprehensive than its title suggests. It is an introduction to the whole purāṇic genre, which it approaches in a new way. Instead of adopting the methods of the text-historical school, which break up purāṇic contents into smaller pieces and arrange them in chronological order so as to show historical development, Bailey takes the Purāṇas as single literary units, and exposes within them the semantic structures which shape their contents, both the surface structure provided by the *pañcalakṣaṇa* formula and the deeper structure of "a *bhakti* ideology and its attendant praxis" (Bailey 1995: 15).

There have been some influential conferences on the Purāṇas during the 1980s and 1990s. The University of Wisconsin's Madison Conference on the Purāṇas in 1985 brought together an international group of scholars whose papers led to the publication of *Purāṇa Perennis* in 1993, while the Dubrovnik International Conference on the Purāṇas and Epics held in 1997 was the first of a continuing series of gatherings. Its proceedings have already been published under the title *Composing a Tradition: Concepts, Techniques and Relationships* (Brockington and Schreiner 1999).

As the twenty-first century begins, the study of the Purāṇas appears to be in good health. No doubt as the century unfolds scholars will receive more and more help from the compilation of electronic texts and other technological developments. Cooperation between text-historical and structuralist approaches may result in a clearer understanding of those features of the Purāṇas which today are puzzling. But in the last analysis the Purāṇas do not belong to the scholarly community, and they will continue to be important even if the latter should neglect them completely. Their rich and variegated mythology creates a total cosmos in which the *bhakti* values of all forms of theistic Hinduism are preserved and flourish. So long as even some of them continue to be recited and heard, so long as the stories which they contain are retold and remembered, they will embody and proclaim these values in the emerging global context in which the planet's religious traditions will share their insights with each other.

References

Bailey, Greg. 1995. *Ganesapurana Part 1: Upasanakhana, Introduction, Translation and Index*. Purana Research Publications Tübingen, vol. 4, part I. Wiesbaden: Harassowitz Verlag.

Biardeau, Madeleine. 1981. *Études de Mythologie Hindoue, Tome 1. Cosmogonies Puraniques.* Paris: École Française d'Extrême Orient.

Bonazzoli, Giorgio. 1983. "Remarks on the Nature of the Puranas," *Purana* 25, no. 1 (Jan.): 77–113.

Brockington, John. 1987. "The Puranas – Priestly or Popular?" *Haryana Sahitya Akademi Journal of Indological Studies* 2.

Brockington, Mary and Schreiner, Peter, eds. 1999. *Composing a Tradition: Concepts, Techniques and Relationships. Proceedings of the First Dubrovnik International Conference on the Sanskrit Epics and Puranas August 1997.* Zagreb: Croatian Academy of Sciences and Arts.

Das, Veena. 1968. "A Sociological Approach to the Caste Puranas: A Case Study," *Sociological Bulletin* 17, 141–64.

Dimmitt, Cornelia and van Buitenen, J. A. B., eds and trans. 1978. *Classical Hindu Mythology: A Reader in the Sanskrit Puranas.* Philadelphia: Temple University Press.

Doniger, Wendy, ed. 1993. *Purana Perennis: Reciprocity and Transformation in Hindu and Jaina Texts.* Albany: State University of New York Press.

Goldman, Robert. 1984. *The Ramayana of Valmiki, Vol. 1, Balakanda.* Princeton: Princeton University Press.

Hardy, Friedhelm. 1983. *Viraha-bhakti – The Early History of Krsna Devotion in South India.* Delhi: Oxford University Press.

——. 1990. "Epic and Puranic Religion," *The World's Religions: The Religions of Asia*, ed. Friedhelm Hardy. London: Routledge.

Kane, P. V. 1977. 1st ed. 1962. *History of Dharmasastra, Vol. 5.* Poona: Bhandarkar Oriental Research Institute.

Kirfel, Willibald. 1979. *Purana Pancalaksana.* Varanasi: Chowkhamba Sanskrit Series Office. 1st Indian ed.; original German ed. Bonn: Schröder, 1927, *Das Purana Pancalakaana. Versuch einer Textgeschichte.*

Lipner, Julius (1994). *Hindus: Their Religious Beliefs and Practices.* London: Routledge.

O'Flaherty, Wendy. 1975. *Hindu Myths.* Harmondsworth: Penguin.

——. 1976. *The Origins of Evil in Hindu Mythology.* Berkeley, Los Angeles, London: University of California Press.

Pargiter, F. E. 1972, 1st ed. 1922. *Ancient Indian Historical Tradition.* Delhi: Motilal Banarsidass.

Rocher, Ludo. 1986. *The Puranas A History of Indian Literature, vol. 2.3*, ed. J. Gonda. Wiesbaden: Otto Harrassowitz.

Schreiner, Peter and Söhnen, Renate. 1987. *Sanskrit Indices and Text of the Brahmapurana.* Purana Research Publications Tübingen vol. 1. Wiesbaden: Otto Harassowitz.

Söhnen, Renate, and Schreiner, Peter. 1989. *Brahmapurana: Summary of contents, with index of names and motifs.* Purana Research Publications Tübingen vol. 2. Wiesbaden: Otto Harassowitz.

Stietencron, H. von, Gietz, K.-P., Malinar, A., Kollman, A., Schreiner, P., and Brockington, M. 1992. *Epic and Puranic Bibliography (up to 1985) Annotated, with Indexes.* Purana Research Publications Tübingen, vol. 3, parts 1 and 2. Wiesbaden: Otto Harrassowitz.

Tagare, G. V., trans. 1976. *Bhagavatapurana, Part 1* (vol. 7 in Ancient Tradition and Mythology Series). Delhi: Motilal Banarsidass.

Wilson, H. H., trans. 1961, 1st ed. 1840. *The Vishnu Purana: A System of Hindu Mythology and Tradition.* Calcutta: Punthi Pustak.

Textual Traditions in Regional Languages

CHAPTER 7

Tamil Hindu Literature

Norman Cutler

While the phrase "Tamil Hindu Literature" may appear to be simple and straightforward, a few moments of reflection reveal that each of its three components are actually rather slippery. What exactly do we mean by Tamil – the relatively formal language associated primarily with writing and public oratory, or the full gamut of regionally and socially based spoken dialects? And even if we were concerned only with the former, we would still have to confront the evolution of the literary language during its 2,000-year history. The slipperiness of the terms "Hindu" and "Hinduism" are well documented in recent scholarship on South Asian religion and culture; and the notion that these terms, as commonly construed, are relatively recent constructions, heavily influenced by India's colonial history, is now widely accepted (Frykenberg 1989). And finally, the term "literature" can be interpreted in various restricted and embracive senses. Within the well established tradition of Tamil grammar and poetics, *ilakkiyam*, commonly translated as "literature," implies a special kind of language usage that is governed by precisely defined rules of grammar and literary convention as well as a particular milieu in which texts were composed and circulated. But the corpus of texts delineated by this term is certainly too narrow for the agenda of this volume.

In this essay the phrase "Tamil Hindu literature" will be interpreted liberally, if not especially rigorously, to include texts conforming to a wide range of linguistic registers and styles, composed at various points in time, and associated with various religious milieux which in modern terms would usually be labelled "Hindu." Further, all of the specific textual types treated here would be viewed as appropriate subjects of study in the curriculum of a Tamil Department in a modern university in Tamilnadu, though they were engendered and originally circulated in a number of different cultural milieux.

Hindu Gods in Classical Tamil Poetry

One of the great achievements of Tamil culture in the field of literature is the corpus of over 2,300 poems collected in the eight so-called caṅkam anthologies. According to legend, the authors of these poems were members of a literary academy (caṅkam) that flourished in the city of Maturai under the patronage of the Pāṇṭiya kings. The legend of the Maturai Tamil caṅkam may or may not be based upon historical fact, but no one who knows these poems can doubt that their authors shared a poetic grammar and vocabulary. The poems presuppose their audience's familiarity with a shared repertoire of dramatic situations, geographical settings, characters, and poetic figures, and these are defined in the earliest extant Tamil treatise on the principles of grammar and poetics, *Tolkāppiyam*. The earliest poems in this corpus were probably composed during the first few centuries CE.

The poems included in five of the eight anthologies are classified as poems of the "interior world" (*akam*). The "interior world" is populated by a cast of characters who are identified only by the roles they play in the dramatized situations represented in the poems. Each poem depicts a moment in the story of two lovers through the words of one of the two or one of several other characters, such as the girl's close friend, the girl's mother, the man's other lover, and a few others. An especially striking feature of many of these poems is their setting. In akam poetry landscape serves as a mirror of mood. Classical Tamil poetics recognizes five landscapes – mountains, forest, seashore, the riverine tract, and arid land – each of which carries a particular emotive association. In the poems mood is signalled by specific features or "germinal elements" (*karupporuḷ*) of these landscapes, which include not only obvious elements such as mountain pools, rivers, coastal backwaters, flora, and fauna, but also human inhabitants of these regions – for instance, fisherfolk and mountain tribes – and their customary beliefs and practices, including the gods they worship.

Complementing the "interior world" is the public "exterior world" (*puṟam*), a world where warriors are acclaimed for their valor, kings are praised for their generosity, and poets instruct their patrons in right action and the nature of life. Puṟam poems, by and large, offer their audience scenes painted in bold, clear strokes, and here the poets generally do not subtly orchestrate features of setting to suggest nuances of mood as in akam poems.

According to *Tolkāppiyam* the gods who preside over the mountains, forest, seashore, riverine tract, and arid land are, respectively, Cēyōṉ, "the Red One," Māyōṉ, "the Dark One," Varuṇaṉ, the god of the sea and wind, Vēntaṉ, "the King," and Koṟṟavai, goddess of war. Cēyōṉ is an alternate name for Murukaṉ, "the Beautiful One," a very popular deity in Tamilnadu, who in the course of time coalesced with the Sanskritic god Skanda, son of Śiva, though the iconography and mythology of Murukaṉ maintains features not generally associated with Sanskritic images of Skanda. Māyōṉ, also known as Māl, "the Great One" or "the Dark One," became identified with Viṣṇu. Finally, Vēntaṉ, "the king," refers to Indra, King of the gods.

It is important to stress that while some poems included in the caṅkam anthologies contain references to these gods or to rites performed in their honor, these are not religious poems in the sense one would ordinarily understand the term. In virtually all cases these poems aesthetically and rhetorically focus on the actions and emotions of human beings in relation to one another and to their natural environment. References to gods and religious practices are subsidiary to these concerns, and when they do occur, they may be tinged with irony. For example, in certain akam poems the heroine or her friend mock Murukaṉ's priest for attempting to cure the ailing heroine through rites of exorcism, when the actual cause for her illness is separation from her lover.

There are however, two significant exceptions to this generalization. The relatively late caṅkam anthology, *Paripāṭal* (ca. fifth century CE), contains a number of poems that celebrate the gods Cevvēḷ (another name for Cēyōṉ/Murukaṉ) and Tirumāl. (The honorific prefix "tiru" is equivalent to Sanskrit "śrī".) And additionally, the caṅkam corpus contains a long "guide poem" (*āṟṟuppaṭai*) in praise of Murukaṉ called *Tirumurukāṟṟuppaṭai* (ca. fifth century). The latter is modeled on guide poems found in *Puṟanāṉūṟu*, the principal caṅkam anthology devoted to puṟam poetry. In these poems a poet praises his patron's realm, his wealth and his generosity in conversation with another poet whom he has met on the road. In *Tirumurukāṟṟuppaṭai*, standard elements of the guide poem genre – poet, patron, patron's realm, patron's gifts – are transposed to a devotional register, becoming, in turn, Murukaṉ's devotee, the god, the six hills which are said to be Murukaṉ's favorite dwelling places in Tamilnadu, and the grace Murukaṉ bestows upon his devotees.

The Canonized Poems of the Tamil Vaiṣṇava and Śaiva Saints

Tirumurukāṟṟuppaṭai, uniquely among the compositions included in the caṅkam poetic corpus, also was canonized in Tamil Śaiva sectarian tradition. (No poems from the caṅkam corpus are included in the equivalent canon of Tamil Vaiṣṇavism.) *Tirumurukāṟṟuppaṭai*'s dual status is a reminder that early Tamil literary practices, which probably flourished in a courtly context, and the somewhat later poetic expressions of devotion for Śiva and Viṣṇu are not unrelated. This is apparent in the large number of canonized bhakti poems that adapt and incorporate literary conventions associated with the caṅkam poems. Most famously, in many Vaiṣṇava bhakti poems the poet assumes a female voice and expresses love for Viṣṇu in an idiom modeled closely on caṅkam akam poems.[1] Nevertheless, the two poetic corpera significantly differ from one another in form, content, or function.

The period extending from the seventh through the ninth centuries was the golden age of bhakti in the Tamil country. During this period temples of Śiva and Viṣṇu became a prominent feature of the Tamil landscape, and communities of bhaktas who hailed from a wide spectrum of social backgrounds and were united by their devotion, became a part of the Tamil social landscape. Also during this period the Tamil Vaiṣṇava and Śaiva saints gave voice to their religious fervor in poetry. The saints and their poems subsequently became defining elements in Tamil Vaiṣṇava and Śaiva sectarian traditions: many of the poems were incorporated in the liturgy of temple worship, and images of the saints were enshrined in the temples along with the images of the gods themselves.

Tamil Vaiṣṇavism recognizes 12 saint-poets, the āḻvārs ("they who are immersed [in their devotion for Viṣṇu]"); and the poems they composed, known collectively as the "four thousand sacred compositions" (*Nālāyirat-tiviya-pirapantam*) are frequently referred to in the tradition as "the Tamil Veda." Beginning around the twelfth century, these poems came to be recited ritually as part of the routine of worship in Tamil Vaiṣṇava temples, and, in keeping with their status as sacred scripture, they also became the object of erudite theologically-oriented commentaries.

In Tamil Śaiva tradition the match between the categories of saint and sacred scripture also overlap, but not quite so precisely. Tamil Śaivism recognizes 63 saints or nāyaṉmār ("leaders") whose legendary life stories are told in the twelfth-century hagiography, *Periya Purāṇam*. *Periya Purāṇam* is included as the twelfth and last of the *Tirumuṟai*, or "sacred compendia" of poems, which carry canonical status in Tamil Śaiva tradition. Like the Vaiṣṇava āḻvār poems, they are considered to be the equal of the Vedas in sacredness. Some, but not all of the nāyaṉmār composed poems that are included in the *Tirumuṟai*, and some, but not all of the poems included in the *Tirumuṟai*, were composed by nāyaṉmār. Also, like the poems of the āḻvārs, poems from the *Tirumuṟai*, were incorporated into the routines of temple worship, but unlike the former, prior to modern times, one does not find written theological commentaries on these poems. Nevertheless, traditional Śaiva scholars often include citations from this corpus in oral discourses on theological topics.

The Tamil bhakti poets utilized many literary models – Tamil caṅkam poems, folksongs, Sanskrit hymns of praise (*stotras*), and even Vedic hymns – thus producing a corpus of great variety with roots in both earlier Tamil and Sanskrit sources. Nonetheless, in broad terms, Tamil bhakti poems can be distinguished as a poetic genre in a number of ways: they employ a relatively simple diction and phraseology modeled after the rhythms of speech; they are filled with allusions to Hindu myths and provide "word pictures" of the Hindu gods in full iconographic detail; they celebrate the sacredness of particular places where local Tamil forms of Śiva and Viṣṇu are enshrined; they are frequently set to music. But perhaps the most distinctive feature of these poems is their emphasis on the poet's own experience and the relationship between poet and God.

Tamil devotees of Śiva and Viṣṇu perceive the saints' poems as spiritual autobiographies in which the saints reveal their innermost experience and set an example for others, or, to make the point somewhat differently, as "verbal embodiments of their authors' experience of divinity" (Cutler 1987: 112). Tamil bhakti poems blur the boundary between devotee and saint by providing a paradigm upon which devotees model their own experience of divinity. From another, but not unrelated, perspective, these poems can be viewed as a poetic corollary of a theology of embodiment. That is to say, just as the presence of divinity is understood to be literally embodied in a properly consecrated stone or metal image of god, the saint's communion with divinity is understood to be embodied in the ritual recitation of his or her poetry. All who participate in the ritual performance of the saint's poem reenact the saint's experience of communion with the deity. And this further highlights the close relationship in Tamil tradition between bhakti poetry and temple worship, in contrast to some later bhakti traditions that express contempt for temples as a relic of a stale religious establishment.[2] This contrast can, in part, be explained historically. Whereas in Tamilnadu the emergence of bhakti coincided with the origins of temple worship (ca. sixth century CE), proponents of some of the later bhakti traditions viewed temples as an established religious institution which had lost its vitality.

Learned Literature of the Court and the Temple

While the poems of the Tamil Vaiṣṇava .and Śaiva saints nowadays are appreciated for their aesthetic as well as for their religious value, prior to modern times the saints' poems were not included in the curriculum of institutionalized literary study and performance where literati found patronage in courtly and temple contexts. The period immediately following the age of the caṅkam poems witnessed the composition of a number of collections of didactic verses, on the one hand, and long narrative poems, on the other.[3] The authors of some of these texts were Buddhists, but an even larger number were Jains. By the twelfth century, however, the influence of Buddhism and Jainism in the Tamil cultural sphere had waned considerably, and Vaiṣṇavism, to some extent, and Śaivism, to an even greater extent, had become powerful forces in Tamil literary culture. Beginning around the ninth century a number of genres came to dominate formal literary composition and education, and these are commonly grouped in two broad categories: *pirapantam* (Sanskrit: *prabandha*) and *kāppiyam* (= *kāvyam*)/*purāṇam* (Sanskrit: *kāvya*/ *purāṇa*). The latter are long narratives in verse. Many are based on the story-lines of the Sanskrit epics and purāṇas, but they are often more poetically sophisticated and elaborate than their Sanskrit counterparts. The former is a very heterogenous collection of genres, some, but not all of which clearly build on the conventions of caṅkam poetry. One common feature of pirapantam poems is that their constituent verses are sequentially related, and this is one feature that distinguishes these works from the caṅkam anthologies. Another feature that distinguishes many (but not all) of these poems from the caṅkam poetry is their focus on Hindu deities and sacred places.

Traditionally the poems of the Tamil bhakti saints and medieval learned literature, even when devoted to religious subjects, inhabited different cultural terrains; but there is one work that belongs to both domains (much as *Tirumurukāṟṟuppaṭai* is included both in the caṅkam corpus and in the Śaiva

Tirumuṟai). This is *Tirukkōvaiyār*, a learned poem attributed to the Śaiva saint-poet Māṇikkavācakar. Though, by historical accident, he is not numbered among the 63 nāyaṉmār,[4] Māṇikkavācakar is nevertheless one of the most highly revered of the Tamil Śaiva poet-saints. The eighth *Tirumuṟai* is composed of his two works: *Tiruvācakam*, a collection of 51 poems of various genres, all of which conform fairly closely to the model of bhakti poetry described above, and a pirapantam poem, *Tirukkōvaiyār*, a much more difficult, learned poem which exemplifies a genre called *kōvai*. The *kōvai*, perhaps more than any other post-caṅkam genre, evolved from the conventional apparatus of caṅkam poetry: the personae and situations represented in verses of a kōvai are lifted directly from the akam poetic tradition.

One feature that sets apart the verses of a *kōvai* poem from those of the caṅkam era anthologies of akam poems is the sequential arrangement of its verses: the storyline which is merely implicit in the akam anthologies becomes the dominant principle of textual structure in *Tirukkōvaiyār*. But there is also another feature that distinguishes the verses of a *kōvai* poem from earlier akam verses: a kōvai celebrates either a human or a divine hero by folding references to this hero into each verse of the poem, for instance, through a simile or through a description of the setting for an incident depicted in the verse. In Māṇikkavācakar's kōvai the hero is Śiva, and thus each of *Tirukkōvaiyār*'s 400 verses contains a Śaiva element. In a certain sense the author of every kōvai poem engages in a balancing act. From one perspective the poetics of akam poetry dominates this genre. The narrative framework of a kōvai poem is a legacy of akam poetry, as are the personae who populate the narrative and the specific situations represented in each verse. But from another perspective the foremost purpose of the author of a kōvai poem is to praise a heroic figure, usually either a king or a deity, and the akam narrative framework serves a means to this end.

The *kōvai* is not the only *pirapantam* genre that facilitates the celebration of either a human or a divine hero(ine). Another genre, popular beginning from the early fifteenth century is called *piḷḷaittamiḻ*, "a Tamil [poem][in praise of] a child." In a *piḷḷaittamiḻ* poem "a poet assumes a maternal voice to praise an extraordinary being (deity, prophet, saint, or hero), envisioning him or her in the form of a baby" (Richman 1997: 3). Not all *piḷḷaittamiḻ* poems are devoted to Hindu subjects, though Hindu gods, goddesses, and saints are well represented in the corpus of *piḷḷaittamiḻ* literature.[5] In keeping with its status as a learned literary genre, the form and content of *piḷḷaittamiḻ* poems are closely governed by convention, though this genre does not, like the *kōvai*, closely model itself on caṅkam poetry. All *piḷḷaittamiḻ* poems are structured in terms of ten sections, called *paruvam*, each of which "takes as its subject matter a specific childhood activity: for example, a child giving the mother a kiss, a little girl bathing in the river, or a little boy beating a toy drum" (Richman 1997: 10).

While one of the Vaiṣṇava bhakti poets, Periyāḻvār (ninth century), adopted a maternal voice in his poems of devotion to the baby Kṛṣṇa, the first piḷḷaittamiḻ poem that fully articulates the paruvam structure is the *Tiruccentūr Piḷḷaittamiḻ* composed by Pakaḻikkūttar (late fourteenth to early fifteenth centuries) in praise of the god Murukaṉ, especially in his association with the seaside town of Tiruccentūr. Paula Richman has summarized the legend that accounts for the composition of this poem:

> According to tradition, Pakaḻikkūttar, originally a Vaiṣṇava devotee, suffered terrible stomach pains for a long time. One day an ancestor who had been a devotee of Murukaṉ (son of Śiva) appeared to him in a dream and asked him to sing a pillaitamil. The poet then saw that sacred ash and a leaf had been bestowed upon him. He awoke to find a palm leaf beside him upon which to compose poetry. After prayer to Lord Murukaṉ cured his illness, he composed his pillaittamil to the deity as manifested at the Tiruccentur shrine. (Richman 1997: 53–4)

One finds here echoes of the legendary life story of Appar (seventh century) which tells how a stomach ailment played a critical role in securing the saint's conversion from Jainism to Śaivism. Since Appar's story was firmly established in the Tamil Śaiva hagiographic tradition prior to Pakaḻikkūttar's lifetime, more likely than not, the similarities in the biographies are not coincidental. But while the echoes of Appar's biography in the later legend establish a linkage between the pirapantam poem and Tamil Śaiva bhakti tradition, the fact that Vaiṣṇavism has replaced Jainism as the non-Śaiva Other, indicates a significant shift in the socio-religious environment in Tamilnadu between the seventh and the fourteenth centuries.

Many Tamil poets, including Hindus, Muslims, and Christians, have composed *piḷḷaittamiḻ* poems. Besides *Tiruccentūr Piḷḷaittamiḻ*, two of the best known *piḷḷaittamiḻ* poems devoted to Hindu subjects are *Maturai Mīṉāṭciyammai Piḷḷaittamiḻ* by Kumarakuruparar (seventeenth century), which praises the goddess Mīṉāṭci, Śiva's consort in the great temple located in Maturai, and *Cēkkiḻār Piḷḷaittamiḻ* by T. Mīṉāṭcicuntaram Piḷḷai (nineteenth century) on Cēkkiḻār, the author of the canonical hagiography of the 63 Tamil Śaiva saints, *Periya Purāṇam* (twelfth century). While the subjects of *piḷḷaittamiḻ* poems, as well as their sectarian and historical contexts, are quite varied, the exemplars of this genre do display certain common features. Most obvious is the paruvam structure and the maternal voice that are central to the definition of the genre. Another feature common to many *piḷḷaittamiḻ* poems is the way poets intersperse images of a god or hero imagined as a child with references to the subject's heroic or gracious acts as an adult. These juxtapositions engender in a poem's audience a simultaneous sense of intimate affection and awe-filled wonder for its subject.[6]

The Tamil literary category of pirapantam is traditionally counterposed to the category of purāṇam or kāvyam (or kāppiyam[7]). In Sanskrit, the category purāṇa, which denotes the primary textual repository of Hindu mythology, is often linked with the category of *itihāsa*, which refers specifically to the *Mahābhārata* and the *Rāmāyaṇa*. While a few of the Sanskrit texts included in the realm of *itihāsa-purāṇa* are noted for their poetic language, by and large these texts are noteworthy more for the stories they tell than for the manner of their telling. In contrast, in the world of Sanskrit arts and letters, the term *kāvya* denotes aesthetically refined poetry, and the "great kāvyas" (*mahākāvya*) are long poems whose verses are embedded in a story line, and in many instances the latter is borrowed from the *itihāsa-purāṇa* corpus.

Some of the Tamil texts which bear the appellation purāṇam are based directly on Sanskrit prototypes, but as David Shulman has observed, "they differ greatly from the Sanskrit originals both in style and in their perspective on the mythological materials; unlike the Sanskrit purāṇas, the Tamil adaptations are polished and compressed, and thus belong, in effect to the *kāvya* genre" (Shulman 1980: 30). The most celebrated of all Tamil kāvya narratives is Kampaṉ's twelfth century rendering of the *Rāmāyaṇa*. While Kampaṉ was familiar with Valmīki's Sanskrit *Rāmāyaṇa*, and his telling of the story corresponds to Valmīki's fairly closely, some episodes are substantially different in the two versions. But more importantly, Kampaṉ distingished himself as a consummate master of the poetic resources of the Tamil language, and in his hands the *Rāmāyaṇa* story became a vehicle for a literary tour de force. Consequently Kampaṉ's Tamil *Rāmāyaṇa* has, for centuries, been honored as much, if not more, for its literary merits as for its choice of subject. This accounts for the attention the text has long received from Tamil literary scholars irrespective of their sectarian affiliations.

Another group of Tamil narratives categorized as purāṇam are closely associated with particular geographical locations, specifically the sites of temples. These texts, known generically as *sthalapurāṇa* ("place purāṇa"), relate legends associated with these sites and the local embodiments of Śiva, Viṣṇu, and other deities enshrined there. The Tamil "place purāṇas" constitute a very large corpus, and the literary quality of these texts is uneven. Many temple sites in Tamilnadu are the subjects of both a Tamil "place purāṇa" and a Sanskrit counterpart, usually assigned to the genre of mahātmya ("greatness"). Traditionally the Sanskrit mahātmya is usually considered to be the source of the Tamil "place purāṇa," but in fact, in many instances the Tamil version may in fact predate the Sanskrit. While the influence of Brahmanic Hinduism is clearly apparent in both Tamil and Sanskrit versions, these texts also include much material that is regionally distinctive. In his landmark study of Tamil Śaiva "place purāṇas" David Shulman describes the myths related in these texts as being "part of the wider world of Hindu mytholgy," while he also points out that the authors of these texts took many of the classical myths "and adapted them to their own purposes, often transforming them considerably in the process" (Shulman 1980: 4).

The Literature of Village Temple Festivals

For the most part, the genres and texts discussed above were originally associated with the culture of the courts of kings and local rulers or with Brahmanic temples. But this is by no means the only literature associated with Tamil Hinduism, broadly defined. The cults of Tamilnadu's village deities are rich in stories, many of which are regularly performed as dramas or as oral discourses, and frequently these are set to music. Often the occasion for these performances is an annual festival observed in a local deity's honor, and in these instances the performance has ritual significance. Two recent studies focus on the cult of Draupadī, which is well represented in the villages of northeastern Tamilnadu and recitation/enactment of the *Mahābhārata* story during the annual festival performed by Draupadī's devotees (Frasca 1988; Hiltebeitel 1988). A third focuses on a genre known as "bow song" (*vil pāṭṭu*), which is traditionally performed during festivals celebrated at the temples of local deities in the far southern region of Tamilnadu. (Blackburn 1988).

Alf Hiltebeitel describes a process, instantiated in the Tamil Draupadī cult, "whereby the *Mahābhārata* is transposed into local, and for the most part village, South Indian traditions" (Hiltebeitel 1988: 131).[8] At the Draupadī festivals celebrated in northeastern Tamilnadu, this transposed *Mahābhārata* is performed in three modes. The first of these, called *piracaṅkam*, the most "textual" of the three, consists of a recitation of episodes from the epic in Tamil by a professional *Mahābhārata* reciter, known as a *piracaṅki* or *pāratiyār*. Richard Frasca has described *piracaṅkam* as a musical narrative amalgamation of song (*pāṭṭu*), musical chant, and exegetical prose" (quoted in Hiltebeitel 1988: 137). More often than not the textual basis for piracaṅkam is the Tamil version of the *Mahābhārata* composed in the fourteenth century by Villipputtūr Āḻvār, though reciters may also drawn upon other Tamil versions of the *Mahābhārata*. The second mode is dramatic enactment, with song and dance, of episodes from the *Mahābhārata* in a style known as "street drama" (*terukkūttu*). According to Hiltebeitel, the *Villi Pāratam* "provides the skein that both genres [piracaṅkam and terukkūttu] follow, but while the dramatists may know of Villi, 'it is doubtful that they ever consult, and unlikely that many of them could consult his *Pāratam*' " (Hiltebeitel 1988: 138). Thus, unlike piracaṅkam, the dramatic enactment of episodes from the *Mahābhārata* at Draupadī festivals is only loosely tied to the classical textual tradition. The third level of performance takes the form of temple ritual, and Hiltebeitel has noted that whereas the piracaṅkam "has as its main task to present the *Pāratam* as a 'whole,' " the street drama "has as its main task to enact those aspects of the *Pāratam* that have the greatest significance in relation to the festival's period of highest ritual intensity" (Hiltebeitel 1988: 140). During such periods it is not uncommon for some festival participants to enter a state of possession and speak with the voices of protagonists in the *Mahābhārata* narrative.

The bow song tradition is found in the far southern region of Tamilnadu. Like the two performance genres associated with the festivals celebrated at Draupadī temples in the northeastern portion of the state, annual village temple festivals provide the occasion for bow song performances. And like the village enactments of the *Mahābhārata*, bow song performances are closely intertwined with temple ritual; and further, at critical junctures in the narrative audience members may become possessed. But there are also salient differences between the two traditions, and these pertain to both the performers and to the narrative they perform. Like piracaṅkam, bow song performances combine both spoken and sung delivery styles, but unlike the pāratiyār of the Draupadī cult, whose recitation is accompanied only by a harmonium player, a bow song ensemble generally includes five members, each of whom both sings and plays an instrument which include a drum, a clay pot, cymbals, and wooden blocks. Additionally, bow song performances do not include dramatic enactment of its narrative repertoire in the manner of the street drama performances associated with the Draupadī cult.

Stuart Blackburn, following local terminology, has designated the two categories that structure the repertoire of stories performed by bow song ensembles as "birth stories" and "death stories." "Birth stories narrate the history or gods and goddesses grouped under the term *teyva piṟavi* ('divine birth') or *teyva vamcam* ('divine descent'); death stories tell the histories of *iṟantuppaṭṭa vātai* ('spirits who were killed') or *veṭṭuppaṭṭa vātai* ('spirits who were cut up') . . . death stories are local histories, stories about people who lived and died (and then became gods); birth stories, on the other hand, are mythic histories of gods and goddesses of divine origin who are not less real than the death story heroes, but who are not men and women either." In his study of the bow song tradition Blackburn describes points of convergence and divergence in the narrative patterns that inform birth stories and death stories in the bow song repertoire. While both conclude with the establishment of a cult, this conclusion is reached via very different paths. In the course of a birth story, a divine being is born in heaven, "completes a series of tasks, wins boons from Śiva, and descends to earth; there the god uses his boons to display his power, usually to wreak havoc among humans and win worship from them." The protagonists of death stories are born on earth, and the birth is a painful one. The story's "protagonist is caught in a conflict over land rights or sexual rights, or both, that leads to his violent death." Whereas the protagonists of birth stories attack people who refuse them worship, the protagonists of death stories attack those responsible for their death. Both types of story end with the deities' victims building a temple and celebrating a festival in their honor, and with this episode the narrative mirrors the occasion for the stories' performance (Blackburn 1988: 31–6).

The performance traditions associated with the Tamil Draupadī cult and the bow song tradition bear comparison by virtue of their roles in village religious life. Both are performed on the occasion of annual temple festivals celebrated to honor deities that are understood to be intimately involved with the well-being of the village. The ritual contexts that frame these performances are similar, and both include incidents of spirit possession at critical moments. However, while many elements of the Draupadī cult may be aptly described (following Hiltebeitel) as transpositions of the epic *Mahābhārata* into a local idiom, the cultic context of the bow song tradition is exclusively local.

Summing Up

While the above overview of genres and texts is far from exhaustive, it should be clear that Tamil Hindu literature is enormously diverse. One might even claim that, like Hinduism itself, it is easier to define this corpus (if indeed this amalgam of texts and performance practices can legitimately be called a corpus) in terms of what it excludes – i.e., Tamil texts that are explicitly affiliated with non-Hindu religious traditions such as Jainism, Buddhism, Islam, and Christianity or non-religious texts – than on the basis of a central doctrine or a uniform world view. Nevertheless, one can identify clusters of shared mythic motifs, ritual affiliations, and attitudes that weave in and out of this corpus, providing it with a kind of informal cohesiveness. Some of the pairings that can be identified through this approach are fairly obvious, others less so. Anyone who is familiar with the poems of the Tamil bhakti saints and with the myths included in the Tamil purāṇic corpus cannot fail to notice their affinities: the saints' poems are filled with allusions to the myths, and the rhetoric of many of the myths promotes a devotional attitude toward their divine protagonists. Perhaps more tenuous, but nevertheless intriguing, would be the connection one might make between descriptions of certain ritual practices, including spirit possession, found in some caṅkam poems and seemingly similar ritual practices that inform the Tamil cults of Draupadī and the bow song deities. The analytic concept of "family resemblance" has been invoked to account for the nature of the relationship among the various beliefs and practices that commonly are identified as "Hindu" (Ferro-Luzzi 1989), and one might do the same when speaking of "Tamil Hindu literature."

Let us then conclude by attempting to profile this wide-ranging corpus by tracing connections with other dimensions of religious life and by reviewing the various textual modalities it encompasses. To begin, some, but not all of these texts are closely intertwined with ritual, especially as performed in the Hindu temples of Tamilnadu. On the one hand, the canonized poems of the Tamil bhakti saints have been incorporated into the liturgy of Brahmanic temples of Viṣṇu and Śiva, where recitation of the saints' poems can be interpreted as a reenactment of the saints' exemplary devotion to these gods. On the other, festival ritual, that in a sense defines the cults of Draupadī and the bow song deities, frames the bow song performances as well as recitation and enactments of episodes from the *Mahābhārata* that are central to these festivals. While the saints' poems may be viewed as verbal embodiments of their authors' devotion, bow song and street drama performances provide occasions for physical embodiments of divine agencies through spirit possession. Other textual genres mentioned in this essay are less directly linked to the ritual domain. We find occasional references to ritual practices in caṅkam poems, but there is no evidence that these poems were themselves performed in a ritual context. Tamil sthalapurāṇas are very much a literature of and about Hindu temples, and while they document the mythological history of specific temple sites and sometimes provide a mythological charter for certain temple rituals, these texts are not themselves deployed as a component of temple ritual. It would take us beyond the scope of this essay to attempt to explicate in any detail the spectrum of specific religious attitudes that are inscribed in these texts. In this regard, however, we should note that sectarian Vaiṣṇavism and Śaivism in Tamilnadu find in these poems the foundation for sophisticated theological systems.

The word "text" has been used as an umbrella term for all of the verbal creations discussed in this essay, but the uniformity of this signifier masks a variety of textual forms. The genres we have considered cover a wide range on the scales of orality and writing, on the one hand, and textual fluidity and fixity, on the other. Until relatively recently, inscribed palm leaves were the predominant medium for recording, preserving, and disseminating texts in South India. But more often than not, even if texts were recorded on palm leaves, they generally were taught, performed and "consumed" in an oral context, with manuscripts serving primarily as an aid to memory. The only evidence we have regarding the original context for the composition and performance of caṅkam poems is found in the legend of an ancient literary academy patronized by early Tamil kings, and in the representation of poets and patrons in some of the poems themselves. This enables us to generalize that this body of poetry originally flourished in a courtly context, but otherwise we know little about the poems' authors and audience and the specific contexts for their performance. The hagiographies of the Tamil bhakti saints would have us believe that the saints composed their poems as acts of service to Viṣṇu and Śiva often in the course of visiting locales associated with specific forms of these gods. The hagiographical literature also accounts for the miraculous events that resulted in the redaction of the saints' poems. Both palm leaf manuscripts and oral transmission – the latter sometimes being of a miraculous nature – are factors in these stories.

The court and the temple continued to serve as the primary loci for learned Tamil literary culture until modern times, and from about the sixteenth century monastic institutions were also an important component of this mix. We are fortunate to have in the autobiography of the great textual scholar and editor U. V. Cāminātaiyar a vivid description of the literary culture that flourished in the monasteries and small towns of nineteenth-century Tamilnadu, and it is likely that the practices he describes were well established for many generations prior to his lifetime. For Cāminātaiyar and many of this contemporaries, pirapantam and purāṇic texts on Śaiva themes were the staple diet of a literary education, and Cāminātaiyar's teacher, Mīṉāṭcicuntaram Piḷḷai was also renowned for composing texts in these genres. Piḷḷai received many commissions from temples, monasteries, and wealthy individuals to compose pirapantam and purāṇam works, and Cāminātaiyar describes how Piḷḷai would orally compose verse after verse while one of his pupils inscribed them on palm leaves. The formal debut of a text, once completed, was always an oral recitation before an audience, though the palm leaf manuscript on which it had been inscribed was also given a place of honor on these occasions.

Though orality is a prominent feature of all of these pre-modern textual varieties, at the same time, there was a strong sense of a fixed text which must be respected in performance. Turning our attention to the texts associated with village temple festivals, the situation is rather different. Within this realm the recitation of the pāratiyār, who often follows the Tamil *Mahābhārata* text of Villipputtūr Āḻvār fairly closely, is based on a textual model not very different from the one mentioned above. But in street drama and bow song performances the "text" is a more fluid entity. Manuscripts of plays and bow song texts circulate among performers, but these serve more as training tools for performers than as authoritative cultural objects in there own right. While performances are based more on what Stuart Blackburn has called "prior preparation" rather than spontaneous composition in performance, still the conventions of these genres leave much room for improvisation, and the "texts" of given narrative may change and have changed over time. We thus find that the material forms of Tamil Hindu literary works are as diverse as their contents.

Notes

1 For a discussion of puṟam elements in Tamil Vaiṣṇava bhakti poetry see Ramanujan and Cutler 1983.

2 This distinction roughly parallels the traditional distinction which is made between saguṇa and nirguṇa bhakti traditions, that is, traditions which conceptualize god as being "with qualities" and those which conceptualize god as being "without qualities." The Tamil bhakti tradition predominantly conforms to the former model, while the Vīraśaiva tradition found in the neighboring Kannada-speaking region conforms to the latter.

3 The most famous text in the first group is *Tirukkuṟaḷ* (ca. fifth century CE), which is sometimes referred to as "the Tamil Bible." Though in modern scholarly circles it is thought to be likely that the text's legendary author, Tiruvaḷḷuvar, was a Jain, this compendium of poetically terse aphorisms on public and domestic life is largely free of specifically sectarian elements. Most famous of the early long narrative poems in Tamil is *Cilappatikāram*, "The Story of the Anklet" (ca. fifth century CE). This text, attributed to the Jain renouncer Ilaṅkō, combines themes of earlier akam and puṟam poetry, goddess worship, and a political vision of a Tamil imperium. In modern times both of these texts have been adopted as emblems of Tamil cultural identity.

4 The paradigm of 63 nayaṉmār begins with a list of saints included in a poem of Cuntaramūrtti (eighth century CE), who predates Māṇikkavācakar (ninth century).

5 Richman includes examples of Muslim and Christian piḷḷaittamiḻ poems in her study of this genre (Richman 1997).

6 Kenneth Bryant has explicated a very similar dynamic in the Kṛṣṇaite poetry of the north Indian bhakti poet Sūrdās (Bryant 1978). Richman points out that, contrary to expectations, there are few Tamil piḷḷaittamiḻ devoted to the subject of baby Kṛṣṇa.

7 Historically, the term kāppiyam is usually applied to a corpus of long narrative poems composed by Buddhist and Jain authors between the fifth and tenth centuries, whereas the preeminent kāvyam poem is Kampaṉ's twelfth-century Tamil version of the *Rāmāyaṇa*. Many Tamil scholars consider the two terms to be etymologically cognate, though some scholars dispute the etymologically link between Sanskrit "kāvya" and Tamil "kāppiyam."

8 This relationship may be thought of as a mirror image of the relationship between the Sanskrit epic and the many Sanskrit mahākāvyas which aim to transform the epic text into refined poetry. For an insightful discussion of the latter relationship see Yigal Bronner's Ph.D. dissertation (Bronner 1999).

References

Blackburn, Stuart. 1988: *Singing of Birth and Death: Text in Performance.* Philadelphia: University of Pennsylvania Press.

Bronner, Yigal. 1999: "Poetry at its Extreme: The Theory and Practice of Bitextual Poetry (śleṣa) in South Asia." Ph.D. dissertation, University of Chicago.

Bryant, Kenneth. 1978: *Poems to the Child-God: Structure and Strategies in the Poetry of Surdas.* Berkeley: University of California Press.

Cutler, Norman. 1987: *Songs of Experience: The Poetics of Tamil Devotion.* Bloomington: Indiana University Press.

Ferro-Luzzi, Gabriella Eichinger. 1989: "The Polythetic-Prototype Approach to Hinduism." In G. D. Sontheimer and H. Kulke, eds., *Hinduism Reconsidered.* New Delhi: Manohar.

Frasca, Richard. 1988: *The Theater of the Mahabharata: Terukkuttu Performances in South India.* Honolulu: University of Hawaii Press.

Frykenberg, Robert E. 1989: "The Emergence of Modern 'Hinduism' as a Concept and as an Institution," in G. D. Sontheimer and H. Kulke, eds., *Hinduism Reconsidered.* New Delhi: Manohar.

Hiltebeitel. Alf. 1988: *The Cult of Draupadi: 1. Mythologies from Gingee to Kuruksetra.* Chicago: University of Chicago Press.

Ramanujan, A. K. and Norman Cutler. 1983: "From Classicism to Bhakti," in Bardwell L. Smith, ed., *Essays on Gupta Culture.* Delhi: Motilal Banarsidass.

Richman, Paula. 1997: *Extraordinary Child: Poems from a South Indian Devotional Genre.* Honolulu: University of Hawaii Press.

Shulman, David Dean. 1980: *Tamil Temple Myths: Sacrifice and Divine Marriage in the South Indian Saiva Tradition.* Princeton: Princeton University Press.

CHAPTER 8

The Literature of Hinduism in Malayalam

Rich Freeman

The development of written literatures in India's regional languages raises fascinating issues of social history and cultural identity for every region where this occurred, at whatever period in the subcontinent's history (Pollock forthcoming). For most of the major regional cultures in India, such literary projects were simultaneously caught up with religious ones, for literature and learning were cast in languages and institutions that claimed an ultimately sacerdotal and even divine authority. Sanskrit, Pali, and Prakrit, though developing in Indo-Aryan speech communities of northern India, rapidly lost their moorings in any local tongue and spread to establish transregional literary cultures primarily in association with Brahmanical Hinduism, Buddhism, and Jainism. These purely learned languages had reached every corner of the subcontinent before the Christian era, prior to the rise of any regional language into written form. For at least the next millennium, until the coming of Islamic polities to many parts of medieval India these religiously sanctioned literary cultures set the framework within which regional literatures had to contend in establishing and maintaining their identities. With the notable exception of Tamil, at the extreme south of India, every major regional literature thus crafted the preponderance of its founding texts as religious works.[1] Even Tamil, the earliest of the regional literary languages, which began through bardic literature of a principally secular nature, was thoroughly transformed through popular Hindu devotionalism, before any other regional literatures of the subcontinent had even appeared (Cutler 1987, Narayanan 1994, Peterson 1991).

The Malayalam literature from the region of Kerala, along India's southwest coast, affords an especially revealing perspective on the intersection of regional identity, local social relations, and the religious institutions of Hinduism in south India. This is because the Kerala tradition emerged out of an earlier Tamil cultural matrix, to develop its own transformations of Sanskrit and indigenous genres, in a complex renegotiation of literary, religious and cultural identity through time. Tamil was itself unique in being the earliest Dravidian language to emerge into literacy, and the only regional speech to develop a "classical" literature (in terms of a formalized grammar, poetics, distinctive genres, and supporting cultural institutions) largely independent of Sanskritic models (Zvelebil 1973).[2] Early Kerala co-authored this Tamil tradition, but then began diverging from it around the twelfth century, to embrace both Sanskrit literary registers, and to develop its own Dravidian poetic and linguistic heritage in different directions. Most of this, however, was prosecuted through textual projects either directly reworking the Sanskrit Epics, Purāṇas, and philosophical treatises of pan-Indic Hinduism, or through local romances that were themselves completely immersed in the temple-culture of Kerala's Hindu social formation (Freeman forthcoming).

In the present chapter, I will attempt to chart the major developments of Kerala's Hindu literature in the local language of Tamil-Malayalam, as a reflection of the particular regional and socio-cultural context of its literary culture.[3] While the particulars of these developments are unique to Kerala, the general task of relating language and literature to those socio-religious cultures we club together under the modern rubric "Hindu" should hold comparative interest for a wider South Asian scholarship.

The Cultural Legacy of the Tamil Tradition in Kerala

The linguistic, cultural and political formation calling itself Tamil, today associated with the modern linguistic state of Tamil Nadu, first emerged in the far south of India in the early centuries, CE, as a triumvirate of territorially based kingdoms. Two of these lines, the Pāṇḍyas and the Cōḻas, divided up what is today Tamil Nadu. The third, the Cēras, ruled the narrow strip of territory today called Kerala along India's southwest coast, comprising the steep, verdant declivities of the Western Ghats, and reaching down from their peaks to the rich littoral rice and coconut tracts along the Arabian Sea. Though comparatively isolated geographically by its formidable mountain borders, this land of the Cēras, (whence, modern *Kēraḷam*), was a vital partner in the wider cultural territory of the Tamils (*Tamiḻakam*). It is around the courts of these Tamil and Cēra kings that India's earliest regionally vernacular literature emerged, the bardic corpus known as Caṅkam literature, after the conclaves (<Skt. *saṅgha*) of royal poets (Hart 1975, Marr 1985, Zvelebil 1973). In keeping with the division of language families between Dravidian southern India and the Indo-Aryan north, the thematic and poetic conventions of this earliest and most southerly Dravidian speech community were markedly different from the productions of classical Sanskrit literature. Representing what is essentially the rapid promotion and codification of an oral tradition into a written corpus, this poetry was thematically bifurcated into domestic themes of romantic love, the "interior" (*akam*) of social life, versus the "exterior" (*puṟam*) of heroism, conquest and warfare.

Both of these thematic divisions of social life were emotionally explored through imaging moods and feelings in a semiotic coding keyed to the flora and fauna of a conventional set of landscapes (*tiṇai*) distinctive to Tamiḻakam (Ramanujan 1967; see pp. 146–7 above).

Most interestingly, in the larger Indian context, this Caṅkam literature seems essentially secular and worldly in terms of its subjective concerns and artistic purpose. Objectively, however, there is considerable reportage of the indigenous forms of religious life in Kerala and the greater Tamil country before the major impact of Sanskritic Puranic culture. While this is not the place for an extended treatment of Caṅkam religion, I will hazard to sketch some of its prominent features, as the substratum of later religious-literary developments in Kerala.[4]

First, religion was not centered on a sacerdotal, priestly class, like the Brahmans, but rather gave prominence to the ritual functions of kings and chiefs on the one hand, and to relatively lower status spirit-possessed oracles and mediums, on the other. The sacred, rather than tending towards the transcendence of Brahmanical Hindu schemes, was thus experienced in the form of immanent powers: immanent to the life of society in the persons of its political leaders, and immanent in the natural powers of life and death, through the oracles. The two formed a related circuit in that kings, as heads of warrior societies, presided over an economy of death that was viewed positively as the fertile basis for social prosperity, while the oracles trafficked in the powers of the resulting heroic dead who were promoted to the status of gods, and whose shrines formed the sites of spirit-possessed worship by the kings. Battle was a form of sacrificial religion, striving to appropriate the life-force (*uyir*) of others, while sacrificial religion was a substitute battle, a celebration of past blood-letting, and the promise and foretaste to ancestral deities of battles to come. This assimilation was lexicalized in the word *kaḷam*, which meant at once the threshing floor for gathering one's agricultural yield, the field of battle, and the sacred space for sacrifice. In the rites of worship, political authorities orchestrated the death-rites of blood sacrifice, while the bodies of mediums became the vehicles for divinized spirits of the ancestral dead who danced, offered oracular pronouncements, and expressed their desires and pleasures.

While this complex of spirit-possessed dancing and blood-sacrifice is viewed in modern times as "folk" religion, for many centuries this was the "classical" religion of high civilization in south India. It has persisted among the rural dominants at a level of formalized worship in this region that is reminiscent of the royal legacy, harboring an alternate sacred order that persists under the later edifice of Sanskritic Hinduism. It is important to keep this in mind because despite the prominence given to Brahmanically Sanskritic models in south India, Brahmans remained a thinly distributed elite atop indigenously organized warrior societies throughout this region, until the latter were dismantled under European colonialism. This was especially so in Kerala, where even the kinship system of the dominant warrior castes was shaped by the exigencies of perpetual warfare.

While the organization of Caṅkam literature around the thematic bifurcation into love and war genres was primarily secular, the powerful emotional complexes of lush eroticism and graphic violence that motivated these carried forward into the Sanskritization of Tamil literature. Known as the "Tamil Bhakti" movement that commenced in the sixth century CE, this literature represented the mapping of mythological themes from the Sanskrit Purāṇas into the indigenous literary forms. As a socioreligious movement, this was coincident with the revival of Tamil kingdoms in new state forms, institutionally centered on the emergence of structural temples, as cultural centers built on and linking together the village structure of these kingdoms' agrarian economies. The originally local deities of these temples were Sanskritized into either the Vaiṣṇava or Śaiva Puranic pantheons, and celebrated in new liturgical song-literatures by poet-saints who revealed the gods' presence through divine visions and inspiration, and who became the subject of their own hagiographies as the saints of Tamil Vaiṣṇavism, the Āḻvārs, and those of Śaivism, the Nāyaṉmārs (Narayanan 1994, Peterson 1991). While the earlier genre distinctions between love and war poetry merged in the new bhakti works, the earlier aesthetic and emotional energies of the Tamil ethos adapted readily to the new religious themes (Cutler 1987). The martial impetus was transferred to the battles of gods with their demonic adversaries (or sometimes with each other), as well as to violence of the god against the devotee, of devotees against sectarian rivals, and of devotees against themselves or their loved ones in acts of self-mutilation and sacrifice (Hudson 1989). Similarly, erotic longings were displaced from human relations to those of longing and devotion between devotee and deity. In many of these saints' poetic utterances, we find clear resonance with the earlier ecstatic mediums, where the longing for bodily and psychic union suggests possession (Yocum 1982). The link between Tamil sovereigns and the deities who represented them likewise remained powerful, though it now accommodated a Brahmanical complement that was specialized in religious pursuits which emerged as a distinctive institutional domain: on the one hand, there was patronage of an essentially Indo-Aryan Vedic ritual cult, and on the other, an increasing Brahmanization of the hybrid temple culture whose roots were in Dravidian ancestral shrines (Hart and Heifetz 1999).

Kerala participated in this new bhakti paradigm to a certain extent, but unlike the earlier Caṅkam tradition, we have only a smattering of Tamil literary sources attributed to Kerala chiefs or kings, and only a dozen or so temple sites in the region that seemed to participate in what became a predominantly eastern Tamil complex. Linguistically, Tamil had shifted from the language of Caṅkam composition into Middle Tamil, and around this time, from the early ninth century, the first Kerala inscriptions attest the divergence of local language into a distinctively regional dialect that anticipates the later emergence of Malayalam (Sekhar, 1953; Ayyar, 1983 [1936]). While there was certainly no "Hundred Years' War" between the Cōḻas and Cēras that an earlier generation of historians invented to account for the political-cultural break between the regions, there can be no doubt that Kerala's cultural divergence from Tamil developments was marked by repeated warring across the Ghats, and that the tenth-century rise of

Cōḻa imperium helped condition and maintain the internal fragmentation of medieval Kerala into a pastiche of feuding sub-kingdoms.[5] This remained the political situation of Kerala down to the advent of the European powers, and formed the social matrix in which Kerala's version of Hinduism and its literary expression arose and developed.

The Early Devotional Mode: Literary Songs of Ritual and War

The first literary writing of Kerala in a recognizably distinctive West coast dialect of the "Tamil" that was to become Malayalam is a commentary on Kauṭilya's *Arthaśāstra* (Sambasiva Sastri, 1972 [1930]). The original work is a Sanskrit treatise on the Indic science of polity, and the commentary is a virtual paraphrase that adds little to the original. What it does show, however, is that Brahmanical Sanskritic treatises were imposing themselves on Kerala society as technical (if improbable) models of political organization and conduct. As with the largely secular focus of Caṅkam literature, there is scarcely anything we might consider of religious import in this text. Unfortunately, the commentary on the various rites of sorcery and magic that are supposed to secure political successes in the final chapter of the work is no longer extant.

Shortly thereafter, in perhaps the thirteenth century, we encounter another very different work, the first religious work in the Malayalam language, the only recently discovered *Tiruniḻalmāla*, the "Garland of the Sacred Shade (or Grace)." Until the discovery and publication of this work in 1980 (Puruṣōttaman Nāyar 1981), the advent of Kerala's literary history was dominated by the *Rāmacaritam*, a roughly contemporaneous and far lengthier retelling of the Sanskrit epic, the *Rāmāyaṇa* (George 1956). While in a very similar linguistic idiom of early Malayalam, however, the *Tiruniḻalmāla* could not be more different, thematically. It is essentially a ritual text, centered on a series of festival rites around the still active temple of Kṛṣṇa at Āṟaṇmuḷa, in south central Kerala. There are a number of interesting aspects to this text that warrant attention. Āṟaṇmuḷa is first of all one of a small number of *divyadēśas*, sacred temple sites known to the Vaiṣṇava bhakti poems of the earlier mentioned Tamil Āḻvārs, to be found in the Kerala country. Furthermore, this text reveals that five of the total thirteen *divyadēśa* temples were included within Āṟaṇmuḷa's jurisdiction, suggesting that Tamil Vaiṣṇavas formed a rather constricted set of colonies in the Kerala country.

More remarkable is the nature of the rites highlighted in this work. While much about the text is clearly embedded in the celebration of Sanskrit gods and their mythology, the focus of the work is not on the Brahmanical rites of worship we would associate with the Sanskritic Āgamic tradition of Tamil temple worship, but rather on the blood rites (*pali* < Skt. *bali*) performed by what are today lower-caste exorcists, known as Malayans.

In modern times, Malayans are found only in far northern Kerala, where both copies of the *Tiruniḻalmāla* were discovered. Malayans, however, intergrade with a caste to their south known as Pāṇar, (from *paṇ*, "melody"), which was the same designation used of bards in the Caṅkam Tamil tradition. Both castes today specialize in sorcery (*mantravādam*) and exorcism rites, for which they perform poetic musical liturgies, and Malayans are perhaps the most accomplished and prominent performers of *teyyāṭṭam* (see the accompanying article). Since, as a polluting caste (*avarṇṇar*), Malayans were banned from Brahmanical temples in later medieval Kerala, it is surprising to find their important role in the great temple center of Āṟaṇmuḷa, and to find them in this role so far south. This suggests that Malayans were once more prominent and widespread, and that the bhakti Vaiṣṇavism of early Kerala temples was more socially inclusive than later, more Brahmanically Āgamic temple culture.

While most of the deities and some of the vocabulary of the *Tiruniḻalmāla* are Sanskrit-derived, the phonological form, patterns of alliteration and metrical structure of the poem are all modeled after classical Tamil. Despite being centered on Viṣṇu, however, a large variety of gods are invoked and worshipped, showing that the sectarianism so characteristic of Tamil bhakti, particularly rivalry between Vaiṣṇavas and Śaivas, was already being deliberately elided in Kerala at this early date. In fact a Malayan performer gives a lengthy recital of the sacred deeds of Śiva (as known to the Tamil tradition) to Viṣṇu before the latter's own shrine, saying, "since there is no difference between the two of you, we have made here an offering (*pali*) to Śiva" (Ln. 302). Later there is a special dance to Kuṟatti, a goddess especially associated with the tribals and mountain ranges of Kerala who survives today in the *teyyam* worship of northern Kerala and other folk festivals.

Though the introduction to the work gives a good idea of the socio-political situation of the temple and its authorities, the bulk of the Tiruniḻalmāla describes the various rites, offerings, and dances of the Malayans. What is quite interesting in this is how the religious function of this worship is perceived, for it is quite clear that the sequence of rituals and offerings over a number of days are essentially a giant exorcism in which the performers remove any noxious spiritual effects that may have accrued to their deity through faulty rituals, enmity, or pollution in worship. Some of these rites must have been quite spectacular, and the following example should give a clear idea that we are not in a normatively "Hindu" ritual milieu here, but one heavily inflected by its Dravidian cultural legacy.

Among the *bali*-rites to deities over successive days and oriented in different directions, that done to the north, the traditional direction for blood sacrifices in battle, is reserved for Kṣētrapālan. For this the Malayans planted a series of gibbets (*kaḻuku*) around the offering ground (*pali-kaḷam*) such as malefactors were traditionally impaled alive on in medieval Kerala. The performers then mounted these contraptions, splayed themselves out, and writhing, had artificial blood (*kuruti*) poured over their chests, and mock entrails pulled from their bodies and draped over the cross-pieces as would be done in disembowelments.

The poem tells us that birds of prey and crows gathered on the gibbets, mistaking this for the real thing. Then amidst a roar of drums like the ocean's waves, Kṣētrapālan was ritually invoked and installed in the site. Summoning the god to witness the sight, they cried, "O Lord, we your slaves, wanting any valuables, have offered the Sacrifice to the North, rending our chests with our hands and taking this to offer on the gibbet" (Lns. 429–30). Even today Malayans recount an exorcism for the gods as their myth of origin that they use in contemporary rites of exorcism for human patrons. Some of these rites still entail the mock self-sacrifice of the performer, and for one of these the Malayans pierce their veins and spew out their own blood as an offering in the awesome *ucca-bali*. Of course today these rites have been demoted to the level of "the folk," but they still live on in the rather robust underground world of Kerala's "sorcery" (*mantravādam*).

The next great work of Hindu affiliation extant in Kerala was the aforenamed *Rāmacaritam*, of the fourteenth century (George 1956). Like the *Tirunil̲almāla*, the phonology, orthography, and metrical structure are largely in conformity with Tamil conventions, but given its modeling on the Sanskrit epic, a somewhat greater portion of the lexicon is Sanskrit-derived. In narrative structure, however, this work effects a unique departure from its original model. The *Rāmacaritam* is narratively framed entirely within the *Rāmāyaṇa's* book of war (the *Yuddha-kāṇḍa*), and reconstructs the earlier parts of the epic through flashbacks and other retellings.

It has long been surmised that the recasting of the *Rāmāyaṇa* entirely around the war may have been related to the militarism of Kerala, suggesting this was a devotional work essentially for the edification of the soldiery. While there is no direct evidence for this, the ethos and tone of the work seem to support this idea. Its occasional reveling in the gore of battle draws images in common with Tamil war poetry, like the dance of the headless corpses. Consider the following description of the effects of Lord Rāma's arrows on the demon hordes that attack him (77.3–5):[6]

> Many shining arrows went swift and continuous
> To plunge in the bodies of those foes who surrounded him to fight.
> They were terrorized, as on every side of the battlefield,
> The gore and corpses mounted through their great destruction.
>
> The earth was thickly adorned with corpses and gore,
> And as the great warriors advanced, striving to search him out and do battle with him,
> They could not even glimpse him, without being struck by this King of king's arrows . . .
>
> Numbers of corpses, severed of their heads, entwined among themselves in a fine, frenzied dance . . .
>
> As their lives were spent on the field of battle,
> And the bodies of those forces were rent in destruction, one on top of another,
> Wherever one turned, the river of blood sent its courses in numbers beyond reckoning.

In another passage, corpses severed of their heads, wander around as if looking for something they've lost (i.e., their heads!), then tiring of the search, sportively join in a *tāṇḍava* dance around the field of battle (20.10). Still another stanza weaves a fantastic trope: as the blood from the rent bodies of demons, the Vānara monkey allies of Rāma, and their various fallen mounts gushes out on the battlefield, it comingles into a river; the rows of faces floating in that river are its lotus flowers; the combatants' crushed teeth (or pearls) are the river's sands; the soldiers' floating trunks are alligators; their viscera are the water-plants; their swishing banners are crocodiles; their parasols are lotus leaves; and the maddened elephants are the river's boulders (23.4).

While the bulk of the separate events and characters in the *Rāmacaritam* closely correspond to the Sanskrit *Rāmāyaṇa*, its narrative restructuring, poetic form, and much of the imagery clearly suggest a different ethos and aesthetic that has recast the work in a classically Dravidian mold of martial devotion. When we pair this with the *Tirunilalmāla* we get a clear sense that the bhakti of early Kerala had a rather different tenor from what the Christian missionaries and modern apologists have rather selectively emphasized in presenting south Indian devotionalism for cosmopolitan consumption.[7] In many ways the myths and ethos of contemporary, and especially lower-caste, folk-forms fit very comfortably with these earlier images of immanent, violent powers, and this suggests a continuity of religious perspective that sits athwart the divide of caste and class-status.

The Early Sanskrit Genre of *Maṇipravāḷam*

Linguistically and poetically, such relative continuities are evident in Kerala literature in those genres that, like the two texts we have just reviewed, conformed to canons recognizably affiliated with Tamil literary models. The first and only premodern linguistic text treating Kerala's language, the fourteenth-century *Līlātilakam*,[8] labels this first style of literary production *Pāṭṭu*. Meaning literally just "song," this suggests its close association with those local performative modes we might later style "folk." At this time, however, *Pāṭṭu* stood as a literary genre contrasted with its highly Sanskritized counterpart, *Maṇipravāḷam*. The name of this latter literary medium literally meant "pearls and coral" after the image of this language as stringing together the different gems of local language forms with those of Sanskrit. Lexically, metrically, and phonologically (through adaptation of the Sanskrit syllabary from the *grantha* script), this Maṇipravāḷam style sought to reshape the local "Tamil" of Kerala on the model of high Sanskrit literature. In fact, the *Līlātilakam* opens by declaring that anything that can be done in the highest Sanskrit literature (*kāvya*), can be literarily accomplished in *Maṇipravāḷam*. But what these accomplishments actually are, in the thematics of the poetry, testifies to the social life of Kerala's literati in a way that becomes an embarrassment to future generations.

It seems relatively clear that the principal authors in the early phase of Maṇipravāḷam were those most intimately acquainted with Sanskrit, namely,

Kerala's Brahmans. It is therefore their literary culture and life-style that were most closely reflected in this literature. The earliest poetic works, in ornately accomplished and highly Sanskritized genres, are poems dealing primarily with erotic themes addressed to their non-Brahman (*Śūdra* caste-grade) mistresses. The earliest of these texts, from perhaps the thirteenth century, is the collection of verses styled the *Vaiśika Tantra* ("The Treatise of the Courtesan"), in the form of a courtesan mother's advice to her daughter (Rāmacandran Nāyar 1969). This is followed in the next century by three major poetic compositions, each in praise of a different named courtesan, and by other collections of short poems on the same topic. Given the prominence of these themes and the voluptuary life-style they portray, the major thrust of later scholarship has been to decry the decadence of Maṇipravāḷam in comparison with the religious themes of the Pāṭṭu literature. Matters, however, are not actually so simple.

A work written in this same milieu, and somewhat before the *Līlātilakam* (which indeed cites it), is the *Anantapuravarṇṇanam* (Ratnamma 1986). This a long descriptive poem on the Viṣṇu temple of Trivandrum and its surroundings. Though similarly in high *Maṇipravāḷam*, and in Sanskrit *anuṣṭhubh* meter, it is clearly religious in its intent. It recounts what a worshipper encounters in visiting all the temples and sacred groves in a circuit around Trivandrum and its subsettlements, culminating in the religious encounter with Viṣṇu as Anantaśayana in the main temple at the heart of the city (vs. 147). Though clearly a work of Vaiṣṇava devotion, such as in weaving an account of the ten incarnations (*daśāvatāra*) of Viṣṇu into the final religious vision, it gives considerable space to descriptions of Śaivite shrines and temples, as well, continuing the earlier nonsectarian impetus *of* the *Tirunilalmāla*. Ethnographically, the work is rich in detail, celebrating the ritual procession of Trivandrum's king into the temple (vs. 115–21) and devoting many stanzas to describing the extensive markets (vs. 41–104). It even eavesdrops on the dialogues between merchants and customers as they haggle over merchandise.

Religiously, the work catches that phase of Kerala's temple culture, in which, in keeping with the Sanskrit idiom, Brahmanically Āgamic ritual had taken over at such royal centers. This is clear from the description of temple rituals, the Brahman "college," and the Brahman mess attached to the temple (vs. 133 ff.; 148–9). It is interesting to note, in the context of sectarian affiliation, that the only other extensive use of the term *Maṇipravāḷam* outside of Kerala was in labeling the contemporary Tamil ŚrīVaiṣṇava literature which used a very similar lexical idiom in terms of combining Tamil and Sanskrit (though only in prose) for commenting on Vaiṣṇava scripture. Putting this together with such evidence as the *Līlātilakam's* celebrating the Tamil Vaiṣṇava *Divyaprabandham* as the "Tamil Veda," and recalling that the Trivandrum temple was one of the sacred centers of Vaiṣṇavism known to the Tamil bhakti corpus, suggests the considerable influence of Śrīvaiṣṇavism at this time. At any rate, the survival of at least several other works in this Kerala-based Maṇipravāḷam, which were exclusively dedicated to religious themes of praising gods or their temples, should caution us against the stereotypic thematic equation of Maṇipravāḷam with Brahmanical eroticism, as against all those works which modern scholars club into the dustbin genre of Pāṭṭu, lending the latter a patina that is at once more indigenous and more piously devotional.

This notion that the erotic was somehow counter to religious perspectives (a notion that one might argue is a back-reading of colonial and postcolonial epistemes) might similarly be eroded even by a closer scrutiny of those works explicitly focused on the courtesan culture. The main works of high Maṇipravāḷam provide descriptive overviews of courtesan manors and their cultural life, which are indeed completely imbricated with the social and religious life of Kerala's medieval temples. Institutionally, the strict primogeniture of Brahmanical inheritance patterns in Kerala worked to regularize recurrent sexual liaisons between junior Brahman males and women of the martial and temple-servant castes. This overlapped with the institution of *Tēvaṭicci*, the *Devadāsī* known elsewhere in India, where women were dedicated to the gods of particular shrines, serving as ritual dancers and entertainers for the gods, and courtesans for higher clientele among the worshippers. In Kerala, I believe these logics fused around Brahmans as simultaneously the chief patrons of the temple arts and of courtesans, as regular genitors among the higher families of royalty and temple-servants, and, as "gods on earth," the intellectual and spiritual heads of the religious culture of temples. Temples and manors of the high-born were thus thoroughly intertwined, with circuits of travel through the landscape of courtesan manors that the Maṇipravāḷam works describe being largely congruent with pilgrimage circuits through the sacred geography of Kerala.

Religiously speaking, these various courtesan works thus contain not just descriptions of many temple-sites and sacred groves, but also dedication verses, descriptions and praises (*stutis*) of many deities, in the context of relations with courtesans. I believe a sustained study of this literature that takes its religious ideologies seriously might demonstrate more pervasive connections between these and the social structuring and sexual politics of caste Hinduism in Kerala. The frequent mapping of religious devotion (*bhakti*) between devotee and deity in gender relationships, the recurrent mythologies of high male deities linked to violently dangerous and militant consort goddesses, and the Śākta or tantric doctrines of liberation through harnessing the libidinal energies of the body cannot, I would argue, be accidental in this historical context. Indeed, I would suspect they were synthesized in the temple cult itself, which was avowedly tantric in its ideology of worship and frequently focused on goddesses who were Sanskritically upgraded versions of local warrior deities. The earliest of these courtesan travelogues, the thirteenth-century *Uṇṇiyaccicaritam*, for instance, ends with a prose description, and then this final stanza of prayer to the goddess of Paḻañcēri (vs. 26):

> Worshipped in fine purity, with her tongue a licking mass of flame, drinking the blood that flows by her shining trident from the bodies of powerful demons, along with the copious nectar that trickles from the crescent moon afflicted by her vigorous battle, may this daughter of Kāma's slayer (Śiva), this Mother who dwells in Paḻañcēri, ever grant us protection.

There is a rich interplay of images here of warfare, blood sacrifice, and consumption, along with the confluence of fiery metabolic energy, female potencies of blood and the seminal emissions of the moon whose tantric overtones are unmistakable. Though research on the development of the tantric tradition in Kerala has been negligible, its doctrines and practices clearly formed a primary nexus in which an official Brahman ideology of worship came to terms with the dominant religious culture of sexual fertility, violent militarism, and spirit possession through the institutionalized rites and festivals of the Hindu temple. In summary, it seems evident that the early phase of Maṇipravāḷam literature contains much of this religious synthesis that has been overlooked in modern scholars' dismissal of and embarrassment at its erotic component, in comparison with that other stream of the so-called Pāṭṭu literature.

Poets of Non-Brahman Bhakti

While the *Tirunil̲almāla* and *Rāmacaritam* are linguistically distinct from the nearly contemporaneous Maṇipravāḷam works in terms of eschewing Sanskrit phonology, grammatical terminations, and massive amounts of vocabulary, the subsequent works classed by modern scholars as Pāṭṭu readily assimilate many of these Sanskritic features of high Maṇipravāḷam. It is on the basis of their narrative dependence on Sanskrit Epics and Purāṇas, and in their Dravidian meters, that they are most readily distinguished from their Maṇipravāḷam counterparts. The next great stage or stratum of production in this tradition comes from the members of a family known as the Niraṇam poets, during the fourteenth and fifteenth centuries.

These poets specialized in condensing the Sanskrit Epics into shorter compendia of stanzas constructed of local Dravidian meters. These meters were based on the same principles as those of Tamil (as opposed to the Sanskrit meters of Maṇipravāḷam), but took simpler and more fluid forms in accordance with their largely performative nature. Linguistically, the adoption of a Sanskritically phonological script brought in the wholesale adoption of Sanskrit vocabulary. This has been the single greatest contributor to the divergence of Malayalam from Tamil down to the present. This script also enabled the Maṇipravāḷam trait of using Sanskrit grammatical terminations, as well, but this was done sparingly, and I am certain this was related to the different social authorship and presumed audience of the Niraṇam poets.

What is most remarkable about the Niraṇam poets is that we know from their recurring title, "Paṇikkar" that they were non-Brahman, most likely of martial caste, and reckoned as mere Śūdras from the Brahmanical perspective. In keeping with their own dedicatory and concluding verses, we can surmise that their linguistic medium, which they craved their audiences "not to despise as mixed language," was intended to bring the salvific powers of Sanskrit religious texts "in some paltry fashion" to their own communities of lower-caste worshippers.[9] On the one hand, this stanza from the introduction to their

Rāmāyaṇam shows the certain hegemony of Brahmanical models over this linguistic and religious community:

> Discarding egotism and such through ascetic meditation, and compassionately given over to peacefulness, restraint, and joy in their dedication to the Veda, considering such incomparable Lords on Earth (i.e. Brahmans) to be my very divinity, by the grace of these Vedic Brahmans will all that I contemplate here by accomplished. (Maṇṇummūṭu 1993: 18)

On the other hand, such lofty praise also implies the establishment of high standards by which to judge Brahmanical conduct, standards which were conspicuously absent in the courtesan literature of Maṇipravāḷam. Furthermore, despite the self-deprecation of this "mixed language" (*bhāṣāmiśram*) and its works as not attaining the elevation of the Sanskrit originals, the Niraṇam tradition authorizes itself in terms of its own "faultlessly pre-eminent great guru, a mighty soul who was a lordly master of both [Sanskrit and vernacular] poetries."[10] If such gurus and their disciples thus chose (or were forced by social convention) to compose in the lower-status local language, the claims to equal spiritual status are nevertheless overt. Their god himself declares to the world in their works, "Be they gods or untouchables, my devotees (*bhaktas*) are alike in my esteem – such is the message of the Lord (Īśvaran),"[11] Lastly, it is interesting that while Vaiṣṇava works take a certain precedence among the Niraṇam poets (including one of the earliest vernacular renderings of the *Bhagavad-Gītā* in India), they also composed a *Śivarātrimāhātmyam* on the greatness of Śiva and vows (*vrata*) kept to him, and their family gods paired the Viṣṇu/Kṛṣṇa of the Malayinkīḻ temple, and the Śiva (as Kapālīśvaran) at Niraṇam itself, to both of whom their poems are repeatedly dedicated.

The Performative Context of Religious Production

While the Pāṭṭu and Maṇipravāḷam streams that later merge to form *Malayāḷam* literature bring Sanskrit myths and deities into written prominence, it is important to realize that the grounds for this mediation into local language were likely laid earlier within the performative features of the Sanskrit tradition itself in Kerala. Traditions of staging Sanskrit dramas were, from the outset, religious events, performed within temple-precincts over many days, as parts of ritual calendars and sponsored in fulfillment of vows. From perhaps the ninth century or earlier, temple-servant castes were occupationally specialized as to their various acting, dancing and musician roles in staging these plays, which were always adapted from the Sanskrit Epics and Purāṇas.[12]

To simplify this picture greatly, what developed within the Sanskrit dramatic tradition were various mediating roles for performers, retelling, glossing, or expanding on the events and characters depicted, first in simpler Sanskrit, then eventually in hybrid language forms that bridged between Sanskrit and the local language. Slots within the performance format were set aside for direct address to the audience, and these developed their own genres ranging from prose retellings (*gadyam*) in a lexically Sanskritic but grammatically local form of Kerala language, to special compositions (*prabandhams*) that mixed Maṇipravāḷam-style verses with prose (a form known as *campu*). The prose, *gadyam* compositions, were apparently recited by the Nambyār caste of temple drummers, while the *campu* works were performed by the somewhat higher-caste actors of the Cākyār caste.

While this interspersing of verse and prose in the *campū* (to use the Sanskrit spelling) emerged at a pan-Indic level in Sanskrit with Bhoja, in the eleventh century, its popularity in south India, and its special adaptation in Kerala, seems closely related to the context of performance and its social moorings there. In the first place, much of the so-called "prose" of the *campus* was in fact in local Dravidian meters. Since these did not qualify as "verse" (*padyam*) under Sanskrit poetic typologies, they had to be smuggled in, as it were, under the label of "prose" (*gadyam*) between the metrically Sanskrit verses of Maṇipravāḷam, to form the matrix of the Malayalam *campu*. These Dravidian "prose" sections seem to be functionally adapted not only to the main description and story line of the Puranic myths, but also to weave in commentary, and especially, social observations and satire, often with the force of recontextualizing the myths in the social setting of contemporary Kerala culture.

This points up several crucial features of the performance traditions of Kerala in relation to Malayalam literature. First, it was such traditions that we think of as the "performing arts" which mediated much of the Sanskrit religious tradition into Kerala culture. It was actors in the temple-theater who seem first to have developed special elaborating sub-genres, as ancillaries to the main performance. With time, these appear to have become more popular, increasingly independent, and eventually to have left the interior of the temple-theater to circulate in the wider society. In this context, we should also keep in mind that while "theater" tends to suggest the primary function of secular entertainment in the modern West, both the Sanskrit theatrical performances and their subsequent transformations were fundamentally religious rituals in Kerala (Jones 1984).

Relatedly, we have to realize that much of what our print-culture thinks of, and therefore receives, interprets, and reconstructs after our book-form as comprising "Malayalam literature," often comprises only the text-artifacts, the mnemonic props of performative genres. Though the *campu* emerges in the fifteenth and sixteenth centuries as the dominant genre of "literature," the degree of borrowing and transposing of whole chunks of composition between works and authors, coupled with frequent direct address to and descriptions of audiences, leaves little doubt that these works were performed in some partly-improvisational, public forum. This public was almost certainly gathered on calendrically ritual occasions, in the context of temple festivals. The Dravidian form of the poetic "prose," coupled with the satiric elements, often with Brahmans and their institutions themselves as the target, suggests that the audience constituency was wider and less exclusive than that of the Sanskritic theater.

This indicates the final, socially significant trajectories of performative context that become more pronounced, finding their way increasingly into literary inscription with time. I refer here to contestatory social forces, both outside Brahmanism and within it, that tend to fragment adherence to any monolithic set of social-literary norms. They derive their strength both from a wider and lower-caste patronage base and literary constituency, conjoined with competitive cleavages among Brahmanical authors who are aligned with different social groups. As an example, during approximately the same period in the fifteenth century when Punam Nampūtiri was composing and performing his great *Rāmāyaṇa Campu*, an artfully woven pastiche of lively Dravidian "prose," high Maṇipravāḷam, and Sanskrit passages from Bhoja's own *campū* form of the epic, Ceṟuśśēri, another Nampūtiri Brahman, had composed his famous *Kṛṣṇa Gātha*.

This latter work is entirely in a simple Dravidian meter of song (*gātha*), explicitly commissioned by a local king of northern Kerala. Its composition in this meter, suggests that it was intended to be sung. While Kerala scholars put it in the Pāṭṭu genre, based on its linguistic and metrical form and its subject-matter on the life of Lord Kṛṣṇa taken from the Sanskrit *Bhāgavata Purāṇa*, other features mark it out as diverging significantly from works like those of the non-Brahman Niraṇam poets. What is firstly always noted as most remarkable in Ceṟuśśēri's work, is that despite its composition in Dravidian meter and vocabulary at the level of content, he has managed to formally work this material into the poetic figures of sound and sense (*alaṃkāra*) that were the hallmark of high Sanskrit literature. The second feature, far more troubling to modern sensibilities, is the amount of erotic sentiment (*śṛṅgāra*) that he seems to develop and savor in this ostensibly devotional project. In this regard the feeling-tone of certain sections is sometimes more like the classically erotic Maṇipravāḷam. While modern scholars tend to either disparage these erotic themes as marring an otherwise fine devotional piece with Brahmanically decadent values, or deny the erotic intention altogether through interpretively subsuming it in a higher form of devotion, I would not rule out the pervasive influence of the tantric milieu (and erotic modes of bhakti, as well) in which sexuality was given an explicitly positive valuation within a religious framework.

A larger point to be noted here is that after the early courtesan romances, the important works of Malayalam, whether in the Pāṭṭu or Maṇipravāḷam styles, are nearly all based on adaptations of Sanskrit Epic and Puranic myths. Being rooted as they are in performative traditions, however, they simultaneously adapt the religious themes of those myths to the particular social context of Kerala, while they offer the mythic models as an interpretive frame for that social context. Moreover, since Kerala society was stratified by partly congruent distinctions of caste, class, and ethnolinguistic affiliation, these performative and literary adaptations bear the internal structural strains of social contestation. Bakhtinian notions of multivocality are clearly in evidence. The initial asides of gloss, commentary, or satire within Sanskrit drama, widen into the wedge of Dravidian "prose," by which all kinds of local myths and context are inserted into Puranic frames. On the Brahmanical side, Ceṟuśśēri seizes on the form and language of his lower-caste predecessors; on the non-Brahman front, from the Niraṇam poets onward, authors lend their local bhakti a Brahmanical veneer with the full lexical embrace of Sanskrit.

The locally Dravidian impulses of the theater finally break out, in the seventeenth century, colonizing the Sanskrit frames themselves with local motifs and language, in the birth of the Malayalam temple-theater form, Kathakaḷi (Zarrilli 2000). Actors need no longer be part of the interior temple-servant castes, but are prominently drawn from the martial castes and bring their themes and narratives in with them. Formerly "demonic" roles may come to overshadow those of the gods (as in the *Rāvaṇavijayam*); the goddess Kāḷi, arrayed as a spirit-possessed hellion from village festivals, leaps from the stage to cavort through the audience; and Narasiṃha enacts the disembowelment of his demonic adversary with simulated bloody entrails, recalling the stunts of the Malayans from their gibbets in the *Tiruniḻalmāla*. While still Sanskritic by the standard of village religious festivals, Kathakaḷi was the genius of locally competing courts, and their martial retainers, yet it brought to the Malayalam language the performative patina of a classical temple-art, still partly sequestered as a high ritual form from the bulk of the "polluting" castes.

The Ferment of Popular Religiosity

In the world outside the temple, in the sixteenth- to seventeenth-century interim between Ceṟuśśēri and the birth of Kathakaḷi, the tradition of *Śūdra* devotionalism found in the Niraṇam poets is taken up by Tuñcattu Eḻuttacchan, often considered the father of Malayalam, proper (Achyuta Menon 1940). While using an array of local Dravidian meters, always in simple couplets, his language effectively effaces any lexical distinction between Maṇipravāḷam and Pāṭṭu styles, wedding them in a medium that seems distinctively modern. His principal work, the *Adhyātma-Rāmāyaṇam*, is taken not from the classical archetype of Vālmīki, but from the fourteenth-century work of popular devotion of the same name. Like its namesake, Eḻuttacchan's work follows the later bhakti interpretation of Rāma as fully empowered godhead incarnate in this world, and teaches the simplistic path of repeating his sacred name as fulfilling all earthly desires and leading to liberation.

While we have no firm historical evidence for the individual, Tuñcattu Eḻuttacchan (his personal name itself being in dispute), we can surmise something of the social import of his work and the new movement he typifies. He was either the founder or star pupil of a religious institution that housed both Brahman and Śūdra literary-religious notables under the patronage of a local chieftain in north-central Kerala. The historical details remain shadowy, but stories report that he was the offspring of a Brahman–Śūdra union. Eḻuttacchan itself is a title (literally "father of letters"), used in recent centuries for schoolmasters, generally of higher Śūdra caste, who imparted basic literacy to the "clean" castes in village settings.

That such literacy became widespread is testified to by the enormous number of manuscripts of the *Adhyātma Rāmāyaṇam*, the largest by far for any premodern work, throughout the region of Kerala. The text itself declares that it was composed by a Śūdra, that "reading and reciting it" frees one from the greatest sins, and that "those who desire learning" will become greatly illumined thereby "with the consent of the Aryan folk" (i.e. the Brahmans).[13] Though grounded in a different milieu than the temple theater and festivals, this text was also clearly performative, by design. The manuscript distributions and the functional implications of the text's structure and content clearly suggest that the context of use was domestic recitation, either privately or on ceremonial occasions. At numerous places the text breaks into metrical lists of epithets and phrases of praise, like it were a kind of breviary for Rāma devotionalism.

The narrative style, using a pastiche of metrical couplets that E̲luttacchan developed, was called Kiḷi-pāṭṭu, the "parrot's song" after the convention he adapted from old Tamil of having a parrot narrate the story to the author. While E̲luttacchan wrote a condensation of the *Mahābhārata* in the same style, a work generally considered of greater literary merit, but less popular than the *Adhyātma Rāmāyaṇam*, most of the other works attributed to him are in dispute. It is clear, however, that he and his followers sparked a whole literary movement, and there are scores of adaptations of Sanskrit works in this genre reaching into modern times.

Some scholars have seen in this marked increase of bhakti literature, with its shift in style and content that supplants and nearly eclipses the earlier Sanskritized, eroticized poetry, a popular upswell, or a "movement." Some attribute it to revolt against a decadent Brahmanism, while others find in it an indigenous response to the incipient colonialism inaugurated by Portuguese involvement in Kerala's mercantile life and ports. Different scholars, however, find and date different bhakti movements (as with the earlier Niraṇam poets or the still earlier *Rāmacaritam*), and in this absence of consensus, I find little convincing historical evidence for anchoring specific texts to specific historical contexts or events at this stage of research, let alone finding clear historical phases or breaks in these developments. I think the movements were too dialogically complex, in terms of caste-strata, linguistic media, and shifting political and religious contexts to demarcate any simple lines of development with the rather patchy evidence we have.

An interesting problem, for instance, is how and why even the highly Brahmanical register of the *campu* (the mixed prose and poetry genre mentioned earlier) shifts from the fifteenth century or so out of a concern with courtesan culture, and into almost exclusively religious literary themes. Many of these works come out of the temple theatre and its various spin-off genres of recitation, and there is some debate as to what the communities or forums of performance actually were for this class of works.

The greatest exemplar of the *campu* proper (other shorter works, called *prabandhams*, having the same mixed prose-poetry form), is the *Rāmāyaṇa Campu* of Punam Nampūtiri, alluded to earlier. This creatively restructures the *Rāmāyaṇa*, weaving together Sanskrit verse, Maṇipravāḷam verse, Dravidian verse (labeled "prose"), and various kinds of quasi-versified prose (*daṇḍakams*, etc.). The composite nature of this "work," the free borrowing of whole passages from other works (and of them from this), as well as repeated references to an audience and to the context of a Rāma festival (*Rāmāvatāra-utsavam*) (Veṅkiṭṭarāma Śarmmā 1967: 104–5), all point to the performance of this and other such works being staged in temple festivals of the higher castes. Another thematically different set of *campus* comes from the sixteenth-century author, Nīlakaṇṭha, who composed three of them, each on the mythology and greatness of a different temple under the patronage of a different king.[14] Being specifically temple-based, these works give an unusual glimpse into the social circles, rites, and patronage base characterizing Kerala's late medieval temples.

A similar shift, though not so marked, comes out of the *sandēśa*, or "messenger poem" genre, in imitation of Kāḷidāsa's great Sanskrit work, the *Meghadūta*. While the bulk of these works in Kerala were in Sanskrit, two well-known ones in Maṇipravāḷam verse seem to chart a similar thematic shift towards religious themes. The late fourteenth-century *Uṇṇunīlisandēśam* sends its narrating messenger over the length of southern Kerala in search of the beautiful damsel Uṇṇunīli, describing a number of courtesans, their physical charms and their associated residential and temple locales (I. Kuññan Piḷḷa, 1985 [1954]). The *Kōkasandēśam* of the next century, however, fails to even name the heroine of its quest, and is given over far more to the description of temples and praise stanzas of their associated gods (Gōpikkuṭṭan 1996). In contrast to these two messenger poems in Maṇipravāḷam, there were scores of them also written in Sanskrit proper, down to the modern era. Their thematics are usually built around literary romances, as with Kāḷidāsa's original, but transposed to the courts, temples and residential palaces of Kerala.

This calls our attention to the fact that throughout the shifts from Maṇipravāḷam and the various early Pāṭṭu works into Malayalam proper (generally reckoned from the era of Eḻuttacchan), and indeed into modernity, Sanskrit literary production continued a parallel life among the Brahmans and royal courts of Kerala. This influence fed into Malayalam in the form of commentaries and digests, particularly on ritual and its ancillary disciplines like astrology, iconology, and architecture, as well as in guides to the complex social rituals of Kerala's Nampūtiri Brahmans. Digests on the tantric rituals of temple worship, for instance, span the fifteenth-century *Puṭayūr Bhāṣa*, down to the eighteenth-century *Kuḻikkāṭṭu Pacca* that was eventually printed and is in common use today.

This technical ritual literature found its didactic, nonritual counterpart in the popular stream of Dravidian song-literature inaugurated by Eḻuttacchan. Thus in addition to the recasting of Sanskrit Epic and Puranic literature discussed earlier, there were a number of highly popular homiletic works that come down from the sixteenth and seventeenth centuries, into modern print editions. Often these were cast in the simple folk-meters like the *pāna* that was named after and used in lower-caste festivals of non-Brahmanical worship. One of the most popular of these, the *Jñāna Pāna*, by one Pūntānam Nampūtiri, fuses simplified Vedantic philosophy with the bhakti approach into a kind of synthetic Hinduism-for-the-masses, imparting basic notions of karma, gnosis, and liberation (Gōpikkuṭṭan 1989). Legend claims that Pūntānam himself was not learned in Sanskrit, and that he came from a lower division of Brahmans not entitled to

Vedic learning. Importantly, this suggests that not all Brahmans shared in the elite structures of socio-religious and political privilege, and it seems likely that many of the déclassé sections among them may have fueled and provided their intellectual capital to the various movements of Śūdra-based, popular religiosity. In keeping with such a reading, there are barbed verses in the *Jñāna Pina* on the social degradation of Brahmans in their competition for courtly honors, their wayward life in the temple, their hunger for women, and the greed that drove their Vedic cultic expertise (Gōpikkuṭṭan 1989: 77–8).

Such works sometimes explicitly aimed to reach the lower castes and women. Pūntānam is also supposed to have rendered the *Kṛṣṇakarṇṇāmṛtam* into Malayalam for his friend of the Vāriyar caste, and another popular and more interesting digest of Vedānta, the *Cintāratnam* (Jewel of Reflection) is explicitly cast as the teaching of a guru to his female disciple (Nārāyaṇapiḷḷa 1967: 7–10). This latter work has also a fascinating Vedantic deconstruction of temple worship, the backbone of Brahmanical and high-caste socioreligious claims to power in Kerala. More antinomian aspects of worship surface more readily in the oral literatures and rich culture of non-Brahmanic folk religion throughout Kerala, with its festivals of spirit possession by local deities, and its rites of liquor offerings and blood sacrifice. In a number of cases from the worship of *teyyams*, for instance, certain Vedantic claims to powers of the mind or tantric notions of bodily powers may be drawn upon and wedded to the empowerment of lower castes in worship. It is further clear, in a number of cases, that higher-caste devotees sometimes helped author such texts, in partnership with the lower-caste performers who transmitted them orally.

From Religion towards Critique and Social Consciousness

Notions of satire and critique in the literate traditions of Kerala Hindu literature, however, reached their highwater mark just at the brink of modernity with the *tuḷḷal* genre of Kuñcan Nambyār in the eighteenth century (Śarmmā 1982). This also represents the culmination of that trajectory we have noted to popularize the temple arts. The legend behind this genre is that Nambyār was a temple musician who was once publicly criticized by his superiors for laxness in his accompaniment of a performance. To avenge his hurt pride, he invented the new performative mode of *tuḷḷal*, and took it out of the temple theater into more pubic spaces where he stole away audiences. Modeled explicitly on the various forms of "dance" in popular low-caste festivals (*tuḷḷal* is literally "jumping," often in the context of spirit-possession cults), Nambyār's performance mode consisted of a single performer dancing and singing, in a colorful costume, head-dress, and make-up, to drummed accompaniment. His sung compositions, however, are cleverly crafted and artful literature. All of them are taken from the Sanskrit narrative materials of Epics and Purāṇas found in the temple theater, but Nambyār's genius was to cast into these roles all the characters found in his contemporary society and hold them up for critique against the projected religious values.[15] The roles of Epic kings, soldiery, and Brahmans, for instance, are filled out by Kerala chieftains, Nāyar-caste militia, and Nampūtiris, with all of their contemporary circumstances and foibles archly displayed. Nambyār wrote at the time when early modern states (most notably Travancore) were developing and crushing the old local orders, and historians can clearly read in his satire the problematic shifts in the agrarian and mercantile order of medieval Kerala that would eventuate in colonialism and modernity. This mode of critique was played out in the language itself, both in overt criticisms of high Sanskritic style, which he states held no charm for the common populace, and in deliberate sporting with different linguistic registers, including hyper-Sanskritic stretches that were clearly playful (Gaṇēś 1996). While modern Kerala literature is most noted for its focus on social problems and reform, it is interesting to consider Nambyār as the harbinger of this trend, sitting on the cusp of the late medieval and early modern periods. In Nambyār's case, though, this observation and criticism of his surrounding society was wrought entirely in the mode of "traditional" Hindu mythology, in frames derived from, but equally subversive of, the high pretensions of Sanskrit.

I conclude my overview in this way with Nambyār, since he is usually considered the last stellar Kerala writer of the premodern period. With the penetration of colonial powers (to which Nambyār already alludes in several places), the entire context of Kerala literature undergoes a series of progressive shifts into modernity. Perhaps the most massively reorienting is the epistemic shift from a frame which assumes that the context of literature is continuous with the institutions of Kerala's Hinduism, to one in which the possibilities of a secular, materially transformative, and revolutionary social vision were opened up, with literature as its sounding board. Yet from another perspective, one could, I think, read the earlier articulation of literature, even in its pervasively Hindu mode, as registering within it all of the tensions of its social and regional context, as these were reconfigured through the forces of history.

In summation, we have seen how the "Hinduism" of Kerala can be traced through a series of literary reworkings in linguistic, poetic, and semantic form and content. From its early origins as part of an autonomously Dravidian religion of the immanent powers of nature and human society, worshipped through the charismatic force of local chiefs, the ancestral dead, and spirit possessed oracles, it developed a bhakti idiom of devotion that accommodated the north Indian gods of Sanskritic Brahmanism and its priestly class of literati to the martial and productive forces of the land. The sociocultural differences were primarily mediated through the temple and its various performative arts, and the articulation of these with popular shrines through religious festivals and the folk-forms. These parallel religious worlds, coinciding with the schism in caste blocs and ritual norms of purity, were equally registered by the split in early Malayalam between two distinctive genres of poetic and thematic form – Maṇipravāḷam and Pāṭṭu. I have suggested, however, that the religious environment of tantrism, entangled with the sexual politics of intercaste relations and the material concerns of sorcery, worked towards synthesis from above, while the impetus of bhakti, exerted a persistent vernacular pressure from below. We have seen how with time, the distance between the strata closed, as newer mediating forms of performance, and new forums of literature, emerged under changed historical circumstances. These were still explicitly religious in their motivation, however, and it is not until the modern transformation that these fundamentally Hindu ideologies and institutions – as internally conflictual as they were – came to be finally eclipsed by the conscious emergence of social relations in their own right as the fount of literary production.

Notes

1 While I take Pollock's point (1998) that we must be cautious in the facile assumption that vernacular literacy was fundamentally driven by a concern with propagating religion in popular milieus – recognizing that literary cultures were just as often imbricated with the political aspirations of regional elites – it seems nonetheless clear that the epistemes that framed these efforts were, almost inevitably, religiously valorized. The challenge is to understand how the political and religious articulated in terms of local social bases, transregional cultural forms, and their histories of interaction.

2 The Dravidian language family comprises the four literary languages of peninsular southern India (Tamil, Malayalam, Kannada, and Telugu), and a score of unwritten tribal languages scattered mostly across southern and central India. These languages are historically unrelated to, and clearly predate the arrival of, Sanskrit and its related Indo-Aryan languages in north India. The distribution of these major languages in the south further coincides with uniquely related institutions of kinship, political and religious culture that were indigenously recognized under the term *Drāviḍa* many centuries before the modern Tamils co-opted the linguistic label, Dravidian, for their contemporary political movements. On the antiquity of these cultural interrelationships, see Trautmann (1981), Freeman (1988), and my accompanying chapter, this volume, on the *teyyam* tradition of Kerala.

3 The standard, and most readily available, histories of Malayalam literature in English are Nair (1967), George (1968), and Chaitanya (1971). Relevant work in Malayalam is extensive, but will be cited here only where I owe a direct debt to an author, and for text-citations. My own attempts to rethink this field in light of my social scientific and historical interests, with fuller Malayalam citations can be found in Freeman (1998, and forthcoming).

4 A thorough and scholarly study of religion in the Caṅkam period is wanting. A number of relevant sections in Hart (1975) and Hardy (1983) are helpful. In the characterization that follows, I rely on these, scattered characterizations through the literature on the Caṅkam traditions, and my own study of the texts.

5 The historical nature of polity in medieval Kerala, particularly around the putatively revived Cēra line of Mahōdayapuram, can only be sketchily reconstructed from a relatively poor inscriptional record and little by way of reliable archeology. While various degrees of formative centralization are argued for this period of the ninth to eleventh centuries, historians (Gurukkal 1992, Menon 1980, Narayanan 1996) all are agreed as to the subsequent fractionated patchwork of independent kingdoms in which all the extant literature we today call Malayalam was produced.

6 References to chapter (*vṛttam*) and verse numbers follow the edition of Kṛṣṇan Nāyar (1979).
7 For instance, one might compare the whole tenor of Dhavamony (1971) with that of Hudson (1989) and the more historically situated sense of south Indian "devotion" in Bayly (1989).
8 See Freeman (1998) for the importance of this text in terms of the history and ideology of language in Kerala of that time. For a descriptive analysis of the text's content and historical context, see Gopala Pillai (1985).
9 Cited from the *Śivarātrimāhātmyam*, vs. 149, in Ś. Kuññan Piḷḷa (1970: 256).
10 From the Uttarakāṇḍam of the *Kaṇṇaśśa Rāmāyaṇam*, cited in Warrior (1977: 106, n. 5).
11 From the *Śivrātrimāhātmyam*, vs. 134, cited in Ś. Kuññan Piḷḷa (1979: 104).
12 For an example of such a Kerala play and its staging with an overview of the tradition, see Jones (1984). A more comprehensive treatment of the tradition of Sanskrit plays in Kerala is in Richmond (forthcoming).
13 Lines 5131–2 in Hariśarma (1980 [1969]: 498).
14 These works are Rājarājavarma (1968), Nīlakaṇṭhakavi (1990), and Rāmacandra Piḷḷa (1987).
15 My reading of Kuñcan Nambyār's work is deeply indebted to the fine historical and discursive analysis by K. N. Gaṇēś (1996).

References

Achyuta Menon, C. 1940. *Eluttacchan and His Age*. Madras: University of Madras.

Ayyar, L. V. R. 1983 [1936]. *The Evolution of Malayalam Morphology*. Thrissur: Kerala Sahitya Akademi.

Bayly, S. 1989. *Saints, Goddesses, and Kings: Muslims and Christians in South Indian Society, 1700–1900*. Cambridge South Asian Studies 43. Cambridge, New York: Cambridge University Press.

Chaitanya, K. 1971. *A History of Malayalam Literature*. New Delhi: Orient Longman.

Cutler, N. 1987. *Songs of Experience: The Poetics of Tamil Devotion*. Bloomington: Indiana University Press.

Dhavamony, M. 1971. *Love of God According to Śaiva Siddhānta: A Study in the Mysticism and Theology of Śaivism*. Oxford: Clarendon Press.

Freeman, R. 1998. "Rubies and Coral: The Lapidary Crafting of Language in Kerala," *Journal of Asian Studies* 57: 38–65.

——. forthcoming. "Genre and Society: The Literary Culture of Pre-Modern Kerala," in S. Pollock, ed., *Literary Cultures in History: Reconstructions from South Asia*. Berkeley: University of California Press.

Gaṇēś, K. N. 1996. *Kuñcan Nambyār: Vākkum Samūhavum*. Śukapuram: Vaḷḷattōḷ Vidyāpīṭham.

George, K. M. 1956. *Rāmacaritam and the Study of Early Malayalam*. Kottayam, Kerala: National Book Stall.

——. 1968. *A History of Malayalam Literature*. New York: Asia Publishing House.

Gopala Pillai, A. R. 1985. *Linguistic Interpretation of Liilatilakam*. Trivandrum: Dravidian Linguistics Association.

Gōpikkuṭṭan. 1989. *Pūntānam Jñānappāna*. Kottayam, Kerala: National Book Stall.

——, ed. 1996. *Kōkasandēśam: Paṭhanavum Vyākhyānavum*. Kottayam, Kerala: Current Books.

Gurukkal, R. 1992. *The Kerala Temple and the Early Medieval Agrarian System*. Sukapuram, Kerala: Vallathol Vidyapeetham.

Hardy, F. 1983. *Viraha-bhakti: The Early History of Kṛṣṇa Devotion in South India*. Delhi: Oxford.

Hariśarma, A. D., ed. 1980 [1969]. *Adhyātma Rāmāyaṇam*. Kottayam, Kerala: Sahitya Pravarthaka Cooperative.

Hart, G. 1975. *The Poems of Ancient Tamil: Their Milieu and their Sanskrit Counterparts*. Berkeley: University of California Press.

Hart, G. L. and H. Heifetz. 1999. *The Four Hundred Songs of War and Wisdom: An Anthology of Poems from Classical Tamil: The Puṟanāṉūṟu*. New York: Columbia University Press.

Hudson, D. 1989 "Violent and Fanatical Devotion among the Nāyanārs: A Study in the Periya Purāṇam of Cēkkiḻār," in A. Hiltebeitel, ed., *Criminal Gods and Demon Devotees: Essays on the Guardians of Popular Hinduism*. Albany: State University of New York Press.

Jones, C. R., ed. 1984. *The Wondrous Crest-Jewel in Performance: Text and Translation of the Āścaryacūḍāmaṇi of Śaktibhadra with the Production Manual from the Tradition of Kūṭiyāṭṭam Sanskrit Drama*. Delhi: Oxford University Press.

Kṛṣṇan Nāyar, P. V., ed. 1979. *Rāmacaritam*. Trichur, Kerala: Kerala Sahitya Akademi.

Kuññan Piḷḷa, I., ed. 1985 [1954]. *Uṇṇunīlisandēśam*. Kottayam, Kerala: Sahitya Pravarthaka Cooperative.

Kuññan Piḷḷa, Ś. 1979. *Kairaḷisamakṣam athavā Agrapūja*. Trivandrum: K. Bhaskaran Nair.

——, ed. 1970. *Malayalam Lexicon*, vol. II. Trivandrum: Government Press.

Maṇṇummūṭu, C. J., ed. 1993. *Kaṇṇaśśa Rāmāyaṇam: Bālakāṇḍam*. Maṇarkāṭu, Kōṭṭayam: C. J. M. Publications.

Marr, J. R. 1985. *The Eight Anthologies: A Study in Early Tamil Literature*. Tiruvaumiyur, Madras: Institute of Asian Studies.

Menon, A. S. 1980. *A Survey of Kerala History*. Kottayam: National Book Stall.

Nair, P. K. P. 1967. *History of Malayalam Literature*, trans. E. M. J. Venniyoor. New Delhi: Sahitya Akademi.

Narayanan, M. G. S. 1996. *Perumals of Kerala: Political and Social Conditions of Kerala Under the Cēra Perumals of Makotai (c. 800–1124 A.D.)*. Calicut: Author.

Narayanan, V. 1994. *The Vernacular Veda: Revelation, Recitation, and Ritual*. Columbia, SC: University of South Carolina Press.

Nārāyaṇapiḷḷa, P. K., ed. 1967. *Cintāratnam: Vēdāntadarśanam*. Kottayam: National Book Stall.

Nīlakaṇṭhakavi, Ś. 1990. *Teṅkailanāthōdayam [Prabandham]*. Trichur, Kerala: Kerala Sahitya Akademi.

Peterson, I. 1991. *Poems to Śiva: The Hymns of the Tamil Saints*. Delhi: Motilal Banarsidass.

Pollock, S. 1998. "The Cosmopolitan Vernacular," *Journal of Asian Studies* 57: 6–37.

——, ed. forthcoming. *Literary Cultures in History: Reconstructions from South Asia*. Berkeley: University of California Press.

Puruṣōttaman Nāyar, M. M., ed. 1981. *Tiruniḻal Māla (Prācīna Bhāṣākāvyam)*. Kottayam, Kerala: Current Books.

Rājarājavarma, V., ed. 1968. *Cellūrnāthōdayam (Bhāṣācampu). Śri Rāmavarma Granthāvali*. Trichur: Kerala Sahitya Akademi.

Rāmacandra Piḷḷa, T. J., ed. 1987. *Nārāyaṇīyam Bhāṣācampu*. Trivandrum, Kerala: State Institute of Languages.

Rāmacandran Nāyar, K., ed. 1969. *Vaiśikatantram*. Trivandrum, Kerala: Author.
Ramanujan, A. K. 1967. *The Interior Landscape: Love Poems from a Classical Tamil Anthology*. Bloomington: Indiana University Press.
Ratnamma, K., ed. 1986. *Anantapuravarṇṇanam (Prācīna Kāvyam)*. Kottayam, Kerala: Current Books.
Richmond, F. forthcoming. *Kūṭiyāṭṭam: Sanskrit Theater of India*. Ann Arbor: University of Michigan Press.
Sambasiva Sastri, K., ed. 1972 [1930]. *Kauṭalīyam: Bhāṣāvyākhyānasahitam*. Trivandrum, Kerala: University of Kerala.
Śarmmā, V. S. 1982. *Thullal: An Audio-visual Art Form of Kerala*. Madras: Distribution Higginbothams.
Sekhar, A. C. 1953. *Evolution of Malayalam*. Poona, India: Deccan College Postgraduate and Research Institute.
Trautmann, T. R. 1981, *Dravidian Kinship*. Cambridge [UK]; New York: Cambridge University Press.
Veṅkiṭṭarāma Śarmmā, V., ed. 1967. *Bhāṣārāmāyaṇa Campu*, 1982 ed. Trichur, Kerala: Kerala Sahitya Akademi.
Warrior, N. V. K. 1977. *A History of Malayalam Metre*. Trivandrum: Dravidian Linguistics Association.
Yocum, G. E. 1982. *Hymns to the Dancing Śiva: A Study of Māṇikkavācakar's Tiruvācakam*. New Delhi: Heritage Publishers.
Zarrilli, P. B. 2000. *Kathakali Dance-drama: Where Gods and Demons Come to Play*. London, New York: Routledge.
Zvelebil, K. 1973. *The Smile of Murugan: On Tamil Literature of South India*. Leiden: E. J. Brill.

CHAPTER 9

North Indian Hindi Devotional Literature

Nancy M. Martin

How to trade in rubies and diamonds,
  My blessed guru has shown me the way.
Rubies lie scattered in the square –
  Worldly people walk over them.

The unknowing cannot discern;
  they leave them and walk away.
But those who understand pick them up –
  My beloved has shown me the way.

The fly sits in the honey
  Bound up in its sticky wings.
So hard to fly away, O Compassionate One,
  From the terrible habit of always wanting more.

In this direction a blind man comes;
  In the other a blind man is going.
Blind man meets blind man –
  Who can show the way?

Everyone is crying, "Ruby, Ruby";
  They all put forward a cloth to receive.
But none unties the knot to see what lies within
  And so they are bereft of all.

Everyone is crying, "Ruby, Ruby";
  But no one has tried to see.
Servant Kabīr has looked,
  and climbed up beyond birth and death.

Though the Hindu saint to whom this song is attributed, Kabīr, was a fifteenth-century resident of Banaras from a Muslim weaver caste, known for his caustic critique of both Hindu and Muslim religious leaders and his advocacy of worshipping God as beyond form and distinction. I recorded this song in 1997 in western Rajasthan. A member of a very low caste of weavers and leather-workers himself, the singer regularly performs this song together with the songs of many other Hindu devotional saints at all-night devotional sessions called *jagarans* – the primary form of religious gathering in rural North India. And such songs, attributed to great devotees of the past, are the central form of devotional literature in North India in the vernacular languages associated with Hindi.

The devotional movements that begin in the Tamil-speaking region of South India in the sixth to the ninth centuries of the Common Era sweep through the Kannada-speaking region in the tenth to the twelfth centuries and up into Marathi-speaking region in the thirteenth and fourteenth centuries and then across the north of India by the fifteenth and sixteenth centuries to generate a vast body of literature of both story and song. Regional dialects were taking shape during this linguistically formative period in the north within a body of vernacular language – the spoken language of everyday interaction in contrast to Sanskrit. Called Hindui or Hindi by Muslims settling in the Delhi region, scholars refer to these emerging regional languages as new Indo-Aryan (McGregor 1992: 3–9). Fluid in their boundaries, they overlapped sufficiently so that songs and stories could travel from devotee to devotee and through the performances of itinerant singers from region to region.

The vernacular traditions of narrative and song in North India belong first and foremost to the devotional or *bhakti* strand of Hinduism, and the sainthood of the songs' composers is conferred not by some religious authority or after rigorous official inquiry but rather through the embrace of subsequent generations of devotees, who have recorded, performed and expanded the traditions that surround them. The saints' exemplary lives and their songs (as well as many more subsequently composed in their names and styles) guide others on the *bhakti* path and ideally cultivate and elicit the expressed all-encompassing love for God in those who hear and perform them. The most famous are the weaver Kabīr with his biting critique, the royal renouncer Mīrābaī, the lover of Kṛṣṇa Sūrdās, the founder of the Sikhs Nānak, Nāmdev of the Vārkarī tradition, the leather worker Raidās, the Rajasthani devotee of the Lord Beyond Form Dādū, and Tulsīdās, the poet of Rāma. But there are literally hundreds more.

North Indian devotional literature is situated within a stream of religious reform. Broadly referred to as the *bhakti* movement, it is in fact a series of movements though *bhakti* or devotion is the defining feature of them all. *Bhaj* – the root of the word *bhakti* – carries multiple meanings, including to apportion, to share, to bestow, to enjoy, to possess, to experience, to practice, to cultivate, to choose, to serve, to honor, to adore, and to love (Ramanujan 1993: 103–4 n. 2). Though translated as "devotion," *bhakti* implies a complex and multi-dimensional relationship between human and divine, including adoration but also partaking of every form of love possible between human beings, from parental love to that of lovers. This love is mediated through the body, experienced through the senses, with devotees employing metaphors of sight, sound, taste, smell, and touch. They even speak sometimes as if they were God, losing all awareness of themselves as separate, in an experience akin to possession by the divine beloved. This passionate and intoxicating love may be spontaneous, seeming to take the devotee by storm, but it is also cultivated through ritual and song (Ramanujan 1993: 103–69; Martin 1999a).

The religious movements that were marked by such love left behind ritual action carried out by priests to focus on personal relationships between individuals and God, with more mature devotees, saints of the past, and even God understood to serve as gurus to those who would deepen this relation. Some movements were radically iconoclastic while others were closely connected to local temples and manifestations of the divine, mapping out mythic events on the regional landscape. In all of them religious expression shifted away from the elite language of Sanskrit to the intimacy of local vernacular languages.

Leadership within the community was based on religious experience rather than heredity (at least in the early stages of the movements), and these leaders composed songs of love, complaint, and praise to their chosen forms of God. Among their number were untouchables and women as well as *brahmans*. All people were recognized as equal in the eyes of God and across rebirths, and communities worshipped and ate together, defying caste rules of purity, although actual social experiments of egalitarian living on a larger scale were admittedly few. The most significant attempt occurred among the Vīraśaivas in the twelfth century in the Kannada-speaking region (present day Karnataka) where a community more than one hundred and ninety thousand strong sought to live without caste distinction, though the wider society did not tolerate this for long (Ramanujan 1973: 62–4). Low-caste saints sometimes had to defend their right to worship and prove their worthiness before God in trials engineered by *brahman* priests outside the movements who felt their own religious authority was being threatened, and women saints faced similar trials before male religious leaders even within the *bhakti* fold, according to the hagiographic accounts.

Institutional structures took shape with time, and hierarchies re-entered. Sects that initially refuted caste became like castes themselves, as their members married only other members and passed religion down as a family heritage rather than an individual choice. Formal liturgies including the songs of particular saints solidified, and elaborate rituals of devotion developed. Lineages of leadership also took hold, sometimes hereditary, sometimes based on a guru's choosing of a successor.

Viṣṇu and Śiva emerged as the primary focus of such devotion, with this same type of organized devotion to the supreme Goddess or Devī developing somewhat later. After the Tamil Āḷvārs, Viṣṇu himself was largely supplanted in direct worship by his *avatārs* – the amorous Kṛṣṇa (who takes birth in Vṛndāvan among the cowherding people of Braj as detailed in Sanskrit in the *Bhāgavata Purāṇa* and who is also the charioteer of Arjuna in the famous dialogue of the *Bhagavad Gītā*) and Rāma (the upholder of the social and religious order and the hero of the epic *Rāmāyaṇa* who must rescue his wife Sītā from the demon king Rāvaṇa). Still others speak of God as beyond form of any kind under the name of Rām, the Formless One, the Imperceptible, and reject images, myths, and the rituals of temple devotion. In many cases the saints sing of both God with form (*saguṇ*) and without or beyond form (*nirguṇ*) and juxtapose the two in a single song that may consider how the Lord who is the reality behind all that is could come to play among his devotees as the child Kṛṣṇa does or could be encountered through a temple image. Nevertheless, movements and saints are often characterized as either practicing *nirguṇ* or *saguṇ* devotion in an oppositional way (Hawley 1995a). Those who worship the *nirguṇ* Lord have been called *sants*, a term which means "one who knows the truth . . . [or] who has experienced Ultimate Reality" (Schomer and McLeod 1987: 2–3). The meaning of the term, however, has been generalized to mean "a good person" or a saint, and thus *sant* is often also used to refer to any member of the larger devotional community, whether his or her orientation is *saguṇ* or *nirguṇ*.

These movements did not develop in a vacuum but built on previous traditions and were in competition with other existing ones. The Nāth tradition was a strong formative influence and continues to be a part of the religious milieu of India (Briggs 1938; Gold 1992: 35–53). Nāth *jogis* looked back to Śiva as the quintessential *jogi* ascetic and practiced *hatha yoga* with the aim of controlling the physical body in an integration of physical and spiritual attainment. Iconoclasm, a radically *nirguṇ* conception of Ultimate Reality, and a defiance of caste are hallmarks of this tradition, and Nāth *jogis* are known for their miraculous powers as well, with Goraknāth being the greatest guru of the sect and an array of songs and stories attached to him and subsequent gurus.

Tantric streams from Hindu and Buddhist sources flowed into the formation of *bhakti* through the Nāths and other sources. The fundamental practices of tantra involve working through the body to unify opposites and overcome all duality; elaborate rituals, diagrams, *mantras*, and visualizations are among the techniques employed (Hess and Shukdev Singh 1983: 139–40). Other strains of Buddhism also had their impact, and particularly in the south, *bhakti* saints saw both Buddhists and Jains as their competitors, and their stories and songs reflect their confrontations.

Muslim traditions were strong in the medieval milieu in which *bhakti* grew as well, Sufis in a very open way and Isma'ilis in more disguised forms (Vaudeville 1974; Khan 1997). The lines between the traditions were fluid with many Muslims devoted to Hindu saints and many Sufi *pīrs* having Hindu followers as well. Low castes converted *en masse* to Islam in order to move out of the hierarchy of caste but often without leaving behind all of their previous Hindu practices and traditions, even as Kabīr's caste may have. Both the Sufis and the *bhakti* saints taught a path of overwhelming love for God, and many of their practices were similar.

Bhakti philosophy and theology developed in opposition to Hindu *advaita* philosophers who argued that Ultimate Reality was an impersonal Oneness to be realized rather than a supreme God to be loved. The *bhaktas* articulated a desire to experience God rather than to become God, whether their orientation was *nirguṇ* or *saguṇ*. Into this fecund mix of religious influences must be added local traditions of worship and manifestations of the divine that played key roles in the development of various regional sects.

Particular movements emerged in different regions at different times, each with its own set of saints, although later movements often included the saints of earlier ones within their clan and all continue to this day. In the Tamil-speaking region the sixth to the ninth centuries were the heyday of the Āḻvārs (those "immersed in God") who were dedicated to Viṣṇu and of the Nāyaṉās whose loving service was directed to Śiva (Ramanujan 1993; Peterson 1989). The songs of both the Āḻvārs and the Nāyaṉās are deeply connected to the Tamil countryside, addressing individually the particular manifestations of Viṣṇu and Śiva in each of its many temples. In the Kannada speaking region in the tenth to twelfth century the Vīraśaiva saints thrived. Theirs was a radically egalitarian tradition, rejecting all manner of outward religious display which might be facilitated by wealth. The body was seen as the most important temple, and Śiva was enshrined within. Devotees wandered as mendicants teaching this way to God. Gender and caste were directly addressed in their songs as only the passing accidents of birth and irrelevant to spiritual attainment (Ramanujan 1973).

North Indian devotional traditions may be said to begin in the Marathi-speaking region (modern day Maharashtra) in the thirteenth century with Jñāneśvar and his saintly brothers Nivṛttināth and Sopan and sister Muktabāī, outcast from society because their father had been a renouncer returned to the householder life. Jñāneśvar's *Jñāneśvari* is recognized as a masterpiece of devotional literature, and together they are seen as the originators of a devotional movement that would be called the Vārkarīs (Ranade 1933). The saint Nāmdev's life overlapped theirs and extended into the mid-fourteenth century, and he sang of the efficacy of reciting the name of God, of singing songs of praise, and of spending one's time in the company of other devotees, all practices affirmed across the spectrum of *bhakti* movements (Callewaert and Lath 1989). He stressed the attitude of the heart over outward acts of worship and addressed his songs sometimes to the incarnate Lord Kṛṣṇa, other times to the One who is beyond human imaginings. Both Nāth traditions and the Mahanubhava sect influenced the development of this sect, and earlier layers of Śaiva tradition were combined with Vaiṣṇava devotion (Vaudeville 1987). Worship focuses on the regional deity Viṭṭhal, recognized as a form of Kṛṣṇa, who first became manifest at Pandharpur (now an essential pilgrimage destination for members of the sect) and whose longing for his devotees is likened to that of a cow separated from her calf. The *brahman* Eknāth added much to the literature of the Vārkarīs in the sixteenth century, including a Marathi translation and commentary on the stories of Kṛṣṇa's life, and the seventeenth-century *śūdra* saint Tukārām sang in coarse and beautiful language of the nature of human existence, the mysteries of God, and the struggles of the devotional path (Chitre 1991).

Poet saints emerged across north India from the fourteenth century onward. Rāmānand is said to be a disciple of the famous *bhakti* philosopher theologian of South India, Rāmānuja, and the guru of a number of renowned low-caste saints, though conflicting accounts are given of his life and religious practices (Burghart 1978). The Rāmānandi tradition or *sampradāy* traces its origins to his teachings, and among his supposed disciples are Kabīr the weaver, Raidās the leatherworker, Sen the barber, and Dhana the butcher.

Kabīr was a fifteenth-century resident of Banaras and member of the *julaha* caste and is the most well-known, particularly for his caustic critiques of all hypocrisy and social and religious hierarchy. He spares no one – both Hindu and Muslim religious leaders and the rulers of the land receive no mercy, and he preaches a path of realization of the One who is beyond all distinctions and limited human categories – the *nirguṇ* Lord. He cries out:

Brother, were did your two gods come from?
Tell me, who made you mad?
Rām, Allah, Keshav, Karim, Hari, Hazrat –
So many names.
So many ornaments, all one gold,
It has no double nature.
(Hess and Shukdev Singh 1983, 50–1)

Again and again he hammers home the point that we must face death and our own mortality if we are going to truly live:

Make your own decision.
See for yourself while you live.
Find your own place.
Dead, what house will you have?
(Hess and Shukdev Singh 1983: 68)

Instead of doing so, we are tied to our senses like an ox to an oil press going round and round on the wheel of life, and we live under delusion, like a dog seeing its own reflection and barking itself to death. And to those who think themselves more pure than others, he reminds us that all bodies are of the same clay and the water we drink, whatever its source, has been the bathing place of humans and animals and passed through corpses and filth on its way to us. And milk?

Trickling through bones, melting through flesh –
Where does milk come from?
That's what you drink after lunch, pandit.
And you call clay untouchable?
(Hess and Shukdev Singh 1983: 57–8)

Who then can claim to be more pure?

Kabīr's message is strident and his language often coarse, and he is above all a preacher, denouncing all outward forms of religious practice as salvific in themselves and calling his hearers into relationship with the One God (Hess and Shukdev Singh 1983: 7–37). Yet the truth is not easily grasped – we must come to hear the unstruck sound and to know its untellable story. Kabīr had both Muslim and Hindu followers, and it is said that at his death they fought over how to carry out his funeral rites. But when they pulled the cover away, they found only flowers where his body had been. These they then divided, the Muslims burying their half and the Hindus burning theirs.

Early records of Kabīr's songs are found in three distinct sources (Hess 1987). The *Bijak* contains only his works (Hess and Shukdev Singh 1983), but his songs are also found in the *Ādi Granth* of the Sikhs and the manuscript collections of the Dādūpanth, another *nirguṇ* "path" or sect founded by Dādū, a cotton-carder (possibly Muslim) living in Rajasthan in the latter half of the sixteenth century who followed in the footsteps of Kabīr (Orr 1947; Callewaert 1988). Among the most important of the latter are the thematic collections of the *Sarvāṅgis* of Rajab and of Gopaldās and the *Pañc-Vāni* collections recording songs of five saints: Dādū, Kabīr, Nāmdev, Raidās, and Hardās (Callewaert 1988; Callewaert and Beeck, 1991; Callewaert 2000a). Both the *Ādi Granth* and these seventeenth-century Rajasthani Dādūpanthi manuscripts provide a gold mine of early songs, especially for *nirguṇ* saints. A sect, the Kabīrpanth, has also been established in Kabīr's name by those who share his low-caste status and for whose adherents Kabīr has reached almost divine status (Lorenzen 1987). A vast oral tradition of song exists as well, performed across North India today, which includes songs of Kabīr together with the songs of many, many other saints (Martin 2000).

Raidās, another of the supposed disciples of Rāmānanda from Banaras, is alternately said to be a pure *nirguṇ* devotee or to blend *nirguṇ* devotion with a *saguṇ* love of Rām (Callewaert and Friedlander 1992). A *camar* (an untouchable leatherworker whose caste-fellows dispose of the bodies of dead animals), he speaks against the hierarchies of purity, approaching God with humility and utter dependence on divine grace and love, relying on the recitation of the name of God to keep his mind and heart focused on his Lord in a world that parades an endless stream of distractions (Hawley and Juergensmeyer 1988: 24–32). His songs too are included in the Sikh and Dādūpanthi collections, and a low-caste religious movement devoted to him and known as the Raidāsis can be found in Banaras (Schaller 1995). There are epic oral song traditions recounting episodes from his life as well, sung among leatherworker communities from Banaras to Rajasthan, which combine social protest with religious devotion, exposing the greed and corruption of rulers and *brahman* priests alike and affirming the dignity and legitimacy of Raidās and thus of other low-caste devotees.

In the lineage of *nirguṇ* Hindu devotion, we also find the founder of the Sikh tradition, Nānak, who lived in the late fifteenth and early sixteenth century in the Punjab region (McLeod 1968). Stories abound of his debates with Nāth *jogis* and his encounters with Hindu and Muslim spiritual teachers. He advocated a *nirguṇ* devotion that focused on the importance of the Lord as guru and on the practice of the repetition of the Name of God. Respected by both Hindus and Muslims, he laid out a path which transcends the particulars of both traditions, preaching adamantly against outward forms of worship including temples and mosques, religious scriptures, pilgrimage, and ritual. Even so the collection of his songs and those of other Sikh gurus was initiated by the fifth guru Arjan in a text that came to be known as the *Ādi Granth* and also included the songs of a number of other earlier saints referred to as *bhagats* (including Kabīr, Raidās, and Nāmdev). This text became the effective guru for the sect's members after their tenth and final human guru Govind Singh passed on, and because of its early date (1604 CE) and clear history, it is a primary source of early *bhakti* literature (Callewaert 2000a, McLeod 1989: 82–101).

Vaiṣṇava devotion and sects were also developing in these centuries. In Andhra Pradesh, Vallabhā was born to a Telegu *brahman* family in the late fifteenth century (Barz 1992). Considered an *avatār* of the mouth of Kṛṣṇa, he was to found the Puṣtimarg, the way of grace, also called the Vallabhā *sampradāy* or "tradition." Known as a great scholar, he traveled widely and bested *advaita* philosophers in debates from a young age, winning the title of *acarya*. His argument was straightforward – a true nondualist philosophy should not divide the world into an illusory phenomenal world and the One reality behind it; rather pure *advaita* (*śuddhādvaita*) would have to acknowledge that all is God – both manifest reality and the Oneness underlying it. The followers of Vallabhā worship Kṛṣṇa, particularly through an image that emerged from Govardhan hill in Vṛndāvan of his mountain-bearing form. The songs of eight poets, called the *aṣṭachap*, constitute the formal liturgy of the *sampradāy*.

The most well-known of the *aṣṭachap* poet-saints is Sūrdās, whose songs of Kṛṣṇa's childhood and adolescence among the cowherding community of Braj draw both singers and listeners inside of the emotional world of that divine drama with its multiple forms of love for the incarnate Lord (Bryant 1978; Hawley 1984). His collected works, the *Sur Sagar* (Sur's Ocean), number over 5,000 songs, and as is the case with all these great medieval poet saints, clearly not all these were composed by a single individual. Indeed the best we can do is to identify an early core of tradition attributed to him, as J. S. Hawley and Kenneth Bryant have done, based on reliable manuscripts. For the most part the manuscripts we have of the saints' songs appear initially to record the repertoires of singers, with all the variation that this might imply. And successive singers have expanded the traditions, the saints' names conferring authority and indicating a particular style of devotion and poetic expression more than actual authorship (Hawley 1988).

Sūrdās is said to have been blind but describes the emotional landscape of Kṛṣṇa's childhood and adolescence in intricate detail. Some of the songs attributed to him speak of the child Kṛṣṇa, articulating the love of parents for children (*vatsalya*) and juxtaposing the Lord of All and the small boy of his incarnation. Having seen him eating dirt as boys are want to do, his mother Yaśoda grows irritated and says:

> "Mohan, won't you spit out the mud?"
> . . . But he wouldn't obey;
> he played a clever trick:
> He opened his mouth,
> and he showed her,
> and the Play unfolded . . .
> (Bryant 1978, 174)

Seeing the divine drama of the cosmos unfold before her as she looks into what is not only the mouth of her son but also of God, she is completely overwhelmed, as the poet takes the hearer also from the ordinary world into sudden recognition of the divine. Other songs recount with wonder how the one who is the Lord of the three worlds is yet unable, in his child's body, to step across the threshold of the house without tripping, and others describe his delightful childish appearance and his mischievous behavior, his miraculous defeat of murderous demons and his propensity for stealing butter (Bryant 1978; Hawley 1983).

Still others speak of his adolescent love play with the young cowherding *gopī* women and particularly with his lover Rādhā – married to another yet unable to resist her Lord; of his irresistible flute playing and his amorous appearance and of the vicissitudes of love. Indeed, transforming the language and emotions of erotic love (*madhurya*) into devotion to God as other devotional saints before him had done, Sūrdās speaks as one of the *gopīs*, describing Kṛṣṇa's (Hari's) appearance to a companion:

> Look, my friend, look at Hari's nimble eyes.
> How could the shimmer of lotuses and fishes,
> Even the darting wagtails,
> Compare in charm with this? . . .
> Look at that beauty: slender, mind-entrancing curls,
> How they ramble uncontrolled
> Over eyebrows just below . . .
> Hari is a mirroring, the image of all desire.
> (Hawley and Juergensmeyer 1988: 106)

Desire and the love of union inevitably yield the pain of separation (*viraha*) which serves as another theme within Sūrdās's songs, some addressing the longing in temporary separation and some set in the time after Kṛṣṇa has left Vṛndāvan and the land of Braj for Mathura, never to return. His companion Uddhāv comes to the *gopīs* to try to persuade them to take up yogic austerities in Kṛṣṇa's absence, but they show him clearly that they have already mastered fasting, sleepless and one-pointed meditation, and more through their undying love. Within the corpus of Sūrdās's songs are also songs of supplication and complaint (*vinaya*) apart from the narrative world of Kṛṣṇa's incarnation (Hawley 1984) in which the poet speaks directly in his own voice, lamenting:

> Life has stumbled, stumbled and unraveled,
> Roped to politics and salary and sons.
> Without my even noticing, my life has ambled off
> And gotten tangled in a snare of illusion so foolproof
> that now I cannot break it or loosen its grip . . .
> (Hawley and Juergensmeyer 1988: 115)

Much of the imagery of these songs and also of the practices of Kṛṣṇa devotion focus on the remembrance and reenactment of the stories of Kṛṣṇa's incarnation and on cultivating the emotions experienced by all the characters who love Kṛṣṇa in various ways within this divine drama – those who serve him, his parents, his companions, and his *gopī* lovers. The Sanskrit *Bhāgavata Purāṇa*, composed in the ninth or tenth century in South India, casts this narrative in a devotional light, particularly in book X which becomes the inspiration for much Vaiṣṇava literature in North India (Entwistle 1987: 22–42). More than a story, this drama becomes map and mirror for divine-human love, an eternal drama in which each devotee has a role. A tradition of religious dramatic performance also develops, with the texts of these plays forming another genre of devotional literature, spiced with humor, social critique, and romance and fully enacted in Vṛndāvan and elsewhere on a regular basis (Hawley 1981; Wulff 1984; Haberman 1988). In his songs Sūrdās invites the hearer inside this world and into the emotions of its characters, taking on multiple personas, as do other Vaiṣṇava poets.

Even as Vallabhācārya's disciples formed the Puṣtimarg in Vṛndāvan, in Bengal another Kṛṣṇa devotee, Caitanya, took birth. An ecstatic saint who often fell into trance and states of divine madness, he is said to have been an incarnation of both Rādhā and Kṛṣṇa. All the possible range of emotions associated with love wracked his body and heart, from the deepest despair at his divine beloved's absence to the supreme bliss of union. He popularized a form of worship involving singing and dancing, and the six Goswamis who were his disciples also went to Vṛndāvan in the early sixteenth century and founded the Gaudiya Vaiṣṇava sect: Rūp, Sanātan, Jiv, Gopal Bhatt, Raghunathdas, and Raghunath Bhatt. The saint Nimbarka had arrived there earlier and founded another *sampradāy* devoted to Kṛṣṇa and named after him, and Hit Harivams, a contemporary of Rūp and Sanātan, was the founding figure of a fourth, the Rādhāvallabh *sampradāy*, which glorified and deified Rādhā, as the songs of its founder clearly articulate (McGregor 1992: 88–9). The convergence of these groups on the site of Kṛṣṇa's legendary incarnation made this a major center of Vaiṣṇava literary production in the sixteenth century, and the language of this region, Braj Bhāṣa, predominated (Entwistle 1987: 136–73).

Sects continued to multiply as the followers of other extraordinary devotees formed new communities to continue their founder's particular teachings, among others the Ramsnehi *sampradāys* in eighteenth-century Rajasthan, advocating a blending of *nirguṇ* and *saguṇ* devotion in their praise of Rām. A tradition of Śaiva devotion had developed in Kashmir, and devotion to the Devī especially in her forms as Durga and Kālī grew, particularly in Bengal. Ramprasad Sen is perhaps the most well-known Bengali poet addressing Kālī (Nathan and Seely 1982), and Lalla the most famous Kashmiri Śaiva poet saint (Odin 1999). Yet there were other saints also in North India who seem to have been appreciated by many but to have stood outside of formal sectarian affiliation, their songs not a part of any official liturgy. Tulsīdās and Mīrābaī are two such saints.

Tulsīdās was an educated *brahman* from eastern India who settled in Banaras. Though he composed a large number of songs in praise to Rām and a small set also for Kṛṣṇa, he is most well-known for his telling of the story of Rām and Sītā entitled the *Ramcaritmanas* or "The Holy Lake of the Acts of Rām," composed in the vernacular language of Avadhi in the latter half of the sixteenth century. More than ten thousand lines in length, this devotional epic poem recounts the adventures of Rām, with an elaborate set of frame stories that allow the incorporation of additional mythic material and further theological reflection as Śiva tells the story to Pārvatī, the crow Bhusundi to Viṣṇu's vehicle Garuḍa, the Upaniṣadic sage Yajñavalkya to Bharadvaj, and Tulsīdās to his audience. Within his telling of the tale, Tulsīdās seeks to cultivate deep devotion to Rāma but also to reconcile and integrate Vaiṣṇava and Śaiva devotion, *nirguṇ* and *saguṇ* perspectives, and *advaita* and *bhakti* religiosity. Situated within a vast stream of both Sanskrit and vernacular literature surrounding Rāma, Tulsīdās is clearly influenced not only by Vālmikī's *Rāmāyaṇa* (though his Rāma is thoroughly divine unlike Vālmikī's great but very human hero) and the South Indian telling of the *Adhyātma Rāmāyaṇa* or "Spiritual Rāmāyaṇa" (incorporating *advaita* ideals with Rām seen as both an incarnation of Viṣṇu and the personification of Ultimate Reality or Brahman and portraying only a shadow of Sītā rather than Sītā herself being abducted by the demon Rāvaṇa) but also by the Kṛṣṇa tradition in his portrayal of Rām's childhood (Lutgendorf 1991; Richmond 1991).

Tulsīdās's *Ramcaritmanas* is extremely popular and the subject of regular recitation, both personal and public, and full-scale enactment as well as an expository tradition of *katha*. The Rāmlīlā carried out every year by the Maharāja of Banaras is the most elaborate, lasting a month with various specific locales on the eastern shore of the Ganges in Ramnagar identified with particular episodes, and all the characters played by carefully selected and prepared young *brahman* boys (Hess and Schechner 1977; Lutgendorf 1991). With this vernacular telling, Tulsīdās made the story of Rāma accessible to all, apparently upsetting some within the *brahman* community of his day in his seeming desecration of a sacred text. Stories attest to the *Ramcaritmanas'* full acceptance as sacred literature of the highest level, however, after the volume rose miraculously to the top of a stack of Sanskrit scriptures under which it had been placed and locked in a temple overnight (Lutgendorf 1991: 8–10).

Though brahmanic opposition may have occurred, Tulsīdās's telling also contains passages that affirm the existing social hierarchy at numerous points, some seemingly aimed at keeping women and *Śūdras* alike "in their place," and also recount some actions on the part of Rām, problematic for one who is said to be God, which generate a literature addressing the resulting doubts that arise (Lutgendorf 1991: 392–409). Tulsīdās is praised and the *Ramcaritmanas* embraced by people of multiple religious orientations, offering a point of meeting between members of divergent *sampradāys*, in line with the synthetic and inclusivist nature of the text.

A second saint who falls outside of the institutional structure of *panths* and *sampradāys* is Mīrābaī, said to have lived in the first half of the sixteenth century.[1] A daughter of a *rājput* royal family in Marwar (western Rajasthan), she was forced to marry into the family of the rulers of Mewar (southern Rajasthan) to cement a political alliance. But her love was only for Kṛṣṇa, and her marital family tried to kill her when she did not behave as a woman of her station should, singing and dancing in public temples and conversing with holy men and people from all castes. In her deeply personal songs she pours out her defiant love and intense longing for her Lord. Not a preacher in the style of Kabīr, she rejects caste and gender restrictions through her actions more than her words, and she need undergo no imaginative change of gender to identify with the *gopīs* as Sūrdās did, giving her words an unmatched emotional directness. Songs attributed to her share some of the imagery of Vṛndāvan but also speak her love in the first person. She draws, as do other poets, on the tropes of classical and folk love lyrics as well as the forms and themes of other folk and women songs, as she declares her love and renounces her royal life and marriage to take up the life of a wandering mendicant.

When she is said to have a guru at all, it is almost always Raidās the leatherworker, but more often she has none, and her behavior as a woman leads to an underlying ambivalence toward her just below the surface of an almost universal admiration. Clearly loved by people of many devotional sects, based on the number who tell her story and record and sing her songs, she is still not formally incorporated into any, perhaps because her challenge to gender norms is too radical, because she is too *saguṇ* in her devotion for the *nirguṇ sampradāys*, or because she acknowledges no authority before Kṛṣṇa, even a guru. We have no early manuscripts of her works, as we do of Kabīr, Raidās, and Sūrdās, and the traditions which surround her are unquestionably composite and stubbornly multiple.

In one song she speaks audaciously of having purchased her Lord whom she calls Govind, the Cowherd, in the market –

> Mother, I bought Govind!
> You say in secret;
> I took him openly,
>   playing a drum.

Some say she paid a high price, but she says no, having weighed him in the balance and given so little in exchange, though she paid with her life. She begs her Lord, the Dark One Syām, to come and dwell in her eyes – they have betrayed her by letting him into her heart, and now she cannot bear to be away from him. She claims to have married him in a dream, bound now irrevocably to him, and she laments his seeming absence, charging him with being a renouncer, a *jogi*, who having seduced her with sweet words now callously walks away. She vows to become a renouncer as well and to go in search of him. In one such famous song, she speaks of the annihilation of self in a union of merger, singing:

> I will build a funeral pyre of sandalwood and aloe;
>   light it by your own hand
> When I am burned away to cinders;
>   smear this ash upon your limbs.
>   . . . let flame be lost in flame.

And in still other songs she addresses the ruler of Mewar, the *rana* (usually identified as her earthly husband though sometimes said to be either her father-in-law or her brother-in-law in order to soften the degree of her rebelliousness). She rejects all that he has to offer her and voluntarily takes on the life of the poor. In successive verses and songs she rejects living in palaces, riding on elephants, eating sweet confections, wearing fine clothes and jewelry, to live in a hut, walk on foot, eat dry scraps of bread, and wear a rough shawl and the white of a widow or the saffron of a renouncer, ornamented only with a string of prayer beads. In a common refrain she sings:

> What can Mewar's ruler do to me?
> If God is angry, all is lost,
> But what can the Rana do?

And what can he do if she does not want anything he has to offer? When such songs are sung within low-caste communities, they provide a clear language of resistance against the values and privileges of the ruling class and upper castes as Mīrābaī stands in solidarity with the underprivileged (Martin 2000; Mukta 1994). Her compelling life story adds a deeper layer of meaning to this and many other songs attributed to her, and the story of her devotion, suffering and triumph is extremely popular, told in almost every conceivable narrative genre from films, comic books, and novels to folk dramas, epic songs, and more standard compendiums of the lives of saints.

Indeed we find the stories of the saints retold in a wide range of vernacular literary genres, with the stories of over 200 appearing first in the *Bhaktamal* or "Garland of Devotees" composed by Nābhadās (a member of the Rāmānandi sect living in Galta, Rajasthan) around 1600 CE (Callewaert and Snell 1994). Nābhadās catches the essence of each saint's life and character in a few short lines of verse and sets the standard for subsequent *bhaktamals* by Dhruvdās (early seventeenth century), Raghavdās (ca. 1713), and others. Commentaries attend each *bhaktamal*, offering fuller narratives, beginning with Priyadās's *Bhaktirasabodhini Tika* (1712) commentary on Nābhadās. The recitation of these texts remains an active part of devotional life, and though each of the composers belonged to a different branch of devotional Hinduism – Nābhadās was a Rāmānandi, Raghavdās a member of the Vaiṣṇava Rādhāvallabhā *sampradāy*, Dhruvdās a *nirguṇ* Dādūpanthi, and Priyadās a follower of Caitanya as well as of Nābhadās – they all honored a broad family of saints devoted to God both with and beyond form. Standard episodes structure the tales – tests the saints must endure imposed by secular and religious authorities, experiences of conversion for male saints, the overcoming of marriage for women saints, and more (Ramanujan 1982; Lorenzen 1995b).

The saints' lives are narrated in the Punjabi *Pothipremabodh* (1693) and the Marathi *Bhaktivijaya* (1762) of Mahipati, and their songs are threaded together with narrative, each composition contextualized in life events, in Nagridas' *Padaprasangmala* (early eighteeth century) (Callewaert 1994: 28–9; Abbott and Godbole 1988). Further, saints' lives are individually the subject of *parcais* by Anantadās, Jangopal, Sukhsaran and others which provide both introductions (*paricay*) and recount the miracles (*paraca*) that surround their lives (Callewaert 1994, 2000b; Lorenzen 1991, 1996). Sikh collections known *janma-sākhīs* or birth stories report anecdotes from the life of Nānak (McLeod 1968: 3–15), and accounts such as the *Caurasi Vaiṣṇavan ki Varta*, the *Accounts of the Eighty-four Vaiṣṇavas* (1620 CE) by Gokulnath, record episodes from the lives of saints of the Puṣṭimarg, thereby illustrating the practical implications of the teachings of Vallabhācārya (Barz 1994).

Further, episodes from the saints' lives appear in the songs of other saints and in some seemingly biographical songs, sometimes attributed to the saints themselves and other times clearly composed by later devotees. There is a sense in which the saints all belong to one devotional community, the *satsang* or "gathering of the true," that transcends time, and so we find stories of their meetings (however historically improbable) and records of extended debates or *gosti* between them (Lorenzen 1996: 153–203). Further, their lives provide the characters and plot for religious dramas called *līlās* performed along with the life of Kṛṣṇa and Rāma with increasing regularity and also for regional folk dramatic forms as well as staged dance performances and films beginning in the silent era.

Among low-caste singers we sometimes also find epic songs telling more extended tales of their lives on a par with the textual traditions but usually with a more humanly realistic and less refined portrayal, as in the *Janma Patri* of Mīrābaī. In this epic song sung by low-caste leatherworkers and weavers, the saint beats her servants as a woman of her high caste might when they bring the wedding garments for the marriage in which she wants no part, and she is cast out by her royal husband specifically because of her association with the *camar* Raidās though she begs him to let her live in a hut within the palace walls and weave his garments, taking on the identity of those who sing this song (Martin 1999b). Stories associated with Raidās and Kabīr also come to life in low-caste communities through the medium of song.

All these narrative genres and the particular songs sung in the saints' names vary dramatically depending on the social, regional, and religious location of both performer and audience, but the saints are well-loved and familiar characters within the world of North Indian devotees and provide the warp and woof with which to weave a wide array of tales and to speak multiple and sometimes divergent truths, emerging out of very different life experiences. The narratives surrounding their lives as well as the tales of Kṛṣṇa, Rāma and other deities, coupled with the full range of emotions and experiences that come with devotion to God, are the primary subjects of the devotional literature of North India, performed and sung as well as written, marked by overwhelming abundance and ongoing creative participation.

Note

1 A comprehensive discussion of the traditions of story and song related to Mīrābaī can be found in my book *Mīrābaī*, forthcoming with Oxford University Press.

References

Abbott, Justin E. and Godbole, N. R., trans. 1988. *Stories of Indian Saints: Translation of Mahipati's Marathi Bhaktavijaya.* Delhi: Motilal Banarsidass.

Barz, Richard. 1992. *The Bhakti Sect of Vallabhacarya.* Delhi: Munshiram Manoharlal.

——. 1994. "The *Caurasi Vaisnava ki Varta* and the Hagiography of the Pustimarg," in *According to Tradition: Hagiographical Writing in India*, eds. Winand M. Callewaert and Rupert Snell. Wiesbaden: Harrassowitz Verlag.

Briggs, George Weston. 1973[1938]. *Gorakhnath and the Kanphata Yogis.* Delhi: Motilal Banarsidass.

Bryant, Kenneth. 1978. *Poems to the Child-God: Structures and Strategies in the Poetry of Surdas.* Berkeley: University of California Press.

Burghart, Richard. 1978. "The Founding of the Ramanandis," *Ethnohistory* 25 (2): 121–39.

Callewaert, Winand M. 1988. *The Hindi Biography of Dadu Dayal.* Delhi: Motilal Banarsidass.

——. 1994. "*Bhagatmals* and *parcais* in Rajasthan," in *According to Tradition: Hagiographical Writing in India*, eds. W. M. Callewaert and Rupert Snell. Wiesbaden: Harrassowitz Verlag.

——. 2000a. "The Adi Granth of the Sikhs: A Canon," in *The Banyon Tree: Essays on Early Literature in New Indo-Aryan Languages*, ed. Mariola Offredi. New Delhi: Manohar, 457–68.

——. 2000b. *The Hagiographies of Anantadas: The Bhakti Poets of North India.* Richmond, Surrey: Curzon.

—— and Friedlander, Peter G. 1992. *The Life and Works of Raidas.* Delhi: Manohar.

—— and Lath, Macund. 1989. *The Hindi Padavali of Namdev.* Delhi: Motilal Banarsidass.

—— and Op de Beeck, Bart. 1991. *Devotional Hindi Literature: Nirgun Bhakti Sagar.* New Delhi: Manohar.

—— and Snell, Rupert, eds. 1994. *According to Tradition: Hagiographical Writing in India.* Wiesbaden: Harrassowitz Verlag.

Chitre, Dilip. 1991. *Says Tuka: Selected Poetry of Tukaram.* New Delhi: Penguin Books.

Entwistle, Alan W. 1987. *Braj: Center of Krishna Pilgrimage.* Groningen: Egbert Forsten.

Gold, Ann Grodzins. 1992. *A Carnival of Parting.* Berkeley: University of Calfornia Press.

Haberman, David. 1988. *Acting as a Way of Salvation: A Study of Raganuga Bhakti Sadhana.* New York: Oxford University Press.

Hawley, John Stratton. 1981. *At Play with Krishna: Pilgrimage Dramas from Brindavan.* Princeton: Princeton University Press.

——. 1983. *Krishna, The Butter Thief.* Princeton: Princeton University Press.

——. 1984. *Sur Das: Poet, Singer, Saint.* Seattle: University of Washington Press.

——. 1988. "Author and Authority in the Bhakti Poetry of North India," *Journal of Asian Studies* 47 (2): 269–90.

——. 1995a. "The Nirgun/Sagun Distinction in Early Manuscript Anthologies of Hindi Devotion," in *Bhakti Religion in North India: Community Identity and Political Action*, ed. David Lorenzen. Albany: State University of New York Press, 160–80.

——. 1995b. "The Saints Subdued: Domestic Virtue and National Integration in Amar Chitra Katha," in *Media and the Transformation of Religion in South Asia*, eds. Lawrence A. Babb and Susan S. Wadley. Philadelphia: University of Pennsylvania Press, 107–34.

—— and Juergensmeyer, Mark. 1988. *Songs of the Saints of India.* New York: Oxford University Press.

Hess, Linda. 1987. "Three Kabir Collections: A Comparative Study," in *The Sants: Studies in a Devotional Tradition of India*, eds. Karine Schomer and W. H. McLeod. Delhi: Berkeley Religious Studies Series and Motilal Banarsidass, 111–41.

—— and Schechner, Richard. 1977. "The Ramlila of Ramnagar," *The Drama Review* 21 (Sept.): 51–82.

——, with Shukdev Singh, trans. 1983. *The Bijak of Kabir.* San Francisco: Northpoint Press; Delhi: Motilal Banarsidass, 1986.

Khan, Dominique Sila. 1997. *Conversions and Shifting Identities: Ramdev Pir and the Ismailis of Rajasthan.* Delhi: Manohar and the Centre de Sciences Humaines.

Lorenzen, David N. 1987. "The Kabir-Panth and Social Protest," in *The Sants: Studies in a Devotional Tradition of India*, eds. Karine Schomer and W. H. McLeod. Delhi: Berkeley Religious Studies Series and Motilal Banarsidass, 281–303.

——. 1991. *Kabir Legends and Ananta-Das's* Kabir Paracai. Albany: State University of New York Press.

——, ed. 1995a. *Bhakti Religion in North India: Community Identity and Political Action.* Albany: State University of New York Press.

——. 1995b. "The Lives of Nirguni Saints," in *Bhakti Religion in North India: Community Identity and Political Action*, ed. D. L. Lorenzen. Albany: State University of New York Press, 181–211.

——. 1996. *Praises to a Formless God: Nirguni Texts from North India.* Albany: State University of New York Press.

Lutgendorf, Philip. 1991. *The Life of a Text: Performing the Ramcaritmanas of Tulsidas.* Berkeley: University of California Press.

Martin, Nancy M. 1999a. "Love and Longing in Devotional Hinduism," in *The Meaning of Life in the World Religions*, eds. Joseph Runzo and Nancy M. Martin. Oxford: Oneworld Publications (Penguin/Houghton Mifflin), 201–19.

——. 1999b. "*Mira Janma Patri* and Other Tales of Resistance and Appropriation," in *Religion, Ritual, and Royalty*, ed. Rajendra Joshi and N. K. Singhi. Jaipur: Rawat Press, 227–61.

——. 2000. "Kabir and Mirabai in Folk Traditions of Western Rajasthan: Meghwal and Manganiyar Repertoires," in *The Banyon Tree: Essays on Early Literature in New Indo-Aryan Languages*, ed. Mariola Offredi. New Delhi: Manohar, vol. 2, 391–418.

——. Forthcoming. *Mirabai.* New York: Oxford University Press.

McGregor, R. S. 1992. *Devotional Literature in South Asia.* Cambridge: Cambridge University Press.

McLeod, W. H. 1968. *Guru Nanak and the Sikh Religion.* Oxford: Claredon Press.

——. 1989. *The Sikhs: History, Religion, and Society.* New York: Columbia University Press.

Mukta, Parita. 1994. *Upholding the Common Life: The Community of Mirabai.* New Delhi: Oxford University Press.

Odin, Jaishree Kak. 1999. *To the Other Shore: Lalla's Life and Poetry.* Delhi: Vitastà.

Orr, W. G. 1947. *A Sixteenth Century Indian Mystic: Dadu and his Followers.* London: Lutterworth Press.

Nathan, Leonard and Seely, Clinton, trans. 1982. *Grace and Mercy in her Wild Hair: Selected Poems to the Mother Goddess* [by Ramprasad Sen]. Boulder: Great Eastern.

Peterson, Indira Viswanathan. 1989. *Poems to Siva: The Hymns of the Tamil Saints.* Princeton: Princeton University Press.

Ramanujan, A. K. 1973. *Speaking of Siva.* Delhi: Penguin.
——. 1982. "On Women Saints," in *The Divine Consort: Radha and the Goddesses of India,* eds. John Stratton Hawley and Donna Marie Wulff. Boston: Beacon Press, 316–24.
——. 1993: *Hymns for the Drowning: Poems for Visnu by Nammalvar.* Delhi: Penguin.
Ranade, R. D. 1983[1933]. *Mysticism in India: The Poet-Saints of Maharashtra.* Albany: State University of New York Press.
Richmond, Paula, ed. 1991. *Many* Ramayanas: *The Diversity of a Narrative Tradition in South Asia.* Berkeley: University of California Press.
Schaller, Joseph. 1995. "Sanskritization, Caste Uplift, and Social Dissidence in the Sant Ravidas Panth," in *Bhakti Religion in North India: Community Identity and Political Action,* ed. David Lorenzen. Albany: State University of New York Press, 94–119.
Schomer, Karine and McLeod, W. H., eds. 1987. *The Sants: Studies in a Devotional Tradition of India.* Delhi: Berkeley Religious Studies Series and Motilal Banarsidass.
Wulff, Donna M. 1984. *Drama as a Mode of Religious Realization.* AAR Academy Series 43. Chico: Scholars Press.
Vaudeville, Charlotte. 1974. *Kabir.* Oxford: Oxford University Press.
——. 1987. "The Shaiva-Vaishnava Synthesis in Maharashtrian Santism," in *The Sants: Studies in a Devotional Tradition of India,* eds. Karine Schomer and W. H. McLeod Delhi: Berkeley Religious Studies Series and Motilal Banarsidass, 215–28.

Major Historical Developments

CHAPTER 10

The Śaiva Traditions

Gavin Flood

Śaiva traditions are those whose focus is the deity Śiva and a Śaiva is a Hindu who follows the teachings of Śiva (*śivaśāsana*). These teachings are thought to have been revealed in sacred scriptures and propagated through the generations in traditions of ritual observance and theology. Many Śaivas have also worshipped the Goddess, Śiva's consort and power (*śakti*), as the esoteric heart of their religion, and it is often impossible to meaningfully distinguish between Śaiva and Śākta traditions. Every culture creates its own forms (Castoriadis 1997: 84) and in the following pages I shall discuss the forms that Śaiva traditions produced and hope to convey something of the Śaiva religious *imaginaire*. This *imaginaire* is distinctive within the Indic traditions and relates to wider cultural and political history, both insofar as it has corroborated and upheld the values and goals of mainstream orthodox society and in the ways it has challenged those norms. On the one hand the Śaiva imagination has been in line with the instituting power of particular regions, on the other it has brought to life a world that undermines that power through its promotion of a vision of the self that transcends social institutions and political stability. It is this ambiguity that shares many of the wider goals of collective life while eroding those goals through promoting a subjectivity external to them that is a characteristic of Śaiva traditions. It is in this truly creative dynamic in which Śaiva values are embedded in social institutions, such as caste and kingship, while simultaneously undermining those values, that the genius of the tradition resides. It is perhaps not a coincidence that this ambiguity is reflected in the ultimate imaginary signification of the tradition, Śiva himself, as the erotic ascetic (O'Flaherty 1981), as family man and vagabond, as form and formless, and as transcendence and immanence.

In this chapter I will focus on early Śaiva traditions, and although I will briefly discuss the fifteenth-century Kerala tradition, I will not venture much past the eleventh century. In effect, largely due to limitations of space I will not deal with developments of Śaivism during most of the last millennium, which includes the Nāth tradition, the traditions of later north India, the Siddha or Cittar tradition in Tamilnadu, nor the Śaiva Vedānta of the Śaṅkarācāryas and their monastic institution (*maṭhas*). I can only justify this exclusion on the grounds that the important doctrinal foundations and practices are established during the earlier period and the later traditions are rooted in these earlier forms. But it is to the indigenous understanding of what a Śaiva tradition is that we must turn first.

The Idea of a Śaiva Tradition

Recent scholarship has problematized the idea of "tradition," particularly in the West, arguing that traditions are not unchanging, historical trajectories, but are rather re-formed and adapted to changing political and social circumstances (Heelas 1996; Hobsbawn and Ranger 1983). The past is constructed to suit the identity needs of each generation. While of course it is true that in a south Asian context traditions change and are particularly challenged by modernity (Smith 2002), perhaps more stable social continuity has meant that until recently traditions have changed at a slower rate. There are certainly traditions of vedic practice that have survived historical contingency, such as the Nambudri vedic recitation, which go back possibly thousands of years (Staal 1963). Śaiva ritual practiced today was certainly extant in early medieval sources and worship of Śiva in some form occurs very early in the history of Hindu traditions. While this is too large a topic to enter into here, involving as it does the question of the relation of ritual to wider social and political history, there are clearly continuities of Śaiva practice that reach back into the past. Rather than looking at Śaiva traditions in terms of the western or western-derived categories of "Hinduism" and "religion," to understand the idea of a Śaiva tradition it is more illuminating to look at indigenous Śaiva classifications.

There is a tension between an externalist understanding that would analyze tradition in terms of history and the way a tradition is constructed in a particular historical circumstance and the indigenous, essentialist understanding of tradition as stemming from a timeless source. This is a large issue and the problem of externalist and internalist discourse is as relevant to Hindu traditions as to Christianity or Islam. While the indigenous view of tradition is clearly legitimate from the insider's perspective and important more generally, it is often challenged by historical, philological scholarship. Certainly living traditions can accept and absorb the findings of philological scholarship (as Christianity has done) and externalist accounts can function as corrective readings of tradition: text-historical accounts are not necessarily incompatible with religious accounts of revelation. This chapter is written from the perspective of externalist, historical-philological scholarship, but which nevertheless regards indigenous claims about tradition to be important and legitimate. At the very least the indigenous account of tradition shows how the transmission of knowledge was perceived in a particular social context. It is also not precisely clear what the relation is between Śaiva accounts of tradition, that is, the Śaiva self-descriptions, and the historical reality of which they are an index. It is therefore important and necessary – particularly in view of the lack of other sources – to begin with the Śaiva concept of tradition. It is largely, but not only, these indigenous self-descriptions that inform my account of the historical trajectory of the traditions, but this account is nevertheless from an external perspective, using the indigenous account to construct a coherent historical narrative.

The Śaiva understanding of tradition has been to see it in terms of a "stream" (*srotas*) or line of transmission of texts and practices, flowing through the generations from teacher to disciple. Another term used is Śaiva *āmnāya*, a Śaiva classification associating traditions of scripture with the four directions or a classification of five emanating from the five mouths of Śiva (Padoux 1994: 35–40; Brunner et al. 2000: 200; Dyczkowski 1988: 66–85). Such a tradition is transmitted through textual commentary and exegesis and through the lineage of teachers, the guru *santāna* or *santati*. Another term used in Śākta or Kula texts is *ovalli*, initiatory lineages (six in number) which are "currents of consciousness" (*jñānapravāha*) flowing from a transcendent source through the founder of the particular lineage (Brunner et al. 2000: 258). The source of such a stream or torrent of transmission in the case of the *āmnaya* is believed to be Śiva. From him the teachings are generally transmitted to the Goddess and from her through a series of divine and semi-divine intermediaries to the human world, for the kind of knowledge revealed through revelation is adapted to the abilities of beings to receive it (MVT 1.24). For example, the ninth- or tenth-century root text of the Kashmiri Śaiva tradition, the *Mālinīvijayottara Tantra* declares itself to be derived from the "mouth of the supreme Lord" (*parameśamukha*) (MVT 1.7), from where it is transmitted through a series of intermediaries, namely the Lord Pareśa to the Goddess (Devī), thence to her son Kumāra, who in turn transmits the teachings to Brahmā's four sons who transmit it to the human world (MVT 1.2–4, 14). The tenth-century Kashmiri theologian Abhinavagupta, likewise traces the guru lineage of the esoteric "family" (*kula*) tradition to the four mythical figures, the Lords Khagendra, Kūrma, Meṣa, and Macchanda, and thence to Śiva (TA 29.29–32; Dyczkowski 1988: 62, 68–9; Goudriaan and Gupta 1981: 5). Similarly, the sage Vasugupta, having received a system of teachings from numerous perfected male and female beings (*siddhas* and *yoginīs*) who made his heart pure, received teachings from Śiva who revealed in a dream that they were inscribed upon a stone on the Mahādeva mountain (namely the *Śiva Sūtras*) (SSV: p. 1). During this transmission process the teachings are believed to become condensed and accessible to the limited understanding of the receivers.

Other examples could be cited, but the point is that tradition in Śaivism is derived from a divine source and is understood in cosmological terms. Indeed, Śaivism could be said to be a cosmological religion in which tradition is not a human construction but is given through a process of transformation through levels of a hierarchical cosmos to the human world. It is the guru who is the embodiment of this tradition and who is the channel of divine grace (*anugraha*) to the community of disciples. The guru lineage or *santāna* is therefore an expression of Śiva's power (*śakti*) (SSV: p. 60) and the guru, at least in monistic Śaivism, is identified with Śiva as one who liberates beings through bestowing initiation (*dīkṣā*) and giving power to mantra (*mantravīrya*) (SN: pp. 52–3). Even in dualistic Śaivism, Śiva enters the guru for the purposes of initiation. The guru becomes the embodiment of tradition, reveals the supreme, liberating truth (*tattva*) to the disciple (SSV: p. 59) and reveals the structure of the hierarchical cosmos. The *Mālinīvijayottara Tantra* defines the guru in these terms:

> He who knows the meaning of the all the levels of the cosmos (*sarva-tattvāni*), is the guru equal to me (*matsamaḥ*) [i.e. Śiva] who has taught the illumination of the power of mantra (*mantravīryaprakāśaḥ*). Men who are touched, spoken to and seen by him with a delighted mind (*prītacetasā*) are released from sin (*pāpa*) even in seven lifetimes. (MVT 3.10–11)

Because of this emphasis on tradition as a stream flowing through the generations from a divine source into the guru, the distinctions between Śaiva and Śākta traditions become blurred. Some texts such as the *Yoginīhṛdaya*, which forms part of the root text of the Śrī Vidyā cult, are clearly Śākta in orientation. What has becomes known as "Kashmir" Śaivism, a nondualistic tradition developing from at least the ninth century, identifies Śiva with undifferentiated consciousness and also identifies this condition with a form of the Goddess Kālī called Kālasaṃkarṣinī (see below). The more esoteric the Śaiva traditions are, the more there is a tendency to focus upon the Goddess.

The implications of this for understanding not only Śaiva traditions but the wider field of Hinduism are great. Firstly, this understanding of tradition and the emphasis on the guru indicates strong decentralizing processes. While the texts of revelation are important, it is above all the revelation as the living tradition of the guru lineage that animates the tradition and through which the grace of Śiva is believed to flow. Here text becomes performance and the texts' teachings embodied in the human guru. Secondly this structure which places such great emphasis on the teacher–disciple relationship, allows for a kind of particularism or individualism which is yet impersonal, insofar as tradition is designed to transcend personality or limited sense of ego (*ahaṃkāra*). It is in this relationship that the transmission of tradition (and the grace of Śiva) occurs. The boundaries of the Śaiva and Śākta traditions are therefore sufficient to ensure transmission through the generations yet are also porous in allowing the influence of other, related traditions. This can be seen by Śaiva theologians quoting from a range of sources and borrowing from different traditions. Abhinavagupta, for example, was initiated into a number of Śaiva systems and the Kashmiri theologian Utpalācārya quotes with approval a text of the Vaiṣṇava Pāñcarātra tradition, the *Jayākhyasaṃhitā* (Span dīp: pp. 6–7). This is not to say, of course, that the Śaiva theologians regarded all revelation as equal; they did not. Rather each new revelation incorporated the earlier within it at a lower level and so, while a text of a different tradition might be quoted with approval, it is generally only regarded as a truth emanating from the level of the cosmos from which it derives. Later, esoteric teachings transcend the previous revelation.

While these traditions maintain a hierarchical structure in the classification of revelation, as we will see, we nevertheless have in the Śaiva understanding of tradition an example of the decentralizing strategies of what we call "Hinduism," which should make us skeptical of the usefulness of the category in a historical context. While Śaiva authors were keen to make totalizing claims about the universal truth of their teachings, the model of tradition shared by all Śaiva schools is inherently pluralistic in the idea of the guru lineage, while simultaneously being hierarchical in its assumption of a graded cosmos or ontology and a graded teaching. These initiatory lineages have been extremely important in the history of Śaivism and have mostly been associated with groups of texts called Tantra. But there has also been a more general temple Śaivism associated with Smārta brahmanism. As Sanderson has shown, the term Śaiva is technically restricted to an initiate into one of the Śaiva systems, while the term Maheśvara has been used for a brahmin worshipper of Śiva within the Smārta domain (Sanderson 1988b: 660–4). It is Sanderson's general mapping of these systems in the early medieval period that I follow here (Sanderson 1985; 1988; 1988) although a more complete mapping of the traditions by him, which will revolutionize our understanding of Śaivism and the history of Indian religions more generally, will have to wait (Sanderson, forthcoming). But before we trace this history a few remarks on the earliest indications of reverence for Śiva and the development of Śaiva traditions are necessary.

Early and Purānic Śaivism

Some scholars maintain that the worship of Śiva goes back many thousands of years in the subcontinent to the Indus valley civilization, where steatite seals have been found suggestive of a deity akin to Śiva. The famous "Paśupati" seal shows a seated, perhaps ithyphallic, horned figure surrounded by animals. Sir John Marshall has claimed that this is a prototype of Śiva as the yogin and Paśupati, the Lord of animals (Marshall 1931: 52). But is not clear from the seals that this is a proto-Śiva figure and Asko Parpola has convincingly suggested that the seal is in fact a seated bull, almost identical to figures of seated bulls found on early Elamite seals of ca. 3000–2750 BC (Parpola 1994: 248–50). It may be, of course, that elements of Śiva's later iconography – such as the crescent moon in his hair – can be traced to this period but unless the Indus Valley script is deciphered, these seals can only be suggestive. There are early textual references to Rudra, arguably a forerunner of Śiva, one of whose epithets is "auspicioius" (*śiva*), in the *Ṛg Veda*. Here three hymns are addressed to Rudra, the "roarer'. He is clothed in an animal skin, brown, with a black belly and a red back. Even at this time he is an ambiguous deity who is like a ferocious beast destroying families and livestock, but yet who is also a benevolent healer of disease (*Ṛg Veda* 2.33, 1.43; 1.114). A famous hymn in the *Ṛg Veda*, the hundred names of Rudra (*śatarudriya*), speaks further of this ambiguous nature, a hymn which is referred to in the *Śiva Purāṇa* and is still recited in Śiva temples today (Gonda 1979: 75–91).

But it is only with the *Śvetāśvatara Upaniṣad*, composed some time prior to the *Bhagavad Gītā*, that a theism focused upon Rudra-Śiva begins to emerge in the literature. This text is important in marking a link between the earlier monistic Upaniṣads and the later theistic traditions. Here Rudra is elevated from the feral deity on the edges of society to the status of the supreme being as the cause of the cosmos, the magician (*māyin*) who produces the world through his power (*śakti*), yet who transcends his creation. He is the Lord who, by his grace (*prasāda*), liberates the soul from its journey from body to body due to its actions. The seeds of Śaiva theology are here and indeed the terms "guru" and "*bhakti*" occur for the first time in the text (*Śvetāśvatara* 6.23), although more than likely this passage is a later interpolation. But certainly the seeds of devotion are implicit in the text's theism.

The formation of Śaiva traditions as we understand them begins to occur during the period from 200 BC to 100 AD. Apart from the *Śvetāśvatara*, we have references to a Śaiva devotee, a *Śiva-bhāgavata*, in the grammarian Patañjali's commentary on the Pāṇini grammar (Pāṇ. 5.2.76). He describes him as a figure clad in animal skins and carrying an iron lance as a symbol of his god, and there are references to early Śaiva ascetics in the *Mahābhārata* (Bhandarkar 1983: 165). There are also suggestions of Śiva worship on the coins of Greek, Śaka, and Parthian kings who ruled north India during this period, bearing a bull, a later symbol of Śiva. While little can be inferred from this, it is probable that adoption of Śaiva traditions of some form accompanied the general "Indianization" of the foreign, barbarian (*mleccha*) rulers (Vallee-Poussin 1936: 239–41).

During the Gupta dynasty (ca. 320–500 AD) the Purāṇas developed along with Smārta brahmin forms of worship (on this see Bühnemann 1988). The Śaiva Purāṇas, most notably the *Liṅga* and *Śiva Purāṇa*, contain standard material on genealogy, caste responsibilities, and cosmology, along with specifically Śaiva topics of installing the symbol (*liṅga*) of Śiva in temples, descriptions of the forms of Śiva and material on early Śaiva sects. The follower of the puranic religion, the Maheśvara referred to by Śaṅkara (*Brahmasūtrabhāṣa* 2.2.37), would at death, having led a life of devotion and responsible enactment of social duties, be transported to Śiva's heaven (*śiva-loka*) at the top of the world egg (*brahmāṇḍa*) and so be liberated. This is the Śaiva equivalent of the Vaiṣṇava heaven *vaikuṇṭha* where the puranic Vaiṣṇava would go at death. Fully orthoprax, the Maheśvara adhered to the Smārta observance of social duties, the *varṇāśrama-dharma*, performed vedic domestic rites and puranic *pūjā*, making vegetarian offerings to orthodox forms of Śiva and using vedic mantras. He followed the brahmanical path in an ordered universe in which his place in the cosmos at death was assured, as had been his social position in life (Sanderson forthcoming).

NON-PURANIC / ATIMĀRGA WANT MOKṢA — VEDIC → PĀŚUPATAS, LĀKULAS → KĀLĀMUKHAS
/ MANTRA MĀRGA WANT SIDDHIS — TANTRIC → DAKṢINA → ŚIVA SIDDHANTA (ORTHOPRAX) DUALIS
VAMA → TRIKA NON-DUALIST
KAULA, KRAMA
PURANIC — SMĀRTA / MAHEŚVARA

In contrast to the brahmin householder who followed the puranic, Smārta injunctions, a number of other Śaiva groups are listed in the Purāṇas which are on the edges of orthopraxy and are even condemned by some texts. These Śaiva sects are classified in quite complex ways in the Purāṇas and other medieval sources – there are references in Śaṅkara's and Rāmānuja's commentaries on the *Brahma Sūtra* and in Yāmuna among others – but four groups in particular emerge as important. These are the Pāśupata, Lākuliśa, Śaiva, and Kāpalika sects. There are variant names for some of these and they are also subdivided (Lorenzen 1991: 1–12; Dyczkowski 1988: 16–19). While the Purāṇas mention these sects and the later Purāṇas contain material which is derived from the nonvedic revelation of the Tantras, they are often hostile to the nonpuranic Śaiva traditions, partly in reaction to the tantric tradition's hostility towards the vedic; the *Kūrma Purāṇa* for instance condemns the Pāśupata system as heretical (*Kūrma Purāṇa* 1.14.30; 1.20.69; see Dyczkowski 1988: 10–11). A picture therefore emerges of a puranic Śaiva tradition, revering the Vedas, with orthoprax social attitudes, being confronted by renunicate Śaiva traditions, at first the Pāśupata sect who threatened puranic tradition, but later by more extreme groups. These alternative Śaiva sects ranged from ascetics who regarded themselves as being within the vedic fold, namely the Pāśupatas and Saiddhāntikas, to groups who consciously placed themselves outside of that sphere such as the Kāpālikas. It is to these nonpuranic groups that I wish to pay some attention, as it is these groups who have formed the majority Śaiva traditions and who are still extant in the subcontinent.

Non-Puranic Śaivism

Sanderson has shown that we can make a broad distinction between the Vedic, Puranic devotee of Śiva on the one hand and the nonpuranic Śaiva initiate on the other. These latter had undergone an initiation (*dīkṣā*) into the cults of their affiliation for the purpose of liberation in this life (*mukti*) and/or obtaining magical power to experience pleasure in higher worlds (*bhukti*). Within this group a distinction can be made between those Śaivas who follow the outer or higher path (*atimārga*) and those who follow the path of mantras (*mantramārga*). The followers of the *atimārga* sought only liberation, while the followers of the *mantramārga* sought not only liberation but power and pleasure in higher worlds (Sanderson 1988b: 664–90). Among the groups of the *atimārga* two are particularly important, the Pāśupatas and a sub-branch, the Lākula, from whom another important sect, the Kālāmukhas, developed.

The Pāśupatas are the oldest named Śaiva group, dating probably from around the second century AD. They are referred to in the *Mahābhārata* (*śantiparvan* 349.64), but the earliest surviving text of the group is the *Pāśupata Sūtra*, pre-tenth century, with a commentary by Kauṇḍinya. This text was regarded as revelation by the Pāśupatas. The myth behind it is that Śiva entered the corpse of a young brahmin that had been cast into a cremation ground and reanimated it as Lakulīśa, the "Lord of the staff," who then gave out the teachings contained in the text to his four disciples.

These teachings present the Pāśupata as an ascetic somewhat on the edges of orthoprax society, even though such an ascetic had to be a brahmin male who should not speak with low castes nor with women (Pāś Sū 1.13). But whereas an ordinary, vedic brahmin would pursue the social norms of adherence to duties regarding caste and stage of life (*varṇāśramadharma*), the Pāśupata had transcended these responsibilities to a higher or perfected (*siddha*) fifth stage beyond the vedic fourth stage of renunciation. To achieve this perfection the ascetic undertook a vow or observance (*vrata*) in three developmental stages. Firstly the Pāśupata should live within the environs of a Śaiva temple, bear the mark (*liṅga*) of a Pāśupata ascetic, namely the ashes in which he bathes thrice daily, and worship Śiva with song, dance, laughter and mantra repetition. Living on alms, the aspirant (*sādhaka*) undertakes the development of virtues such as not stealing, celibacy, and not harming creatures by straining water, and so on (Pāś Sū 1.2–11 and commentary). He thereby gradually purifies himself and enters the second stage of his practice in which he discards external signs of his observance, leaves the temple, and undertakes various forms of antisocial behavior. These include pretending to be asleep in public places, making his limbs tremble as though he were paralyzed, limping, acting as if mad, and making lewd gestures to young women (Pāś Sū 3.12–17). Such practices, the text claims, are doors to the acquisition of merit, for in behaving in this way the ascetic will attract verbal and physical abuse whereby his sin (*pāpa*) will be passed over to his abusers and their merit (*sukṛta*) passed over to him (Pāś Sū 3.8–9). In the third stage of the practice the sādhaka withdraws from the public eye to a deserted house or cave, lives off alms, and devotes himself to meditation upon the five sacred mantras of Śiva along with the syllable oṁ (Pāś Sū 5.21–4). Through this he unites his soul with Śiva and gains uninterrupted union for a period of six months (Pāś Sū 5.9–12). Finally the ascetic withdraws to become a resident in a cremation ground (*śmaśāna-vāsī*), where he lives on whatever is available (Pāś Sū 5.30–2), and dies reaching union with Śiva (*rudrasāyujya*) and the end of sorrow through his grace (Pāś Sū 5.33, 40).

There were more extreme forms of Pāśupata religion. The Lākula ascetic imitated the terrible form of his god Rudra, carrying a cranium begging bowl, a skull-topped staff, a garland of human bones, ash covered, with matted hair or shaved head (Sanderson 1988b: 665–6). This kind of Śaiva had taken the "great vow" (*mahāvrata*) or penance for killing a Brahmin in the Dharma Śāstras, namely living beyond the pale of vedic society and carrying the skull of his victim for 12 years (*Manu* 11.73). This practice is reinforced by a myth in which Śiva as the terrible Bhairava decapitates Brahmā's fifth head with his left-hand thumb, because Brahmā had attempted incest with his daughter. The skull sticks to Bhairava's hand and he wanders as the beggar Bhikṣāṭana until he reaches Banaras where the skull falls at Kapālamocana, a site of pilgrimage (*tīrtha*) (Eck 1984: 119). The Lākula sect gave rise to a further subsect, the Kālāmukhas, who were especially dominant in Karnataka during the eleventh to thirteenth centuries. Indeed they were an important group here, attracting donations and political patronage for Kālāmukha temples and monastic centers (*maṭhas*) (Lorenzen 1991: 97–140). The Kālāmukhas' in turn probably gave rise to the important Liṅgayat or Vīraśaiva tradition, still extant in Karṇāṭaka, famous for devotional poetry (Ramanujan 1973).

With these groups of the higher path we have the beginnings of a tendency away from orthodox forms of religion and adherence to the vedic social order. Although brahmins within the vedic order, the Pāśupatas believed their teachings to transcend that order. They went beyond the four stages on life's way (*āśrama*) into a fifth stage beyond the fourth vedic order, they also saw themselves as being within that order. Similarly, the Kālāmukhas in seemingly rejecting the vedic world, vividly symbolized by their great vow as a consequence of brahminicide, were yet at the center of the social order in Karṇāṭaka, supported by kings, with well-funded centers of practice and learning. The relationship between these groups and the established hierarchy is therefore complex and cannot be seen in terms of a simple rejection of vedic values by a heterodox or excluded community. The issue of the relation of these groups to the wider society and to vedic orthopraxy becomes even more sharply delineated with the traditions of the *mantramārga*, all of which revered a body of scripture distinct from the Veda, known as the Tantras.

The Tantras

The Tantras are a vast body of literature in Sanskrit, composed mostly between the eighth and eleventh centuries AD, claiming to have the status of revelation and claiming to supercede the Vedas. Some Tantras acknowledged the Vedas while others rejected them. The Tantras were composed in a number of traditions where they are sometimes known by the name of Āgama in the Śaiva Siddhānta and Saṃhitā in the Vaiṣṇava tantric tradition or Pāñcarātra. There are also a very few Jain Tantras, a vast body of Buddhist Tantras, mostly preserved in Tibetan and Chinese translations, and Tantras to the Sun, none of which have survived (Sanderson 1988b: 660–1). As the Buddhist Tantras were translated into Tibetan, so some of the Śaiva Tantras were translated into Tamil and are used as the basis for temple rituals in south India to this day. All of the Śaiva traditions of the *mantramārga* accept the Tantras, or rather different groups of Tantras, as their textual basis, although some Śaiva traditions have been more closely aligned to orthoprax, brahminical practice than others.

While there are specific traditions and the language of the Tantras is often obscure, partly because these texts would have been accompanied by a living, oral tradition, and partly because they regarded themselves as secret and heavily symbolic, they nevertheless share common features. They are concerned with practice (*sādhana*) involving ritual and yoga undertaken after initiation (*dīkṣā*) by a guru, but also contain sections on temple building, architecture, and occasional rites such as funerals. Indeed, each Tantra of the Śaiva Siddhānta theoretically rests on the four "feet" (*pāda*) of doctrine (the *vidyā* or *jñāna pādas*), yoga, ritual (*kriyā-pāda*), and behavior (*cārya-pāda*), although most texts do not follow this rather artificial scheme. The majority of the tantric corpus is concerned with ritual of some kind and the texts follow a common ritual structure, as we shall see, for the purposes of attaining liberation and above all, magical power and pleasure in higher worlds. These rituals involve the enacting of elaborate hierarchical cosmologies, are concerned with the divinization of the body, with divine energy or power (*śakti*), and with possession (*āveśa*) and exorcism.

We do not yet have a full picture of the groups of ascetics and the social context in which the Tantras originated, although Sanderson's work on manuscript sources will clarify the picture (Sanderson 1985, 1988, forthcoming). Any statements are therefore preliminary and must remain conjectural and provisional until the publication of Sanderson's more recent work. The Tantras probably originated with groups of ascetics similar to the Lākula Pāśupatas, on the edges of brahminical society who were supported by low castes, although the low-caste origins of Tantra is contentious as the Tantras are linked to courtly circles and royal power (Sanderson, forthcoming). Cremation ground asceticism is a very old tradition in the subcontinent and meditation on death is an important feature in the meditation practice of early Buddhist monks (e.g. Norman 1973: 123). The Tantras became more popular and tantric images and ideas became pervasive in later Hindu traditions. Although generally distancing themselves from the Tantras, the Purāṇas nevertheless absorb tantric elements (Hazra 1983; Dyczkowski 1988: 8) and tantric ideas and practices become absorbed by the eleventh century into mainstream, brahminical society and courtly circles. The divine power (*śakti*) of the Goddess becomes identified with the power of the King in different regions such as Vijayanagara. But it is in Kashmir, above all, where we see this process of the brahmanization of tantric ideology and practice. This history has been traced by Sanderson through the sequences of texts and the divisions of the Śaiva tantric canon. It is to this canon and the traditions it expresses that we now turn.

The path of Mantras can be divided into the texts and teachings of the Śaiva Siddhānta on the one hand and the teachings of Bhairava of non-Siddhānta groups on the other. While the former, although accepting 28 "dualist" Tantras, adhered to vedic social practice and made generally vegetarian offerings to a milder form of Śiva known as Sadāśiva, the latter accepted a large body of texts which were often hostile to vedic orthopraxy. This distinction between orthoprax and heteroprax Śaivism is identified in the sources, as Sanderson has shown, as a distinction between traditions of the right (*dakṣina*), namely the Śaiva Siddhānta, and traditions of the left (*vāma*), namely the non-Saiddhāntika traditions (Sanderson 1995: p.18). While the Śaiva Siddhānta is a dualistic tradition, maintaining a distinction between the soul and the Lord, the non-Saiddhāntika groups, especially the tradition known as the Trika, are nondualistic, claiming that the self and Śiva are identical. This dualistic and nondualistic distinction also applies to the ritual realm where the Śaiva Siddhānta accepted the vedic distinction between purity and impurity, remaining within the vedic rules of purity, whereas the non-Saiddhāntika rejected this distinction (Sanderson 1995: 17).

These Śaiva, tantric traditions not only permeated the subcontinent but became royal religions, along with Buddhism, in southeast Asia and beyond to Java and Bali during the medieval period. Here kings modeled themselves on south Asian kings, Sanskrit became the sacred language, and Brahmin priests officiated at rites of royal consecration. In Java, for example, there are early Śaiva inscriptions (732 CE) and eighth-century Śaiva temples seemed to have followed ritual patterns found in the subcontinent of bathing the Śiva liṅga (Dumarçay 1986). In Bali Śaiva temple priests still perform daily rites in which the priest symbolically becomes Śiva through uttering the five-syllabled mantra "homage to Śiva" (*namaḥ śivāya*) (Goudriaan and Hookyas 1971). There are important tantric Buddhist texts of Indonesia, such as the *Kuñjarakarṇadharmakathana*, depicting Śaiva elements but in a Buddhist context (Nihom 1994: 119–41).

The Śaiva Siddhānta

The Śaiva Siddhānta forms the fundamental Śaiva system, providing the template for ritual and theology of all other Śaiva groups within the Path of Mantras. The tradition may have originated in Kashmir where it developed a sophisticated theology propagated by theologians such as Sadyojoti, Bhaṭṭa Nārāyanakaṇṭha and his son Bhaṭṭa Rāmakaṇṭha (ca. 950–1000 AD). It spread to the South where the Sanskrit scriptures are complemented with Tamil texts. Here the gnostic, ritual system becomes infused with an emotional devotionalism (*bhakti*) characteristic of southern Śaiva Siddhānta, through the Tamil poetry of the Śaiva saints or Nāyaṉārs. Ritual and devotion are accompanied here by theology in works by Bhojadeva (eleventh century) and Aghoraśiva (twelfth century) (Gengnagel 1996).

The Śaiva Siddhānta is dualistic (*dvaita*), maintaining a distinction between the self and Śiva and claiming that there are three distinct ontological categories, the Lord (*Pati*), the self (*paśu*), and the bond (*pāśa*). The Lord or Śiva in his form as five-faced Sadāśiva, performs the five acts (*pañcakṛtya*) of the creation, maintenance, and destruction of the universe, concealing himself and revealing himself to devotees (Tat Prak 1.7). The self or "beast" (*paśu*) is eternally distinct from Śiva and bound within the cosmos or "bond" (*pāśa*), in the cycle of birth and death by impurity (*mala*), action (*karma*), and the material substratum of the cosmos (*māyā*). Śiva performs the five acts for his play (*krīḍā*) and for the liberation of beings (Tat Prak 6.1). This liberation is attained with the grace (*anugraha*) of Śiva through initiation (*dīkṣā*) by a teacher in whose body Śiva has become established (*ācāryamūrtistha*) (Tat Prak 1.15; Hulin 1980: 115–17). Through initiation and the subsequent actions of daily an occasional rituals performed throughout his life, the impurity, which is a substance (*dravya*) covering the soul, is gradually removed and the aspirant finally achieves liberation a death through the descent of Śiva's grace (*śaktipāta*). Once liberated, the soul does not merge with Śiva, because of their ontological distinction, but rather becomes equal to Śiva (*śivatulya*), possessing all of Śiva's powers of omniscience and omnipotence, but remaining eternally distinct (Sanderson 1995: 39–40; Davis 1991: 83–111).

There were two initiations which the Śaiva Siddhāntin would undergo, the lesser initiation into the cult ritual and scriptures (*samaya-dīkṣā*) and the liberating initiation (*nirvāṇa-dīkṣā*) ensuring the soul's final release (Brunner 1975: 411–43). While initiation was open to all classes, it was not open to women who could only participate in Śaiva worship vicariously through the actions of their husbands and so at death rise up to Śiva's abode (Sanderson 1995: 35–6). The daily ritual acts of the Śaiddhāntika were performed at the junctures of the day (dawn, midday, sunset) and involved the standard tantric ritual structure of the purification of the body through its symbolic destruction (*bhūtaśuddhi*), the creation of a divine body through imposing mantras upon it (*nyāsa*), mental or inner worship (*antarayāga*) in which offerings are made mentally to the deity, in this case Sadāśiva, and external worship in which external *pūjā* is performed. In the Śaiva Siddhānta, the form of Sadāśiva worshipped is consortless, possessing 5 faces with 3 eyes, 10 arms, holding a trident, and covered in a tiger skin (Ne T 9. 19c–25), and in the *Īśānaśivagurudeva-paddhati* is represented as a beautiful sixteen year old youth (ISG 3. 14. 5d), although there is some variation in the objects held in his ten hands (ISG 3. 1–11). This ritual structure is standard, found in both primary scriptures and in ritual manuals such as Īśānaśivagurudeva's and Somaśambhu's *paddhatis* (twelfth century) (SSP 1963, 1968, 1977, 1998; ISG 1988). The ritual structure in these texts is also found outside the Siddhānta, showing that some degree of ritual invariance occurs across the tantric traditions in spite of divergent theologies and deities (Sanderson 1988b: 660–704; Padoux 1990: 330–8; Brunner 1975: xxi–xxii; Flood 2002).

But while the ritual of the Śaiva Siddhāntin is very closely aligned with the normative, vedic rites of the Smārta brahmins (Sanderson 1995: 27–38) and the Saiddhāntika followed a straightforward path of fulfilling *dharma* along with performing ritual enjoined by his initiation, there was another path that could be followed. This was the path of power and the enjoyment of pleasure in higher worlds that required a distinct consecration (*sādhakābhiṣeka*) after the *nirvāṇa-dīkṣā* (Brunner 1975). In contrast to one who simply desired liberation at death (*mumukṣu*), one desiring powers (*bubhukṣu*), technically referred to as a *sādhaka*, could take on supererogatory rituals. While this distinction between the *mumukṣu* and the *bubhukṣu* does not directly map on to the distinction between the Śaiva Siddhānta followers of the right and the non-Saiddhāntika groups of the left, because the *sādhaka* path was an option also within the Siddhānta, it is nevertheless the case that the non-Saiddhāntika traditions are more concerned with attaining power in this sense. Indeed, the obtaining of various forms of magical power through the practice of yoga and the performance of rituals for a desired end (*kāmya*) are integral to the Tantras. The *Svacchanda Tantra*, for example, describes rituals for the Sādhaka to attain the goals of causing the death of enemies (*maraṇa*), ruining his enemies (*uccāṭana*), the subjugation of women (*vaśikaraṇa*), the power of attraction (*ākaṣaṇa*), and the tranquilising of supernatural forces (*śānti*) (Sva TUd 9. 46. On these powers see Goudriaan 1978: 251–412) through the worship of a particular ferocious form of the god Svacchanda called Koṭarākṣa or Aghorahṛdaya (Sva TUd 9. 2). For example, the destruction of enemies and subjugation of a desired woman are achieved through establishing their names in a magical diagram (*yantra*), visualizing the enemy or desired person, and repeating certain mantras (Sva T 9. 65c-70). These kind of rites are an important part of the Tantras of the left often associated with the cremation ground traditions.

Non-Saiddhāntika Śaivism

In contrast to the orthoprax Śaiva Siddhānta, the second major division of the path of Mantras comprises the Bhairava Tantras and their various subdivisions. These texts are concerned with the Śaivas who worshipped a ferocious form of Śiva called Bhairava and which originated in ascetics groups living in cremation grounds. These groups are generally known as Kāpālikas, the "skull-men," so called because, like the Lākula Pāśupata, they carried a skull-topped staff (*khaṭvāṅga*) and cranium begging bowl. Unlike the respectable brahmin householder of the Śaiva Siddhānta or Smārta tradition, the Kāpālika ascetic imitated his ferocious deity, covered himself in the ashes from the cremation ground, and propitiated his gods with the impure substances of blood, meat, alcohol, and sexual fluids from intercourse unconstrained by caste restrictions (Sanderson 1985: 200–2). He thereby flaunted impurity rules and went against vedic injunctions. His aim was power through evoking deities in the rites associated with his particular system, especially ferocious goddesses. In Hindu drama the Kāpālika was often lampooned, but his continued existence, although in small numbers, into the present in the form of the Aghorī ascetics of Banaras, bears witness to the power of this tradition (Parry 1994: 251–710).

Within this broad purview of Kāpālika Śaivism or the Śaivism of the left, a number of distinct traditions developed during the early medieval period, especially the Kaula, Krama, and Trika traditions, which form part of the Kula ensemble. These originated in cremation ground asceticism but became incorporated into householder life. As Sanderson has clearly demonstrated, while for the Krama and Kaula there was no conformity to vedic ritual purity, for the Trika there was some conformity for the householder, although transcendence of vedic orthopraxy remained at the tradition's esoteric heart where transcendence is achieved through transgression (Sanderson 1995: 21–3). But in order to understand the distance of these Śaiva groups from the Siddhānta let us look at the Krama tradition first.

The Krama or "gradation" tradition existed in Kashmir where it is known about through the works of the author Abhinavgupta (ca. 975–1025 AD) and the anonymous *Mahānayaprakāśa* (*The Illumination of the Great Way*) which can be dated between the late tenth and thirteenth centuries. In contrast to the Śaiva Siddhānta in which Sadāśiva is worshipped without a consort, in the Krama system the Goddess is worshipped without a male consort as a form of Kālī (Kālasaṃkarṣiṇī), surrounded by a retinue of 12 identical forms (Sanderson 1988: 197–8). Within the Krama system these forms are identified with emanations of pure consciousness and Abhinavagupta describes the process of the projection of pure consciousness into apparent manifestation as objects of knowledge and its contraction back into itself. The expansion (*vikāsa*) of the cosmos in manifestation is the contraction (*saṃkoca*) of consciousness, while conversely the contraction of manifestation becomes the expansion of consciousness (TS 29–30; see also Silburn 1975: 134–90, 193–4). The explanation of existence is to be found in these goddesses who are the impulse (*udyoga*) for experience, its manifestation (*avabhāsana*), the tasting of it (*carvaṇa*), and finally its destruction (*vilāpana*) (Sp Nir p. 6). In consonance with this idealism, the Krama denied the vedic distinction between purity and impurity in its rituals.

Closely associated with the Krama are the Trika and Kaula traditions which merge at the higher levels of their initiatory hierarchy. The Trika is a particularly important form of Śaivism which came to dominate Kashmir, and is generally understood as "Kashmir" Śaivism. This form of Śaivism was absorbed into the householder life in Kashmir and developed a sophisticated theology that became known as the recognition school (*pratyabhijñā*). It was strongly influential on the Śaivism of the south and on the Goddess tradition of the Śrī Vidyā. The root text of the tradition is the *Mālinīvijayottara Tantra*, around which text Abhinavagupta centered his monumental exposition, the *Tantrāloka* ("Light on Tantra"), and two other works, the *Tantrasāra* ("Essence of Tantra") and his commentary on the text (Mal Vart, Hanneder 1998). Abhinavagupta claimed that the text is the essence of the nondualist Tantras, although Sanderson has argued that the text itself is in fact dualistic in its orientation (Sanderson 1993: 291–306). Sanderson observes that Abhinavagupta's basing his teaching on this text shows his desire to ground his idealism in a text that had wide circulation and appeal (Sanderson 1995: 22). This idealism comprised the central claim that all manifestation, including the self, is identical with the pure consciousness (*saṃvit, caitanya*) of Śiva and to therefore qualify the Saiddhāntika distinction between Lord, self and bond. Liberation is not becoming equal to Śiva, as the Siddhānta believed, but rather the realization of the nondistinction between self and Śiva or Kālī as absolute consciousness.

To show that this realization is the overall goal of practice (*sādhana*), Abhinavagupta adopted the Trika pantheon of three goddesses, Parā, Parāparā, and Aparā, from where the tradition derives its name, showing that they are all manifestations of consciousness. Consciousness is at the esoteric heart of the Trika which Abhinavagupta identified with the Krama Goddess Kālasaṃkarṣiṇī, and this rejection of dualism at a theological level is reflected in the rejection of the dualism of purity and impurity at a ritual level. Abhinavagupta distinguished between two ritual systems, the normative rite of the Trika householder (the *tantra-prakriyā*) and the optional esoteric rites which flaunted vedic purity rules (the *kula-prakriyā*). The former was enjoined on the Trika initiate and involved the worship and internalization of a ritual diagram in the form of a trident (*triśūlābja-maṇḍala*) whose prongs were identified with the three goddesses stemming from pure consciousness of the fourth goddess Kālasaṃkarṣinī (Sanderson 1988). This normative Trika rite followed the pattern of Saiddhāntika daily worship. But for the suitable person (*adhikārin*) the supererogatory rite of the *kula-prakriyā* was possible in order to achieve gradual perfection (*siddhikrama*) which would otherwise take thousands of years with floods of mantras (TA 29.1–3). This rite involved making offerings of meat, wine and sex (TA 29.97–8), ritually anathema to the orthoprax brahmin, with a partner or "messenger" (*dūtī*) who was regarded as the sādhaka's "door" (*dvāra*) to realizing the wonder (*camatkāra*) of pure consciousness (TA 29.115b–117; Silburn 1988: 219; Flood 2002: 281–301). The sādhaka and his ritual partner thereby recapitulated the union (*yāmala*) of Śiva and his female power or Śakti and the pleasure of their union reflected the universal joy (*jagadānanda*) of liberation. The deities in these esoteric levels of the Trika and Krama demanded to be appeased by impure substances, such as offerings which included drops of the five substances, urine, semen, menstrual blood, faeces, and phlegm, along with other substances polluting to the brahmin such as garlic and onions (Sanderson 1995: 82). The Trika goddesses were so powerful that they must be placated with offerings of blood and alcohol, only after which could ordinary offerings of flowers and incense be made (TA 26.51c–53b from Sanderson 1995: 81). The secret Kula rites were available only to the Trika initiate who would also maintain outward, vedic responsibilities. Thus Abhinavagupta could say that the Trika initiate should be internally a Kaula (i.e. a practitioner of the secret rite), externally a Śaiva and vedic in his social practice (TAV 3: 27, 277–8 from Sanderson 1985: 205).

The Trika was very successful in Kashmir and its theologians succeeded in making their interpretation of the scriptures predominant. With Moslem invasion in the eleventh century the tradition became greatly eroded, but there is still a Śaiva householder tradition in Kashmir (Madan 1987) and until recently a living representative of the Recognition school in Swami Lakshman Joo. But while the Trika and Krama schools were important within ascetic and intellectual circles, the majority of Śaivas followed less demanding forms of religion in the popular cults of Śiva.

Popular Śaivism

Alongside the Trika was the popular worship of Śiva in the Kashmir valley as Svacchandabhairava. His cult, expressed in the *Svacchandabhairava Tantra*, has continued to the present, and is closely connected with the cult of the Lord of the eye (Netranātha) found in the *Netra Tantra*. Both of these texts show concerns with special rites of protection, exorcism and rites for a desired goal (*kāmya*) such as the destruction of enemies or seduction of a desired person. While both the Netra and Svacchanda cults conformed to the ritual purity of the Śaiva Siddhānta, the latter contained the worship of impure forms of the deity. The majority of all Śaivas were probably followers of these cults rather than the more esoteric and demanding Trika and Krama (Sanderson 1995: 22–3). Although popular, these texts present quite complex systems of visualization (Brunner 1974) and their deities as emanations of Netranātha tend to be ferocious, a characteristic of the Kāpālika cults. The *Netra Tantra*, although the text itself has connections with royalty, also bears witness to popular possession and exorcism rites which were probably pervasive among lower social levels. Indeed, one of the main tasks of the orthoprax brahmin was to prevent possession. These "demons" (*bhūta*) and powerful female deities or "mothers" (*mātṛ*) enter through the "hole" (*chidra*) of the shadow of impure men and women whose behaviour is bad (*durācāra*), and who have neglected their ritual obligations, so causing the evil eye (*dṛṣṭipāta*) to fall upon them (NT 19. 34, 45–6).

The classification of possessing beings in the sources is a fascinating example of the way in which cosmological taxonomies link in to Śaiva cosmological structures. The *Netra Tantra* and the Kashmiri Śaiva theologian Kṣemarāja's commentary list several classes of being who possess and who must be appeased through different ritual offerings. These beings include a class of female deities called "mothers" (*mātṛ*), the "removers" (*vināyakas*), "demon-grabbers" (*bhūtagraha*), and others (NT 19. 55–80 and commentary), who are classified in a broader scheme depending upon their motives for possession. Thus there are those desirous of meat offerings (*balikāma*), those desirous of sexual pleasure (*bhoktukāma*) and those desiring to harm and kill (*hantukāma*) (N TUd 168). These malevolent powers are within the cosmic hierarchy assumed by the Śaiva systems. They exist within a family (*kula*) of powers with a deity at the head and are indeed, particles or fragments (*aṃśa*) of that higher being. Through appeasing the Lord of the family of the possessor, the possessor leaves the possessed person (NT 19.80b–81a). For example, if possessed by the Vināyakas, one worships their Lord Vighneśa (i.e. Gaṇeśa), offering him sweetmeat, meat, and plenty of alcohol (NT 19. 63–5). Or if possessed by the innumerable mothers (*mātṛ*) who desire to do harm, then one should perform worship (*prapūjayet*) for the great mothers (*mahāmātṛ*), namely the famous seven or eight goddesses Brahmī, Maheśvarī and so on, from whose wombs they have originated (NT 19. 55–6). The lower beings in the hierarchy are emanations or particles of the higher. Once the higher being is appeased with offerings of flowers, rice, and the four kinds of meat from domestic and wild, aquatic and flying animals (N TUd 9. 59–61a, p. 166), then also are the lower manifestations.

While the *Netra Tantra* is from the north, similar concerns are shown in the Śaiva Siddhānta ritual treatise, probably composed in Kerala, the *Īśānaśivagurudeva-paddhati*. This is the only Saiddhāntika text that I am aware of that deals with possession and exorcism and contains a typology of supernatural beings, although the Kerala medical text the *Tantrasārasaṃgraha* knows the same typology (TSS 12. 9–11). The text has eighteen types (ISG 2. 42.1) of powers who can possess, although the typology is different from that of the northern text. Īśānaśivagurudeva does classify them broadly into those desiring sexual pleasure (*ratikāma*) and those wanting to kill (*hantukāma*). These beings are everywhere, in rivers, gardens, mountains, lakes, empty places, cremation grounds and in temples (ISG 2. 42. 3b–4). The text goes on the describe the kinds of people these beings attack, usually people on the social margins or in vulnerable situations; for example, children, those alone in the night, those whose wealth has been lost, those wishing to die, and those separated from their loved ones. But especially vulnerable are women when naked, who have bathed after menstruation, who are filled with passion, intoxicated, pregnant, or prostitutes (ISG 2. 42. 5b–8). That is, possession happens to those who are or are potentially outside of social control, as women's sexuality was perceived to be by the male oriented Śaiva Brahmanism. Indeed, women's sexuality was a threat to brahmanical order because, according to the *Pāśupata Sūtra*, it is beyond the control of the scriptures (Pāś Sū 9, comm. p. 66). The *Īśānaśivagurudeva-paddhati* also makes clear that possession is caste-related. Thus there are demons who specifically possess Brahmins (*brahmarākṣasa*), warriors (*kṣatriyagraha*), and so on (ISG 2. 42.26–9), and one of the symptoms of possession is somebody from one caste taking on the roles or pretending to perform the duties of another.

There are specific cures or rituals to enact a cure, prescribed in the text. For example, the exorcist should nail the tuft of the possessed person to a tree and the *bhūta* will then go (ISG 2. 43. 3) or he should make an ersatz body of the possessor and pierce it with sharp sticks (ISG 2. 43. 11–12), and so on. All of these rites involve the use of mantras, ritual diagrams, and offerings, such as the substitute blood (*raktatoya*) so common in Kerala rites (ISG. 2. 43. 28–30). The construction and use of mantras is a striking feature of this tradition and for exorcising especially powerful beings, the text gives distorted or garbled mantras (ISG 2. 43. 83). In dealing with local, possessing deities, the text also thereby express the concerns of those in lower social strata. Not only do the texts articulate the dominant ideology, they also express divergent voices which can be heard in the places dealing with possession and which can be read in terms of social protest (Lewis 1971).

The Śaiva cults of possession and exorcism are an important aspect of the tradition which show links between religion, healing and social comment. Possession is linked to the diagnosis of disease and the prescription of mantras; the *mantravāda* in Kerala, for example, is related to the Ayurveda. Indeed, it is these aspects of tradition which, while being local in origin, have traveled to other areas. The Śaiva exorcist deity Khaḍgarāvaṇa, for example, in the text of the *Kumāra Tantra*, while originating in the north, became popular in Tibet and southeast Asia (Filliozat 1937). Where these topics are dealt with we move away from the ordered world of temple and domestic ritual, into a world of the lower levels of the supernatural order and so of lower levels of the social order. But although the *Īśānaśivagurudeva-paddhati* is concerned with possession and exorcism, most of the text is devoted to the more usual concerns of the Śaiva Siddhānta, its temple ritual and deities.

The Southern Śaiva Siddhānta

By the eleventh century Śaiva Siddhānta had faded in Kashmir but developed in Tamilnadu, where it exists to the present time. Here in the south the dualist tradition merged with the Tamil devotionalism of the 63 Śaiva saints, the Nāyaṉars. Śaivism took on a distinctive flavor and the Sanskritic ritualism and theology of the northern tradition combined with Tamil poetry and devotion to produce a distinctively southern Śaiva religious *imaginaire*. This devotional poetry is still sung in temples throughout South India. It was in the south that Śaivism had royal patronage in the Cōḻa dynasty (ca. 870–1280 AD), with the great Śaiva temples at Cidamabaram, Tanjavur, Darasuram, and Gangaikondacolapuram thriving, and the famous Cōḻa bronzes developed. At Cidamabram, for example, wealthy donors' inscriptions made in the temple walls show how the temple supported and legitimized royal power in the region (Younger 1995: 125–58). This power was not centralized as in a modern state, but pervaded through a segmented hierarchy, whose basic unit was the locality or *nāṭu* (Stein 1980). But even here where Śaivism became aligned with an ideology of royal power and the king was thought to embody the power (*śakti*) of the Lord, Śaivism not only upheld vedic norms, but simultaneously undermined them in a devotionalism where the devotee transcends his birth to fall in love with his Lord. It is these two aspects of Śaiva Siddhānta in the south that I wish to briefly examine.

Tamilnadu developed an extensive temple culture in which large, regional temples became not only places of worship, but centers of political power and also great centers of learning. In Tamilnadu a distinctive sense of the sacredness of place and temple buildings develops (Shulman 1980). Perhaps this is nowhere seen more vividly than in the temple city of Cidambaram, the "sky of consciousness," where Śiva is installed, not as in all other Śiva temples in the aniconic form of the *liṅga*, but as the dancing Śiva (Naṭarāja). Here he is installed along with a bronze icon of his consort Śivakāmasundarī, and in contrast to fixed icons, is paraded on festival occasions (Smith 1996: 10). Like other Śaiva temples, Cidambaram had a group of texts associated with it, extolling its virtues and narrating its mythology, namely the twelfth-century *Cidambara Mahātmya* along with four *sthalapurāṇas*, a Tamil translation of the former text and Umāpati Śivācārya's hymn of praise to Naṭarāja (Smith 1996: 8–9). Through these texts and the popular imagination, Cidambaram became incorporated into the sacred geography of Tamilnadu.

Although the Śaiva Siddhānta has been the predominant form of theology and ritual in southern Śaivism, and Cidambaram was an important center for this theology, the temple and its rites are not sectarian in a strict sense. Indeed, the community of Brahmins who perform six daily rituals to Naṭarāja claim that they follow vedic practice rather than tantric or āgamic. They thereby differentiate themselves from the hereditary priests at other Śaiva Siddhānta temples, the *arccakaṇs*, who follow the tantric or āgamaic rites of the texts we have discussed. The Dīkṣitas (Tamil Dīṭcitars), as they are called, are an endogamous community, who perform rites accompanied by Smārta Brahmins or Aiyars who are qualified to perform recitation of the Vedas (Younger 1995: 133–24). These rites are quite elaborate and involve the performance of *pūjā* to a crystal *liṅga* transported out from the inner sanctum of the bronze Naṭarāja to an outer porch where ablutions are made over it (*abhiṣeka*). It is then returned to the inner shrine and *pūjā* to the icon of Naṭarāja himself is performed, involving the offering of lights (*dīpa*), sound, and, at certain times of the day, food (*naivedya*). During one of the evening *pūjās* low caste singers, the Ōtuvārs, sing Tamil devotional hymns before the icon, as they do elsewhere throughout Tamilnadu.

While Tamil Śaivism is strongly associated with royal power and the upholding of orthoprax values, as we can see at Cidambaram, it simultaneously undermines those values through its emphasis on popular devotion. We can see this in the context when a caste of singers, the Ōtuvārs, sing hymns to the icon of Śiva and during the great festival when the icons of Nāṭarāja and his consort are paraded through the streets by Vēḷāḷas, outside of brahmanical control (Younger 1995: 60–3). In one sense festival transgression of formal boundaries can serve to reinforce those boundaries but in another sense the carnival disrupts hierarchy and in it we can hear voices otherwise occluded. Indeed, it is these other voices that are articulated in much of the devotional poetry of the Nāyaṉars, which partly developed against the oppression of the lower castes in the feudalism of the southern kingdoms.

The Nāyaṉars were often low caste themselves, composing love songs to Śiva in his icons at different temples. In the love or *bhakti* presented in these Tamil sources what is important is the direct, unmediated relationship between the devotee and the Lord in which the devotee can become mad (*piccu, uṉmatta*) with devotion. The texts of the Nāyaṉars are incorporated into the canon of the southern Śaiva Siddhānta, the *Tirumurai*, which also contains Śaiva Siddhānta Śāstras in Tamil (Zvelebil 1975; Peterson 1991: 52–9). Among the Nāyaṉars represented, the most famous is Māṇikkavācakar dated by tradition to the fifth century, who composed the "sacred verses" (*Tiruvācakam*) and whose 20-verse hymn, the *Tiruvempāvai*, is still recited in temples today. Māṇikkavācakar is the most revered saint of Tamil Śaivism. He was a court official in Madurai but retired to a life of meditation at Cidamabaram where, tradition maintains, he entered the inner sanctum never to return and merged with his god (Younger 1995: 194–201). Other texts are also recited by the Ōtuvārs, particularly the later *Tēvāram* (Peterson 1991). The following is an example from the Nāyaṉar Appar, who expresses a devotional sentiment specific to place, to the particular temple in which Śiva dwells:

When I think of the skullbearer
who wears a wreath of flowers in his hair,
the Lord with the white moon who likes to live
in Veṇṇis ancient city,
a flood of ambrosia
wells up in my tongue.
(Peterson 1991: 210)

This kind of devotionalism, so typical of the *bhakti* movement, spread from Tamilnadu to neighbouring Karnataka where the Liṅgayat or Vīraśaiva sect were founded by Basava (ca. 1106–67 AD), although there was some continuity with the Kālāmukha sect (see above). As in Tamilnadu this form of Śaivism is highly devotional and the *bhakti* movement instigated by Basava was against asceticism (as would have been practiced by the Kālāmukhas), against caste, and against formal, temple worship, preferring instead an immediate relationship between devotee and Lord symbolised by a small *liṅga* worn around the neck. As in Tamilnadu, beautiful devotional poetry was composed in Kanada to Śiva and his forms (Ramanujan 1973). The fusion of *bhakti* with tantric ritual as occurred in the Tamil Śaiva Siddhānta and Liṅgayats of Karnataka has provided a rich mix that gave expression to both a popular religiosity and to formal, brahmanical, tantric ritual. There is a fusion of the two in that the personal religion of *bhakti* becomes formalized and incorporated into temple ritual structure.

Śaiva Siddhānta temple ritual found its way into Kerala where the Nambudri Brahmins, akin to the Tamil *arccakars*, developed a distinctive form of temple Tantrism based on a fifteenth century *Tantrasumuccaya* ("Compendium of Tantra") by Cenasnambudri, although some families use the *Īśānaśivagurudeva-paddhati* (Freeman 1997). This tradition is not strictly Śaiva, but rather a synthesis of traditions focusing on the temple worship of Śiva, Viṣṇu, Gaṇeśa, Devī, and low-caste regional goddesses.

In the Śaiva Siddhānta of the south and in the related Kerala Tantrism, we see traditions which formally align themselves with adherence to vedic worship and social mores (*varṇāśrama-dharma*) but which in practice perform worship according to the Tantras. The southern tradition absorbed lower-caste devotion and succeeded in all but eradicating the ascetical traditions of Buddhism and Jainism from the region and successfully aligned the tantric tradition with the vedic. This alignment is achieved in ritual where the Śaiva Siddhānta and Kerala traditions absorb vedic elements into the tantric ritual structure that then forms a common pattern in both temple and private cults. Having taken this survey of Śaiva history so far, it is to the patterns of Śaiva practice that we must now turn.

Śaiva Temple Ritual

While personal yoga and private ritual for both liberation and power must not be forgotten in Śaiva traditions, it is the ritual life of the temple that provides its wider social coherence. The Śaiva Siddhānta is the basic ritual and theological structure to which the other tantric traditions respond and build. Many of the Śaiva Siddhānta Tantras and manuals are concerned with temple ritual, such as the *Rauravottarāgama*, while others, such as the *Mṛgendra*, are not concerned with temples but rather with personal practice under the direction of a teacher. The *Rauravottara* describes various styles of temple, the rites for the installation of the temple, and for the installation of deities within it (*pratiṣṭhā*). The deities of the directions (*diṅmūrti*) are first established and then others may be installed in the vicinity of the central shrine, namely the gods Gaṇeśa, Dakṣiṇāmūrti, Viṣṇu, Brahmā, and Durgā. Finally the *liṅga* is installed as the central icon of Śiva. The *liṅga* is regarded as the highest, undifferentiated (*niṣkala*) form of Śiva in contrast to the anthropomorphic form which is differentiated (*sakala*). The *liṅga* with a face or faces is a mixture of both (*sakalaniṣkala*) (Davis 1991: 121–2).

There are different kinds of *liṅga* for different kinds of temple, and an elaborate typology is offered in the *Rauravottara* (Rau A ch. 15). Abhinavagupta offers an esoteric interpretation of the *liṅga* as being unmanifest where it is equated with absolute consciousness or the "supreme heart of tranquility" (*viśrāntihṛdayam param*), manifest-unmanifest (*vyaktāvyakta*) when identified with the body, and manifest (*vyakta*) as an outer symbol (TA 5 117a). It is with the outer symbol and its worship that the Śaiva Siddhāna is mainly concerned. Having made the icon of wood, metal or stone, the eyes are opened and the icon is purified by being immersed in water, the altar (*vedikā*) constructed, firepits (*kuṇḍa*) placed around it, the deity invoked in the icon, the icon bathed (*abhiśeka*), priests honored and brahmins fed (Bhatt 1982: cxii). Daily rites are thereafter performed involving bathing the icon (*abhiṣeka*), its decoration, the offering of vegetarian food (*naivedya*) to the accompaniment of ringing bells, the vision (*darśana*) of the deity for devotees, and the offering of light (*dīpa*).

Daily domestic rites of the Śaiva Siddhānta initiate involve a similar pattern of making offering to a *liṅga*. This will involve the tantric pattern of the devotee bathing, purifying the body through its symbolic destruction (*bhūtaśuddhi*), re-creating a divine body through the imposition of mantras (*nyāsa*), mental worship (*antara/mānasa-yāga*), followed by external worship (*bahya-yāga*) with offerings into the fire pit (Davis 1991: 51–60; 148–62. For a complete account of daily ritual see SSP vol. 1, 1963 and Brunner-Lachaux's introduction). As we have seen, the initiate into the tantric systems of the "left," while conforming to orthodox society, after his initiation undertook worship of the trident maṇḍala in his imagination (Sanderson 1985) and made offerings of impure substances in the Kaula system (*kula prakriyā*). But even within the Śaiva Siddhānta there are varying levels of commitment and expectation. The texts speak of four kinds of devotee: the *samyin* who has simply undergone the basic initiation or *samāya dīkṣā* discussed above; the *putraka*, who has also undergone the *nirvāṇa-dīkṣā*; the *ācārya* who can perform initiations and has undergone a special consecration called the *ācāryābhiṣeka*; and the *sādhaka* who desires to follow the path of power and has undergone the *sādhakābhiṣeka* (see Brunner 1975). The *Mataṅgapārameśvarāgama* says that the samayin should serve his teacher in order to eventually be granted liberation, the putraka should be detached with eveness of behavior, and serve his teacher, his god, and the sacred fire, while the sādhaka is an ascetic (*tapasvin*) whose consciousness is one-pointed in his repetition of mantra to attain his goal. The ācārya must teach and so cannot spend too much time on his practice of repetition and meditation (Mat. Caryāpāda 4. 2–17). Although this is a schematic structure, it does have some bearing on the social world, although the sādhaka, as Brunner has observed, is a "personnage oubliée" in modern India. Private practice is nevertheless still important on the Śaiva path and not only ritual, but yoga and meditation are a part of this.

Private Yoga

While it is often not meaningful to draw a hard distinction between private ritual and yoga, there are nevertheless practices beyond the basic daily ritual structure that can be undertaken. Many dualistic Tantras have sections on yoga (the *yogapāda*), often virtually identical to the yoga of Patañjali, and some Śaiva Siddhānta texts are devoted to yoga, such as Jñānaprakāśa's *Śivayogaratna* (Michaël l 1975). But in nondualistic Śaivism there is a particular emphasis on various kinds of yoga practice beyond the ritual obligations of the initiate. These practices are categorized into four methods or ways (*upāya*): the "non-means" or the pathless path (*anupāya*), the divine means (*śaṃbhāvopāya*), the way of energy (*śāktopāya*), and the individual means (*āṇavopāya*) (see Dyczkowski 1987: 163–218). This structure, the oldest description of which is in the *Mālinīvijay-ottara Tantra* where they are called "immersions" or "possessions" (*samāveśa*) (MVT 2.21–3), was used by the monistic Śaivas Abhinavagupta and Kṣemarāja as a lens through which to view the earlier tradition. Thus Kṣemarāja uses the scheme as a way of organizing the *Śiva Sūtras*. The classification of the three *upāyas* relates to the three perceived human and divine faculties of desire or will (*icchā*), cognition (*jñāna*), and action (*krīyā*). Thus the *śaṃbhāvopāya* is linked to desire or will as the sudden upsurge of emotion and instinct that shatters thought construction, thereby enabling the adept to perceive the nonduality of consciousness. This can be achieved through extreme situations of fear or through inducing pain by scratching the arm with a sharp instrument (VB 93), through the arising of sexual desire (VB 41, 73) and so on. Abhinavagupta even says that thought-shattering energy (*vīrya*) can arise in the heart upon seeing a loved one unexpectedly (PTV p. 16). In fact any emotional situation is potentially transformative.

The *śāktopāya*, in contrast to the *śāmbhava*, which is without thought construction (*nirvikalpa*), is achieved by using the faculty of cognition. By focusing on a pure thought construction (*śuddhavikalpa*) that corresponds to a true state of affairs, such as "I am Śiva" or "I am omnipresent" (VB 104), the mind is gradually purified until the truth of the claim is existentially realized.

In contrast to the *śāktopāya* which develops a pure thought unsupported by any practices external to it, the *āṇavopāya* develops thought supported by external phenomena, namely mantra, meditation on the body, and external objects. The *āṇavopāya* also includes yoga practices. *Mālinīvijayottara Tantra* defines the individual means as being supported by the breath, postures, visualization, the rotation of syllables (*varṇa*) in the breath, and focusing on an external place. Abhinavagupta says this external place refers to the body, breath, and external ritual objects such as the ritual area, the ritual diagram (*maṇḍala*), the chalice for offerings (*pātra*), the rosary, and flowers (MVT 2.21; TS p. 45). All external ritual, mantra practice and meditation on the breath are supports of consciousness and means of purifying it to realize the nondistinction between the self and Śiva for the monistic Śaiva. Within the *āṇavopāya* is also the practice of Kuṇḍalinī yoga. The Goddess Kuṇḍalinī is the power (*śakti*) dwelling within the body at the base of a central channel thought to pervade it, who, once awakened, rises up through this vertical axis of power to the crown of the head, whereupon the yogi awakens to the truth of his identity with Śiva (Silburn 1988). As she rises, she pierces various centers of power (*cakra*) located along the body's axis. These centers became codified as six or seven (including the thousand-petaled lotus at the crown) and pervade later Hinduism although there is a fluidity in the earlier texts; the system of six being probably originally peculiar to a tradition focused on the goddess Kubjikā (Sanderson 1985: 164). The *āṇavopāya* therefore develops the faculty of action (*kriyā*) rather than cognition or will.

While the *Mālinīvijayottara* says that the ways are identical as to goal but differ as to method (MVT 2.25a), Abhinavagupta and his commentator Jayaratha claim that the *upāyas* form a graded hierarchy (TA 13. 157, *upāyayogakramatā*), with the individual means at the bottom and the nonmeans at the top. But Abhinavagupta also observes elsewhere that because of his extreme monism, there cannot really be any hierarchical gradation; any hierarchy (*uttaratva*) contains the delusion of dualism (PTV p. 8). This idea is reflected in the last method, which is no method. The *anupāya* is the realization of the nonduality of self and Śiva that is a sudden realization, because the path and the goal are the same. This realization without any method (other than the guru who is not a method) is understood as an intense descent of power (*śaktipāta*) and realization that consciousness was never bound. From this nondual perspective, the very idea of a path, which implies a journey from one place to another, is erroneous. Even the idea of a descent of power is problematic in this context. Abhinavagupta writes in an eloquent passage:

> The supreme Lord is the essence of his own light and our own self. By what means then is he to be achieved? Due to his own light he cannot be known. Due to his eternity his essence cannot be attained. Due to the non-existence of a covering, there cannot be the cessation of a covering (of consciousness). What then is the means? If it is distinct then it cannot be accomplished. Therefore the totality is a single reality of consciousness only, undivided by time, unlimited by space, unclouded by constraints, unobstructed by forms, unsignified by word, and unmanifested by means of knowledge. (TS pp. 8–9)

Because there is only the reality of pure consciousness in this tradition, a practice cannot lead to a goal that implies a distinction between self and object of attainment. The web of paths (*upāyajāla*) cannot illumine Śiva (TS p. 9). The monistic Śaivism of Kashmir regarded this as its highest truth. If there is one reality only, there can be no distinction between knower (*vedaka*) and object of knowledge (*vedya*) and nothing which is impure (SSV p. 8). Abhinavagupta is certainly aware of this problematic. If the lord is equidistant from all points does it make sense to also claim that he crowns a hierarchy? But while the tradition claimed this nondual awareness to be the supreme realization, the tradition nevertheless cultivated an elaborate ritual structure and sought to defeat its opponents, the dualist Saiddhāntikas and the Buddhists, in theology.

Śaiva Theology

Śaivism developed a sophisticated theology articulated in commentaries on its sacred texts. The Śaiva Siddhānta's most important theologians in its early years were Sadyojoti (eighth century), Bhaṭṭa Rāmakaṇṭha (ca. 950–1000 AD), and Bhojadeva (eleventh century). These theologians through their textual hermeneutics argued for a dualism regarding the self and Lord which the nondualist theologians of the Pratyabhijñā attempted to refute. There was rigorous debate between these two theologies, although the monists succeeded in supplanting the Siddhānta in Kashmir. Debate focused particularly on two issues: the first was the nature of the self, the second was the nature of matter, both of which had consequences for practice.

For the Saiddhāntikas the self is quite distinct from the Lord and from matter. The self is in fact trapped or bound by matter from which it must break free through its own efforts, but ultimately through the grace of Śiva, whereupon it will achieve equality with him and not be reborn again. In his *Nareśvaraparīkṣa* Sadyojoti argues against his theological rivals to establish this position regarding the self. The self is the knower and actor who experiences the fruits of his action (Nar 1.2) and is constituted by cognition itself. The self knows sense objects (he uses the typical Sanskrit expression "such as blue and so on") as distinct, and does not perceive an undifferentiated field (Nar 1.13). He thereby argues against the monists from a pragmatic perspective of common experience as well as against the Buddhist view that there is no self but only a series of momentary perceptions. Sadyojoti also goes on the argue, against the Mīṃāmsā, for the authorship of the Veda by the Lord, arguing that the Veda is a sound which is a product and so must be produced from one whose knowledge transcends the human for it takes effort for us to understand it (Nar 3.76). This view of the self as distinct is constantly refuted by the nondualists of the Pratyabhijñā who systematically present a nondual interpretation of sacred scripture and argue their position in independent treatises. Perhaps the best introduction to this theology is Kṣemarāja's *Pratyabhijñāhṛdaya* ("the Essence" or "Heart of Recognition"), a commentary on his own verses arguing against other theological positions.

Apart from the nature of the self and its relation to the divine, the second major area of disagreement between the Śaiva Siddhānta and the Pratyabhijñā was over the status of matter or rather the substrate of matter, *māyā*. Both regard *māyā* as that which constitutes the cosmos. In the higher levels or pure creation of the cosmic hierarchy, comprising a number of levels or *tattvas*, it is called, by the Saiddhāntikas, *mahāmāyā* or the "drop" (*bindu*), while in the lower or impure creation it is called *māyā*. For the Siddhānta *māyā* is an eternal substance (*dravya*) as real as the self and the Lord, upon whom the Lord acts through his regent Ananta and other higher beings (the Vidyeśvaras) to create the cosmos. *Māyā* is thus the material cause of the universe (*upadānakāraṇa*) whereas Śiva is only the efficient cause (*nimittakāraṇa*). For the Pratyabhijñā, by contrast, *māyā* is not a substance, but is a manifestation of pure consciousness or is, indeed, identical with pure consciousness. The consequences of these doctrines were the theological justification of their practices. For the Siddhānta liberation is the removal of impure substance from the self which, because it is a substance, can only be done through action (i.e. ritual action). For the Pratyabhijñā liberation is not the removal of substance but the recognition of the self's identity with the absolute, and so is the highest knowledge and not action (see Sanderson 1992: 282–7).

The methods whereby these doctrines were established were generally through commentary on sacred texts. The doctrinal neutrality of some texts was such that they lent themselves to both dualistic and monistic interpretations. Much of the language of these texts is in bad Sanskrit and the commentators, such as Kṣemarāja on the *Svacchanda Tantra* and Bhaṭṭa Rāmakaṇṭha on the *Kiraṇa Tantra*, excused this "language of the Lord" (*aiśa*) as a kind of disruption of language due its sacredness (Goodall 1998: lxv–lxxi). Through their commentaries the Śaiva theologians clarified the doctines of their own schools by drawing upon a full apparatus of techniques open to Indian philosophical analysis. For example, as Sanderson and Kahrs have shown, Abhinavagupta and Kṣemarāja use a method called *nirvacana*, an interpretive device whereby the name of a thing is analysed into its component parts to reveal its true nature (Sanderson 1995: 59–65). Through this method Kṣemarāja inteprets the names of deities and their mantras in an esoteric sense, thereby linking language and metaphysics. For example, Kahrs cites Kṣemarāja's analysis of the term "Bhairava" in his commentary on the *Svacchanda Tantra* to embrace a variety of meanings, such as he who is the inner nature of yogins, who destroys transmigratory existence and so on. In this way monistic doctrines could be injected into the text if they were not there already.

Conclusion

This survey of Śaiva history, practice and doctrine, shows the diversity of the traditions. Yet it also shows a distinctive religious *imaginaire* that sets Śaivism apart from other Indic traditions. I have focused on what I would regard as the most important developments, but this treatment is not, of course, exhaustive or even comprehensive. For example, there is a fascinating history of groups of yogis known as Nāths or Siddhas which has been strongly influenced by Śaivism and a rich history of Śaiva tradition in Southeast Asia (see White 1996). Until the last thirty years or so Śaivism was often only given cursory treatment in the history of Indic religions. This was partly due to scholarly ignorance of these traditions and partly due to not taking seriously their major sources, namely the Tantras. The situation has changed with groups of scholars working on this material, particularly in Pondichery, Oxford, Paris, and Rome. In Pondichery the Centre d'Indologie has continued to edit and publish Tantras of the Śaiva Siddhānta and scholarly interest in Śaivism exists at many major centers of learning. The study of Śaivism has contributed to our wider understanding of Hindu traditions in showing the importance of nonvedic, tantric tradition and the incoherence of the term "Hinduism" in a historical context.

As regards Śaivism itself, the Śaiva Siddhānta still provides the ritual template of temple worship in the South and is a form of Śaivism that has come to America in a new form as the Church of the Śaiva Siddhānta. The nondualistic Śaiva traditions have been eroded over time, although the Pratyabhijñā still has some followers and has become a tradition in the west, where it has influenced a number of contemporary groups, particularly Siddha Yoga and the Nityananda Institute of Swami Cetanananda. The image of Śiva is now deeply embedded as a cross-cultural icon. It remains to be seen the extent to which traditional forms of Śaivism will be eroded in India and to what extent it will be transformed in the global, new religious context.

Abbreviations and Primary Texts

ISG *Īśānaśivagurudevapaddhati*, ed. Ganapati Sastri, 4 vols. Trivandrum Sanskrit Series, 1920–5.

Kir T *Bhaṭṭa Rāmakaṇṭha's Commentary of the Kiraṇatantra*, ed. D. Goodall, vol. 1: chs. 1–6. Pondichery: École Française d'Extrême Orient, 1998.

KSTS Kashmir Series of Texts and Studies.

Kur P *Kūrma Purāṇa*, Sri Ahibhusan Bhattacharya et al. (eds. and trans.). Varanasi: All India Kashi Raj Trust, 1972.

Mat *Mataṅgapārameśvarāgama (Kriyāpāda, Yogapāda et Caryāpāda) avec le commentaire de Bhaṭṭa Rāmakaṇṭha*. Pondichery: Institut Français d'Indologie, 1982.

MVT *Mālinīvijayottara Tantra*, ed. M. S. Kaul (Srinagar: KSTS 37, 1922).

MVTvart *Mālinīvijavārtikā*, ed. M. S. Kaul. Srinagar: KSTS 31, 1921. Ed. with an English trans. by J. Hanneder, *Abhinavagupta's Philosophy of Revelation: An Edition and Annotated Translation of Mālinīślokavārttika I, 1–399*. Groningen Oriental Series, 1999.

Nar *Nareśvaraparīkṣa of Sadyojoti with Commentary by Ramakantha*, ed. M. K. Shastri. Srinagar: KSTS 45, 1926.

NT *Netra Tantra*. See N TUd

N TUd	*Netratantram: Srimatksemarajaviracitodyotakhyavyakhyopetam*, ed. Vrajavallabha Dviveda. Delhi: Parimala Publications, 1995.
Pāṇ	*Astadhyayi of Panini*, Katre, Sumitra M. (trans.). Delhi: MLBD, 1989.
Pāś Sū	*Pāśupata-Sūtras* with *Pañcārthabhāṣya* of Kaundinya, ed. R. A. Sastri. Trivandrum Sanskrit Series, 143, 1940.
PH	*Pratyabhijñāhṛdaya* by Kṣemarāja, ed. J. C. Chatterji. Srinagar: KSTS 3, 1911.
PTV	*Parārātriṃśikāvivarana* by Abhinavagupta, ed. M. S. Kaul. Srinagar: KSTS 18, 1918.
Rau A	*Rauravottarāgama*, ed. N. R. Bhatt. Pondichery: Institut Français d'Indologie, 1983.
Span dīp	*The Spandapradīpikā, a Commentary on the Spandakārikā* by Utpalācārya, ed. Mark S. G. Dyczkowski. Varanasi, private publication, 1990.
Sp Nir	*Spandanirṇaya* by Kṣemarāja, ed. and trans. M. S. Kaul. Srinagar: KSTS, 42, 1925.
SSP	*Somaśambhupaddhati*, ed. and trans. H. Brunner-Lachaux, 4 vols. Pondichery: Institut Français d'Indologie, 1963, 1968, 1977, 1998.
SSV	*Śivasūtravimarśinī* by Kṣemarāja, ed. J. C. Chatterjee. New Delhi: Biblioteca Orientalia, 1990 [1911].
Sva T	*Svacchandabhairava Tantra* with *uddyota* by Kṣemarāja, 4 vols. Delhi: Sanskrit Gian Sansthan, 1986.
Sva TUd	*Svacchanda Tantra Uddyota*
SVT	*Śvetāsvataropaniṣad*, trans. P. Olivelle, *Upaniṣads*. Oxford: Oxford University Press, 1996.
TA	*Tantrāloka* by Abhinavagupta, eds. R. C. Dwivedi and N. Rastogi, 8 vols. Delhi: MLBD, 1987. French trans. and commentary on chs. 1–5 by L. Silburn and A. Padoux *Abhinavagupta – La Lumière sur les Tantras: chapitres 1 à 5 du Tantrāloka*. Publications de l'Institut de Civilisation Indienne Fasc. 66. Paris: de Boccard, 1998.
Tat Prak	*Tattvaprakāśa* by Bhojadeva with *tātparyadīpikā* by Śrīkumāra. Trivandrum Sanskrit Series, 68, 1920.
TS	*Tantrasāra* by Abhinavagupta, ed. M. M. R. Sastri. Delhi: Bani Prakashan, 1982.
TSS	*Tantrasārasaṃgraha* by Nārāyaṇa with commentary, ed. M. Duraiswami Aiyangar. Madras: Government Oriental Library, 1950.
VB	*Vijñānabhairava Tantra* with commentaries of Kṣemarāja and Śivopādhyāya, ed. M. R. Sastri. Srinagar: KSTS 8, 1918.

References and Secondary Works Cited

Bhandarkar, D. R. 1983 [1913]. *Vaiṣṇavism, Śaivism and Minor Religious Systems*. New Delhi: Asian Educational Services.

Bhatt, N. R. 1982. "Introduction," *Mataṅgapārameśvarāgama (Kriyāpāda, Yogapāda et Caryāpāda) avec le commentaire de Bhaṭṭa Rāmakaṇṭha*. Pondichery: Institut Français d'Indologie.

Brunner, H. 1974. "Un Tantra du Nord: Le Netra Tantra," *Bulletin de l'École française d'Extrême-Orient* 61: 125–96.

——. 1975. "Le Sādhaka, personnage oublié de l'Inde du Sud," *Journal Asiatique*: 411–43.

Bühnemann, Gudrun. 1988. *Pūjā: A Study in Smārta Ritual.* Vienna: Publications of the De Nobili Research Library.
Castoriadis, C. 1997. *World in Fragments: Writings on Politics, Society, Psychoanalysis, and the Imagination.* Stanford: Stanford University Press.
Davis, Richard. 1991. *Ritual in an Oscillating Universe: Worshipping Siva in Medieval India.* Princeton: Princeton University Press.
Dumarçay, J. 1986. *The Temples of Java,* trans. M. Smithies. Oxford: Oxford University Press.
Dyczkowski, Mark. 1987. *The Doctrine of Vibration.* Albany: SUNY Press.
——. 1988. *The Canon of the Śaivāgama and the Kubjikā Tantras of the Western Kaula Tradition.* Albany: SUNY Press.
Eck, Diana. 1984. *Banares: City of Light.* London: Routledge and Kegan Paul.
Filliozat, Jean. 1937. *Le Kumāratantra de Rāvaṇa et Les Textes Parallèles Indiens, Tibétains, Chinois, Cambodgien, et Arabe.* Paris: Imprimerie Nationale.
Flood, G. 2002. "The Purification of the Body in Tantric Ritual Representation," *Indo-Iranian Journal* 45(1): 25–43.
Freeman, Rich. 1997. "Possession Rites and Tantric and the Tantric Temple: A Case Study from Northern Kerala," in Dieter B. Kapp, ed., *Proceedings of the First International Conference on Dravidian Studies.* Koln: Institut für Indologie.
Gengnagel, Jorg. 1996. *Māyā, Puruṣa und Śiva: Die dualistische Traditions des Śivaismus nach Aghoraśivācarya* (Beiträge zur Kenntnis südasiatischer Sprachen und Literaturen 3). Weisbaden: Harrassowitz.
Gonda, Jan. 1979. "The *Śatarudriya,*" in M. Nagatomi, B. K. Matilal, and J. M. Masson, eds., *Sanskrit and Indian Studies: Essays in Honour of Daniel H. H. Ingalls.* Dordrecht: Reidel, 75–91.
Goodall, D. 1998. "Introduction," *Bhaṭṭa Rāmakaṇṭha's Commentary of the Kiraṇatantra,* vol. 1: chs. 1–6. Pondichery: Institut Français d'Indologie.
Goudriaan, T. 1978. *Māyā Divine and Human.* Delhi etc.: Motilal Barnasidass.
——, ed. 1992. *Ritual and Speculation in Early Tantrism: Studies in Honor of André Padoux.* Albany: SUNY Press.
—— and S. Gupta. 1981. *Hindu Tantric and Śākta Literature.* Weisbaden: Harrassowitz.
—— and C. Hookyas. 1971. *Stuti and Stava (Bauddha, Śaiva and Vaiṣṇava) of Balinese Brahmin Priests.* Amsterdam: Verhandelingen ser Konilijke Nederlandse Akademie van Wetenschappen.
Hanneder, J. 1998. *Abhinavagupta's Philosophy of Revelation. An edition and annotated translation of Mālinīślokavārttika I, 1–399.* Groningen: Egbert Forsten.
Hazra, R. C. 1983 [1940]. *Studies in the Purāṇic Records on Hindu Rites and Customs.* Delhi: MLBD.
Heelas, Paul, ed. 1996. *Detraditionalization: Critical Reflections on Authority and Identity.* Oxford: Blackwell.
Hobsbawn, E. and T. Ranger, eds. 1983. *The Invention of Tradition.* Cambridge: Cambridge University Press.
Hulin, M. 1980. *Ṃgendrāgama: Sections de la Doctrine et du Yoga, avec la vṛtti de Bhattnārayanakaṇṭha et le dīpikā d'Aghoraśiva.* Pondichery: Institut Français d'Indologie.
Kulke, Hermann. 1970. *Cidamaramahātmya: Eine Untersuchung der religionsgeschichtlichen und historischen Hintergrunde für die Entstehlung der Tradition einer sudindischen Tempelstadt.* Freiburg Beitrage zur Indologie, vol 3. Wiesbaden: Otto Harrassowitz.
La Vallée Poussin, Louis de. 1930. *L'Inde aux Temps des Mauryas et des Barbares, Grecs, Scythes, Parthes et Yue-Tchi.* Paris: de Boccard.

Lewis, I. O. 1971. *Ecstatic Religion*. Harmondsworth: Penguin.
Lorenzen, D. N. 1991 [1972]. *The Kāpālikas and Kālamukhas: Two Lost Śaivite Sects*. Delhi: MLBD.
Madan, T. N. 1987. *Non-Renunciation*. Delhi: Oxford University Press.
Marshall, J. 1931. *Mohenjo-Daro and the Indus Civilization*. London: Oxford University Press, 3 vols.
Michaël, Tara. 1975. *Le Joyau du Śiva-Yoga: Śivayogaratna de Jñānaprakāśa*. Pondichery: Institut Français d'Indolgie.
Nihom, Max. 1994. *Studies in Indian and Indo-Indonesian Tantrism: The Kuñjarakarṇadharmakathana and the Yogatantra*. Vienna: Publications of the De Bobili Research Library.
Norman, K. R. 1973. *The Elder's Verses*, vol. 11. London: Luzac.
O'Flaherty, W. D. 1981. *Śiva, the Erotic Ascetic*. New York: Oxford University Press.
Padoux, A. 1990. *Vāc: The Concept of the Word in Selected Hindu Tantras*. Albany: SUNY Press.
——. 1994. *Le Coeur de la Yoginī: Yogninhṛdaya avec le commentaire Dīpika d'Amṛtānanda*. Paris: E. de Bocard.
Parpola, A. 1994. *Deciphering the Indus Script*. Cambridge University Press, 1994.
Parry, J. 1994. *Death in Banares*. Cambridge: Cambridge University Press.
Peterson, Indira V. 1991. *Poems to Śiva: The Hymns of the Tamil Saints*. Delhi: MLBD.
Ramanujan, A. K. 1973. *Speaking of Śiva*. Harmondsworth: Penguin.
Sanderson, Alexis. 1985. "Purity and Power Among the Brahmans of Kashmir," in M. Carrithers et al., eds., *The Category of the Person: Anthropology, Philosophy, History*. Cambridge: Cambridge University Press, 190–216.
——. 1988 a. "Maṇḍala and the Āgamic Identity of in the Trika of Kashmir," in A. Padoux, ed., *Mantras et Diagrammes Rituels dans l'Hindouisme*. Paris: E. De Boccard, 169–207.
——. 1988b. "Śaivism and the Tantric Traditions," in S. Sutherland et al., eds., *The World's Religions*. London: Routledge, 660–704.
——. 1992. "The Doctrine of the *Mālinīvijayottaratantra*," in T. Goudriaan, ed., *Ritual and Speculation in Early Tantrism: Studies in Honour of André Padoux*. Albany: SUNY Press, 283–312.
——. 1995. "Meaning in Tantric Ritual," in A.-M. Blondeau and K. Schipper, eds., *Essais sur le Rituel*. Louvain, Paris: Peeters, 15–95.
——. Forthcoming. "Śaivism: Its Development and Impact" (unpublished paper).
Silburn, L. 1975. *Hymnes aux Kālī, La Roue des Énergies Divines*. Paris: De Boccard.
——. 1988. *Kuṇḍalinī: The Energy of the Depths*. Albany: SUNY Press.
Shulman, D. 1980. *Tamil Temple Myths: Sacrifice and Divine Marriage in the South Indian Śaiva Tradition*. Princeton: Princeton University Press.
Smith, D. 1996. *The Dance of Śiva: Religion, Art and Poetry in South India*. Cambridge: Cambridge University Press.
——. 2002. *Hinduism and Modernity*. Oxford: Blackwell.
Staal, F. 1961. *Nambudri Veda Recitation*. The Hague: Mouton.
Stein, B. 1980. *Peasant, State and Society in Medieval South India*. Delhi: Oxford University Press.
White, D. G. 1996. *The Alchemical Body: Siddha Traditions in Medieval India*. Chicago University Press.
Younger, P. 1995. *Home of the Dancing Śivaṉ: The Traditions of the Hindu Temple in Citamapram*. Oxford: Oxford University Press.
Zvelebil, Kamil V. 1975. *Tamil Literature*. Leiden, Cologne: Brill.

CHAPTER 11

History of Vaiṣṇava Traditions: An Esquisse

Gérard Colas

Introduction

The present chapter will focus on the history of "Vaiṣṇava traditions" that is, of organized and institutionalized Vaiṣṇava movements, mainly on the basis of religious literature and epigraphy. We will use the term "Vaiṣṇava" in the rather anachronistic way in which it is often used today among scholars, namely as denoting those who worship Viṣṇu and his different aspects as well as the traditions which they follow. While "Vaiṣṇava" meant only "related with the god Viṣṇu" in the early period, it also assumed another denotation, namely an affiliation with the religion of which Viṣṇu is the god from around the fifth century AD, for instance, in the title *paramavaiṣṇava* found on the coins of Traikūṭaka kings Dahrasena and Vyāghrasena. Kings of the eighth century continued to use the title *paramavaiṣṇava*. The *Pauṣkarasaṃhitā*, one of the ancient Pāñcarātra saṃhitās, also refers to *paramavaiṣṇavas* (Jaiswal 1967: 204; Matsubara 1994: 19–20; von Stietencron 1978: 11). The term Vaiṣṇava evokes a conception of an overarching and syncretic religion for it includes the worshippers of all aspects considered as those of Viṣṇu, like Kṛṣṇa, Narasiṃha, etc. although a devotee of Kṛṣṇa, who is classified as a Vaiṣṇava, probably feels more a Kṛṣṇaite than a Vaiṣṇava.

Indian literature employs many terms (like *sampradāya*, *pantha*, *mata*, *siddhānta*, *paramparā*, etc.) which could be translated more or less precisely as "tradition" and which are sometimes translated as "sect," "system," "school." But a historical study of these Indian terms which often take particular shades of meaning according to the context is beyond the scope of this chapter. We will avoid using the term "sect," not only because this term, which has been used by scholars to signify socioreligious realities of great diversity, in an Indian context would need a lengthy discussion, but also because the very status of Indian religious traditions and the definition of their members are often obscure and in any case evolved over the course of time. The use of "school" in this essay will be reserved for Vaiṣṇava doctrinal systems of the Vedānta which were often accompanied by socioreligious counterparts.

We will neither follow nor examine ancient Indian doxographical views on Vaiṣṇavism. Nor shall we study the relations of Vaiṣṇava with non-Vaiṣṇava traditions and with non-exclusivist milieux which, like Smārtas, worshipped several gods including Viṣṇu. This chapter is not a history of Vaiṣṇavism, which should discuss all facts and literatures related to the god Viṣṇu and the divine aspects retrospectively considered as his manifestations. Therefore we will not consider iconographical data, whose links with a specific Vaiṣṇava tradition are often difficult to demonstrate, nor fluid oral traditions associated with Vaiṣṇavism. A special emphasis is laid on the rather neglected Vaikhānasa tradition. The social and political background, for which we have a scanty and uneven documentation, is not examined.

This chapter does not claim to be exhaustive. It only discusses traditions which exercised some influence and it is limited by the state of research on the subject. Many Vaiṣṇava traditions still need a critical examination and study of their history and their literary sources. The views of scholars remain bound by the image which each tradition wished to project of itself and of other Vaiṣṇava traditions under specific historical circumstances. Research also focused on the aspects which these traditions themselves brought forward – rites with predominantly ritualistic traditions, doctrine with theologizing ones, devotion with devotional currents – though most of these traditions were not without specific views on each of these aspects. The chronology of several Vaiṣṇava traditions covers such a long period of time and shows such contrasted phases that we found it convenient to periodize their history according to the successive tendencies to which they gave shape.

Early Bhāgavatism

Bhāgavata aristocratic patrons (second century BC *to eighth century* AD*)*

Bhāgavatism is the first "Vaiṣṇava" tradition to appear distinctly in history. The earliest known use of the term *bhāgavata* (literally "relating to Bhagavant," that is, the Lord) is clearly associated with aristocratic patrons. Several inscriptions from the second to first century BC, all of them found in a limited area of the present Madhya Pradesh and Rajasthan states, except one from Maharashtra, record the existence of a Bhāgavata cult promoted by local rulers and men of political importance. This cult, associated with Nārāyaṇa, Vāsudeva (=Kṛṣṇa) and sometimes Saṃkarṣaṇa (=Balarāma, Kṛṣṇa's elder brother), all "Vaiṣṇava" divine aspects, is often marked by the erection of a Garuḍa-pillar (in front of a temple according to an inscription from Besnagar). In these early inscriptions, the Bhāgavata faith is not in contradiction with the patronage of Vedic rituals but they do not show with certainty a ritual admixture between these two tendencies, contrary to what has been sometimes interpreted (Meth Srinivasan 1997: 196, about Ghosundi inscription).

The most famous of these epigraphs is the Garuḍa pillar inscription of Besnagar (near Sanchi, Madhya Pradesh) usually dated second or first century BC (Sircar 1942: 90). Its Prakrit text relates the setting up of a Garuḍa pillar in honor of Vāsudeva by a Greek ambassador Heliodora (=Hēliodōros) of Ta[khkha]silā (=Taxila), the Bhāgavata. It mentions that three steps to immortality, when well practiced, lead to heaven: self-control, generosity, and vigilance (*dama, tyāga,* and *apramāda*), three virtues also extolled in the Mahābhārata (Brockington 1998: 266). Another inscription from Besnagar, in probably the same period, records the setting up of the Garuḍa pillar of an "excellent temple" (*prāsādottama*) of the Lord (Bhagavat) in the twelfth regnal year of a king named Bhāgavata (here a proper name, not the name of a religious tradition), usually identified with a Śuṅga king (Jaiswal 1967: 153).

An inscription of Pratapgarh (not far from Besnagar and today in the Chitorgarh District of Rajasthan) dated probably second century BC records, in a sanskritized Prakrit, the erection of a pillar by Utararakhita who is said to be a sacābhāgavata, "true[?] bhāgavata" (Salomon 1998: 240). The Ghosundi stone inscription in Sanskrit dated first century BC (on the basis of its script) was found near Nagari (Chitorgarh District). This inscription, usually read with the help of the Hathibada inscription which bears a similar text, records the building of a "stone-enclosure for the place of worship" (*pūjāśilāprākāra*) called "the enclosure of Nārāyaṇa" for the gods Saṃkarṣaṇa and Vāsudeva by a Bhāgavata king Sarvatāta, performer of an *aśvamedha* sacrifice (Sircar 1942: 91–2).

The Nanaghat cave (Maharashtra) inscription of the Sātavāhana queen Nāyanikā, usually dated second half of the first century BC, though not explicitly using the term bhāgavata, begins with an invocation to various gods including Saṃkarṣaṇa and Vāsudeva and records the sacrificial fees given to priests for the queen's husband's sacrifices (including an installation of Vedic fires, two *aśvamedhas* and a *rājasūya*) (Sircar 1942: 186–90).

By contrast with that early period, the extant epigraphic documents of the first three centuries of the Christian era do not seem to specifically mention Bhāgavatas nor any other particular "Vaiṣṇava" tradition. In this regard, textual sources are the only possible evidence for this period. The Bhagavad-gītā (probably first century AD) (Brockington 1998: 147) has been assumed to correspond to a Bhāgavata tendency or even affiliation (Esnoul 1956: 155; Matsubara 1994: 2). However it does not contain the word bhāgavata. The Harivaṃśa, a "supplement" (*khila*) to the Mahābhārata (usually dated third to fourth, sometimes first to third centuries AD), mentions a *kṣatriya* devotee, Akrūra, paying hommage to Ananta (the lord of the serpents) who is qualified as Bhāgavata, with "Bhāgavata mantras," an expression which could refer to sacred formulas of a Bhāgavata religious community (Couture 1986: 224–5; Couture 1991: 77;

Brockington 1998: 326). The Nārāyaṇīyaparvan of the Mahābhārata, dated third to fourth/fifth century AD (Brockington 1998: 152; Schreiner 1997a: 1; Oberlies 1997: 86), does not associate any particular meaning with the term *bhāgavata*: the reference to *bhāgavatapriyaḥ* in verses 327.2 and 331.43 is too general, the Poona edition accepts *bhāgavataiḥ* in 332.16 but as an uncertain reading and rejects the term *bhāgavata* as a variant reading in 322.22 and 324.1.

The term *bhāgavata* reappears in epigraphy with the Gupta period mainly in the compounds *paramabhāgavata* ("supreme bhāgavata") and *mahābhāgavata* ("great bhāgavata"), current epithets of monarchs and rulers. The Gupta emperors from Candragupta II (fourth century) onwards styled themselves as Paramabhāgavatas. The same epithet was applied to Dhruvasena I (fifth century) in Saurashtra, Saṃkṣobha (early sixth century) in Central India, Caṇḍavarman and Nandaprabhañjanavarman, Kaliṅga monarchs of Orissa in the late fifth and early sixth centuries (Jaiswal 1967: 201 sqq.), several kings of the so-called Śarabhapurīya dynasty (seventh to eighth centuries) (von Stietencron 1978: 11), and king Śrīvijaya Nandivarman of the Śālaṅkāyana dynasty who ruled over the regions of Godavari and Kṛṣṇa in Andhra in the second half of the fifth century AD (Jaiswal 1967: 205). A Badami (Southern Deccan) sixth-century cave inscription records the patronage of the founding of a cave temple and the consecration of an image of Viṣṇu in it by king Maṅgaleśa, a Mahābhāgavata born in the family of the Calkya-s (=Cālukyas) who performed sacrifices like *agniṣṭoma*, *agnicayana*, *vājapeya*, *pauṇḍarīka*, *bahusuvarṇa*, and *aśvamedha* (Sivaramamurti 1966: 204–6). It appears from this sixth-century inscription that as in the earlier period, the aristocratic followers of Bhāgavatism did not see any contradiction between their performance of Vedic sacrifices and the worship of the image of Viṣṇu. It may be noted that the Tamil text Paripāṭal (fifth or sixth century) which depicts Kṛṣṇa with Balarāma, also mentions Garuḍa's banner and Tirumāl (=Viṣṇu or Kṛṣṇa) as manifesting himself in the Vedic sacrificial post and fire (Gros 1968: xlix). But this text does not contain any explicit reference to Bhāgavatism.

It however remains difficult to evaluate from the above evidence to what extent the aristocratic patrons of Bhāgavatism from the second century BC to the eighth century AD were personally engaged in this tradition or religion. We do not know whether Bhāgavata gods were merely their tutelary deity or whether these patrons underwent an initiation, nor do we have any precise information on the type of rite they performed. No documentation enables us to know whether Bhāgavatism had a popular basis and whether it was an independent tradition with organized institutions.

Bhāgavata priests in fifth- to sixth-century sources

The term *bhāgavata* was also applied to a group of priests in charge of ritual installation of images of Viṣṇu in epigraphical and textual sources from the fifth to sixth century AD. But this does not imply that all Bhāgavatas were priests. A fifth-century Sanskrit inscription of southeast Asia found in the ruins of the monument of Prasat Pram Loven of the Fu-nan (a kingdom which comprised the Mekong delta), mentions Bhāgavatas among those who should enjoy the gift which Guṇavarman donated to a newly installed footprint of Viṣṇu named Cakratīrthasvāmin. These Bhāgavatas are probably the priests of that image (Cœdès 1931; Bhattacharya 1961). The Bṛhatsaṃhitā of Varāhamihira (sixth century) prescribes that the ritual installation of an image should be performed by those devoted to that god – Bhāgavatas in the case of Viṣṇu – according to their own rule (*svavidhi*) (chap. 60, verse 19, in Kern's edition). An earlier verse (12) in the same chapter stipulates that during this installation, the "twice-born" (*dvija*) priest should sacrifice into the fire with the mantras which correspond to the god to be installed. We may infer from this that in the case of Viṣṇu, a twice-born Bhāgavata sacrifices with Vaiṣṇava mantras.

Yogic and Ascetic Traditions (third to ca. fifth century AD)

Besides the Bhāgavata worship evidenced mainly through epigraphy, Sanskrit literature from around the third century AD, attests a tendency which stresses asceticism and yoga in association with devotion for Nārāyaṇa. The existence of organized Vaiṣṇava ascetic communities in this period cannot be excluded, though documentation to sustain this hypothesis is scanty. The early Pāñcarātra and Vaikhānasa traditions promoted this yogico-ascetic-cum-devotional tendency. A main trait of the early Pāñcarātra view of ritual is non-injury, perhaps in answer to the Buddhist criticism of Vedic rites. The Vaikhānasa tradition, especially as represented in its Smārtasūtra, transformed Vedic types of rite and included image worship. This probably answered the questions which arose about the nature of ritual itself, on what the relations between Vedic rite and *pūjā* could be, and, perhaps, how far they could be combined in a devotional context.

Early Pāñcarātra and the Nārāyaṇīyaparvan of the Mahābhārata

Scholars are not unanimous about the origin of the term *pāñcarātra* as applied to a Vaiṣṇava tradition. Some trace it to the Śatapathabrāhmaṇa (13.6.1) (usually dated between tenth and seventh centuries BC), which contains the oldest available occurrence of the term "pañcarātra": this passage describes the god Nārāyaṇa performing a *pañcarātra* ("five nights") *puruṣamedha* sacrifice, after which he is said to have surpassed all beings and become the entire universe. Modern scholars have proposed various explanations of the name (van Buitenen 1971: 6 sqq.; Neevel 1977: 8–10; Brockington 1998: 299–301). Pāñcarātra has also been said to be connected with the Ekāyana, a lost Vedic *śākhā* ("school"). Old Pāñcarātra texts mention Ekāyana mantras and Ekāyana adherents (Matsubara 1994: 54; Bhattacharya 1967: 206). But the Nārāyaṇīyaparvan

(NP) of the Mahābhārata (12, 321–39) does not seem to mention the word *ekāyana*, although it refers to Pañcarātra (Schreiner 1997 (ed.), Lemma-Index). Some scholars consider the link of the Pāñcarātra tradition with this Ekāyanaśākhā as a late fiction (Renou 1985a: 205).

The NP is the oldest known source to record several theological and ritual characteristics of an ancient Pañcarātra tradition, though it does not explicitely originate from the Pāñcarātra milieu. Devotion (*bhakti*), omnipresent in the NP, is addressed to the god Nārāyaṇa, who also bears other names like Hari, Vāsudeva, and Viṣṇu. Without being anti-Vedic or Tantric in character, it tends to subordinate Vedic rituals to its own renunciative ideology which upholds non-injury (*ahiṃsā*) and rites without animal sacrifice. The NP does not refute the way of ritual action (*pravṛtti*), but harmonizes it with suspending ritual activity (*nivṛtti*) and replacing it by yogic devotional practices. All sacrifices, whether executed with the expectation of fruits or not, are said to ultimately go to Nārāyaṇa in whom the "exclusive worshippers [of Nārāyaṇa]" (*ekāntins*) finally enter. It has been suggested that the NP perhaps evokes a concept equivalent to that of release while living (Schreiner 1997b: 178).

The term *bhāgavata* which seems to refer to devotees of Nārāyaṇa in general in the NP does not appear to be synonymous with the term *pañcarātra* in this text. Sātvata (which originally referred to the clan of Kṛṣṇa and later to his worshippers) appears more or less as an equivalent of *pañcarātra* in chapter 336, which belongs to the later part of the text (chapters 327–39, probably completed by the fourth to fifth centuries according to Schreiner 1997a: 1). This is not certain in chapter 322, which belongs to the earlier part (chaps. 321–6, probably written in ca. 200–300 AD, ibid., and Oberlies 1997a: 86). Verses 17–25 of chapter 322 depict the domestic rites and conduct of King Uparicara Vasu who practiced non-injury towards all beings, and being a devotee of Nārāyaṇa, considered himself, his kingdom and his possessions as belonging to Nārāyaṇa. He worshipped the Lord of the gods following the Sātvata method (*vidhi*) of worship promulgated by the Sun god, he then worshipped the ancestors with the rest of the previous worship. He distributed the rest of the ancestor worship to vipras (Brāhmaṇas or priests?) and others and consumed that which remained. In verses 23–4, the king is said to have performed "the best rites" (*paramakriyāḥ*), optional (*kāmya*), periodical (*naimittika*), and daily (*yajñīya*), following the Sātvata method. He used to feed in his house the knowers of the Pañcarātra (*pañcarātravit*), a group which may or may not be different from the Sātvatas. But in another passage of the older part of the NP (324, 28), King Uparicara Vasu is described as offering the five *kālas* to Hari, an expression which could be understood as referring to the Pāñcarātra way of worship. This could either mean that the king practiced two ritual systems or that Sātvata is the same as Pañcarātra or, as it has been suggested, that Sātvata could be a branch of Pañcarātra (Schreiner 1997a: 10).

According to the NP, the Pañcarātra-knowers who have attained the state of *ekānta* enter Hari (337, 67). The Pañcarātra is said to be a "great upaniṣad" which subsumes the four Vedas, Sāṃkhya, and Yoga into itself (326, 100). The

NP refers to two concepts which became essential in later Pāñcarātra: the four-emanation theogony and the five-*kāla* worship. The four emanations bear the names of divine aspects known in mythology and iconography long before the NP: Kṛṣṇa-Vāsudeva, Saṃkarṣaṇa (Kṛṣṇa's elder brother), Pradyumna (Kṛṣṇa's son by Rukmiṇī), and Aniruddha (Pradyumna's son). The specificity of the Pāñcarātra teaching is its reinterpretation of these divine aspects in a cosmological perspective. While, at a later time, Pāñcarātra saṃhitās name these emanations as vyūhas, the NP employs the terms *mūrti* (326, 66–70) and *mūrticatuṣṭaya* (326, 43) to refer to them, though it uses the name *vyūha* in verse 336, 53, where Hari is said to consist of one, two, three, or four *vyūhas*. Chapter 326 (31–41) describes the unborn, unperishable Vāsudeva, supreme soul, *puruṣa* beyond qualities (*guṇa*), entering the five elements which together are said to be his body. Thus Vāsudeva is said to be born and is named *jīva* (soul), the "knower of the field" (*kṣetrajña*) and is called Saṃkarṣaṇa. From this soul proceeds Pradyumna who is the mind (*manas*) of all beings and into which all beings disappear at the time of dissolution. From this arises Aniruddha who is the ego (*ahaṃkāra*) as well as agent, effect and cause (*kartṛ, kārya, kāraṇa*) and from whom sentient and insentient beings come into existence. Saṃkarṣaṇa, Pradyumna, and Aniruddha as well as the entire universe arise from and dissolve into Vāsudeva. Verses 68–9 mention the four emanations and the creation which ensues from them, Brahmā the creator of the world being born of Aniruddha. Chapter 332 describes the four *mūrtis* in the path of release: having become minute, the "best of the vipras" enter the divine being (*deva*) from which they reach and stay in Aniruddha's body. Having become mind, they enter Pradyumna. Leaving Pradyumna they enter Saṃkarṣaṇa who is the *jīva*. Then, freed from the three *guṇas* and pure, they enter *kṣetrajña* who transcends the *guṇas*. Practicing penance and having attained *ekānta*, they finally enter Vāsudeva who is the abode of all beings (14–19).

The NP refers to the practice of *pañcakāla*. This characteristic Pāñcarātra notion, current in the Pāñcarātra Saṃhitās, refers to five observances of the day: *abhigamana* ("approaching [of the god]," that is, morning prayer, ablutions, etc.), *upādāna* (collection of material of worship), *ijyā* ("sacrifice," that is, worship), *svādhyāya* (textual study), and *yoga* (meditation) (Gonda 1977: 72). The NP qualifies the *ekāntin* worshippers of Hari as "knowers of the five kālas" (*pañcakālajña*) (323, 42). King Uparicara Vasu is described as offering the five *kālas* to Hari after he fell into a ravine because of non-observance of *ahiṃsā* (324, 28). Pañcakālakartṛgati, that is, "the one who is the resort of the performer of the *pañcakāla*," is one of the 171 epithets of Nārāyaṇa, who is also designated as *pañcarātrika* (325, 4).

Early Vaikhānasa tradition

Although an often discussed passage of the Chāndogya-upaniṣad (3.17.6) (which mentions a Kṛṣṇa) and comparatively late Vedic texts are associated to some degree with Vaiṣṇavism, no Vedic *śākhā* is so closely and exclusively connected with Vaiṣṇavism as the Vaikhānasa *śākhā* is. Two medieval Vaikhānasa texts, the Ānandasaṃhitā and Ādisaṃhitā, ascribe the Vaikhānasa *śākhā* to the Yajurveda. The first identifies Vaikhānasa with Aukhya *śākhā*, whereas the second considers them as distinct. Dharmaśāstras often consider Vaikhānasas, like Phenapas and Vālakhilyas, as hermits (*vānaprasthas*), those who enter the third stage of life in the *varṇāśrama* system. In the NP, the Vaikhānasa seers are the second group after the Phenapas to receive the Ekāntadharma (336, 14), Soma is the third to receive it, and Vālakhilya seers are the fourth. However the Vaikhānasasmārtasūtra itself does not mention a category of hermits named Vaikhānasas unless the Vairiñca category mentioned in that text should be identified with Vaikhānasa hermits.

Both Vaikhānasa Vedic *sūtras* namely, *śrauta* and *smārta* (probably later than the fourth century and earlier than the eighth century) are attributed to a sage Vikhanas by the Vaikhānasa tradition. The oneness of their authorship is upheld by Caland in his posthumous edition of the Vaikhānasaśrautasūtra (1941: xxv). Their South Indian origin is sometimes questioned but with no serious arguments.

Several passages of the Vaikhānasaśrautasūtra reveal a strong tendency towards devotion to Viṣṇu or Nārāyaṇa. Meditation on these two divine aspects accompanies the performance of several ritual acts. The *ūrdhvapuṇḍra*, a main emblem in later Vaiṣṇavism, which the patron of the sacrifice should draw on several parts of his own body, is eulogized. Some of the mantras which the text prescribes do not belong to known Vedic collections, but their full text seems to be lost. The Vaikhānasasmārtasūtra which consists of both Gṛhya and Dharma parts, frequently mentions devotion to and meditation on Viṣṇu or Nārāyaṇa. It prescribes the installation and daily worship of Viṣṇu's image at home, in a temple (perhaps private), or in a sacrificial pavilion which contains ritual fires. These rites involve the recitation of two mantras: the 8-syllable (*oṃ namo nārāyaṇāya*) and 12-syllable (*oṃ namo bhagavate vāsudevāya*) mantras which became very important in the later Vaiṣṇavism. They also include elements which figure prominently in later medieval Vaikhānasa rituals, like the invocation of the four aspects of Viṣṇu, that is, Puruṣa, Satya, Acyuta, and Aniruddha and the introduction of divine power (*śakti*) into the image before worship.

The Vaikhānasasmārtasūtra is the only known text of its kind to prescribe a ceremony of entry into the hermit stage of life. It describes hermits devoted to Viṣṇu and practicing a *yoga* which involves 10 external observances (*niyama*) (bathing, cleanliness, study, ascesis, generosity etc.) and 10 internal observances (*yama*) (truthfulness, kindness, sincerity, etc.). The practice of *yoga* is still more important in the fourth stage of life, that of the renouncer who aims at uniting his self with the Supreme Self. Besides the practice of the varṇāśrama duties which culminates in renunciation, the Vaikhānasasmārtasūtra also describes yogic paths leading to the Brahman without qualities. It contrasts action "with desire" (*sakāma*) that is, seeking fruits in this world and the other, with "desireless" (*niṣkāma*) action that is, the disinterested performance of what is prescribed. Desireless action is of two kinds: "activity" (*pravṛtti*) and "disengagement" (*nivṛtti*). "Activity" signifies yogic practices and procures yogic powers, but does not procure release from further births. "Disengagement" characterizes those *yogins* for whom the only reality is the Supreme Self and who, having abandoned householder life, realize the "union [*yoga*] of the individual self with the Supreme Self." The Vaikhānasasmārtasūtra distinguishes three classes of these *yogins*, Sāraṅga, Ekārṣya, and Visaraga (or Visaraka), the first two classes comprising respectively four (*anirodhaka, nirodhaka, mārgaga, vimārgaga*) and five (*dūraga, adūraga, bhrūmadhyaga, asaṃbhakta, saṃbhakta*) categories. The *anirodhakas* only practice meditation on Viṣṇu, while the rest of the Sāraṅgas employ methods known from the classical Yogaśāstra. Among the Ekārṣyas, the *dūragas* meditate on the occult body with its subtle veins (*nāḍikā*), whereas the *adūragas* meditate on the Supreme Self (*paramātman*). The *asaṃbhakta* conceives the deity as the unique object of his sensorial perceptions: he contemplates the deity in its form, enjoys its perfume, and salutes it, a devotional attitude reminiscent of the Āḻvārs, the Tamil Vaiṣṇava saints.

Several groups of *yogins* are disapproved or even rejected. The *vimārgagas* are "those who go the wrong way," probably because they distort the (right) object of the meditation (which is the Supreme Self, *paramapuruṣa*, according to a late commentary), although they practice "eight-limbed" (*aṣṭāṅga*) *yoga*, consisting of *yama, niyama, āsana*, etc. which the Yogasūtras describe. The *bhrūmadhyagas* are said to be "without authority" (*niṣpramāṇa*). The *visaraga* class of *yogins* which groups adherents of various currents and doctrines, is condemned. Qualified as "beasts" (*paśu*) and said to follow the "wrong path" (*kupatha*), they reject the possibility of release in their current lifetime. This suggests that the author of the Vaikhānasasmārtasūtra believes in what is generally known as release while living. This viewpoint as well as the primacy of Brahman without quality (*nirguṇa*) over Brahman with quality (*saguṇa*) differs from the position of the later Vaiṣṇava Vedāntic school of Viśiṣṭādvaita (Colas 1996: 17–44).

Ritualistic and Devotional Traditions (Sixth to Thirteenth Centuries)

From the sixth century onwards, several Vaiṣṇava currents gradually built up a textual corpus which helped them to fix and define their own tradition.

Āḻvārs

The 12 Āḻvārs, Tamil poet-saints, composed devotional poems (collected under the title Nālāyira-divyaprabandham in the tenth century) from about the sixth or the early seventh to about the ninth century. Although they did not form a homogenous tradition, their influence on other Vaiṣṇava currents gives them an important place in the history of South Indian Vaiṣṇavism. We know nothing of their affiliation to any specific Vaiṣṇava tradition, if they had any. Periya-āḻvār and Toṇṭaraṭippoṭi may have been temple priests, but the ritual system (Vaikhānasa, Pāñcarātra, or other) they practiced is not known. Like other devotees of their time, the Āḷvārs were probably often engaged in pilgrimage, since their poems praise the presiding deities of 97 south Indian Vaiṣṇava temples. These poems exhibit a high degree of learning and literary skill and can hardly be termed as "popular literature."

Yogic practices like meditation play an important role in the Divyaprabandham. The earlier Āḷvārs, Poykai, Pūtattu, Pēy and Tirumaḻicai sing of the mystic union with Māyōṉ (Kṛṣṇa) attained through meditation and temple worship. Nammāḻvār (Caṭakōpaṉ), a later Āḷvār (seventh or early eighth century), is presumably the first to express devotion to Māyōṉ in terms of the passionate love of a girl for her beloved (Hardy 1983: 307). Several poems of the Divyaprabandham seem to show a kind of nondualism between the individual soul and God and even the notion of release obtained while alive (Hardy 1983: 440–1). Though they cannot be said to illustrate a particular theological system, they could be considered as poetical formulations of attitudes comparable to those found in the NP and in the Vaikhānasasmārtasūtra.

Soon after the last Āḷvār, South Indian Vaiṣṇava traditions encouraged the diffusion of the Divyaprabandham. Hagiography credits (Śrīraṅga-)Nāthamuni (probably tenth century) with the rediscovery of these poems. From his time onwards, the 4,000 stanzas of the Divyaprabandham were canonized and recited in the Shrirangam temple, a practice which spread to other Vaiṣṇava temples in South India. The Kōyil Oḻuku, chronicle of the Shrirangam temple, describes the duties of the Araiyars or Viṇṇappaṉ-ceyvār, literally "supplicants" who were and still are, in charge of chanting and illustrating (by stylized gestures) the Divyaprabandham and enacting simple religious dramas. The oldest known inscription mentioning the Araiyars goes back to the end of the eleventh century. Today, male descendants of hereditary lineages of Araiyars perform in three temples of Tamil Nadu (Shrivilliputtur, Shrirangam, and Alvar-tirunagari) and in the temple of Melkote in Karnataka (Hari Rao 1961: 78–9, 90; Vēṅkaṭarāmaṉ 1985).

Sāttvatas and Bhāgavatas

cf SAIVAS + MAHEŚVARAS IN SAIVITE TRADITION

Sāttvatas and Bhāgavatas formed groups which are difficult to identify since the meaning of these terms changed according to the historical context. Though Sāttvata (sometimes in the orthography Sātvata) sometimes appears to be synonymous with Pāñcarātra (Matsubara 1994: 60–2), it may not always have been the case as we saw in a passage of the NP. A ninth-century Cambodian inscription (stele of Prasat Komnap) which records the foundation by Yaśovarman I of a Vaiṣṇava monastery (vaiṣṇavāśrama) designed to feed Vaiṣṇavas, mentions three denominations among them: pañcarātra, bhāgavata, and sāttvatas, but it does not yield any precise definition of sāttvata (Cœdès 1932: 88–112).

Several scholars consider that the term *bhāgavata* refers to a group of Vaiṣṇava Smārtas which was already in existence in the sixth century AD and was still widespread in south India at the beginning of the twentieth century. These Bhāgavatas are said to adhere to nondualism and worship the five gods Viṣṇu, Śiva, Durgā, Sūrya, and Gaṇeśa, consider Viṣṇu equal to Śiva, by contrast with other Smārtas who prefer Siva to Viṣṇu. Their main scripture is said to be the Bhāgavatapurāṇa and their mantra *oṃ namo bhagavate vāsudevāya* (Farquhar 1967: 142–3; 181; 233; 297–8). A "Bhāgavatasampradāya" group of Vaiṣṇavas having the above characteristics was known until recently in the Kannaḍa country. Its priests officiate in temples, several of them in Udipi. Curiously, they follow the Śaivāgama (not the Pāñcarātrāgama) ritual, though they seem to have integrated Pāñcarātra ritual elements (Siauve 1968: 11–12). Bhāgavata is also the name of Brahmin actors of *kūcipūḍi* who enact plays on Vaiṣṇava themes in the Telugu country (Sastry 1991: 64).

The significance of the term *bhāgavata vis-à-vis* the term *pāñcarātra* fluctuated from the seventh century onwards. It signified devotee of the Lord in general including Pāñcarātrins or referred to the follower of a specific Bhāgavata tradition or was taken as synonymous with Pāñcarātrin. Bāṇa's Harṣacarita (seventh century) clearly mentions Bhāgavata and Pāñcarātrika as distinct groups. Vaikhānasa texts of around the tenth century set the Bhāgavatas and Pāñcarātrikas apart. They describe Bhāgavatas as "tonsured," their doctrine being "secondary" and their scriptures being "mixed" (Colas 1996: 173). But by the eleventh century Viśiṣṭādvaitins like Yāmuna and Rāmānuja identify Bhāgavatas with Pāñcarātrins.

Evidence from Cambodian epigraphy shows that a Bhāgavata could be one who performs temple rites and perhaps also a Pāñcarātra expert or one who resides in a Vaiṣṇava monastery. The mid-seventh-century deteriorated inscription of the stele of Baset found at Battamban records that the *ācārya* Dharmapāla who was born in a Bhāgavata family installed an image of Acyuta and mentions his (?) expertise in Pāñcarātra (Cœdès 1942: 193–5). A ninth-century inscription of Prasat Kok Po relates the ritual installation of an image of Hari in 857 AD by a "Bhāgavata kavi" named Śrīnivāsakavi who was the preceptor of Jayavarman III. It also mentions a member of Śrīnivāsakavi's family, Amṛtagarbha, who bore the title Bhāgavata (Cœdès and Dupont 1937: 389–90). The above-mentioned ninth-century inscription of Prasat Komnap lists the qualifications of those Bhāgavatas who are eligible to reside in the Vaiṣṇava monastery: they practice the three *sandhyā* rites, observe good conduct and textual study, are not householders, restrain their senses, have nowhere to stay during the rainy season, and eat one meal a day.

The expansion and influence of the Pāñcarātra system

The early history of the Pāñcarātra and of its corpus after the NP (see above) still remains uncertain (Matsubara 1994: 17 sqq.). Modern scholarship tends to ascribe the oldest extant Pāñcarātra texts to the sixth century at the earliest, but still discusses the region of their compilation (Gonda 1977: 56; Gupta 1972: xxi; Matsubara 1994: 18–21). The Jayākhyasaṃhitā, one of the Pāñcarātra ancient texts, mentions the Vaikhānasa group which is presumably of south Indian origin (Colas 1996: 22 n. 1; 53 n. 1).

Bāṇa (seventh century) mentions the Pāñcarātrikas. The Advaitin Śaṅkara (eighth century) refers to the adherents of the Pāñcarātra (*pāñcarātrasiddhāntins*) in his commentary on Brahmasūtra 2, 2, 44. His criticism of their tenets proves that the Pāñcarātra doctrine was well-known in his time in south India. In spite of the importance of the Pāñcarātra tradition, inscriptions referring to it are scanty (Smith 1968). A Tirumukkudal (Chengalpattu district of Tamil Nadu) inscription of Vīrarājendra Cōḻa (1063–9) records a donation to the Vaikuṇṭhaperumāḷ temple partly for the maintainance of a Vedic college where Mahāpāñcarātra and Vaikhānasa, among other subjects, would be taught (Sankaranaranayan 1983: 18–19). A Tiruvarur (Tanjore district of Tamil Nadu) inscription of the twelfth century mentions the Pañcarātrasaṃhitās as authoritative in matters of architecture besides Vaikhānasa scriptures, Śaivāgamas, etc. (cf. S.I.I. 17: 270).

In fact, Cambodian epigraphy provides a comparatively larger and earlier documentation on Pāñcarātra (often in the orthography Pañcarātra). The seventh-century Thvar Kdei inscription mentions the well-known Pāñcarātra *caturvyūha* concept. This notion, though not the term *vyūha*, apppears in inscriptions of Koh Ker (during the reign of Jayavarman IV, 921–41 AD), Pre Rup (961 AD, Rājendravarman), Prasat Kok Po (during the reign of Jayavarman V, 968–1001 AD) (Bhattacharya 1961: 98). The already mentioned Baset inscription (between 648 and 657 AD) informs us about a person who performs the five sacrifices (*yajña*), follows the five timely observances (*pañcakālābhigāmin*), and knows the five elements "of those well-versed in the meaning of Pañcarātra doctrine." These observances probably refer to those of Pañcarātra, and *abhigāmin* in the compound *pañcakālābhigāmin* perhaps alludes to the first of them, *abhigamana*, that is, morning prayer, ablutions, etc. (Bhattacharya 1964: 50; 1965). A later inscription from the reign of Rājendravarman (944–68 AD) mentions a priest "proficient in Pañcarātra" and "knower of the five timely observances (*pañcakāla*)" (Cœdès 1953: 121). The already mentioned Prasat Komnap stele inscription (late ninth century) mentions knowers of the Pañcarātra precepts (*pañcarātravidhānajña*) among guests to be honored, which means perhaps that they were not permanent residents of the Vaiṣṇavāśrama (Cœdès 1932: 88–112, esp. 98). The Kup Trapan Srok stele in Khmer records the activities of a sacerdotal family, an ancestor of whom, named Kavīśvarapaṇḍita, followed the Pañcarātra observances, was the head of four hermitages, installed an image of Bhagavatī (in 1003 AD) and a *liṅga*. Other members of his family installed various non-Vaiṣṇava representations like Caṇḍī and *liṅgas* (Cœdès 1942: 129–33). Could this indicate a tolerant or syncretististic Vaiṣṇavism which would be peculiar to ancient Cambodia?

These inscriptions demonstrate the influence of Pāñcarātra in this part of southeast Asia as early as the seventh century, that is, not much later than the composition of the oldest known Pāñcarātra *saṃhitās*. Pāñcarātra rituals and doctrine often inspired such systems as Viśiṣṭādvaita, Dvaita, and later Vaiṣṇava schools. Important Pāñcarātra texts were still being written in India in the seventeenth century (Matsubara 1994: 34–5).

Vaikhānasa corpus of temple rituals

By contrast with the influential Pāñcarātra corpus, Vaikhānasa scriptures, their *sūtras*, and the texts which govern their temple rites (here called "medieval corpus" for the sake of convenience), remained comparatively less known to non-Vaikhānasas. This may be partly due to the fact that the Vaikhānasa tradition was reputed as a Vedic *śākhā* and not as a group to which one adhered through initiation. Nevertheless it greatly contributed to the growth of public temple worship in South India before the reforms of Rāmānuja who is said to have favored the Pāñcarātra method of worship.

The evolution of the Vaikhānasa community from its renunciative traits to professional priesthood practicing temple rites aiming at the prosperity of the society is not well known. It appears in a Karnataka copper-plate dated 828 AD that Vaikhānasas also worshipped non-Vaiṣṇava deities: this inscription mentions that a Vaikhānasa named Devaśarman of the Kāśyapa clan was commissioned to worship the image of a sword-bearing goddess for King Rājamalla II. Later south Indian inscriptions (especially from the eleventh century onwards), however, record Vaikhānasas as priests in Vaiṣṇava temples. One of them, an edict of the Cōḻa King Rājarāja I, applicable to Cōḻa, Toṇṭai, and Pāṇḍya regions, allows villagers to confiscate and sell properties on which Vaikhānasas (among others) have not paid due taxes, thus indicating the affluence of the Vaikhānasas of that period. Epigraphic evidence attests that in the eleventh to twelfth centuries the Vaikhānasa tradition was considered both as a Vedic *śākhā* and reputed for the architectural and iconographic teachings of its scriptures (Colas 1996: 58–64).

The main part or totality of the medieval corpus of Vaikhānasas was probably composed in a rather short period between ninth and thirteenth/fourteenth centuries, that is, much later than their *sūtras*. Vaikhānasas considered it as a continuation with their *sūtra* corpus and forming with it what they call the Vaikhānasaśāstra. Its designation by the late expression "Vaikhānasāgama" is anachronistic. Vaikhānasa tradition lists as many as 28 texts in the medieval corpus and attributes them to Vikhanas's four disciples: Bhṛgu, Kāśyapa, Atri, and Marīci, and sometimes to a fifth author, Aṅgiras, also often identified with Marīci. By 1997 nine texts of the corpus and the corresponding collection of mantras were published fully or in part.

Though the published texts mainly deal with ritual, they also provide some gnostic and theological teaching. The Vimānārcanākalpa contains a complete gnosis (*jñāna*) section. Its physiology which involves mystical centers and a complex "vein" (*nāḍī*) system differs from that of such texts as the Haṭhayogapradīpikā (probably composed after the fourteenth century). Its metaphysical speculations consist of a kind of theistic Sāṃkhya with the emanation of successive "principles" (*tattva*) from the Primordial Matter (*pradhāna, prakṛti*), but this Matter ontologically depends on Viṣṇu. Its teachings are similar to those of the Viṣṇusmṛti and it borrows certain passages almost verbatim from the Bhagavadgītā. Certain ritual passages of the corpus also prescribe meditations on complex metaphysical notions, for example the visualization by the performer of the god from his "undivided" (*niṣkala*) aspect to his aspect "with divisions" (*sakala*). Mantric texts like the Ekākṣara, the Ātmasūkta, and the Pāramātmika contain the conception of an Ātman or Viṣṇu, both the creator of the universe and omnipresent in it.

The major Vaikhānasa theogonical notion is the group of "Five Manifestations" (*pañcamūrti*): Primordial Viṣṇu, Puruṣa, Satya, Acyuta, and Aniruddha, already announced in the Vaikhānasasmārtasūtra. The medieval corpus provides abundant instructions for the installation of this group of Manifestations in a temple. It considers the last four of these Manifestations as fractions of the Primordial Viṣṇu and as incarnating his four qualities (*dharma, jñāna, aiśvarya,* and *vairāgya*), four Vedas, four cosmic ages, etc. Puruṣa etc. are sometimes identified with Viṣṇu, Sadāviṣṇu, Mahāviṣṇu, and Nārāyaṇa (or Vyāpin) (also mentioned in Pāñcarātra texts), and sometimes they are said to arise respectively from them. The medieval corpus contains frequent and long descriptions of the iconography and ritual installation of Viṣṇu's incarnations (*avatāra*), sometimes divided into *āvirbhāvas* (Matsya, Kūrma, Varāha, Nṛsiṃha, and Vāmana) and *prādurbhāvas* (Paraśurāma, Rāghavarāma, Balarāma, Kṛṣṇa, and Kalkin).

While the Vaikhānasaśrautasūtra, in common with Vedic and Mīmāṃsaka texts, did not recognize Śūdras (the fourth class of the society) and Anulomas (groups born from fathers of a higher class than that of the mother) as qualified to be *yajamānas*, that is, institutors of Vedic sacrifices, the medieval corpus accepts them as *yajamānas* of several major temple rites like the installation of an image, festivals, marriage of the god with Śrī and Bhū. This admission was conditioned by the presence of devotion to Viṣṇu in the patron and by the ritual intermediary of a "king" (*rājan*), that is, of an economically and/or politically eminent person (though perhaps not specifically a person of a Kṣatriya class which was absent from south Indian society). An initiation called Nigamadīkṣā which Vaikhānasas conferred to non-Vaikhānasas served as a ritual recognition of the presence of devotion. This positive reevaluation of the role of Śūdras and Anulomas perhaps corresponded to the growing economic and social importance of these potential temple patrons. They could not be classified as twice-born, as was the case with Veḷḷāḻas, often agriculturists, whom inscriptions of the eleventh century mention as donors to Vaikhānasa temples. The rather rigid social pattern which the corpus prescribes is also mitigated by the omnipresence of devotion, ritualized or not, in the masses, for instance during the Festival (*utsava*), when strict rules against social promiscuity were lifted at least temporarily.

The medieval Vaikhānasa corpus was addressed to Vaikhānasas who were temple priests. Their qualification for this office was conditioned by their undergoing of the personal sacraments (*saṃskāras*) which the Vaikhānasasmārtasūtra enjoined and, in more recent texts of the corpus, the "initiation in the maternal womb" (*garbhadīkṣā*). The corpus limited temple priesthood to householders (*gṛhastha*) and Brahmanical students (*brahmacārin*), hermits and renouncers being denied this right (except in rare cases), thus making a remarkable shift from the ascetic values which the Vaikhānasasmārtasūtra promoted. While Vaikhānasas of this corpus considered themselves and were considered by outsiders as belonging to a Vedic *śākhā* (which signifies that they belonged to the Brāhmaṇa community), they perhaps practiced endogamy, as they do today, thus forming a "caste."

The medieval corpus while situating its tradition among Vedic *śākhās*, provides an interesting though somewhat confused picture of these *śākhās*. It also classifies cultic and doctrinal systems (*siddhānta*, *mata*, and *śāstra*, and *samaya* for "non-*vaidika*" systems). It claims Vaikhānasa tradition to be "*vaidika*," peaceful (*saumya*), bringing about enjoyment here and in other worlds as well as release, and procuring general well-being. By contrast, Pāñcarātra is considered as "*avaidika*," *tāntrika* and sometimes as "cruel" (*krūra*), meant for ascetics and for those who search exclusively for release, and is to be practiced in places outside villages and towns. This stern doxographical standpoint perhaps denotes a wish to restrain the influence of Pāñcarātra in public temple worship. Current practice, however, was probably less rigorous, for the corpus itself prescribes a ritual expiation in the case of admixing Pāñcarātra and Vaikhānasa systems of worship, which implies that admixing was not infrequent. Although allocating the main ritual functions exclusively to Vaikhānasas, it permits the employment of Pāñcarātrins as ritual assistants (*paricāraka*).

The word *dīkṣā* bears several meanings in the corpus. Firstly, *dīkṣā* refers to a pseudo-Vedic practice consisting mainly of a series of ascetic commitments like fasting, supposed to prevent the pollution of the priests and patrons which would occur due to birth or death in their families during the performance of several long rituals (Colas 1999). Secondly, it refers to an "initiation in the maternal womb" (*garbhadīkṣā*) prescribed to all Vaikhānasas. According to the Vaikhānasasmārtasūtra, the sacrament of *sīmantonnayana* (tracing a furrow in the hair of a woman in the eighth month of her pregnancy) is followed by an offering of rice cooked in milk to Viṣṇu and feeding the rest of it to the Vaikhānasa pregnant wife. The rather late Ānandasaṃhitā adds an initiation which consists of branding this rice with hot metallic forms of a disk and a conch (symbols of Viṣṇu) before it is fed to the pregnant Vaikhānasa wife. There is no evidence for this practice being current at the time of the older and intermediate texts of the corpus, and the very expression "*garbhadīkṣā*" which the Ānandasaṃhitā employs to refer to it may be still later than the introduction of this ceremony. Vaikhānasas may have introduced this device perhaps under the pressure of Pāñcarātrins, as a proof of their Vaiṣṇavahood which they proclaim to be innate.

The corpus also prescribes two kinds of initiation (*dīkṣā*) to non-Vaikhānasas: the Nyāsacakradīkṣā and the Nigamadīkṣā. The Nyāsacakradīkṣā seems to be mentioned and described only in the Ānandasaṃhitā. Meant for non-Vaikhānasa hermits, it consists of the application of a santal paste etc. with forms of a conch and a disk on the arms of the disciple with the recitation of non-Vedic formulas. The Nigamadīkṣā, also called *taptacakrāṅkaṇa* ("branding with a hot disk"), is mentioned only in two texts, namely the Samūrtārcanādhikaraṇa, which is ancient in the corpus, and the Ānandasaṃhitā, probably a more recent one. According to the Samūrtārcanādhikaraṇa, this ceremony gives Śūdras and Anulomas the ritual qualification of offering a sacrifice and also enables non-Vaikhānasas to be employed as cooks and ritual assistants in temples of Vaikhānasa ritual, when born Vaikhānasas are not available for these tasks. According to the Ānandasaṃhitā, candidates to this initiation may be twice-born or Śūdras or belong to a "mixed class" (i.e., be Anulomas or Pratilomas). It describes this ceremony which, like the Pāñcarātra initiation, consists of five sacraments: branding the arms of the initiand with hot metallic forms of a conch and a disk, directing him to wear the Vaiṣṇava emblem (*ūrdhvapuṇḍra*) on 12 parts of his body, attributing him a Vaiṣṇava name, teaching him a mantra (on which details are not given), and introducing him to the Vaiṣṇava "sacrifice," that is, the worship of Viṣṇu.

While the corpus naturally extolls its own ritual, it nevertheless allows traditional and local customs to operate with regard to temples of "nonhuman" origin. Its rules are supposed to be applied to temples identified as those founded by human beings, but not to temples of "nonhuman" origin that is, those supposed to correspond to a direct manifestation of Viṣṇu, or to have been founded by other gods, or by a Seer or which are mythological (*paurāṇika*). The texts thus leave a large scope for innovation since the human origin of a temple may be obliterated within a few years of its actual foundation.

The main subject of the corpus, however, are the prescriptions relating to worship in public temples, for it is said that the all-pervasive Viṣṇu manifests himself in the image out of compassion for his devotees. The older texts of the corpus distinguish between domestic worship (*gṛhārcā*) and temple worship (*ālayapūjana*), that is, in a public shrine, more on the basis of the importance of the ritual than of its nature. More recent texts differentiate between worship performed "for one's own self" (*svārtha or ātmārtha*), which brings fruits to the performer, and that performed "for others" (*parārtha*), which benefits the patron who finances it. The notion of *yajamāna* which the corpus applies to the patron echoes the Vedic division between the ritual patron and actual performers of the rite. Temple rites and the results which they produce are often equated with Vedic rites and their results in a hyperbolic way. Temple worship is not only said to be an extension of Vedic rites, but also to last even after the *yajamāna* disappears and to benefit the whole village including those who do not practice the domestic fire-sacrifice.

Vaikhānasa temple worship consists of three aspects: yogic practices, pseudo-Vedic rites, and ceremonies performed to the material representation of the deity.

Though not numerous, yogic practices are not altogether absent from temple worship. Meditation plays an essential role at precise moments in the ritual performance and the priest is often enjoined the practice of breath-control (*prāṇāyāma*). The Vimānārcanākalpa contains a section on *yoga* which is intended for the Vaikhānasa temple priest though not exclusively for him. The final goal of *yoga* is *samādhi*, a state of release while living (*jīvanmukti*), a notion which the Vaiṣṇava Vedānta school of Viśiṣṭādvaita rejects. The Vimānārcanākalpa prescribes the classical pattern of an eight-limbed (*aṣṭāṅga*) *yoga*. Its description of *yoga* bears close similarities with two chapters of the Ahirbudhnyasaṃhitā, a Pāñcarātra text. It however conceives *brahmacarya* which forms part of *yoga* practice as fidelity to his spouse for the householder and sexual abstinence for those in the other three stages of life, while the Pāñcarātra text understands it as complete sexual abstinence even with one's own spouse. Temple rites also involve procedures which, though rather Tantric in character, can be understood as yogic broadly speaking. Mystical gestures (*mudrā*) are very rare in the corpus but imposition (*nyāsa*) of mantras and germ-syllables (*bīja*) are prescribed (more often on the image than on the ritual performer's body). The Khilādhikāra enjoins a "purification of the elements" (*bhūtaśuddhi*) of the performer's body through meditation, a procedure not found in the oldest texts of the corpus, but current in Pāñcarātra and Śaiva ritual traditions. Ritual conceptualization of the divine power (*śakti*), also found, for instance, in Śaivāgama, plays an important role in the corpus, since the installation of divine power in the image is a condition *sine qua non* for its worship.

Vedicized ceremonies often run parallel to ceremonies devoted to the image. They are borrowed from the Vaikhānasa Śrauta and Smārta Sūtras but are often transformed. Fire-sacrifices have a secondary importance during festivals and daily worship but they are numerous and elaborate during the solemn installation of an image in a temple. The fire-pavilion of the Vaikhānasaśrautasūtra was rectangular in shape; that of the medieval corpus is made square to suit ritual transformations. The five *śrauta* fires and a sixth lotus-shaped fire called Pauṣkara are installed around a central altar on which the image to be installed, and vases are placed. Each of these fires is identified with a world and with a divine Vaikhānasa manifestation. Domestic fires prescribed by the Vaikhānasasmārtasūtra are also sometimes added to these six fires. Fire-procedures, from their preparation and kindling to their abandonment or their keeping for daily worship, form a ritual cycle almost independant of image worship, though the corpus sometimes attempts to connect them through the notions of fire and divine power (Colas 1996: 280–3).

The worship of the image of Viṣṇu, his different aspects, and attendants is the most prominent feature of temple ritual. The corpus contains a great quantity of iconographic descriptions of the numerous deities to be installed ideally in large temples with several enclosures. The same divine aspect can be represented by as many as five images (*dhruva, kautuka-arcā, autsava, snāpana, balibera*), each of them fulfilling a specific function. For instance, the fixed (*dhruva*) image, said to represent the immovable and undivided (*niṣkala*) form of the god, is the reserve of divine power. The mobile image of worship (*kautuka, arcā*) which receives the essential of the daily worship but draws its power from the fixed image, is said to represent the movable and divided (*sakala*) form of the god.

The main rituals are similar to those found in Pāñcarātra and Śaiva ritual traditions. The initial rite is the installation (*pratiṣṭhā*) of a new image in a new temple, a long rite in which major ceremonies are the opening of the eyes of the image and the final shower of water imbibed with divine power on the installed image(s). It could last several years because it is closely connected with the material construction of the temple. The daily rite of worship (*nityapūjā*) of the *kautuka* image is usually performed three times in the day (morning, midday, and evening before sunset). There are many varieties depending on the number of homages it includes. The rite of the festival (*utsava*) may be the regular yearly one (*kālotsava*) or motivated by faith (*śraddhotsava*) or of an exceptional character (*naimittikotsava*). It may last between one and 21 days. The texts of the Vaikhānasa corpus also prescribe expiatory rites (*prāyaścitta, niṣkṛti*) and different kinds of solemn baths which are purificatory or expiatory in nature. They often contain one or several chapters devoted to minor and optional festivals, thus giving a complete and vivid picture of the liturgical calendar of a south Indian temple around the tenth century.

The production of religious literature by Vaikhānasas did not cease with their medieval corpus but continued well into the twentieth century. Apart from *belles-lettres* works, this later literature consists of ritual manuals, hymns, commentaries on the Vaikhānasasūtras and Brahmasūtras, on medieval texts and parts of the mantra collection. The Mokṣopāyapradīpikā by Raghupati Bhaṭṭācārya (twentieth century?), for example, extolls the role of worship as a means of release.

Vaikhānasas also tried to impose themselves as a third division of Śrīvaiṣṇavism on a par with Teṉkalai and Vaṭakalai. This later doctrinal dependance of Vaikhānasas on Śrīvaiṣṇavism, even while they preserved their ritual specificity, reflects a major departure from their tradition as represented in the medieval corpus (Goudriaan 1965; Colas 1988, 1995, 1996).

The Rise and Development of Vaiṣṇava Schools of Vedānta

The tenth to thirteenth centuries saw the rise and development of three Vaiṣṇava schools of Vedānta which gave theistic interpretations of Upaniṣadic doctrines: Viśiṣṭādvaita, Dvaita, and Dvaitādvaita, to which modern scholars often add Viṣṇusvāmin's school. Though these early Vaiṣṇava Vedāntic schools are often grouped together, their destinies varied much in terms of geographical expansion and influence. We do not have any extant text of Viṣṇusvāmin's system. The other three schools produced articulated philosophical systems. They emphasized the role of devotion as a means of attaining release (by contrast with Śaṅkara's Advaita which considered knowledge as the sole means) and greatly influenced directly or indirectly the later Vaiṣṇava traditions. Each was accompanied and more or less supported by a specific network of religious institutions, particular ritual systems and modes of transmission. Viśiṣṭādvaita and Dvaita developed and received a religious basis first and mostly in South India. There is no testimony of the influence of Nimbārka, the Dvaitādvaita founder, and of Viṣṇusvāmin in south India, though hagiography places their birth in this part of the subcontinent.

The school of Viśiṣṭādvaita

While Viśiṣṭādvaita ("nondualism of what is qualified") refers to a certain doctrine, the term Śrīvaiṣṇavism (to be differentiated from the more general word Vaiṣṇavism) could be said to refer to the socioreligious manifestation of this doctrine as it was integrated and promoted by Viśiṣṭādvaita in south India. Modern scholarship does not seem to have yet brought out a clear historical definition of this term. In fifteenth-century epigraphy the term *śrīvaiṣṇava* is used to qualify a Vaiṣṇava group known as Sāttāda. It is today often taken as referring solely to a group of Brahmins called Aiyaṅkārs, but it is admitted that the use of the word may have not been so exclusive in the past (Jagadeesan 1977: 323; Lester 1994: 44, 47, 48; Hardy 1998: 101). The word *śrī* in the expression Śrī-vaiṣṇava is sometimes explained as stressing the role of Śrī, the spouse of Viṣṇu, in this tradition (Renou 1985a: 652; 1985b: 22). Developed in south India, Viśiṣṭādvaita came to be known later as Śrīsampradāya in north India.

Viśiṣṭādvaita is also called Ubhayavedānta since it refers to both (*ubhaya*) Vedānta doctrine written in Sanskrit and the mystical experience recorded in the Āḻvārs songs in Tamil as its sources. Viśiṣṭādvaita usually considers Nāthamuni (probably born at the beginning of the tenth century) as its first teacher. According to hagiography, Nāthamuni was born in a Brahmin family in Vīranārāyaṇapuram (near Cidambaram) where he officiated in the temple of Rājagopāla. His role in the rediscovery and early propagation of the Divyaprabandham has already been mentioned. His instauration of the practice of singing the Divyaprabandham in the Shrirangam temple gave these hymns the status of Vedas. Scholars have argued for or against his being a follower of Pāñcarātra ritual (Mesquita 1979; Neevel 1977). Renowned for his yogic capacities, he is attributed with several doctrinal works in Sanskrit which are known only through quotations in later texts. His Nyāyatattva, quoted by Yāmuna and Vedānta Deśika, is considered as the first treatise which systematized Viśiṣṭādvaita doctrine. His main disciple was Puṇḍarīkākṣa (Uyyakoṇṭār), himself succeeded by Rāma Miśra (Maṇakkāl Nampi). The works of these authors are known only through quotations.

Yāmuna (Āḻavantār, eleventh century) is the first *ācārya* whose several complete works are preserved. He was the grandson of Nāthamuni and like him a native of Vīranārāyaṇapuram. He is said to have become an ascetic after several years of marriage. Hagiographical accounts relate that under the guidance of

Rāma Miśra, he left a life of luxury in the Cōḻa capital Gangaikondacholapuram and settled in Shrirangam as a renouncer. He wrote the Stotraratna and the Catuḥśloki, two well-known poems, and the Gītārthasaṅgraha, a summary of the teachings of the Bhagavadgītā. His Siddhitraya explains the Viśiṣṭādvaitic conception of the individual soul, the Supreme being, and knowledge. His Āgamaprāmāṇya which is the first extant Viśiṣṭādvaitic work to defend the authoritativeness of the Pāñcarātra texts, argues that these texts are revelations of the God and are equal to Vedas (Srinivasachari 1970: 512–16; Neevel 1977: 17).

Rāmānuja (Uṭaiyavar, said to have died in AD 1137) is the best known among Viśiṣṭādvaitin teachers. According to traditional accounts, he was born in Shriperumbudur near Kanchipuram in a Brahmin family. He was taught in Kanchipuram by one Yādavaprakāśa, probably an Advaitin, also sometimes identified with the Yādavaprakāśa, who propounded the Bhedābheda philosophy. He received instruction on the Divyaprabandham, Rāmāyaṇa, and the true meaning (*rahasya*) of mantras from five of Yāmuna's disciples. It is said that when Tirukoṭṭiyūr Nampi (Goṣṭhīpūrṇa) taught Rāmānuja the secret meaning of the eight-syllabled mantra (*oṃ namo nārāyaṇāya*), Rāmānuja immediately revealed it from the Tirukoshtiyur temple tower out of compassion for the crowd gathered in the shrine. Rāmānuja left the life of a householder, became a renouncer, and was called to preside over the activities of the Shrirangam temple. It is said that during his north Indian pilgrimage he read in Kashmir a manuscript of the Bodhāyanavṛtti, a commentary of the Brahmasūtras, which later formed the basis of his own commentary. To escape the persecution of Vaiṣṇavas by the Cōḻa king Kulottuṅga I, a fanatical follower of Śaivism, he fled from Shrirangam to Karnāṭaka where he converted the Jain Hoysala king Biṭṭideva (Viṣṇuvardhana) to Vaiṣṇavism. He is said to have returned to Shrirangam in 1118 where, as administrator of the temple, he replaced the Vaikhānasa mode of worship with that of the Pāñcarātra. He is also said to have established the Pāñcarātra system of worship in many other Vaiṣṇava temples. There is, however, no historical basis for this.

Rāmānuja's Śrībhāṣya, a commentary on the Brahmasūtras, established Viśiṣṭādvaita as a full-fledged philosophical school. Its main conception is that the Brahman has the individual souls (*cit*) and the insentient world (*acit*) as his modes (*prakāras*). Both these modes are as real as the Brahman and dependent on him as the body is dependent on the soul. Rāmānuja also wrote short treatises on these *sūtras*, the Vedāntasāra and the Vedāntadīpa, as well as a commentary on the Bhagavadgītā. His Vedārthasaṃgraha refutes nondualist and dualist doctrines and explains seemingly contradictory Upaniṣadic passages. The attribution to Rāmānuja of the Nityagrantha, which gives instructions for the personal daily worship of an image, has been challenged. Three devotional poems are attributed to him (Vaikuṇṭhagadya, Śaraṇāgatigadya, Śrīraṅgagadya) (Hari Rao 1961: 45; Srinivasachari 1970: 516–21; Carman 1981: 24–64).

Piḷḷai Lokācārya and Vedānta Deśika are two major figures of Viśiṣṭādvaita after him. Piḷḷai Lokācārya seems to have flourished during the second half of the thirteenth century. His works mainly written in a highly sanskritized Tamil (Maṇipravāḷa), are compiled under the title Aṣṭādaśarahasya, 18 texts of which the Tattvatraya, the Arthapañcaka, and the Śrīvacanabhūṣaṇa are well-known. Maṇavāḷamāmuṉi (also named Varavaramuni and Ramyajāmātrimuni, fourteenth century), a celebrated commentator of the works of Piḷḷai Lokācārya, also wrote the Yatirājaviṃśati, a well-known hymn on Rāmānuja. Following the preceptors of Shrirangam, he was actively engaged in expounding the devotional teachings contained in the hymns of the Āḻvārs. Vedānta Deśika (Veṅkaṭanātha), born and educated in Kanchipuram, was a younger contemporary of Piḷḷai Lokācārya whom he controverts in his works. He is credited with 130 works in Sanskrit, Tamil, and Maṇipravāḷa which contain commentaries on the works of Yāmuna and Rāmānuja, independent treatises, devotional hymns, and literary works. A brilliant logician, he not only perfected the doctrine of Viśiṣṭādvaita and refuted the doctrines of rival schools but also developed Viśiṣṭādvaita logic based on the works of Viṣṇucitta, Nāthamuni, and others. He gave a theistic interpretation of the Pūrvamīmāṃsāsūtras which he considered as forming one work with the Brahmasūtras. He emphasized the role of "self-surrender" (*prapatti*, the attitude whereby the soul surrenders the responsibility of its protection to God) towards release and defended the authority of Pāñcarātra scriptures. True to the spirit of Ubhayavedānta, he summarized Nammāḻvār's hymns in Sanskrit (Singh 1958).

MONKEY / ŚRI = VIṢṆU

The schism between the Vaṭakalai ("the Northern division") which traces its origin to Vedānta Deśika and the Teṉkalai ("the Southern division") which traces its origin to Piḷḷai Lokācārya and Maṇavāḷamāmuṉi is not attested before the late sixteenth century (Mumme 1988: 2). Some scholars explain this split as resulting from the Vaṭakalai preference for the Sanskrit tradition and the Teṉkalai preference for the Tamil Divyaprabandham (Appadurai 1977: 56). However the differences between these two divisions are based not so much on linguistic grounds as on doctrinal principles (Mumme 1988: 6–7). One of the principal differences (which later texts believe to be 18 in number) concerns the definition of *prapatti*. The Vaṭakalai, according to which the soul is required to make an effort to be saved by Viṣṇu, is often described as the school of the monkey's baby, which clings to its mother. By contrast, the Teṉkalai, according to which God alone chooses those whom he wants to save, believes that the soul should abandon all effort. It is known as the school of the kitten, for the kitten lets its mother carry it around in her mouth. Another subject of doctrinal dissension was the role of Lakṣmī. The two schools stress her role as an intermediary between God and the devotee, but the Vaṭakalai believes that she is infinite and ontologically of the same level as Viṣṇu while the Teṉkalai holds that she is only a soul (*jīva*) which is ever liberated. Vaṭakalai followers give more importance to ritual performance than the Teṉkalai. Both the divisions consider the initiation by the five sacraments (*pañcasaṃskāras*) indispensable, but while the Teṉkalai followers do not see the need of a further formal initiation into *prapatti*, the Vaṭakalai consider it to be necessary. In the course of time the antagonism between the two divisions expressed in such minor details as the shape of the

Vaiṣṇava emblem (*ūrdhvapuṇḍra*) applied on the body and the order of dishes served during a meal (Siauve 1978, Mumme 1988, Jagadeesan 1977: 171–208, Varadachari 1983). Quarrels between them even occasioned lawsuits throughout the eighteenth and until the twentieth centuries (Hari Rao 1964: 117–28). This split which concerned devotees who financed the temple rites affected the current administration of temples and minor aspects of rituals, but not the core of the rites which Vaikhānasa or Pāñcarātra priests continued to perform according to their own ritual tradition, even as the particular emblem of one of the two divisions was imposed on the walls of the shrine, its main idol, or its priests (Colas 1995: 124, 125–6).

The notion of lineage (*paramparā*) has a special importance in Śrīvaiṣṇavism in which various currents continuously tried to define themselves through distinct lines of affiliation, because during the daily ritual, a Śrīvaiṣṇava recites the names of teachers in an order of priority which reflects his spiritual lineage. Two types of lineages are invoked: the Ācārya- (or Samāśrayaṇa-)paramparā, that is, lineage of the initiating preceptor, and the Grantha-paramparā, that is, the lineage of the preceptor-commentator of sacred texts. Rāmānuja is said to have appointed 74 disciples called the Siṃhāsanādhipatis to spread Viśiṣṭādvaitic teachings. Prestigious Śrīvaiṣṇava families like the Uttamanampis and the Tātācāryas still claim that their religious honors and privileges originate from his time. Several Śrīvaiṣṇavas who did not belong to any line of preceptorial succession acted as masters and initiated disciples (Jagadeesan 1977: 42–3, 47, 51, 113–14).

The Kōyil Oḻuku (probably eighteenth-century in its present form) attributes Rāmānuja with the assignment of religious functions to Śūdra groups, not a revolutionary step, given the role already played by Śūdras as patrons in Vaiṣṇava temples. Among them, Sāttādas (also named Sātānis), identified as Veḷḷāḷas (that is ranked among Śūdras) but also sometimes as Brāhmaṇas, officiated as administrators of feeding houses for pilgrims at Shrirangam, Tirupati, and Kanchipuram during the fifteenth and sixteenth centuries. They also were in charge of providing flowers and other ingredients for temple worship and participated in the recitation of the Divyaprabandham. Even today Sāttādas have the religious privilege of performing similar services in temples in Tamil Nadu, Karnataka, and Andhra Pradesh. Some of them also officiate as priests in small temples (Hari Rao 1961: 50, 90; Lester 1994).

The late fourteenth century saw the rise and development of Śrīvaiṣṇava monasteries (*maṭhas, mutts*). It is not known with certainty which part Yāmunācārya and Rāmānuja (also named *yatirāja*, "king of renouncers") played in the origin of Śrīvaiṣṇava ascetic orders, though both of them are said to have embraced an ascetic life. Viśiṣṭādvaitin renouncers (*saṃnyāsins*) are usually called "three-staffed" (*tridaṇḍin*) by contrast with the "single-staffed" (*ekadaṇḍin*) Advaitins who considered that the triple-staff custom is meant for lower classes of renouncers (Olivelle 1986: 53). Apart from Brahmin *saṃnyāsins*, Śrīvaiṣṇavism also comprised of non-Brahmin renouncers called *ekākī/ekāṅgī* and known from fifteenth-century inscriptions. Heads of Śrīvaiṣṇava monasteries generally were (and still are) Brahmins and bore the title of *cīyar* (Jeer, Jiyar), though there are historical instances of non-Brahmin Ekāṅgī cīyars. These monasteries were instrumental in the conversion to Śrīvaiṣṇavism of lower castes and even of non-Hindu tribes, according to some sources. Several monasteries like the Ahobilam Maṭha and the Parakāla Maṭha (which initiated the seventeenth-century rulers of Mysore into Śrīvaiṣṇavism) belong to the Vaṭakalai division or were later affiliated to it. Among the well-known Teṉkalai monasteries, mention should be made of the Vānamamalai Maṭha (which had a special importance for the Rāmānandasampradāya, a Vaiṣṇava tradition of north India), the Tirukkurungudi Maṭha and the Śrīraṅganārāyaṇa-cīyar Maṭha which were probably founded about the fourteenth century (Appadurai 1977; Jagadeesan 1977: 147–68; Lester 1992; Clémentin-Ojha 1999: 74).

The school of Dvaita

Madhva (probably 1238–1317), also named Ānandatīrtha, Ānandajñāna, Ānandagiri, and Pūrṇaprajña, is the founder of the Dvaita, that is, dualistic school of Vedānta later known as "Brahmasampradāya" in the north Indian Vaiṣṇava milieux. Information about his life comes mainly from the Madhvavijaya, a hagiography by Nārāyaṇapaṇḍitācārya, the son of one of his direct disciples. Born of Tuḷu brahmin parents in the village of Pājakakṣetra near Udipi in Karnataka, Madhva became a renouncer at the age of 16 as an unmarried perpetual religious student (*naiṣṭhikabrahmacārin*). He acknowledged no other teacher than the mythical Vyāsa, but according to hagiography an Advaitin ascetic, Acyutaprekṣa (Puruṣottamatīrtha), was his master and initiated him. Though Madhva refused his doctrine, he succeeded him as the head of his monastery. The debates he had with scholars in the course of his tours all over India strengthened his conviction against Advaitic doctrine and he converted his master to his own views. He installed an image of Kṛṣṇa in Udipi and promoted several ritual reforms like the substitution of a flour-made sacrifice animal (*piṣṭapaśu*) in the place of a living one. The prestige of his school increased notably after the conversion of Trivikrama, a then-famous Advaitin and probably the court-pandit of King Jayasiṃha, to Dvaita.

Thirty-seven works are attributed to Madhva. Several of them consist of commentaries on basic texts of the Vedānta (Upaniṣads, Brahmasūtras, and Bhagavadgītā), on the Mahābhārata and the Bhāgavatapurāṇa, a text to which, unlike Rāmānuja, Madhva gave much importance. His *tātparyas* on Bhagavadgītā, Mahābhārata, and Bhāgavatapurāṇa, give the essential teachings of these texts important to Dvaita school. Madhva summarizes his main doctrinal principles in 10 very brief treatises called the Daśaprakaraṇas. Several devotional hymns are attributed to him. He also wrote several ritual treatises like the Yatipraṇavakalpa, which explains how to enter the renunciative way of life.

Madhva's works often quote from Pāñcarātra texts which he considers as authoritative as the Veda because, according to him, these two originally formed one tradition (Siauve 1968: 16). His Tantrasārasaṅgraha seems to follow the Pāñcarātra mode of temple worship.

Madhva maintains that the Brahman is the only independent (*svatantra*) entity; the world consisting of sentient beings (*cit* or *jīva*) and insentient (*acit*) objects does not have an existence independent of the Brahman (they are *asvatantra*). The five differences (*pañcabheda*) which exist between God and matter, God and sentient beings, matter and sentient beings, between sentient beings, and between material objects, prove the reality of multiplicity. While Madhva insisted on the absolute superiority of Viṣṇu on Śiva and other deities, his works and his hagiography do not show conflicting relations with Śaivas. Several Mādhva followers composed hymns in honor of Śiva. Till today, some Mādhva families maintain a Śaiva domestic temple. These facts seem to confirm ancient connections of the milieu of Madhva with Śaiva worship. His family may have belonged to a Smārta group (today known as the Bhāgavatasampradāya) (Sharma 1960; Siauve 1968: 1–36). Other major authors of Dvaita are Jayatīrtha (1365–88) and Vyāsarāya (Vyāsatīrtha, 1460–1539). The latter's mastery of *śāstras* won him great fame. Called to the Vijayanagar court, he may have been the preceptor (*guru*) of Kṛṣṇadevarāya (Sharma 1961: 30).

According to the Madhvavijaya, Madhva ordained his brother and seven other disciples as renouncers, directing them to perform the worship of Kṛṣṇa at the Maṭha founded by him in Udipi. These eight ascetics established their own lines of succession by ordination which resulted in the foundation of eight monasteries (*maṭhas*) in Udipi. Until today the heads of these monasteries are in charge of the worship in Kṛṣṇa Maṭha in turn for two years each, an arrangement known as *paryāya*. Other direct or later disciples are attributed with the foundation of monasteries outside the Udipi region. The Mādhva tradition had a following mostly in the Tuḷu country (today a part of Karnataka), but in the eighteenth and nineteenth centuries a rather significant number of people converted to the Mādhva tradition in Tamil Nadu and in Kerala, including several local rulers and members of the Nambudiri Brahmin community (Sharma 1960; 1961; Hari Rao 1964: 133).

The Haridāsakūṭa (to be distinguished from Haridāsasampradāya, a later north Indian tradition) was closely associated with the Mādhva tradition. These wandering devotees spread all over the Kannaḍa region, held Viṭṭhala, the image of the temple of Pandharpur (in the southern part of the present Maharashtra) as their deity. They praised devotional, moral, and renunciative values in an easy nonliterary Kannaḍa language which appealed to the common man. While the Haridāsakūṭa tradition is said to have started with Acalānanda Viṭṭhala (ca. 888 AD) and others before Madhva, the earliest known poet-saint connected with the Haridāsakūṭa is Naraharitīrtha (fourteenth century), perhaps a direct disciple of Madhva. Like him, many prominent figures of the Haridāsakūṭa were distinguished Sanskrit scholars and held high positions in Mādhva monasteries.

Purandaradāsa (sixteenth century), who contributed greatly to Carnatic music, was a follower of the Haridāsakūṭa (Sharma 1961: 314–26).

The school of Dvaitādvaita

Nimbārka (Nimbāditya, Niyamānanda), the founder of the Dvaitādvaita ("Dualism-cum-nondualism") or (Svābhāvika-)Bhedābheda ("(natural) identity in difference") school (later referred to as Sanakādisampradāya in north India), probably flourished in the thirteenth century. His date and life still remain a subject of discussion among scholars. The earliest hagiography, the Ācāryacarita, probably does not predate the sixteenth century. Hagiographical accounts locate Nimbārka's birth in various places in the Telugu country, in Vrindavan or a nearby village, in a Brahmin family. His school traces Nimbārka's spiritual lineage to Viṣṇu's incarnation as a swan, through the four spiritual sons of Brahmā (Sanaka, Sananda, Sanātana, and Sanatkumāra) who in turn taught Nārada, whom Nimbārka acknowledges as his guru. Nimbārka, like Madhva, is said not to have received his doctrine from any historical teacher. Like Madhva again, he is said to have remained an unmarried perpetual religious student.

Nimbārka's main work is the Vedāntapārijātasaurabha, a brief commentary on the Brahmasūtras. Except this and probably the Daśaślokī, 10 verses which summarize his doctrine, the authorship of most of the works attributed to him like the Rahasyamīmāṃsā of which we know two sections only (the Mantrarahasyaṣoḍaśī and the Prapannakalpavallī), several hymns and several unpublished works (R. Bose 1943: 8–12, 16) still need to be confirmed. In the Vedāntapārijātasaurabha, Nimbārka recognizes three principles: the sentient (*cit*), the nonsentient (*acit*), and the Brahman. Their relation which is natural (*svābhāvika*) and not caused by any condition (*anaupādhika*) is neither of absolute nondifference (*abheda*), since they are distinct by nature, nor absolute difference (*bheda*), because *cit* and *acit* are inseparable from the Brahman. The Vedāntapārijātasaurabha does not mention the notion of *prapatti* which the post-Rāmānuja Viśiṣṭādvaita emphasized, but the Prapannakalpavallī describes it in terms similar to those of later Viśiṣṭādvaita. The path of *prapatti* or total surrender to the Lord is open to all including Śūdras, but does not imply absence of any effort on the part of the surrendering devotee, for he is required to lead a life of devotion and service. The Mantrarahasyaṣoḍaśī advocates complete self-surrender not directly to the Lord, but to the preceptor (*gurūpasatti*) and the abandonment of all other practices (R. Bose 1943: 54–7). These two attitudes are reminiscent respectively of the Vaṭakalai and Teṉkalai views on *prapatti*.

There is no historical proof that Nimbārka and the first 28 preceptors of this tradition settled in Braj in and around Mathura before the end of the fifteenth century. Keśava Kāśmirī Bhaṭṭa (born in 1479), the 29th *ācārya*, is the first whose historical association with the Braj area is certain. His direction is marked by the revival of the Nimbārka tradition and the propagation of its teachings all over India. He composed doctrinal texts, devotional hymns, and an elaborate ritual treatise the Kramadīpikā, which influenced Caitanyaite authors. His successor, Śrī Bhaṭṭa, is the first *ācārya* of the Nimbārka school known to have written in Braj *bhāṣā*, the vernacular of the Braj region. His Yugalaśataka describes the divine loving couple of Kṛṣṇa and Rādhā, a theme which became increasingly popular also among several other Vaiṣṇava traditions from the sixteenth century onwards (Clémentin-Ojha 1990: 333–8, 374).

Śrī Bhaṭṭa's disciple, Harivyāsadevācārya (probably sixteenth century), who wrote in Braj *bhāṣā* as well as in Sanskrit, had a strong influence on the organization and theology of Nimbārka's tradition. This tradition developed into 12 branches based in 12 monasteries. A number of subdivisions later arose, progressively weakening its cohesiveness. While in its early stages, the Nimbārka tradition stressed the ascetic values, however initiating lay members into its fold. Under Harivyāsadevācārya, lay members received the right of initiating others and transmitting this right to their male descendants. These householder preceptors were later called gosvāmīs and the wealth which they accumulated significantly contributed to the developement of the tradition (Clémentin-Ojha 1990: 346–8).

The school of Viṣṇusvāmin

Information on Viṣṇusvāmin and on his school, later referred to as Rudrasampradāya by north Indian Vaiṣṇava traditions, is very scanty. Viṣṇusvāmin predates Vallabha (sixteenth century) and is often said to have lived in the thirteenth century. Vallabhite hagiography describes him as the son of a south Indian priest. None of his works including commentaries on Bhāgavatapurāṇa and Brahmasūtras have survived. According to Mādhava's Sarvadarśanasaṃgraha (fourteenth century) the followers of Viṣṇusvāmin's school maintained that the body of Nṛsiṃha (Viṣṇu's incarnation as man–lion) is eternal. It cites a verse from the Sākārasiddhi of a Śrīkāntamiśra which pays hommage to Nṛsiṃha whose body is made up of existence, consciousness, and continual inconceivable bliss, and who is esteemed by Viṣṇusvāmin. Some scholars mention that according to the Sarvajñasūtra attributed to Viṣṇusvāmin, God, whose principal incarnation is Narasiṃha, takes a form consisting of existence, consciousness, and bliss, is accompanied by his knowledge which is named *hlādinī* and has *māyā* at his disposition (Shukla 1971: 12). Śrīdhara (fourteenth to fifteenth centuries) refers to Viṣṇusvāmin in his commentary on Bhāgavatapurāṇa. In his commentary on the same text Vallabha differentiates Viṣṇusvāmin's views from his own. Viṣṇusvāmin's followers are said to have *oṃ rāmakṛṣṇāya namaḥ* and *oṃ rāmakṛṣṇahari* as mantras, the Gopālatāpanīya-upaniṣad and the Gopālasahasranāman as manuals. Farquhar claims to have met several ascetic followers of this school in Allahabad in 1918 (Farquhar 1967: 239, 304; Dasgupta 1975: 382).

North Indian Traditions from Thirteenth Century

While the four Vaiṣṇava schools of Vedānta were building or achieving their systems, other traditions of Vaiṣṇavism developed from the thirteenth century onwards in the Deccan and northern India. They crystallized around the pious personalities, and sometimes around the devotional works of poet-saints. Their origin and chronology often remains uncertain. Our knowledge of these traditions depends on mostly biased and anachronistic documentation. Several of these movements were closely associated with the then developing literature in New Indo-Aryan (NIA) languages. Two other traditions, those of Vallabha and Caitanya, which began in the late fifteenth century, expressed their doctrinal views and their devotion both in Sanskrit and in NIA languages.

Traditions associated with New Indo-Aryan literatures

The devotional fervor which nourished the traditions of NIA expression was in fact not so much Vaiṣṇavite properly speaking as Rāmaite and Kṛṣṇaite, that is, directed to Rāma and Kṛṣṇa which are however aspects of Viṣṇu. The practices and concepts which they valued and which since have long existed in Hinduism and Buddhism converged to some extent with several similar mystic techniques and notions of Islam and Sufism: ecstatic forms of worship, collective singing (*bhajan* and *kīrtan*), repetition of holy names (and devotion to them), notion of divine love, etc. Other means of release were devotion to the "Good preceptor" (*satguru*) who is God in human form, and the "company of the good" (*satsaṅg*), that is, of the poet-saints, but more generally of pious devotees. The social ideology of these traditions is difficult to circumscribe. They initially rejected caste barriers and were indifferent or even hostile to Brahmanic learning and to ritualism. They have sometimes been presented as revolutionary currents but they did not specifically denounce social structures (except perhaps Mahānubhāvas, who isolated themselves from mainstream Hinduism), nor did they seem to have raised strong opposition from the Brahmanical side. The figures around whom these traditions developed were often of a humble social origin, yet their following belonged to all strata of society including Brahmins. Though not professing formal renunciation, they often insisted on nonviolence (*ahiṃsā*), strict vegetarianism, and sexual restraint. Similar tendencies arose in south Indian Śaiva milieux, as illustrated by Basava (thirteenth century) who wrote in Kannaḍa and Vēmana (fifteenth century) who wrote in Telugu. Some North Indian Vaiṣṇava traditions which developed from the late fifteenth century frequently around a *guru* and left a literature in NIA languages, remain rather obscure. for example, the Caranadāsīs (whose tradition Caranadāsa founded at Delhi around 1730) who worshipped god in the form of Rādhā and Kṛṣṇa, and the Rāmasnehīs, a tradition founded in the eighteenth century which spread mostly in Rajasthan (Farquhar 1967: 344–6; Renou 1985a: 660). Only those that are relatively better documented will be mentioned here. Vaiṣṇavism from Gujarat, of which Narasiṃha Mehatā (fifteenth century) is a main personality, is the subject of another chapter in the present volume.

Of the two Vaiṣṇava traditions of Maharashtra, the Mahānubhāvas (or Manbhaus), literally "those who have a great experience" and the Vārakārīs, "those who perform the tour," that is, the pilgrimage to Pandharpur, the first is probably older. Cakradhara (thirteenth century) is said to be its founder, and he was succeeded by Nāgadeva. During the leadership of Paraśarāmabāsa (which began in the late fourteenth century), the tradition isolated itself from the common fold of Hinduism and divided into 13 currents (*āmnāya*), each with its own line of initiating preceptors and particularities of doctrine and practices. Reduced to two *āmnāyas* in the twentieth century, it reopened itself to the surrounding Hinduism and revealed its scriptures which until then had been encoded and kept secret. The Sūtrapāṭha and the Līḷācaritra, which record Cakradhara's life and sayings, as well as the Smṛtisthaḷa, which describes the activities of Cakradhara's followers during the time of Nāgadeva, all in Old Marathi and of uncertain date, are among well-known texts of the Mahānubhāvas. The Mahānubhāvas direct their devotion to Parameśvara, the sole source of release who is said to have incarnated in five *avatāras* called "the Five Kṛṣṇas," who are Cakradhara, his teacher, his teacher's teacher, the god Dattātreya, and the god Kṛṣṇa. Their books prescribe mental exercises rather than external and ritual forms of worship (*sevā*). The main religious practice is the "recollection" (*smaraṇa*) of the names, deeds (*līḷās*), and manifestations of the above five incarnations, a recollection stimulated by pilgrimages to places which they are said to have visited and veneration of the relics of these incarnations, including objects used or touched by them. The Mahānubhāvas rejected social categorization in terms of *varṇas* and castes and several pollution rules. This institution is divided between lay disciples and wandering renouncers (*saṃnyāsīs*) initiated into ascetic life through a ceremony called *bhikṣā* (a term which also conveys the ordinary meaning of begging in the Mahānubhāva texts). In the early period of this tradition women were eligible for this initiation as well as for instructing and initiating others (Feldhaus 1983: 3–68; Feldhaus and Tulpule 1992: 3–53).

The Vārakarīpantha is more a devotional current associated with the god Viṭṭhala (or Viṭhobā, also called Pāṇḍuraṅga) of Pandharpur (Maharashtra) than a homogenous and organized tradition. In the eighteenth century its followers claimed a spiritual lineage of 50 Sants (holy men) (Schomer 1987: 4). They believe that Jñāneśvara (a Marathi author and saint of the end of the thirteenth century) established the Vārakarīpantha, but Nāmadeva was probably the founder of their movement (Vaudeville 1987b: 218, n. 9). A tailor by profession, Nāmadeva (1270 to 1350 according to tradition) could be assigned to the beginning of the fifteenth century from the linguistic analysis of his songs. Two other major Maharashtrian Sants, Ekanātha (a Brahmin, second half of the sixteenth century) and Tukārāma (a Śūdra, 1607–49) belonged to this movement.

Rāmadāsa (1608–81), an ascetic follower of the Vārakarīpantha, founded his own tradition (the Rāmadāsasampradāya) and became the preceptor of king Śivājī. Vārakarī Sants consider the god Viṭṭhala of Pandharpur as "father and mother" and often address him as a loving mother. According to the followers of the Vārakarīpantha this image of Viṭṭhala is the very form (svarūpa) of Viṣṇu-Kṛṣṇa (Vaudeville 1987a: 28–9; see chapter 9).

By contrast with the above Marathi poet-saints who were Vaiṣṇava devotees, the "Northern Sants," from the northwestern states of Panjab and Rajasthan and the Hindi-speaking area, are generally associated with devotion to a formless God conceived as being beyond the three *guṇas* of *sattva, tamas,* and *rajas* (*nirguṇabhakti*) and with the notion of nonduality of the individual soul with God. But at least three of these "Northern Sants," Rāmānanda, Dādū, and Haridāsa, are considered by traditions distinctly Vaiṣṇava as their founders.

The most basic details of Rāmānanda's life remain unknown. Modern scholarship tends to assign him to the fifteenth century (Pollet 1980: 142). Hagiography records that he reconverted to Hinduism persons who had previously been converted by force to Islam, and recruited women and intouchable castes in the tradition which bears his name and which enjoins devotion to Rāma. However, it is not even sure that he founded that tradition (Burghart 1978). Rāmānanda is attributed not only with a number of poems in the vernacular but also with several texts in Sanskrit. Most of the often undatable texts of this tradition are written in northern Indian languages, not in Sanskrit (Burghart 1978: 121, 124–5).

Special mention must be made in this context of the Bhaktamāla which Nābhādāsa (or Nābhājī) of the Rāmānanda tradition composed in the late sixteenth or early seventeenth centuries (Burghart 1978: 129; Pollet 1980: 142). This important text, very rich in hagiographical stories, declares that Rāmānanda was the disciple of Rāghavānanda, himself an indirect disciple of Rāmānuja (stanza 35), a statement which remains unproven.[1] It also declares that Hari (Viṣṇu) manifested himself as four vyūhas in this Kaliyuga: Śrīrāmānuja, Viṣṇusvāmin, Madhvācāraja (=Madhva=Madhukara in stanza 29), and Nimbāditya (=Nimbārka), each having established a "sampradāya" (28), named respectively Janma, Karma, Bhāgavata, and Dharma. The *paddhatis* ("paths") – Ramā-, Tripurāri-, Mukhacāri-, and Sanakādikā- – belong respectively to these four *sampradāyas* (29). Sindhujā (another name of Śrī) is called the *sampradāyaśiromaṇi*, the "summit of the *sampradāya*" to which Rāmānuja and others belonged (30). Nāma (=Nāmadeva of the Vārakarīpantha?) and Vallabha are said to belong to the Viṣṇusvāmisampradāya (48).

The nineteenth-century followers of Rāmānanda were called Rāmānujīs and claimed to be under the authority of the head of the Śrīvaiṣṇava Teṉkalai monastery of Vanamamalai. But in the early twentieth century, the Rāmānanda tradition no longer traced its historical origin to Śrīsampradāya which corresponds to the tradition of Rāmānuja, but designated itself as Rāmānandasampradāya (Burghart 1978: 133; Clémentin-Ojha 1999: 74). In about the sixteenth and seventeenth centuries, the tradition combined a devotional and a

Tantric heritage and its following consisted of twice-born Hindus as well as untouchables, women, and converted Muslims (Burghart 1978: 124, 133). At the end of eighteenth century the Rāmānandī ascetics formed a militant order (*akhāṛā*), gathering ascetic-warriors named *nāgās* in view of retaining or regaining control over several pilgrimage centers against the concurrence of Daśanāmī ascetics (Burghart 1978: 126). By the nineteenth century, the tradition comprised of several lineages (some of them consisting of ascetic-warriors like the Bālānandīs) associated with different monasteries, of which the head bore the title of Mahant. Each lineage owned its own temples, villages, and territories (Clémentin-Ojha 1999: 73).

Several groups arose out of the Rāmānandī tradition. Two of them originated from Varanasi: the Rāidāsī group, a religious corporation of tanners, organized by Rāidāsa (or Ravidāsa) (fifteenth century) and the Sadhanapantha founded by a butcher named Sadhana (seventeenth century). The Senāpantha which claims the barber Senā (or Senānanda) (fifteenth century) as its founder and the Malūkadāsī group said to have been founded by Malūkadāsa in the seventeenth century also belong to the Rāmānandī fold (Farquhar 1967: 323–30; Renou 1985a: 655).

Dādū (Dādū Dayāla) (1544–1604) was born in Ahmedabad (Gujarat) according to the hagiographical work of his direct disciple, Janagopāla. He probably belonged to a family of humble origin. Having experienced several mystical visions in his youth, he left home in around 1562 and became an itinerant preaching ascetic. He is said to have married and become a cotton-carder. He died in Naraiṇā (near Jaipur) which continues to be the center of his tradition. The Dādūpantha developed soon after his death. One of Dādū's disciples, Rajjab, is said to have compiled his sayings (*bānī*), which consist of religious didactic verses and devotional songs in Braj *bhāṣā*. Another disciple, Sundaradāsa, composed many devotional hymns and short religious poems in a highly Sanskritized Braj *bhāṣā*. His Jñānasamudra integrated a yogic heritage from the system of Gorakhanātha and from the Pātañjalayoga, and was perhaps influenced by Caitanyaite theology. According to the Dādūpantha doctrine, devotion consisting of chanting God's name, etc., leads to a state of union with God who is the object of devotion. In this state of nonduality, the devotee becomes fully conscious of his total dependance on God (*dāsatva*). While Dādū himself converted members from all strata of society, Hindus and Muslims alike, to his way, the Dādūpantha today only accepts persons identified as twice-born. It is followed by laymen and by religious ascetics, mostly men, who are designated as *viraktas*. The Dādūpantha is divided into two main branches, Khālsā which is attached to the center of Naraiṇā and to Dādū's immediate disciples and Uttarādhā which traces its lineage to those preceptors of the Dādūpantha who migrated to northern regions after Dādū's death. While the *viraktas* of the Uttarādhā branch sometimes exercise a profession in society, the Khākhi ("ash-smeared") *viraktas*, another group of Dādūpantha ascetics, lead a life of complete renunciation. The Dādūpanthī Nāgās were originally organized as a militant group perhaps around the mid-seventeenth century, but today consist of laymen and ascetics (Thiel-Horstmann 1983).

Haridāsa belongs to the sixteenth century according to modern research. His hagiography seems generally unreliable. The canon of the Haridāsa tradition contains the poems of its successive heads of the organization till around 1750–60, and two works which are attributed to Haridāsa: the Kelimāla, a devotional poem which depicts the love sports of Rādhā and Kṛṣṇa, and the Aṣṭādaśasiddhānta, a brief didactic poem which warns against worldly life which is an illusion, emphasizes the value of meditation on God (Kuñjabihāri) and absolute devotion to him. The *sādhu* Bihārinidāsa (probably late sixteenth to early seventeenth century), a prolific writer, produced the main code of worship of this tradition. The two main subdivisions of the tradition could have originated from two disciples of Haridāsa: the Gosvāmīs, who are in charge of the main temple of this tradition, claim to have descended from Jagannātha, a married Panjabi Brahman, while Sādhus, renouncers who practice worship in which singing devotional hymns (*saṃkīrtana*) is of the utmost importance, trace their spiritual lineage to Vīṭhalavipula. In the early eighteenth century, in response to the organization of Vaiṣṇava groups into four main traditions (*catuḥsampradāya*) by Savai Jaisiṅgh, the Sādhu Pītāmbaradāsa defended the thesis that the Haridāsa tradition stemmed from the school of Nimbārka, while the Gosvāmīs claimed an affiliation with Viṣṇusvāmin's school. A schism occurred between these two subdivisions in the second quarter of the eighteenth century, after which Sādhus lived secluded in monasteries, a disposition which continued till the end of the nineteenth century. Apart from Sādhus and Gosvāmīs, the Haridāsa tradition has a following of lay people who receive varied types of initiation with different mantras from a preceptor of either of the two groups (Haynes 1974; Rosenstein 1997).

Sanskritizing traditions from the late fifteenth century

The fifteenth and sixteenth centuries which saw the growth of the traditions of NIA expression also witnessed the rise of two Sanskritizing Vaiṣṇava traditions, those of Vallabha and Caitanya, both closely associated with a devotion to images perceived as the very form (*svarūpa*) of Kṛṣṇa and with the mythology of Kṛṣṇa's life as described in the Bhāgavatapurāṇa. These two teachers (who lived around the same time) or their immediate disciples, identified several places in the Braj region as Gokula and as sacred sites of Vrindavan which mythology associates with Kṛṣṇa's life. The Vallabha tradition, from the time of Viṭṭhalanātha, glorified the role of Rādhā, Kṛṣṇa's favorite cowherd girl (*gopī*), and Caitanya tradition (and connected traditions) stressed the worship of the divine couple (*yugala*) which they formed (Barz 1992: 90–1). This mode of worship was not new but received a great impetus during the sixteenth century in traditions of NIA expression (like the Haridāsa tradition) as well. This was also associated with the revival of the Nimbārka tradition (Clémentin-Ojha 1990: 351–75). Both Vallabha's and Caitanya's traditions, like that of Madhva, gave great importance to the Bhāgavatapurāṇa. They held devotion superior to knowledge and built religious doctrines rather than scholastic philosophies on the lines of the Vaiṣṇava schools of Vedānta of the tenth to thirteenth centuries. The importance which the Vaiṣṇava schools of Vedānta gave to devotion which could be practiced by all, irrespective of their social status, did not affect their social conservatism. By contrast, Vallabha's and Caitanya's traditions which held the same position with regard to access to devotion had to envisage integrating backward classes, women, and other converts in a congregation of devotees which implied social promiscuity.

Vallabha's tradition, called Vallabhasampradāya, consists of a doctrine, the Śuddhādvaita ("Nondualism of the pure," that is, of Śrīkṛṣṇa-Parabrahman), and a religious path guided by it, the Puṣṭimārga. According to hagiography, Vallabha was born in 1479 in a family of Telugu Brahmans in a village on the Godavari river. He passed his childhood in Varanasi, studied Vedas, Śāstras, and Purāṇas and spent 19 years debating with scholars and spreading his doctrine during pilgrimage tours. In 1493–4 he is said to have identified at Kṛṣṇa's command, an image on the Govardhana Hill in Braj as Śrīgovardhananāthajī, the very form (*svarūpa*) of Śrīkṛṣṇa whose worship became an important feature of his tradition. This image was later moved to Nāthadvāra in Rajasthan and is now known as Śrīnāthajī. In 1494 again, according to Vallabha himself, Śrīkṛṣṇa revealed to him the *brahmasambandha* (direct relation with the Brahman who is Śrīkṛṣṇa). This initiation is said to remove the impurities (*doṣas*) of the soul, who then proceeds to worship Śrīkṛṣṇa by dedicating all actions and possessions to him. According to hagiography, Vallabha, who was celibate, married in around 1502 under the order of the image of Viṭṭhala of Pandharpur. His tradition does not consist of ascetics and all preceptors and laymen are householders. In 1531 Vallabha became a renouncer and retired to Varanasi where he died (Barz 1992: 16–55).

Eighty-four Sanskrit works are ascribed to Vallabha, among which Subodhinī and Aṇubhāṣya commentaries on the Bhāgavatapurāṇa and Brahmasūtras, the Tattvārthadīpa, based on the Bhāgavatapurāṇa, the Ṣoḍaśagrantha, 16 tracts which discuss dedication to God and the three obstacles to it, are considered as important. According to Vallabha, sentient beings and insentient world are the real manifestations of Śrīkṛṣṇa-Parabrahman. Sentient beings are nondifferent from Śrīkṛṣṇa in nature but do not realize it due to ignorance (*avidyā*) imparted to them by Śrīkṛṣṇa himself. Their release (*uddhāra*) too is bestowed by the god himself through his grace (*anugraha*) and out of his own free will (*icchā*). Śrīkṛṣṇa appears in different incomplete divine "descents" (*avatāras*) in sport (*līlā*) and out of compassion for his devotees but his only complete *avatāra* is that of Śrīkṛṣṇa who lived in Braj and whose deeds are described in the Bhāgavatapurāṇa. The institutional and doctrinal connections which hagiography ascribes between his tradition and that of Viṣṇusvāmin remain uncertain (Barz 1992: 45).

Vallabha's elder son Gopīnātha, and later his younger son Viṭṭhalanātha, succeeded him at the head of the organization. Viṭṭhalanātha (died in 1586) received several grants from Emperor Akbar, one of which was used to found a new village at Gokula near Mathura, where he settled with his family and his followers. He delegated the guidance of the Vallabha tradition among his seven sons, each of them in charge of one or several divine images of temples in different places in the present Uttar Pradesh, Rajasthan, and Gujarat states. These charges were transmitted to further generations through the eldest male descendants of Viṭṭhalanātha's sons. Vallabha and Viṭṭhalanātha initiated Muslims, women, and untouchables (Barz 1992: 47).

The Vallabha tradition produced a vast literature in Sanskrit (Dasgupta 1975: 373–81) and also developed a devotional literature of high quality in Braj *bhāṣā*. Four disciples of Vallabha, Sūradāsa (1483–1563, the author of the Sūrasāgara), Kumbhanadāsa, Paramānandadāsa, and Kṛṣṇadāsa, and four disciples of Viṭṭhalanātha who wrote and sang the glory of the image of Śrīgovardhananāthajī, are known as the *aṣṭachāpa*. Their songs (*kīrtanas*) form part of the disinterested service rendered to the god, called *sevā*. *Sevā* consists of collective praise of the god before his image, donation of wealth to the temples of the tradition, and finally constant contemplation of Śrīkṛṣṇa. This form of worship is characteristic of Vallabha's Puṣṭimārga, built around the notion of Śrīkṛṣṇa's grace. It is to be distinguished from the *maryādāmārga*, considered as inferior, that is, the conventional mode of worship such as *pūjā* and observance of scriptural injunctions. In Puṣṭimārga, where external and mundane actions represent divine events, meditation on and physical enactment of Kṛṣṇa's games (*līlās*) played an important role from the time of these poets (Barz 1992: 46 sqq., 52, 97–104).

Viśvambharamiśra, the future Caitanya, was probably a younger contemporary of Vallabha, but his exact dates (usually said to be 1486–1533) remain uncertain. Sanskrit and Bengali hagiographies written soon after Caitanya's death provide a detailed though often unreliable picture of his life. It is said that Viśvambharamiśra, born in a Vaiṣṇava Brahmin family of Navadvīpa (Nadiā) in Bengal, grew up in a milieu in which Kamalākṣa Bhaṭṭācārya (also named Advaitācārya) was influential. Kamalākṣa Bhaṭṭācārya was the disciple of Mādhavendra Purī who seems to have taught a Śaṅkarite nondualism combined with devotion. Viśvambharamiśra had a traditional *śāstric* education and was a householder who remarried on the death of his first wife. At the age of 22 he is said to have received in Gayā an initiation with Kṛṣṇamantra from Īśvara Purī (perhaps another disciple of Mādhavendra Purī), which debuted his mystical life. On his return to Navadvīpa, he organized the collective singing of *kīrtanas* with music and ecstatic dancing. Singing processions in the city (*nagarakīrtana*) were also organized with the agreement of the local Mohammedan authority. Possibly in 1510, Viśvambharamiśra was initiated into renunciation by Keśava Bhāratī (perhaps an Advaitin renouncer, De 1961: 20) and received his name Śrīkṛṣṇacaitanya, abbreviated to Caitanya. After many years of pilgrimage he settled in Puri, but continued to visit holy places, especially Vrindavan where he is said to have identified certain sites as places connected with Kṛṣṇa's life. Caitanya is said to have spent the rest of his life in ecstasy and in the worship of Jagannātha, the image of the main temple of Puri (De 1961: 17, 20, 30–2, 67–110; Hardy 1974: 37–40).

Caitanya's affiliation with the Mādhva tradition is a late construction. His followers came to be known as Gauḍīyavaiṣṇavas, that is, Vaiṣṇavas from the Gauḍa region (situated in present South Bengal). After his death an important group gathered around Nityānanda, an early companion of Caitanya (and perhaps previously an Avadhūta ascetic), who remained in Navadvīpa. Nityānanda seems to have accepted members of all social classes more easily than Caitanya, who allowed equal access to worship and to the role of preceptor but held a rather conservative view with regard to social rules. He became a householder and had two wives. Another group formed in Vrindavan around six of Caitanya's disciples, called Gosvāmins. Apart from these two main branches other smaller groups arose around several personalities and sometimes against certain teachers (De 1961: 13–15, 77–8, 107–9, 111 sqq., 84 n. 2; Majumdar 1969: 260–9).

Caitanya did not write any work except perhaps the Śikṣāṣṭaka, a collection of eight verses describing his intense joy of devotion to Kṛṣṇa (De 1961: 113). The Six Gosvāmins composed the basic scriptures of the tradition. Sanātana and Rūpa, two brothers, and their nephew Jīva, the most prolific of the three, are the authors of main literary as well as ritual and theological works. According to them Bhagavant, that is, Śrīkṛṣṇa, is the ultimate reality who possesses infinite powers and creates the universe which is real and ever dependent on him. He has an undifferentiated aspect (Brahman) in which his powers lay in a latent form and another aspect in which he is the inner controller of all creation (Paramātman). The individual soul (*jīva*) is neither different from Bhagavant (it forms a part of him) nor nondifferent from him (it retains its individuality in release which can be obtained either during his lifetime or after death). Devotion to Kṛṣṇa is the sole means of release. This devotion (*bhāva*) which is ever present in all beings is aroused by practice (*sādhana*) which comprises *rāgānugā* (spontaneous attachment to God) and *vaidhī* (practice of the injunctions of the Scriptures). Constant practice of devotion in all its aspects or the grace of Kṛṣṇa lead the soul to the experience of divine love (*preman*). An essential feature of the doctrine is the explication of devotion through the notion of aesthetical emotion (*rasa*) and its utilization of the terminology of Sanskrit poetics (De 1961: 166–244).

The other three Gosvāmins are Raghunātha Bhaṭṭa, Raghunāthadāsa, and Gopāla Bhaṭṭa. No work of Raghunātha Bhaṭṭa is extant. Raghunāthadāsa composed devotional hymns imbued with mysticism expressed in an erotic fashion and centered on the worship of the couple Rādhā-Kṛṣṇa. The well-known Haribhaktivilāsa is attributed (though with some uncertainty) to Gopāla Bhaṭṭa (Joshi 1959). It codifies the behavioral and ritual rules of the Caitanya tradition, is influenced by Purāṇic, Pāñcarātra, and Tantric texts. Its prescriptions include the possibility of also initiating Caṇḍālas, but with Tantric mantras (De 1961: 454). Besides doctrinal and ritual texts, the Caitanya tradition produced a large quantity of Sanskrit poems, dramas, and biographical works. Its early literature also comprised devotional songs in Bengali. Caitanya directly or indirectly inspired a number of traditions, the most important being the Rādhāvallabhīs and the Sahajiyās.

Little is known about Hitaharivaṃśa (1502–52) and the tradition of the Rādhāvallabhīs (mentioned in Nābhādāsa's Bhaktamāla) which claims him as its founder. Hagiography describes him as born in a rich family near Mathura. He is said to have settled in Vrindavan at the age of 32 where he founded the Rādhāvallabha tradition. The Rādhāsudhānidhi in Sanskrit and two Hindi works are attributed to him. On his death, his son Kṛṣṇadāsa (probably born in 1531) became the head of the organization. He constructed a temple for the image of Rādhāvallabha which had been discovered by Hitaharivaṃśa, and the worship of this image formed one of the features of this tradition. This temple was destroyed by Aurangzeb (Shukla 1971: 21–2). Works attributed to Kṛṣṇadāsa reveal a strong influence of the Caitanya tradition, especially of Rūpa Gosvāmin. They consist of a Padāvali in Braj *bhāṣā* and 13 Sanskrit texts, several of which were commented upon in Braj *bhāṣā* by later authors. His Karṇānanda, a poem on the sports of Rādhā and Kṛṣṇa, with his own commentary is his main work (Shukla 1971: 22–3, 68–91). The works of Hitaharivaṃśa and Kṛṣṇadāsa show no interest in religious practices or philosophical discussions. Their main theme is the constant and eternal union of Rādhā and Kṛṣṇa. The contemplation of this union by the individual soul who is said to be the female friend (*sakhī*) of Rādhā, gives rise to an emotion of joy (*hita*) which forms the aim of devotion to Rādhā and Kṛṣṇa and is considered as release (Shukla 1971: 24 sqq.). The Sakhībhāva group, where men dressed and behaved like Rādhā's female friends, may have been a branch of the Rādhāvallabha tradition (Renou 1985a: 647).

The links of the Bengali Vaiṣṇava Sahajiyā (from *sahaja*, "innate," "natural") tradition with the Buddhist Sahajiyā tradition (which flourished in Bengal at least three centuries before Caitanya) are uncertain. Though modern scholarship does not rule out a Sahajiyā influence on Caitanya himself (through his direct disciples Rāmānanda Rāya, Nityānanda, and Jahnavī, Nityānanda's wife, who are said to have been Sahajiyās) (Dimock 1966: 46–55), it seems more probable that the Caitanya tradition influenced Sahajiyās.

Sahajiyā followers had no regard for Vedic texts, but accepted texts written by Vaiṣṇava authors (Dimock 1966: 185–6). The Vaiṣṇava Sahajiyā tradition produced a vast amount of literature often kept secret by its followers (M. M. Bose 1930: 261–302). It contains a great number of lyric songs, the date of which modern scholarship has not yet fixed. Its Tantras (of which 79 titles are known) were written in Bengali, in an obscure and coded language (*sandhā-bhāṣā*), between the early seventeenth and nineteenth centuries (Dimock 1966: 38, 124; Gupta 1981: 177, 201). They adopted the Caitanya theology besides their own views. Sahajiyās considered Caitanya as the teacher of their doctrine and believed he was incarnated as both Rādhā and Kṛṣṇa in a single body. Besides the conventional mode of devotion, they prescribed mystic worship in order to realize the divine presence of Rādhā and Kṛṣṇa and their union in one's own self (Dimock 1966: 228). Their mystical physiology, influenced by Tantric traditions, insisted on the role of chastity and the control of *rasa* (semen) (Dimock 1966: 157) in a spiritual progress which is said to be divided into three stages. During the first stage the adept learns certain mantras from an initiating preceptor and conducts such practices as the repetition of Kṛṣṇa's names. The second stage involves ritualized copulation with meditation on the divine couple. In the third stage the adept, transcending all physical desires, experiences the eternal divine union of Rādhā and Kṛṣṇa which is pure bliss (M. M. Bose 1930, *passim*; Dimock 1966: 124–248). Though it had no consideration for orthodox social conceptions and believed in the personal evaluation of moral principles, the Sahajiyā tradition with its esoteric rituals conducted in secrecy did not enter into conflict with society (Dimock 1966: 105, 121). The Sahajiyā tradition is said to no longer exist, but the possibility of its continuation in contemporary India is evoked (Dimock 1966: 249).

Other minor movements inspired by the Caitanya tradition remain less well known due to a lack of documentation. Kartābhājās recognized Kartābābā (end of the eighteenth century) of Navadvīpa and his descendants as their only deity. The Spaṣṭadāyakas, followers of Rūparāma Kabirāja, lived in celibacy in monasteries which gathered men and women (Renou 1985a: 646–7). A group of Vaiṣṇavas of Orissa, called the *pañcasakhās*, "the five friends," who worshipped the formless Kṛṣṇa, are also said to have been followers of Caitanya (Majumdar 1969: 240; Mukherjee 1978: 313–14).

Except Vallabha's, Caitanya's, and related traditions, mention must also be made of Śaṅkaradeva (1449–1548). The tradition which claims him as its founder was independent from the Caitanya tradition though seventeenth-century hagiography mentions a meeting of both the religious leaders. It remained confined mostly to Assam. Twenty-seven works, written in Sanskrit and Assamese, are attributed to Śaṅkaradeva. Among them six plays (called *nāṭas*, *nāṭakas*, and *yātrās*) still extant show that the extensive use of dramatic performances was from the beginning a main feature of his tradition. His teachings were based on devotion as explained in the Bhāgavatapurāṇa. He and his first disciple, Mādhava, a main propagandist of the tradition, were *kāyasthas*. Śaṅkaradeva's granddaughters and great-granddaughters played an important role in the creation of its monasteries, called *sattras*, where monks and married devotees lived in separate quarters. Soon after Śaṅkaradeva's death the tradition subdivided into several currents; the four main ones are usually counted Brahma-, Nikā-, Puruṣa-, and Kāla-saṃhatis. The ceremony of conversion to this tradition is called *śaraṇa*. The main object of worship is a book (normally the Bhāgavatapurāṇa) while the use of images is not strictly forbidden. Objects used by the gurus of the tradition are also worshipped (Neog 1965).

Late Vaiṣṇava Tantras

Apart from Pāñcarātra texts, several Tantric works were of special importance for the different Vaiṣṇava traditions. The Rāmānanda tradition favored the use of several texts, like an Agastyasaṃhitā (different from the Pāñcarātra text of the same title and probably from the twelfth century) for their worship of Rāma. The sixteenth-century Caitanya texts quote the Gautamīyatantra as their authority. Later tantras like the Īśānasaṃhitā and the Ūrdhvāmnāyasaṃhitā either mention Gaurāṅga, that is, Caitanya, or promote him as the main object of worship (Goudriaan 1981: 105 sqq.). Several ritual Tantric texts, tentatively called "Kālī-Viṣṇu Tantras," like the Kālīvilāsatantra, the Utpattitantra, the Kāmadhenutantra, tried integrating Vaiṣṇavism into Śāktism by claiming Kṛṣṇa to be a son of Kālī. They seem to be associated with the Vaiṣṇava revival which arose in northeastern India from the sixteenth century onwards (Goudriaan 1981: 82–4).

Late Modern and Contemporary Vaiṣṇava Traditions and Groups

New Vaiṣṇava movements developed in the nineteenth and twentieth centuries. The Svāminārāyaṇa tradition (nineteenth century) from Gujarat promoted both social and religious reforms. The Assamese reformist movements that arose in the 1930s, like the Haridhaniyas (or Nama Kirtaniyas), the Mahākīyas, etc., may also be mentioned in this context (Cantlie 1985). At the end of the nineteenth century, Bengal saw a revival of Vaiṣṇavism inspired by the Caitanya devotional current. While reformist movements like Brāhmo Samāj and Ārya Samāj scorned this tradition, several historical personalities illustrate the opposite tendency. For instance, Bijoy Krishna Goswami (born in 1841), previously an ardent and influential missionary of the Brāhmo Samāj, left it in 1889 and became a follower of Caitanya. He had several disciples like Bipincandra Pāl whom he initiated, but did not found any organized movement (Jones 1989: 39–41; Lipski 1971). By constrast, Kedārnāth Datt (1838–1914) founded a branch of the Caitanya tradition, the International Society for Kṛṣṇa Consciousness, which spread outside India and is popularly known as Hare Kṛṣṇa movement. Serving as a magistrate in the British Government, in 1868 he discovered the Caitanya tradition into which he had been born and subsequently wrote and edited around a hundred books on the subject. He took the Vaiṣṇava *saṃnyāsin* Jagannātha Dāsa Bābājī as his master and received the name of Bhaktivinoda Ṭhākura from the Gauḍīya Gosvāmīs in 1887. In the same year he established a printing press in Calcutta to help circulate Vaiṣṇava texts. He was initiated as a renunciate in 1908. His son Bhaktisiddhānta Sarasvatī succeeded him at his death in 1914. He reestablished the use of the sacred thread in the tradition (which his father had abolished) as a symbol of "real brahminhood" for every initiate irrespective of his caste or origin. A. C. Bhaktivedānta Svāmī, who succeeded Bhaktisiddhānta in 1937, aimed at spreading the message of Caitanya among English-speaking people and undertook a translation of the Bhāgavatapurāṇa. Having become a renouncer in 1959, he visited New York in 1965 at the age of 70 and died in 1977 (Hopkins 1984, *passim*).

Conclusion

Vaiṣṇava traditions did not develop in themselves and by themselves. They were under constant pressure from political and socioeconomic powers which considerably influenced them as protectors, as in the case of the early Bhāgavata tradition, but sometimes also as controllers. For instance, the fortunes of rival Śrīvaiṣṇava tendencies may have varied according to the support of Vijayanagar kings (Appadurai 1977). Another illustration is the political instrumentalization of the notion of *catuḥsampradāya* ("fourfold tradition" of Vaiṣṇavism which refers to the traditions of Rāmānuja, Viṣṇusvāmin, Nimbārka, and Madhva) by the rulers of Rajasthan in the eighteenth and nineteenth centuries (Clémentin-Ojha 1999).

The perception of Vaiṣṇavism as a single religion with an homogenous development can only be an ideal view. The notion of Vaiṣṇavism partly corroborated by comparatively late Indian doxographies and adopted by modern scholarship, corresponds in fact to the aggregation of a multitude of varied traditions. The above overview shows the successive rise of Vaiṣṇava traditions (and sometimes, their reappearance in another form) and their multiple aspects. This is because these traditions had to cater for a variety of human needs in terms of devotion, rituals, doctrine, and these furthermore towards a chosen divine aspect. Again, our comprehension of Vaiṣṇavism according to its successive tendencies depends on extant historical evidence which project to forefront merely fragmented and crystallized images of Vaiṣṇava traditions. This should not hide the fact that such trends as asceticism, devotion, image worship probably coexisted at the same time in Vaiṣṇavism, though the texts do not give them equal importance.

Only critical research can disentangle a historical perspective from textual views. A comprehensive study of the multifarious and often biaised descriptions and classifications of Vaiṣṇava traditions in Vaiṣṇava Sanskrit and vernacular texts, as well as a complete historical study of such vital themes as the notion of *guru* or of initiation in the different Vaiṣṇava traditions, are required. A methodical evaluation of the influence of these traditions on each other and on other traditions, as well as that of the non-Vaiṣṇava traditions on Vaiṣṇava traditions, would help to locate them more precisely in Indian religions.

More or less institutionalized traditions form only a part of religious culture. These structures which we tried to circumscribe are, so to say, superficial. Larger socioreligious realities in fact nourish them: patrons and devotees form the core of historical Vaiṣṇavism. This continuously changing social substance facilitated influences and conversions and partly explains the growth and decay of these traditions.

Acknowledgments

I would like to thank C. Clémentin-Ojha for her observations on a first draft of this chapter. Unfortunately M. Rastelli's article on the *pañca kālas* (*Wiener*

Zeitschrift für die Kunde Südasiens 44: 101–34) was published after I had submitted the manuscript of my chapter (April 2000) so could not be included for discussion here.

Note

1 Another text, the Rāmārcanapaddhati, sometimes dated to the fifteenth century (Burghart 1978: 127), also contains this declaration, but more recently it has been assigned to the late nineteenth or early twentieth centuries (Bakker 1986: 120).

Short Bibliography and Abbreviations

Appadurai, A. 1977. "Kings, Sects and Temples in South India, 1350–1700 AD," *Indian Economic and Social History Review* 14: 47–73.

Bakker, H. 1986. *Ayodhyā*. Groningen.

Bāṇa. *Harṣacarita*, eds. K. P. Parab and Dh. P. Vaze. Bombay, 1892.

Barz, R. 1992. *The Bhakti Sect of Vallabhācārya*. Delhi (1st ed. 1976).

BEFEO: *Bulletin de l'École Française d'Extrême-Orient.*

Bhattacharya, K. 1961. *Les religions brahmaniques dans l'ancien Cambodge d'après l'épigraphie et l'iconographie*. Paris.

——. 1964. "Recherches sur le vocabulaire des inscriptions sanskrites du Cambodge," *BEFEO* 52: 1–70.

——. 1965. "Sur une stance d'une inscription sanskrite du Cambodge," in *JA* 253: 407–8.

——. 1967. "Le 'védisme' de certains textes hindouistes," *JA* 255: 199–222.

Bose, M. M. 1930. *The Post-Caitanya Sahaji[y]ā Cult of Bengal*. Calcutta.

Bose (born Chaudhury), R. 1940, 1941, 1943. *Vedānta-pārijāta-saurabha of Nimbārka and Vedānta-kaustubha of Śrīnivāsa (Commentaries on the Brahma-sūtra)*, vol. III: *Doctrines of Nimbārka and his followers*. Calcutta.

Brockington, J. 1998. *The Sanskrit Epics*. Leiden/Boston/Köln.

van Buitenen, J. A. B. 1971. *Yāmuna's Āgama Prāmāṇyam or Treatise on the Validity of Pañcarātra*. Sanskrit text and English trans. Madras.

Burghart, R. 1978. "The Founding of the Ramanandi Sect," *Ethnohistory* 25: 121–39.

Caland, W. 1929. *Vaikhānasasmārtasūtram. The Domestic Rules and Sacred Laws of the Vaikhānasa School Belonging to the Black Yajurveda* [trans.]. Calcutta.

Cantlie, A. 1985. "Vaishnava Reform Sects in Assam," in R. Burghart and A. Cantlie, eds., *Indian Religion*. London and New York, pp. 134–57.

Carman, J. B. 1981. *The Theology of Rāmānuja. An Essay in Interreligious Understanding*. Bombay (reprint).

Clémentin-Ojha, C. 1990. "La renaissance du Nimbārka Sampradāya au XVIe siècle: Contributions à l'étude d'une secte kṛṣṇaïte," *JA* 278, pp. 327–76.

——. 1999. *Le trident sur le palais: une cabale anti-vishnouite dans un royaume hindou à l'époque coloniale*. Paris.

Cœdès, G. 1931. "Études cambodgiennes: XXV. – Deux inscriptions sanskrites du Fou-nan," *BEFEO* 31 (1931): 1–23.

Cœdès, G. 1932. "Études cambodgiennes: XXVIII–XXX," *BEFEO* 32: 71–112.

——. 1942. *Inscriptions du Cambodge*, vol. II. Hanoi.

——. 1953. *Inscriptions du Cambodge*, vol. V. Paris.

—— and Dupont, P. 1937 "Les inscriptions du Pràsàt Kôk Pô," *BEFEO* 37: 379–411.

Colas, G. 1988. "Le yoga de l'officiant vaikhānasa," *JA* 276: 245–83.

——. 1995. "Cultes et courants du vishnuisme en Inde du Sud. Quelques observations à partir des textes," in M.-L. Reiniche and H. Stern, eds., *Les ruses du salut. Religion et politique dans le monde indien*. Paris, Collection Puruṣārtha 15, pp. 111–38.

——. 1996. *Viṣṇu, ses images et ses feux. Les métamorphoses du dieu chez les vaikhānasa*. Paris.

——. 1999. "The Reworking of 'Vedic' Paradigms in Medieval Liturgies," in J. Assayag, ed., *The Resources of History: Tradition, Narration and Nation in South Asia*. Paris/ Pondichéry: École Française d'Extrême-Orient/Institut Français de Pondichéry, pp. 41–50.

Couture, A. 1986. "Akrūra et la tradition Bhāgavata selon le Harivaṃśa," *Studies in Religion/Sciences Religieuses* 15, pp. 221–32.

——. 1991. *L'enfance de Kṛṣṇa*. Paris.

Dasgupta, S. 1975. *A History of Indian Philosophy*, vol. IV. Delhi (reprint).

De, S. K. 1961. *Early History of the Vaiṣṇava Faith and Movement in Bengal from Sanskrit and Bengali Sources*. Calcutta (2nd ed.).

Dimock, E. C. 1966. *The Place of the Hidden Moon: Erotic Mysticism in the Vaiṣṇava-Sahajiyā Cult of Bengal*. Chicago & London.

Eschmann, A., H. Kulke, and G. C. Tripathi, eds. 1978. *The Cult of Jagannāth and the Regional Tradition of Orissa*. Delhi.

Esnoul, A.-M. 1956. "Le courant affectif à l'intérieur du brahmanisme ancien," *BEFEO* 48: 141–207.

Farquhar, J. N. 1967. *An Outline of the Religious Literature of India*. Delhi (1st ed. 1920).

Feldhaus, A. 1983. *The Religious System of the Mahānubhāva Sect: The Mahānubhāva Sūtrapāṭha*. Ed. and trans. with an intro. Delhi.

—— and S. G. Tulpule. 1992. *In the Absence of God: The Early Years of an Indian Sect. A Translation of Smṛtisthaḷ with an Introduction*. Honolulu.

Gonda, J. 1977. *Medieval Religious Literature in Sanskrit*. Wiesbaden.

Goudriaan, T. 1965. *Kāśyapa's Book of Wisdom (Kāśyapa-jñānakāṇḍaḥ). A ritual handbook of the Vaikhānasas*. London–The Hague–Paris.

——. 1981. "Hindu Tantric Literature in Sanskrit," in Goudriaan and Gupta 1981, pp. 1–172.

—— and S. Gupta. 1981. *Hindu Tantric and Śākta Literature*. Wiesbaden.

Gros, F. 1968. *Le Paripāṭal, texte tamoul, Introduction, traduction et notes*. Pondichéry.

Gupta, S. 1972. *Lakṣmī Tantra, A Pāñcarātra text, Translation and notes*. Leiden.

——. 1981. "Tantric Śākta Literature in Modern Indian Languages," in Goudriaan and Gupta 1981, pp. 173–213.

Hardy, F. 1974. "Mādhavêndra Purī: A Link between Bengal Vaiṣṇavism and South Indian Bhakti," *Journal of the Royal Asiatic Society of Great Britain and Ireland* 1974: 23–41.

——. 1983. *Viraha-bhakti: The Early History of Kṛṣṇa Devotion in South India*. Delhi/Oxford/New York.

——. 1998. "South Indian Viṣṇu Temples and the Performing Arts," *South Indian Research* 18: 99–114.

Hari Rao, V. N. 1961. *Kōil Oḻugu. The Chronicle of the Srirangam Temple with Historical Notes* [trans. of the Kōyil Oḻuku]. Madras.

——. 1964. "Vaishnavism in South India in the Modern Period," in O.P. Bhatnagar, ed., *Studies in Social History (Modern India)*, pp. 116–35.

Haynes, R. D. 1974. "Svāmī Haridās and the Haridāsī Sampradāy." Ph.D. thesis, University of Pennsylvania.

Hopkins, T. J. 1984. "Hindu Sects in America: the Kṛṣṇa Consciousness Example," in P. Gaeffke and D. A. Utz, eds., *Identity and Divisions in Cults and Sects in South Asia.* Philadelphia, pp. 174–88.

JA = Journal Asiatique.

Jagadeesan, N. 1977. *History of Sri Vaishnavism in the Tamil Country (Post-Ramanuja).* Madurai.

Jaiswal, S. 1967. *The Origin and Development of Vaiṣṇavism (Vaiṣṇavism from 200 BC to AD 500).* Delhi.

Jones, K. W. 1989. *Socio-religious Reform Movements in British India.* Cambridge.

Joshi, R. V. 1959. *Le rituel de la dévotion kṛṣṇaïte.* Pondichéry.

Lester, R. C. 1992. "The Practice of Renunciation in Śrīvaiṣṇavism," *Journal of Oriental Research, Madras* 56–62: 77–95.

——. 1994. "The Sāttāda Śrīvaiṣṇavas," *Journal of the American Oriental Society* 114: 39–53.

Lipski, A. 1971. "Bipincandra Pāl and Reformed Hinduism," *History of Religions* 11: 220–35.

Majumdar, A. K. 1969. *Caitanya. His Life and Doctrine. A Study in Vaiṣṇavism.* Bombay.

Matsubara, M. 1994. *Pāñcarātra Saṃhitās & Early Vaiṣṇava Theology with a Translation and Critical Notes from Chapters on Theology in the Ahirbudhnya Saṃhitā.* Delhi.

Mesquita, R. 1979. "Zur Vedānta- und Pāñcarātra-Tradition Nāthamunis," *Wiener Zeischrift für die Kunde Süd-Asiens* 23: 163–93.

Meth Srinivasan, D. 1997. *Many Heads, Arms and Eyes: Origin, Meaning and Form of Multiplicity in Indian Art.* Leiden.

Mukherjee, P. 1978. "Caitanya in Orissa," in A. Eschmann, H. Kulke, and G. C. Tripathi 1978, pp. 309–19.

Mumme, P. Y. 1988. *The Śrīvaiṣṇava Theological Dispute: Maṇavāḷamāmuni and Vedānta Deśika.* Madras.

Nābhājī (=Nābhādāsa). *Śrībhaktamāla, with the commentary Bhaktirasabodhinī of Priyādāsa and a (modern) commentary Bhaktisudhāsvāda of Sītārāmaśaraṇa Bhagavānprasāda Rūpakalā.* Lakhnaü (Lucknow): Tejakumāra Book Depot, 1977.

Neevel, W. G. 1977. *Yāmuna's Vedānta and Pāñcarātra: Integrating the Classical and the Popular.* Missoula.

Nārāyaṇīya Parvan in *Śāntiparvan (=12,321–39)* of the *Mahābhārata, Part III: Mokṣadharma B*, ed. S. P. Belvalkar. Poona: Bhandarkar Oriental Research Institute, 1954.

Neog, M. 1965. *Śaṅkaradeva and His Times.* Gauhati.

NP = Nārāyaṇīyaparvan.

Oberlies, T. 1997. "Die Textgeschichte der Śvetadvīpa-Episode des Nārāyaṇīya (Mbh 12,321–326)," in Schreiner 1997, pp. 75–118.

Olivelle, P. 1986. *Renunciation in Hinduism, Volume 1: The Debate and the Advaita Argument.* Vienna.

Paripāṭal: see Gros 1968.

Pauṣkarasaṃhitā, ed. Sree Yatiraja Sampathkumara Ramanuja Muni. Bangalore, 1934.

Pollet, G. 1980. "The Old Braj hagiography of Nābhādās," in W. M. Callewaert, ed., *Early Hindi Devotional Literature in Current Research.* Leuven, pp. 142–9.

Renou, L. 1985a. "Les sectes," in L. Renou, J. Filliozat et al., *L'Inde classique. Manuel des Études indiennes, Tome I.* Paris (1st ed. 1947–9), pp. 620–61.

——. 1985b. "Le Vedānta," in L. Renou, J. Filliozat et al., *L'Inde classique. Manuel des Études indiennes, Tome II*, Paris (1st ed. 1953), pp. 16–33.
Rosenstein, L. L. 1997. *The Devotional Poetry of Svāmī Haridās*. Groningen.
Salomon, R. 1998. *Indian Epigraphy*. New York–Oxford.
Sankaranarayanan, S. 1993. "Sanskrit education in ancient Tamil country (An Epigraphical Survey)," *Adyar Library Bulletin* 57: 7–33.
Sastry, V. V. 1991. "Ancient Classical Telugu Theatre," *The Samskrita Ranga Annual* 9 (1988–90), Madras, pp. 62–7.
Schomer, K. 1987. "Introduction," in K. Schomer and W. H. McLeod 1987, pp. 1–19.
—— and W. H. McLeod, eds. 1987. *The Sants: Studies in a Devotional Tradition of India*. Delhi.
Schreiner, P., ed. 1997. *Nārāyaṇīya-Studien*. Wiesbaden.
——. 1997a. "Introduction," in Schreiner, ed., 1997, pp. 1–29.
——. 1997b. "'Schau Gottes' – ein Leitmotiv indischer Religionsgeschichte?," in Schreiner, ed., 1997, pp. 159–96.
Sharma, B. N. K. 1960. *A History of the Dvaita School of Vedanta and its Literature*, vol. I: *From the Earliest Beginnings to the Age of Jayatīrtha (c. 1400 AD)*. Bombay.
——. 1961. *A History of the Dvaita School of Vedanta and its Literature, vol. II: From the 15th Century to Our Own Time*. Bombay.
Shukla, N. S. 1971. *Le Karṇānanda de Kṛṣṇadāsa*. Pondichéry.
Siauve, S. 1968. *La doctrine de Madhva: dvaita-vedānta*. Pondichéry.
——. 1978. *Aṣṭādaśabhedanirṇaya [. . .] de Śrī Vātsya Raṅganātha*. Pondichéry.
Singh, S. 1958. *Vedānta Deśika: His Life, Works and Philosophy: A Study*. Varanasi.
Sircar, D. C. 1942. *Select Inscriptions bearing on Indian History and Civilization*, vol. I: *From the Sixth Century BC to the Sixth Century AD*. Calcutta.
Sivaramamurti, C. 1966. *Indian Epigraphy and South Indian Scripts*. Madras (repr.).
Smith, H. D. 1968 "Relevance of Epigraphic Evidence for the Pancaratra Studies," in R. Nagaswamy, ed., *Seminar on Inscriptions 1966*. Madras, pp. 15–18.
Snell, R. 1991. *The Eighty-four Hymns of Hita Harivaṃśa: An Edition of the Caurāsī Pada*. Delhi.
Srinivasachari, P. N. 1970. *The Philosophy of Viśiṣṭādvaita*. Madras.
Stietencron, H. von. 1978. "The advent of Viṣṇuism in Orissa: An Outline of its History according to Archaeological and Epigraphical Sources from the Gupta period up to 1135 AD," in Eschmann, Kulke, and Tripathi 1978, pp. 1–30.
Thiel-Horstmann, M. 1983. *Crossing the Ocean of Existence: Braj Bhāṣā Religious Poetry from Rajasthan. A Reader*. Wiesbaden.
——. 1991. "On the Dual Identity of the Nāgās," in D. L. Eck and Fr. Mallison, eds., *Devotion Divine: Bhakti traditions from the Regions of India. Studies in Honour of Charlotte Vaudeville*. Groningen–Paris, pp. 255–71.
Varadachari, V. 1983. *Two Great Acharyas: Vedānta Desika and Manavala Mamuni*. Madras.
Varāhamihira, *Bṛhatsaṃhitā = The Bṛhad Saṃhitā of Varāha-Mihira*, ed. H. Kern. Calcutta, 1865.
Vaudeville, C. 1969. *L'Invocation. Le Haripāṭh de Dñyāndev*. Paris.
——. 1987a. "Sant Mat: Santism as the Universal Path to Sanctity," in Schomer and McLeod 1987, pp. 21–40.
——. 1987b. "The Saiva–Vaishnava Synthesis in Maharashtrian Santism," in Schomer and McLeod 1987, pp. 215–28.
Vēṅkaṭarāmaṉ, Cu. 1985. *Araiyar cēvai*, Ceṉṉai. [=Madras]: Tamiḻpputtakālayam.
White, C. 1977. *The Caurāsī Pad of Śrī Hit Harivaṃś*. Hawaii.
[Yāmunacarya]. *Āgamaprāmāṇya of Yāmunācārya*, ed. M. Narasimhachary. Baroda, 1976.

CHAPTER 12

The Renouncer Tradition

Patrick Olivelle

Shaven-headed and clad in yellow-orange robes – whether they are Buddhist monks in Thailand, Sadhus in the Indian countryside, or Hare Krishnas in American airports – that is the enduring image of Indian religion that many westerners carry in their minds. The cultural institution behind these modern manifestations, an institution which we have chosen to call the "renouncer tradition," is very old. It goes back to about the middle of the first millennium BCE and took shape along the mid-Gangetic plane in roughly what is today the state of Bihar.

The image of Indian religion as essentially world-renouncing and ascetic (Dumont 1960), however, is grossly inaccurate. Yet, behind that image lies a kernel of truth: the renouncer tradition has been a central and important ingredient in the sociocultural mix that contributed to the formation of the historical religions in India. As any human institution, nevertheless, that kernel and the Indian religions themselves changed over time and space.

The earliest historical information about the renouncer tradition comes from the Upaniṣads and other vedic writings, as well as from Buddhist literary sources. Given the uncertainly of their dates, however, it is impossible to give a precise or certain date to the origin of that tradition: hence, my vague reference to "the middle of the first millennium BCE." The earliest datable source that attests to the existence of the renouncer tradition is the Aśokan inscriptions of the middle of the third century BCE. Around this time, if I may be permitted to generalize, two competing ascetic traditions appear to have crystallized: *anchorites* living settled lives in forest hermitages cut off from social intercourse, and *renouncers* living itinerant lives in the wilderness but in interaction with towns and villages from which they begged their food.

An ancient Brahmanical law book describes the normative lifestyle of anchorites:

> An anchorite shall live in the forest, living on roots and fruits and given to austerities. He kindles the sacred fire according to the procedure for recluses and refrains from eating what is grown in a village. He may also avail himself of the flesh of animals killed by predators. He should not step on plowed land or enter a village. He shall wear matted hair and clothes of bark or skin and never eat anything that has been stored for more than a year. (*Gautama Dharmasūtra*, 3.26–35)

The anchorite's life is marked by his refusal to avail himself of any product mediated by human culture. His clothing and food come from the wild; he is not permitted to step on plowed land, the symbol of human culture and society. The anchorite has *physically* withdrawn from society, even though he continues to participate in some of the central religious activities of society, such as maintaining a ritual fire and performing rituals. At least some of the anchorites may have lived in family units; we hear often of wives and children living in forest hermitages.

The renouncer, on the other hand, lives in proximity to civilized society and in close interaction with it.

> A mendicant shall live without any possessions, be chaste, and remain in one place during the rainy season. Let him enter a village only to obtain almsfood and go on his begging round late in the evening, without visiting the same house twice and without pronouncing blessings. He shall control his speech, sight, and actions; and wear a garment to cover his private parts, using, according to some, a discarded piece of cloth after washing it. Outside the rainy season, he should not spend two nights in the same village. He shall be shaven-headed or wear a topknot; refrain from injuring seeds; treat all creatures alike, whether they cause him harm or treat him with kindness; and not undertake ritual activities. (*Gautama Dharmasūtra*, 3.11–25)

The renouncer's withdrawal from society is not physical but ideological. He does not participate in the most central of socioreligious institutions: family and sex, ritual fire and ritual activities, a permanent residence, and wealth and economic activities. He is a religious beggar, depending on social charity for his most basic needs.

Of these two ascetic institutions, the one that became central to the development of Indian religions and cultures was the renouncer tradition. The hermit culture became obsolete at least by the beginning of the common era and lived on only in poetic imagination; some of the most beloved of Indian poetry and drama, including the two great epics, *Rāmāyaṇa* and *Māhābhārata*, center around hermit life in the forest. Śakuntalā, the famous Indian heroine immortalized by the Sanskrit playwright Kālidāsa, was a girl living in a forest hermitage. But it had little historical influence on Indian religion.

The Origins

There is a longstanding and ongoing scholarly debate regarding the origin of the renouncer tradition. To simplify a somewhat intricate issue, some contend that the origins of Indian asceticism in general and of the renouncer tradition in particular go back to the indigenous non-Aryan population (Bronkhorst 1993, Pande 1978, Singh 1972). Others, on the contrary, see it as an organic and logical development of ideas found in the vedic religious culture (Heesterman 1964).

It is time, I think, to move beyond this sterile debate and artificial dichotomy. They are based, on the one hand, on the false premise that the extant vedic texts provide us with an adequate picture of the religious and cultural life of that period spanning over half a millennium. These texts, on the contrary, provide only a tiny window into this period, and that too only throws light on what their priestly authors thought it important to record. It is based, on the other hand, on the untenable conviction that we can isolate Aryan and non-Aryan strands in the Indian culture a millennium or more removed from the original and putative Aryan migrations. It is obvious that the ancient Indian society comprised numerous racial, ethnic, and linguistic groups and that their beliefs and practices must have influenced the development of Indian religions. It is quite a different matter, however, to attempt to isolate these different strands at any given point in Indian history (Olivelle 1993, 1995b).

It is a much more profitable exercise to study the social, economic, political, and geographical factors along the Gangetic valley during the middle of the first millennium BCE that may have contributed to the growth of ascetic institutions and ideologies (Olivelle 1993, Gombrich 1988). This was a time of radical social and economic change, a period that saw the second urbanization in India – after the initial one over a millennium earlier in the Indus Valley – with large kingdoms, state formation, a surplus economy, and long-distance trade. Ambition, strategy, drive, and risk-taking all played a role in both a king's quest for power and a merchant's pursuit of wealth. A similar spirit of individual enterprise is evident in a person's decision to leave home and family and to become a wandering mendicant. The new social and economic realities of this period surely permitted and even fostered the rise of rival religious ideologies and modes of life.

The Formative Period of Indian Religions

The second half of the first millennium BCE was the period that created many of the ideological and institutional elements that characterize later Indian religions. The renouncer tradition played a central role during this formative period of Indian religious history.

Renouncers often formed groups around prominent and charismatic ascetic leaders, groups that often developed into major religious organizations. Some of them, such as Buddhism and Jainism, survived as major religions; others, such as the Ājīvakas, existed for many centuries before disappearing. Renunciation was at the heart of these religions.

Even though the ideal of homeless wandering is often maintained as a theological fiction, many of these renouncer groups, such as the Buddhist and the Jain, organized themselves into monastic communities with at least a semi-permanent residence. These communities vied with each other to attract lay members, donors and benefactors, and for political patronage.

A significant feature of these celibate communities is that they were voluntary organizations, the first such religious organizations perhaps in the entire world, and their continued existence depended on attracting new members. Another was the admission, at least in some traditions such as the Buddhist and the Jain, of women and the creation of female monastic communities. If voluntary celibate communities that rejected marriage were remarkable even for men, they must certainly have been revolutionary in the case of women.

The influence of renouncer practices and ideologies was not limited to what we have come to regard as non-Hindu or "heterodox" traditions; their influence can be seen within the Brahmanical tradition itself. Indeed, during this early period of Indian history the very division into "orthodox" and "heterodox" is anachronistic and presents a distorted historical picture. Scholars in the past have argued that some of the changes within the Brahmanical tradition, such as the creation of the *āśrama* (orders of life) system, was instituted as a defense mechanism against the onslaught of renunciation. Evidence does not support such claims. The Brahmanical tradition was not a monolithic entity. The debates, controversies, and struggles between the new ideologies and lifestyles of renunciation and the older ritualistic religion took place as much within the Brahmanical tradition as between it and the new religions (Olivelle 1993). This struggle created new institutions and ideas within that tradition, the *āśrama* system being one of the more remarkable and enduring.

Some of the fundamental values and beliefs that we generally associate with Indian religions in general and Hinduism in particular were at least in part the creation of the renouncer tradition. These include the two pillars of Indian theologies: *saṃsāra* – the belief that life in this world is one of suffering and subject to repeated deaths and births (rebirth); *mokṣa/nirvāṇa* – the goal of human existence and, therefore, of the religious quest is the search for liberation from that life of suffering. All later Indian religious traditions and sects are fundamentally ideologies that map the processes of Saṃsāra and Mokṣa and technologies that provide humans the tools for escaping saṃsāric existence. Such technologies include different forms of yoga and meditation. An offshoot of these ideologies and technologies is the profound antiritualism evident in most later traditions. In the areas of ethics and values, moreover, renunciation was principally responsible for the ideals of non-injury (*ahiṃsā*) and vegetarianism.

Several of the renouncer movements that turned into major religions were founded by people who had renounced the world, Gautama Buddha and the Jina Mahāvīra in the case of Buddhism and Jainism. Within these religions the monastic communities are at the center of both theology and ecclesiastical structure.

Within the Brahmanical tradition, on the other hand, the situation was more complex. In the old vedic religion, the Brahmin was the ritual specialist and religious leader, but these very functions required that he get married and father children, activities diametrically opposed to renunciation. We will examine diverse attempts to integrate the ideals of these two poles of the tradition at both the institutional and the theological levels. The tension between the two ideals of religious living, however, continued to exist throughout the history of the Brahmanical and Hindu traditions.

Values in Conflict

The debate on the conflicting value systems of renunciation and the society-oriental vedic religion is recorded in many early texts and revolved especially around the male obligation to marry, father offspring, and carry out ritual duties. These obligations were given theological expression in a novel doctrine, probably the result of that very debate on values. The "doctrine of debts" posited that a man is born with three debts – to gods, ancestors, and vedic seers – debts from which one can be freed only by offering sacrifices, begetting offspring, and studying the Vedas. An ancient text waxes eloquent on the importance of a son, who is viewed as the continuation of the father and the guarantor of his immortality:

> A debt he pays in him,
> And immortality he gains,
> The father who sees the face
> Of his son born and alive.
>
> Greater than the delights
> That earth, fire, and water
> Bring to living beings,
> Is a father's delight in his son.
> (*Aitareya Brāhmaṇa*, 7.13)

And in what appears to be a dig at ascetic claims, the same text continues:

> What is the use of dirt and deer skin?
> What profit in beard and austerity?
> Seek a son, O Brahmin,
> He is the world free of blame.

The proponents of ascetic and renunciatory values, on the other hand, dismiss these claims for sons and rituals. Their view of immortality and liberation is centered not on outward activities but on inward self-cultivation. Sons, sacrifices, and riches only guarantee the return to a new life of suffering within the wheel of saṃsāra. An Upaniṣad comments on the futility of sacrifices:

> Surely, they are floating unanchored,
> these eighteen forms of the sacrifice,
> the rites within which are called inferior;
> The fools who hail that as the best,
> return once more to old age and death.
> (*Muṇḍaka Upaniṣad*, 1.2)

The Upaniṣads also devalue the importance of marriage and progeny:

> This immense, unborn self is none other than the one consisting of perception here among the vital functions. It is when they desire him as their world that wandering ascetics undertake the ascetic life of wandering. It was when they knew this that men of old did not desire offspring, reasoning "Ours is this self, and it is our world. What then is the use of offspring for us?" (*Bṛhadāraṇyaka Upaniṣad*, 4.4.22)

This conflict in values and ideologies is often presented as a contrast between village and wilderness, the normative geographical spaces of society and renunciation. People inhabiting these spaces are destined to vastly different paths after death, the villagers returning back to the misery of earthly existence and ascetics proceeding to immortality:

> Now, the people who know this, and the people here in the wilderness who venerate thus: "Austerity is faith" – they pass into the flame, from the flame into the day, from the day into the fortnight of the waxing moon, from the fortnight of the waxing moon into the six months when the sun moves north, from these months into the year, from the year into the sun, from the sun into the moon, and from the moon into lightning. Then a person who is not human – he leads them to *brahman*. This is the path leading to the gods.
>
> The people here in villages, on the other hand, who venerate thus: "Gift-giving is offerings to gods and to priests" – they pass into the smoke, from the smoke into the night, from the night into the fortnight of the waning moon, and from the fortnight of the waning moon into the six months when the sun moves south. These do not reach the year but from these months pass into the world of the fathers, and from the world of the fathers into space, and from space into the moon. This is King Soma, the food of the gods, and the gods eat it. They remain there as long as there is a residue, and then they return by the same path they went. (*Chāndogya Upaniṣad*, 5.10.1–2)

The theological debates concerning the two value systems took place as much within the Brahmanical circles as between the so-called orthodox Brahmanism and the heterodox sects. The intense discussion between Kṛṣṇa and Arjuṇa in the *Bhagavad Gītā* on the issue of the relative value of renunciation and engagement in one's socially appointed duties is a classic example of such controversy and debate.

The *Āśrama* System

The system of four *āśramas* (orders of life) was an early attempt to institutionalize renunciation within Brahmanical social structures. Created probably around the fourth century BCE, the system in its original form proposed four alternate modes of religious living that young adults could pursue after they had completed their period of temporary studentship following vedic initiation. These were: continuing to be a student until death, getting married and setting up a household, withdrawing to the forest as a hermit, or becoming a renouncer (Olivelle 1993). This system, first recorded in the early Dharmasūtras composed between the second and third centuries BCE, envisaged a free choice among the *āśramas*, which were viewed as permanent and lifelong vocations. Here is one of the oldest descriptions of the *āśramas*:

> There are four orders of life: the householder's life, living at the teacher's house, the life of a sage, and that of a forest hermit. If a man remains steadfast in any of these, he attains bliss. A common prerequisite for all is to live at the teacher's house following one's initiation, and all are required not to abandon vedic learning. After he has learnt the rites, he may undertake the order that he prefers.
>
> Following the rules of a novice student, a student should serve his teacher until death, leaving his body in his teacher's house.
>
> Next, the wandering ascetic. From that very state, remaining chaste, he goes forth. With regard to him they admonish: "He should live as a silent sage, without fire or house, without shelter or protection." Speaking only when he is engaged in private vedic recitation and obtaining food from a village to sustain himself, he should live without any concern for this world or the next. Discarded clothes are prescribed for him. Some say that he should go completely naked. Abandoning truth and falsehood, pleasure and pain, the Vedas, this world and the next, he should seek the Self. When he gains insight, he attains bliss.
>
> Next, the forest hermit. From that very state, remaining chaste, he goes forth. With regard to him they admonish: "He should live as a silent sage with a single fire, but without house, shelter, or protection." Let him speak only when he is engaged in private vedic recitation. Clothes made of materials from the wild are prescribed for him. (*Āpastamba Dharmasūtra*, 2.21.1–22. 1)

The term *āśrama* is somewhat new in the Sanskrit vocabulary and was probably coined to express a new reality. Contrary to the common perception, the term did not refer to ascetic habitats or modes of life, if by "ascetic" we understand values and institutions that oppose Brahmanical values centered around the householder. On the contrary, *āśrama* is a fundamentally Brahmanical concept and is absent outside Brahmanical discourse. It referred originally to habitats and life styles of exceptional Brahmins living apart from society and devoted solely to austerities and rituals.

The creators of the *āśrama* system took this term and concept and extended it to all the legitimate modes of life, especially to celibate asceticism. Evidence does not support the common assumption that the system was created by conservative Brahmins with the intention of resisting the new religious movements and of safeguarding Brahmanical religion by incorporating the renunciatory lifestyle into a scheme that would lessen its impact and reduce or eliminate the conflict between it and the life of the householder. Elements of such a motive may be detected in the later "classical" form of the system I will discuss below. But the original system gives equal weight to all *āśramas* and, quite contrary to the normal Brahmanical attitude, gives the candidates total freedom of choice among the competing modes of life. Permitting choice, indeed, placed renunciation and celibacy on an equal footing with household life. The authors of the system in all likelihood came from the antiritualistic tradition within Brahmanism, a tradition that finds expression in some of the Upaniṣads. In light of the socioeconomic conditions of northern India during this time with possibly the beginning of the Maurya empire, I am inclined to believe that the *āśrama* system was an urban invention, or at least reflects the openness of an urban mentality. This is reflected in the very nature of the original *āśrama* system. It envisaged the *āśramas* as voluntary institutions. People are free to choose what they want to be as adults. The same principle was the basis of other voluntary organizations of the time, such as Buddhist and Jain monastic orders.

This novel proposal did not go unchallenged. Indeed, some of the earliest sources that record the *āśrama* system present it as an opponent's view that is to be rejected. One important argument used against the *āśrama* system was the theology of the three debts. The obligation to father offspring is clearly stated in the authoritative texts of the Veda. This injunction contradicts the central provision of the *āśrama* system permitting a man to become a celibate renouncer prior to marriage.

By the beginning of the common era, however, the *āśrama* system underwent drastic changes that culminated in its classical formulation. The *āśramas* are now envisaged not as alternate modes of life but as stages an individual goes through as he grows old. The first *āśrama* in the new scheme is identified with the temporary period of study following vedic initiation. After completing this stage, a young adult got married and raised a family; this is the second *āśrama*. When the householder had settled his children, he withdrew into the forest as a hermit. After a period of time in this stage, the man became a renouncer during the final years of his life. Here *āśramas* are temporary modes of life corresponding to different age groups, and choice is eliminated. This formulation reasserts the centrality of the householder; the productive years of an adult's life are spent as an economically productive head of a household. The classical formulation also avoided the problems posed by the theology of debts. In the new system a man only took to renunciation and celibacy after he had fulfilled his obligations to get married, beget offspring, and offer sacrifices. In effect, the classical *āśrama* system transformed renunciation from a life's calling into an institution of old age, a form of retirement.

Both these formulations of the system contained aspects of artificiality. They answered to the requirements of theological and legal minds demanding order; they did not reflect the usually chaotic reality of social or religious institutions. In the original system the choice of *āśramas* was limited to a single moment of a young adult's life; in reality, as we know from numerous contemporary sources, married people did leave their families and became renouncers. The classical system limited renunciation to old age; in reality people of all ages became renouncers. In time riders were attached to the classical system permitting individuals with extraordinary zeal and detachment to become renouncers early in life.

Attempts to blunt the opposition between domesticity and celibate asceticism were at best only partially successful. Proponents of asceticism objected especially to the fact that the grand compromise of the *āśrama* system relegated asceticism to old age, equating it thereby with retirement. The urgency of personal salvation could not brook such postponement. An example comes from a *Life of the Buddha* written in the first century CE by Aśvaghoṣa, a Brahmin who converted to Buddhism and became a Buddhist monk. Although the setting is formally Buddhist, the dialogue between the future Buddha and his father, Suddhodana, captures the controversy both within and outside the Brahmanical mainstream regarding the proper age for becoming an ascetic. When the future Buddha informs his father of his intention to leave the world, Suddhodana tells him:

> Give up this plan, dear child; the time is not right for you to devote yourself to religion (*dharma*). For in the first period of life, when the mind is unsteady, the practice of religion, they say, can cause great harm.
>
> His senses easily excited by sensual pleasures, a young man is incapable of remaining steadfast when confronted with the hardships of ascetic vows. So his mind recoils from the wilderness, especially because he is unaccustomed to solitude.

The future Buddha replies:

> I will not enter the penance grove, O king, if you will be the surety for me in four things. My life shall not be subject to death. Sickness shall not rob me of my health. Old age shall not strike down my youth. And misfortune shall never plunder my wealth.
>
> Given that separation is certain in this world, is it not better to separate oneself voluntarily for the sake of religion? Or should I wait for death to separate me forcibly even before I have reached my goal and attained satisfaction. (Aśvaghoṣa, *Buddhacarita*, tr. E. H. Johnston, 5.30–8; selections)

The rejection of the compromise proposed in the classical *āśrama* śsystem is presented vividly also in a conversation recorded in the *Mahābhārata* (12.169:

selections) between a father, the guardian of the old order, and his son, representing the troubled and anguished spirit of the new religious world. This story, appearing as it does in Jain (*Uttarādhyayana*, 14) and Buddhist (*Jātaka*, 509), and later Brahmanical (*Markaṇḍeya Purāṇa*, ch. 10) texts as well, probably belonged to the generic ascetic folklore before it was incorporated into the *Mahābhārata*. This text, just like the story of the Buddha, points to the ascetic rejection of societal attempts to convert asceticism into an institution of old age. To the son's question regarding how a person should lead a virtuous life, the father replies:

> First, learn the Vedas, son, by living as a Vedic student. Then you should desire sons to purify your forefathers, establish the sacred fires, and offer sacrifices. Thereafter, you may enter the forest and seek to become an ascetic.

The son retorts:

> When the world is thus afflicted and surrounded on all sides, when spears rain down, why do you pretend to speak like a wise man?
>
> The world is afflicted by death. It is surrounded by old age. These days and nights rain down. Why can't you understand?
>
> When I know that death never rests, how can I wait, when I am caught in a net.
>
> This very day do what's good. Let not this moment pass you by, for surely death may strike you even before your duties are done.
>
> Tomorrow's task today perform. Evening's work finish before noon, for death does not wait to ask whether your duties are done.
>
> For who knows whom death's legions may seize today. Practice good from your youth, for uncertain is life's erratic path.
>
> The delight one finds in living in a village is truly the house of death, while the wilderness is the dwelling place of the gods – so the Vedas teach.
>
> The delight one finds in living in a village is the rope that binds. The virtuous cut it and depart, while evil-doers are unable to cut it.
>
> In the self alone and by the self I am born, on the self I stand, and, though childless, in the self alone I shall come into being; I will not be saved by a child of mine.

The text concludes:

> Of what use is wealth to you, O Brahmin, you who must soon die. Of what use are even wife and relatives. Seek the self that has entered the cave. Where have your father and grandfather gone? (Translation from Winternitz 1923)

Textual Traditions

Renouncer groups both within and outside the Brahmanical tradition developed their own literature, especially texts that dealt with their modes of life and rules of conduct. The Buddhist and Jain textual traditions are well known. Within Brahmanism itself we have evidence of renouncer texts. The fourth century BCE grammarian Pāṇini (4.3.110–11), for example, mentions the *Bhikṣusūtras* composed by Pārāśarya and Karmandin. The *Baudhāyana Dharmasūtra* (2.11.14; 3.3.16) mentions a treatise on forest hermits.

None of these early texts has survived. One of the reasons may have been that discussions of ascetic life became incorporated in the Dharmaśāstras within the context of the *āśrama* system. Some of their sections dealing with renouncers and forest hermits may, indeed, be fragments from early handbooks for these ascetics. The epic *Mahābhārata*, likewise, contains similar fragments of ascetic literature (Winternitz 1923). Sections of some of the early Upaniṣads may reflect renouncer influence or literature.

Within the Brahmanical tradition, nevertheless, the only surviving literature dealing with renunciation is embedded within the Dharmaśāstras. It was not until the early middle ages that independent compositions dealing with the life of renouncers were composed. These fall into the category called Nibandha, that is, scholarly texts dealing with one or several elements of Dharma with copious quotations from earlier Dharmaśāstric treatises. One of the earliest surviving texts of this class is the *Yatidharmasamuccaya* by Yādava Prakāśa (twelfth century CE; Olivelle 1995a). Numerous other texts dealing with the rite for becoming a renouncer, his daily life and activities, rules governing his life, and his funeral were composed during medieval times. Most of these have not been edited or printed and only exist in manuscript (Olivelle 1976–7, 1987).

Saṃnyāsa: Abandoning Fire and Ritual

I have already alluded to an important aspect of renunciation that cuts across sectarian divides: the refusal to use fire and the rejection of ritual activities centered on the sacred fire. This led to another central feature of renunciation: mendicancy. Renouncers begged cooked food and not dry rations; without a fire they were not able to cook. At least in some traditions, likewise, renouncers did not follow the normal social custom of cremating their dead but instead buried them. One of the reasons given for this practice is again their refusal to use fire.

Although present also in Buddhist and Jain traditions, the abandoning of the fire became a central feature especially in the Brahmanical understanding of renunciation. The sacred fire and the rituals connected with it are a central feature in the vedic and Brahmanical religion. The very first word of the very first hymn of the very first text of the Veda, namely the *Ṛgveda*, is "Agni," Fire – a celebration of the fire god as the priest who conveys oblations to the gods, who is the mouth of the gods in which all oblations are deposited. Abandoning this paramount symbol of vedic religion, therefore, received special attention in this tradition.

Sometime toward the end of the first millennium BCE a new word was coined to express this significant element of Brahmanical renunciation. The word was *saṃnyāsa*, which in later times became the most common term in the

Brahmanical/Hindu vocabulary for the institution of renunciation. In the early years, however, the term had a more restricted meaning, referring primarily to the abandonment of the fire and ritual during the rite of renunciation. This ritual is often referred to simply as *saṃnyāsa*.

A medieval definition of renunciation captures the central meaning of this term: "*Saṃnyāsa* is the abandonment of daily, occasional, and optional rites found in the Veda and in the texts of tradition, rites known though injunctions, an abandonment carried out by reciting the Praiṣa formula" (Olivelle 1975).

The Praiṣa formula is the central act in the ritual by which a person becomes a renouncer. It consists of saying three times the words "I have renounced" (*saṃnyastaṃ mayā*), first softly, second in a moderate voice, and the third time aloud. The ceremonies leading up to this climax begins the day before with a series of offerings to ancestors and the shaving of the head and beard of the candidate followed by a bath. On the day of renunciation, the candidate offers a final sacrifice in his sacred fire and extinguishes the fire. The abandonment of the fire is interpreted within the tradition as an internalization. The fire is deposited in the renouncer, who carries it within himself in the form of his breaths. There are five types of sacred fires in the vedic ritual, and there are five types of breaths within the human body. Thus, the two sets dovetailed nicely; after his renunciation the five breaths are his five fires, and whenever a renouncer eats he offers an internal sacrifice in the fires of his breaths.

The final act of the renunciatory ritual is the taking possession of the emblems of his new state: ochre robe, water pot, begging bowl, pot hanger, and staff. The new renouncer places himself under the tutelage of an experienced teacher.

The medieval theological tradition of Advaita Vedānta made renunciation central in its understanding of the path to liberation. Advaita was a monistic system of philosophy that looked upon the world of multiplicity as in some way illusory. Taking this illusion that constitutes one's own individual existence and the external world as reality is ignorance, the cause of our suffering and of our bondage to repeated births and deaths. The first step in the direction of true knowledge is to give up all activities (*karma*) that are the driving force of the universe, and the most potent of such acts are the ritual acts, which are also called *karma*. Thus, the giving up of the ritual and the ritual paraphernalia, especially the ritual fire, was considered in Advaita Vedānta as a prerequisite for spiritual progress.

Renunciation as Penance

The Dharmaśāstra of Manu (first to third centuries CE) contains a significant verse, which was probably a proverb current during that period: "What needs cleansing is cleansed by using earth and water; a river is cleansed by its current, a woman with a defiled mind by her menstrual flow, and a Brahmin by means of renunciation" (5.108). Here we find renunciation compared to other methods of purification; renouncing is an act of purification from sin and defilement.

Now, the normal method for getting rid of sin in the Hindu tradition is by performing an appropriate penance, which is called *prāyaścitta*. The most common form of penance is fasting. Sometimes penitential acts are carried out as a vow, which is called *vrata*. Beginning about the fifth century CE and with increasing frequency, the literature on Dharma subsumes renunciation under these two categories of religious acts. The early texts of Dharma generally discuss renunciation and ascetic modes of life under the *āśrama* system. Later texts, for example the Dharmaśāstra of Yājñavalkya and medieval legal digests (*nibandha*), on the other hand, place them within the section dealing with penances (*prāyaścittakāṇḍa*). According to this understanding, the difference between normal penitential acts and renunciation is that the former are undertaken for a limited, often brief, period of time, whereas the latter is undertaken for life.

This connection between penance and renunciation influenced both the religious practices of ordinary people and the behavior of renouncers, a process that I have referred to as the domestication of renunciation (Olivelle 1995a). This process is most evident in the handbook on renunciation written by Yādava Prakāśa. He integrates ascetic life into the normal ritual life of Brahmanism. In dealing with the daily practices of a renouncer, for example, he concludes that any practice not mentioned in connection with ascetics should be gathered from corresponding practices of householders and vedic students. Penances for renouncers, likewise, are the same as those for householders, except that they are sometimes more intense. So, for example, the common lunar fast (*cāndrāyaṇa*), which consists in reducing and increasing by one mouthful the intake of food according to the waning and the waxing of the moon, has a more severe ascetic counterpart called *yaticāndrāyaṇa* which not only ascetics but also ordinary people can perform. Reading Yādava's work closely, one gets the distinct impression that the Brahmanical renouncer is a very exalted type of householder rather than a figure who contradicts the value system represented by domestic life.

Renunciation in Later Religions

The leadership provided by renouncers in founding and propagating sects, already evident in the case of Buddhism and Jainism, continued well into the middle ages and modern times. The French social anthropologist, Louis Dumont, has drawn attention to the close connection between sects and renunciation (Dumont 1960). Many of the founders of both Śaiva and Vaiṣṇava sects were renouncers, and the organization of sects often accorded renouncers a central position.

Most of the medieval Indian sects, however, had devotional theologies and liturgies that asserted the centrality of love and devotion to its particular god as the sole means of attaining liberation. These theological and religious traditions are collectively referred to as "*bhakti*." Most *bhakti* sects accepted the institution of renunciation, often redefining its meaning as withdrawal from worldly concerns so as to focus solely on devotion to god. Nevertheless, the internal logic of *bhakti* contradicted the elitism inherent in the institution of renunciation. Renouncers were religious virtuosi; and in theologies where mystical quests and ascetic discipline were central, the claim could be made that only renouncers were able to achieve the highest goal of religion, namely liberation. Love, on the other hand, is egalitarian; anyone can love. Indeed, *bhakti* literature is filled with examples of poor and ignorant men and women who gain divine favor by the intensity of their love.

Bhakti contained the potential for radicalism both in religion and in society, even though not all *bhakti* tradition espoused radical social or religious change. Most were, in fact, rather conservative, acknowledging caste and gender differences within religion. There were some, however, that did draw radical conclusions from the premise that all humans are alike in the eyes of god, and the only thing god requires from humans is complete and unconditional love and surrender. It was not necessary to go to Benares to see god; he is present in one's heart. For a person who loves god, his or her front yard is Benares. There is no need to leave home and family and to become a world renouncer in order to love god; a poor farmer can love god more intensely while pursuing his lowly tasks than an arrogant renouncer surrounded by a throng of disciples.

The seeds of this challenge was already sown in the *Bhagavad Gītā*. Standing in his chariot with Kṛṣṇa, the incarnation of Viṣṇu, in the middle of the two armies ready for battle in the great Bhārata war, Arjuna is struck with remorse at the imminent destruction of kith and kin. There they stood, fathers and sons, uncles and nephews, grandfathers and grandsons, teachers and pupils, ready to kill each other for the petty comforts of royal power. In disgust and dejection, Arjuna throws down his bow and says, "I will not fight!" Kṛṣṇa, god and upholder of social order, uses every argument possible to convince Arjuna that it is his duty as a warrior to fight, to kill and to be killed. The author of the Gītā, subtly but effectively transforms Arjuna's refusal to fight into the broader theological dispute over engagement in and withdrawal from activity, living in society and renouncing it. What is better? To act or not to act?

Kṛṣṇa's response amounts to a redefinition of renunciation, which is called *saṃnyāsa* in the Gītā. Renunciation, Kṛṣṇa points out, is not simply the running away from society, the refusal to act – for whether we like it or not, our very nature forces us to act. "True" renunciation is not the mere withdrawal from action, which is impossible in any case, but the abandonment of any desire for the fruits, the results, of one's actions. This true renunciation is an internal attitude and habit; not an external institution with specific rules and emblems. Kṛṣṇa calls it "continuous or perpetual renunciation"; unlike institutional renunciation which is carried out on the day that one performs the ritual of renunciation, here one has to continuously fight inner longings and give up desire for fruits every time one engages in any activity. Finally, this inner and true renunciation is not a simple negativity, a giving up of desire; desire is given up so that one can offer to god one's actions as an offering, as a token of one's love.

This new understanding of renunciation pervades later *bhakti* discourse. Most often, it only supplements the more traditional understanding of renunciation. Debates raged between competing traditions in medieval India about renouncers and renunciation – from lofty theological arguments about the nature and the function of renunciation in the path to liberation to what appears to the outside observer as petty squabbles about the dress, food, and emblems of a renouncer, even whether they should carry a single bamboo staff or three bamboos tied together (Olivelle 1986–7).

In some of the more radical sects and traditions, however, we find the explicit rejection of renunciation. The Sikh religion that emerged in north India in the sixteenth century rejecting both Muslim and Hindu identities – "There is neither Hindu nor Muslim" – does not have a place for renouncers within its institutional structures. The fifteenth-century *bhakti* saint Kabir is at his sarcastic best when he rails against the holier-than-thou ascetics:

> Go naked if you want, put on animal skins; what does it matter till you see the inward Ram? If the union yogis seek came from roaming about in the buff, every deer in the forest would be saved. If shaving your head spelled spiritual success, heaven would be filled with sheep. And brother, if holding back your seed earned you a place in paradise, eunuchs would be the first to arrive. (Hawley and Juergensmeyer 1988)

Down the centuries the Hindu traditions have been caught in an internal and unresolved conflict not just between two institutions – married household life and celibate renunciation – but also between the two value systems represented by these two institutions. We have seen many and repeated attempts to bring these two poles of the tradition together, always with limited success. This long debate, with echoes in the ancient Upaniṣads, epics, Dharmaśāstras, and medieval theological tracts, continues in India today, as exemplified in this 1978 speech by the then Vice-President of India, whose view of householder as "true renouncer" goes back to the Bhagavad Gītā:

> Who is better – the householder or the sanyasi? Of course, the householder, according to Vice-President B. B. Jatti. While the householder willingly renounces all that he earns to his wife and children for their love and affection, the sanyasi depends on others for his milk and fruits. Parasites, who are a mere burden on society, are sinners. If man has to progress, everybody must work. (*Indian Express*, May 8, 1978)

Bibliography

Basham, A. L. 1951. *History and Doctrines of the Ājīvikas: A Vanished Indian Religion.* London: Luzac.

Bradford, N. J. 1985. "The Indian Renouncer: Structure and Transformation in the Lingayat Community," in R. Burghart and A. Cantlie, eds., *Indian Religion*. London: Curzon Press.

Bronkhorst, J. 1993. *The Two Sources of Indian Asceticism*. Schweizer Asiatische Studien, Monographien 13. Bern: Peter Lang.

Cantlie, A. 1977. "Aspects of Hindu Asceticism," in J. Lewis, ed., *Symbols and Sentiments*. London: Academic Press.

Deo, S. B. 1956. *History of Jaina Monachism from Inscriptions and Literature*. Deccan College Dissertation Series, 17. Poona.

Dumont, L. 1960. "World Renunciation in Indian Religons," *Contributions to Indian Sociology* 4: 33–62.

Dutt, S. 1960. *Early Buddhist Monachism*. Rev. ed. London: Asia Publishing House.

Ghurye, G. S. 1964. *Indian Sadhus*. 2nd ed. Bombay: Popular Prakashan.

Gombrich, R. 1988. *Theravada Buddhism: A Social History from Ancient Benares to Modern Colombo*. London: Routledge & Kegan Paul.

Hawley, J. S. and J. Juergensmeyer. 1988. *Songs of the Saints of India*. New York: Oxford University Press.

Heesterman, J. C. 1964. "Brahmin, Ritual and Renouncer," *Wiener Zeitschrift für die Kunde Südasiens* 8: 1–31.

Jaini, P. S. 1991. *Gender and Salvation: Jaina Debates on the Spiritual Liberation of Women*. Berkeley: University of California Press.

Kaelber, W. O. 1989. *Tapta Mārga: Asceticism and Initiation in Vedic India*. Albany: State University of New York Press.

Lorenzen, D. N. 1972. *The Kāpālikas and Kālāmukhas: Two Lost Śaivite Sects*. Australian National University Centre of Oriental Studies, Oriental Monograph Series, XII. New Delhi: Thompson Press.

——. 1978. "Warrior Ascetics in Indian History," *Journal of the American Oriental Society* 98: 61–75.

Miller, D. M. and D. C. Wertz. 1976. *Hindu Monastic Life: The Monks and Monasteries of Bhubaneswar*. Montreal: McGill-Queen's University Press.

Olivelle, P. 1975. "A Definition of World Renunciation," *Wiener Zeitschrift für die Kunde Südasiens* 19: 75–83.

——. 1976–7. *Vāsudevāśrama Yatidharmaprakāśa: A Treatise on World Renunciation*. Vol. 1: critical edition; vol. 2: annotated translation. Vienna: Institute for Indology, University of Vienna.

——. 1986–7. *Renunciation in Hinduism: A Medieval Debate*. Vol. I: *The Debate and the Advaita Argument*. Vol. II: *The Viśiṣṭādvaita* Argument. Vienna: Institute for Indology, University of Vienna.

——. 1992. *The Saṃnyāsa Upaniṣads: Hindu Scriptures on Asceticism and Renunciation*. New York: Oxford University Press.

——. 1993. *The Āśrama System: History and Hermeneutics of a Religious Institution*. New York: Oxford University Press.

——. 1995a. *Rules and Regulations of Brahmanical Asceticism* (critical ed. and trans. of Yādava Prakāśa's *Yatidharmasamuccaya*). Albany, NY: State University of New York Press.

——. 1995b. Review of Bronkhorst 1993 in *Journal of the American Oriental Society* 115: 162–4.

——. 1996. *The Upaniṣads*. World's Classics Series. Oxford: Oxford University Press.

Pande, G. C. 1978. *Śramaṇa Tradition: Its History and Contribution to Indian Culture.* Ahmedabad: L. D. Institute of Indology.

Singh, S. 1972. *Evolution of Smṛti Law: A Study in the Factors Leading to the Origin and Development of Ancient Indian Legal Ideas.* Varanasi: Bharatiya Vidya Prakasana.

Skurzak, L. 1948. *Études sur l'origine de l'ascétisme indien.* A, no. 15. Wroclaw: Societé des Sciences et de Lettres.

Sprockhoff, J. F. 1976. *Saṃnyāsa: Quellenstudien zur Askese im Hinduismus. I – Untersuchungen Über die Saṃnyāsa-Upaniṣads.* Abhandlungen für die Kunde des Morgenlandes 42,1. Wiesbaden: Franz Steiner.

Winternitz, M. 1923. "Ascetic Literature in Ancient India," *Culcutta Review*, October: 1–21.

CHAPTER 13

The Householder Tradition in Hindu Society

T. N. Madan

Defining the Terms

To write about the householder tradition in Hindu society, it seems desirable that we begin with a brief clarification of the key terms "householder," "tradition," and "Hindu society" as employed in this chapter.

A household is a group of persons who own or "hold" a house: they are the householders. They may as well be seen as a group that is held together, as it were, in or by a house. The idea of ownership is mutual and dynamic: it is a durable relationship made of many strands. A house is of course a building of some kind intended for human habitation, but in many cultural settings, including the Hindu, it is more than that. Besides a material (architectural, allodial) aspect, it has ritual, symbolic, and emotional significance, establishing richer bonds between the house and the householders, and among the householders, than those of mere co-residence in a dwelling.

Co-residence is, however, a crucial aspect of the life of the householders. It arises from the ties of kinship, which may be biological or fictive but modeled on the biological, and of marriage. To elaborate, the household comprises at least a married couple and their naturally born or adoptive children. In preindustrial societies the household is usually more ramified structurally and may even include distantly related or unrelated helpers and dependants. In such societies, the family and the household usually are, unlike in contemporary western society, differentiated. A family usually comprises many households which live in separate sections of a house or in separate houses. The houses may be built around a compound or may be scattered. The failure to recognize the embedded character of the household within the family has given rise to the somewhat misleading notion of the Hindu "joint" family (Madan 1962). Some perceptive scholars have rightly observed that from the Hindu perspective the western household, which is also the immediate family, may well be characterized as being "restricted."

Apart from having a structural or formal aspect, the household also has functional and cultural aspects. Householders do many things together. Most notably they produce and socialize children. They act as an economic group engaged in productive and distributive activities, and marked by a division of labor on the basis of (among other considerations) age and sex. They participate in domestic rituals focused on particular household members (e.g. birth, marriage, and death rites) or on other religious concerns (e.g. propitiation of supernatural "beings"). They gossip, tell tales, sing and dance together. All these and other related activities comprise a significant part of the way of life of the householders – their culture. What they do not only fulfills certain practical needs, but also bestows meaning and significance on their lives. The practical and the symbolic aspects of the householders' lives, their interests and values, are closely intertwined. They are a legacy that is ever being reaffirmed and reformulated.

This brings us to the second term, "tradition," which is used here to denote the established ways of living in a society, and their underlying principles and values, accumulated over time. Traditions may be written or they may be oral. All that is remembered may not, however, be currently alive, nor may it be dead, for it may be revived and in the process reinvented. The householder tradition in Hindu society today had its beginnings in the so-called vedic age about 3,000 years ago, and has inevitably undergone many significant changes. Given such a length of time, what is remarkable is perhaps not the extent of change, but the measure of continuity.

This continuity, however, is often questioned because the very idea of Hindu society is said to be relatively recent. What, then, do we mean when we write of Hindu society in this chapter? Existentially, Hindu society comprises all those Indians who consider themselves Hindus and make public acknowledgment of this identity, for example when the decennial census is taken. It accounts for four-fifths of the population of India of nearly one billion. If the so-called Scheduled Castes of officialese, or Dalits (the oppressed) of popular discourse, formerly known as the "Untouchables," are excluded – as some vocal Dalit intellectuals demand (see Ilaiah 1996) – Hindus still account for over two-thirds of the population.

The word "Hindu" is of course not new: even as term of self-ascription it has been employed at least since the fifteenth century (Thapar 1989: 224). The idea of a large, multimillion-strong, community of subcontinental distribution, however, emerged only in the nineteenth century in response to the western colonial and Christian missionary challenges, and as a result of improved means of transport and communication. Such an encompassing idea brought together, but did not merge into one, a multitude of communities identified by regional culture and language, religious belief and practice, hereditary occupation and caste, and other criteria.

Thus, Bengali Brahmans, Tamil Śaivas or Vaiṣṇvas, Gujarati Patidars, north Indian Kayasthas, and numerous other communities acquired an additional shared identity as Hindus. The immediate significance of this development was primarily political. It also highlighted a sense of cultural togetherness in terms of the recognition of a common textual tradition of long duration, beginning with the Vedic corpus and including the later Purāṇas and Epics. The extent and nature of the knowledge of this tradition was (and is) variable, being derived from the texts themselves or their exegeses among the literate elites, or received through verbal exposition by professional story tellers and family elders among the nonliterate, largely rural populace.

It has been suggested that acknowledgment of the ultimate authority of the Veda may well be the minimum definition of Hinduism and Hindu identity today (Smith 1989: 13–14), irrespective of how much or how little is known about it. But Hinduism is not identical with Vedism or Brahmanism (Flood 1996). In its growth other sources too, notably the folk traditions – some of them predating the Vedic period – have contributed significantly. In fact, a two-way flow has been at work. Elements of the textual ("Great") tradition have been restated and reenacted in the idiom of the folk ("Little") traditions (the process has been called, somewhat infelicitously, "parochialization"). Likewise local beliefs and practices have been built into the textual tradition through "universalization" (Marriott 1955). Other process of communication or combination have also been at work, such as the identification of critical resemblance between different traditions (Hiltebeitel 1999).

In short, both existentially and historically one can speak and write of Hindu society meaningfully. Its boundaries are flexible, however, and even at its center "an inner conflict of tradition" (Heesterman 1985) has been manifest. One of the most significant of such antagonisms is between householdership (*gārhasthya*, firmly embedded in society, and renunciatory withdrawal from social obligations (*saṃnyāsa*). And this dichotomy is as old as the Vedic tradition itself.

"Gārhasthya": Way of Life or Stage of Life?

Domestic groups of one kind or another are a cultural universal. Even food-gathering and nomadic tribes periodically settle down to rest and residence in open camps or covered huts before they set out again in search of food for themselves and their domesticated animals. Relatively permanent households are generally but not always associated with cultivation of the soil. They are characterized by rites and symbols that, among other things, valorize domesticity.

Among the Vedic Aryans the domestic fire was more than a hearth for cooking food: it was also the locus of rites of various kinds and thereby acquired a symbolic character. The Aryan householder (*śālīna*, from *sālā*, "hall") did not, however, immediately qualify for the performance of the prescribed *śrauta* sacrifices that occupied a central place in his and his household's life. For this purpose he had to establish several fire altars. The first of these (*agnyādheya*) was lit with fire taken from the domestic hearth but, after some ceremonial cooking of grain, it was extinguished. One then set out from home to relight it elsewhere with a fire drill after a lapse of time, say a year. More altars (two or four) were set up subsequently. The process completed, the *śālīna* became the *āhitāgni*, that is, one who has made the transition from the world in which he was born to one that is transcendent. Two options were apparently available.

The householder could choose to settle down in the second abode, after leaving the first, and establish the sacrificial fires there, and acquire the various accoutrements of a householder, namely a fixed residence, grain, cattle, and other kinds of wealth including servants. Alternatively, the householder could opt for the life of a wanderer (*yāyāvara*). Although he might not have settled down long anywhere, his wandering had a clear purpose, namely the performance of the very same *śrauta* sacrifices to which the householder devoted himself. Indeed, the wanderer traveled to acquire the means, by force if necessary, to do so. Those from whom he took included the settled householders, whose antagonist he would have seemed to be. But his ultimate aim, after the years of wandering and violence, apparently was to settle down to the life of a peaceful householder. Although less glamorous it was regarded as a welcome way of life.

In the event, the *śālīna* and the *yāyāvara* were really not opposed to each other in their aims but only in their methods. The householder does leave home once to become the *āhitāgni* householder, and the wanderer eventually settles down to domesticity. Both are united in the role of the *śrauta* sacrificer, who is a householder although, paradoxically, he also performs rituals that are extrasocial. Making their appearance in the vedic texts, the householder and the wanderer are present in the Dharma literature also as two types of householders.

Jan Heesterman, on whose discussion of the original Sanskrit sources the foregoing account is based (see Heesterman 1982 and 1985), points out that while all Dharma texts prescribe the departure of the *śālīna* from home before he may establish the sacrificial fires, the *yāyāvara* emerges as the renouncer (*saṃnyāsa*) in some of them. Like the *śrauta* sacrifice, renunciation is an act that transcends society. But while the sacrificer periodically reverts to the life of the householder (after each sacrificial performance), or even does so for good, the renouncer turns his back on both the domestic and the sacrificial fires. According to Heesterman, the renouncer better fulfills "the inner logic" of the vedic tradition, wherein the desire for breaking away from society is first articulated. The wish for transcendence, however, never wholly repudiates the human world but rather encompasses it. "The householder adds an extra-social dimension to his quality by becoming a *śrauta* sacrificer and finally withdraws from society into a renunciatory mode of life. But even then he retains the quality of *gṛhastha* and [of] *āhitāgmi*" (Heesterman 1982: 268).

Patrick Olivelle, another authority on the subject, is even more emphatic in presenting the early primacy of the householder's way of life. He writes: "The ideal and typical religious life within the vedic ideology is that of a married householder. The normative character of that life is related to the two theologically central religious activities: offering sacrifices and procreating children"

(Olivelle 1993: 36). The scope of sacrifice was vast with cosmo-moral significance and included the three (or five) daily obligations of the householder in redemption of the "debts" mentioned in vedic literature. These number three in some texts and five in others: the debts to goods, seers, and fathers, and additionally to all men and nonhuman creatures. To discharge the debt to the ancestors, adult men of the "twice-born" (*dvija*) classes (*varṇa*) were expected to marry and beget sons. Implicit in the notion of the discharge of debts was an enlarged conception of the moral agent, comprising not only the male sacrificer but also his wife ("one half of the husband") and their offspring. From the *Ṛgveda* down (in time) to the *Manusmṛti* this idea of the man–wife–son triad holds ground and idealizes the life of the householder. Through the performance of sacrifices and by begetting a son, a householder achieves the prized goal of immortality.

The foregoing view of life underwent a radical transformation as a result of both an inner dynamism and significant socioeconomic changes between the sixth and fourth centuries BCE. The latter included the introduction of wetland rice cultivation in the lower regions of the Ganges valley resulting in the generation of an agricultural surplus that facilitated an increase in population and the emergence of urban settlements. With the latter came the merchant class, the notion of kingship, and an individualistic spirit. "The freedom to choose" that one would associate with individualism was, according to Olivelle, "at the heart" of the challenge to "the vedic religious ideal," which led to the formulation of "the original *āśrama* system that permitted a choice among several modes of religious life" (Olivelle 1993: 58).

The alternatives to the life of the married man and the householder that now became available comprised the life of the celibate and the ascetic respectively. For the ascetic and the renouncer the ultimate aim of moral striving was liberation from the cycle of birth, death, and rebirth in place of the Vedic householder's quest for immortality. Comparing the ideology of the early āśrama system to that of the *varṇa* and caste systems, Olivelle observes: "The creators of the *āśrama* system intended to do to the diversity of religious life styles what the creators of the *varṇa* system did to the diversity of social and ethnic groups": instead of "eliminating" it, they accommodated "the diversities within an overarching system" (Olivelle 1993: 101).

The *āśrama* system as originally conceived was, however, transformed by the beginning of the common era into what Olivelle calls the classical *āśrama* system. Whatever the reasons for this transformation, which can only be speculative and do not directly concern us here, it comprised two significant elements. The alternative modes of life of the worldly householder and the ascetic renouncer now became stages in the life of the moral agent. Of the four stages of studentship (*brahmacarya*), householdership (*gṛhastha*), retreat (*vānaprastha*), and renunciation (*saṃnyāsa*), the first three were by the very nature of the scheme temporary (each stage leading to the next), and the last one permanent as long as one lived. Moreover, a sense of obligation in the pursuit of ideals, which had been overtaken by the notion of choice, was revived.

To quote Olivelle again, "the four *āśramas* came to be regarded as constituting four ideals of the Brahmanical ethic" that were, "as far as possible," to be "realized by each individual" (Olivelle 1993: 129–30). And each stage was inaugurated by the rites of passage appropriate to it. The Brahmans were less tolerant of choice than their ancestors and provided an ideological back-up to the scheme of stages through the notion of *svadharma*, that is, *dharma* appropriate to each stage of life and, concomitantly, each *varṇa*. It was thus that the compound notion of *varṇāśrama-dharma* came to be the definition of the religiomoral life of the Brahmans and derivatively of the other twice-born *varṇas*.

While the notion of the life of the householder as a choice for life is present in the Dharmasūtras, the later notion of *āśramas* as stages of life is elaborated in the Dharmaśāstras, belonging to the first five centuries of the common era. Of these the most frequently cited, perhaps, is the *Mānava Dharmaśāstra*, also known as the *Manusmṛti* and believed to have been in existence already in the second century (see Bühler 1964: xiv). The householder's stage in the life of the individual is prescriptively introduced early in the text: "When, unswerving in his chastity, [the student] has learned the Vedas, or two Vedas, or even one Veda, in the proper order, he should enter the householder stage of life" (Manu 3.2 in Doniger and Smith 1991: 43).

One notices a certain urgency here, a desire not to postpone too long the inauguration of the householder's life. Appropriately, the making of a proper marriage is taken up first (Manu 3.4–66). The qualities of a woman that make her a good wife are listed. Eight forms of marriage and their *varṇa*-wise appropriateness are described. Exhortations on the duties of spouses and the respect due to women follows. The men of the household are advised to "revere" and "adorn" women if they wish for "good fortune": "The deities delight in places where women are revered . . . and [the family] thrives where women are not miserable" (Manu 3.55–8).

The law book then proceeds to prescribe the establishment of the domestic fires for cooking food and performing "five great sacrifices" as well as other domestic rituals. These sacrifices, it is explained, enable the householder to expiate the sins that are daily committed as a matter of necessity at the five slaughterhouses of the home, namely the fireplace, the grindstone, the broom, the mortar and pestle, and the water jar (Manu 3.68). The expiatory rites are: "The study (of the Veda) is sacrifice to ultimate reality, and the refreshing libation is the sacrifice to the ancestors; the offering into the fire is for the gods, the propitiatory offering of portions of food is for the disembodied spirits, and the revering of guests is the sacrifice to men" (Manu 3.70). The continuity of the tradition from the vedic sacrifices (mentioned earlier in this chapter) down (in time) to Śāstric rituals is noteworthy.

The argument is enlarged to bring in the other three orders (corresponding to the other stages of life): "since people in the other three stages of life are supported every day by the knowledge and food of the householder, therefore the householder stage of life is the best" (Manu 3.78).[1] In the giving of offerings and alms nobody is left out, not even dogs, those who have fallen, "Dog-cookers," those whose evil deeds have made them ill, birds, and worms (Manu 3.92).

Guests come in for detailed mention, and even a deserving Vaiśya or Śūdra, approaching a Brahman's house in the proper manner, must be given food, although only alongside the servants (Manu 3.112). Not everyone qualifies to be a guest, however; certainly not Brahman householders in their own village, who can only be called foolish, for they run the risk of being reborn as "the livestock of those who have given them food" (Manu 3.104). It is only after one and all have been fed that the pious householder shall himself eat. "The householder should eat the leftovers only after he has revered the goods, the sages, humans, ancestors, and the household deities. The person who cooks only for himself eats nothing but error [sin], for the food left over from the sacrifice is the food intended for good men" (Manu 3.117–18).

A large part of the third book of *Mānava Dharmaśāstra* (122–286) has *śrāddha*, the sacrifice to the ancestors, for its theme. The central rites consist of offering rice balls (*piṇḍa*) to specified deceased ancestors and feeding invited Brahmans who represent them.

The fourth book attends to the issue of the means of subsistence of the householders. An interesting classification is presented. Subsistence by gleaning corn and gathering grains is "lawful"; unsolicited gifts are "immortal" and acceptable; farming, although the "deadly" mode of life, is legitimate; trade is "simultaneously good and unlawful" and yet permissible. But servility must be avoided for it is "the dog's way of life" (Manu 4.5–6). Detailed rules of behavior not only in respect of diet but the whole range of natural and legitimate activities are listed.

Altogether, a view of the householder's life is presented in which a great deal is permitted including profit and pleasure, so long as it is lawful, prudent, generally acceptable to good people, and in conformity with tradition (see e.g. 175–80). What is more, the conception of the householder's life presented in the *Manusmṛti* is inclusive and incorporates through subtle devices "the values of other *āśramas* without abandoning home and family" (Olivelle 1993:140).

The conflict between the two views of *gārhasthya* – as a permanent alternative to other ways of life, notably that of the renouncer, or as a temporary stage in the life of a twice-born man – was apparently never completely resolved in the textual tradition of the Dharmaśāstras and subsequently. What is clear, however, is that, even when the idea of *āśramas* as stages of life prevailed, the virtues of the householder's way of life were uniformly eulogized. Thus the *Mahābhārata*, which is a truly oceanic source of the precepts and practice of *dharma*, endorses "the superiority of the householder" and promotes the idea that renunciation of the householder's life is appropriate only in old age (Olivelle 1993: 148–51).

Although Olivelle argues persuasively that the notion of choice in the original *āśrama* did not completely disappear from subsequent formulations, contemporary Indological literature has generally favored the idea of an ordered sequence of stages. This is true of both earlier works and the more recent ones, but Olivelle's seminal work is bound to generate rethinking on the subject. The prevailing consensus regarding *āśramas* as stages of life may be illustrated by referring to two widely read studies of Hinduism by Zaehner (1962: 146–50) and Flood (1996: 61–5, 87–90). In considering the householder's state the very foundation on which the other states rest, contemporary scholarly opinion follows the standard reading of *Mānava Dharmaśāstra*.

The influence of Indology on social-anthropological studies of the family and household in Hindu society has been negligible. Indeed many anthropologists and sociologists writing in the 1950s and 1960s emphasized the desirability of freeing ethnographic inquiry from Indological assumptions about the character of the Hindu family and the household (see e.g. Shah 1973). The one major dissenter was Louis Dumont, who maintained that the sociology of India should lie at the confluence of the findings of Indology and the sociological vantage-point (1957: 7). Following this methodological perspective, he produced a seminal essay on world renunciation in Indian religions in which he suggested that "the secret" (or core principle) of Hinduism (and the structure of Hindu society) may be found in "the dialogue between the renouncer and the man-in-the-world" (Dumont 1960: 37–8).

As Heesterman has pointed out, "In the classical Brahmanic view the pivotal actor on whom the *dharma* turns is the typical man-in-the-world, the substantial 'twice-born' householder, the *gṛhastha*" (Heesterman 1982: 251). He disagrees with Dumont regarding the notion of the dialogue because, according to him, the renouncer and the householder lack a common ground, and stand for genuinely dichotomous, mutually antagonistic – rather than complementary – lifestyle choices. What interests us here is that both recognize the traditionally central position of the householder in Hindu society.

Taking that agreement as the point of departure, we now turn to an examination of the ethnographic evidence accumulated in the recent past.[2]

The Householder in Ethnography

In the clarification of the definitional conventions (in the first section of this chapter), the attention paid to the house may have seemed somewhat excessive. In the classical textual tradition, the building of temples, royal palaces, and cities expectedly received much more attention than ordinary houses (Rowland 1953), but some of the basic principles (concerning, for example, the choice of the site and the size and orientation of the building) were the same. The applicability of these principles to house building varied according to the *varṇa* of the household, more choices being open to the Brahmans and Kṣatriyas than to the others. The abundance or meagerness of the material resources of the household also was a significant factor influencing if not determining the choices that were made. Some of the traditional considerations have survived until today; indeed there is today a resurgence of interest in urban India in vedic architectural principles of house-making.

The folk traditions are not lacking in this respect. Indeed, there are not only explicit guidelines about house-making, which combine ritual and practical considerations, but a vast lore about the character of the houses, and its significance for the well-being of the household also exists.

Thus, among the Brahmans of the Kashmir Valley, widely known as the Pandits (Madan 1989),[3] the house is the abode of gods as well as human beings. It has a guardian deity (*gṛhadevā*) who is identified (through the rituals associated with him) with Vāstupati, the vedic lord of the earth. The bonds between the house, the deity, and the household are intimate. It is noteworthy that, traditionally, a Kashmiri Pandit household never sold or bought a house. On building a new house, the protective deities would be ritually reinstalled there before entering it, and the old house would then be demolished or, rarely, abandoned.

The sentiments of love, sharing, and solidarity that characterize interpersonal relations in a well integrated household are, in the Pandits' estimation, the highest ideals of human conduct, the acme of morality. The house is loved and valued because of the sanctity and the sentiments associated with it and not merely because of its material value. It is regarded as a moral space *par excellence*. The home is said to be neither the place for the indulgence of one's physical appetites (*bhogaśālā*), nor for the performance of austerities (*yogaśālā*, Madan 1989: 256–7). In other words, it is the narrow middle ground, the "razor's edge" of the Upanisads.

An even richer conception of the house in relation to the householders than among the Pandits is found in Tamil Nadu. Here houses are material structures like they are everywhere, but they also partake of the properties of personhood. Valentine Daniel writes:

> Not only are houses, as are [village] and persons, [made of] substance that can be contaminated and changed by mixing with other substances (hence the concern with what kind of substance crosses the vulnerable thresholds – windows and doors – of the house and affects its own substance and that of its inhabitants) but houses are also "aware" of their vulnerability. They have personlike needs for companionship, and experience loneliness and fear when isolated. (Daniel 1984: 114)

Houses here are believed to have a life cycle: they are conceived and born, they grow, and may eventually die. Houses like human offspring have astrological significance and may bring good or bad fortune to the household. They have feelings and attitudes. It is not therefore without trepidation that the decision to build a house is taken. To minimize the risks and uncertainty strict rules are followed in the selection of the site. It must be judged to be auspicious, and appropriate rituals (e.g. Vāstu Puruṣa *pūjā*, although everybody is not sure who Vāstu is) may be performed.

Conception is said to occur when a corner post or cornerstone is installed by a member of the artisan caste who is traditionally entrusted this work. While at work, he must observe rules pertaining to himself. For example: he must eat only vegetarian food or else ghosts and evil spirits will take possession of the house under construction; he must avoid bodily contact with members of lower *jātis* or goods in the house will disappear; he must abstain from sexual intercourse or else the house will be eaten by white ants. Another set of rules concerns the construction. Scarecrows must be planted in the four cardinal directions to ward off the evil eye. When the roof is laid, only an odd number of beams must be used, as a result of which it is deemed to be incomplete. Incompleteness is a blemish and helps in warding off the evil eye. Moreover, incomplete houses may be expected to grow further.

When a house is ready for occupation, it is said to have been born. A horoscope is cast for it to figure out what the future holds for it. In addition to the nine planets of horoscopes for human beings, the influence of the qualities of the first occupants also are crucial for a house. Houses acquire the same *jāti* status as the householders and must observe the same rules of intercaste conduct as is applicable to them. In short, there is a structural homology between the human body and the house which is culturally constructed.

That the house–householder relationship is an intrinsic one is well illustrated by the distinction that Bengali Hindus make between the *bāsā* ("nest," abode) of a man, his wife and children, and the *bāṛī* (also called *gṛha*, house) in which his parents (and other family members) live. Until his father's death he and his immediate family are deemed to be part of the larger family and he may not claim to have his own separate *bāṛī*. Needless to add, not all sons may live away from the parental home (Inden and Nicholas 1977: 7).

The Bengalis think of a house as shared space, and this makes room for unrelated dependents (for example, servants) to live in it along with those who constitute the family and who share bodily substance. The Kashmiri Pandits make a similar distinction between one's *gara* (house, home) and *ḍera* (place of temporary residence), but the latter may be *gara* to someone else. Moreover, a son may establish his own household even during the life time of his mother, but this normally does not happen while the father is alive.

The issue here is the manner in which a household is constituted. Among the Pandits the family (*kutumb*) usually comprises a number of households, each living in a house or a part of a house, and known as *chulahs* (hearth, hearth group). They make a clear distinction between those members who are born into the family/hearth group (*zamat*), and those who are married into it (*āmati*, "incomers"). Consanguinity and affinity are mutually exclusive principles. Besides birth and marriage, fictive kinship in the form of adoption also is a recognized mode of recruitment to the family. At the household level unrelated persons may also be present, in some cases on a permanent or quasi-permanent basis (Madan 1989: chs. 5 and 6). Moreover, families are not thought and spoken of in terms of a beginning and an end, but the household is subject to a developmental cycle. Births and marriages are the incremental events; deaths and partitions result in the loss of members. A household may even die as when the surviving spouse of a childless couple, or a couple that have only daughters who have moved out on marriage (Madan: ch. 4).

Although parental love, filial piety, and fraternal solidarity are said to be the foundation of the householder's life, abandonment of joint living as one *chulah*, and complete or partial partition of the jointly owned estate, are commonly expected to occur among the Pandits (see ibid.: ch. 8). In terms of the ideology of the householder, fraternal strife is considered morally reprehensive, but practical considerations are allowed to override morality. Moreover, the blame for intrahousehold bickering is cleverly placed on the shoulders of the wives who are, of course, the *āmati* and not the *zāmati*. And the decline of morality in the dark age of *kaliyug* is always cited as a cause of things that should not happen.

In this context it is noteworthy that the domestic scene two thousand years ago was essentially the same as it is today in most Hindu homes. Thus, we read in the *Mānava Dharmaśāstra*): "After the father and mother (are dead), the brothers [may] assemble and divide the paternal estate equally, for they have no power over two of them while they are alive" (Manu 9.104 and 111). More significantly, apropos the contention of the decline of morality: "They [the brothers] may live together in [mutual respectfulness], or they may live separately if they wish for religious merit; for religious merit increases in separation, and so separate rituals are conducive to religious merit" (Doniger and Smith 1991: 209, 210). It is, of course, questionable how much considerations of religious merit count in contemporary times, but division of jointly owned estates does often occur with a view to reducing the income tax burden.[4]

The question of religious merit apart, performance of rituals is indeed a major concern of Brahman and other upper caste households even if only as a matter of convention. There are two main types of domestic rituals. Firstly, those associated with life-cycle events (notably birth, initiation, marriage and death), known as *saṃskāra*, and those that affirm the bonds between ancestors and descendents, called the *śrāddha*. Secondly, there are the rituals that seek to establish purposive and meaningful communication between householders and supernatural "beings." These may be supplicatory in character as is the daily worship to one's chosen deities, or contractual, or even coercive. The rituals performed by lower caste Hindu households may not be an exact replica of upper caste rituals, and may not involve the specialist services of a Brahman priest, but they too fall into the two categories mentioned above. Work-related rituals also take place in artisan and peasant households.

Sustained by economic activity, reinforced by religious observances, the life of the Hindu householder is nourished and legitimized by the values of love, sharing, and solidarity. It has been explicated that, while "authority, rights and duties, land, inheritance, the distribution of resources within the joint family, prestations, reproduction, and so forth" are critical factors in the construction of interpersonal relations in Bengali households, often providing the basis for conflict, love (*prīti, prema*) holds them together. "If kinsmen have the proper kind of love for one another then they will enjoy well-being and they will not be divided by greed, selfishness, or envy" (Inden and Nicholas 1977: 87–8).

A variety of loves is said to be discernible, namely conjugal, filial, fraternal, parental, and the love between brothers and sisters. Love may be egalitarian or hierarchical. In all cases, it is expressed through spontaneous and selfless feelings of caring (*pālana*), nourishing (*poṣaṇa*), and supporting (*bharaṇa*) for one another. Delight (*ananda*), gratification (*tṛpti*), and contentment (*santoṣa*) are the fruit of such feelings (Inden and Nicholas 1977: 21).

An elaborate ideology of love in Tamil Nadu comprises the ideas of *anpu* (love), *pācam* (attachment), *ācai* (desire), *kāppu* (bonding), *paṭṭu* (devotion), etc. These are articulable, and sometimes articulated, in explication of how the members of a household relate to one another (Trawick 1996: ch. 3). Anpu is a complex notion that connotes a multitude of emotions and moral judgments. Thus, love must be contained (*aḍakkam*, containment), for excess is harmful; moreover "love grows in hiding." Even a mother's love for the child must be "kept within limits," for "letting love overflow its bounds could be harmful not only to the recipient, but to the giver as well" (Trawick 1996: 94). While the legitimacy and power of sexual love and pleasure *inpam*, "sweetness") may not be denied, the love of spouses is also best contained to the point of concealment. Such concealment takes diverse forms including, particularly among the lower castes, the derogation of the husband by the wife.

Love is a force, but its essence is tenderness. It grows slowly by habituation; indeed it becomes a habit (*paṛakkam*) that even death does not destroy. The loved person becomes a part of oneself. *Paṛakkam* implies friendliness, easiness, and grace (Trawick 1996: 100). But it has its emotional costs. Love and attachment have a cruel aspect, for they produce restlessness. Moreover, being parted from the loved person is painful; it is like having a part of oneself severed. Love makes one do strange and even improper things, such as defiance of the rules of purity: picking up the leaf from which someone has eaten, and which is therefore impure, is an act of love and meritorious. It conveys a message of union and equality. Love teaches humility (*pani*). "In acts of love, the humble became proud, the servant became master, the renouncer became possessed" (Trawick 1996: 106). Love normally produces servitude (*adima*), a sense of being controlled by another person, but then this feeling itself is "a powerful expression of love" (111). Ultimately, love means that the members of the household "are all one" within the "four walls of the house." As a Tamil householder (a woman) has put it, "In order for you to understand my heart, you must see through my eyes. In order me to understand your heart, I must see through yours" (115, 116).

There is a gentle and authentic simplicity about the manner in which the Tamil villager articulates the place of love in the ideology of the householder. There are other values too that are generally affirmed elsewhere by other Hindu communities, but raised above them all is the ideal of domesticity itself. The Kashmiri Pandits are the self-aware ideologues of *gārhasthya* within the value framework of Hinduism, expressed, for example, in the notion of *puruṣārtha* comprising the goals and orientations of *dharma*, *artha*, and *kāma*. The Pandit ideology of the householder is lukewarm about the fourth *puruṣārtha* of *mokṣa*, and explicitly negative about renunciation as a way of life or as the last stage of life. As a householder, a Pandit may legitimately seek joy and plenitude, but ideally this endeavor should be subordinated to *dharma* and combined with detachment (*virakti*) and the love of one's chosen personal deity (*iṣtadeva, iṣtadevī*). As a well-known Pandit poet, Krishna Razdan (1850–1925), who was a devout Vaiṣṇva, put it: "Why should we renounce the lovely world?/ Our love of Him is our austerity . . ." (Cook 1958).

The Pandit's ideology of the householder is, in fact, more than just that: it is their ideology of humanity. While all sentient beings are born (and die), human beings are made and matured through the *saṃskāras* and achieve different degrees of moral perfection by their conduct. A boy attains the ritual status of an adult when he receives the girdle (*mekhalā*) and the holy neck threads (*yajñopavīta*). In the case of girls, it is marriage that bestows similar status on them. Marriage is crucial for men as well as women for it is only through it that they become householders. Bachelors, childless widowers, and widows are normally members of households but not themselves *gṛhastha*, and are therefore considered unfortunate. The greatest desire of a Pandit, whether man or woman, is to be a full-fledged householder.

The Pandit ideology of the householder is constructed around men. Women and children are spoken of in relation to them. But the men themselves recognize that in the reality of everyday life women are significant role players. They are referred to as *gṛhasthadhārinī*, the upholders and the bearers of the burden of *gārhasthya*. A man works out his destiny as a Pandit and a human being in the company of women: without them his ritual, personal and social life is incomplete. Among the most coveted meritorious acts that a Pandit may perform, the giving away of his daughter in marriage (*kanyādāna*) ranks very high. Men are hierarchically superior to women, but it is together with them that they constitute the core of the life of the householder.

Being a Pandit is as much a concern of women as it is of men. In the domain of domestic activity, however, women's roles are different, and their work in the kitchen as well as their participation in religious rites is severely but discretely restricted during the periods of menstruation. Moreover. women do not offer water and food to ancestors; they do not have the ritual status and authority to initiate their sons into adulthood or give their daughters in marriage. And yet the wife is always present by the husband's side on all major ceremonial occasions. She is one-half of his self (*ardhāṇginī*).

The ideology of the householder clearly establishes the Pandit as the man-in-the-world. Such a person's prime concern in the midst of worldly activities is with the maturation of his self. This is ensured if he organizes his domestic life in strict conformity with traditional purposes (*puruṣārtha*), employing appropriate procedures for their achievement. Release from the chain of transmigration (*saṃskāra*) is a high but frankly distant goal – so distant indeed as to be virtually beyond reach. A prudent person concentrates on the slow but steady accumulation of merit by the conscious effort to lead a disciplined life.

Renouncers are conspicuous by their absence in Pandit society. Self-styled renouncers are distrusted as men who, with a failed domestic life behind them, make a virtue of necessity. At a deeper level, however, one might detect a fear of the renouncer, for he poses a threat to the ideology of the *gārhasthya*. The *saṃnyāsī* is too powerful an adversary to be contemplated with equanimity. Individual renouncers, if judged to be genuine, will be accorded respect. But renouncers as a category are caricatured: that the caricature is only too often an accurate enough portrait of the "holy men" one actually meets is another matter through not totally irrelevant. The real point seems to be that only when the renouncer is thus portrayed may he be convincingly employed as a foil to highlight the virtues of the life of the householder. These are said to flow from "detachment in enjoyment," which is the essence of renunciation. *Gārhasthya* is not to end in renunciation, but it should be guided by the values of *saṃnyāsa*. For the rest, everything is dependent upon divine grace (*anugraha*).[5]

The foregoing summary of the Pandit ideology of the householder is based on my fieldwork in the village of Utrassu-Urnanagri (southeast Kashmir) carried out mainly in 1957–8. It is noteworthy that, despite over 500 years of life lived as a small minority (about 4 percent of the population in the 1950s) amongst Muslims – who are mainly descendants of Hindus converted to Islam *en masse* in the fourteenth century – and under Muslim rule between the early fourteenth and mid-nineteenth centuries, the Pandits have managed to preserve many core ideas and values of the Brahmanical tradition via oral transmission. In an essay based on Sanskrit texts of the medieval period (ninth to thirteenth centuries) unknown to the rural Pandits among whom I engaged in fieldwork, Alexis Sanderson observes:

> The Brahmanism of the middle ground . . . offered the Brahman householder a monism for the ritual agent which admitted renunciation but tended to confine it to the last quarter of a man's life (after the payment of the three debts), and at the same time made it an unnecessary by propagating a doctrine of gnostic liberation within the pursuit of conformity to the householder's dharma. . . . [Moreover, the householder] was to protect himself through disinterested conformity to God's will manifest as his dharma. (Sanderson 1985: 197–8)

Needless to emphasize, it is the continuities between the ideas of the two periods (pre-Muslim and Muslim) that are remarkable rather than the differences, which are essentially those of emphasis. It follows that in the study of the householder tradition in Hindu society, the bringing together of the perspectives of Indology and sociology is not only justifiable but indeed imperative.

Concluding Observations

The two most characteristic institutions of Hindu society are caste and the family/household. Kane in his monumental survey of the Dharmaśāstras concludes that the overall tendency "is to glorify the status of an householder and push into the background the two *āśramas* of *vānaprashtha* and *saṃnyāsa*, so much so that certain works say that these are forbidden in the Kali age" (Kane 1941: 424). Ethnographic evidence also underscores the importance of the life of the householder in contemporary Hindu society.

Looking back over time, it is noteworthy that various developments in the history of Hinduism have reinforced the householder tradition. Thus, many of the major protestant sectarian movements of medieval times, which today have millions of followers, emphasized the virtues of disciplined domesticity as against renunciation. Basava (ca. 1106–67), the founder of the Vīraśaiva (or Lingayat) sect in Karnataka (in the south), himself moved to and fro between withdrawal from and participation in worldly activities, but his followers have remained wedded to the householder's life. In Punjab (in the north) all but one of the ten Sikh Gurus were married men with families, and explicitly opposed the renunciation of the householder's life. (The eighth guru died during his boyhood.) Similarly, Vallabha (ca. 1479–1531), promulgator of *puṣṭi marga* ("the way of abundance"), whose followers are found mainly in western India, was a householder, and so are his followers. Although Caitanya (ca. 1485–1533), founder of the Gaudiya movement in the east, devoted to Rādhā-Kṛṣṇa worship, did himself abandon family life in his exultation of divine, conjugal love, his followers include householders as well as ascetics, All these sects extoll domesticity as the preferred state so long as it is an affirmation of the bliss of the union of the devotee and the deity.

In popular imagination, however, particularly outside India, the renouncer looms large. This may be so because he is a magnificent, even theatrical figure, who gives away all his possessions, performs his own mortuary rites to proclaim the severance of all social bonds, and lives a highly disciplined life of austerities (see Madan 1987: 1–16 *et passim*). Although he may be impressive, the renouncer is not the only actor on the Hindu stage of life; in fact, he is not on the stage at all, but looks at it from the outside. That his gaze is powerful may not be, however, denied. The figure in the center of the stage is the homely householder. If not exactly cast in a heroic mould, he is not a shadowy figure either. And, in his own manner, he is a fighter.

The everyday life of the householder is marked by temptations that he must resist. On the one hand, he hears on his front door the knock of the *saṃnyāsī*, who stands there in the guise of the mendicant asking for alms, but also suggests the possibility of an alternative way of life. On the other hand, the *bhogī* ("enjoyer") knocks on his back door, as it were, inviting him to a life of pleasures. The values of *gārhasthya* are challenged and threatened by both the visitors. The householder's success lies in his ability to resist the extremist alternatives and to tread the middle ground, combining the values of domesticity and detachment. For the Hindu, of whatever caste or sect, domesticity is marked by the feelings of well-being and happiness."[6] It embodies the values of righteousness and action, purity and auspiciousness, and purposefulness and contentment. It is the good life.[7]

Notes

1 In the original: *yasmāt trayo 'pvāśramiṇo jnānenānnena mānhavam/gṛhasthenaiva dhāryante tasmājjyeṣṭhāśramo gṛhi.*

2 We may briefly note here the reading of the tradition by the scholars of what is known as "Hindu law" (a product of British colonial administration). Thus, it is stated that, "the joint and undivided family is the normal condition of Hindu society. An undivided Hindu family is ordinarily joint not only in estate, but also in food and worship" (Desai 1998: 314). From the sociological point of view this statement suffers from the conflation of two analytically and often empirically distinct groups, namely the family and the household. The law qualifies the foregoing characterization by maintaining that, "the existence of joint estate is not an essential requisite to constitute a joint family and a family, which does not own any property, may nevertheless be joint" (Desai 1998: 314). It is obvious that it is a larger grouping than the household to which the law refers; it is equally clear that without constituent households, there would be no joint families. The foundational nature of the household in relation to Hindu society is thus implicitly recognized in Hindu law.

3 Virtually all but 5,000 to 10,000 persons of this community of about 300,000 persons have been driven out of Kashmir following the eruption of a Muslim militant, secessionist movement in 1989. The refugees live in temporary camps in Jammu and Delhi, or have taken up residence in various towns and cities of India, mainly in the north. The hope that they will be able to return to their homes are not bright. In describing aspects of their domestic life, the present tense has been retained here.

4 The Hindu undivided family has tax-saving privileges that may be availed by individual members. These are not available to non-Hindu households (see Gulati and Gulati 1962).

5 A negative attitude towards renouncers is widespread, and may go so far as to ascribe a malignant influence to them, responsible for misfortune among householders, as do the residents of the village Ghatiyali in Rajasthan. For them the *saṃnyāsī* is the threatening outsider (see Gold 1988: 53). But there are exceptions. In Rajasthan itself, the pastoral Raikas consider renouncers auspicious, even like gods, and their blessings are valued by householders. The householder–renouncer relationship is not antagonistic here but "intertwined" (Srivastava 1997: 266).

6 For vignettes of domestic life among four castes of north India (Brahman, farmer, carpenter, and oil-presser), which show interesting similarities and differences, see Wiser 1978.

7 That would be a neat way to conclude this chapter, but we must note (at least in a note) that the values by which many secularized, Hindu, urban households live today come from sources other than traditional culture. The process of change had already become manifest in the late nineteenth century in cities such as Calcutta and Bombay. Individualism was on the rise and large households were being viewed negatively by social reformers. The process of social transformation has deepened and become more widespread, particularly since independence. More and more people of means in urban India today live in rented apartments, have small "households," affirm the values of individual choice and achievement, and gender equality, and generally participate in a global culture of western origin. But, as the ethnographic content of this chapter shows, the old household tradition is by no means dead, particularly in the rural areas, where three-quarters of the people of India live.

References

Bühler, G. 1964. *The Laws of Manu*. Delhi: Motilal Banarasidass.

Cook, Nilla Cram. 1958. *The Way of the Swan: Poems of Kashmir*. Bombay: Asia.

Daniel, Valentine. 1984. *Fluid Signs: Being a Person the Tamil Way*. Berkeley: University of California Press.

Desai, S. T. 1998. *Mulla: Principles of Hindu Law*, 2 vols. New Delhi: Butterworths.

Doniger, Wendy and Brian K. Smith. 1991. *The Laws of Manu*. New Delhi: Penguin Books.

Dumont, Louis. 1957. "For a Sociology of India," in *Contributions to Indian Sociology* I: 7–22. Repr. in Dumont 1970: 2–18.

——. 1960. "World Renunciation in Indian Religions," in *Contributions to Indian Sociology* IV: 33–62. Repr. in Dumont 1970: 33–60.

——. 1970. *Religion, Politics and History in India*. Paris: Mouton.

Flood, Gavin. 1996. *An Introduction to Hinduism*. Cambridge: Cambridge University Press.

Gold, Ann Grodzins. 1988. *Fruitful Journeys: The Ways of Rajasthani Pilgrims*. Berkeley: University of California Press.

Gulati, I. S. and J. S. Gulati. 1962. *Undivided Hindu Family and its Tax Privileges*. Bombay: Asia.

Heesterman, J. C. 1982. "Householder and Wanderer," in T. N. Madan, ed., *Way of Life: King, Householder, Renouncer*. New Delhi: Vikas.

——. 1985. *The Inner Conflict of Tradition*. Chicago: University of Chicago Press.

Hiltebeitel, Alf. 1999. *Rethinking India's Oral and Classical Epics: Draupadi among Rajputs, Muslims and Dalits*. Chicago: University of Chicago Press.

Ilaiah, Kancha. 1996. *Why I am not a Hindu: A Śūdra Critique of Hindutva Philosophy, Culture and Political Economy*. Calcutta: Samya.

Inden, Ronald B. and Ralph W. Nicholas. 1977. *Kinship in Bengali Culture*. Chicago: University of Chicago Press.

Kane, Pandurang Vaman. 1941. *History of Dharmaśāstra*. Vol. II, pt. I. Poona: Bhandarkar Oriental Research Institute.

Madan, T. N. 1962. "The Joint Family: A Terminological Clarification," *International Journal of Comparative Sociology* 3: 1–16.

——. 1987. *Non-renunciation: Themes and Interpretations of Hindu Culture*. Delhi: Oxford University Press.

——. 1989. *Family and Kinship: A Study of the Pandits of Rural Kashmir*, 2nd ed. Delhi: Oxford University Press.

Marriott, McKim. 1955. "Little Communities in an Indigenous Civilization," in M. Marriott, ed., *Village India*. Chicago: University of Chicago Press.

Olivelle, Patrick. 1993. *The* āśrama *System: The History and Hermeneutics of a Religious Institution*. New York: Oxford University Press.

Rowland, Benjamin. 1953. *The Art and Architecture of India: Buddhist, Hindu, Jain*. London: Penguin Books.

Sanderson, Alexis. 1985. "Purity and Power among the Brahmans of Kashmir," in Michael Carrithers et al., eds., *The Category of the Person*. Cambridge: Cambridge University Press.

Shah, A. M. 1973. *The Household Dimension of the Family in India*. New Delhi: Orient Longman.

Smith, Brian K. 1989. *Reflections on Resemblance, Ritual and Religion*. New York: Oxford University Press.

Srivastava, Vinay Kumar. 1977. *Religious Renunciation of a Pastoral People*. Delhi: Oxford University Press.
Thapar, Romila. 1989. "Imagined Religious Communities? Ancient History and the Modern Search for Identity," *Modern Asian Studies* 23 (2): 209–31.
Trawick, Margaret. 1996. *Notes on Love in a Tamil Family*. Delhi: Oxford University Press.
Wiser, Charlotte V. 1978. *Four Families of Karimpur*. Syracuse: Syracuse University.
Zaehner, R. C. 1962. *Hinduism*. Oxford: Oxford University Press.

Regional Traditions

CHAPTER 14

The Teyyam Tradition of Kerala

Rich Freeman

The tradition of worshipping *teyyams*, the local deities of northern Kerala, through costumed spirit possession and dance, is surely one of the most performatively engaging and sociohistorically profound of those Hinduisms we call "folk" found anywhere in India. Performatively, these hundreds of gods each have their unique costuming, make-up, and insignia, and they are danced as part of annual festivals in public rituals of worship by spirit-possessed professionals who incarnate them in thousands of family, caste, and community shrines across this region. Historically, *teyyams* literally enshrine the legacy of the way local deities, often themselves the apotheoses of human ancestors, have alternately contested or come to terms with caste-Hinduism, as their lives are liturgically recounted and ritually enacted from a largely subaltern religious perspective.

The *teyyam* tradition illumines a number of interesting issues for the student of Hinduism, whether from the perspective of the history of religions or from that of the social sciences. Regionally speaking, *teyyam* worship is demonstrably part of those ancient and cognate patterns of institutionalized spirit possession that were shared as a religious paradigm across the cultural zone of south India that we identify in kinship and linguistic terms as "Dravidian" (Trautmann 1981). In its ritual and institutional stability, *teyyam* exemplifies how south Indian cults of possession and ancestor worship may have articulated with, and synthetically given rise to, the local cultural form of temples and enshrined images associated with high Hinduism. It further suggests how those beliefs and practices labeled "tantric," which are generally recognized to underlie the Āgamic ideology of temple-installation and worship, served historically and in the present to mediate between high Hindu practice and possession-worship (Freeman 1998).

From the vantage point of social science, *teyyam* affords an equally fascinating perspective on the caste-dynamics of this process, both ethnohistorically, through *teyyam* narratives and recitations, and ritually, through the organization of worship, the various constituents and modes of the rites themselves, and the spatial and social arrays they configure and map. Finally, all of this is centrally brought to bear on the transformations of personhood that form the phenomenological core of spirit possession, with all the implications of mimesis and deification enacted by lower-caste practitioners in a rigorously hierarchical system. The chapter that follows will attempt a broad and descriptive overview of *teyyam* worship, in a way that such aspects of widest scholarly interest are contextualized and brought to the fore.[1]

Possession Worship in its Sociohistorical Context

In the Malayalam language of Kerala, *teyyam* most literally refers simply to the "god" or "deity" (cognate with the Sanskrit *deva* or *daiva*) whose elaborately costumed form is donned for the rites of its possessed worship. These rites themselves, and the festivals built around them, are called *teyyāṭṭam*, or "god-dance." The ambiguity of this compound itself, however, points to the central ideology of possession, for the usual interpretation is not that the performers are dancing the gods, but rather that the gods themselves are dancing, through the bodies of the mediums that they have possessed for the occasion. This is borne out most dramatically at the close of the dance-sequence, where the *teyyam* (the costumed performer, we would say), walks among the gathered devotees, interacting with them, hearing various complaints, receiving offerings, and granting blessings in the direct voice and behavior and person of the god.

This kind of institutionalized possession as a central paradigm of worship is anciently attested in south India from the Tamil Caṅkam literature of the first few centuries CE, the earliest literature of any surviving Indian vernacular language (Zvelebil 1974). Ancient Kerala was culturally and linguistically a part of this early Tamil country, and it is clear from the structural and ritual features of worship described in the Caṅkam corpus, that there are clear continuities with *teyyāṭṭam* and similar Dravidian modes of worship. The ancient Tamils worshipped apotheosized ancestors and fallen martial heroes whose spirits they installed into stone monuments (*naṭukal*). These spirits were then periodically invoked into costumed dancer-mediums who spoke as oracular embodiments of the deity, and received the same offerings of liquor and blood before similarly described altars that one finds in *teyyam* worship today (Kurup 1982). The principal title of the ancient oracle, Vēlan, even survives as the caste-name of one those communities who perform *teyyams* today in Kerala, as does the caste of Pāṇar exorcist-musicians, whose title was anciently used of Caṅkam bards (Hart 1975).

As stated earlier, similar cults of possession abound in south India, where they are almost always confined to those castes that were traditionally of *Śūdra* or lower status in the Brahmanical, Sanskritic reckoning. Throughout south India, however, the *Śūdra* category has always included many of those dominant, martial, and landed castes that would elsewhere in India have been reckoned in the royal or *Kṣatriya varṇa*. This seems consonant with the fact that possession worship received royal patronage in Caṅkam times (Hart 1975), and that many socioeconomically and politically dominant castes in south India have continued to patronize such practices into recent times, often in worship of their own family, clan, and caste deities (*kula-dēvatā*). This, I believe, is historically linked with a qualitatively different ethnographic patterning one finds in possession cults across south India as compared with the north. There are often greater institutional investment, social organizational stability, and caste-based hereditary lines of possession-priesthoods across south India, whereas such cults tend to be more idiosyncratically personalistic, popularly contingent, and institutionally marginal across much of north India. At any rate we find that while many (especially urban) sections of the dominant and upper castes have Brahmanized in terms of embracing temple culture and Sanskritic norms of worship, many landed, village-based dominants have also continued their ancestral investment in local temple and shrine establishments that give prominence to possessed worship. This is all the more the case for the bulk of those lower castes who were traditionally excluded from temple entry, with the combined result that possession often retains a level of ritual formalization and socially structured entitlement one would associate with higher-caste priestly office in the north. *Teyyam* worship exemplifies these points with great clarity, and further suggests how tantric doctrine and practice mediated between the Brahmanical and more localized religious complexes in the south.

We have little by way of hard historical documentation for *teyyam* from the premodern, but the internal references, traditions, and subject-matter of the *teyyam* liturgies as oral literature, conjoined with the areal spread of its ritual forms, particular gods, shrine networks, and social entitlements, would all indicate that it existed in substantially its contemporary form from at least the period of the late medieval kingdoms of northern Kerala, from perhaps the fifteenth century. The deities and their shrines distribute with clear ritual and social cleavages in conformity with boundaries of the old kingdoms of Kōlattunāṭu, Nīlēśvaram, and Kumbaḷam (covering today's Kannur and Kasargode Districts). Major events recounted in the liturgies go back to probably the thirteenth century, and the distribution of cognate dance and possession forms, both further south, throughout Kerala, and further north, in the *bhūta* worship of the Tuḷu country in Karnataka (Claus 1978, Nambiar 1996), suggest the much older distribution of possession worship, as clearly fundamental to the religious organization of medieval society.

The dominant kingly line in the *teyyam* region of Kerala, that of the Kōlattiri Rāja, still celebrates its own lineage goddess in the form of a *teyyam*, in concert with an amalgam of other local *teyyam* deities at its royal, family temple in a popular regional festival. This is despite the fact that, of course, the Kōlattiris also worshipped at and extended their patronage to a variety of exclusively higher-caste, Brahmanical temples and establishments throughout their domain. Moreover, all of their subordinate chiefs similarly had their own *teyyāṭṭam* shrines, with similar amalgams of family and local *teyyam* gods, and the festivals of these regional and sub-regional pantheons were calendrically coordinated in conformity with political precedence and boundaries of religious-political jurisdiction throughout northern Kerala. Further south of old Kōlattunāṭu, in the territory of the more powerful Sāmūtiri or "Zamorin" of Calicut, that king presided over a similar network of deities called *tiṟas*, which most people do not distinguish from *teyyams*, and whose forms have regularly migrated into the *teyyam* region, where they have intermingled with the *teyyāṭṭam* pantheons.

Despite royal patronage of a number of local gods represented in *teyyam* form, some of whom are apotheosized chiefly warriors, one of the centrally organizing social facts of *teyyāṭṭam* is that all of the actual performers are from castes traditionally considered polluting, the *avarṇar*, or Kerala's former "Untouchables." This means that much in the *teyyam* deities' liturgies, costuming, and ritual forms was authored by and is in the custody of communities that Indian researchers today might label subaltern or Dalit, in other contexts. Indeed, since the substantial numbers of *avarṇa* castes in Kerala (perhaps a numeric majority in some locales) were all excluded from entry into Brahmanically regulated temples, *teyyam* shrines and temples were *the* principal institutional form of religion for all these peoples. *Teyyams* were their only manifest gods, and *teyyāṭṭam* was their form of "Hindu" worship.

Since the caste constituency of *teyyam* worshippers covers a far wider spectrum of society than that of the actual performers, however, it means that the social provenance of *teyyam* deities is similarly wide. While we have thus seen that some deities are of higher caste origins, representing socially powerful warriors or their tutelaries, others find their origins among the lower castes, being the apotheoses of local *avarṇa* culture-heroes and heroines, as well as their versions of more *sui generis* supernatural spirits and powers. The result of this is that the associations of *teyyam* gods to caste, both as to their particular origins and worshipping communities, weave complexly across the whole of Kerala Hindu society, drawing sharp social distinctions in some cases, while articulating a larger ritual order across the lines of pollution-status in others.

The legend of how the current form and distribution of *teyyāṭṭam* was established in the Kōlattiri's domains illustrates something of the caste and status mediations and the challenges these posed in Kerala's late medieval social order. The creation and establishment of the 39 chiefly *teyyams* of this realm is attributed to one Maṇakkāṭan Gurukkaḷ, a powerful sorcerer-magician of the then Untouchable Washerman caste, the Vaṇṇāns. His fame was such that his chief disciple and attendant, against the norms of caste-pollution, was even a member of the chiefly Nāyar caste.

Eventually the notoriety of the Gurukkaḷ's supernatural accomplishments brought him to the attention of the Kōlattiri Rāja, who summoned him to his palace. While *en route* and at court, Maṇakkāṭan was subjected to a number of natural and supernatural tests by the king and his agents, in all of which he handily triumphed. His final trial was to single-handedly perform the *teyyāṭṭams* of 39 different gods in the span of a single night. He not only succeeded in this, but the king was so impressed that he commanded these *teyyams* to be established throughout his territories. These 39 comprise some of the most prominent *teyyams* connected with notable lineages and their territorial centers, including that of the king's family, though they also include more rustic and, from a Brahmanical perspective, even quasi-demonic beings. Given the social affinities, depth, and spread of *teyyāṭṭam*, there is little likelihood that this legend relates to its actual origins; rather, it seems clear that this represents a movement of consolidation, in which a core of the *teyyam* tutelaries of prominent lineages (many of which were upwardly mobile from humbler origins) were organized into the ritual network of this king's polity, with the royal cult at the center.

The caste tensions inherent in such incorporations, however, are evident in the conclusion to the legend. Having shamed the king and his nobles through the course of his meteoric rise, Maṇakkāṭan determined to pre-empt the ignominy of their almost certain attempts at vengeance. Like the Caṅkam heroes of old, he therefore sat facing the north, in a rite of deliberately relinquishing his mortal life (cf. Hart 1975). Though Maṇakkāṭan Gurukkaḷ is not himself celebrated as a *teyyam* (his empowering family goddess, however, is), his final resting place is surmounted by a monument of laterite stone, dedicated by the king, in which his living presence still resides. There he is regularly worshipped through vows and periodically offered liquor and massive blood sacrifices in collective calendrical rites. While the formal aspects of *teyyam* worship are different, we can see in the social dynamics of Maṇakkāṭan's life-story, demise, and subsequent worship a theme of subaltern defiance and elevation common to many *teyyam* liturgies.

The Social Organization of Worship

Teyyāṭṭam festivals are commonly celebrated on a yearly basis in the grounds of shrines and temples where a particular group of one or more deities are housed. Festivals may be held less often at some shrines, though as with the annual celebrations, the dates are astrologically fixed by tradition. Shrines were, and usually still are, owned or managed along specific family, lineage or clan, and therefore caste lines, though generally during the festivals, all who wish may come to worship in a regulated fashion, according to traditional precedence. The castes sponsoring such shrines run all the way from the highest Brahmans, to the lowest of the traditional *avarṇa* castes, though not surprisingly, there are differences in means, structural and ritual elaboration, and behavioral norms associated with these levels of worship.

A specific cluster of named and individuated *teyyam* deities are hereditarily installed in any given shrine, and designated lineages within specific castes of performers have exclusive, hereditary rites to perform each particular *teyyam* deity in any given locale. *Teyyam* shrines are often still the prominent, and sometimes the only, community religious institution among the lower castes. For the middle and upper castes, however, *teyyam* shrines may be attached as adjuncts to a larger temple structure for Brahmanically worshipped deities, sometimes structurally set apart, sometimes accommodated within the walls of the former.

In addition to the lower-caste *teyyam* performers who come to incarnate a deity during a *teyyāṭṭam*, most of the lower and middle castes have additionally members of their own particular caste who serve as priests to *teyyam* images in the shrine, ministering to them several times a month, or even daily. A class of these, called *Veḷiccappāṭus* or *Kōmarams*, are themselves possession mediums for their *teyyam* deities, dedicated each to his particular deity, usually for life. They undergo ritually induced possession when worshippers come to the shrine at set times once or twice a month to consult the *teyyam* deities, though a few undergo more spontaneous episodes of possession outside of the ritual context. They also frequently perform their oracular rites in conjunction with the regular *teyyam* forms during the annual festival. In contrast to the elaborate costuming and make-up of *teyyāṭṭam* dancers during the annual festivals, these priests always have only a light and standardized costume of a few ornaments, weapons, and other ritual insignia. Depending on their caste traditions, they may have special red waist-cloths for these occasions of possession. Others wear only the regular bleached cloth (*muṇḍu*) of daily wear, but in most cases there are preparatory baths and purification rites before the onset of possession.

A typical lower or middle-caste shrine complex generally consists of a laterite walled compound, with one or more free-standing wooden shrine-rooms, slatted, brightly painted, fronted with wooden carvings of supernaturals, and roofed in tile. Each shrine room is generally dedicated to one, though sometimes more, *teyyam* deities, whose spiritual power may be installed in a full image of metal, a flat icon, a metal mirror, or simply a sword standing on a masonry platform or a wooden stool. Except for the nightly lighting of lamps outside the shrines, most *teyyam* images are activated in worship only during the *teyyāṭṭam* festivals or bi-monthly priestly rites, and so at other times these shrine-rooms are closed and locked. Subsidiary *teyyams* often have their own loci in simple stone or laterite altars, placed at other points in the compound, before which performers dedicated to those deities incarnate their gods.

Some of the traditionally lowest castes, and those presently or formerly of "tribal" designation, may have only a small altar in a forest clearing, or only a clearing itself, into which a ritual stool (*pīṭham*) will be brought and set up for a *teyyam* performance. Occasionally these clearings are adjuncts to fuller *teyyam* shrines of higher castes, the lower *teyyams* being done in conjunction with larger and higher caste *teyyams* nearby, with rites of interaction between the deities. In other cases, such clearings are for communities with their own relatively autonomous performances and deities.

For the more prominent, permanently structural shrines, the occasion of the regular *teyyam* festival is conjoined with the caste or community that owns the shrine conducting its own *pūja* rites on the enshrined images. These are usually carried out by its own shrine priests, including the ecstatic oracles dedicated to each god, though for the higher castes, a Brahman or other priest of the temple-servant castes may be brought in for special *pūjas* as well. In any case, only these priests will be allowed inside the shrine-rooms to handle and minister to the images, and these rites are closely modeled on the tantric or Āgamic worship common to Kerala and south India generally (Davis 1991, Diehl 1956).

Often there are relations of traditional hierarchical subordination of the castes sponsoring a *teyyāṭṭam* to one or more higher castes in the vicinity. In that case the *teyyam* festival is inaugurated by lamps in the *teyyam* shrine being lit with a flame brought by shrine priests from the temple that is associated with these higher castes. Thus the social hierarchy is mirrored in the divine energy of the gods flowing down the chain of authority, from the temple gods to the *teyyam* shrine through the medium of the flame. In any case, however, it is the flame used in worship of the *teyyam* shrine's images that will be passed out by the priests, (and through insulating intermediaries in the case of higher caste priests) to the *teyyam* performers. This represents the actual spiritual energy or power (*caitanyam* or *śakti*) of the enshrined images being transferred to the lower-caste dancers. As we shall see below, the ritual elaborations that this transfer takes are significant.

The Rituals of Worship and Possession

Once the particular performers from the families entitled to perform a particular shrine's gods have been appointed for that year's festival, they will each approach the shrine in a fixed order during their inaugural rites. Each separate performing caste will have their own caste-segregated make-up rooms where they will take up residence for the duration of the festival, which may run from one or several days to an entire week. The gods are performed in a traditionally stipulated order for each shrine, each in a preliminary and more simply costumed form on the first night, to be followed on the next or subsequent days with the more highly elaborated and individuated full-*teyyam* costume.

There are actually two generic kinds of these preliminary forms, and every *teyyam* god will have one or the other form exclusively associated with it. The simpler of the two forms is called *tōṟṟam*, which is also the name for the *teyyam* songs generally, and consists only of a special red waist-cloth, a vertically rising frontlet tied across the brow, belled anklets and various other ornaments and jewelry. The more complex form, the *veḷḷāṭṭam*, has warrior-style pleated waist-cloths and leggings, a wooden waist-piece, a winged wooden crown, and a crude but standardized pattern of facial and body make-up.

The various gods all have the same basic costume and appearance in the *tōṟṟam* or *veḷḷāṭṭam* phase, whereas the fuller *teyyam* form, donned later by the same consecrated performer for that deity, is highly differentiated and individuated, with its particular configuration of elaborate costuming and crown, facial and bodily make-up, and insignia that mark it as an immediately recognizable and distinct being. If we range the various forms of possessed dancer associated with *teyyam* deities on a continuum we thus find a steady progression of increasing ornamentation and complexity from the shrine oracle priests, through the *tōṟṟam* to the *veḷḷāṭṭam* and into the iconographically elaborate *teyyams* proper. This suggests that historically either distinct earlier forms of costume merged into *teyyāṭṭam*, or that earlier forms of possessed worship have undergone this iconographic elaboration in partial emulation of the fixed images of the high temple (though influence in the opposite direction is clear as well).

Since the ritual transformation of the performer into the god is the most centrally significant aspect of the *teyyāṭṭam*, I wish to dwell on a few of the most important elements of these rites to mark some larger points. For the *tōṟṟam* celebration of a particular deity, each dancer comes individually before the opened shrine in which the priests have been performing *pūja* to receive from them a folded banana leaf containing sandalwood paste and a ritual vessel of water (*kiṇḍi*). The dancer uses these to sprinkle himself and daub the paste over specified parts of his body in a prescribed fashion, starting with his head and ending at his feet. This sandalwood paste comes from the deity and being co-substantial with it, helps to transubstantiate the body of the dancer into that of the god. The places the paste is daubed are additionally said to correlate with the significant nodes and portals of the body according to the physiological conceptions of *tantra*, through which the performer absorbs, and is purified by, the divine energy. Some compared this explicitly with the ritualized bodily purification, the *deha-śuddhi* rites of tantric priests (cf. Flood 2000).

Following this, a second folded leaf is passed out which contains raw rice, five burning wicks, five betel leaves, and pieces of areca nut. The performer reverently tosses some grains of rice into his mouth, over his head and towards the shrine, then wafts the flames thrice towards his brow, inhaling the vapors. This leaf kit is then carried to a special masonry altar off to the north of the shrine, called the *kalaśa-taṟa*, or toddy-pot altar, and there the five leaves are laid out, reverenced, and their essences ritually circulated through the dancer.

As informants said of these rites, "the conception behind this is not just that when the *teyyam* performer gets this (leaf-packet) he is made worthy to put on the costume; rather, through that lamp's flame, he is actually being given the divine power . . ." Aside from the evident continuation of the theme of absorbing the god's energy through consumption of the god's rice and of the divine flame's energy, the rites at the toddy-pot altar have added significance. This structure is a sacrificial altar, named for the pot of alcoholic toddy (*kalaśam*) that sits atop it and that will later be carried with the *teyyam* in procession by a special priest of the toddy-tapper caste whose presence is mandatory at all *teyyams*. It is also the altar where blood sacrifices will later be offered, liquor and blood being potent substances of empowerment in the non-Brahman worldview. In these preliminary rites, the five wicks laid out are said to represent the five vital forces or life's breaths (*prāṇa*) of the performer, with which he at once offers up his own substance as a sacrifice (areca nut being a regular substitute for a body in tantric rites), and absorbs the life's energies of the god in their stead. Some performers indeed referred to the system of inner vessels or *nāḍis* known to tantric physiology, along which this energy is conducted through the body.

Completing these rites, and tying on a headband representing the tradition's gurus along with a frontlet, the dancer comes before the main shrine and begins to sing the *tōṟṟam* songs of the deity. The first of these songs is significant, for it is the invocation, the *vara-viḷi* (literally "call to come"), addressed to the deity. Rather like the *āvāhana* or invocation of a standard temple *pūja*, it summons the god into one's presence, but like the tantric variety of ritual to which it is akin, the site of that divine presence is one's own body–mind complex. This becomes clearer in the progression of the main *tōṟṟam* songs that are then sung by the dancer and his support troupe.

In archaic or sometimes Sanskritized varieties of Malayalam, these *tōṟṟam* songs variously recount in fixed compositions for each specific god its biographical life and deeds (often as a former human being), its origins and migrations in terms of the various locales and shrines where it was established (culminating with the place of current performance), and poetic descriptions of its costumed appearance, or imaginative enhancements built on the same. All of these themes converge in their common performative purpose, in that they work to recreate the actual presence of the deity in the body and person of dancer, through verbally repeating the highlights of its genesis and development as a person, and then ritually indexing these to the current context and bodily site of possessed enactment. This is the very force of the word, *tōṟṟam*, where the root meaning is "to seem" or "appear," but with a transitive force of agency and effective creativity that lacks any simple English equivalent (unless we perhaps conjoin the separate physical and mental significations of our word, *conceive*).

This transformative trajectory culminates in a final song of actual possession (*uṟaccal tōṟṟam*), which may narratively conclude with the death and apotheosis of the now divine protagonist, whom the dancer now becomes. Ritually, this culmination of the song is signified by the performer receiving a mirror into which he peers (figure 14.1). The force of this act is universally acknowledged by performers, as in the following explanation:

> When he looks into the mirror, the conception will arise, "This is not my form – this is the actual form of the goddess that I am seeing" . . . The act here is the seeing of the sacred face by the sacred face, a divine occasion in which they are fused through seeing each other.

The songs and rituals that bring on the possession state are basically the same for the preliminary *tōṟṟam* or *veḷḷāṭṭam* of the god as for the full *teyyam* form. The latter, more elaborate *teyyam* rituals are always done by the same dancer consecrated for the preliminary rites, generally the next day. The costuming for the full form, which takes place in the make-up room, is generally quite elaborate and complex, the facial make-up alone taking sometimes several hours to

Figure 14.1: The teyyam dancer reflexively experiences his transformation into the deity through the mirror-gazing rite

apply. The costuming may include elaborate configurations of pleated cloth, and lacquered and gilt wooden pieces, in addition to sometimes valuable ornaments and items of jewelry. The make-up room itself (*aṇiyaṟa*) accordingly becomes a locus of the prolonged ritual transformation of the dancer, where empowering liturgical verses may be sung (*aṇiyaṟa-tōṟṟams*), in addition to those performed before the main shrine. When the costuming is nearly completed, save for the placement of the crown, the performer is led from the make-up room before the shrine, where he usually sits on a ritual stool (*pīṭham* – again a term and concept of tantric significance), for the singing of the final *tōṟṟam* songs. As the verses that bring on possession are sung, the crown is fitted and tied into place, the *teyyam* is handed the weapons of the deity from within the shrine, and the god's power is brought out as before in the form of the shrine's flame, and reflexively fixed and acknowledged through the dancer gazing into the mirror. Shrine officials throw rice grains over the crowned deity from within the shrine, an act of royal and divine consecration.

With the onset of possession, the dancer begins to tremble and shake, and finally gives way to dance. The dances (*āṭṭam*) for which the *teyyāṭṭam* festival is named interweave several phases of dance proper, interspersed with various other rites in interaction with shrine officials and worshippers. There is a generally mandatory procession of the god from the toddy-pot altar, led by a priest of the toddy-tapper (*Tīyya*) caste carrying the colorfully decked toddy-pot on his head, accompanied by attendants with chowries, canopies, and tasseled ornamental umbrellas. At various points there are rites that, like the initial receipt of the shrine's weapons and flame, periodically recharge or reconfirm the flow of divine power to the *teyyam*. Such transfers of symbolic media with the priests inside the shrine-room include rice, burning lamps, the god's own weapons, and other sacred insignia such as woven umbrellas. In dances with the shrine's own oracle-priests, this divine *śakti* may be tangibly passed back and forth between possessed priest and *teyyam*, making the recipients alternately reel or leap spasmodically in place, or leading them into concertedly controlled joint dances of wonderful precision and power.

At the close of the main dance phase personal interactions, first with shrine officials, then with gathered devotees begin, the *teyyam* speaking in the first-person voice of the deity itself. Blessings are given out, contributions are received, and disputes may be presented before the god for settlement. Additionally, there may be an extended procession of the dancer out of the shrine compound and on a journey through the neighboring settlement to visit worshippers' families and other temple-sites, as the god itself. Finally, the deity returns to its shrine and to the toddy-pot altar, where, depending on the nature of the particular god, it may preside over a chicken sacrifice before a large cauldron of artificial blood (*kuruti*). This is alternately interpreted as a great blood sacrifice either to the deity itself, or to the numerous ghostly hordes in its charge, depending on the degree of Sanskritization at the shrine and among the performers. After a final round of blessings before the main shrine, the dancer removes his crown and retires to the make-up room. If this is his last dance as the god during this festival, this final rite is accompanied with a ceremonial return of the divine energy back out of the performer's person and into the custody of the shrine officials.

Where a shrine houses a number of such deities, they are sequenced over one or more days, with repeat performances of the lesser deities on successive days, culminating in the final and grandest performance by the principal deity of the shrine. Not surprisingly, this will generally be the leading family deity of the most powerful lineage who founded or who presently controls the shrine.

The Social Place of Divine Beings and Powers

The range of types of *teyyam* deities is quite great, reflecting their origins at various levels in the social hierarchy and under different sets of historical circumstances. All of the data as to their various origins, natures, and histories are preserved in the fixed liturgies which are sung to invoke their presence for worship, and, to a lesser extent, in the ancillary legends that worshippers circulate about them. (There is, however, a fairly strict hierarchy of expert knowledge operative here, where worshippers routinely refer one to, or cite, the liturgies and professional performers or oracle-priests as the authentic sources of truth in these matters.)

Many *teyyams*, those who represent the original prototype, I would argue, derive from the apotheosis of formerly living human beings. In apparent contrast, others are represented, from their birth, as gods, usually as localized incarnations of Puranic Hindu deities, created for some special purpose in local circumstances. The "human" *teyyams* themselves, however, seem to undergo apotheosis, often after miraculous deeds and violent death, only because of the divine power already inherent within them. Relatedly, many of the originally godly *teyyams*, likewise, are reported to have wandered about in human form, interacting with other human characters as members of their social communities. The essential point suggested here is that there is no clear ontological break between the human and the divine in this cultural context, but rather a continuum of expressions of powers, always divine to the extent they manifest an awesomely heightened effectiveness, and always human, to the extent that they emerge from social relations in a narratively historical context. This narrative continuum of the human–divine power spectrum is fully consonant with, and perhaps even necessary, as the discursive support for a performative mode of worship whose whole rationale is the demonstrated transformation of low-caste human beings into the tangible embodiments of living gods.

The worldview of *teyyam* clearly implies that the entirety of human life at its various levels – physical, social, and political – is suffused with unseen powers. The varying organizational scale and levels of *teyyam* rites indicate as much, for they range from occasions of individually contingent vows, consummated with *teyyāṭṭams* performed in family homesteads, to prominent temple festivals, of intricate social organization and calendrical coordination (sometimes planned over decades), drawing on communities over an entire region. It is in the narrative content of the liturgies themselves, however, that the varied levels of origin and pertinence of divine powers are most clearly in evidence. *Teyyams* who originate in the political context of rule and warfare range from the tutelary goddess of the Kōlattiri Rāja, who defeated an arch enemy-demon to secure the kingdom, down to the apotheoses of local chiefs, warriors, and military henchmen. Other *teyyams* have a more caste-specific focus, representing milieus special to a particular lifestyle, and sometimes in conflict with other castes in terms of social authority or status relations around ritual purity and pollution. Familial levels of concern generate *teyyam* deities as well, around authority and social controls within the family, around peculiarly marked ancestral figures, and, significantly, in terms of the oppression and wrongful deaths of various women who become goddesses subsequent to their deaths. Finally, there are various individuals who set themselves apart in special achievements that entail the quest for and control of divine powers: healers, scholars, sorcerers (*mantravādis*), martial arts experts, hunters, and even traders who operate in dangerous territories, may all be singled out as individuals whose surfeit of power marked them as divine.

This spectrum of human–divine powers, being arrayed in an inherently hierarchical system of social dominance, frequently takes on an agonistic and contestatory character, lending *teyyam* its characteristic narrative and performative violence. Among those *teyyams* of human derivation, as earlier noted, some clearly have their origins in the vengeful ghosts of lower-caste victims of social or political oppression, or of women, often murdered by their own male kinsmen in the enforcement of gender hierarchy. Others arise from great hunters or martial champions, whose low-caste origins and rise to power clearly harbored elements of challenge to the sociopolitical *status quo*. Still others are powerful warriors to begin with, who murder and conquer other peoples, establishing their own new order of power relations at the cost of pre-existing polities (figure 14.2).

Similarly for those of even initial godly status, there are usually relations of social hierarchy or conflict that lead to violence against their often demonized Others, in which social elements of relative status, power, and imputations of impurity drive supernatural struggles that inevitably draw human characters into the fray, establishing charters for lasting institutions and relationships. A typical example might be the case of Kuṇḍōṟa Cāmuṇḍi (figure 14.3). She is initially created by Śiva to kill the demon Dārikan in the Kerala-specific recasting of a standard Puranic theme. Since this Cāmuṇḍi, however, is polluted from the carnage of her successful battle, she is banished from Śiva's presence and ordered to travel to local holy bathing spots (*tīrtha*), where she must seek purification. Instead of finding the enjoined purity, however, in visiting such places she forms agonistic relations with Brahmans, whose rites she disrupts, and who accordingly struggle, unsuccessfully, to banish and exorcise her. She similarly afflicts a local king and his kingdom, committing cow-slaughter in his barns to feed her appetite for blood, attacking the local temples in her demands for a place as a deity, and finally killing the Brahman priests when this is refused. Through such acts she eventually extorts acts of placation from the populace, is promoted to the status of a goddess, and is enshrined by a Brahman chief of Kuṇḍōṟa (whence her name), under the patronage of the king. As I have demonstrated at length in my larger work (Freeman 1991), such narratives frequently recall real political and social struggles, in our historical sense, as well as forming divine

Figure 14.2: Vairajātan, a teyyam who embodies the martial violence of the traditional military hero (*vīran*)

charters, both locally and in extended regional networks, that sanction ongoing relations of authority, community and worship. Kuṇḍōṟa Cāmuṇḍi is today a popular *teyyam*, performed by the traditionally polluting Vēlan caste, in which they offer liquor and blood sacrifice to placate this goddess, even as they perform her in the compounds of Brahman sponsors. The narrative tension of the myth around issues of caste, social control, and relations of pollution is thus preserved

Figure 14.3: The goddess Kuṇḍōṟa Cāmuṇḍi confronts a small child in her shrine compound

today in the rituals themselves, and chartered by continuing links to prominent families and shrines, on the one hand, and to historically Untouchable and impoverished dancer-priests, on the other, that keep the tensions alive in the present relations of patronage and performance.

It should be clear from such cases and others I have alluded to, therefore, that though the distribution of *teyyams*, as embodiments of divine power, runs the social institutional gamut of worship from the highest castes to the lowest, *teyyam* narratives and performances may also harbor within them a contestatory and symbolically violent set of claims against traditional authority structures. There is thus a major strain of resistant religion that informs *teyyāṭṭam*, in keeping with its largely subaltern performative province and community organization. Some intellectuals identifying themselves with the Dalit resurgence have even recently enlisted *teyyam* myths as representative of their struggles (Ayrookuzhiel 1996).

Related Traditions in the World of Teyyam: Tantra and Mantravādam

In the wider culture of this region, however, two earlier mentioned religious complexes that span and link the caste order, cannot be severed from the context of *teyyāṭṭam*, or from each other. These are the traditions of Kerala's tantric mode of temple worship and that of *mantravādam*. Kerala's prominent Brahman caste, the Nambūtiris, are avowedly tantric in terms of the rites by which they conduct the installation and worship of temple images throughout Kerala. By tantric, I mean in this context, that the Kerala priest relies on classic tantric teachings of the psychophysical powers immanent in the human body, to first invoke the deity of worship into his own body, and only then to transfer its power, through his own metabolic life's energy or breath (*prāṇa*) into the fixed image in the temple's sanctum. As I have written at length elsewhere (Freeman 1998), it is not a great stretch to posit that a long and complex historical relation underlies the prominence of tantric worship as official Hinduism in Kerala – essentially involving a mini-possession each time the god is invoked in daily worship – and the eminence that overt possession, epitomized in *teyyāṭṭam*, as a dominant popular mode of worship in south India has enjoyed over at least the past two millennia. The paradigm of Brahmanical worship as essentially a muted form of possession thus reflects, on the high end of the social scale, an historical mediation whose results we also saw in the incorporation of a tantric rationale for the ritual acts of *teyyam* possession reviewed earlier, at the lower end of the spectrum.

Similarly, the whole complex of *mantravādam*, problematically rendered as "sorcery" or "magic," runs the gamut of the social hierarchy. In the Brahmanical register, rites of *mantravādam* are essentially contingent and private rites of controlling, marshalling, or exorcising various gods and demons through rites of tantric worship that are closely cognate to those used in the temple, but with generally temporary sites of invocation and various props and effigies for manipulating sacred powers (Freeman 1999). In the traditionally low-caste register, those castes who perform *teyyāṭṭam* practice similar rites of *mantravādam* for similarly personal purposes, in which they additionally take on the costumed forms of special *teyyams* to invoke and control these same divine and demonic powers. Again this suggests a long period of historical interaction and synthesis between the various castes, in which similar conceptions of divine and demonic powers, and similar technologies of control through animate and inanimate mediums of "possession," get differently realized according to contrastively more Sanskritic, versus more indigenous, linguistic and ritual idioms. Here *teyyāṭṭam* grades into lower-caste *mantravādam*, just as surely as Brahmanical tantric practice informs the *mantravādam* of higher castes.

Thus the larger point to grasp in the relation of *teyyāṭṭam* to both tantric doctrines and to *mantravādam* is that popular religion and magic in south India are both predicated on immanent local powers whose worship entails ritually intensifying that immanence through divine "possession," whether of normally animate humans or through their inanimate surrogates. The natural immanence of these powers is revealed in the fluidity of boundaries between the divine and human, the living and the dead. Since these powers are immanently human, they are also social, and thus we can see how *teyyāṭṭam*, putatively "low-caste" religion, is actually and pervasively "popular" Hinduism. It was of course intimately and integrally part of the life-world of all the laboring castes, but it was simultaneously a powerful index of martial prowess and authority for all those involved in traditional polity, and it also epitomized the dreaded Other of low-caste religious power against which Brahmanism defined itself, and which it therefore came to assimilate in veiled, but unmistakable ways.

Premodern Gods in Postmodern Kerala

One of the most remarkable aspects of *teyyam* for the historian of religion is the extent to which belief-structures, ritual practices, and social forms from premodern south Indian life-worlds seem to be stubbornly maintained, and even celebrated, in the midst of modern, globalizing Kerala. Officially secular educational systems, where science and technology are at a premium, socially egalitarian institutions which deny, in principle, the relevance of caste, and a political scene largely shaped, and frequently dominated, by a putatively Marxist party, all sit cheek-by-jowl with *teyyāṭṭam*. We have reviewed the extent to which divine and magical powers, their ritual harnessing and manipulation, the continued life and presence of the ancestral dead, and their channeling through incarnate possession vehicles all point to sustaining a worldview very different from the empirical scientism of high modernity.

While there have been some avowedly "progressive" attempts to administratively integrate and re-organize some *teyyam* shrines at a wider "community" level, in my experience, these are for the most part rhetorical and symbolic; the majority of these institutions remain clearly associated with hereditary lineage control within particular castes, with offices, titles, insignia, and powers that devolve in ancestral lines and that link them to the very historical identity of the gods enshrined there. And in any case, these managerial concerns are largely a matter of administering the economic resource-base of the shrine during festival times. When it comes to the enduring ritual offices themselves, the shrine priests, officiants, and of course, the *teyyam* performers are all filling their titled roles according to a highly regulated hereditary, caste protocol. Different caste names and conventions of address according to caste status from the medieval order all apply in the rites themselves, in and through the very voice of the god's possessed vehicle. Even the demarcations of ritual space still create zones of caste inclusion and exclusion, keyed to accord with the traditional purity norms of the controlling shrine members. Discriminations, supposedly extinct, that would create revolt in other, more secular public forums, reappear and are embraced as ancestrally charged and potent mandates for accessing divine powers in this religious context.

In a wider extension of these same kinds of relations, we find former political organizing principles and institutions resurfacing as well. While the largely Marxist movements have gone far in refiguring patterns of land control and associated social inequalities at many levels we would consider "political," the earlier order in which religion and polity were intertwined in a more pervasively felt set of institutional ritual "norms" (*ācāram*), is preserved in relations between and across the network of *teyyam* shrines. Thus, hierarchical relations between Brahmanical temples and lower-caste *teyyam* shrines still find overt ritual expression, as with the earlier mentioned rite of transferring flames from temples' lamps to their subordinate shrines. Processional prestations (*kāḻca*) of produce and goods are routinely made from former subjects and their shrine representatives to their former overlords as part of the celebrations. Former tenants seek ritual "permission" from their historical landlords and chiefs to conduct their festivals and accord them special honors and dignities in the shrines. Reciprocating ritual visits persist between former martial allies and dependants during each others' *teyyam* festivals. These and many other complex relations of "traditions and rites" (*ācārānuṣṭhānaṅṅaḷ*) reenact, without apparent protest or embarrassment, many of the so-called "feudal" sociopolitical hierarchies that Kerala so prides itself on having eradicated in secular forums. Many of the shrine ritual offices and the various dignities of the *teyyam* dancers themselves are still ritually ratified and their "ritual names" (*ācārappēr*) conferred by the descendants of kings, who become once again "rājas" for the occasion, at their "palaces" (*kōṭṭārams*). This culminates in the fact that the territorial norms that regulate and define different sub-traditions within the practice of *teyyam*, still largely conform to the territorial boundaries of the otherwise defunct medieval kingdoms.

For the historian, humanist, and social scientist alike, the persistence of this whole complex obviously raises perplexing problems for the construct of "modernity" itself, and the place of religion and tradition within it. The perennial vigor of traditions like *teyyam* suggest ways that secular modernity itself may sometimes be relativized by a fundamentally religious reframing. It is clear, in any case, that the Hindus of northern Kerala maintain the prominence of *teyyam* in their social lives not as a mere curiosity or relic of tradition. In addition to the motives we may problematically recognize as religious, my sense is that for many *teyyam* also defines the space of an alternate worldview and hedge against their continued colonization by Western epistemes that purport to be global in their reach and penetration.

Note

1 The author's dissertation (1991) would still seem to provide the most comprehensive cultural and historical coverage of *teyyam* worship in English (there are numbers of studies in Malayalam cited therein); other general treatments in English include Kurup (1973), Ashley and Holloman (1990), Pallath (1995), Nambiar (1996), and a nice pictorial selection in Shah and Sarabhai (1994). See also Menon (1994) for the modern historical context, and the recent documentary film on one particular deity (de Maaker 1998).

References

Ashley, W. and R. Holloman. 1990. "Teyyam," in *Indian Theatre: Traditions of Performance*, eds. F. Richmond, D. Swann, and P. Zarrilli, pp. 131–50. Honolulu: University of Hawaii Press.

Ayrookuzhiel, A. 1996. "Chinna Pulayan: The Dalit Teacher of Sankaracharya," in *The Emerging Dalit Identity: The Re-assertion of the Subalterns*, ed. W. Fernandes. New Delhi: Indian Social Institute.

Claus, P. 1978. "Oral Traditions, Royal Cults and Materials for a Reconstruction of the Caste System in South India," *Journal of Indian Folkloristics* 1: 1–26.

Davis, R. H. 1991. *Ritual in an Oscillating Universe: Worshiping Śiva in Medieval India*. Princeton, NJ: Princeton University Press.

de Maaker, E. 1998. *Teyyam: The Annual Visit of the God Vishnumurti* (film). Watertown, MA: Documentary Educational Resources.

Diehl, C. 1956. *Instrument and Purpose: Studies on Rites and Rituals in South India*. Lund: Gleerup.

Flood, G. 2000. "The Purification of the Body," in *Tantra in Practice*, ed. D. White. Princeton: Princeton University Press.

Freeman, R. 1991. *Purity and Violence: Sacred Power in the Teyyam Worship of Malabar*. Ph.D. dissertation, Dept. of Anthropology, Universtiy of Pennsylvania. Ann Arbor, MI: University Microfilms Incorporated.

——. 1998. "Formalised Possession among the Tantris and Teyyams of Malabar," *South Asia Research* 18: 73–98.

——. 1999. "Dynamics of the Person in the Worship and Sorcery of Malabar," in *Possession in South Asia: Speech, Body, Territory*, Special Ed. of *Puruṣārtha* 21. Eds. J. Assayag and G. Tarabout, pp. 149–81. Paris: École des Hautes Études en Science Sociales.

Hart, G. 1975. *The Poems of Ancient Tamil: Their Milieu and their Sanskrit Counterparts*. Berkeley: University of California Press.

Kurup, K. K. N. 1973. *The Cult of Teyyam and Hero Worship in Kerala*. Indian Folklore Series no. 21. Calcutta: Indian Publications.

——. 1982. "Memorial Tablets in Kerala," in *Memorial Stones: A Study of their Origin, Significance, and Variety*, eds. S. Settar and G. D. Sontheimer. Heidelberg and New Delhi: South Asia Institute, University of Heidelberg.

Menon, D. M. 1994. *Caste, Nationalism, and Communism in South India: Malabar, 1900–1948*. Cambridge South Asian studies no. 55. Cambridge (UK) and New York: Cambridge University Press.

Nambiar, S. 1996. *The Ritual Art of Teyyam and Bhūtārādhane*. New Delhi: Indira Gandhi National Centre for the Arts & Navrang.

Pallath, J. J. 1995. *Theyyam: An Analytic Study of the Folk Culture, Wisdom, and Personality*. New Delhi: Indian Social Institute.

Shah, P. and M. Sarabhai. 1994. "Teyyam," in *Performing Arts of Kerala*, pp. 82–99. Ahmedabad: Mapin.

Trautmann, T. R. 1981. *Dravidian Kinship*. Cambridge (UK) and New York: Cambridge University Press.

Zvelebil, K. 1974. *Tamil Literature*. Vol. 10, fasc. 1. *A History of Indian Literature*. Wiesbaden: Otto Harrassowitz.

CHAPTER 15

The Month of Kārtik And Women's Ritual Devotions to Krishna in Benares

Tracy Pintchman

Oh Krishna, go to Benares
Bring a packet of bracelets for the bride
Bring them in either your pocket or your purse
Climb into bed and gently put the bracelets on the bride's hand

Oh Krishna, go to Benares
Bring a packet of *bindis* for the bride
Bring them in either your pocket or your purse
Climb into bed and gently attach one to the forehead of the bride

Oh Krishna, go to Benares
Bring a packet of ankle bracelets for the bride
Bring them in either your pocket or your purse
Climb into bed and gently put the ankle bracelets on her

Oh Krishna, go to Benares
Bring a necklace for the bride
Bring it in either your pocket or your purse
Climb into bed and gently put the necklace on her

Oh Krishna, go to Benares
Bring a packet of toe rings for the bride
Bring them in either your pocket or your purse
Climb into bed and gently put the toe rings on her

Oh Krishna, go to Benares.[1]

Those familiar with Krishna devotional traditions might find some elements of the song text quoted above rather surprising. Predominant Krishna traditions, for example, tend to associate Krishna primarily with Braj, a region just south of Delhi on the Gangetic plain of North India. According to Sanskritic textual traditions, Krishna grows up in the Braj countryside living among cowherds and frolicking on the banks of the Yamuna river. In later life, he leaves Braj to take up residence in Dvaraka, which lies on the coast in the contemporary state of Gujarat. In this song, however, Krishna is enjoined to go to the city of Benares, famously situated on the banks of the Ganges River well to the southeast of Braj, a city that has been associated primarily not with Krishna, but with Shiva (Eck 1982: esp. 94–145). Krishna traditions also tend to associate Krishna with the goddess Radha, widely understood to be not Krishna's wife, but his lover: their relationship is an illicit one, for Radha is married to another. But in this song, Krishna is a new groom, enjoined to come join his bride in their nuptial bed and to decorate her body "gently" (*dhīre se*) with the adornments that mark her new status as a *suhāgin*, an auspiciously married woman. Furthermore, the bride in question is not Radha: it is Tulsi, the basil plant widely associated with the worship of Vishnu and his forms as the deities Krishna and Ram.

I recorded this song in the city of Benares in the autumn of 1998, during the lunar Hindu month known as Kārtik. I had returned to Benares for the third time in the space of four years to complete research on the religious dimensions of Kārtik, particularly focusing on women's devotional traditions associated with the month.[2] During Kārtik, many Hindu women living in and around Benares gather together in groups along the banks of the Ganges River and perform ritual devotions that they refer to collectively as Kārtik *pūjā* (Kārtik worship). It is in the context of these devotions that I heard female devotees sing this song, beseeching Krishna to come to Benares and join his new bride, Tulsi, in their marital chamber. The image of Krishna as Tulsi's gentle groom and the nature of women's religious practices concerning this sacred marriage are deeply embedded in broader devotional traditions pertaining to Kārtik.

Kārtik as a Sacred Month

When measured against the solar calendar commonly used in the West, the first day of Kārtik in Benares usually falls sometime in mid-October, although this varies from year to year.[3] Kārtik is considered the second month of the two-month autumn season and the last month before the onset of winter. Sandwiched between the hot and humid rainy season and the chilling cold that often comes in late December and January, Kārtik is widely associated in Benares with pleasant and hospitable weather. From the perspective of traditional Indian medicine, the change of season that occurs at this time of year is unhealthful, leaving the body vulnerable to illnesses, and in Benares I heard people attribute all kinds of medical problems to the change in the weather. Yet many people also declare that autumn is the best season and that during Kārtik the climate is more pleasant than at any other time of year.

In addition to being welcomed for the change of season that it marks, Kārtik is also one of the most religiously important months in the Hindu calendar. It is associated primarily with the worship of Vishnu and hence is most meaningful to Vaiṣṇavas (those whose devotional life centers on Vishnu). At least in Benares, however, some Śaivas (devotees of Shiva) and Śāktas (devotees of the Goddess) also participate in month-long devotional observances associated with Kārtik, although they appear to be outnumbered by Vaiṣṇavas. Distinctive narratives, practices of text recitation, and month-long ritual observances bring the month to life in Benares in people's homes, in temples, and along the *ghāṭs*, the stone steps that line the banks of the Ganges river at the edge of the city.

The merits of Kārtik are especially lauded in sections of the Skanda and Padma Purāṇas that both go by the name "Kārtik Māhātmya" (Glorification of Kārtik).[4] The two Kārtik Māhātmyas are not exactly the same, but they do share a good deal of content. Significant portions of material appear in both texts in identical or nearly identical form, and some narrative sections that are elaborated at length in the Padma Purāṇa's version of the text are recounted in abbreviated form in the Skanda Purāṇa's version. Some portions of the Kārtik Māhātmya of the Skanda Purāṇa that are not reproduced in the Padma Purāṇa's version of the text are found elsewhere in the Padma Purāṇa in similar or identical form, and vice versa. During the month of Kārtik the Kārtik Māhātmyas are recited aloud in homes and temples all over Benares, and it is considered to be highly meritorious to recite daily a portion the Kārtik Māhātmya in the original Sanskrit, have it recited by a Brahmin priest, or at least listen to it. Of the two versions, that of the Padma Purāṇa is by far the one most popularly recited in Benares, and it is also the one most familiar to the women with whom I performed *pūjā* throughout the month. Both versions of the Kārtik Māhātmya include passages glorifying Kārtik, explanations of its religious importance, descriptions of ritual practices that should be undertaken during Kārtik, narrative material related to the month and its observances, and passages lauding those who recite the text or listen to its recitation.

The month of Kārtik is also associated with a month-long votive observance known as the Kārtik *vrat* (Skt. *vrata*). Mary McGee describes the term *vrat* as it is generally used in contemporary Hindu culture as referring to "a religiously sanctioned votive observance, that is, a rite performed at a particular time with a particular desire in mind" (McGee 1987: 17). McGee also notes that central to the practice of *vrats* in contemporary India is the notion of *niyam* (Skt. *niyama*), "rule" or "restriction," which underscores an emphasis in the *vrat* tradition on practices that inculcate self-discipline and restraint of the senses (50, 93–5). In keeping with this emphasis, the month-long Kārtik *vrat* includes a number of injunctions for actions and behaviors that are to be upheld throughout the entire month and that focus on disciplines and restraints pertaining to the mind, body, and personal conduct.

Food restrictions figure prominently in votive observances, and the Kārtik *vrat*, too, entails abstention from certain types of food for the entire month, including eggplant, white radish, and certain types of pulses. The key observance of the Kārtik *vrat*, however, is Kārtik *snān* (Skt. *snāna*), daily ritual bathing before sunrise in a river or other publicly accessible body of water. In Benares the goal for most Kārtik bathers is the Ganges River. The Ganges is considered a goddess in liquid form and is held to be a holy river, eternally pure and purifying. While bathing in the Ganges at any time of year is thought to be meritorious, in Benares the months of Kārtik, Māgh, and Vaiṣākh are all recognized as especially meritorious months for daily Ganges bathing.

The Benarsis with whom I spoke about Kārtik and its merits tended to describe Kārtik as a highly auspicious month. Generally speaking, auspiciousness is a desired value in the Hindu tradition associated with well-being and happiness. Ronald Inden lists several Sanskrit terms often translated to mean "auspicious" and describes them as including that which is "pleasant, agreeable, propitious, favorable, salutary, better, fortunate, prosperous, desirable, beautiful, handsome, good, charming, radiant, beneficial – and, yes, auspicious" (Inden 1986: 30). Frederique Marglin's work on auspiciousness in Hindu culture has emphasized its connection to fertility, prosperity, happiness, and worldly well-being, values generally associated with householdership (Marglin 1985). While Inden and Marglin focus on auspiciousness largely as it pertains to worldly pursuits, Vasudha Narayanan further ramifies the discussion by calling for a clear recognition of two levels of auspiciousness. In her work on Śrī Vaiṣṇavism, she identifies one level of auspiciousness that has to do with everyday life and householder values and pertains to things like prosperity, happiness, or the longevity of a husband – values that are encompassed under the general rubric of auspiciousness as Marglin describes it. But Narayanan also emphasizes another level of auspiciousness that encompasses the pursuit of spiritual liberation or *mokṣa* and is associated with the life of renunciation (Narayanan1985: 62). This second level pertains to the achievement of spiritual advancement, renunciation of the world, and pursuit of the divine.

Kārtik exemplifies and promotes auspiciousness on both of the levels that Narayanan describes. Much of the symbolism that pervades the month can be interpreted as conducive to either spiritual or worldly boons, or both, depending on the devotee, and the line between the two is quite fluid. Many auspiciousness-related images, themes, and practices that permeate the month are not unique to Kārtik, but during the month they assume distinctive forms that uniquely contextualize auspiciousness while embodying more general themes of auspiciousness in Hindu culture.[5]

Kārtik's auspiciousness is exemplified by the month's strong association with Lakshmi, quintessential goddess of auspiciousness. The full-moon night with which Kārtik begins, Śarat Pūrṇimā or "Autumn Full Moon," marks a festival dedicated to Lakshmi. This celebration is known as Kojāgarī, and in Benares, as elsewhere, celebrants perform a special form of worship to Lakshmi and ask for her blessings. The goddess is said to roam the earth on this night asking, "*Ko jāgarti?*" ("Who is awake?"), and those who remain awake are considered most likely to win her blessings. Lakshmi roams the earth again, of course, on Divālī, an important and well-known festival that takes place at the junction between Kārtik's dark and light fortnights in the middle of the month. Lamps are lit in great abundance during Divālī to show Lakshmi the path to people's homes, filling the city with light. Light is popularly associated with Lakshmi: it is a form of the goddess, and as such it embodies auspiciousness. The lighting of lamps is actually important throughout the entire month of Kārtik, however, not just on Divālī. Every evening throughout the month, small lamps called "sky-lamps" are placed in baskets and then hoisted to the top of bamboo poles. These sky-lamps are displayed mainly on the *ghāṭs* constructed along the banks of the Ganges. The Kārtik Māhātmya of the Skanda Purāṇa claims that Lakshmi herself comes to view these lamps throughout the month (7.118–20), and the Dharmasindhu proclaims that by offering sky-lamps during Kārtik, one obtains Lakshmi, i.e., auspicious boons associated with Lakshmi, such as wealth, good health, and abundance (205).

Light also has esoteric connotations and can be interpreted as symbolic of spiritual processes. One finds such an interpretation of the sky lamps, for example, in a 1995 volume of the booklet, *Rāmānand Prakāsh*, "The Light of Rāmānand," published at Śrī Maṭh, a Vaiṣṇava monastery located at the Pañcagaṅgā Ghāṭ in Benares. Śrī Maṭh is home to a number of monks of the Rāmānanda tradition, a celibate Vaiṣṇava order. Śrī Maṭh is very active during Kārtik and is a major organizational and financial power behind many of Benares's public Kārtik celebrations. Here the sky lamps are attributed a spiritual meaning:

> These lamps hidden inside wicker baskets hanging from bamboo have probably been lit for gods. They have become a mediator between people "down below" and "people" "up there." . . . But heaven is nowhere up there, nor do the gods reside somewhere "up there." . . . Hanging the lamp in the sky means awakening consciousness in one's mind. . . . These sky lamps are nothing but an effort to elevate this consciousness. The gods reside only inside us, and whatever good there is in the outside world is nothing but an expansion of this inner divinity. (32)

The lighting of lamps each evening during Kārtik also occurs in conjunction with the worship of Tulsi, the basil plant. Tulsi is specifically associated with Vishnu, and Vaiṣṇavas are bid to maintain a Tulsi plant in their homes during this month in particular, honoring it every evening by burning a small lamp at its base. Tulsi is considered to be an auspicious, purifying, life- and health-enhancing herb, and many informants in Benares advised me to consume it for all manner of ills, from upper respiratory problems to an upset stomach. Tulsi is also considered a goddess, and during Kārtik she comes to be elevated to the status of God's bride. In Benares Tulsi's wedding is performed at the appropriate time in homes and temples all over the city.

Tulsi is wed to her divine groom on the eleventh of Kārtik's light fortnight. This day also marks the end of the *cāturmāsa*, a four-month period that is considered to be inauspicious. The *cāturmāsa* begins right after eleventh of the bright fortnight of *ṣāḍh*, a day known as Śayanī Ekādaśī, "sleeping eleventh." It is believed that on this day Vishnu retires to sleep, floating in a vast ocean on the back of his serpent Ananta. For the duration of his slumber, which lasts for four months, auspicious life-cycle rituals, like marriages, are suspended.

Vishnu awakens on the eleventh of Kārtik's bright fortnight, a date known as Prabodhanī Ekādaśī, "waking eleventh."[6] Tulsi's wedding takes place on this very day, not only marking the end of the inauspicious *cāturmāsa*, but also establishing the opening of the marriage season for Hindus in North India. From this day forward until the next Śayanī Ekādaśī, auspicious life-cycle rituals, including marriages, are resumed.

The Kārtik Māhātmyas describe the eleventh of Kārtik's light fortnight as the day of Tulsi's marriage to *Vishnu*, and they enjoin devotees to ritually reenact the marriage. In this regard, Tulsi acts as a double of Lakshmi, Vishnu's other auspicious wife. For the women of Benares, however, Tulsi is wed not to Vishnu, but to *Krishna*. Such a distinction might at first appear trivial – Krishna and Vishnu are, after all, different forms of the same deity, and the female devotees I interacted with often referred to Krishna, Vishnu, and Ram interchangeably as "Bhagavān" (Lord). While the distinction between Krishna and Vishnu might not be terribly important *theologically* in this instance, however, it is quite important *mythologically*, for distinctive narrative traditions associated with Krishna come into play in, and are shaped and transformed by, the particular context of Benarsi women's Kārtik celebrations.

Krishna and Kārtik

Like Vishnu, Krishna, too, figures prominently in the month of Kārtik. Not only is daily *pūjā* to Krishna advocated in the Kārtik Māhātmyas, but various events associated with Krishna's life are also celebrated and commemorated throughout the month. For example, some popular sources associate the day preceding Divālī with Krishna's victory over the demon Naraka (e.g., Vālā: 157; Gautam: 168). The first day of Kārtik's light fortnight marks the celebration of Govardhan *pūjā*, worship of the lord of Mount Govardhan (Cow-Dung Wealth), a mountain located in Braj that is associated with Krishna mythological traditions.[7] And the eighth of Kārtik's light fortnight, Gopāṣṭamī (Cowherd Eighth), is cited in some contemporary sources as the day that Krishna began not only to graze cattle in the forest, but also to slay demons (Bharatīyā and Raṇvīr: 161; Gautam: 185).

Several informants associated the month of Kārtik with the sum total of Krishna's life as a cowherd in Braj, from his birth until his eventual departure for Dvaraka, even insisting that all the major events of this period of his life took place during the month of Kārtik. This association is reinforced in Benares in a series of performances occurring during this month that are known as "Krishna Līlā." These performances take place every evening on Tulsi Ghat beginning on the twelfth of Kārtik's dark fortnight and ending just after the month concludes. The term *līlā* means "play," and it encompasses a number of meanings: it refers not only to theatrical performance, but to Krishna's "play" in Braj, that is, the sum total of his life from birth until his departure to Dvaraka. Krishna Līlā reenacts all the major events of this period of Krishna's life.[8]

One of the most famous images associated with Krishna is that of the *rāsa-līlā*, the "circle dance," where Krishna, surrounded by the circle of cowherdesses, or *gopīs*, in the forest, not only dances with all of them, including Radha, but also multiplies himself many times over so that he can take each one of them into his intimate embrace. Some contemporary textual sources link Kārtik with the *rāsa-līlā* episode, citing in particular the night of Śarat Pūrṇimā, the full moon night with which the month begins, as the night that the *rāsa-līlā* took place in ancient times, or locating it during the last day or days of the month (e.g., Underhill 1921: 83; Mukherjee 1989: 210ff; Raghavan 1979: 172). The Devī-Bhāgavata Purāṇa maintains that the Ganges herself first appeared in the *rāsa-maṇḍala* (the dance circle) on the last night of Kārtik, the night of Kārtik Pūrṇimā (full-moon), and remains in the *rāsa* circle on that night (851; 854–5). Popular traditions in Benares, however, tend to associate the entire month of Kārtik with the *rāsā-līlā* episode.

Participants in Kārtik *pūjā*, the *pūjā* that Hindu women perform on the banks of the Ganges River throughout the month, consider it to be a version of the *rāsa-līlā* transfigured into a form appropriate for human women and enacted each year in celebration of the earthly *rāsa-līlā* of ancient times. The songs sung during the *pūjā* tend to invoke the term *sakhī* or "female friend," a term used to refer to the *gopī* companions who accompany and serve Radha and Krishna in their love play, and in the *pūjā* circles women refer to themselves and each other with the same term. In interviews, several informants compared their role in the *pūjā* to that of the *sakhīs* and described themselves as repeating or imitating the *sakhīs*' devotions to Krishna.[9] As one informant explained it,

> Krishna-jī did *rās* with the *sakhīs*, and that is why all we *sakhīs* get together and make Bhagavān and put Him in the middle. . . . Whatever they did in the past, we are doing the same thing in the *pūjā*. Without *sakhīs*, this *pūjā* cannot be done. . . . In reality, we cannot get Lord Krishna himself, so we do this. It is the very same thing (as *rās-līlā*). Bhagavān is in the middle of us, and we are doing *rās* all around him. We say that we are Krishna's *sakhīs* and that we are doing *rās*, we are doing his *līlā*.

This informant draws a clear link between the *pūjā* and the circle dance episode. It was not uncommon, however, for informants to use the term "*rāsa-līlā*" to refer not only the specific episode of the *rāsa-līlā*, but also to Krishna's entire *līlā*, his entire playful life on earth, and they understand their role in the *pūjā* as related to this more expansive sense of the term as well.[10] Several informants likened their role in the *pūjā* to that of the *gopīs* who cared for and played with Krishna throughout his many years in Vrindavan. Within Kārtik *pūjā*, this role takes on a progressive character and concludes in the arrangement and celebration of Krishna's wedding to Tulsi. Hence while the understanding of *rāsa-līlā* as the circle dance that facilitates the love-play between Krishna and Radha in the forests of Vrindavan remains, it is here supplemented by a vision of the *rāsa-līlā* as the nurturing of Krishna from childhood to adulthood, a nurturing that culminates in the fulfillment of parental responsibility through the arrangement and execution of his marriage to a socially acceptable wife.

Kārtik *Pūjā* and Krishna's Wedding to Tulsi

Women who participate in Kārtik *pūjā* are Kārtik *vratīs*, those observing the month-long Kārtik *vrat* by bathing in the Ganges River very early in the morning. Following their morning ablutions, they gather together in groups along the *ghāṭs* at the river's edge. Participants construct several icons, called *mūrtis*, out of Ganges clay, including those of Vishnu and Lakshmi, Shiva, Ganesha, Radha-Krishna, Tulsi, the moon-god Candrama, the Sun-god Surya, and the Ganges herself. Forming a circle around the *mūrtis*, they perform *pūjā* while singing devotional songs, called *bhajans*, particular to this occasion.

Many deities are represented and honored, but several of the *bhajans* sung during the *pūjā* focus specifically on Krishna, and informants told me that the *pūjā* itself is largely dedicated to Krishna with the other deities called to be present chiefly so that they, too, can participate as devotees. In the first song, the gods are awakened by their consorts so that they can attend the *pūjā*: Pārvati wakens Shiva, Lakshmi wakens Vishnu, and Radha wakens Krishna. Then while making devotional offerings to all the icons, *pūjā* participants themselves waken Krishna with song, inviting him to arise, cleanse himself, and eat his breakfast. A subsequent *pūjā* song celebrates Krishna's form, enjoining all the *sakhīs* to focus their gaze on him and enjoy his physical beauty:[11]

> Having bathed and cleaned himself, good Govinda is walking: look at him!
> He has a golden pot and is offering water: look at him!
> He is playing a golden flute in his hand: look at him!
> He has a golden anklet on his ankle and is making a ringing sound with it: look at him!
> He has a golden basket, from which he is offering flowers: look at him!
> He has a shiny, golden *seharā*[12] on his head: look at him!
> The *pītāmbar*[13] that he is wearing is flapping: look at him!
> He is chewing *pān*[14] in his mouth: look at him!
> He has put black eyeliner (*kājal*) on his eyes: look at him!
> He is wearing golden sandals and tapping them: look at him!
> Oh Krishna, Oh Narayan, take away my worries!

Several other *bhajans* sung specifically to or about Krishna are also included in the *pūjā*, along with *ārati* songs to the Ganges, the sun-deity Suraj, Tulsi, Annadev (the goddess of food), and Shiva.

After the main section of the *pūjā* is completed, participants narrate several devotional stories. The first story focuses on Ganesha, Lord of Obstacles, and ideally is followed by four other stories, including at least one story related to the particular day in question. Since Friday is associated with the Goddess, for example, then on Fridays a devotional story related to the Goddess is narrated; on Thursdays, a story related to Vishnu; and so forth. There is no official storyteller in the groups, although some women are more knowledgeable and outgoing than others and hence tend to recount more devotional narratives than other women. Stories narrated include, among others, those related to Kārtik, Tulsi, the Ganges, and Krishna, all of which are of central importance in the *pūjā* itself.

Participants in Kārtik *pūjā* consider Krishna to be in child form for the first half of the month. During this period, when the daily *pūjā* comes to an end, participants gather together all the clay icons in the cloth on which the *pūjā* is performed. They then swing the baby Krishna, along with all the other deities involved in the *pūjā*, offering Krishna milk and singing a special swinging song to pacify him. After this, the clay icons, cloth, and all items offered during the *pūjā* are immersed in the Ganges River. Most participants remain and sing several other *bhajans* before dispersing. The final end of the *pūjā* is marked with a declaration about the auspicious fruits of Kārtik bathing, chanted in chorus:

> Ram-ji told us to bathe in Kārtik. So we bathe in Kārtik. Why? For food (*ann*), for wealth (*dhan*), for an ever-filled food storage room (*bharal bhaṇḍār*), for marital happiness (*suhāg*), for going to Heaven (*Vaikunth*).

This basic rhythm defines the course of the *pūjā* for approximately the first 20 days of the month.

On the fifth or eighth of Kārtik's light fortnight, however, there is a shift. *Pūjā* participants have a priest come to their *pūjā* circle to perform Krishna's *janeū*, the ceremony marking his investiture with the sacred thread, which designates Krishna's transformation from child to young man. For this occasion, as for the marriage itself, a brass *mūrti* (icon) is used in place of the usual clay one. *Pūjā* participants lovingly bathe Krishna in Ganges water and turmeric, dress him in finery, and sing *janeū* songs in order to prepare Krishna for his *janeū*. The priest is then called to utter the *mantras* appropriate to the occasion.

In some *pūjā* circles, the swinging song is no longer sung after this point, since Krishna is no longer thought to be a child, and there is bawdy joking and dancing on this day as women begin to look forward to the impending marriage. In the *pūjā* circle that my friend and research assistant, Sunita Singh, attended in 1997, Krishna's transition to manhood after the *janeū* was marked by the reworking of the clay Krishna *mūrti* from a reclining position to a seated one that explicitly displayed his newly mature male features, accompanied, apparently, by a good deal of laughter and off-color joking.

For several days following the *janeū*, women sing marriage songs in the *pūjā* circle before beginning the *pūjā* itself, marking the impending marriage. During the intervening days, *pūjā* participants assume the roles of family members on both bride's and groom's sides, discussing wedding arrangements, arguing about dowry, and so forth. Designated participants gather money from the entire *pūjā* circle to purchase gifts and other necessary items for the wedding as well. A special ritual is then performed on the ninth of Kārtik's light fortnight, a special *vrat* day known as Akṣaya Navamī, "indestructible ninth."

In Benares, women execute a special *pūjā* on Akṣaya Navamī, which Kārtik *pūjā* participants do right after they have finished the Kārtik *pūjā*. Facing the river and the newly risen sun, women use turmeric to draw on the ground a ritual diagram consisting of thirty squares, called *koṭhā*. Various offerings are placed in the squares, and a pandit is called over to recite the appropriate *mantras*. As one *votary* explained to me, observers of the *vrat* symbolically fill up the *koṭhā* with spiritual merit, since it is said that any good deed done on this day carries with it indestructible merit (hence the name, "indestructible ninth"). Kārtik *pūjā* participants, however, use this particular ritual to exchange wedding invitations among Kārtik *vratīs*. In Benares, some kind of food gift may accompany a wedding invitation, especially if you greatly desire the person's presence at the wedding. After the Akṣaya Navamī *pūjā* is completed, participating women offer each other *prasād* from the *pūjā* as a food gift while orally inviting one another to the upcoming wedding.

For many Benarsi women, the marriage of Tulsi and Krishna is inextricably woven into the devotional fabric of Kārtik of the whole. Some, for example, interpret food restrictions associated with the Kārtik *vrat* as commemorating the fast that Tulsi undertook in ancient times to attain Krishna as a husband. One informant described the festivities associated with Śarat Pūrṇimā, the full-moon night that ushers in the month of Kārtik, as a celebration of Tulsi's engagement to Krishna. On this night, it is said that nectar rains down from the moon, and at nighttime many Benarsis place out on their rooftops white foods, especially *khīr* (rice pudding), to catch the nectar. The *khīr* and other foods are then shared among family members the next day as *prasād*, a practice that this informant described as sealing Tulsi's engagement to her future husband. Several informants claimed that Kārtik *pūjā* imitates a *pūjā* that Tulsi herself performed in ancient times to win Krishna as a husband. Hence, many *pūjā* participants interpret the entire month of Kārtik in relation to the marriage of Krishna and Tulsi, and when the day of the marriage finally arrives on the eleventh of Kārtik's second fortnight, they celebrate it with great fanfare.

On the day of the wedding, after concluding the daily *pūjā*, participants clear and purify a space for the *mandap*, the marriage pavillion, which is decorated with bamboo branches. The groom, represented in this context by a brass *mūrti*, is brought to the *pūjā* circle, bathed, and dressed in finery. The bride, a potted Tulsi plant, is also brought to the circle, dressed in a red wedding sari, and adorned with tinsel, small mirrors, and other decorations. Gifts are placed before the bride and groom and displayed as dowry offerings, and participants engage in a raucous round of *gālī* – abusive, often crudely sexual songs that women sing at marriages. As in the *janeū*, a male pandit is called in briefly to recite the appropriate *mantras* and to collect the dowry items as *dān*. The participants then sprinkle *sindūr* on the bride's "head" to mark her new, married status and throw puffed rice at the newly wed couple.

Krishna's wedding to Tulsi takes place on the eleventh of Kārtik's light fortnight, so the full-moon night that marks the end of the month is still several days away. In Benares this is the period of the Bhiṣmapañcak, the five days of Bhishma, when large, clay effigies of the hero are made and worshipped on *ghāṭs* all over the city. For many Kārtik *pūjā* participants, however, these five days mark the period between Tulsi's marriage to Krishna and her departure with her new husband to her *sasurāl*, her in-laws' house, where the newlyweds are to take up residence. Most of the *pūjā* participants with whom I spoke understand the *sasurāl* to be Vaikunth, the Vaiṣṇava heaven that is usually associated not with Krishna, but with Vishnu. During this time, women's daily *pūjā* continues, but no *mūrtis* are made; the *pūjā* is done instead with a plastic or metal box. This period ends on Kārtik Pūrṇimā, the full-moon night with which Kārtik draws to a close. Kārtik Pūrṇimā is celebrated with great fanfare in Benares as Deva-Divālī, the Divālī of the gods. As the full moon rises over the Ganges River, thousands of lamps light the *ghāṭs* up and down the river along the city's edge, and boatloads of spectators float along the Ganges's waters to enjoy the remarkable sight.

Women who participate in Kārtik *pūjā* interpret the five days from Tulsi's marriage to Kārtik Pūrṇimā as related to both the wedding itself and the ensuing *suhāgrāt*, the night on which the marriage is consummated. According to many informants, these days mark the period that Krishna and Tulsi spend in the specially prepared Kohabar, a room in the house that is decorated in a special way for the wedding and set up for wedding-related *pūjā*. In some Benaras households, newlyweds exchange *dahi-guṛ*, yogurt mixed with raw sugar, in the Kohabar of the bride's natal home after the wedding before departing for the bride's *sasural*. I was also told that in parts of Bihar, the groom remains at the bride's house for nine days, and the *suhāgrāt* is celebrated in the Kohabar. Other informants insisted that this period had nothing at all to do with the Kohabar: instead, they said, Tulsi is too young to leave for her *sasurāl* at the time of her wedding, so she remains at her natal home until Kārtik Pūrṇimā, the night of her *gauna*, when the bride is ceremoniously brought from her natal home to her huband's home. In any case, many informants insisted that Krishna and Tulsi consummate their marriage and depart for Vaikunth on the night of Kārtik Pūrṇimā.

Tulsi, Radha, and Realms of Auspiciousness

Many of the women I interviewed in connection with the Kārtik *pūjā* insisted both that Kārtik is the time of *rāsa-līlā* with Radha and the *gopīs* and that Krishna leaves Radha for the month to spend the time with Tulsi and then marry her, apparently without feeling that these two versions of events might be mutually incompatible. In casual conversation, informants even tended to collapse the two into a single goddess and name them interchangeably as Krishna's blushing bride. Nevertheless, songs and stories associated with the *pūjā* paint a picture of tension between Radha and Tulsi and describe their competition over Krishna. Consider the following song, for example, which I recorded from the *pūjā* in 1997. In the song, Krishna appears wearing the garb and ornaments of a groom, and Radha becomes suspicious.

Oh, my heart, worship Krishna.[15]
Laughing, sweet Radha asked, "Krishna, how did that red *tilak* (auspicious mark) get on your forehead?"
Krishna said, "Listen, dear Radha, I got the *tilak* when I went to bathe in the Ganges river."[16]
Laughing, sweet Radha asked, "Krishna, how did that *kājal* (eyeliner) get on your eyes?"
Krishna said, "Listen, dear Radha, when I picked up a pen, the ink (from the pen) got on my eyes."
Laughing, sweet Radha asked,"Krishna, how did that red color get on your mouth?"
Krishna said, "Listen dear Radha, my friends fed me *pān*, and because of that my mouth has gotten red."[17]
Laughing, sweet Radha asked, "Krishna, how did that red color get on your feet?"
Krishna said, "Listen, dear Radha, my heel has become red from walking on a henna-leaf."
Laughing, sweet Radha asked, "Krishna, how did your *dhoti*[18] get yellow?"
Krishna said, "The washerman (*dhobi*) must have changed the *dhoti*."
When sweet Radha heard these things, she called the washerman immediately.
"Listen to what I have to say, Washerman: How is it that Krishna's *dhoti* got exchanged for this one?"
The washerman said, "Listen, sweet Radha, Krishna and Tulsi have gotten married."
When sweet Radha heard these words, she bolted the door from inside
Krishna said, "Dear Radha, open the door! Tulsi will be your servant (*dāsī*)."

The following song is even more explicit about the tensions between Radha and Tulsi:

In back of me, there is a Clove tree; cloves fall down from it all night long.
My father cut down that clove tree and made a bed frame, and father wove a bed out of silk.
The groom Shri Krishna and Queen Rukmini sleep on that bed
Radha and Rukmini sleep there, one on each side, and Shri Krishna sleeps between them.
Radha asks, "I am asking you, Sister Rukmini, what is it that I smell?"
Krishna is talking and laughing; Tulsi stands just at his head
(Rukmini says,) "That is Tulsi's fragrance wafting in."
(Radha says,) "If I get a hold of Tulsi now, I will pull her out by the roots, and I will throw her into the Ganges River! Then all of my troubles will go away!"
(Tulsi says,) "Go ahead, Radha, go to the Ganges River (and throw me in); Krishna will bathe in the river. I will touch Krishna's feet, and my life will be fulfilled (*suphal*)."
(Radha says,) "If I get a hold of Tulsi now, I will pull her out by the roots, and I will throw her in the cooking fire. Then all my troubles will go away!"
(Tulsi says,) "Okay, go ahead and throw me in the cooking fire. Then I will become fire in the month of Māgh. In Māgh and Pūs, everyone is cold.[19] Krishna will warm himself by that fire, and my life will be fulfilled."

The tension between Tulsi and Radha that is exemplified in these songs has larger symbolic resonances. Krishna's proper marital relationship to Tulsi, culminating in their departure for Vaikunth, forms a symbolic counterpoint to the relationship between Krishna and Radha, whose love-play in Vrindavan is widely understood as always remaining outside the bounds of marriage. In Vrindavan, Krishna is eternally at play, and his erotic sport is not bound by *dharmic* conventions (Kinsley 1979: esp. 56–121). Vaikunth, on the other hand, where Krishna and Tulsi are widely believed to go when they leave the earthly realm at the end of Kārtik to take up residence as husband and wife, is the domain of Vaiṣṇava kingship and marriage, both of which are subject to the demands of *dharma*. When Krishna marries Tulsi and becomes her proper husband, he counts Vaikunth, not Vrindavan, as his home. This is the Krishna summoned to Benares in the song with which this chapter begins.

In his work on performances of Krishna *līlā* in Braj, John S. Hawley invokes symbolism of auspiciousness to contrast Vrindavan and Vaikunth (Hawley 1983: 305–6). Krishna's play in Vrindavan, Hawley contends, is the realm of dispersed auspiciousness, where auspiciousness flows in all directions and is "made available to all who thirst." Vaikunth, on the other hand, represents the realm of stable auspiciousness, embodied in the goddess Lakshmi – for whom Tulsi acts as a "double" in the context of Kārtik *pūjā* – and exemplified in the marital relationship. Frédérique Marglin contrasts the playful realm of the young Krishna of Vrindavan, which is characterized by sweetness, with the later, princely realm of Krishna's Dvaraka, which is characterized by sovereignty (Marglin 1985: 195–216). According to Marglin, the eternally lush, forested bowers of Vrindavan represents a transcendent type of auspiciousness that never wanes; this is not true of Dvaraka, however, where auspiciousness is temporally bound, and, in accordance with the demands of sovereignty, acquisition of auspiciousness remains a chief concern. As the divine realm of Vaiṣṇava sovereignty, Vaikunth is the heavenly counterpart of Dvaraka.

In Benarsi women's Kārtik celebrations, Vrindavan and Vaikunth, sweetness and sovereignty, transcendent auspiciousness and temporally bound auspiciousness all come together at the Ganges's edge. The world of Kārtik *pūjā* celebrates the youthful Krishna's Vrindavan *līlā* and the tasting of dispersed auspiciousness; but it also welcomes the sovereign glory of Vaikunth and the stabilizing of auspiciousness that Krishna's marriage to Tulsi suggests. While the former realm embodies sacred ideals pertaining to religious devotion, however, the latter realm reflects and is allied more closely with the concrete, worldly concerns of Hindu women.

David Kinsley (1979) has described the nature of Krishna's play in Vrindavan as embodying the bliss of the divine realm, a bliss that transcends worldly concern. The call of Krishna's flute to summon the *gopīs*, Kinsley notes, "cares nothing for this world and its moral and social laws. . . . It comes from another world where this-wordly morality and conduct have no place" (99–100). Such perceptions of the divine permeate the world of Kārtik *pūjā*, where participants assume the role of the *sakhīs* and, in their hearts, frolic with Krishna on the banks of the Ganges. Yet the devotional realm of Krishna's carefree sport is far removed from the realm of real human relations that tend to occupy the space of Hindu women's lives. Krishna's marriage to Tulsi, celebrated so enthusiastically on the banks of the Ganges, reflects the world of values and conventions that shape and inform human conjugal relations. When Krishna comes to Benares to adorn his new bride with the ornaments of a *suhagin*, a properly married woman, he enters that world.

In her analysis of women's symbols, Caroline Walker Bynum notes that women's images and symbols tend to continue or enhance women's ordinary experience rather than break with that experience (Walker 1996: 74). The imagery surrounding Krishna and Tulsi that is invoked in the *pūjā* – raising Krishna to marriageable age, then arranging and participating in his wedding to Tulsi – has deep social resonance for Hindu women, whose lives revolve to a great extent around their roles as brides, wives, and mothers. The child Krishna frolics eternally in Vrindavan; yet the sons and daughters of women who participate in Kārtik *pūjā* grow up, and when they do, their weddings have to be arranged. The erotic love play between Radha and Krishna expresses the yearning of the soul for intimacy with the Divine; yet human women marry, and when they do, they yearn for a proper husband with whom they can share the earthly joys of marriage and family. Like Tulsi, many of the married women in Benares who participate in the *pūjā* were also carried off after marriage to an uncertain future in their in-laws' house; their daughters, similarly, grow up and leave their natal homes to take up residence in their husbands' villages and towns. Kirin Narayan observes that in Kangra, Himachal Pradesh, where Tulsi's wedding during Kārtik is also performed, some women make an explicit link between Tulsi's life and the lives of human women, identifying Tulsi's marriage and subsequent uprooting with human women's marriage and departure for the in-law's house (Narayan 1997: 37). In Benares, too, the marital drama unique to women's Kārtik traditions is continuous with the norm of women's lives, representing in ideal form the marital and parental destiny of numerous Hindu women in contemporary India.

Notes

1 The epithet used here for Krishna is "Mohan Rasiyā." The epithet "Mohan" indicates Krishna's nature as divine "enchanter." The epithet "Rasiyā" points to his nature as an "enjoyer" or "taster" of the emotions associated with devotion. Each line of song text is repeated twice. In this chapter, all songs are translated in ways that emphasize clarity of meaning, not literal accuracy.

2 This chapter is based on a larger book project currently in process. Support for this project was supplied by the American Institute of Indian Studies, the National Endowment of the Humanities, the American Academy of Religion, Loyola University of Chicago, and Harvard University, which granted me a position as research associate and visiting lecturer in the Women's Studies in Religion Program

in 2000–1 so that I could work intensively on this project. I am grateful to all these organizations and institutions for their support.

Very special thanks to Sunita Singh, friend and research associate, without whom I could not have conducted the research on which this chapter is based. Special thanks as well to my husband, William C. French, who helped me conduct interviews and collect film footage about Kārtik and Kārtik *pūjā* in autumn of 1998.

3 Normal discrepancies between lunar and solar calendars mean that dates calculated by the solar calendar will not consistently correspond year after year to particular dates calculated by the lunar calendar. In addition, since the lunar year is about ten days shorter than the solar year, an intercalary month is inserted into the lunar year every two to three years to correct the discrepancy. When this happens the month of Kārtik can fall quite a bit later than it does in years that are not intercalated.

4 Skanda Purāṇa 2.4.1–36; Padma Purāṇa 6.88–6.117.

5 For more on Kārtik and auspiciousness, see Pintchman 1999.

6 For more on the *cāturmāsa*, see McGee 1987: 729–31 and 774–8. McGee also notes that the twelfth (*dvādaśī*) and full moon are also acceptable beginnings for the *cāturmāsa*.

7 For more on Govardhan and Govardhan *pūjā*, see Toomey 1994; Vaudeville 1989; and Hawley 1999.

8 For more on Krishna Līlā/*līlā* as both playful activity and dramatic reenactment see Hawley 1981 and Kinsley 1979.

9 This type of religious practice in which devotees assume the identities of the *gopīs* or other divine actors involved in the drama of Krishna's life is in keeping with many other forms of Krishna devotionalism, which also emphasize role playing or play-acting as a vehicle for expressing one's devotion. See Kinsley 1979, especially chapter three (122–204), and Haberman 1988.

10 In John S. Hawley's research on *rāsa-līlā* performances in Braj, the term *rāsa-līlā* is also used to indicate both the *rāsa-līlā* episode itself and the entire *līlā* of Krishna's life enacted in liturgical drama. See Hawley 1981 and 1983, chs. 6 and 7.

11 Kinsley notes an emphasis on bodily appearance in Krishna devotion (1979: 77): "In every Vaiṣṇava-Krishna work, be it devotional, poetic, or theological, Krishna's physical appearance is doted upon. . . . The attitude of the devotee should be like that of the *gopī* who cursed the creator for having given her eyelids that prevented her seeing Krishna constantly."

12 The *seharā* is a type of headpiece that grooms wear at the time of the wedding. The mention of the *seharā* here suggests Krishna's upcoming wedding.

13 *Pītāmbar* is a type of yellow garment associated especially with Krishna.

14 *Pān* is a mixture of betel nut, spices, and other additives rolled up in a betel leaf and chewed for enjoyment. Benares is particularly known for its excellent *pān*.

15 *Bhaju man Govinda, bhaju Gopāl.* This refrain repeats throughout the song. For stylistic reasons, however, I have chosen to omit the repetitions.

16 Krishna here is indicating that a *pujari* (a ritual functionary) residing on the banks of the Ganges River put the *tilak* on his forehead.

17 Chewing *pān* releases a red-colored juice that stains whatever it touches, especially the *pān*-chewer's mouth and teeth.

18 A *dhoti* is a type of cloth that is wound around the hips; one end is passed between the legs and tucked in at the waist. The implication here is that Krishna is wearing his *pītāmbar*, a garment that the song implies is suitable for a groom to wear.

19 These are the months falling from roughly mid-December to mid-February.

References

Bharatīyā, Rūpakiśor and Kārṣṇi Raṇvīr Brahamacārī. 1974. *Bārahoṅ mahīne ke sampūrṇ vrat aur tyauhār*. Mathura: Govardhan Pustakālaya.

Carman, John B. and Frédérique Marglin. 1985. *Purity and Auspiciousness in Indian Society*. Leiden: E. J. Brill.

Eck, Diana L. 1982. *Banares: City of Light*. Princeton, NJ: Princeton University Press.

Gautam, Camanlāl. 1982. *Bārah māsoṅ ke sampūrṇ vrat evaṁ tyauhār*. Baroli: Saṁskṛti Saṅsthān.

Haberman, David L. 1988. *Acting as a Way of Salvation: A Study of Rāgānugā Bhakti Sādhana*. New York: Oxford University Press.

Hawley, John S. 1981. *At Play With Krishna: Pilgrimage Dramas From Brindavan*. Princeton, NJ: Princeton University Press.

——. 1983. *Krishna, the Butter Thief*. Princeton, NJ: Princeton University Press.

——. 1999. "Govardhan *Pūjā*: When Krishna Worships Krishna," *Journal of Vaiṣṇava Studies* 7 (2): 37–63.

Inden, Ronald. 1985. "Kings and Omens," in J. Carmen and F. Marglin, eds., *Purity and Auspiciousness in Indian Society*. Leiden: E. J. Brill.

Kinsley, David. 1979. *The Divine Player: A Study of Krishna Līlā*. Delhi: Motilal Banarsidass.

Marglin, Frédérique. 1985. *Wives of the God-King: The Rituals of the Devadasis of Puri*. Delhi: Oxford University Press.

McGee, Mary. 1987. "Feasting and Fasting: The *Vrata* Tradition and Its Significance for Hindu Women." Th.D. dissertation, Harvard University Divinity School.

Mukherjee, A. C. 1989. *Hindu Fasts and Feasts*, 2nd ed. Gurgaon: Vintage Books.

Narayan, Kirin. 1997. "Sprouting and Uprooting of Saili: The Story of the Sacred Tulsi in Kangra," *Manushi* 102: 30–8.

Narayanan, Vasudha. 1985. The Two Levels of Auspiciousness in Śrivaiṣṇava Ritual and Literature," in J. Carman and F. Marglin, eds., *Purity and Auspiciousness in Indian Society*. Leiden: E. J. Brill.

Pintchman, Tracy. 1999. "Kārttik as a Vaiṣṇava *Mahotsav*: Mythic Themes and the Ocean of Milk," *Journal of Vaiṣṇava Studies* 7 (2): 65–92.

Raghavan, V. 1979. *Festivals, Sports, and Pastimes of India*. Ahmedabad: B. J. Institute of Learning and Research.

Toomey, Paul. 1994. *Food From the Mouth of Krishna: Feasts and Festivities in a North Indian Pilgrimage Centre*. Delhi: Hindustan Publishing Corp.

Underhill, M. M. 1921. *The Hindu Religious Year*. Calcutta: Association Press.

Vālā, Rajanī, ed. n.d. *Hinduoṅ ke varṣbhar ke vrat aur tyauhār*. Delhi: Sumit Publication.

Vaudeville, Charlotte. 1989. "Multiple Approaches to a Living Hindu Myth: The Lord of the Govardhan Hill," in G. Sontheimer and H. Kulke, eds., *Hinduism Reconsidered*. Delhi: Manohar, pp. 105–25.

Walker, Caroline Bynum. 1996. "Women's Stories, Women's Symbols: A Critique of Victor Turner's Theory of Liminality," repr. in Ronald L. Grimes, ed., *Readings in Ritual Studies*. Upper Saddle River, NJ: Prentice Hall, pp. 71–86.

PART III
Systematic Thought

The Indian Sciences 345

Introduction
Frits Staal 346

16 The Science of Language 348
Frits Staal

17 Indian Mathematics 360
Takao Hayashi

18 Calendar, Astrology, and Astronomy 376
Michio Yano

19 The Science of Medicine 393
Dominik Wujastyk

Philosophy and Theology 410

20 Hinduism and the Proper Work of Reason 411
Jonardon Ganeri

21 Restoring "Hindu Theology" as a Category in Indian Intellectual Discourse 447
Francis Clooney, SJ

22 Mantra 478
André Padoux

The Indian Sciences

Introduction

Frits Staal

Europeans discovered China during the Enlightenment and India during the Romantic Period. They are therefore predisposed to find in China science and in India religion. But the Indian scientific tradition is strong and contributions were made to it by Jainas and Buddhists as well as Hindus – a term that may be used by default to denote its etymological equivalent "Indian."

The modern world is totally permeated by science but the concept itself has recently become controversial. Many people, not only readers of books on religion, but also scientists who use the expression "modern science" in other contexts as a kind of yardstick, maintain at the same time that the concept of science reflects a particular culture – "our own." This is not the place to discuss the universality of science, but it can be determined by studying the history of science cross-culturally as Joseph Needham has done in his monumental *Science and Civilization in China*. These 18 volumes demonstrate that the notion of science is universally valid even if particular sciences and the classification of sciences are not. For India, we do not have a single Needham but the literature on the sciences is vast (see our Bibliographies below) and Needham's conclusion is confirmed by the Indian scientific tradition which is as rich as the Chinese. (The Chinese were interested in Buddhism not merely because of religion but because of sciences – from logic to medicine – that are contained in the extensive Buddhist canons; Arab authors were later interested in India, and Europeans in Arabic, primarily for the same reason.)

To understand Indian (or any other ancient or classical) science, we cannot presuppose Euro-American classifications and must give to the notion of science a wide extension, including all forms of systematic knowledge of ourselves and the universe in which we live. From the modern, Anglophone point of view, a striking feature of the Indian scientific tradition is that it makes no principled distinction between "human" and "natural" sciences. This should not surprise us for that distinction is confined to English and reflects a very particular, if not peculiar, cultural development. Its chief source lies in the confused ideas of the nineteenth century German philosopher Wilhelm Dilthey, who was primarily a historian and student of civilization but knew little or nothing of mathematics or physics. After Dilthey had introduced the distinction between natural sciences (*Naturwissenschaften*) and sciences of culture (*Kulturwissenschaften*), C. P. Snow, a physicist and successful author, who did not know anything about human sciences, did the rest. Much discussion followed, including a book on "Literature and Science" by Aldous Huxley, but the upshot has been that modern English, on both sides of the Atlantic, restricts the term *science* to the *natural* or *exact sciences*, and balks at the notion of *human sciences*. In continental Europe or Japan, the term *Wissenschaft* and its various equivalents continue to be used without qualification. Only the latter perspective enables us to study the Indian sciences adequately.

That no distinction between "human" and "natural" sciences was made in India is apparent throughout. It starts with the earliest known Indian classification of sciences which dates from the end of the Vedic period. Anticipated by the *Chāndogya Upaniṣad* (7.1.2) and therefore later than the fifth century BC, six sciences are classified there as auxiliaries or "limbs" of the Veda (*vedāṅga*). The first is *kalpa* "ritual"; the next four deal with language: *sik ṣā* "phonetics and pronunciation, " *nirukta* "etymology," *vyākarana* "grammar" and *chandas* "prosody"; and the last is *jyotiṣā* "astronomy."

Many other Indian sciences are not included in this Vedic classification. Our section does not cover all the sciences of India but we offer what we like to regard as a representative selection in four sections: 1) The Science of Language along with some notions from the Science of Ritual which developed at roughly the same time and in the same milieu and to which it is in some respects similar; 2) Mathematics, which first manifested itself in various disciplines such as ritual, prosody, cosmography, calendar-making, accounting and commerce; and then developed through interaction with horoscopic astrology and spherical astronomy; 3) Astronomy, which started as calendar making and astrology and, after the introduction of Hellenistic science, developed into mathematical astronomy; 4) The Science of Medicine, which offered an empirical system of observations and theories that enabled physicians and patients to maintain positive health, to understand the causes of diseases and, where possible, to provide appropriate therapies.

General Bibliography

Chattopadhyaya, Debiprasad. 1986–96. *History of Science and Technology in Ancient India*. 3 vols. New Delhi: Firma KLM Private.

Pingree, David. 1970–94. *Census of the Exact Sciences in Sanskrit*, Series A, vols. 1–5. Philadelphia: American Philosophical Society.

Rahman, A., ed. 1999. *History of Indian Science, Technology and Culture: AD 1000–1800*. D. P. Chattopadhyaya Imprint: Oxford University Press.

Subbarayyappa, B. V. and S. R. N. Murty. 1988. *Scientific Heritage of India*. Bangalore: The Mythic Society.

CHAPTER 16

The Science of Language

Frits Staal

The assertions and propositions of many Indian sciences are formulated by means of brief expressions called *sūtra*, literally "thread" and often translated as "rule." The earliest *sūtras* are the *Śrauta Sūtras* of the science of ritual (*kalpa*); the most perfect *sūtras* are those of Pāṇini's grammar of Sanskrit. Both sciences include, along with the notion of rule, those of *paribhāṣā* or "metarule," that is, a rule about rules; and of *rule order*, a requirement often formulated by means of a metarule of the form "Rule A precedes Rule B." A simple example from ritual is that the rules about lighting the ritual fire precede those that describe how oblations are made into it.

Some of the early discoveries of ritualists and grammarians anticipate rules or techniques in modern linguistics, logic, mathematics or computer science. An example is the notion of *default*. The ritual *Āpastamba Śrauta Sūtra* (24.1.23–6) singles out default options for oblations, priests, and implements. It specifies that the default *oblation* is clarified butter; the default *priest*, the Adhvaryu; and the default *implement*, the *juhū* ladle. There are degrees of default: when the *juhū* is already used, and no other implement is specified, the oblation is made with the help of the *sruva*. The notion of multiple default echoes or is echoed by Pāṇini's metarule 2.3.1 which deals with *kāraka* or syntactic relations: "(the following rules apply) when it [i.e., the *kāraka*] is not (already) expressed."

Using metarules and rule order, the ritual and grammatical systems express *recursiveness*, that is, they describe an infinite domain of facts with the help of a finite number of rules. Pāṇini's commentator Patañjali compares the expressions of language to rituals of infinite duration and explains (by telling a story about Bṛhaspati, Professor of the Gods, trying to teach Sanskrit to Indra) why an attempt to enumerate all the forms of language can never reach an end. He concludes that "a work containing rules has to be composed."

Rules can only operate on units that are clearly demarcated. This requirement was met in the oral transmission of the Vedas: for Vedic mantras are recited in one breath, the caesura at the end being marked by a pause or the particle *iti*. Vedic Brahmins continue to the present day to recite *mantras* in this manner. Ritualists and reciters generally do not know – and need not know – their *meaning*; but they know their precise *form* along with their accents and modes of recitation which incorporate a good measure of linguistic analysis.

For the Vedas to be orally transmitted, its sentences were analysed "word-for-word." This is not easy because Sanskrit possesses *sandhi* or "junction" (literally "putting together"). Sandhi is common in spoken English but uncommon in writing where, for example: the indefinite article "a" is replaced by "an" when a *vowel* follows so that we have: "*a* book" but "*an* apple." (The rule could be formulated the other way round depending on what is taken to be the default option: "an" is replaced by "a" when a *consonant* follows.) In Sanskrit, *sandhi* is all-pervasive, for example:

> *orvaprā amartyā nivato devyudvataḥ* (*Rigveda* 10.127.2)
>
> "The immortal Goddess has pervaded wide space, depths and heights"

The CONTINUOUS RECITATION of this *mantra* is called *saṃhitā-pāṭha* (the word for "continuous", *saṃhitā*, is related to *sandhi*, and *pāṭha* means "recitation"). The WORD-FOR-WORD ANALYSIS, called *padapāṭha* (from *pada* "word"), is:

> *ā / uru / aprāḥ / amartyā / ni-vataḥ / devī / ut-vataḥ //*
>
> ("per / wide / vaded / immortal / depths / goddess / heights")

This analysis goes deeper than *words*: the "pre-verb" *ā* is separated from the verb *aprāḥ* (in the translation: "per" from "vaded"). Later rules express *sandhi* transformations, e.g.:

ā + uru > *oru*

uru + aprāḥ > *urvaprāḥ*,

where the arrow ">" may be read as: "has to be replaced by", "changes into," or "becomes."

Generalizations of such rules are the *sūtras* with which the linguistic study of language or "grammar" (*vyākaraṇa*) began. I shall subdivide its history into four parts or periods: (1) PADAPĀṬHA or "word-for-word" analysis; (2) PRĀTIŚĀKHYA or treatises that formalize these procedures; (3) PĀṆINI; and (4) LATER SCHOOLS.

1 Padapāṭha

The first system we know of is Śākalya's *Padapāṭha* of the Rigveda but it contains ideas and techniques that may go back to an older period (also preserved in the

Iranian *Avesta*). The Padapāṭha "word-for-word" analysis separated words and other elements, insuring their proper pronunciation, including accents (which I omit from our discussion) and orally fixed the corpus or "text" thus contributing to *canon formation* during the late Vedic period in eastern India (Videha around 600–500 BC).

There are several stages in the development of this analysis which depict a gradual extension or generalization, i.e., scientific progress. At first the separation between words or stems and suffixes was marked by a brief pause in the recitation as in the above example from *Rigveda* 10.127.2 or in *ṛṣi-bhiḥ*, "by the seers." This method was extended to nominal compounds: *saptaputram* > *sapta-putram* "seven sons." It was called *avagraha*, "separation" and we express it by a hyphen though no writing was known in India at this period. Since "separation" was used in each analysis only once, a problem arose: many compounds consist of more than two members.

Śākalya's solution was inspired by semantics: *daśapramatīm* is analyzed as *daśa-pramatīm* "ten protectors" (i.e., fingers), not *daśapra-matīm* which would correspond to the equally meaningless "tenpro-tectors." More complex cases were taken care of with the help of two other methods of analysis: *pragraha*, "marking," e.g., *saptaputram iti*; and *parigraha*, "marking-and-separation," e.g., *saptaputram iti sapta-putram*.

The Padapāṭha is an analysis of the *Saṃhitāpāṭha* or "continuous recitation," but by isolating words from each other, it facilitated the opposite of what was intended: the *forgetting* of single words. Special patterns of repetition or *vikṛtis* were constructed to minimize this risk. The question arises whether these procedures were *prescriptive* or *descriptive* – a relevant question for the historian of science since science is presumably descriptive. How can we find out?

If we represent the words of the Saṃhitāpāṭha as: 1 2 3 4 . . . and the Padapāṭha as: 1 / 2 / 3 / 4 / . . . , the next two *vikṛti* variations may be represented as follows:

> *Kramapāṭha* "Step-by-step recitation": 1 2 / 2 3 / 3 4 / . . .
>
> *Jaṭāpāṭha* "Plaited recitation": 1 2 / 2 1 / 1 2 / 2 3 / 3 2 / 2 3 / . . .

The *Kramapāṭha* does not introduce any new *sandhi* combinations: all its expressions belong to the Vedic Saṃhitā and are *ārṣa*, i.e., they were used by the "seers" (*ṛṣi*); but the *Jaṭāpāṭha* (called after plaited or matted hair) introduces "2 1" and "3 2" which are reversals of the original order: they introduce something that was not in the Veda and therefore "not from the seers" (*anārṣa*).

The *Kramapāṭha* of the first words of our first example of Sanskrit *sandhi* is straightforward:

> *ā* + *uru* / *uru* + *aprāḥ* / *aprāḥ* + *amartyā* > *oru* / *urvaprāḥ* / *aprā amartyā* / . . .

The *Jaṭāpāṭha* is plaited. It begins: *ā* + *uru* + *uru* + *ā* + *ā* + *uru* which becomes: *orvurvoru* – a real tangle. Worse, it contains an element that does not come from the Saṃhitā of the Vedic seers: *uru* + *ā* > *urvā*. However, *urvā* is not an artificial *pre*scription because the reciters *de*scribe the regular form that would result from *uru* followed by *ā* in their ordinary speech, that is, the contemporary Sanskrit they spoke and were familiar with. The form *urvā*, which happens to be absent from the finite corpus of the Vedas, is *grammatical*: it belongs to the infinitely many expressions of language that a native speaker is able to produce. The so-called *anārṣa* forms, then, which do not come from the Vedas, are Sanskrit and *descriptive*. They are, in fact, the precursors of Pāṇini's description of a form of the spoken language that he regarded as exemplary.

2 Prātiśākhya

The practice of the Padapāṭha was formalized in the *Prātiśākhya* compositions, in principle one for each *śākhā* or "Vedic school." The earlier name *pārṣada* suggests that they belonged to a community (*pariṣad*) which orally transmitted and discussed the contents of their *śākhā*. The relationship between *continuous recitation* and *word-for-word* analysis is expressed ambiguously by the Sanskrit sentence *padaprakṛtiḥ saṃhitā* which may be taken to mean: "The Saṃhitā is the base of the Pada" or: "The Saṃhitā has the Pada as its base." The *Prātiśākhya* generally adopt the second interpretation, puzzling from a historical perspective, but signalling a return to the original composers who put words together in their inspired speech just as any user of language puts words together when speaking or writing. This illustrates that Indian grammarians regarded language as *unchanging*, an erroneous assumption which led, however, to the linguistically productive *synchronic* analysis that was advocated in Europe more than two millennia later by Ferdinand de Saussure.

The *Prātiśākhyas* are early because of their structure and function, not because of the forms that survive and may have been influenced by Pāṇini or other grammarians. Their original aim was completeness. Whitney noted on a section of *Taittirīya Prātiśākhya* that he could not discover any case of a retroflex nasal arising in the *Taittirīya Saṃhitā* from a dental nasal in the *Taittirīya Padapāṭha* "that was not duly provided for." Weber used the term "complete" (*vollständig*) and a century later, Surya Kanta called the *Rik-Prātiśākhya* "*entirely* free from all oversights." To be complete is only possible when we deal with a *finite* corpus of *utterances*, (copies of) unique events in space and time such as the extent of a Vedic *śākhā*. A living language consists of *sentences* which cannot be enumerated because they are infinite in number as Patañjali knew. Following Suryakanta, we postulate that the *Prātiśākhya*s originally produced exhaustive listings (*gaṇas*) of examples, showing patterns of linguistic structure, and proceeded only later to generalizations explained by *sūtra* rules. This dichotomy of ideal types does not always survive in the texts as they have come down to us because these have been influenced by Pāṇini or other grammarians.

The *Prātiśākhyas* introduced the metalinguistic use of case-endings, at first the Nominative and Accusative as formulated by the metarule:"the expression 'this (Nom.) that (Acc.)' means 'becoming-that' with reference to the sound which stands nearest to it" *(Rik Prātiśākhya* 1.14); and later simply as: "a change is expressed as an Accusative" (*Vājasaneyi Prātiśākhya* 1.133).

The Padapāṭha discovered the differences between sentences, words, stems, pre- and suffixes, roots, etc., but the Prātiśākhya added an almost perfect analysis of the sounds of language into vowels, consonants, semi-vowels, stops, dentals, velars, nasals, etc. They placed these sounds in a two-dimensional configuration, developed from the square or *varga of* five-by-five series (also called *varga*) of syllables that begin with a stop followed by a short *a*:

ka	*kha*	*ga*	*gha*	*ṅa*	
ca	*cha*	*ja*	*jha*	*ña*	
ṭa	*ṭha*	*ḍa*	*ḍha*	*ṇa*	
ta	*tha*	*da*	*dha*	*na*	
pa	*pha*	*ba*	*bha*	*ma*	(1)

These sounds are marked in our modern transcription by diacritics which we need because our alphabet cannot express all the sounds of Sanskrit. It is not necessary for the reader to know how exactly they are pronounced (but see below); however, we need to know that all the vowels *a* in the syllables of the table are *short* (like the first *a* of *aprāḥ*). A bar above a vowel (like the second *a* of *aprāḥ*) indicates that it is *long*, that is, lasts twice as long as the short.

The 5 × 5 *varga* "square" was extended and completed with fricatives or sibilants, semi-vowels and vowels. One should not look upon the resulting inventory as the *beginning* of linguistics or compare it to our haphazard "ABC's" to which there is no rhyme or reason. Like Mendelejev's Periodic System of Elements, the *varga* system was the result of centuries of analysis. In the course of that development the basic concepts of phonology were discovered and defined.

In the *mental* representation of a such a square, it does not matter what is its spatial orientation and whether *varga* denotes a row or a column. The configuration remains the same when the square is rotated around its diagonal. Proximity and distance are also the same whatever the direction. Since two directions are met with, this shows that these squares were composed and transmitted orally. Renou and Filliozat (1953: 668) had already made a more significant general observation: "One is forced to observe in this context that a Semitic type of writing would have hindered phonetic studies if it had existed at the time in India, because it would have provided a model of analysis of the sounds of language that was practical but not scientific." The Indian science of language, in other words, did not originate *in spite of* the absence of writing but *because* of it.

3 Pāṇini

The "Eight Chapters" (*Aṣṭādhyāyī*) of Pāṇini's grammar of Sanskrit (early to mid fourth century BC) consist of rules, metarules, and defining rules. In the area of phonology, they are sometimes similar or almost the same as some Prātiśākhya rules, e.g., the definition of "homorganic":

> (Homorganic is) having the same place, producing organ, and effort of articulation in the mouth. (2)

Here "place" refers to "throat," "palate," "teeth," etc., "producing organ" means "tip of the tongue," "rolling back the tip of the tongue," "tip of the teeth," "middle of the jaw," etc. "Effort of articulation" refers to "closed," "semi-closed," "open," etc. – all Prātiśākhya concepts. Pāṇini (or earlier grammarians eclipsed by him) added to the study of phonology that of morphology, syntax and semantics. Pāṇini then freed himself from the notion of a finite corpus like that of the Vedic mantras, and began to treat Sanskrit as a creative and infinite *energeia* in the sense in which that Greek concept is now associated with von Humboldt or Chomsky.

Pāṇini started his grammar with a new classification of sounds, the result of an at first sight surprising overhaul of the Prātiśākhya classification. He replaced the two-dimensional *varga* system by a linear sequence, later called the *Śivasūtra:*

> a i u Ṇ / ṛ ḷ K / e o Ṅ / ai au C /ha ya va ra Ṭ / la Ṇ / ña ma ṅa ṇa na M / jha bha Ñ / gha ḍha dha Ṣ / ja ba ga ḍa da Ś / kha pha cha ṭha tha ca ṭa ta V / ka pa Y / śa ṣa sa R / ha L // (3)

The sounds I have expressed here by small letters are the sounds of the Sanskrit object-language. They consist of vowels and consonants (including semivowels), the latter followed by a short *a*. Capitals are part of the metalanguage: they refer to metalinguistic markers to which I will return. The five vowels with which (3) starts may be long or short (*ṛ* and *ḷ* in their short form sound approximately like *ry* in "crystal" and *li* in "Clinton").

Pāṇini used short vowels (*a*, etc.) to refer to both short and long vowels (*a* and *ā*, etc.) because of an important generalization that he would otherwise miss. It happens to be a fact about Sanskrit (and some other languages) that many rules of grammar that apply to vowels, apply to them whether they are long or short. For example, *a* + *a*, *a* + *ā*, *ā* + *a* and *ā* + *ā*, all become long *ā* (e.g., *atra* + *agni* > *atrāgni* "here, Agni!", *vā* + *agni* > *vāgni* "or Agni," etc.).

To express this by four rules would not only be unwieldy; it would be unnatural for it would fail to express a generalization that captures a feature of the language. Pāṇini, therefore, uses *in his metalanguage* a single vowel to express the short and long forms of *the object language.* This enables him to express by a single rule of the form "*a* + *a* > *ā*", all four combinations of long and short. He generalizes further, because this lenghtening applies to the other vowels: e.g., the *i* in *dadhi* + *indra* > *dadhīndra* ("milk, Indra!"). We shall see in a moment how he expressed these facts.

What happens to grammatical rules that apply to a short or long vowel only? Pāṇini marks them with *T* in accordance with metarule (4):

A vowel followed by *T* denotes its own length. (4)

This means: "aT" denotes *a*, "āT" denotes *ā*, "uT" denotes *u*, etc.

Kātyāyana, another early grammarian, objected to (4), that "long" and "short" are merely habits of speech: some people speak fast and others slow. Patañjali retorted that this objection pertains to *dhvani*, "speech sound," not to the subject matter of linguistics which is *sphoṭa*, the meaningful unit of expression. Patañjali is right because, in Sanskrit, as in many other languages, the difference between short and long may affect meaning. Patañjali's concept of *sphoṭa* is concerned with *competence* of the language; speakers' habits such as rapid or slow speech belong to the psychological domain of *performance*. This is one of several cases where rules of Pāṇini's grammar have logical, psychological, or philosophical implications.

We are ready to return to the metalinguistic "indicatory markers" indicated by the capitals "Ṇ," "K," "Ṅ," etc. in (3). Their use is explained by metarule (5):

An initial sound joined to a final (indicatory) sound (denotes the intervening sounds as well). (5)

Thus, aṆ denotes "*a i u*," aK denotes "*a i u ṛ ḷ*," iK denotes "*i u ṛ ḷ*," yaṆ denotes "*ya va ra la*," and aC denotes vowels. The expression aṆ may denote "*a i u*" or the class of all vowels and semivowels because the indicatory marker "Ṇ" occurs twice as the reader will have noted. I shall not discuss whether this is a flaw or a particular merit of the system but Patañjali and other commentators pay plenty of attention to such problems. They do not assume that Pāṇini was perfect and reject what he said if they find that it contradicts the data or does not work.

Pāṇini needs the notations aṆ, aK, yaṆ etc. as elements of his artificial language, because phonology requires many combinations of sounds that cannot be simply or naturally expressed in the *varga* system of (1) or in any form of (3) without metalinguistic markers. The notations of (5) enable him to express how two vowels combine into a single long one as follows:

aK is lengthened when followed by a homorganic vowel. (6)

Another rule is needed to express the fact that the vowels *i*, *u*, *ṛ* and *ḷ* are replaced by the semivowels *y*, *v*, *r* and *l*, respectively, when followed by a heterorganic (i.e., nonhomorganic) vowel: e.g., *dadhi* + *atra* > *dadhyatra* ("milk here!"), *madhu* + *atra* > *madhvatra* ("honey here!"), etc. (compare the contrast in English between *penniless* and *penny arcade*). Using (5), Pāṇini's first step may have been to formulate this fact as: "iK is replaced by yaṆ when a heterorganic aC follows." But "heterorganic" is omitted by default because (5) already took care of the homorganic cases.

Why does *dadhi* + *atra* becomes *dadhyatra* and not **dadhvatra*? I have expressed it by using the English term "respectively." Pāṇini uses a metarule:

Reference to elements of the same number is in the same order. (7)

Therefore, $i > y$, $u > v$, etc., but not, e.g., $i > v$. The rule we need may now be expressed as:

iK is replaced by yaṆ when aC follows. (8)

Expressions such as these are extremely common. Most phonological rules, and many others, are of the form:

After A, in the place of B, substitute C, when D follows. (9)

Pāṇini expresses this formula and captures this generalization about language by introducing an artificial expression that makes metalinguistic use of the cases of the Sanskrit of his object language, a method inspired by Sanskrit usage and introduced by the Prātiśākhyas as we have seen. Pāṇini's starting point is the subject of the rule, i.e., the element which is substituted and therefore expressed by the Nominative Case. The metalinguistic uses of three other Cases are laid down by three metarules which refer to the Genitive, Locative, and Ablative Cases:

> The Genitive case ending is used for that in the place of which (something is substituted);
>
> when something is referred to by the Locative ending, (the substitute appears) in the place of the preceding element;
>
> when (something is referred to) by the Ablative ending, (the substitute appears in the place) of the following. (10)

Applying these rules, Pāṇini formulates (9) as:

> A + Ablative ending, B + Genitive ending, C + Nominative ending, D + Locative ending. (11)

Applying this to the sandhi rule we have been discussing, where there is no restriction on the left so that there is no need for the Ablative ending, we arrive at:

iK + Genitive, yaṆ + Nominative, aC + Locative,

which in Sanskrit becomes:

ikaḥ yaṇ aci

to which sandhi is applied, producing the actual rule as it occurs in Pāṇini's grammar:

iko yaṇ aci. (12)

As it happens, a language consists of sentences, not just of words. From the perspective of the history of science, therefore, Pāṇini's step is momentous because it resulted not just in the creation of artificial expressions but of an artificial metalanguage. Rule (12) is not merely an artificial expression but an element of an artificial language like the artificial languages of algebra that came into being much later through Arab and European efforts. Pāṇini demonstrates in passing that artificial languages need not be written.

Patañjali refers to Pāṇini's first step of generalization by declaring: "this science pertains to all the Vedas" or "this science is a Parṣad = Prātiśākhya for all the Vedas" (*sarvavedapāriṣadam idam śāstram*). Actually, Pāṇini's Vedic rules are haphazard and incomplete while his rules for the spoken language are almost perfect, if not in syntax, at least in phonology and morphology. Claims like these sound like cheap commercials but are substantiated by comparing his grammar with linguistic usage as we know it. It is sometimes said that "Pāṇini was, of course, aided in his analysis by the extraordinary clarity of the Sanskrit language," but John Brough observed: "We are apt to overlook the possibility that this structure might not have seemed so clear and obvious to us if Pāṇini had not analysed it for us."

The perfection of Pāṇini's grammar is not only due to its high degree of formalization. His science is as empirical as it is formal. The *locus classicus* on the importance of empirical description is the laconic expression *lokataḥ* "on account of (the usage) of the people." "The people" are the native speakers as illustrated by Patañjali: "He who needs a pot for some purpose goes to the house of a potter and says: 'You make a pot. I need a pot for some purpose.' No one who wants to use words goes to the house of a grammarian and says: 'You make words. I want to use them.' (On the contrary,) having brought something to mind, without further ado, he uses words."

4 Later Schools

Patañjali's "Great Commentary" of around 150 BC seems to have been followed by a lull of several centuries. In the fifth century AD, the great grammatical philosopher Bhartṛhari broke the silence by composing an original subcommentary on Patañjali. By that time, Jainas and Buddhists had also begun to use Sanskrit for their canonic writings and this resulted in several new grammars, at first practical manuals, but increasingly systematical and scientific treatises. Devanandin and Candragomin, Jaina and Buddhist grammarians, respectively, also of the fifth century, adopted Pāṇini's system and metalanguage and sought to simplify or abbreviate his expressions, sometimes introducing innovations. Candragomin refers to Middle-Indic forms that had been used in earlier Buddhist writings as *ārṣa*, "belonging to the seers," just as the Prātiśākhya authors had done with respect to Vedic *mantras*.

A later development of Sanskrit grammar benefited from the "new logic" (*navya nyāya*) that had originated in Bengal with Gangeśopādhyāya (thirteenth century). This development continued, at least, through the eighteenth century when Nāgojī Bhaṭṭa wrote a treatise on Pāṇini's metarules and philosophical works in which he combines Bhartṛhari with the Indian philosophy of language – a discipline not included in the present sketch.

Grammatical concepts and techniques from the Sanskrit tradition influenced the early (second century BC?) grammar of Tamil *Tolkāppiyam* which is, in other respects, very different in outlook and structure. Sanskrit models were followed more closely in later Dravidian grammars as well as grammars of Persian, Marathi, and other languages. Tibetan grammars were inspired by the Sanskrit tradition but it took almost 500 years (from the ninth to the fourteenth century AD) before they fully captured the power and sophistication of the Indian originals.

The Indian grammatical tradition influenced not only a few grammarians but much of Asian civilization. We have seen that the first scientific classification of the sounds of language, that of the *varga* sysem of the Prātiśākhyas, was due to an *oral* analysis. It is not surprising that this classification was taken into account when the first Indian scripts evolved, but it went much further and served, for millennia to come, as a sound foundation for most of the numerous scripts and writing systems of south, southeast and east Asia – from Kharosthi, Khotanese, Tibetan, Nepali, and all the modern scripts of India (except the Urdu/Persian) to Sinhalese, Burmese, Khmer, Thai, Javanese, and Balinese. In south and southeast Asia, the *shapes* of earlier Indian syllables inspired some of these inventions, but it is the *system* of classification that was of enduring significance wherever it became known. In east Asia, the bastion of Chinese characters could not adapt it; but in Japan it led to the creation of the *hiragana* and *katakana* syllabaries during the Heian period (794–1185), and in Korea it inspired the world's most perfect script, *han'gul*, developed in 1444 by a committee of scholars appointed by the emperor Sejong. All these Asian scripts are a far cry from the haphazard jumble of the "ABC" and the countless spelling problems that result from it in English and other modern languages that use the alphabet.

The Indian Science of Language influenced modern linguistics primarily through Franz Bopp (1791–1867) who was inspired by the Sanskrit grammar of Charles Wilkins of 1807, based in turn upon Pāṇini. But Bopp did not use *rules* and the celebrated nineteenth-century sound laws were discovered by others. That rules could be formal had been discovered by Aristotle but remained confined to logic. The equations of algebra, another formal science from Asia, were restricted to mathematics and the natural sciences. That linguistics could be a formal science was perceived, or at least envisaged, by de Saussure, who predicted in 1894, that the expressions of linguistics "will be algebraic or will not be." Leonard Bloomfield was familiar with Pāṇini and used ordered rules once (*Menomini Morphonemics* of 1939). Formal rules were used extensively by Noam Chomsky and his school, and finally replaced by more abstract principles.

In classical India, "the arrangement of forms and speculation on forms reveal most clearly their content – they ultimately are the content itself." I translate this phrase from Charles Malamoud who adopted it from Louis Renou, the foremost twentieth-century scholar of ancient Indian civilization. Attention to form is a characteristic of all science and even the Mīmāṃsā system of ritual philosophy declares: "when a visible result is possible, it is improper to postulate an invisible one" (*Mīmāṃsā Paribhāṣā*).

To the modern age, the most important contribution of the Sanskrit grammatical tradition is its construction of linguistics as a formal science. The study of language, the most characteristic feature of the human animal, is as formal as that of the so-called natural sciences. The need of an artificial, formal language shows that natural language is unable to express adequately the structures not only of the nonhuman universe but also those of human language itself. When linguistics is an exact science, the distinction between human and natural sciences falls to the ground and it becomes far-fetched to assert that humans stand isolated in the universe – a postulate that has never been popular in India.

Bibliography

Boehtlingk, Otto. 1887. *Pāṇinis' Grammatik*. Leipzig. Reprint Hildesheim 1964.

Brough, John. 1951. "Theories of General Linguistics in the Sanskrit Grammarians," *Transactions of the Philological Society*. London: 27–46. Reprinted in Staal 1972: 402–14.

Cardona, George. 1976. *Pāṇini: A Survey of Research*. The Hague: Mouton. Reprint (1980) Delhi: Motilal Banarsidass.

Deshpande, Madhav M. 1997. *Śaunakīyā Caturādhyāyikā*. Cambridge and London: Harvard University Press.

Faddegon, Barend. 1926. "The Catalogue of Sciences in the *Chāndogya-Upaniṣad*," *Acta Orientalia* 4: 42–54.

Jha, V. N. 1976. "Stages in the Composition of the Ṛgveda-Prātiśākhya," *Bulletin of the Deccan College Research Institute* 35: 47–50; also in Jha 1987: 101–5.

——. 1987. *Studies in the Padapāṭhas and Vedic Philology*. Delhi: Pratibha Prakashan.

Joseph, George Gheverghese. 1990. *The Crest of the Peacock: Non-European Roots of Mathematics*. London: Penguin Books.

Joshi, S. D. and Roodbergen, J. A. F. 1986. *Patañjali's Vyākaraṇa-Mahābhāṣya: Paspaśāhnika*. Pune: University of Poona.

Kielhorn, Franz. 1876. *Kātyāyana and Patañjali: Their Relation to Each Other and to Pāṇini*. Bombay: The Educational Society. Reprint 1965: Osnabruck: Otto Zeller.

Kiparsky, Paul. 1979. *Pāṇini as a Variationist*. Cambridge, London, Pune: MIT/Poona University Press.

Renou, Louis. 1960. "La forme et l'arrangement interne des Prātiśākhya," *Journal asiatique* 248: 1–40.

——. 1963. "Sur le genre du sūtra dans la litterature sanskrite," *Journal asiatique* 251: 165–216.
——. 1969. "Pāṇini," *Current Trends in Linguistics* 5: 481–98.
——. 1978. *L'Inde fondamentale: Etudes d'indianisme réunies et présentées par Charles Malamoud*. Paris: Hermann.
—— and Filliozat, Jean. 1953. *L'Inde classique: Manuel des études indiennes*, vol. II, Paris: Imprimerie Nationale/Hanoi: Ecole Française d'Extrême Orient.
Ruegg, D. S. 1959. *Contributions à l'histoire de la philosophie linguistique indienne*. Paris: E. de Boccard.
Scharfe, Hartmut. 1977. *Grammatical Literature*. Wiesbaden: Otto Harrassowitz.
Staal, Frits (ed.). 1972. *A Reader on the Sanskrit Grammarians*. Cambridge, MA: MIT.
——. 1988. *Universals: Studies in Indian Logic and Linguistics*. Chicago and London: University of Chicago Press.
——. 1989. "The Independence of Rationality from Literacy," *European Journal of Sociology* 30: 301–10.
——. 1989, 1993. *Rules Without Meaning: Ritual, Mantras and the Human Sciences*. New York etc.: Peter Lang.
——. 1992. "Sūtra," in Vatsyayan, ed., 303–14.
——. 1993, 1994. *Concepts of Science in Europe and Asia*. Leiden: International Institute of Asian Studies.
——. 1995. "The Sanskrit of Science," *Journal of Indian Philosophy* 23: 73–127.
——. 2000. "Vyākaraṇa and Śulba in the Light of Newton's Lesson," in R. Tsuchida and A. Wezler, eds., *Volume in Honour of Professor Minoru Hara*. Reinbek.
Surya Kanta. 1968. *Atharvaprātiśākhya*. Delhi: Mehar Chand Lachman Das.
——. 1970. *Ṛktantra*. Delhi: Mehar Chand Lachman Das.
Thieme, Paul. 1935. *Pāṇini and the Veda: Studies in the Early History of Linguistic Science in India*. Allahabad: Globe Press.
Vatsyayan, Kapila (ed.). 1992. *A Lexicon of Fundamental Concepts in the Indian Arts*. New Delhi: Indira Gandhi National Centre for the Arts.
Verhagen, Pieter C. 1996. "Tibetan Expertise in Sanskrit Grammar – A Case Study: Grammatical Analysis of the Term *pratītiya-samutpāda*," *The Journal of the Tibet Society* 8: 21–48.
Weber, Albrecht. 1873. "Ueber den padapāṭha der Taittirīya-Saṃhitā," *Indische Studien* 13: 1–128.
Wezler, Albrecht. 1972. "Marginalien zu Pāṇini's Aṣṭādhyāyī I: *sthānin*," *Zeitschrift für vergleichende Sprachforschung* 86: 7–20.
Whitney, William D. 1871. "The Taittirīya-Prātiçākhya with its Commentary, the Tribhāshyaratna," *Journal of the American Oriental Society* 9: 1–469.
Witzel, Michael. 1997. "The Development of the Vedic Canon and its Schools: The Social and Political Milieu," in Witzel, ed., *Inside the Texts/Beyond the Texts: New Approaches to the Study of the Vedas*. Cambridge: Harvard University Press.
Wujastyk, Dominik. 1993. *Metarules of Pāṇinian Grammar*, 2 vols. Groningen: Egbert Forsten.

CHAPTER 17

Indian Mathematics

Takao Hayashi

I Vedic Mathematics

I.1 Vedas

Since the *Vedas* are religious texts produced by poets, we cannot expect in them enough information for systematically describing the mathematical knowledge of those times. We can only gather scattered terms for whole numbers, for basic fractions, and for simple geometric figures.

The *Ṛgveda* contains a number of numerical expressions. The Vedic poets were particularly fond of three and seven as holy numbers, and often used their multiples such as 3×7, 33 ($= 3 \times 11$), 3×50, 3×60, 3×70, $3 \times 7 \times 70$, and 333 ($= 3 \times 111$). It has been argued that the number of gods, 3339, mentioned in *Ṛgveda* 3.3.9, is the sum of three numbers, namely, 33, 303, and 3003. Although it has not been proved that the Vedic Indians had a place-value notation of numbers, this summation itself must have not been difficult for them since their numeration system was basically decimal. They used the words *eka*, *daśa*, *śata*, *sahasra*, and *ayuta*, for 1, 10, 10^2, 10^3, and 10^4. For multiples of 10^3 and of 10^4 they often used expressions based respectively on 10^2 and on 10^3 as well; for example, $2 \times 10^3 = 20$ (*víṃśati*) $\times 10^2$ (*śata*), $3 \times 10^4 = 30$ (*triṃśat*) $\times 10^3$ (*sahasra*), etc. The words for "hundred" and "thousand" are sometimes employed in the sense of "a number of." Thus, Indra is said to have destroyed a hundred old fortresses of Śambara and slain a hundred thousand (*śataṃ sahasraṃ*) brave men of Varcin (ibid. 2.14.6). The number sixty seems to have had a certain weight with the Vedic poets since we come across expressions like "a thousand and sixty (1060) cows" (ibid. 1.126.3), "sixty thousand and ninety-nine (60099) kings" (*ibid.* 1.53.9), and "sixty thousand *ayuta* ($60 \times 10^3 \times 10^4 = 6 \times 10^8$) of horses" (*ibid.* 8.46.22), but its significance is not known.

There are also references in the *Ṛgveda* to the basic unit-fractions 1/2 (*ardha* or "a half"), 1/4 (*pāda* or "a foot," from the 4 "feet" of a quadruped), 1/8 (*śapha* or "a hoof," from the 8 "hooves" of a cow), and 1/16 (*kalā* or "a digit," from the 16 "digits" of the moon).

The Vedic people seem not to have felt much difficulty in performing the addition, subtraction, and, perhaps, multiplication of whole numbers, but division appears to have troubled them when it left a remainder, for only Indra and Viṣṇu are said to have succeeded in dividing a thousand cows into three. According to the *Śatapathabrāhmaṇa* (3.3.1.13, 4.5.8.1), they correctly obtained 333 for the quotient with the remainder 1. This story is believed to be implicitly alluded to already in *Ṛgveda* 6.69.8.

By the time of, at latest, the *Yajurvedasaṃhitā*, the Indians had extended their list of the names of powers of ten up to 10^{12}. In *Vājasaneyisaṃhitā* 17.2, they are used for counting the numbers of bricks. In *Taittirīyasaṃhitā* 7.2.11–20, they constitute part of the sacrificial formulas (*mantras*) to be uttered on the occasion of an *annahoma* or "food-oblation rite," which is performed at a certain stage in the *aśvamedha* or "horse-sacrifice rite." In the *annahoma*, a priest makes a series of oblations of ghee, honey, rice, barleycorns, etc. to the fire (*agni*) called *āhavanīya* through the night until sunrise, while uttering *mantras* in which a unit formula, "the dative case of a numeral + *svāhā* (hail to)," is repeated.

The first *mantra* reads: "Hail to one, hail to two, hail to three, . . . , hail to nineteen, hail to twenty, hail to twenty-nine, hail to thirty-nine, . . . , hail to ninety-nine, hail to one hundred, hail to two hundred, hail to all (*sarva*)." The numbers that actually occur in this *mantra* are:

1, 2, 3, 4, 5, 6, 7, 8, 9, 10, 11, 12, 13, 14, 15, 16, 17, 18, 19, 20, 29,
39, 49, 59, 69, 79, 89, 99, 100, 200;

but this seems to be an abbreviation of a series of natural numbers from 1 to 200 or more. According to the traditional interpretation, "one" represents Prajāpati ("lord of creatures" or creator), the rest being all things in the world which have evolved from him. The *mantras* that follow consist of arithmetical progressions such as odd numbers, even numbers, multiples of 4, etc., some of which are accompanied by an additional number either at the end or at the beginning. Then comes the last *mantra*, which contains the decimal names from *śata* (10^2) to *parārdha* (10^{12}): "Hail to *śata*, hail to *sahasra*, hail to *ayuta*, . . . , hail to *parārdha*, hail to the dawn (*uṣas*), hail to the twilight (*vyuṣṭi*), hail to the one which is going to rise (*udeṣyat*), hail to the one which is rising (*udyat*), hail to the one which has just risen (*udita*), hail to the heaven (*svarga*), hail to the world (*loka*), hail to all." The four phrases beginning with "hail to the dawn" are uttered immediately before the sunrise, and the four beginning with "hail to the one which has just risen" immediately after that. Some regard the last seven terms, *uṣas* to *loka*, as the names of 10^{13} to 10^{19}, but there is no support for this conjecture.

It has been conjectured that zero is indicated by the word *kṣudra* (lit. petty, trifling) in the *Atharvaveda* (19.22.6 = 19.23.21), and a negative number by *anṛca* (lit. without a hymn) (*ibid.* 19.23.22). But this conjecture still awaits a proof.

It is probable that the Pythagorean Theorem (the sum of the areas of the squares on the two sides of a right-angled triangle is equal to that on its hypotenuse), which was explicitly stated and utilized by the authors of the *Śulbasūtras*, had already been known at latest in the times of the Brāhmaṇas.

The *Śatapathabrāhmaṇa* (10.2.3.18) speaks of successive increases of the areas of the fire altars (*agni*): the basic fire altar, called the "seven-fold *agni*," has the area of seven and one half square *puruṣas* (one *puruṣa* or "man" is the height of the sacrificer with his hands stretched upwards), and it is increased, in subsequent rites performed by the same sacrificer, by one square *puruṣa* each time up to the "one hundread and one-fold *agni*." The augmentation of area was made most probably by means of the Pythagorean Theorem.

The inverse case of the Pythagorean Theorem (if the sum of the areas of the squares on two sides of a triangle is equal to that on the remaining side, then the first two sides contain a right angle) is also possibly referred to in the *Śatapathabrāhmaṇa*.

The *Vājasaneyisaṃhitā* (30.20) and the *Taittirīyabrāhmaṇa* (3.4.15) include the word *gaṇaka* ("a calculator") in their lists of people to be sacrificed on the occasion of the *puruṣa-medha* ("human-sacrifice rite"). The *gaṇaka* in the former list, who is sacrificed for the divinity of a sea animal, is usually taken to be an astrologer, but this interpretation seems not to be decisive at all since an astrologer called *nakṣatradarśa* ("a star-gazer"), who is sacrificed for the divinity of wisdom, is listed prior to it in the same list (30.10). The *gaṇaka* in the latter list, who is sacrificed together with a *vīṇā* player for the divinity of songs, is presumably related with music.

I.2 Śulbasūtras

Śulbasūtras, which constitute part of, or appendices to, the *Śrautasūtras*, are basically practical manuals meant for the preparation of the sites of śrauta rituals, the main topic being the construction of fire altars with burned bricks. A sacrificer (*yajamāna*) had to strictly follow the regulations affecting the sizes and shapes of the sites and altars, because otherwise he was supposed to lose the merit to be attained through the specific ritual he was performing. Hence follows the connection between rituals and geometry. But it would be wrong to suppose only practical geometry like the measurement of land in the *Śulbasūtras*. The geometry conceived by the śulba mathematicians already has theoretical aspects as will be seen below.

The two oldest *Śulbasūtras*, those of Āpastamba and Baudhāyana, can be each divided into two parts. The first part treats geometry in general terms. The topics dealt with in this geometry are certainly related to the construction of ritual sites, but it contains few words which indicate rituals. The second part treats the construction of ritual sites including various altars. It is mostly devoted to the description of various fire-altars (*agni*) to be employed in the *agni-cayana* ("fire-altar-construction rite"). For the construction of a standard *agni*, the following requirements had to be satisfied: (1) an *agni* consists of five layers of 200 bricks each with the total height equal to the knee-height of the sacrificer; (2) the odd-numbered and the even-numbered layers each have one and the same arrangement of bricks, and no brick should coincide with the one above or below it; and (3) an *agni* should occupy an area of seven and one half square *puruṣas*. The area of an *agni* was increased by one square *puruṣa* each time the same rite was repeated by the same sacrificer.

The topics dealt with in the geometric portion of the *Śulbasūtras* of Āpastamba (abbr. A) and Baudhāyana (B) are as follows.

Linear measures (B 1.3–21; A provides them in later chapters at need).
Construction of geometric figures (A 1.2–3, 1.7–2.3; B 1.22–44, 46–7).
Relationships between the diagonal and the side of a rectangle (oblong and square).

Pythagorean Theorem (A 1.4–5, B 1.45, 48–9).
Computation of the diagonal of a square (A 1.6, B 1.61–2).

Sum and difference of two squares (A 2.4–6, B 1.50–1).
Equi-area transformation of geometric figures (A 2.7, 3.1–3, cf. 12.5, 12.9, 15.9; B 1.52–60).
Relationship between the area and the side of a square (A 3.4–10).

The tools used for drawing figures in the *Śulbasūtras* are a rope called *rajju* or *śulba* and pegs or posts called *śaṅku*. A bamboo rod is sometimes used instead of a rope. By means of these tools, one can draw a straight line, cut out a line segment having any desired length, and draw a circle or an arc with any desired radius.

No specific rules are given for the drawing of a line, a circle, and an arc; these can be easily obtained by a rope and pegs. The main problem for the śulba geometers, who were required to construct geometric figures like a square, a rectangle, and a trapezium, was how to draw a line orthogonal to, or parallel to, a given line.

The most important mathematical motif of the *Śulbasūtras* is the area. The core of the Śulba mathematics is concerned with the religious requirement that one should construct altars in varoius shapes with a given area, a requirement which seems to have originated from agriculture where a harvest greatly depends on the area of the land (*bhū* or *bhūmi*).

The *Śulbasūtras* contain the earliest extant verbal expression of the Pythagorean Theorem in the world, although it had already been known to the Old Babylonians. It is stated in exactly the same words by Āpastamba (1.4), Baudhāyana (1.48) and Kātyāyana (2.7): "The diagonal rope (*akṣṇayā-rajju*) of an oblong produces both which the flank (*pārśvamānī*) and the horizontal (*tiryaṅmānī*) ⟨ropes⟩ produce separately." What "the ropes produce" are not explicitly mentioned, but are no doubt the square areas constructed on them.

Highlights of the śulba mathematics are transformations of geometric figures with their areas kept unchanged. This theme was originally related with the practical requirement of drawing altars in various shapes with a given area, but the Śulba makers seem to have taken a step forward and tried to treat the theme with a theoretical perspective in mind.

Baudhāyana deals with seven transformations. Five out of them are concerned with transformations from a square to a circle, a rectangle, an isosceles trapezium, an isosceles triangle, and a rhombus, while the other two are those from a rectangle and a circle to a square. All these, except the last one, can be put into the following scheme for constructing various figures.

a rectangle → a square → a circle, etc.

This scheme consists of three steps. Given an area A:

1 Construct a rectangle having the area A.
2 Transform it into a square having the area A.
3 Transform it into the desired figure (a circle, etc.) having the area A.

For example, in order to draw a circle with the area A, one first constructs a rectangle with the two sides a and A/a for any rational number a, and then transforms the rectangle into a square and the square obtained into a circle. In fact, for the śulba mathematicians, this was the most natural way of constructing a circle with a given area, since they did not know the formula, $A = \pi r^2$, from which we would compute r to draw a circle with the radius r.

An apparent gap between śulba mathematics and later Indian mathematics used to puzzle scholars, and this made some suppose Western influence upon the latter. But now we know some links between the two.

The word, *karaṇī*, used in later mathematics to denote a square number and the square root of a number, originated from its use in the *Śulbasūtras*.

In order to draw a line measured by $\sqrt{n}$, Brahmagupta constructs an isosceles triangle, whose base and two sides are measured respectively by $(n/m - m)$ and by $(n/m + m)/2$, where m is any optional number. Its perpendicular is the line to be obtained (*Brāhmasphuṭasiddhānta* 18.37). This is a generalization of Kātyāyana's rule (6.7), where $m = 1$.

The square nature or an indeterminate equation of the second degree of the type, $Px^2 + t = y^2$, which was to be investigated in detail by Brahmagupta and others, presumably has its origin in the śulba mathematicians' investigation of the diagonal of a square or $\sqrt{2}$.

Two root-approximation formulas used in Jaina works and in the *Bakhshālī Manuscript*, seem to have been obtained by algebraically (or numerically) interpreting *Śulbasūtras* geometric rules for the rectangle-squaring transformation.

Āryabhaṭa I's terminology for series, *citi*, etc., too, is probably related to the *Śulbasūtras*, whose main theme was the piling (*citi*) of bricks for Vedic altars.

II Gaṇita (Mathematics)

II.1 Up to the 5th century – prologue

It is but natural that one who calculates most in a society is called a calculator. Before the introduction and spread of horoscopic astrology and mathematical astronomy to the Indian subcontinent, the occupation that, in Indian society, required calculations most seems to have been that of the accountant, since he was called either *gaṇaka* or *saṃkhyāyaka*, both meaning "a calculator." In the *Mahābhārata* (2.5.62) the sage Nārada recommends to the king Yudhiṣṭhira that he make his calculator (*gaṇaka*) and scribe (*lekhaka*) report to him the revenue and expenditure every morning. Kauṭilya's *Arthaśāstra* (1.19.9), too, refers to the same daily task of a king. The salary of a king's calculator and scribe is 500 *paṇas* each, while the highest salary, 48,000 *paṇas*, is paid to a minister, a prince, etc., and the lowest, 60 *paṇas*, to a servant who takes care of animals (*ibid.* 5.3.3–17). The superintendents of governmental departments are said to be assisted by five persons, namely, calculators (*saṃkhyāyakas*), scribes (*lekhakas*), inspectors of coins (*rūpa-darśakas*), receivers of balances (*nīvī-grāhakas*), and supervisors (*uttarādhyakṣas*) (ibid. 2.9.28). According to a later law book, the *Bṛhaspatismṛti* (1.1.81–90), a court consists of ten elements including a *gaṇaka*, who calculates money and assets, and a *lekhaka*, who writes sentences.

The 107th story, *Gaṇakamoggallānasutta*, of the *Majjhimanikāya* narrates a discourse of the Buddha with a brāhmaṇa *gaṇaka* named Moggallāna, from which we know: (1) that a *gaṇaka* lived on calculation (*gaṇanā*), (2) that a *gaṇaka* took live-in pupils (*antevāsins*) and taught them calculation (*saṅkhāna*), and (3) that a *gaṇaka* first taught his pupils to count from one to one hundred. The *gaṇanā* and the *saṅkhāna* in this story seem to mean respectively calculation (or mathematics) in general and a relatively elementary skill of computation beginning with the counting of numbers.

According to the *Arthaśāstra* (1.2–5), a prince learns *lipi* (writing) and *saṃkhyāna* after his hairdressing rite, and then, after his initiation rite, learns the four disciplines (*vidyās*), namely, philosophy, the *Vedas* with related fields, practical knowledge like agriculture and commerce, and politics. This *saṃkhyāna* is perhaps as elementary as the *saṅkhāna* of Moggallāna, although a calculator in general is called not a *gaṇaka* but a *saṃkhyāyaka* in the *Arthaśāstra*.

In the *Mahābhārata* (3.70), the king Ṛtuparṇa is proud of his ability in *saṃkhyāna* in addition to that in dice, when he correctly estimates, without counting, the number of nuts, 2095, on two branches of a Vibhītaka tree (*Terminalia bellerica*). This *saṃkhyāna*, therefore, contains a sort of statistical estimate of the quantities of nuts, crops, etc. The *saṅkhāna* of the Jaina canonical text, *Ṭhāṇaṃga*

(747), consists of ten topics, which presumably cover the entire mathematics known to the Indians of those days. They are: basic computation (*parikamma*), procedure or applied mathematics (*vavahāra*), rope (*rajju*), quantity (*rāsi*), reduction of fractions (*kalāsavanna*), "as many as" (*jāvaṃtāvati*), square (*vagga*), cube (*ghana*), square of square (*vaggavagga*), and choice (*vikappa*, combinatorics). The Jainas played an important role in the making of Indian mathematics.

It was, however, neither *gaṇanā* nor *saṃkhyāna* but *gaṇita* that was used later as the most general term for mathematical science. Āryabhaṭa I, in the first verse of his *Āryabhaṭīya* (AD 499 or a little later), enumerates the three subjects to be dealt with in its subsequent chapters, namely, *gaṇita*, *kāla-kriyā* (time-reckoning), and *gola* (spherics).

The Vedic numerals continued to be used in later Hindu society as well, while the Buddhists and the Jainas each developed their own systems of numerals for numbers greater than a thousand.

Apart from the Indus script, the earliest extant script in India is the one called Karoṣṭhī of, probably, Aramaic origin. Its use was restricted to north-western India and central Asia from the fourth century BC to the fourth century AD. At nearly the same time, in the Aśokan edicts, appeared another script called Brāhmī which was to become the origin of many varieties of south and south-east Asian scripts. Its relationship to the former is not certain. These scripts had their own numerical symbols, but in both systems particular symbols were used not only for units but also for tens, hundreds, thousands, etc., and some of them were made by the principle of addition, and others by the principle of multiplication. The numeral systems in both scripts were therefore not based on a place-value system, and the Brāhmī, non-place-value, numerals continued to be used in epigraphy even after the place-value system was introduced in daily calculations and in mathematical literature in the early centuries of the Christian era.

The oldest datable evidence of the decimal place-value system in India is found in the *Yavanajātaka* (AD 269/270) of Sphujidhvaja, a book on astrology. It is not certain if the decimal place-value notation in India had a symbol for zero from the beginning. We have to keep it in mind that, historically, not all place-value notations were accompanied by a zero symbol as the sexagesimal notation of the Old Babylonians proves. There is no reference to zero in the *Yavanajātaka*. In Piṅgala's *Chandaḥsūtra* (8.28–31), a work on Sanskrit prosody, zero (*śūnya*) and two (*dvi*) are used as signs for the multiplication by two and for the squaring, respectively, in the computation of powers of two, which occurs in the right-hand side of the equation, $2 + 2^2 + 2^3 + \ldots + 2^n = 2 \times 2^n - 2$. The date of the work is controversial: some ascribe it to ca. 200 BC but others to the third century AD or later. The oldest datable evidence of zero as a symbol as well as of that as a number are found in Varāhamihira's *Pañcasiddhāntikā* (ca. AD 550).

II.2 The fifth to sixth centuries – beginning

Āryabhaṭa I is so called to distinguish him from another astronomer of the same name, the author of the *Mahāsiddhānta*, who is called Āryabhaṭa II.

Āryabhaṭa I was one of the most influential mathematicians and astronomers in India through his two works, *Āryabhaṭīya* and *Āryabhaṭasiddhānta*. The latter work is not extant but has been referred to by many later scholars. The work mainly influenced northwestern India. It is also known to have had some influence upon the Sasanian and Islamic astronomy. The *Āryabhaṭīya*, on the other hand, mainly influenced south India.

Āryabhaṭa I was born in AD 476. This is known from his own statement in the *Āryabhaṭīya* (3.10): "When sixty of sixty years and three quarters of the Yuga had passed, then twenty-three years had passed here from my birth." That is, he was 23 years old in AD 499 (= 3600 − 3101, since the last quarter, called Kaliyuga, of the current Yuga began in 3102 BC). The year mentioned here, AD 499, is usually taken to refer to the date of the composition of the *Āryabhaṭīya*.

The *Āryabhaṭīya* is divided into four "quarters" (*pādas*), that is,

1 Quarter in Ten Gīti verses,
2 Quarter for Mathematics (*gaṇita*, in 33 Āryā verses),
3 Quarter for Time-Reckoning (*kālakriyā*, in 25 Āryā verses), and
4 Quarter for Spherics (*gola*, in 50 Āryā verses).

Chapter 1 consists of 13 verses. The first verse contains the author's salute to God Brahmā and refers to the three fields to be treated in the next three chapters. The second verse defines an alphabetical notation of numbers. The next ten verses (the words, "ten Gīti verses," in the title of this chapter refer to this part) contain tables of astronomical parameters and of sine-differences expressed in that notation. For example, the number of the sun's revolutions in a *yuga*, 4320000, is expressed as *khyughṛ* $= (2 + 30) \times 10^4 + 4 \times 10^6$.

Chapter 2 of the *Āryabhaṭīya* is the oldest extant mathematical text in Sanskrit after the *Śulbasūtras*. Although the chapter does not have a clear division into sections, it may be divided into four parts:

i. Rules for basic computations (vv. 2–5),
ii. Rules for geometric figures (vv. 6–18),
iii. Rules for both figures and quantities (vv. 19–24), and
iv. Rules for numerical quantities (vv. 25–33).

Āryabhaṭa gives the names of the first 10 decimal places, and says: "⟨Each⟩ place shall be ten times greater than ⟨the previous⟩ place."

Problems of proportion were solved by means of the *trairāśika* or "the ⟨computation⟩ related to three quantities." The *trairāśika* was not only indispensable for astronomy but also essential for monetary economy. The first of the seven examples for the *trairāśika* supplied by the commentator, Bhāskara I, is this: "Five *palas* of sandal-wood were bought by me for nine *rūpakas*. Then, how much of sandal-wood can be obtained for only one *rūpaka*?" The *pala* and the *rūpaka* are units of weight and money, respectively.

The last rule provides a general solution called *kuṭṭaka* or "pulverizer" to an indeterminate system of linear equations of the following type: "When a certain unknown integer, N, is divided by a set of integers, $\{a_1, a_2, \ldots, a_n\}$, one by one, the remainders are $\{r_1, r_2, \ldots, r_r\}$. What is that number, N?"

Varāhamihira is one of the most famous authorities on astrology in India. He flourished in Avantī (modern Ujjain) in the sixth century AD.

He divided the "astral science" (*jyotiḥśāstra*) into three major "branches" (*skandhas*), namely, (1) mathematics including mathematical astronomy (*gaṇita* or *tantra*), (2) horoscopic astrology (*horā*), and (3) natural astrology or divination in general (*saṃhitā*) (*Bṛhatsaṃhitā* 1.8–9, 2.2, 2.19), and wrote several books each in the second and third branches. His only work in the first branch, *Pañcasiddhāntikā*, is a compendium of the texts of five earlier astronomical schools, and no work on mathematics proper is known to have been written by him, but his works are important from the view point of the history of mathematics as well.

In the *Pañcasiddhāntikā*, zero occurs as a number, that is, the object of mathematical operations like addition, subtraction, etc. For example, he states the mean daily velocity of the sun in each of the 12 zodiacal signs beginning with Aries as follows: "The daily velocity of the sun is in order 60 ⟨minutes⟩ minus 3, 3, 3, 3, 2, 1; plus 1, 1, 1, 1; and minus 0, 1" (*Pañcasiddhāntikā* 3.17).

Presumably, the existence of both the zero symbol for vacant places in the place-value notation and calculations by this notation brought about the concept of zero as a number, because we cannot calculate, for instance, $15 + 20 = 35$ without the rule, $5 + 0 = 5$. This is not the case with an abacus where no symbol exists for vacant places.

He expressly stated the "graphic procedure" for constructing a sine table, a method which had been only alluded to by Āryabhaṭa I, and gave a sine table for the radius, $R = 120$ (ibid. 4.1–15).

In a chapter on the combination of perfume of his work on divination, *Bṛhatsaṃhitā* (76.22), he provided a rule for calculating the number of combinations, ${}_nC_r$, when r things are taken at a time from n things, and a method called "spread by token" (*loṣṭaka-prastāra*) for enumerating all the possible combinations correctly. In the same chapter he gave the correct numbers, 84 and 1820, of ${}_9C_3$ and ${}_{16}C_4$ respectively, but he mistakenly regarded $4! \times 4 \times {}_{16}C_4 = 174720$ as the number of possible combinations when 4 are taken at a time out of 16 ingredients for perfumes, in the ratio, 1:2:3:4 (ibid. 76.13–21); the correct number should be ${}_{16}P_4 = 16 \times 15 \times 14 \times 13 = 43680$.

In the same chapter he utilized a magic square of order four in order to prescribe the perfumes called "good for all purposes." It consists of the four rows: 2, 3, 5, 8; 5, 8, 2, 3; 4, 1, 7, 6; and 7, 6, 4, 1 (ibid. 76.23–6). This is the oldest magic square in India. It is irregular because it is made not of the numbers 1 to 16 but of two sets of the numbers 1 to 8, but it is "pan-diagonal" in the sense that not only the two main diagonals but also all the "broken" diagonals each amounts to the magic constant, 18 in this case. Presumably, Varāhamihira first constructed a regular magic square with the numbers 1 to 16, and then modified it by subtracting 8 each from the numbers greater than 8 to arrive at his irregular square.

II.3 The seventh to eighth centuries – restructuring

The seventh century saw a restructuring of Indian mathematics. It was divided into two major fields, that is, arithmetic with mensuration and algebra, which were later called *pāṭī-gaṇita* ("mathematics of algorithms") and *bīja-gaṇita* ("mathematics of seeds"), respectively. The "seeds" here means algebraic equations (*samīkaraṇa*, lit. "to make ⟨both sides⟩ equal"), which, just like seeds of plants, have "the potentiality to generate" the solutions of mathematical problems. A work for *pāṭī-gaṇita* usually consists of two categories of rules often accompanied by examples, that is, *parikarman* (basic operations) and *vyavahāra* (practical or applied mathematics).

Brahmagupta included two chapters corresponding to these two fields in his astronomical work, *Brāhmasphuṭasiddhānta* (AD 628), and began to use the word *gaṇaka* ("calculator") in the sense of one who knows mathematical astronomy.

According to his own words, Brahmagupta, son of Jiṣṇu, wrote the *Brāhmasphuṭasiddhānta* in 25 chapters at the age of 30 in Śaka 550 = AD 628. This means that he was born in AD 598. He was still active at the age of 67 (AD 665), when he composed another work on astronomy, the *Khaṇḍakhādyaka*.

In the *Brāhmasphuṭasiddhānta*, five chapters are particularly concerned with mathematics. They are: chap. 12, "Mathematics," on arithmetic and mensuration, chap. 18, "pulverizer," on algebra (the title has simply been taken from the name of the first topic in the chapter), chap. 19, "Knowledge about Gnomon and Shadow," on measurements of shadows and lights, chap. 20, Answer to <the Problems of> Piling of Meters" (*chandaścityuttara*, on combinatorics concerning prosody, and a small section called "sine-production" (*jyā-utpatti*) in chap. 21 ("Spherics") on trigonometry.

It is in chap. 12 that he gives his famous theorem on the diagonals of a cyclic quadrilateral. In chap. 18, he prescribes rules for surds, negative quantities, zero, and unknown quantities, and provides rules called *varga-prakṛti* ("square nature") for quadratic indeterminate equations of the type, $Px^2 + t = y^2$.

Bhāskara I flourished in the first half of the seventh century in Saurāṣṭra, perhaps in Valabhī near modern Bhāvnagar, and composed three works as the expositions of the teachings of Āryabhaṭa I, "based on the continuity of tradition" (*sampradāya-avicchedāt*). They are, in chronological order, *Karmanibandha* ("Treatise on ⟨Astronomical⟩ Computation") alias *Mahābhāskarīya* ("Large ⟨Book⟩ of Bhāskara"), a prose commentary on the *Āryabhaṭīya* (written in Śaka 551 = AD 629), and an abridged version of the first work also called *Karmanibandha* alias *Laghubhāskarīya* ("Small ⟨Book⟩ of Bhāskara").

Particularly important for the history of Indian mathematics is the second work, that is, the commentary on the *Āryabhaṭīya*, which provides valuable information on, among other things, mathematical procedures and expressions of his time.

A vacant place (*kha*) in the decimal place-value notation was indicated by a small circle (*bindu*, lit. "a dot"), which was also put on the right shoulder of a negative number. A fraction was expressed, just like our fractions, by placing the numerator above the denominator (without a bar between them), and the fractional part of a number was put below its integer part. Thus, for example, the diameter of the reference circle of Āryabhaṭa's sine table whose circumference is 21600 is

$$\begin{array}{c}6875\\625\\1309\end{array}$$

since Āryabhaṭa's value of π is 62832/20000, and the circumference of the earth, whose diameter is 1050 *yojanas* according to Āryabhaṭa, is

$$\begin{array}{c}3299\\8^{\circ}\\25\end{array}$$

($= 3299 - \frac{8}{25}$) *yojanas*. The value of the linear measure, *yojanas*, varies from time to time and from place to place. Āryabhaṭa equates it with 8000 *nṛs* ("men"), where 1 *nṛ* = 4 *hastas* (cubits) = 96 *aṅgulas* ("fingers").

In geometry, Bhāskara I probably knew a proof of the Pythagorean Theorem, because he provides a square figure (figure 17.1) divided into 8 equal right-

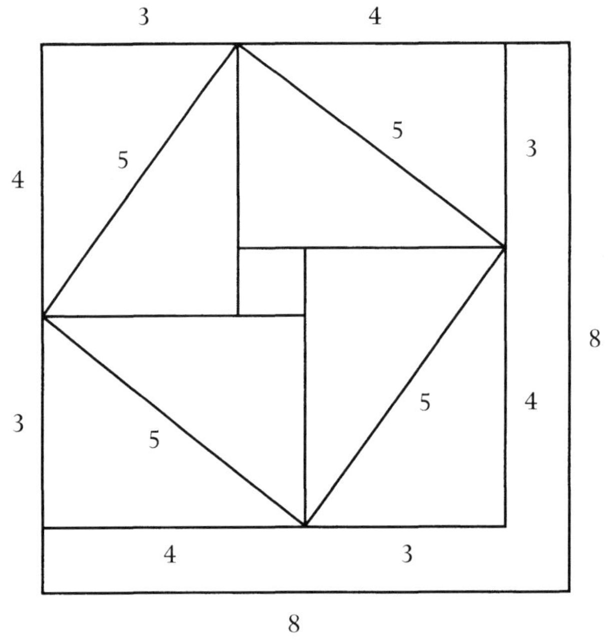

Figure 17.1: Diagram by Bhāskara I, probably used for a proof of the Pythagorean Theorem.

angled triangles and a central square, while discussing the validity of Āryabhaṭa's statement, "A square (*varga*) is an equi-quadri-lateral ⟨figure⟩" (*Āryabhaṭīya* 2.3). Bhāskara's square demonstrates that $4 \times (ab/2) + (a - b)^2 = c^2$, from which he would easily obtain the equation, $a^2 + b^2 = c^2$, numerically.

The *Bakhshālī Manuscript*, whose original title is not known, is the oldest extant manuscript in Indian mathematics. It was unearthed in a deteriorated condition at Bakhshālī near Peshawar (now in Pakistan) in 1881 and is now preserved in the Bodleian Library at Oxford University. The extant portion of the manuscript consists of 70 fragmentary leaves. It is written on birchbark with the earlier type of the Śāradā script, which was used in the northwestern part of India from the eighth to the twelfth centuries AD. The language is Sanskrit but it has largely been influenced by the vernacular(s) of those regions.

The work is a loose compilation of mathematical rules and examples collected from different works. They are written in verse, and the examples are solved in prose commentaries on them and are often given verifications of the answers.

The dates so far proposed for the Bakhshālī work vary from the third to the twelfth centuries AD, but a recently made comparative study has shown many similarities, particularly in the style of exposition and terminology, between the Bakhshālī work and Bhāskara I's commentary on the *Āryabhaṭīya*. This seems to indicate that both works belong to the nearly same period, although this does not deny the possibility that some of the rules and examples in the Bakhshālī work date from anterior periods.

The rules that occur in the extant portion of the Bakhshālī work are: (1) arithmetical operations such as addition, etc.; (2) general rules applicable to different kinds of problems such as the rule of three, *regula falsi*, etc.; (3) rules for purely numerical problems such as algebraic equations and arithmetical progressions; (4) rules for problems of money such as buying and selling, etc.; (5) rules for problems of travelers such as equations of journeys, etc.; and (6) rules for geometric problems such as the volume of an irregular solid. The Bakhshālī work employs a decimal place value notation with a dot for zero.

Śrīdhara, who flourished between Brahmagupta and Govindasvāmin, is one of the earliest mathematicians who wrote separate treatises for the two major fields, *pāṭī-gaṇita* and *bīja-gaṇtia*, although his work on the latter is known only from a quotation. He included many new topics such as combinations of the six tastes, the hundred fowls problem, the cistern problem, etc., in his *Pāṭīgaṇita*.

II.4 The ninth to fourteenth centuries – later developments

A follower of the Āryabhaṭa school of mathematics and astronomy, Govindasvāmin flourished in the first half of the ninth century in Kerala. His commentaries on Bhāskara I's *Mahābhāskarīya* and on the latter half of Parāśara's *Horāśāstra* (between 600 and 750) are extant, but three works of his, *Govindakṛti* on astronomy, *Govindapaddhati* on astrology, and *Gaṇitamukha* on mathematics, are known only from references and quotations by later writers.

Govindasvāmin shows a keen interest in the logical foundations of the rule of three. He provides a definition, with a detailed explanation, of the four terms (*pramāṇa, pramāṇa-phala, icchā,* and *ichhā-phala*) of the rule of three in his commentary on the *Mahābhāskarīya* (1.7), and, in three verses cited by Śaṅkara, compares these four terms to the constituent parts of the inference (*anumāna*) of Indian logicians. A typical inference according to them is as follows: "That mountain has fire because of its having smoke. That which has smoke has fire, like a kitchen." According to Govinda, the four terms of the rule of three correspond in order to the smoke and fire in the kitchen and the same two in the mountain, and thus the rule of three can be regarded as an inference.

A Jaina mathematician, Mahāvīra wrote a book for *pāṭī-gaṇita* entitled *Gaṇitasārasaṃgraha* during the reign of King Amoghavarṣa (ca. 814/815–80). The work is quite voluminous and comprises more than 1130 verses for rules and examples. He seems to be the first in India who admitted two solutions of a quadratic equation.

Bhāskara II was born in AD 1114 to a family which produced a number of scholars and literary men before and after him. He lived in Vijjaḍaviḍa at the foot of the Sahya mountain situated at the northern end of the Western Ghats, and completed his main work, *Siddhāntaśiromaṇi*, when he was 36 years old (AD 1150). He also wrote an astronomical manual, *Karaṇakutūhara*, in AD 1183, and a commentary (date unknown) on Lalla's *Śiṣyadhīvṛddhidatantra*. The *Siddhāntaśiromaṇi* consists of four parts. Two of them, *Līlāvatī* and *Bījagaṇita*, are on mathematics, and the other two, *Grahagaṇitādhyāya* and *Golādhyāya*, on astronomy. These four parts were often regarded as independent works.

The most popular among them was the *Līlāvatī*, which is a well organized textbook of *pāṭī-gaṇita* written in a plain and elegant Sanskrit. It circulated all over India and was commented upon in Sanskrit and in north Indian languages (such as Marāṭhī and Gujarātī) by a number of persons and translated not only into Indian languages of the north and of the south (such as Kaṇṇaḍa and Telugu) but also several times into Persian.

Bhāskara II included a whole theory of the pulverizer in the *Līlāvatī*, a book of *pāṭī*. This was possible because it required neither algebraic symbolism nor "intelligence" (*mati*) which were essential for *bīja-gaṇita* or algebra according to Bhāskara II.

The last chapter, "the nets of digits," deals with permutations of numerical figures. The last problem, for example, reads as follows: "How many varieties of numbers are there with digits placed in five places when their sum is thirteen? It should be told, if you know."

The *Bījagaṇita* is the culmination of Indian algebra. Bhāskara II's main contribution to algebra is his treatment of various types of equations of order two or more (up to six) with more than one unknown. The equations of higher orders are solved by reducing them to quadratic equations. In his solutions, the square nature and pulverizer, as well as the "elimination of the middle term" (which is the name given to the solution procedure of quadratic equations), play important roles.

Nārāyaṇa Paṇḍita wrote, in AD 1356, a book for *pāṭī-gaṇita*, *Gaṇitakaumudī*, in which he developed, among other things, theories of factorization, of partitioning, of combinatorics, and of magic squares. His work for *bīja-gaṇita*, *Bījagaṇitāvataṃsa*, seems, judging from its extant portion, to have been modeled after Bhāskara II's *Bījagaṇita*.

II.5 The fifteenth to seventeenth centuries – a new wave in the south

South India in this period produced many talented mathematicians and astronomers. Particularly important is the academic lineage headed by Mādhava of Saṅgamagrāma (fl. 1380/1420), which is often called the Mādhava school.

Mādhava, a resident of Saṅgamagrāma near Cochin in Kerala, was one of the most brilliant mathematicians in the world. His name is, and will be, remembered for his discovery of a power series expansion of π at least and perhaps also of those of trigonometric functions such as sine, cosine, versed sine, and arctangent. The verses that state these series are found not in his extant astronomical works but in the works of his successors.

In his commentary on the *Līlāvatī*, Śaṅkara explicitly ascribes two methods for calculating the circumference of a circle to Mādhava. Śaṅkara also cites Mādhava's verse which expresses, in the word-numeral notation (*Bhūtasaṃkhyā*), an approximation to π correct to 11 decimal places, $2827433388233/(9 \cdot 10^{11})$.

Nīlakaṇṭha Somayāji, son of Jātavedas, was born ca. 14 June 1444 in Kuṇḍapura near Tirur, Kerala, and studied under Dāmodara, son of Parameśvara, at Ālattūr, Kerala.

He wrote an elaborate commentary on the *Āryabhaṭīya* in about 1510. It shows his great talent in mathematics as well as in astronomy. To cite a few examples, he rediscovered the correct meaning of Āryabhaṭa's rule for sine-differences. He expressly states the incommensurability of the diameter and the circumference of a circle, although whether he has proved it or not is not known. He cites and proves Mādhava's formulas for interpolation in the sine table, and for the sum and difference of sines. He died after 1542.

Indian mathematics thus made unique, remarkable progress up to the sixteenth century. It was only in the 1720's that Jagannātha (1652–1744), at the request of his patron, Jai Singh Sawai (1688–1744), produced the first Sanskrit version of Euclid's *Elements* under the title *Rekhā-gaṇita* (Mathematics of Lines) from the Arabic version of Naṣīr al-Dīn al-Ṭūsī.

Bibliography

For more bibliographical information, see Pingree 1970–94 and 1981 and Hayashi 2000.

Amulya Kumar Bag, 1979, *Mathematics in Ancient and Medieval India*, Varanasi: Chaukhambha Orientalia, 1979.

Henry Thomas Colebrooke, 1817, *Algebra with Arithmetic and Mesuration from the Sanscrit of Brahmegupta and Bháscara*, London: John Murray, 1817. Reprinted Wiesbaden: Martin Sändig, 1973.

Bibhutibhusan Datta and Avadhesh Narayan Singh, 1962, *History of Hindu Mathematics: A Source Book*, part 1: *Numerical Notation and Arithmetic*, Lahore 1935, part 2: *Algebra*, Lahore: Motilal Banarsidass, 1938. Reprinted in one volume, Bombay: Asia Publishing House, 1962. Repr. in 2 vols., Delhi: Bharatiya Kala Prakashan, 2001.

—— and Avadhesh Narayan Singh, 1980, "Hindu Geometry", revised by K. S. Shukla, *Indian Journal of History of Science*, 15, 1980, pp. 121–188.

—— and Avadhesh Narayan Singh, 1983, "Hindu Trigonometry", revised by K. S. Shukla, *Indian Journal of History of Science*, 18, 1983, pp. 39-408.

—— and Avadhesh Narayan Singh, 1984, "Use of Calculus in Hindu Mathematics", revised by K. S. Shukla, *Indian Journal of History of Science*, 19, 1984, pp. 95-404.

——, 1932, The *Science of the Śulba: A Study in Early Hindu Geometry*, Calcutta: University of Calcutta, 1932.

——, 1991, "Vedic Mathematics", revised anonymously, in Priyadaranjan Ray and S. N. Sen (ed.), *The Cultural Heritage of India*, vol. 6: *Science and Technology*, Calcutta: The Ramakrishna Mission Institute of Culture, 1986, reprinted 1991, pp. 18–35.

Julius Eggeling, 1963–88, *The Śatapatha-Brāhmaṇa according to the Text of the Mādhyandina School*, 5 vols., Sacred Books of the East, ed. by F. Max Müller, vols. 12, 26, 41, 43, and 44, Oxford: Clarendon Press, 1882–1900. Reprinted, Delhi: Motilal Banarsidass, 1963/66/72/78/88.

Radha Charan Gupta, 1937, "South Indian Achievements in Medieval Mathematics", *Gaṇita Bhāratī*, 9, 1987, pp. 15–40.

Takao Hayashi, 1994, "Indian Mathematics", *Companion Encyclopedia of the History and Philosophy of the Mathematical Sciences*, edited by I. Grattan-Guinness, London/New York: Routledge, 1994, vol. 1, pp. 118–130.

——, 1995, *The Bakhshālī Manuscript: An Ancient Indian Mathematical Treatise*, Groningen Oriental Studies 11, Groningen: Egbert Forsten, 1995.

——, 2000, "Indian Mathematics", *The History of Mathematics from Antiquity to the Present: A Selective Annotated Bibliography*, edited by Joseph W. Dauben, New York: Garland, 1985. Revised edition, on CD-ROM edited by Albert C. Lewis in cooperation with the International Commission on the History of Mathematics, Providence: American Mathematical Society, 2000.

Edward Washburn Hopkins, 1894, "Numerical Formulae in the Veda and Their Bearing on Vedic Criticism", *Journal of the American Oriental Society*, 16, 1894, pp. 275–281.

Georges Ifrah, 1981, *Histoire universelle des chiffres*, Paris: Segher, 1981; translated into English by Lowell Bair as *From One to Zero: A Universal History of Numbers*, New York: Penguin Books, 1985.

George Gheverghese Joseph, 2000, *The Crest of the Peacock: Non-European Roots of Mathematics*, London: Penguin Books, 1992. Reprinted, New Delhi: Affiliated East-West Press, 1995. Revised, Princeton: Princeton University Press, 2000.

A. P. Juschkewitsch, 1964, *Geschichte der Mathematik in Mittelalter.* Translated from the 2nd edition of the Russian original by V. Ziegler. Leipzig: Teubner, 1964.

Raghunātha Puruṣottama Kulkarṇī, 1983, *Geometry according to Śulba Sūtra*, Poona: Vaidika Saṃśodhana Maṇḍala, 1983.

Axel Michaels, 1978, *Beweisverfahren in der vedischen Sakralgeometrie: eine Beitrag zur Entstehungs-geschichte von Wissenschaft*, Alt- und Neu-indische Studien, Ed. 20, Wiesbaden: Franz Steiner, 1978.

David Pingree, 1970–94, *Census of the Exact Sciences in Sanskrit*, ser. A, vols. 1–5, Philadelphia: American Philosophical Society, 1970/71/76/81/94.

——, 1978, "History of Mathematical Astronomy in India", in C. C. Gillispie (ed.), *Dictionary of Scientific Biography*, 16 vols., New York: Charles Scribner's Sons, 1970–80, vol. 15, 1978, pp. 533–633. Reprinted in an eight-volume edition, 1981.

——, 1981, *Jyotiḥśāstra: Astral and Mathematical Literature*, in Jan Gonda (ed.), *A History of Indian Literature*, vol. 6, fasc. 4, Wiesbaden: Otto Harrassowitz, 1981.

K. Kunjunni Raja, 1963, "Astronomy and Mathematics in Kerala (An Account of the Literature)", *Brahmavidyā*, 27, 1963, pp. 118–167. Repr. Madras: Adyar Library and Research Center, 1995.

C. T. Rajagopal and M. S. Rangachari, 1978, "On an Untapped Source of Medieval Keralese Mathematics". *Archive for History of Exact Sciences*, 18, 1978, pp. 89–102.

Ludo J. Rocher, 1953/54, "Euclid's Stoicheia and Jagannātha's Rekhāgaṇita", *Journal of the Oriental Institute, Baroda*, 3, 1953/54, pp. 236–256.

Arion Roşu, 1989, "Les carrés magiques indiens et l'histoire des idées en Asie", *Zeitschrift der Deutchen Morgenländischen Gesellschaft*, 139, 1989, pp. 120–158.

T. A. Sarasvati Amma, 1979, *Geometry in Ancient and Medieval India*, Delhi: Motilal Banarsidass, 1979.

K. Venkateswara Sarma, 1972, *A History of the Kerala School of Hindu Astronomy (In Perspective)*, Vishveshvaranand Indological Series 55, Hoshiarpur: Vishveshvaranand Institute, 1972.

A. Seidenberg, 1978, "The Origin of Mathematics", *Archive for History of Exact Sciences*, 18, 1978, pp. 301–342.

S. N. Sen and A. K. Bag, 1983, *The Śulbasūtras of Baudhāyana, Āpastamba, Kātyāyana and Mānava*, with text, English trsl. and comm., New Delhi: Indian National Science Academy, 1983.

——, 1971, "Mathematics", in D. M. Bose, S. N. Sen, B. V. Subbarayappa (eds.), *A Concise History of Science in India*, New Delhi: Indian National Science Academy, 1971, pp. 136–212.

C. N. Srinivasiengar, 1967, *The History of Ancient Indian Mathematics*, Calcutta: The World Press, 1967.

Frits Staal, 1983, *Agni: The Vedic Ritual of the Fire Altar*, 2 vols., Berkeley: Asian Humanities Press, 1983.

George Frederick Thibaut, 1984, *Mathematics in the Making in Ancient India* (reprints of *On the Śulvasūtras* and *Baudhāyana Śulvasūtras*), ed. by Debiprasad Chattopadhyaya, Calcutta/Delhi: K P Bagchi, 1984.

CHAPTER 18

Calendar, Astrology, and Astronomy

Michio Yano

Another title of this chapter could be *jyotiḥśāstra*, or "science of heavenly bodies." Sometimes mathematics (*gaṇitaśāstra*) is regarded as a part of *jyotiḥśāstra*, but an independent chapter is given to mathematics in this book (see chapter 17). Thus, what is touched on in this chapter is *jyotiḥśāstra* minus mathematics proper. The remainder can be expressed in the three words in the title of this chapter. Topics are limited to those which would be useful for the students of Hinduism.

1 Vedāṅga Calendar

Even taking into account the refined taste of Vedic poets who refrained from describing natural phenomena in a direct manner, observational records of heavenly phenomena are scarce in the Vedic *saṃhitā* literature. Of course the poets were interested in the sky as nature, but they were less eager to engage in mathematical formulation of the periodic changes in the starry heaven. So there is nothing systematic in the *saṃhitā* texts that can be called mathematical astronomy. What we find in them is the hymns to the Sun and the Moon, and *nakṣatras*. It is even doubtful whether they knew the five planets as such (*grahas* in later texts), namely, as a special class of stars which are distinguished from the fixed stars.

It was as one of the six auxiliary branches (*aṅga*) for the pursuit of Vedic rituals that the earliest astronomical knowledge of ancient India was systematically described. This branch was called *jyotiṣavedāṅga*. The word *jyotiṣa* comes from *jyotiḥ*, "light (in the sky), luminary." The text of the *jyotiṣavedāṅga* survived in two recensions: that of the *Ṛgveda*, which is older and ascribed to a Lagadha belonging to the fifth century BC, and that of the *Yajurveda*, which belongs to somewhat later period (Pingree 1981: 10). The two recensions, consisting of 36 and 44 verses respectively, have many verses in common.

The following quotation is from the Ṛgvedic recension:

> The Vedas advanced for the sake of sacrificial rituals. And the sacrificial rituals were prescribed in the order of time. Therefore one who has known this science of prescription of time, namely, astronomy, has known sacrificial rituals. (Ārcajyautisam 33, in Dvivedin 1907)

This verse gave a strong motivation to those who devoted themselves in the study of astronomy. Thus, for instance, Bhāskara II, the author of the *Līlāvatī* and one of the most popular astronomer-mathematicians in India, wrote in the middle of the twelfth century:

> First of all the Vedas advanced through the activities of sacrificial rituals, while sacrificial rituals are said to be dependent on time. Since knowledge of time is from this science, therefore astronomy is said to be a branch of Vedic studies. (Siddhāntaśiromaṇi; Grahagaṇitādhāya 1.1.9)

The main purpose of the *jyotiṣavedāṅga* was the preparation of a calendar in order to fix the date of sacrificial rituals. Nothing is written on planets. The calendar described here represents the earliest stage of Indian calendrical tradition. Almost all the important elements which characterize the Indian calendar are already found in this literature. The main feature of this calendar is the five-year cycle which is clearly stated as:

> A year is 366 days, 6 seasons, 2 *ayanas*, and 12 solar months. This, multiplied by five, is a *yuga*. (Yājuṣajyautiṣam 28cd, in Dvivedin 1907)
>
> (The number of) *sāvana* months, lunar months, sidereal months (in a *yuga*) are 61, 62, and 67 (respectively). A *sāvana* [month] has 30 days. A solar year is a turn of the stars. (Yājuṣajyautiṣam 31)

This statement can be tabulated as follows. Items in [ ] are not explicitly stated.

1 year	= 366 days	= 6 seasons	
	= 2 *ayanas*	= 12 solar months	
1 *sāvana* month		=30 days	
5 years	= 60 solar months		[= 1,800 solar days]
	= 61 *sāvana* months		[= 1,830 *sāvana* days]
	= 62 synodic months		[= 1,860 *tithis*]
	= 67 sidereal months		

This system requires two intercalary months (*adhimāsas*) in every five years, in other words, one intercalation in every two and a half years. This is clearly mentioned in Kauṭilya's *Arthaśāstra* (2.20.66). We can interpret the word *sāvana* here as equivalent to the modern adjective "civil", although there were different meanings of this word and this verse has been subject to different interpretations.[1]

With our interpretation it follows that

62 synodic months = 1,830 days, i.e., 1 synodic month ≈ 29.515 days.

Since this value is not very accurate (the modern value is 29.530589 days), the ancient Indian ritualists should have put an adjustment rather frequently – addition of one day is necessary about every 64 months – in order to keep the relation of the date of rituals and the lunar phases. But there are many textual evidences which show the use of this five-year *yuga*, for instance, the *Arthaśāstra* as mentioned above, the medical text *Suśrutasaṃhitā*, the Buddhist text *Śārdūlakarṇāvadāna*, and the Jain text *Sūryapannatti*. It was only after the introduction of Hellenistic astronomy that the calendrical values were improved to a useful degree.

2 *Nakṣatra* and Lunar Astrology

2.1 Two systems of nakṣatra

Sometime in the later Vedic period the meaning of the word *nakṣatra* shifted from its original sense of "star" in general to its narrower sense, namely, one of the 28 or 27 groups of stars which were regarded as the lunar stations along the ecliptic. The earliest list of *nakṣatras* in this sense is found in the *Taittirīyasaṃhitā* (Macdonell and Keith 1912: 409–31). The names of the *nakṣatras* show some variations and their grammatical forms do not always agree. In table 18.1 the most commonly used forms are given. When 28 *nakṣatras* are counted, Abhijit is put between Uttarāṣāḍhā and Śravaṇa. The most important difference between the 28 *nakṣatra* system and the 27 *nakṣatra* system is that in the latter each *nakṣatra* occupies an equal space of 13°20′ while in the former the distance is irregular. When, therefore, we find a *nakṣatra* name in Sanskrit texts, we should know which of the two system is intended. Since similar systems of unevenly spaced 28 lunar mansions are found in Chinese and Islamic astronomy, there have been disputes concerning their origin. In my view, the Chinese and Indian systems are independent while the Islamic *manāzil al-qamar* (stations of the moon) should have been influenced by the Indian *nakṣatras*.

The identification of stars comprising each *nakṣatra* poses even more difficult problems, but some secure identification can be made: for example, Kṛttikā is a group of stars corresponding to Pleiades, and Citrā is α Virginis (= Spica).

In the earlier Sanskrit texts *nakṣatras* are counted from Kṛttikā, while in the later period Aśvinī (β and γ Arietis) became the first mansion. The shift of the starting point of the *nakṣatra* system can be ascribed to the precession of the equinoxes. The time when Pleiades was near the vernal equinox is about

2300 BC. This is one of the reasons that some people claim the high antiquity and originality of Indian astronomy. There is also an attempt at deciphering some of the Indus scripts as the names of *nakṣatra*. Such attempts are not utterly impossible, but we must remember the difference between the *nakṣatra* as a well-defined coordinate system and the *nakṣatra* as a star or a group of stars in general.

According to the *jyotiṣavedāṅga* the sun's northern course (*uttarāyaṇa*) begins at its entry into the first point of the *nakṣatra* Dhaniṣṭhā, which, therefore, was regarded as the winter solstice. Since the *jyotiṣavedāṅga* used the equally spaced 27 *nakṣatra* system, it turns out that the vernal equinox was assumed to be at Bharaṇī 10°, which is 23°20′ distant from the first point of Aśvinī which, in the later period, was equated with the first point (*meṣādi*, i.e. "the beginning of Aries") of the ecliptic longitude. If this difference were accepted as the amount of the precession, and if we could admit that the accurate observation was made in the *jyotiṣavedāṅga* period, the text might be dated about 1,600 years before the time when Indian *nakṣatra* coordinate system was fixed. This would put the date of the *jyotiṣavedāṅga* in about 1300 BC. But here I should remind the reader of what I already said about Kṛttikā. What we can say about the date is only relative.

The *nakṣatra* system played a very important role in some aspects of Indian culture, i.e., calendar making, astrology and ritual.

2.2 Nakṣatra *in calendar and astrology*

The lunar month was named after the *nakṣatra* where the full moon is located. Thus, for instance, Caitra is the month during which the full moon is stationed in Citrā. The relation of the *nakṣatras* and the month names is shown in table 18.1. This naming system must have been one of the reasons that the sidereal (*nirayaṇa*) position of the Sun and the Moon was more important than their tropical (*sāyana*) position. In this way the relation of month names to seasons could not but be sacrificed by the effect of the precession of equinoxes.

The *nakṣatras* played the central role in the earlier period of Indian astrology, namely, the period before the introduction of horoscopic astrology from the west. Predictions were made according to the *nakṣatras* where the moon is located. To each *nakṣatra* a deity from the Indian pantheon was assigned, for example, Agni to Kṛttikā and Prajāpati to Rohiṇī, etc. (see table 18.1). Thus *nakṣatra* worship became an important part of Indian rituals. Since little attention was paid to the position of planets nor to the solar position, I would call this type of astrology "lunar astrology" in contrast to horoscopic astrology where the planetary position against the background of the zodiacal signs is more important. Among the texts preserving this old lunar astrology are the *Śārdūlakarṇāvadāna* and the *Sūryapannatti* which we have mentioned above, and the *Pariśiṣṭa* of the *Atharvaveda*.

Table 18.1: Nakṣatras

No.	*Nakṣatra*	*Deity*	*Month name*
1	Kṛttikā	Agni	Kārttika
2	Rohiṇī	Prajāpati	
3	Mṛgaśīrṣa	Soma	Mārgaśira
4	Ārdrā	Rudra	
5	Punarvasu	Aditi	
6	Puṣya	Bṛhaspati	Pauṣa
7	Āśleṣā	Sarpa	
8	Maghā	Pitaras	Māgha
9	Pūrvaphālgunī	Bhaga	
10	Uttaraphālgunī	Aryaman	Phālguna
11	Hasta	Āditya	
12	Citrā	Tvaṣṭṛ	Caitra
13	Svāti	Vāyu	
14	Viśākhā	Indrāgnī	Vaiśākha
15	Anurādhā	Mitra	
16	Jyeṣṭhā	Indra	Jyaiṣṭha
17	Mūla	Nirṛti	
18	Pūrvāṣāḍhā	Toya	Āṣāḍha
19	Uttarāṣāḍhā	Viśvadeva	
	(Abhijit)	Brahmā	
20	Śravaṇa	Viṣṇu	Śrāvaṇa
21	Dhaniṣṭhā	Vasu	
22	Śatabhiṣaj	Varuṇa	
23	Pūrvabhadrapadā	Ajapāda	Bhādrapada
24	Uttarabhadrapadā	Ahirbudhnya	
25	Revatī	Pūṣan	
26	Aśvinī	Aśvin	Āśvina
27	Bharaṇī	Yama	

3 Nine *Grahas*

3.1 Grahas *in medical texts*

Most Hindu temples have a shrine which contains the images of *navagraha*, i.e. nine planetary gods. How and when Indian people began worshiping planets, after being indifferent to them for a very long time, is an interesting but difficult question.

The word *graha* is used in medical texts referring to the demons which possess children and cause mental diseases. For instance, there is a chapter devoted to "nine *grahas*" in the *Suśrutasaṃhitā*, which was compiled sometime around the third to fourth century AD. The nine *grahas* enumerated in this context have nothing to do with planets. Whether the coincidence of the number nine is accidental or not is yet to be investigated. That the *graha* in some other contexts in medical texts can be properly interpreted as a heavenly body complicates our problem. In one passage of the *Carakasaṃhitā* (3.3.4), *graha* is mentioned along with *nakṣatra*, which means that *graha* here is one of the heavenly bodies. It should be remembered that in this context the Sun and the Moon are separately enumerated and thus they are excluded from the group of *grahas*.

In three passages of the *Suśrutasaṃhitā* (1.6.19, 1.32.4, and 6.39.266cd–267ab) *grahas* as heavenly bodies are mentioned. Especially deserving attention is the second passage, because here we find the word *graha* along with *horā* in the enumeration of bad omens (*nimittas*) leading to a patient's death. The word *horā* is a phonetic transcription of the Greek word ὥρα which denotes (1) a spatial unit of half a zodiacal sign or (2) a temporal unit of the 24th part of a day, or (3) the first astrological place (ascendant). In Sanskrit texts on astrology this word became one of the basic technical terms.

This brief summary of *grahas* in medical texts would suffice to reveal the complicated nature of Sanskrit texts. One and the same word was used in different meanings according to the context, and new ideas were sometimes incorporated into the older text. Even if we limit our topic to the *grahas* as heavenly bodies, they are subject to a variety of meanings, as will be shown below.

3.2 Grahas *as planets*

Semantic change The concept of *graha* (etymologically meaning "one which seizes") as a heavenly body experienced at least the following stages of development.

1 A demon which eclipses the Sun and the Moon was called *svarbhānu* and, probably, *graha*.
2 The demon got the name Rāhu and, somewhat later, the tail of the truncated Rāhu was called Ketu.
3 Five planets were regarded as *grahas*.
4 The Sun and the Moon joined the *grahas*, and a group of seven or nine *grahas* was established, though without fixed order.
5 The week-day order of the seven *grahas* and the concept of the nine *grahas* were established.

This process shows an interesting semantic change where the Sun and the Moon, which were originally considered as "one which is seized" finally turned to be "seizer" (*graha*). The chronological order of the stages 2 and 3 is difficult to decide.

Eclipse demon Since a solar or lunar eclipse is one of the most conspicuous heavenly phenomena, it is difficult to imagine that it escaped attention of the

Vedic poets. In fact a demon called Svarbhānu in the *Ṛgveda* 5.40.5 seems to have been regarded as the cause of eclipses. This is the only occurrence of *svarbhānu* in the *Ṛgveda* and there is no evidence that this demon was identified as *graha*. In epics, however, *svarbhānu* is explicitly called "*graha*" (*Mahābhārata* 6.13.40ab and *Rāmāyaṇa* 3.22.11cd).

Old references to planets In one passage of the *Atharvaveda* a *graha* appears as an eclipse demon. The oldest text which mentions Rāhu as an eclipse demon is the *Chandogya-Upaniṣad* (8.13). The *Maitrāyaṇī-Upaniṣad* (7.6) enumerates Rāhu and Ketu along with Saturn (*śani*) as one of the semi-deities. But the date of these passages is problematical.

It is only after the period of Greek settlement in Bactria (third century BC) that explicit references to planets are attested in Sanskrit texts.

The *Arthaśāstra* is one of the oldest texts which clearly mentions Jupiter and Venus by the name Bṛhaspati and Śukra, respectively:

> Its ascertainment (is made) from the position, motion and impregnation of Jupiter, from the rising, setting and movements of Venus and from the modification in the nature of the Sun. From the Sun (is known) the successful sprouting of seeds, from Jupiter the formation of stalks in the crops, from Venus rain. (*Arthaśāstra* 2.24.7–8)

The data of the text has not been well established. Probably its oldest part was composed about two hundred years before Christ. It is evident that this passage concerns weather prognostics. Pingree (1981) regards such prognostics as of Babylonian origin.

Nine grahas without fixed order The *Gārgyajyotiṣa* (between BC and AD)[2] arranges the nine *grahas* in a strange order: Moon, Rāhu, Jupiter, Venus, Ketu, Saturn, Mars, Mercury, and Sun. Here Ketu (almost always in plural form) is not yet the tail of Rāhu but comets. The great epic *Mahābhārata* abounds in the enumeration of *grahas*,[3] but the order of the enumeration is not fixed, nor is the weekday order attestable. Ketu is not always included in the group of *grahas*. Often it is called *dhūmaketu* ("smoke-bannered") and no reference to the single "Ketu" without similar modification is found in the *Mahābhārata*. This evidence shows that there was a period in India when all the nine *grahas* were known but the order was not yet fixed.

To this period belongs the *Śārdūlakarṇāvadāna*. The passage which concerns us runs as follows:

> Now, oh Puṣkarasārin, I will talk about *grahas*. Hear about them. They are Venus, Jupiter, Saturn Mercury, Mars, Sun, and the Lord of the stars (Moon). (Mukhopadhyaya 1954: 53)

The *Modengqie Jing*, one of the Chinese translations of the *Śārdūlakarṇāvadāna*, adds in this context Rāhu and comets (or a comet) to the seven luminaries and regards "nine" *grahas* as making one group. What is more interesting is that the week-day order of seven *grahas* is attested in a passage of this Chinese translation (Taisho Daizôkyô, vol. 21: 410). It is quite puzzling to find the week-day order here, because the Chinese translation is said to have been made in the early third century AD. This was the time when the notion of the week-day was just introduced into India. In order to settle this puzzle we must hypothesize either (1) that the Chinese translators got some new information directly from the west or (2) that this passage was inserted in a somewhat later period.

Week-day order of grahas It was only after the transmission of Hellenistic astrology that the order of planets in India was fixed in that of the seven-day week. This order is the outcome of the combination of the Greek cosmological idea of concentric spheres and the Egyptian belief of the planetary gods presiding over the 24 hours (ὥρα mentioned above). In order to get the present order of week-day, the concentric spheres must be arranged in the order of Saturn, Jupiter, Mars, the Sun, Venus, Mercury, and the Moon. This order was known sometime in the second century BC. But the evidence of the earliest use of the week-day belongs to a considerably later period.

The first evidence of the introduction of Greek astrology in India is the *Yavanajātaka*. The text was translated into Sanskrit prose in AD 149/150 and it was versified in AD 269/270 by a Sphujidhvaja. Only the verse version is extant (Pingree 1978). Sphujidhvaja's version enumerates seven planets on many occasions, but it is only towards the end of the work (chapter 77) that the week-day order is attestable. This order does not seem to have been widely spread in that period in India. Neither Rāhu nor Ketu appears in this text. About a quarter century later, however, Mīnarāja in his *Vṛddhayavanajātaka* (about AD 300–25) describes planets in the week-day order, together with Rāhu, although he does not mention Ketu (Pingree 1976). Varāhamihira (mid-sixth century) does not regard Ketu as the tail of Rāhu but as comets.

The oldest Indian inscription which gives a date with a week-day is that of Thursday, 21 July, AD 484 (Fleet 1877: 80–4). The first astronomical text which defines the week-day is the *Āryabhaṭīya* of Āryabhaṭa (born AD 476). His definition is:

> These seven Lords of *horā* beginning with Saturn are (more and more) speedy in this order (of concentric spheres). Every fourth by the order of swiftness is the Lord of the day (which begins) with the sunrise. (ABh. 3.16)

What we can safely say is, therefore, that the week-day and the order of the days of the week gradually became known to Indian people at the end of the third century and it became wide spread about a century later.

Thus all the passages in Sanskrit texts which describe planets in the week-day order should be dated later than the end of the third century.

Graha worship section of the Gṛhyasūtras Many variations of the order of the nine *grahas* are found in the section of the rite of worshiping *grahas* (*grahayajña*) in the *Gṛhyasūtras*. Thus the time in which this rite originated belongs to the fourth stage mentioned above. Even in one and the same text we can find different orders of enumeration. In some texts the seven planets are arranged in the order of Sun, Mars, Moon, Mercury, Jupiter, Venus, and Saturn. Some texts presuppose the week-day order using the word *krameṇa* or *kramāt* ("by the order (of week-day)"). Such texts or at least this part of such texts must be considered as belonging to the later period.[4] Old elements are of course preserved and repeatedly appear in the later texts, so we cannot use such elements as the means of fixing the lower limit of the date of a document, while new elements can surely serve as the criterion to judge the upper limit of the text, or at least the part of the text which contains them.

4 Classical Period

4.1 *New aspects*

Zodiacal signs A great change of the *jyotiḥśāstra* resulted from the introduction of Hellenistic astrology and astronomy into India. The most remarkable element in this was the important role played by the seven planets. Other new elements transmitted to India were the twelve zodiacal signs beginning with Aries and the twelve astrological places beginning with the ascendant. The first point of Meṣa (a translation of the Greek word corresponding to Aries) was equated with the first point of the *nakṣatra* Aśvinī. With the relation 27 *nakṣatras* = 12 zodiacal signs (i.e., 9/4 *nakṣatras* = 1 zodiacal sign), one zodiacal sign was equated to "nine quarters" of a *nakṣatra*.

Referring system The Sanskrit names for zodiacal signs are translations of the Greek words and in some texts we finḍ phonetic transliterations from Greek. However, there is a remarkable difference between the western zodiacal signs and Indian signs (called *rāśi*). In Indian astronomy the precession (*ayana*) of equinoxes was not taken into account and the initial point of the ecliptic coordinates was fixed sometime about AD 285.[5] This is the so-called *nirayaṇa* system. In the course of time, therefore, the true vernal equinox (V.E. in figure 18.1), moving backward, separated from the initial point (*meṣādi*) of the *nirayaṇa* longitude. The amount of this difference, called *ayanāṃśa*, has accumulated to some 23.5 degrees in modern times. This is the reason why the day of

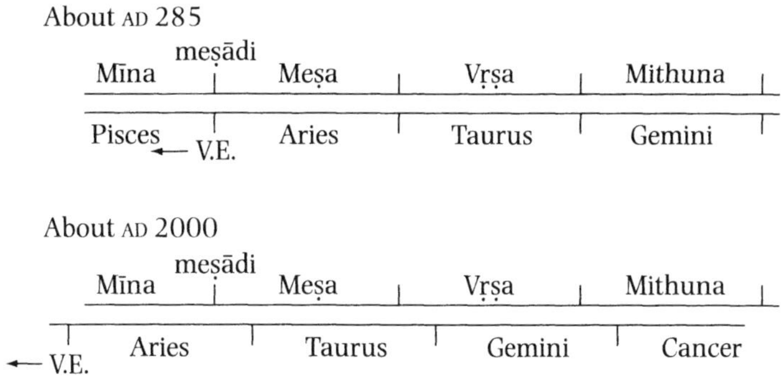

Figure 18.1: Precession of equinoxes.

Table 18.2

Saṃkrānti	*Present date*	*Lunar month*
Meṣa (Aries)	April 14	Caitra
Vṛṣa (Taurus)	May 14	Vaiśākha
Mithuna (Gemini)	June 15	Jyaiṣṭha
Karkaṭa (Cancer)	July 16	Āṣāḍha
Siṃha (Leo)	August 16	Śrāvaṇa
Kanyā (Virgo)	September 17	Bhādrapada
Tulā (Libra)	October 17	Āśvina
Vṛścika (Scorpion)	November 16	Kārttika
Dhanus (Sagittarius)	December 15	Mārgaśira
Makara (Capricorn)	January 14	Pauṣa
Kumbha (Aquarius)	February 13	Māgha
Mīna (Pisces)	March 14	Phālguna

Meṣasaṃkrānti, which was originally equivalent to the vernal equinox, now falls on around April 14. This also explains the date of Makarasaṃkrānti, the festival of winter solstice, falling on around January 14.

4.2 *Calendar system*

Month names The traditional Indian calendar is essentially luni-solar, although the solar calendar is also used additionally in some regions. In order to keep the relation of the lunar months with the change of seasons, the lunar month name was related to the solar month. First of all the solar month was determined by the "entry" (*saṃkrānti* or *saṃkramaṇa*) of the sun into each of the zodiacal signs. The relation between *saṃkrānti* and the lunar month names is shown in table 18.2. Thus, for example, the lunar month Caitra is defined as the month which contains the Meṣasaṃkrānti and Vaiśākha is the month which contains the

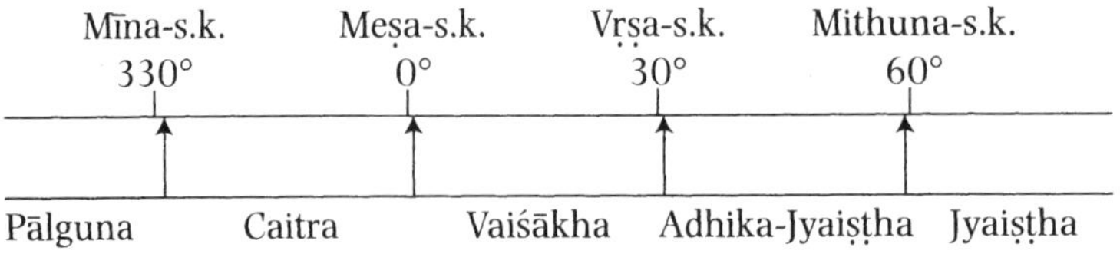

Figure 18.2: *Adhimāsa* (amānta system).

Vṛṣasaṃkrānti, etc. For the sake of the reader's convenience the approximate date of *saṃkrāntis* in the modern calendar is given in the second column.

Amānta and Pūrṇimānta One should remember that there are two different systems of naming the month, i.e. *amānta* ("new moon ending") and *pūrṇimānta* ("full moon ending"). In the bright half month (*śukla-pakṣa*) nothing is different, but in the dark half month (*kṛṣṇna-pakṣa*), the *pūrṇimānta* month name is ahead of the *amānta* month name by one. Roughly speaking, south Indian calendars follow the *amānta* method, while in north India the *pūrṇimānta* system has been used since ancient times.

Intercalary month (adhimāsa) Since a lunar month (synodic month) is a little shorter than a solar month, sometimes there occurs a lunar month which does not contain any *saṃkrānti*. Such an additional month (*adhimāsa*) was called by the name of the following month prefixed by *adhika-*. In the example of figure 18.2 the month after Vaiśākha is called Adhika-Jyaiṣṭha. An *adhimāsa* was regarded as inauspicious and no religious ceremony was performed during this month. Thus it is also called *malamāsa* ("impure month").

Omitted month (kṣayamāsa) In very rare cases there occurs a month which contains two *saṃkrāntis*. In such cases the second *saṃkrānti* does not contribute to the naming of the month and it is omitted as *kṣayamāsa*. When such a case happens there are inevitably two *adhimāsas*, one before and the other after the *kṣayamāsa*. In such years the first *adhimāsa* is called *saṃsarpa* and the rituals can be performed as usual. The month containing two *saṃkrāntis* is called *aṃhaspati*, while the second *adhimāsa* is the *adhimāsa* proper when rituals are not performed (see Kane 1962: vol. 5, p. 671).

The possibility of *kṣayamāsa* was first mentioned by Bhāskara II in his *Siddhāntaśiromaṇi*. He correctly remarks that a *kṣayamāsa* usually occurs in every 141 years and sometimes after the interval of 19 years. According to him, *kṣayamāsa* is possible only during the three months beginning with Kārttika. In figure 18.3 I have shown the case where Pauṣa is omitted. The *kṣayamāsa* shows the theoretical nature of the Indian calendar.

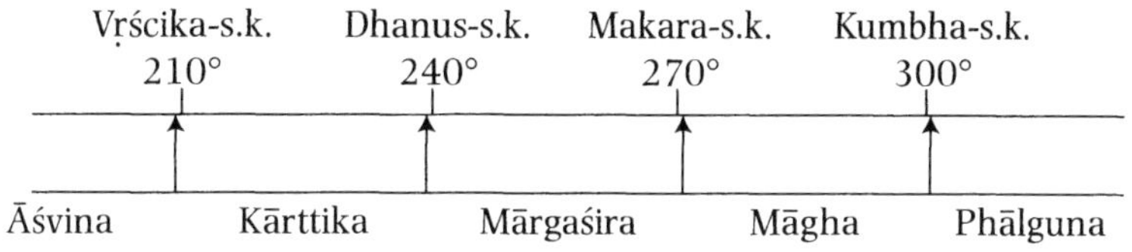

Figure 18.3: *Kṣayamāsa* (amānta system).

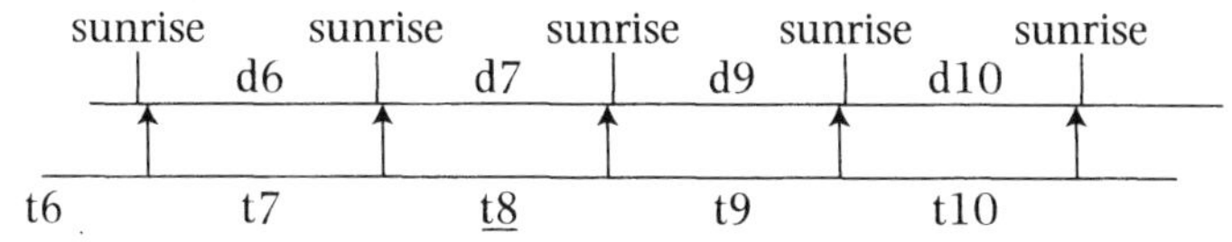

Figure 18.4: *Kṣayadina.*

Omitted day (kṣayadina) Since the average length of a synodic month is about 29.5 days, a month in a lunar calendar consists of either 29 days or 30 days. In the Indian calendar the concept of *tithi* plays an important role in order to determine whether a month contains 29 days or 30 days.

In the earlier period, a *tithi* was simply defined as one-thirtieth of a lunar month, but later it was more exactly defined as the period of time in which the increment of the lunar longitude over the solar longitude becomes 12 degrees. In both definitions one month consists inevitably of 30 *tithis*. A month is divided into two halves (*pakṣas*), a bright half (*śuklapakṣa*) and a dark half (*kṛṣṇapakṣa*) each having 15 *tithis*. Since the sunrise is the beginning of a civil day, the ordinal number of a civil day in a half month is determined by the *tithi* which is current at the sunrise. For instance, as in figure 18.4, if the sixth *tithi* (t6) is current at a sunrise, the day is called "sixth day" (d6). In this example, however, the next day (d7) contains two ends of *tithi* (t7 and t8) and at the sunrise of the following day the ninth tithi (t9) is current. Thus the eighth *tithi* does not contribute to the naming of the civil day. The eighth day (d8), therefore, is omitted from this half month. This omitted day is called *kṣayadina*.

Additional day (adhikadina) Quite opposite to the omitted days, sometimes it happens that a *tithi* contains two sunrises. In such case the same date is repeated and the second one is called *adhikadina*. In the example of figure 18.5 the eighth day (d8) of this half month is repeated.

Pañcāṅga The traditional Indian calendar is called *pañcāṅga*, i.e., "that which is consisting of five elements." The five elements are *vāra* (days of week), *tithi*, *nakṣatra*, *karaṇa*, and *yoga*. The *karaṇa* is a time unit of half of *tithi*, and the

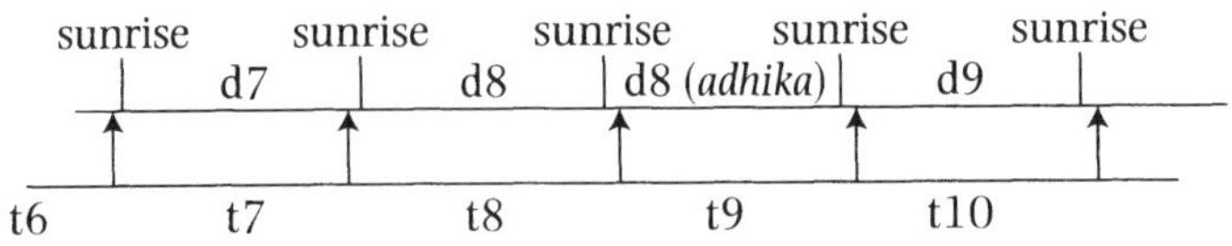

Figure 18.5: *Adhikadina.*

yoga is based on the "sum" of the longitude of the Sun and the Moon. The present author has written a computer program for *pañcāṅga* based on the *Sūryasiddhānta*. The program is available at my web page (http://www.kyoto-su.ac.jp/~yanom/).

4.3 Mathematical astronomy

Sanskritization The planetary astrology of Hellenistic origin gave a strong motivation for Indian people to learn Greek astronomy. How they got access to Greek astronomical texts and which texts were studied are not known yet. When the first Sanskrit astronomical text based on Greek astronomy appeared it was already in a well established form. The text was the *Āryabhaṭīya* of Āryabhaṭa (born in AD 476). During the interval of 300 years between the first *Yavanajātaka* and the *Āryabhaṭīya* Indian astronomers must have been occupied with the task of Indianizing and Sanskritizing Greek astronomy. The astronomical texts of this period were all lost, but fortunately we have Varāhamihira's *Pañcasiddhāntikā* (Neugebauer and Pingree 1970) where the five astronomical schools which were known in his time were summarized. They are: the *Paitāhamasiddhānta*, the *Vasiṣṭhasiddhānta*, the *Romakasiddhānta*, the *Pauliśasiddhānta*, and the *Sūryasiddhānta*. Varāhamihira evaluates them by the following words:

> The Pauliśa is accurate, that which was pronounced by Romaka is near it; the Sāvitra (i.e. the Sūrya) is more accurate; the remaining two have strayed far away (from the truth). (PS 1.3; Neugebauer and Pingree 1970: 27)

In fact the *Paitāmahasiddhānta*, belonging to the *vedāṅga* tradition, was obsolete already in Varāhamihira's time. What characterizes the *Vasiṣṭhasiddhānta* is period relations and linear zigzag functions which are probably of Babylonian origin. No geometrical method is used in these two older schools of astronomy. The *Pauliśa* and *Romaka*, which are highly regarded, are of western origin as the names suggest. These two texts were, according to Varāhamihira's own statement, commented upon by a Lāṭadeva. The author of the *Sūryasiddhānta*, the most accurate of the five *siddhāntas*, is not known. This text is different from the later and more popular *Sūryasiddhānta*.

Table 18.3

Fixed stars	R_s	1,582,237,828
Solar years	Y	4,320,000
Civil days	$D = R_s - Y$	1,577,917,828
Sidereal months	R_m	57,753,336
Synodic months	$M = R_m - Y$	53,433,336
Intercalary months	$A = M - 12Y$	1,593,336
Tithis	$T = 30 \times M$	1,603,000,080
Omitted days	$K = T - D$	25,082,580

Pre-Ptolemaic system What is to be stressed here is that the Greek astronomy transmitted to India was not the system of Ptolemy who was active in the middle of the second century in Alexandria, but that of certain schools belonging to the earlier period. This can be shown from several technical aspects: for example, the effect of the evection (second anomaly) in lunar motion, the equant point in the planetary model, and the spherical trigonometry, which were first used by Ptolemy, are all absent in Indian astronomy.

It is interesting that Indian astronomy preserved some older elements of Greek astronomy which disappeared in their homeland. One of the good examples in this respect is trigonometry. It was by tracking backward along this line of transmission that the first chord table ascribed to Hipparchus (fl. 150 BC) was recovered by G. J. Toomer (Toomer 1973: 6–28) from an Indian sine table. Toomer showed that some numerical values ascribed to Hipparchus in Ptolemy's *Almagest* could be explained by hypothesizing the use of this reconstructed table. It does not follow, however, that the Indian astronomers were only uncritical receivers of Greek astronomy. Rather, they introduced the foreign elements in a very limited time through a very small number of texts, and after this initial stage of introduction all the developments were made by themselves without foreign influence.

With the introduction of Greek astronomy, Indian astronomical constants were greatly improved. After Āryabhaṭa the constants were given as the rotations in a *mahāyuga* (4,320,000 years) or in a *kalpa* (4,320,000,000 years).

The number of civil days (D) in a *mahāyuga* is the difference between the number of the rotations of fixed stars (R_s) and those of the Sun (Y). Similarly, the number of lunar months (M) is the difference between the Moon's rotations (R_m) and those of the Sun. As we have seen in the *jyotiṣavedāṅga*, the difference between the number of lunar months and that of solar months ($12Y$) is the number of intercalary months (A). In the same way the difference between the number of *tithis* (T) and that of civil days is the number of omitted days (K).

Let us give a set of these numbers according to the later *Sūryasiddhānta*, belonging to about the eighth or ninth century. From table 18.3 we can get the length of a solar (i.e. sidereal) year and that of a synodic month:

$$\text{solar year} = \frac{D}{Y} = 365.258757,$$

$$\text{synodic month} = \frac{D}{M} = 29.530588.$$

These numbers are good enough to prepare a calendar. This is why there still survive some traditional calendars which are based on the *Sūryasiddhānta* and which give almost the same results as my computer program mentioned above.

Kali yuga epoch Since the mean positions of the Sun and Moon and the planets are the function of time, one should assume a certain time as the initial point of calculation. The class of astronomical literature called *karaṇa* is characterized by the use of an epoch which is not very far back from the time of the text, while the *siddhānta* texts employed an epoch in a very remote past where all the planets were assumed to be in mean conjunction at the starting point of the ecliptic coordinates. The epoch was sought by means of indeterminate equations of the first degree – at a certain time true positions were observed and they were converted into mean positions, while the mean motions of all the planets had been somehow known. The epoch arrived at by this method was midnight of February 17/18 in 3102 BC according to the midnight (*ārdharātrika*) school, and the sunrise of February 18 (Friday) of the same year according to the sunrise (*audayika*) school. That the epoch was very accurately chosen can be demonstrated by the fact that even today we can get a fairly good calendar using this epoch and the constants of the *siddhānta* texts.

Planetary theory The numbers for the rotations of planets are also given in astronomical texts. They vary slightly according to the schools (Pingree 1981: 15). Let us give here (table 18.4) those from the later *Sūryasiddhānta*.

Table 18.4

Rotations in a Mahāyuga	
Fixed stars	1,582,237,828
Saturn	146,580
Jupiter	364,212
Mars	2,296,832
Sun	4,320,000
Venus's *śīghra*	7,022,364
Mercury's *śīghra*	17,937,076
Moon	57,753,336
Moon's apogee	488,203
Moon's node	–232,246

The "rotations of the fixed stars" in this table is the "rotations of the earth on its axis" according to *Āryabhaṭa*, because he thought that the earth was moving while the stars were fixed. But no Indian astronomers followed his idea until Nīlakaṇṭha of the sixteenth century. The different behaviors of the outer planets (Saturn, Jupiter, and Mars) and the inner planets (Venus and Mercury) were known to Indian astronomers. The numbers given for the outer planets are their sidereal rotations and those of their *śīghra* (literally "swift one") are equal to that of the Sun. Those numbers for the inner planets are the rotations of the *śīghra*, while their sidereal rotations are equal to that of the Sun. From modern astronomical point of view, therefore, the *śīghra* can be interpreted as the mean Sun. Since, however, ancient Indian planetary theory was geocentric, they regarded the *śīghra* as rotating on the geocentric orbit of the planet and constantly drawing the planet in its direction.

After computing the longitude of the mean planets as the function of time since epoch, the true position was obtained by means of the eccentric-epicyclic theory. Here is a remarkable difference from Ptolemy's theory. Ptolemy combined two effects which cause the irregular motions of planets, namely, that of eccentricity and that of anomaly, and put them together in a single geometric model. In doing so he had to introduce a controversial point, which was later called the "equant," outside the center of the eccentric circle. In India, on the other hand, the two effects were kept separate and no unified model was conceived. One was called the *manda* (literally "slow one") epicycle which explains, in modern words, the combined effects of the eccentricities of the Sun and the planet, the other was called the *sīghra* epicycle as mentioned above. The effects of these two elements for each planet were separately tabulated. The procedures of using the two tables in order to get the final equation (*antyaphala*) show some variations depending on the school. Thus we can say that Indian planetary theory is not totally geometrical. Once they introduced geometrical models from the west, they developed their own functional method.

It is worth mentioning that Āryabhaṭa's school survived in south India, especially in Kerala, and was revived as the Mādhava school in the fourteenth century. The culmination of this school is Nīlakaṇṭha (1444 to after 1542), who tried to combine the two effects in a single geometrical model, and the result was quite similar to the partial heliocentric model of Tycho Brahe.

Notes

1 I follow Dr. Ohashi's interpretation. Cf. Yukio Ohashi, 1993.

2 *Yugapurāṇa*, a part of the *Gārgya-jyotiṣa*, was edited and translated by John E. Mitchiner, Calcutta 1986.

3 MBh.2.11.20; 3.3.19; 6.3.11–17; 13.151.12 etc. Thanks are due to my friend, Prof. M. Tokunaga by whom the whole text of the *Mahābhārata* has been digitalized.

4 Some other examples are: *Rāmāyana* 1.17 (Rāma's horoscope), *Mudrārākṣasa* 4.19 (horoscopic prediction), and a part of the *Atharvaveda-pariśiṣṭa*.

5 The time when the longitude of α Virginis was 180°. Cf. Chatterjee 1998.

References

Chatterjee, S. K. 1998. *Indian Calendric System*. New Delhi.

Dvivedin, S., ed. 1907. *Ārcajyautiṣam* 33. *The PANDIT*, new Series, vol. 29, Benares.

Fleet, J. F. 1877. *Corpus Inscriptionum Indicarum*, vol. 3. Calcultta.

Kane, P. N. 1962. *History of Dharmaśāstra*. Delhi.

Macdonell, A. A. and A. B. Keith. 1912. *Vedic Index of Names and Subjects*, vol. 1. London.

Mitchiner, John E., ed. 1986. *Yugapurāṇa*, a part of the *Gārgya-jyotiṣa*. Calcutta.

Mukhopadhyaya, S. 1954. *Śārdūlakarṇāvadāna*. Santiniketan.

Neugebauer, O. and D. Pingree. 1970. *The Pañcasiddhāntikā of Varāhamihira*, 2 parts. Copenhagen.

Ohashi, Yukio. 1993. "Development of Astronomical Observation in Vedic and Post-Vedic India," *Indian Journal of History of Science* 28 (3): 186–251.

Pingree, David, ed. 1976. *Vṛddhayavanajataka*. Gaekward Oriental Series nos. 162 and 162. Baroda.

——. 1981. *Jyotiḥśāstra*. Vol. VI, fasc. 4 of *A History of Indian Literature*. Wiesbaden.

——. 1987. *Yavanajātaka*. Harvard Oriental Series no. 48, 2. vols. Cambridge, MA.

Toomer, Gerald J. 1973. "The Chord Table of Hipparchus and the Early History of Greek Trigonometry," *Centaurus* 18: 6–28.

CHAPTER 19

The Science of Medicine

Dominik Wujastyk

The Beginnings of Medical Science

Indian medicine, as a systematic and scholarly tradition, begins historically with the appearance of the great medical encyclopedias of Caraka, Suśruta and Bhela about two thousand years ago.[1] These are the oldest Indian medical texts we have, and also the most influential. Just as Pāṇini's famous linguistic study of Sanskrit leaps into the historical record fully formed, like the Buddha from Queen Maya's side, so the medical encyclopedias too emerge with a learned medical tradition in an almost fully articulated form.

The antecedents

In the case of Pāṇini, we do have some preceding literature, which shows us traditional Indian linguistics in its childhood, so to speak, notably the *Nirukta* of Yāska, as well as the various *śikṣā* and *prātiśākhya* texts. But in the case of medicine far less precursory material has survived. Early medical texts which are now known only by name include the *Jatūkarṇatantra*, the *Hārītasaṃhitā*, the *Parāśarasaṃhitā*, and the *Kharanādasaṃhitā*, all of which apparently existed at the time of Śivadāsa who commented on the *Carakasaṃhitā* in the fifteenth century. Other lost works include the *Viśvāmitrasaṃhitā*, the *Atrisaṃhitā*, the *Kapilatantra*, and the *Gautamatantra* (Roy 1986: 157–9 and Meulenbeld 1999–2002: Ia.145–79, 369–71, 689–99). But even before these specialist treatises on medicine, there is a certain amount of material on the history of medicine which can be recovered from earlier, chiefly religious, texts.

Medicine in Vedic times It is often claimed that āyurveda evolved organically from the medical traditions discernible in Vedic literature. The respected scholar Mira Roy, for example, draws attention to several areas of apparent continuity between the Vedic concepts, especially from the *Atharvaveda*, and the āyurvedic compendia (1986:6.155f.). One of the examples she cites is the fact that five vital breaths are mentioned in both the *Atharvaveda* and the *Carakasaṃhitā* (AV 10.2.13, Ca.sū.12.8).

But on closer examination, all of these supposed parallels break down. Thus, it is true that Caraka's *Compendium* does have a discourse on the five vital breaths. This discourse is put into the mouth of a scholar called Vāyorvida ("he who knows about air"), who presents his theory as a cornerstone of physiology. As soon as he finishes his description, another scholar, Marīci, disputes his statement impatiently, saying (Ca.sū.12.9):

> Even if this is so, what is its general relevance to the purpose of this discussion or with knowledge of medical science? This is a discussion on the subject of medical science!

Vāyorvida tries to defend his point of view briefly, but without introducing any new ideas, and Mārica proceeds to put forward his own view that fire (*agni*) is the cornerstone of medicine. This too is superseded by the sage Kāpya with yet another view that *soma* is the cornerstone, and so the discussion continues. The conclusion presented by the chairman of the debate, Punarvasu Ātreya, is that while he regrets contradicting anyone, health ultimately comes down to a balance of the three humors (*doṣas*) (Ca.sū.12.13).

All we can really deduce from these passages is that a doctrine of five breaths existed at the time of the composition of the medical encyclopedias. Of course this is well known: the five breaths are already discussed in the much earlier literature of the Upaniṣads and Brāhmaṇas. But although the doctrine of the breaths is mentioned in the early medical texts, it does not become an important part of medical thought or practice until the composition of a much later work called the *Āyurvedasūtra*. This synthetic work, probably written in the early seventeenth century, tries for the first time to combine doctrines from āyurveda and a form of tantric yoga (Meulenbeld 1999–2002: IIa.499ff.).

Roy herself finally concludes that in spite of some superficial similarities,

> Āyurveda, which incorporates different traditions [from the Veda], has a distinct place alongside of the Vedas. . . . Although glorified as an appendage of Vedic literature, Āyurveda as such is not mentioned there. (1986:6.156)

Roy points out that although a later Vedic text, the *Ṛgvedaprātiśākhya* (16.54), refers to a medical treatise called *Good Medicine* (*subheṣaja*), it is the *Mahābhārata* that first refers to medicine as a science of eight parts (*cikitsāyāṃ aṣṭāṅgāyāṃ* 2.50.80), and uses the word "āyurveda" as the name of the science of medicine (12.28.44, 12.328.9, 12.330.22).

The *Compendium* of Caraka contains a passage in which the physician is advised on how to respond, when pressed by questioners on the subject of which Veda his science belongs to (Ca.sū.30.21). He should answer that he is devoted to the *Atharvaveda* because that Veda prescribes rituals and prayers to enhance and prolong life, and this is the purpose of medicine too. The context suggests that this passage should be read as a slightly knowing suggestion, in which the physician is being advised to claim allegiance to a Veda because his interlocutor requires it of him, and as part of a didactic strategy, rather than for any more fundamental reason connected with real historical connections. It is tempting to read Roy's arguments above, and others like them, as adhering to exactly this ancient recommendation.

If āyurveda does not derive from Vedic medical traditions, what then are its antecedents?

This has been one of the most outstanding problems for the history of āyurveda for most of the last century. One serious suggestion which has recurred in the literature on āyurvedic history is that some of the the innovative doctrines of āyurveda were taken from Greek physicians in Gandhāra. Jean Filliozat tested this idea in his book on classical Indian medicine, and indeed found parallels between Indian and Greek thought, especially regarding the doctrines of breath (Skt. *prāṇa*, Grk. *pneuma*) (Filliozat 1964). But Indian medical literature has no loan-words from Greek, and is in this respect quite different from the Indian astral sciences (*jyotiḥśāstra*) which have borrowed many items of Greek vocabulary. There are philologically puzzling words in āyurveda, for example *jentāka*, meaning a steam bath or sauna. This is almost certainly not a Sanskrit word in origin, but it is not from the Greek either, and its origin has not yet been traced. In fact, Michio Yano has, as reported elsewhere in this volume, discovered one Greek word in the early Sanskrit medical corpus. The word *horā* (ὥρα) occurs in Suśruta's *Compendium* (Su.sū.32.4) in a passage listing omens which foretell the death of a patient. If the patient's zodiacal sign (*horā*) has burning lights or meteors in it, the patient is doomed. This proves that the compiler of this part of the text was already aware of the Hellenistic astrology that became available in India during the second century CE. But this makes it even more striking that not one Greek loanword for a medical term appears in Sanskrit medical literature. Indian physicians almost certainly had the opportunity to imbibe Greek medical ideas, but apparently no motive.

Until recently, few other serious ideas had been mooted for the origin of āyurveda. The conjecture that āyurveda embodies traditions that somehow came from the Indus valley civilization is tempting, of course, but impossible to establish. Scholars working within a traditional framework have tended not to engage with the problem, because of the strong traditional belief that āyurveda is indeed a continuation of medicine from the Vedic *saṃhitās*. Many texts on the history of āyurveda, even written by contemporary scholars, start by repeating the mythological accounts given in the beginning of the saṃhitās in which medicine is passed from the gods to the humans through a chain of divine beings and spiritual teachers. Such scholars seem unable or unwilling to see such an account for what it is, a common frame for initiating any orthodox śāstra, which occurs in variant forms at the beginning of a number of other major texts, such as the *Bṛhajjātaka*, and in various places in purāṇic literature (Pollock 1985; Zysk 1999).

Accounts of origins cast as historical discourses can be considered as having two dimensions: a horizontal and a vertical, rather as Ferdinand de Saussure divided linguistic study into orthogonal diachronic and synchronic dimensions. The horizontal dimension is that of mundane time: history in this dimension is a narrative of the events of past times. The vertical dimension measures closeness to God: the history of this dimension is the account of how the present manifest situation has evolved, or descended, from an original, pristine world of absolute unity. When at the start of a Sanskrit text we are told by the author, as so often happens, that the work once consisted of millions of verses, but was handed from the original omniscient sages to human scholars only in abbreviated form, we must understand that we are dealing with vertical history. This is the story of how knowledge – which is essentially of God – has come to us mere mortals. Such a spiritual narrative is not to be confused or conflated with horizontal history, although the narrative may be cast in the language of past tenses and linear teacher–pupil descent. What we are being told is how the present work is an imperfect reflection of divine omniscience, a mirror – and many Sanskrit texts are called "Mirrors" of this or that subject – of what is known in heaven. So when, at the start of the foundational texts of Sanskrit medicine, we are told of the passage of medical knowledge from the gods to ancient sages such as Dhanvantari and Ātreya, and thence to other humans such as Agniveśa and Suśruta, to Caraka and Nāgārjuna, we do not necessarily need to try to grasp all these figures as historical personages in the horizontal dimension. We are in the presence, rather, of a kind of *apologia*, an explanation of how something which was (past tense!) perfect, is now presented, brought into the present, in the blemished, mundane form of a textbook. It is an account of how knowledge which was once privileged is now commonly accessible.

It was Debiprasad Chattopadhyaya who first began to grapple with the sociology of Indian medical history in his fascinating book *Science and Society in Ancient India* (Calcutta, 1977). In that text he presented strong arguments for considering the early medical encyclopedias to be nonreligious, empirically oriented works which had undergone a secondary process of "Hinduization," in order to make them into works acceptable to a Hindu brahmin elite. Chattopadhyaya, writing from a Communist perspective on Indian history, had his own motivations for discovering materialist and empirical traditions wherever possible in Indian intellectual history, and this probably biased many readers against accepting his conclusions about the history of Indian medicine. In the case of āyurveda, however, there is much to commend his arguments. But even Chattopadhyaya was not able to suggest where this empirical tradition came from.

Medicine in the Buddhist community Evidence for the beginnings of a systematic science of medicine in India appears first in the literature of the earliest Buddhists, with many medical tales being recounted in the *Tripiṭaka*. The Buddha instructed his monks to care for each other in sickness, since they had abandoned the social structures which would have provided them with treatment if they had not left their families to become monks.

> You, O bhikkhus, have neither a mother nor a father who could nurse you. If, O bhikkhus, you do not nurse one another, who, then, will nurse you? Whoever, O bhikkhus, would nurse me, he should nurse the sick. (*Mahāvagga* 8.26.3, cited in Zysk 1998: 41)

The earliest Buddhist monks seem to have concentrated on providing medical help only for each other, but before long the lay community started to request help from the monks. Zysk (1998) has collected evidence to show that early Buddhist monasteries included infirmaries and had standing instructions to aid all those who were sick, not only monks.

Buddhist monks thus seem to have taken an active attitude to their own health and that of their lay supporters. This attitude may have been encouraged by the many medical epithets and turns of phrase attributed to the Buddha in the recorded sermons. In his parables he often used images such as "removing the arrows of suffering." One of the forms in which the Buddha has been revered since at least the first century CE is as the "Medicine Buddha" (*bhaiṣajyaguru*), and there is even a sūtra devoted to him under this name (Zysk 1998: 62).

Zysk's research into the medical materials recoverable from the Buddhist canon has revealed close similarities with the classical Sanskrit sources on medicine. It now seems almost certain that the foundations of classical āyurveda were being laid at the time of early Buddhism in the Buddhist and other ascetic communities.

In the centuries of Buddhist missionary expansion, Indian medical doctrines were carried across the Himalayas into Central Asia and beyond, as well as into Sri Lanka. The rare manuscripts that have survived from this diaspora, such as the Bower Manuscripts, share a common character: they are practical handbooks, manuals listing ailments and explaining the herbs and compounds that should be administered to cure them (Wujastyk 2001: ch. 4). There is little theory, little explanation, little philosophy. In this they differ from the classical compendia of āyurveda.

It is also possible that some important authors of Sanskrit medical texts, such as the famous Vāgbhaṭa, were Buddhists.

The Medical Body

The medical system which evolved from this ascetic milieu contained a sophisticated set of doctrines, supported by close observation and long experience of treating patients.

The body to which Indian medicine addresses itself is the physical body as understood to the senses and to empirical examination. In particular, āyurveda knows no *cakras*, nor the spinal conduits of breath (*prāṇa*) known from tantric literature. The concept of the *cakras* has today entered public consciousness world-wide, and is widely viewed as an ancient and immutable element of the Indian world view. This view needs to be qualified in two directions. First, the idea of the *cakras* is a relatively recent development in Indian tantric thought. It is datable only to the tenth century CE, making its appearance in texts such as the *Kubjikāmatatantra* and the *Mālinīvijayottaratantra* (Heilijgers-Seelen 1990). Secondly, the *cakras* make no appearance whatsoever in āyurveda. Notwithstanding the contemporary growth of various forms of massage and therapy focussed on the *cakras*, there is no such theme in the classical Sanskrit literature on medicine. The *cakras* really are an idea specific to *tantra* and yoga, and it is not until relatively recent times that this idea has been synthesized with medical thought and practice.

With a customary Indian interest in itemization (Smith 1994), the āyurvedic literature is keen to enumerate the receptacles, ligatures, conduits, orifices, and tissues which can be found in the human body. The *Śārṅgadharasaṃhitā* (ca. 1300) offers a fairly standard and clearly-presented version of such a list (Wujastyk 2001: 322–8). There are: 7 receptacles (*āśaya*); 7 body tissues (*dhātu*); 7 impurities of the body tissues (*dhātumala*); 7 subsidiary body tissues (*upadhātu*); 7 membranes (*tvac*); 3 humors (*doṣa*); 900 sinews (*snāyu*); 210 ligaments (*sandhi*); 300 bones (*asthi*); 107 lethal points (*marman*); 700 ducts (*sirā*); 24 pipes (*dhamanī*); 500 muscles (*māṃsapeśī*); 20 extra ones for women; 16 tendons (*kaṇḍarā*); 10 orifices of the male body; 13 orifices of the female body. Although these items may not in all cases be organs in the modern biomedical sense (Zimmermann 1983), there is a definite sense that āyurveda views the body as a locus of medical organs and processes which would be recognizable in general terms to a modern anatomist. After making his own much earlier enumeration of anatomical parts, Caraka noted, perhaps wistfully, that (Ca.śā.7.17),

> The parts of the body cannot, however, be counted because they are divided into tiny atoms (*paramāṇu*), and these are too numerous, too minute, and beyond perception. The cause of the conjunction and separation of these tiny atoms is wind (*vāyu*) and an innate disposition to action (*karmasvabhāva*).

This demonstrates an acute sense of the limits of possible scientific investigation, but at the same time contains fascinating and plausible suggestions about the nature of these "tiny atoms." Throughout medical and scientific discourse in Sanskrit, "wind" often appears in contexts which would, in early European scientific discourse, require the word "force."

The metabolic process

The central process of the body is digestion. The Sanskrit words for the processes of digestion (*pācana, dīpana*) all imply "cooking" or "burning." And the digestive force itself is simply called the "fire" (*agni*), or "fire in the belly" (*jāṭharāgni*). Once food has been eaten and cooked by this digestive fire, it turns into the first of the seven "body tissues" (*dhātu*), namely chyme or chyle (*rasa*), the pulpy juice to which food is reduced in the stomach. Then the other principle of heat in the body, choler (*pitta*), goes to work and the chyle is transformed into the next body tissue in the chain, blood. Blood transforms into flesh, and similarly the remaining tissues, fat, bone, and marrow; are converted one into the next, until the seventh and highest essence of the body is generated: semen. This, of course, suggests a purely male view of the body, and āyurveda's picture of women's metabolism includes no obvious equivalent to semen: the evolution of the chain of body tissues does not seem to fit the substances in a woman's body. One passage in Suśruta's *Compendium* locates menstrual blood in the place of semen; another seems to suggest a certain degree of homology between male semen and female breast-milk. Yet another passage suggests that two women having intercourse may "somehow" (*kathaṃcana*) produce semen (Su.ni.10.18–23ab, Su.śā.2.47). Āyurveda understands conception as the union of male semen and female menstrual blood (there is no concept of "ovum"). It is the woman's blood discharged during menstruation, but retained during pregnancy (when it is transformed into breast-milk), which joins with male semen and goes towards building a child's body.

Suśruta's *Compendium* gives the time scale for this principle metabolic process (Su.sū.14.10–16). The nutritive juice (*rasa*) spends about 108 hours in each of the body tissues. Thus, it takes a lunar month for the nutritive juice to become semen, or menstrual blood. The total time spent in metabolizing is 648 hours. In a curious and interesting verse, Suśruta notes that, "This nutritive juice (*rasa*) flows throughout the whole body like a tiny particle, in a manner similar to the propagation of sound, light, and water."[2] However, this is not the normal āyurvedic conception of how fluids are transported around the body. How then is the irrigation of the body – a metaphor used by Suśruta – carried out?

Fluids and their conduits

The types of fluid in the āyurvedic body include blood (*rakta*), milk, semen, breath (*prāṇa*), the juice of digested food (*rasa*), and the humors wind (*vāta*), bile (*pitta*), and phlegm (*kapha*).

These fluids are transported from place to place by three principle types of conduit: ducts (*sirā*), pipes (*dhamanī*), and tubes (*srotas*). Given the importance of this system of fluid distribution to the āyurvedic physiology, surprisingly little work has been done on clarifying what these conduits do, and how they are explained in āyurvedic theory (exceptions include Dasgúpta 1969: ii.13 and Kutumbiah 1999: ch. 2).

Ducts (sirā) According to the *Suśrutasaṃhitā*, the function of the 700 ducts is to carry wind, bile, phlegm, and blood around the body, starting from their origin in the navel. In a vivid pair of metaphors, one agricultural and one botanical, Suśruta's text describes the ducts as follows (Su.śā.7.3):

> As a garden or a field is irrigated by water-carrying canals, and each part receives nourishment, so the ducts provide nutrition to the body by means of their contraction and dilation. Their branches are just like the veins on a leaf.

A point of special interest is that the ducts are colored according to what they carry: those carrying wind are yellowish brown (*aruṇa*), those carrying bile are dark blue, those carrying phlegm are white, and those carrying blood are red (Su.śā.7.18). It seems likely that these distinctions are based on the observation of different-colored vessels under the surface of the skin. In yet another simile, Suśruta likens the distribution of these ducts from the umbilical center through the body to the spokes radiating from the center of a wheel (Su.śā.7.7).

Pipes (*dhamanī*) There are said to be 24 pipes in the body (Su.śā.9). Like the ducts, they originate in the navel. From there, 10 go up, 10 down, and 4 sideways.

Those which go up from the navel support the body by carrying particular items (*viśeṣa*) such as sound, touch, vision, taste, smell, out-breath (*praśvāsa*), in-breath (*ucchvāsa*), yawning, sneezing, laughter, speech, crying, etc. These 10 pipes go from the navel to the heart and there each one divides into 3 branches, thus producing 30 pipes. Ten of these are devoted to carrying the humors, wind, bile, and phlegm, as well as blood and nutritive fluid (two pipes for each substance). Eight more carry sense impressions: sound, form, taste, and smell (again, two pipes each). Two pipes are used for speech (*bhāṣā*), two for making sound (*ghoṣa*), two for sleeping, and two more for waking up. Two pipes carry tears. Two pipes connected to the breasts carry women's breast-milk; curiously, in men the same two pipes are said to carry semen from the breasts.

Those pipes which go down from the navel carry substances such as wind, urine, feces, semen, and menstrual blood. In between the receptacles of raw and digested food, the pipes divide into three branches, as before. The first 10 pipes have the same functions as the first 10 upward pipes. The next two carry food to the intestines, and another two carry water. Two carry urine to the bladder. Two generate and transport semen, and two make it ejaculate. In women, the same four pipes carry and discharge menstrual blood. Two pipes are connected to the intestines and function in defecation. The remaining 8 pipes supply sweat to the horizontal pipes.

Each of the four pipes which run sideways are said to subdivide hundreds of thousands of times, holding the body together in a network. Their ends are connected to the hair follicles, and through these sweat is carried out and nutritive juice is carried in. This is how massage oils, showers, and ointments can move through the skin and affect the body internally. They are also the means by which pleasant and unpleasant sensations of touch are experienced.

Tubes (*srotas*) According to Suśruta, there are initially 22 tubes in the body, 2 for each of 11 substances. Two of the tubes (*srotas*) carry breath (*prāṇa*), and are joined to the heart and the pipes (*dhamanī*) which carry nutritive juice. Two more carry food, and are joined to the food-carrying pipes and the stomach. Two carry water and are joined to the palate and the lung (*kloman*). Two carry nutritive juice and are joined to the same places as those carrying breath. Two carry blood, and are joined to the liver, the spleen, and the pipes which carry blood. Two carry flesh, and are joined to the ligaments, skin, and pipes which carry blood. Two carry fat and are joined to the waist (*kaṭī*) and the kidneys. Two carry urine and are joined to the bladder and penis. Two carry feces and are joined to the receptacle of digested food and the rectum. Two carry semen and are joined to the breasts and testicles. Two carry menstrual blood and are joined to the womb and the pipes which carry menstrual blood. (There is no suggestion that these last pairs are specific to either gender.) Caraka adds three more categories of tube: two carrying bone, two carrying marrow (completing the set of 7 basic body elements (*dhātu*)), and two carrying sweat. He omits menstrual blood. Like the horizontal pipes, the tubes in the body divide and subdivide into innumerable tiny branches.

In contrast to the ducts and pipes, the description of these tubes is embedded in a discourse of injury, and the symptoms arising from damage to them are listed.

Suśruta records the existence of an ancient disagreement amongst physicians as to whether the pipes, ducts, and tubes are really separate types of vessel, and in particular whether there is a significant difference between pipes (*dhamanī*) and tubes (*srotas*). He argues that there is indeed a difference between these three types of vessel: they look different, have different connections, and different functions. The authoritative tradition of medical science also asserts their difference. It is merely because of their close proximity, similarity, and small size that they are conflated. Caraka also testifies to contemporary debates about the nature of these vessels; he records – and rejects – an extreme view that the human body consists only of a conglomeration of tubes.

Diagnosis

Another disagreement in the early medical tradition concerns the methods of diagnosis. Caraka uses the traditional scheme of the three "epistemological standards" (*pramāṇa*) as the basis for his diagnostic scheme. Diseases are discovered by means of the combined application of authoritative testimony, direct perception, and inference. The tradition of medical learning and science counts as authority. Direct perception means examining the patient using all the senses, although Caraka is distinctly squeamish about the sense of taste, and offers several ways of avoiding the need to taste the patient. Finally, inference is used to deduce the state of nonvisible features of the patient's body and functioning.

Using a simpler approach, Suśruta first records the tradition that there are three methods a physician should use to examine a patient: touching, looking, and questioning. But he then argues that a doctor has five senses, and that he should use all of them when examining a patient. For some reason, this common-sense view did not prevail in later medical textbooks, nor did Caraka's complex system. Later medical tradition normally reproduces Suśruta's triple-examination method.

Pulse

Debate and questioning on the topic of diagnosis probably continued, for by the late fifteenth century a new set of diagnostic methods had emerged as standard, the "examination of the eight bases" (*aṣṭasthānaparīkṣā*): pulse, urine, eyes, face, tongue, faeces, voice, and skin. These methods are first mentioned as a fixed set in the *Jvaratimirabhāskara* of the Mewari physician Cāmuṇḍa (fl. ca. 1474–1538; Meulenbeld 1999–2002: IIa.165), and become a standard in later medical textbooks.

The diagnosis of disease by pulse first appears in Sanskrit in the fourteenth-century *Compendium* of Śārṅgadhara (Wujastyk 2001: ch. 7). He begins by describing the pipe (*dhamanī*) on the hand at the base of the thumb as "an indicator of life," and notes that an expert can tell the well-being or ill health of the body by its behavior. He then connects various humoral conditions with different movements felt in the tube (*nāḍī*). Thus, inflamed wind feels like the movement of a leech or a snake; inflamed bile feels like the gait of a sparrow-hawk, crow or frog; inflamed phlegm feels like the gait of a swan or pigeon. The tube is also characterized as feeling weak or strong, cold or hot, firm or sluggish (Wujastyk 2001: 318).

In Śārṅgadhara's text, and until the advent of influences from European medicine, the understanding and use of pulse is closely tied to prognostication techniques. The ability to foretell the course of a patient's illness has formed a part of āyurvedic medicine from the earliest times. Caraka, for example, devotes a section of his *Compendium*, the *Indriyasthāna*, to the various signs by which a doctor can read the impending death of a patient. Thus, a patient who is about to die is called blossomed (*puṣpita*), partly because of the metaphor of a flower inevitably preceding a fruit, and partly because a dying person may produce unusual and unexpected smells, including the smell of various flowers. In looking for signs of death, the physician is advised to feel the patients body for temperature, perspiration, and resilience. He should also look for changes in the breathing and in the pulsations at the nape of the neck (Ca.ni.3.6). Thus, when the examination of the pulse appears in āyurveda, it fits well into a preceding tradition of prognostication. In a medical tradition which does not know of the pumping function of the heart or of the circulation of the blood, one has to ask what the physicians thought they were feeling in the pulse (cf. Kuriyama 1999). The position of the first historical description of āyurvedic pulse lore, in Śārṅgadhara's text, immediately precedes his sections on the interpretation of omens and dreams. This context sheds important light on how this new diagnostic technique was understood.[3]

Disease Etiology

The question of disease etiology in *āyurveda* is of great interest, and is far more sophisticated than the simple idea that "disease is an imbalance of the humors," although this statement is certainly part of the classical tradition. One of the central etiological ideas in *āyurveda* is the "abrogation of wisdom" (*prajñāparādha*), the idea that we fall ill through actions that follow lapses of judgment.[4] This "judgment" (*prajñā*) consists of the combined work of three mental faculties: intelligence (*dhī*), will-power (*dhṛti*), and memory (*smṛti*).[5] As an example of impaired intelligence, the classical authors cite errors such as mistaking something permanent as temporary, or something harmful as helpful, etc. Poor will-power would be exemplified by a lack of self-control in the face of sensual enjoyments which are unhealthy. Faulty memory is exemplified when a person's mind becomes so confused by passion or darkness, that they cease to be able to see things as they really are, and they cannot remember what should be remembered. The concept of memory is expanded elsewhere in Caraka's *Compendium* into a full-blown doctrine of yogic self-remembering, strongly reminiscent of the Buddhist mindfulness (*sati*).[6] Erroneous mental processes are likely to lead a person to engage in several types of faulty action. The person may misuse or abuse their senses, body, speech, or mind in various ways, and this abuse leads to sickness.

A related cause of illness is the suppression of natural urges. Urges related to urine or feces, semen, wind, nausea, sneezing, clearing the throat, and yawning should always be obeyed, without hesitation. So should the urgings of hunger and thirst, tears, sleep, or the panting induced by exertion. The suppression of any of these natural urges can lead to disease and is another example of a lapse of good judgment. Of course, bad urges, such as to impetuous or dishonorable deeds, should be suppressed, and this applies also to extreme feelings of negative emotion, the vocal expression of hatred or criticism, or physical violence.

Yet another disease etiology is the operation of karma: diseases afflict people due abrogations of their good judgment in the past. In the medical texts, the workings of karma are described in more detail than is usual. The karma one created oneself during a previous embodiment shows itself in the present as good or bad luck. Added to that is the further karma one creates in the present lifetime. These two kinds of karma may be graded according to strength or weakness: karma can be low, medium, or superior. A combination of the superior kinds of the two karma types gives rise to a long and happy lifetime. A combination of the low ones brings about a short and miserable life, and a combination of medium karmas is expected to result in an average lifespan.[7] The literature of "the ripening of deeds" (*karmavipāka*) develops these ideas, sometimes in great detail, with personal case histories exemplifying diseases and their karmic antecedents (Pingree 1997; Wujastyk 1999).

Demonic interference and possession was viewed as another valid cause of illness. Women and children are particularly vulnerable to such possession, which is also often presented as a punishment for bad deeds (Wujastyk 1999). Disease contagion is not a standard feature of the āyurvedic understanding of how illness arises (Zysk 2000; Das 2000), but interestingly a form of spirit-contagion is described in Kāśyapa's *Compendium*, in which a demon (*graha*) which has taken up abode in one unfortunate person may be transferred to another by means of touch (Wujastyk 2001: ch. 5).

Therapy

Āyurveda recommends a wide range of therapeutic techniques, including herbal drugs, massage, sauna, exercise, diet (including the use of meat broths and other non-vegetarian and alcoholic tonics), blood-letting (including leeching), simple psychotherapy, and surgery. One important group of five therapies (*pañcakarman*) became established early. According to Caraka, these were: emetics, purgation, two types of enema, and nasal catharsis. Suśruta replaced one of the enema treatments with bloodletting. Other authors introduced sweating and massage, as well as other therapies, into what became historically an increasingly important and elaborate complex of treatments.

Almost every other therapeutic application in āyurveda is preceded by a standard regime of oiling and sweating. "Oiling" usually consists of taking oils or fats by mouth, often with food. But it can also consist of oil enemas, nasal drops, bodily anointing, gargling, or the application of oils to the head, eyes, or ears. "Sweating" can mean warming the body by any of a range of methods: with a hot cloth, a warm metal plate, or the hands, the application of hot poultices, taking a traditional steam sauna, or the pouring of infusions of herbs and meats over the patient from a kettle. These preliminaries help to open the channels in the patient's body and to liquefy the humors which have been causing blockages, enabling them either to flow out of the body through the digestive tract, or to return to their proper locations in the body.

Surgery

The discussion of surgery in early āyurveda is most highly developed in the *Compendium* of Suśruta. There are many chapters here on such topics as the training of the surgeon, the preparation and maintenance of a wide range of scalpels, probes, pincers, and other surgical tools, and the diagnosis of medical problems which are to be treated specifically by surgery. Elaborate and varied surgical techniques are described, including perineal lithotomy, ophthalmological couching for cataract, the reduction of dislocations, the lancing of boils, the piercing of earlobes, the removal of obstructions and foreign bodies of all kinds from the flesh and orifices, rhinoplasty and the repair of hare-lip, and the suturing of wounds (Mukhopādhyāya 1913; Majno 1975; Wujastyk 2001: ch. 3). Suśruta's surgical chapters are justly famous. Why such an extraordinarily advanced school of surgery should have arisen so early in India, and why its work should have been recorded in Sanskrit, remain unanswered questions. The vibrant tradition evidenced by Suśruta's text did not survive as part of professional medical practice, although isolated techniques such as cataract couching did continue to be performed by barber-surgeons in a tradition apparently unsupported by a learned literature or formal training.

Materia medica

A large part of the āyurvedic literature, including general works, monographs, and dictionaries, is devoted to herbal medicine and materia medica generally. Several thousand plants are known and described in terms of a pharmacological typology based on flavorings (six types), potency (usually two: hot and cold), post-digestive flavorings (usually three), and pragmatic efficacy (used when the effect of a medicine is not adequately defined by the earlier categories). This typology is keyed to the system of humors and other physiological categories as expressed through the vocabulary of pathology. The system of humors functions in medicine in somewhat the same manner as the "case function" (*kāraka*) system in Pāṇinian grammar. Just as the six case functions provide the grammarian with a set of categories though which the urge to express a meaning (*vivakṣā*) can be related to morphological units of grammar, so the three medical humors provide a set of mediating categories through which diseases can be related to herbal medicines.

Rules of interpretation

There are certain rules of interpretation (*paribhāṣā*) which are applied when using herbal medicines, and these exemplify the important notion of "default values" which Frits Staal has highlighted elsewhere in this volume in the context of ritual and grammar. Thus, unless otherwise stated, the time of any action is dawn, the part of a plant is the root, the quantity of substances is equal, the container is made of clay, the liquid is water, and the oil is from sesame. By default, herbs should be fresh, not dried, and fresh herbs should be used in double the specified measure (Wujastyk 2001: ch. 7). There are many other standard defaults which are silently applied in medical situations, including a set of more than 30 subtle and interesting rules called "the logic of the system" (*tantrayukti*) which are to be used when interpreting medical statements (Su.ut.65, Ca.si.12.41–48).[8]

Medical Philosophy

Several modern authors have written about the interesting philosophical passages which occur in the early medical literature, especially in Caraka's *Compendium* (e.g., Dasgupta 1969: ii.13; Larson 1993). Caraka's use of Sāṃkhya and Vaiśeṣika concepts is of particular interest: his extensive treatment of the theory and practice of formal argument (Ca.vi.8) led Dasgupta to argue that the medical literature preserved perhaps the earliest stratum of Nyāya thought. Less attention has been paid to Caraka's version of the Yoga system (Ca.śā.1 esp. 137 ff.). Comba (2001) has shown that this chapter of Caraka's work cites several passages from the *Vaiśeṣikasūtra*. For Caraka, yoga and liberation (*mokṣa*) are both states in which all sensations (*vedanā*) cease. In liberation, however, this cessation is complete, while in yoga it is a goal. Quoting from the *Vaiśeṣikasūtras*, Caraka asserts that yoga arises when the mind is concentrated steadily on the self; in that state, the contact between the self and the sense organs, etc., ceases to exist, and several special powers arise. These are the standard eight siddhis of yoga and Indian magic. Caraka then focuses on the concept of mindfulness or remembering, in particular the memory of reality (*tattvasmṛti*), which both gives rise to a serious and soteriologically oriented lifestyle, and is produced by it. The full emergence of this special kind of memory (*smṛti*) results in freedom from suffering. At this point, Caraka presents his own unique eightfold path of yoga, which is quite different from the classical scheme of Patañjali. The path is aimed at developing memory, and consists of the following eight elements: understanding causes, forms (*nimittarūpagrahaṇa*), similarity (*sādṛśya*), and difference (*viparyaya*); adherence to purity (*sattvānubandha*), practice (*abhyāsa*), the yoga of knowledge (*jñānayoga*), and repeated listening (*punaḥśruta*). The mindfulness of reality (*tattvasmṛti*) produced by these eight practices leads to the identification of the self with *brahman*.

The Wider Influence of Āyurveda

Classical Indian medicine, āyurveda, has exerted a long and pervasive influence on other indigenous traditions in India, as well as on those of foreign countries. The fields of dharmaśāstra, arthaśāstra, tantra, alchemy, kāmaśāstra, and other sciences were all influenced by āyurveda in varying degrees. Āyurvedic treatises, such as the toxicological tract which is embedded in Suśruta's *Kalpasthāna*, became famous in Arabic translations from a very early period (Wujastyk 2001: 123). The Tibetan translation movement from the eighth century onwards resulted in many āyurvedic works becoming an integral part of the Tibetan healing tradition, and āyuvedic manuscripts recovered from the oasis towns of the Taklamakan desert testify to its importance in Central Asia. The Persian *Kitāb Firdaws al-ḥikma* by 'Alī ibn-Sahl aṭ-Ṭabarī, written in 850, included a detailed account of āyurveda, based on already existing Persian and Arabic translations of the āyurvedic classics. The great Muslim physician Muḥammad ibn-Zakariyyā" ar-Rāzī (d. 925) frequently cited Arabic translations of Caraka (Ullmann 1978: 19). Later, through the works of da Orta (1563), van Rheede (1678–1703) and Linnaeus (1748, 1753), āyurvedic traditions exerted an important and lasting influence on the development of botanical science in Europe (Grove 1995: ch. 2). During the twentieth century, āyurveda has been supported at the national level in post-independence India, with hospitals, colleges, clinics, and a thriving āyurvedic pharmaceutical industry. And a process of globalization – similar to that which took place earlier with yoga – has begun to occur also with āyurveda. As might be expected, āyurveda "in diaspora" is changing and adapting, as it moves from its premodern role as the only learned medicine available to the population to a new position as one part of a portfolio of alternative and complementary therapies offered alongside modern biomedicine.

Notes

1 Abbreviations used in this chapter: Ah. = *Aṣṭāṅgahṛdayasaṃhitā* (Kuṃṭe et al. 1995), Ca. = *Carakasaṃhitā* (Ācārya 1981), Su. = *Suśrutasaṃhitā* (Ācārya 1992). All translations are my own unless otherwise stated.
2 Su.sū.14.16: *sa śabdārcirjalasantānavad aṇunā viśeṣeṇānudhāvaty evaṃ śarīraṃ kevalam.*
3 I am grateful to Anupam Goenka, with whom these ideas were discussed and developed (Goenka 2001).
4 For accessible introductions to the concept of *prajñāparādha*, see Dasgupta (1969: II, 415–18 *et passim*) and Weiss (1980).
5 Ca.śā.1.98–109.
6 Ca.śā.1.137–55. Cf. Thera 1996.
7 Ca.Vi.3.29.
8 These same rules also appear in the *Arthaśāstra*.

References

Ācārya, Jādavji Trikamji, ed. 1981. *Carakasaṃhitā, śrīcakrapāṇidattaviracitayā āyurvedadīpikāvyākhyayā saṃvalitā*. New Delhi: Munshiram Manoharlal, 4th ed.

——, ed. 1992. *Suśrutasaṃhitā, śrīḍalhaṇācāryaviracitayā nibandhasaṃgrahākhyavyākhyayā nidānasthānasya śrīgayadāsācāryaviracitayā nyāyacandrikākhyapañjikāvyākhyayā ca samullasitā . . . Ācāryopāhvena trivikramātmajena yādavaśarmaṇā . . . saṃśodhitā*. Vārāṇasī, Delhi: Caukhambhā Oriyanṭāliyā, 5th edn.

Chattopadhyaya, Debiprasad. 1979. *Science and Society in Ancient India*. Calcutta: Research India Publication. Repr. of original 1977 ed.

Comba, Antonella. 2001. "Carakasaṃhitā, Śārīrasthāna I and Vaiśeṣika philosophy," in Gerrit Jan Meulenbeld and Dominik Wujastyk, eds., *Studies on Indian Medical History*, ch. 3, pp. 39–55. Delhi: Motilal Banarsidass, 2nd ed.

Conrad, Lawrence I. and Dominik Wujastyk, eds. 2000. *Contagion: Perspectives from Pre-modern Societies*. Aldershot, Burlington USA, Singapore, Sydney: Ashgate.

Das, Rahul Peter. 2000. "Notions of 'Contagion' in Classical Indian Medical Texts,' in Conrad and Wujastyk (2000), pp. 55–78.

Dasgupta, Surendranath. 1969. *A History of Indian Philosophy*. Cambridge: Cambridge University Press. 5th repr. of 1922 ed.

Filliozat, Jean. 1964. *The Classical Doctrine of Indian Medicine*. New Delhi: Munshiram Manoharlal.

Goenka, Anupam. 2001. "The Nadi is Not the Pulse: Different Ways of Knowing the Body," History of Medicine B.Sc. dissertation, UCL, London.

Grove, Richard. 1995. *Green Imperialism: Colonial Expansion, Tropical Island Edens and the Origins of Environmentalism, 1600–1860*. Cambridge: Cambridge University Press.

Heilijgers-Seelen, Dory. 1990. "The Doctrine of the Ṣaṭcakra According to the Kubjikāmata," in Teun Goudriaan, ed., *The Sanskrit Tradition and Tantrism*, vol. 1 of *Panels of the VIIth World Sanskrit Conference*, pp. 56–65. Leiden: Brill.

Kuṃṭe, Aṇṇā Moreśvara, Kṛṣṇaśāstrī Navare, and Hariśāstrī Parādkar, eds. 1995. *Aṣṭāṅgahṛdayam, śrīmadvāgbhaṭaviracitam, śrīmadaruṇadattaviracitayā "sarvāṅgasundarākhyā" vyākhyayā hemādripraṇītayā "āyurvedarasāyanāhvayā" ṭīkayā ca samullasitam*. No. 4 in Kṛṣṇadāsa Āyurveda Sīrīja. Vārāṇasī: Krishnadas Academy. Reprint.

Kuriyama, Shigehisa. 1999. *The Expressiveness of the Body and the Divergence of Greek and Chinese Medicine*. New York: Zone Books.

Kutumbiah, P. 1999. *Ancient Indian Medicine*. Bombay, etc.: Orient Longman, rev. 1969 ed. First published 1962.

Larson, Gerald James. 1993. "Āyurveda and the Hindu Philosophical Systems," in Thomas P. Kasulis, Roger T. Ames, and Wimal Dissanayake, eds., *Self as Body in Asian Theory and Practice*, ch. 5, pp. 103–21. New York: SUNY.

Linnaeus, Carolus. 1748. *Flora Zeylanica sistens plantas Indicas Zeylonae Insulae, quae olim 1670–1677 lectae fuere a Paulo Hermanno, prof. Bot. Leydensi*. Amstelædami: Wetstenium.

——. 1753. *Species plantarum, exhibentes plantas rite cognitas, ad genera relatas, cum differentiis specificis, nominibus trivialibus, synonymis selectis, locis natalibus, secundum systema sexuale digestas*. Holmiae: Impensis Laurentii Salvii, 2 vols.

Majno, Guido. 1975. *The Healing Hand: Man and Wound in the Ancient World*. Cambridge, MA: Harvard University Press.

Meulenbeld, Gerrit Jan. 1999–2002. *A History of Indian Medical Literature*. Groningen: Egbert Forsten, 5 vols.

Mukhopādhyāya, Girindranāth. 1913. *The Surgical Instruments of the Hindus, with a Comparative Study of the Surgical Instruments of the Greek, Roman, Arab, and the Modern Eouropean* (sic) *Surgeons*. Calcutta: Calcutta University, 2 vols., illustrated.

da Orta, Garcia. 1563. *Coloquios dos simples, e drogas he cousas mediçinais da India. . . .* Goa: J. de Endem.

Pingree, David. 1997. "Two *Karmavipāka* Texts on Curing Diseases and Other Misfortunes," *Journal of the European Āyurvedic Society* 5: 46–52.

Pollock, Sheldon. 1985. "The Theory of Practice and the Practice of Theory in Indian Intellectual History," *Journal of the American Oriental Society*, 3 (105): 499–519.

van Rheede, Henricum. 1678–1703. *Hortus Indicus Malabaricus. . . .* Amstelaedami: J. van Someren, J. van Dyck. 12 vols.

Roy, Mira. 1986. "Āyurveda," in Priyadaranjan Ray and S. N. Sen, eds., *The Cultural*

Heritage of India, vol. 6: Science and Technology, ch. 11, pp. 152–76. Calcutta: Ramakrishna Mission Institute of Culture, 2nd ed, 6 vols.

Smith, Brian K. 1994. *Classifying the Universe: The Ancient Indian Varṇa System and the Origins of Caste.* New York, Oxford: Oxford University Press.

Thera, Nyanaponika. 1996. *The Heart of Buddhist Meditation.* York Beach, ME: Samuel Weiser. First published by Rider & Co., London, 1962.

Ullmann, Manfred. 1978. *Islamic Medicine*, vol. 11 of *Islamic Surveys*. Edinburgh: Edinburgh University Press.

Weiss, Mitchell G. 1980. "*Caraka Saṃhitā* on the Doctrine of Karma," in Wendy Doniger O'Flaherty, ed., *Karma and Rebirth in Classical Indian Traditions*, pp. 90–115. Berkeley: University of California Press.

Wujastyk, Dominik. 1999. "Miscarriages of Justice: Demonic Vengeance in Classical Indian Medicine," in John Hinnells and Roy Porter, eds., *Religion, Health, and Suffering*, pp. 256–75. London: Kegan Paul International.

——. 2001. *The Roots of Āyurveda: Selections from Sanskrit Medical Writings.* New Delhi: Penguin, 2nd ed.

Zimmermann, Francis. 1983. "Remarks on the Conception of the Body in Ayurvedic Medicine," in Beatrix Pfleiderer and Guenther D. Sontheimer, eds., *Sources of Illness and Healing in South Asian Regional Literature*, vol. 8 (1979) of *South Asian Digest of Regional Writing*, pp. 10–26. Heidelberg: South Asia Institute, Dept. of Tropical Hygiene and Public Health, Dept. of Indology, Heidelberg University.

Zysk, Kenneth G. 1998. *Asceticism and Healing in Ancient India: Medicine in the Buddhist Monastery.* Indian Medical Tradition, vol. 2. Delhi: Motilal Banarsidass, 2nd ed. First published 1991.

——. 1999. "Mythology and the Brāhmanization of Indian Medicine: Transforming Heterodoxy into Orthodoxy," in Folke Josephson ed., *Categorisation and Interpretation*, pp. 125–45. Göteborg: Meijerbergs institut för svensk etymologisk forskning, Göteborgs universitet.

——. 2000. "Does Ancient Indian Medicine have a Theory of Contagion?," in Conrad and Wujastyk (2000), pp. 79–95.

Philosophy and Theology

CHAPTER 20

Hinduism and the Proper Work of Reason

Jonardon Ganeri

1.1 Early Recognition of a "Practice of Reason"

Reason can be used or abused. A cautionary episode in the *Mahābhārata* illustrates the point. Bhīṣma tells Yudhiṣṭhira that there is nothing more worth having than wisdom. Wisdom, he declares, is the greatest good, the refuge of all living things, the ultimate acquisition, and is considered by the virtuous to be heaven itself (12.173.2). But then, in case his point should be misunderstood, he recounts the story of Indra appearing in the form of a jackal (12.173.45–8):

> I used to be scholarly [says Indra], a reasoner, a scorner of the Veda. I was pointlessly fond of critical inquiry and the science of argument. I used to make declarations on the basis of logic; in assemblies, speaking with reasons, I harangued the brahmins and was rude during the Vedic recitations. I was an unbeliever, sceptical about everything, and though stupid, I thought myself wise. The status of a jackal that I have obtained is the result, Kāśyapa, of my misdeeds.

The terms in which Indra deprecates himself are important ones, for they gradually came to be associated with the practice of philosophy itself in India. Indra was a "reasoner" (*haituka*), he was addicted to the study of critical inquiry (*ānvīkṣiki*) and to the science of argument (*tarka-vidyā*). That free thinking of this sort was seen as embodying a danger to the stability of orthodox brahminical learning is only too clear. In another epic narrative, the *Rāmāyaṇa*, Rāma advises his brother Bharata to steer well clear of such people (2.94.32–33):

> You must not associate with those "worldly" (*lokāyata*) brahmins, dear brother. Their only skill is in bringing misfortune; they are fools who think themselves wise. In spite of the pre-eminent treatises on right conduct (*dharma*), these ignorant people derive their ideas from critical inquiry, and make declarations without any point.

These "reasoners" represent a challenge and a threat to the existing tradition. They will assent to the deliverances of reason whether or not it agrees with the scriptures and the authorities on what is considered to be proper conduct. The lawmaker Manu therefore advises that a brahmin who has adopted the science of reasoning, treating with contempt the twin authorities on proper conduct (the scriptures and the texts on right conduct or *dharma*), should as an "unbeliever" and a "scorner of the Vedas" be driven from the company of the virtuous.[1]

It is not that in the great epics reason as such is condemned, but only its capricious use. The "reasoners" are condemned for lacking any goal other than the use of reason itself; they believe in nothing and are skeptical of everything. They use reason to criticize the scriptures, but have no doctrines of their own. Reason, the message seems to be, is misapplied when it is used in a purely negative, destructive way. In other words, the proper use of reason should be to support, and not to undermine, one's beliefs, goals, and values, The objection to the reasoners, as they are represented in the epics, is that for them the use of reason has become an end in itself. It is goalless, capricious, ungrounded.

The idea that the use of reason must be purposeful or goal-directed is taken up in the *Treatise on Gains* (*Arthaśāstra*), a famous book on government, politics, and economics which dates from around 300 BC. Its author is Kauṭilya, supposed to have been the chief minister in the court of Candragupta, a Mauryan ruler who came to power at about the time of Alexander's death. The period following Alexander's campaign in India was in fact a time of intimate and extended contact between India and Greece. The ancient Greek chronicler Megasthenes frequently visited the court of Candragupta and in his *Indica* he presented to the Greeks a vivid account of the Indian society of those times. Fragments of this lost work quoted by later writers reveal Megasthenes to have been greatly impressed by similarities between Greek and Indian ideas, especially about space, time, and the soul.[2] He is also said to have carried messages between Candragupta's son Bindusāra, the father of Aśoka, and Antiochus I. Bindusāra indeed asked Antiochus to send him Greek wine, raisins, and a Sophist to teach him how to argue. Antiochus replied by sending the wine and raisins, but regretted that it was not considered good form among the Greeks to trade in Sophists!

Kauṭilya's purpose in writing the *Treatise on Gains* was to educate future kings in the necessary skills required for a successful and prosperous rule. He states that there are four branches of learning in which a young prince should be trained: the religious canon composed of the three Vedas; the sciences of material gain, primarily trade and agro-economics; the science of political administration and government; and finally *ānvīkṣikī*, the discipline of critical inquiry, of which *sāṃkhya*, *yoga*, and *lokāyata* are listed as the principal divisions. Significantly, he rejects explicitly the claim of Manu and others that the study of critical reasoning is tied exclusively to a religious study of the self and its liberation (*ātmavidyā*). Critical inquiry is an autonomous discipline (1.2.11):

> Investigating by means of reasons, good and evil in the Vedic religion, profit and loss in the field of trade and agriculture, and prudent and imprudent policy in political administration, as well as their relative strengths and weaknesses, the study of critical inquiry (*ānvīkṣikī*) confers benefit on people, keeps their minds steady in adversity and in prosperity, and produces adeptness of understanding, speech and action.

He reiterates an old couplet (1.2.12):

> The study of critical inquiry is always thought of as a *lamp* for all branches of knowledge, a *means* in all activities, and a *support* for all religious and social duty.

Shortly after the rediscovery and publication of the *Treatise on Gains* in 1909, Hermann Jacobi wrote an article arguing that Kauṭilya had to all extents distinguished and defined "philosophy" in India.[3] Kauṭilya's separation of a study of "critical inquiry" (*ānvīkṣikī*) from theological studies was enough, he conjectured, to justify the identification of "critical inquiry" with philosophy. This rather important conjecture has been strongly disputed, on the grounds that critical inquiry as described by Kauṭilya consists simply in the art of investigating by reasons, and this is something that is practiced in *all* branches of learning. Paul Hacker[4] makes the point that this "critical inquiry" is not necessarily an independent system of thought, but is sometimes rather a *method*. In the same vein, it has very plausibly been conjectured[5] that the early references to *sāṃkhya*, *yoga*, and *lokāyata* are not to well-defined schools of philosophical speculation, but reflect instead a methodological division. Thus *sāṃkhya* labels the methods of inquiry that rest on the intellectual enumeration of basic principles, *yoga* the methods of spiritual practice, and *lokāyata* the methods of worldly or empirical investigation.

We can agree with these conjectures without having to identify philosophy as a discipline with the having or inventing of a system of thought. Philosophy is circumscribed by adherence to a certain methodology and body of problems. Broadly, it is the *a priori* analysis of the interconnections and distinctions between groups of concepts to do with the nature of value, thought, existence, and meaning. It is indeed possible to hear in Kauṭilya's remark about "investigating . . . good and evil in the Vedic religion, profit and loss in the field of trade and agriculture, and prudent and imprudent policy in political administration" a suggestion that a reasoned investigation is an inquiry into the nature of the distinction between good and evil, the proper goals of political institutions, and so on. But the intended domain of application for critical inquiry seems to be much wider than that. It encompasses any situation in which one sets about achieving one's aims in a reasoned way. There is a reasoned way to go about making a profit, a reasoned way to rule a country. The study of what such reasoning consists in is one thing, the *philosophical* investigation of the nature of profit or rule quite another. So *ānvīkṣikī* in Kauṭilya's sense is a study of the generic concept of rationality, as that concept features in questions about how rationally to think, how rationally to act, and how rationally to speak.

Kauṭilya's conception of rationality is goal-oriented and instrumental. The interest is in the reasoned way to achieve some goal, whatever that goal may be. The use of reason does not tell us for which goals one should strive, but only how rationally to strive for them. The *Arthaśāstra* is, after all, a manual of instruction for princes. The discipline Kauṭilya calls that of critical inquiry is the one which trains the prince in the way for him to fulfill his projects, having once decided what those projects are to be. The other sciences, of trade and agriculture, of policy-making and government, train him in the skills of choosing one objective rather than another. A person is rational when he uses rational methods to reach his aims. (Kauṭilya wanted kings to become philosophers, not as Plato that philosophers be made kings.) It is not enough to be rational that the aim be in some sense a "worthy" one, for even worthy goals can be striven for by irrational means.

Bertrand Russell[6] said that "reason" "signifies the choice of the right means to an end that you wish to achieve. It has nothing to do with the choice of ends." The epic horror of the reasoner concerned the *aimless* use of reason, using reason capriciously or solely to subvert the goals of others. Kauṭilya's defence makes rationality instrumental and therefore goal-directed. It follows, however, that a tyrant can be just as rational as a ruler who is beneficent, an atheist as rational as a believer. If rationality is instrumental, then to act rationally is not the same as to act well. Followers of reason alone still face the charge of immorality, hereticism, and untruth.

1.2 Rationality in the *Nyāyasūtra*

Gautama Akṣapāda's *Nyāyasūtra*, the redaction of which took place in the first or second century AD, deals with such themes as the procedures for properly conducting debates, the nature of good argument, and the analysis of perception, inference, and testimony in so far as they are sources of knowledge. There is a detailed account of the causal structure of the mind and the nature of its operation. Certain metaphysical questions are addressed, notably the reality of wholes, atoms, and universals. At the beginning of his commentary on this remarkable work, Vātsyāyana Pakṣilasvāmin (ca. AD 400) wonders what it is that makes the Nyāya system distinctive. He answers as follows:

> Nyāya is the examination of things with the help of methods of knowing (*pramāṇa*). It is an inference supported by observation and authority. This is called a "critical proof" (*anvīkṣā*). A "critical proof" is the proof of things desired, supported by observation and authority. The discipline of critical inquiry is the one which pertains to it, and is also called the science *of nyāya* or the writings on *nyāya*. But an inference that contradicts observation and authority is only a bogus-*nyāya*.[7]

Vātsyāyana agrees with Kauṭilya that the study of critical inquiry is one of the four branches of study, but he insists that it has its own procedures or methodology. He claims that if critical inquiry did not have its own procedures then it would "merely be a study of the soul's progress, like an Upaniṣad." This is a rather important remark. Reasoned inquiry and scriptural studies are now claimed to have the same eventual goal or purpose; where they differ is in method. That marks a departure from Kauṭilya's purely instrumental conception of rationality, in which the use of reason could equally well serve any end. For Vātsyāyana wants to claim that there can be rational goals, as well as rational means, and so to distance the Nyāya system from the free-thinkers in the epics.

Let us first see that Vātsyāyana shares the epic horror of *aimless* reason. Reason, he says, can be used in one of three ways. One may employ it in a good and proper way (*vāda*), as one does when one's goal is to ascertain the truth of the matter. One may employ it in a bad or improper way (*jalpa*), as when one's goal is to defend one's position at all costs, using any intellectual tricks one can think of. Finally, one might employ reason in a negative and destructive way (*vitaṇḍā*). Here one has no goal other than to undermine one's opponent. People who use reason in this way are very like the sceptics and unbelievers of the epics, and Vātsyāyana disapproves. He claims indeed that to use reason in this way is virtually self-defeating:

> A *vaitāṇḍika* is one who employs destructive criticism. If when questioned about the purpose [of so doing], he says "this is my thesis" or "this is my conclusion," he surrenders his status as a *vaitāṇḍika*. If he says that he has a purpose, to make known the defects of the opponent, this too is the same. For if he says that there is one who makes things known or one who knows, or that there is a thing by which things are made known or a thing made known, then he surrenders his status as a *vaitāṇḍika*.[8]

Vitaṇḍā is the skeptic's use of reason. Vātsyāyana's point is that someone who presents an argument against a thesis has at least that refutation as their goal, and so commits himself to the machinery of critical examination. But a *vaitāṇḍika* who accepts this gives up his claim to use reason aimlessly, without commitment. So the aimless use of reason is not just pernicious, it is self-defeating!

The salient point here is that reason must have a purpose, and the question is what that purpose should be. Vātsyāyana's answer is clever. He argues that a goal is a rational one if it is the rational means to some further goal. And he claims that whatever one's eventual goal is, the rational way to achieve it is through the acquisition of knowledge – knowledge about one's goal and how it might be achieved. So the acquisition of knowledge is always a rational goal. Indeed it is the rational goal *par excellence*, for knowledge is instrumental in the rational pursuit of any other goal:[9]

> Since there is success in one's activities when the awareness of one's object is produced by an accredited method of knowing (*pramāṇa*), the method of knowing is connected with the object. Without a method of knowing, there is no awareness

> of the object. Without an awareness of the object, there is no success in one's activities. But the knower, having grasped the object in thought by some suitable method, either desires it or wants to avoid it. His "activity" is the effort prompted by his desire for or aversion of it. "Success" is the coming together of that activity with its reward. Desiring the object, or wanting to avoid it, one either makes an effort to obtain it or else to avoid it. One's "object" is the contentment [one feels] and the cause of that contentment, or the disdain and the cause of that disdain.

Let me take a simple example. Suppose my goal is to acquire a piece of silver. To succeed, I need to know where silver might be found, and how to recognize it; I need to be in a position to know, of some object, that it is made of silver. I need to know other things as well, such as that I have some way of acquiring the silver once identified. So the reasoned way for me to go about acquiring a piece of silver is to seek to acquire knowledge of the identifying traits, whereabouts, and means of acquiring of silver objects. The acquisition of such knowledge becomes itself a goal, subsidiary to my principal aim of acquiring silver.

In the translation, I have tried to retain an ambiguity in the Sanskrit word *artha*, in rendering it as "object." It can mean both one's goal, such as acquiring silver, and also the thing which that goal concerns, the silver itself. It is the target of one's endeavor, both as the piece of silver, and equally well as the acquiring of that silver. Vātsyāyana suggests that it can also denote the satisfaction one feels on achieving one's goal, or the irritation of not doing so. Later on,[10] he stresses that, in virtue of the connection that exists between knowledge of the object and success or failure in one's goals concerning it, one should employ some suitable method of knowing if one wants to succeed. The theory of rationality in this way depends on a theory of the proper means of acquiring true beliefs.

Kauṭilya said that the study of critical inquiry is the study of the notion of "investigating with reasons." Vātsyāyana tells us what a "reason" (*hetu*) is. It is a method of acquiring knowledge, a *pramāṇa*. For a "reasoned" inquiry is one which is based on the acquisition of knowledge. The early Nyāya writers look closely at the characteristic method that constitutes a rational inquiry. The opening verse in the *Nyāvasūtra* is a list of 16 items which, according to its author, comprise the subject matter of the Nyāya system. The first two items are the various methods of knowing and the domain of knowables. They constitute the Nyāya epistemology and metaphysics. The next seven are the theoretical components in the process of critical inquiry: doubt, purpose, observational data, doctrinal bases, extrapolative demonstration, suppositional reasoning, and a final decision. The final seven are terms of art in the theory of debate. *Nyāyasūtra* 1.1.1:

> The highest goal in life is reached through knowledge about the nature of:
>
> (a) knowables, methods of knowing,
> (b) doubt, purpose, observational data, doctrinal bases, the parts of a demonstration, suppositional reasoning, final decision,

(c) truth-directed debate, victory-directed debate, destructive debate, sophistical rejoinders, tricks, false reasons, defeat situations.

A properly conducted inquiry, adds Vātsyāyana, is that process by which we move from an initial uncertainty about the nature of the thing or concept under investigation, to an ascertainment of its properties. The inquiry is permitted to draw upon such data as are incontrovertible or accepted by both parties in the dispute, and it proceeds by adducing evidence or reasons in support of one side or the other. The first element here is the existence of a doubt (*saṃśaya*) which initiates the investigation. A doubt is said to be a mental state whose content is of the form "Does this object have a certain specified property or not?" Typical doubts discussed in the *Nyāyasūtra* (is the soul eternal or non-eternal?, is a whole object identical with the sum of its parts?) tend to be philosophical conjectures or hypotheses, but the method applies just as well to the resolution of empirical questions.

An inquiry must have a purpose. The assumption is that any form of rational behavior must have some motivating purpose, the point for which one wishes to resolve the doubt. The inquiry can appeal to shared background doctrinal principles and empirical data. Here, by "empirical data," what is meant are the observational facts to which all parties can appeal. The background principles are called "doctrinal bases" or "proved doctrines," and might also include a category of *a priori* truths or principles. Gautama actually mentions several kinds of doctrinal base. In particular, there are those which everyone must accept, for example that objects of knowledge are established via means of knowing. Other doctrinal principles are in the form of conditionals, where both parties agree on the truth of the conditional, but dispute the truth of the antecedent. Also mentioned are assumptions which are made merely for the sake of argument. One or both sides might grant some principle, simply to facilitate the inquiry. In any case, having initiated an inquiry for some purpose, and taken into consideration both empirical evidence and such doctrinal or *a priori* considerations, the investigation concludes with the decision, which is a resolution of the initiating doubt.

Similar characterizations of the general structure of problem-solving are offered in the contemporary literature on formal heuristics.[11] There a problem is defined as one in which the following features are specified and delimited: *a goal* – a criterion of judging outcomes; *an initial state*, consisting of a situation and the resources available for the solution; a set of *admissible operations* for transforming states; *constraints* on states and operations; and *an outcome*. It would seem that the Nyāya account fits rather nicely this characterization of the structure of a problem-solving set-up. The doubt is an initial state of uncertainty, the purpose is the goal, the admissible operations are the sanctioned methods of reasoning by extrapolative demonstration (section 1.6) and supposition (*tarka*), the constraints are the observational data and doctrinal bases to which all parties agree, and the outcome is the final decision. A critical inquiry, then, is a formal heuristic for problem-solving.

Nyāyasūtra 1.1.1 makes a further demand on the type of proof procedure admissible in a critical inquiry. It insists that the inquirer be able explicitly to set out for others the piece of knowledge so acquired as the conclusion of a precisely formulated demonstration (*avayava*). In its general schematic form, a demonstration scheme has five steps:

i) Preliminary statement of the thesis to be proved.
ii) Citation of a reason.
iii) Invoking an example.
iv) Application to the present case.
v) Assertion with confidence of the conclusion.

For example: (i) There is a fire on the mountain. (ii) Because there is smoke there. (iii) As in the kitchen. (iv) The mountain is the same. (v) Therefore, there is fire there. I will look in detail at the structure of such argument schemes in a later section (1.7). I am interested here in what the demand for demonstration tells us about the nature of critical inquiry, an investigation "with reasons." The early Nyāya writers want to explicate the notion of a reason. Since the rational way to achieve one's goals is by acquiring knowledge about its constituents, it might seem that a reason is any method of acquiring knowledge (*pramāṇa*). However, the insistence now is that the rational inquirer be able to set out his reasoning in an explicit and canonical way. And a "reason" is the premise or evidence (*hetu*) in such a suitably formulated argument. Vātsyāyana explains that the various means of acquiring knowledge have a subsidiary role here. They enter the account as the means by which each step in the explicitly formulated demonstration is proven:[12]

> The means of acquiring knowledge reside in those [demonstration steps]. The preliminary statement of the thesis is an item of testimony (*āgama*). The reason (*hetu*) is an item of inference. The example is an item of perception. The application is an item of "analogical comparison." The final conclusion exhibits the possibility of all these coming together in a single thesis. Such is a *nyāya par excellence*. With the help of this alone can truth-directed, victory-directed and destructive debate techniques be employed, never otherwise. Fixing the truth depends on this. The steps in the demonstration are sentences, and as such are included among the objects of knowledge; but they are mentioned separately for the above reasons.

Vātsyāyana's systematizing idea is that the three strands out of which the Nyāya system is formed – theory of knowledge, study of critical inquiry and art of debate – can be brought together into a single discipline. In doing so, he introduces a new condition on a rational inquiry: that it be capable of being made public through verbal demonstration. A rational inquiry is, to be sure, a procedure for reaching one's goal which exploits knowledge about that goal and the most effective way to achieve it. But it must also be knowledge of the sort that can be displayed. It must be knowledge that is backed up by reasons of the sort that are potentially capable of convincing others, something that can stand up to the scrutiny of a debate.

There is a conflict here between two accounts of the source of rational norms. On the one hand, to proceed rationally is to proceed by acquiring knowledge of an appropriate sort. But on the other hand, to proceed rationally is publicly to adduce reasons and arguments for the knowledge one purports to have. The first is an epistemic conception of norms, while the second grounds norms in the public conventions of the debating hall. The early Naiyāyikas, drawing on their roots in the systematization of debating theory, insist that rationality must be a public affair, an explicit demonstration in the five-step format, but they try to merge this idea with another, that the norms of reason are the norms of warranted belief. The tension between these two concepts of reason will manifest itself again as we examine in later sections other paradigms of rationality in the *Nyāyasūtra*.

1.3 Rationality and the Ends of Life

The early Naiyāyikas have linked the pursuit of rational inquiry with the final ends of life: *Nyāyasūtra* 1.1.1 states that it is by understanding the nature of reasoned inquiry, epistemology and debating theory that one attains the "highest goal" (*niḥśreyasa*). *Nyāyasūtra* 1.1.2 amplifies the point, adducing an exact sequence of causal relations between knowledge and liberation (*apavarga*).

The final aim of life is the permanent elimination of *duḥkha*. Duḥkha is a difficult term in Indian soteriology. Its meaning is: suffering, pain, discontent, frustration, displeasure. What then is the source of all this discontent? One source has already been mentioned by Vātsyāyana in the passage quoted before – the frustration of one's plans. Obtaining one's goals is an end in itself, but so too is the pleasure or contentment that success instils. It is not just that in obtaining the piece of silver, I gain as well the pleasures that go with possessing a valuable thing. It is also that fulfilling one's projects is a form of satisfaction in its own right. Vātsyāyana stresses, however, that the final aim of life must involve a separation from pleasures as well as pains. For pleasure is invariably attended by pain, as if it were honey mixed with poison! So the ultimate aim in life consists in the elimination of any attachment to the success or failure of one's projects, or the rewards or discomforts such projects bring.

Can a life of reason help one achieve this? Kauṭilya perhaps thought so, for he said that pursuing one's goals by means of rational inquiry helps to keep the mind steady in both adversity and prosperity. The Naiyāyika thinks so too (NS 1.1.2):

> Liberation results from the removal of the next member when the immediately preceding member is removed in the sequence of: wrong belief, bad qualities, actions, birth, suffering.

This is the pan-Indian *karma* theory, a causal theory of moral retribution. There is a direct causal link between the moral quality of one's present actions and one's future contentment or frustration in this birth or another (a commentator[13] points out that by "actions" here what is meant is righteous and unrighteous conduct, since it is such conduct that is the cause of birth and rebirth). We observed earlier that with a purely instrumental conception of rationality, it is no more rational to do good than to do evil. To be rational is simply to set about one's aims in a reasoned way. In the context of a causal theory of moral retribution, however, it is rational to strive to do good. For given that one's final aim in life is to avoid frustration (presumably including the frustration of one's future plans), one has a reason to behave well now and do good. At least, one has a reason as long as one knows that there is a direct causal link of the sort described. After all, acquiring knowledge about the sources of frustration and suffering is the rational way to accomplish one's aim of eliminating them!

The rational life is a life best suited to eliminate at least one source of suffering, namely the frustration of having one's plans fail. So if one's ultimate end in life is to avoid suffering, and the main source of suffering is due to the frustration of one's plans, one has a reason to live a rational life. Moreover since, when one examines the general causes of suffering and frustration, what one finds is that future frustration is caused by past immoral deeds, one has a reason to have only moral deeds as one's goal. Someone who believes in the *karma* theory of moral retribution has a reason to strive to do good and not to do evil. One final link is needed to complete the picture. It is that bad or immoral deeds are the result of false beliefs. Once one knows this, one has a reason to strive for only true beliefs. For if one has only true beliefs, then one cannot do wrong, cannot incur the moral cost of future frustration, and so will succeed in life's ultimate goal of eliminating such frustrations. One has, therefore, a reason to strive to minimize false beliefs, and so to study the sources of true belief and knowledge. And, in so far as a study of the Nyāya system is the best method of achieving one's highest goals, one should study it through repeated reflection, discussion with others and by engaging in friendly debates (NS 4.2.47–9).

This then is the reason why the study of epistemology and critical inquiry, in short of the Nyāya philosophy, is instrumental in achieving one's final aims. There is an elegant explanatory closure here. One might not be inclined to agree with every step in the explanatory chain. While it is plausible that there is a dependency between the degree of success or failure of one's plans and the extent of falsity in one's beliefs, it is less easy to see that the dependency is mediated by the *moral* value of one's actions. Even if one were tempted to omit that link, or regard the tie between rationality and moral behaviour differently, the explanatory scheme affords a marvelous account of the relationship between the study of philosophy and the quest for life's final ends.

1.4 Perception

The Buddhist asserts that perception of objects is itself a rational activity. One does not, properly speaking, perceive the object at all, but only patterns of color, sound, touch, smell, and taste. From their sequence in time and arrangement in space, one infers the presence of an object of one kind or another. Reason here is a mental faculty of construction, synthesis, and superimposition. It brings order to the array of sensory data. The early Naiyāyika, however, has tied reason to explicit demonstration and proof. He has no place for the idea of reason as an inner mental faculty of sensory integration. Since there is no logical connection between the capacity to see an object and the capacity to describe it, one is led instead to the idea that objects enter *directly* into the content of perceptual experience. The Naiyāyika rightly worries that if reason has a role in the construction or synthesis of the *objects* of perception, then realism about those objects is threatened. However, he allows reason to have a role in the *organization* of the totality of one's perceptions. Kalidas Bhattacharya accurately, if enigmatically, assessed the idea when he said that "thought as judgement, according to Nyāya, is either the perception of a passive unity of different data in substantive-adjective relation, or, going beyond perception, conscious management of data through actual use of language."[14]

I begin with the *Nyāyasūtra* definition Vātsyāyana would later classify the *sūtras* into three kinds: "naming" *sūtras*, which introduce a topic or concept for analysis; "defining" *sūtras*, which offer a definition of the concept in question; and "critical" *sūtras*, which examine and evaluate the adequacy of the proposed definition. A definition is a property co-extensive with the concept to be defined. A definition is faulty if it is either too wide or too narrow – showing that it has neither of these faults is the purpose of the "critical" *sūtras*. The Nyāya method here is not very different from the technique of finding necessary and sufficient conditions. Notice however that it does not tell us what the essence of the thing defined is, but rather gives us a syndrome, a criterion for distinguishing between it and all other kinds of thing.

Nyāyasūtra 1.1.4 is a "defining" *sūtra*. It is the definition of perception:

> Perception is an awareness which, produced from the connection between sense-organ and object, is nonverbal, non-errant, and determinate in nature.

A perception is an awareness that stands in a certain special relation to its object. The attempt is to define that relation in purely noncognitive terms. If the attempt is successful, then perception is a physical anchor between the subject and the external world. It is not itself cognitive, but rather supplies the raw material for cognition and so for reason.

What constraints are there on the physical relation that obtains between a perceiver's perceptions and the object perceived? A first constraint is just that the relation be physical, so that it is not explicated in terms of semantic relations such as that of denotation. This is what is meant by the assertion that perception is "nonverbal." Second, the relation has to have the right extension: it needs to hold between perceptions and the sorts of object one is normally regarded as capable of perceiving. Uddyotakara (ca. AD 500) has a clear discussion of this point.[15] He notes that the relation must be capable of obtaining between the perceiver's perceptions and objects which are both nearby and far away; it must be a relation capable of obstruction by solid, opaque objects; it must connect the perceiver not only with the objects themselves, but also with their perceptible properties such as color and shape, as well as with the perceptible properties of those properties; it must connect the perceiver not only with the front surface of a whole object, but with the object as a whole (for one sees the table and not just its surface); and finally, he asserts that it connects the perceiver with the *absences* of things, for apparently one can say that one *sees* the absence, and not merely that one fails to see.

It is hardly surprising that the Naiyāyikas find themselves unable to describe a single physical relation which obtains in all (and only) these circumstances, but perhaps they do not need to. For if it is part of the concept of perception only that it is grounded in a physical relation with a certain extension, then an adequate physicalist theory of perception needs only to specify what the extension of the underlying physical relation is. The discovery of the way that relation is realized in actual human perception might be a task assigned to the psychologist of perception, not to the philosopher.

The real interest in the *Nyāyasūtra* attempt to give a physical description of perception lies in the remaining two conditions. The point is that, no matter how well one succeeds in describing the underlying physical connection, there will be cases where that connection obtains, but the resulting awareness is not genuinely perceptual. Vātsyāyana points to cases of perceptual illusion and perceptual confusion:

> During the summer the flickering rays of the sun intermingled with the heat radiating from the surface of the earth come in contact with the eyes of a person at a distance. Due to this sense–object contact, there arises an awareness as of water. Such an awareness might be (mis-)taken as perceptual; hence the clause "non-errant." An errant one is of that wherein it is not. A non-errant one is of that wherein it is – this is a perception.
>
> Perceiving with the eyes an object at a distance, a person cannot decide whether it is smoke or dust. Such an indecisive awareness resulting from sense–object contact might be (mis-)taken as perceptual; hence the clause "determinate in nature."

These ambiguous passages led to a "vortex of controversy" (Matilal 1995: 310) and eventually to a sophisticated theory of content. It is alleged that a person witnessing a mirage does not see the refracted sun's rays, even if in the right sort of physical connection with them. Neither does he see water, for there is none to be seen. Someone witnessing a mirage does not *see* anything, but only seems to see water. And a person who witnesses a ball of dust in the distance does not *see* the dust if he is uncertain whether it is dust or smoke. An object is not seen if it is not seen distinctly.

In both cases there is a natural temptation to say that the person does see something, but does not understand or know what it is that they see, or that they misconstrue what it is that they see, or that their perceptual appearance is nonveridical. One sees the refracted rays of light, but mistakes them to be water; one sees the ball of dust, but fails to determinate it as such. To say this would be to concede that the existence of an appropriate physical connection is sufficient for object perception. The difficulty with such a move is that, although it does indeed extrude rationality from the perceptual, it does it so completely that the perceptual cannot be a basis for rational thought. The "objects" of perception are merely things in which one stands in a certain special physical relation, on a par with other objects one comes into physical contact with (e.g. by standing on or picking up). However, if perception is to be a foundation for rationality, there must be a way in which it is understood as making objects available in thought, as placing them within the ken of the observer.

Might we analyze the two additional clauses in terms of belief? If a person witnessing a mirage does not see the refracted rays of the sun, perhaps it is because he falsely believes them to be water. Similarly, one can perhaps say that the person looking at the ball of dust does not see it because he does not believe that it is dust (does not know whether it is dust or not). We might then think of taking the additional clauses as defining the perception of an object in terms of a physical connection, together with the absence of a belief that it is something it is not, and the absence of doubt or disbelief that it is something that it is. That is:

S's perception is of object *x* iff:

1) S's perception stands in a relation R with *x*.
2) R is physical (nonverbal).
3) for all *F*, if S believes that *Fx* then *Fx*.
4) for all *F*, if *Fx* then S does not disbelieve that *Fx*.

There are two objections to such a proposal. First, clauses (3) and (4) are much too strong. It is clearly possible to perceive an object and at the same time have false beliefs about it. I might, for example, perceive the table and yet believe that it is made of space-filling infinitely divisible stuff. Second, since belief implies rationality, the definition of perception in terms of belief is contrary to the attempt to extrude reason from perception.

The proper implication of the *Nyāyasūtra* definition is that the perception of objects is *modulo* a property. When I see an object (my desk, for instance) I do not simply see it, but I see it *as a table.* Here, the clause "as a table" is to be read as an adverbial modifier of the seeing relation R. I stand in a "table-seeing" relation to the object. The relativization of the seeing relation by a property allows a reconstruction of Vātsyāyana's cases. The person who witnesses a mirage stands in a "water-seeing" relation to the refracted rays. The errancy lies in the fact that they are seeing the refracted rays *as water*, when in fact the rays are not. And the person who witnesses a ball of dust, but fails to distinguish it as dust or smoke stands neither in a dust-seeing relation to the dust-ball, nor in a smoke-seeing relation, but equivocates. The correct way to read the definition then is:

S's perception is of object x iff:

4) for some F, S sees x as an F, where

S sees x as an F iff:

1) S's perception stands in a relation R with x.
2) R is physical (nonverbal).
3) Fx.

Cause (4) excludes the case of the ball of dust, for since there is no definite way by which the person sees the dust, the person does not see any object. It is necessary for object perception that the object is seen in some definite way. Clause (3) excludes the case of the mirage, for the person attempts to see the rays *modulo water* but the rays are not water. Notice here that "non-errancy" signifies simply an absence of warping, a lack of discord between the perception and its object, and is not explicated in terms of a correspondence between the object and a perceptual content. We should think of this absence of warping as a property of the perceptual relation, much as transparency is a property of clear glass. Both are characterized in terms of the lack of a distortion or corruption of what is seen, and not in terms of representational correspondence. The passivity of perception is preserved; perception remains free from interpretation and construction.

It follows from the definition that if one perceives an object, and one does so by seeing it *modulo* its having a certain property, then it does indeed have that property. This is so even though one does not see *that* the object has the property. Perceiving x as F does not imply believing that x is F, but it does imply that one would be justified were one to believe that x is F. Perception is an evidential support for reason, without itself being reasoned (an idea echoed in Roderick Chisholm's critical cognitivism[16]). Later Nyāya writers draw a distinction between perception that is "with imagination" and perception is "without imagination." Bimal Matilal explains the philosophical use here of the term "imagination" or *vikalpa* as standing "for anything that, let us say, the mind adds to, or recognises in, the 'given.'"[17] In the Nyāya theory the object perceived (x) and also the mode under which it is perceived (F) constitute the perceptual given. It is the work of the "imagination" to bring them together into a propositional judgment (x is F).

Buddhist objections to the Nyāya definition focus on instances where perception does seem to imply belief and inference. There is the case of Uddyotakara's rather remarkable claim that we perceive absences. I am looking for a pot. I look in the kitchen and see no pot. Uddyotakara says: I see the kitchen as qualified by absence-of-pot and thereby see the absence. The Buddhist Dharmakīrti objects that this is really a piece of reasoning, an inference from nonobservation. The inference runs thus. None of the objects which I perceive in the kitchen is a pot. If there were a pot in the kitchen, I would see it, for my perceptual faculties are working normally and all other *ceteris paribus* conditions for perception are met. Therefore, there is no pot in the kitchen. Dharmakīrti's point is well taken, but it does not constitute a refutation of the theory. We may simply give up the strange claim that absences can be perceived.

Nyāyasūtra 2.1.31 rehearses an argument, apparently again due to Buddhists, which if sound *would* constitute a refutation. The argument is that our ordinary perceptual claims are disguised inferences. I cannot see the whole table from any one place. When I say that I see the table, what I mean is that I infer that there is a whole table on the basis that I have seen a part (its front surface). We never see wholes, but infer their existence from our more immediate perceptions. If the argument is that all perception is inferential, then Gautama's counter in *Nyāyasūtra* 2.1.32, that we see at least front surfaces, is conclusive. If the argument is that all perception of wholes is inferential, the Nyāya reply is that the whole is present in each of its parts. So we can perceive a whole just as we can perceive a property. One says that one sees the colour or shape of the flower in virtue of seeing the flower; so too one sees the whole in virtue of seeing a part.

What is at stake is the amount of work done in perception by reason. The Buddhist presses the Naiyāyika on the point that there is, in perception, an extrapolation and interpretation of what is immediately given. Allowing properties to enter the (nonconceptual) content of perceptual experience as adverbial modifiers offers a way of avoiding the unpalatable consequence that the perception of a whole is an inference. Attention is drawn to two kinds of properties of wholes: those that are properties of the whole without being a property of any its parts, and those that are properties of the whole only because they are properties of every part. The second sort "saturate" the object, in rather the same way that sesame oil saturates the sesame seed. The property being-a-table or being-a-cow, on the other hand, applies to the whole, but not to any of its parts. It follows that seeing modulo such a property is seeing the whole and not its parts. This Nyāya rejoinder to the Buddhist criticism depends on one's being able to regard the property being-a-cow as an entirely objective feature of the perceived situation, not as itself a mere concept or mental construct. It is for this reason that, in the war for hegemony between the Buddhist and Nyāya philosophical views, some of the severest battles were those over the reality of universals and wholes.[18]

1.5 Mind, Attention, and the Soul

Is the mind rational? Is it conscious? That depends on what we mean by "mind." The Naiyāyika, as generally for thinkers in classical India, sees in the mind (*manas*) something distinct from the soul (*ātman*). It is the soul alone which is the seat of reason, *qua* thinker, perceiver, enjoyer of pleasures and sufferer of pains. The mind is a mere instrument of the soul. It is that by which the soul controls the senses. The mind is given a second function: it is also that by which the soul perceives its own mental states. So the mind is both an inner sense and the controller of the outer senses, but all the while entirely directed by the soul. The mind is mechanical.

An enduring metaphor for the senses, due at least to Praśastapāda, is as windows onto the world. In a room with a window on every wall, each one represents a possibility of sensory contact with some aspect of the world. But only a possibility: in order to see out, one has to direct one's attention to one window rather than another. In the case of the senses, this role is assigned to the mind. It is a faculty of attention, that by which the soul directs its gaze through one sense rather than another. Another metaphor is helpful here. Think of the senses as converging railway tracks, meeting at a point and becoming a single track. The mind is the set of points at the junction. It is that by which the controller (the soul, the signalman) channels its attention in one direction rather than another.

A perception arises in the soul when there is a causal chain: from object to sense, from sense to mind and from mind to soul.[19] Uddyotakara observes that if this role of the mind in perception seems to have been forgotten in the *Nyāyasūtra* definition of perception, it is because a mind–soul link is not something *special* to perception, while a mind–sense link is *implied* by the mention of the sense–object connection.[20]

The existence of the mind as an intersensory switching device follows from an alleged deficiency in the powers of the conscious soul. This is that the soul can attend to at most one thing at a time. There is a strict sequence in the temporal order of thought. If the senses are functioning simultaneously, but one can entertain no more than one thought at a time, then one must have within oneself a capacity to choose between the deliverances of the senses (NS 1.1.16, NS 3.2.56). In reply to the obvious objection that we do seem to be able to attend to more than one thing at once, Vātsyāyana claims that this is an error produced by our inability to discriminate events which happen in very quick succession. He cites (NS 3.2.58) the illusion of a circling firebrand, appearing as if it were a continuous hoop, and more interestingly, the way one hears a sentence as a whole even though the letters and words are uttered in sequence.

This account of the mind is smooth. But a worry now presents itself. If the conscious soul fails to notice the distinctness in a sequence of perceptions, it seems to follow that the mind after all has a certain autonomy in operation. For if the soul is not quick enough to follow the mind's switchings from one perception to the next, how can it be controlling them?[21] And yet there is no question of assigning consciousness (*caitanya*) to the mind. *Nyāyasūtra* 3.2.38 is explicit:

> It [consciousness] is not a property of the mind, for reasons already given, and because of its being ruled by another, and because [there would then follow an] acquiring of the benefits of actions not performed.

The "reason already given" is simply the definition itself of the soul, as the exclusive abode of thought, will, pleasure and pain (NS 1.1.10). The idea of "benefits of actions not performed" is a reference to the *karma* theory of moral retribution. If the soul and the mind were distinct consciousnesses, then the future contentments or frustrations of the soul would depend on the present deeds of another, the mind. This contradicts the fundamental principle of the *karma* theory, that the benefits and costs of one's present actions accrue to oneself and not to someone else. Vātsyāyana uses the same line of reasoning against the Buddhist reduction of a person to a "sum and series" of consciousness-moments (NS 3.2.39). If a person is a series of distinct consciousnesses, then the deeds of one reach their fruition in the contentments and frustrations of another, an injustice incompatible with the hypothesis of *karma*.

The more important assertion is that the mind is "ruled by another." It does not act independently, but only as directed by the conscious soul. It therefore cannot itself choose which sense to connect with. How then can the soul be unaware of its operation? A solution to the puzzle begins to emerge when we remember that the mind has another function, along with that of intersensory switch. It is also an inner sense, the means by which the soul perceives its own mental states. Vātsyāyana:[22]

> Memory, inference, testimony, doubt, intuition, dreams, suppositional argument, and perception of pleasure and pain are the proof of mind.

One conclusion we can draw from this is that the soul is not immediately aware of its own thoughts, for it requires an inner sense to perceive them. Thoughts, just like external events, can appear and disappear unperceived. So the mere fact that a thought occurs does not imply that it is taken notice of in consciousness. Once the point has been made that the mere occurrence of a thought is not sufficient for its being *noticed*, we see that the switching function of the mind need not determine which thoughts are noticed, but need only ensure that thoughts occur in succession. We can think of the mind as scanning the senses, constantly switching from one to the next. Its movement so conceived will be very swift, but entirely automatic and mechanical. Perceptions from all the senses occur rapidly, but sequentially in the soul.

To attend to something then, is not to direct the mind *qua* intersensory switch towards one rather than another sense faculty, but rather to direct it *qua* inner sense to some occurrent perception. The rapid movement of the mind need not be something of which the soul is aware. There is still a problem. If a perception comes before consciousness only if one chooses to direct the mind towards it, how can it be that one's attention is sometimes drawn by the perception itself? Standing on a thorn or a chip of stone will draw the attention even of a person whose mind is fastened on some other thing (NBh. under NS 3.2.32). The worry is that I will not notice the pain in my foot unless I direct my mind to attend to the deliverances of my tactile sense, but that there need be no motivation for me to do this in advance of noticing the pain. Unless it occurs to me to check whether my foot has been injured, I will not notice the pain! Even this, however, can be squared with a mechanistic conception of the mind. Let us say simply that some perceptions are so intense as to force the mind in their direction, not because it chooses to direct itself towards them, but simply because it is driven to do so by the intensity of the perception. A conception of the mind as entirely mechanical in operation has room to allow that this could happen. The "movement" of the mind is an automated scanning of the senses, potentially diverted by the occurrence of intense perceptions and by the controlling influence of the soul. The mind is not itself a rational agent, and it is only in a relatively weak sense that the Indian soul–mind division is what one would now call a "divided mind" hypothesis.[23]

What now is the place of reason in perception? The function of the soul is to integrate the content of distinct perceptions across times and between sensory modalities (NB 3.1.1). It has the power to identify the object of some past perception and an object currently being perceived. The identity "this is the same as that" is not *given* in perception, but discovered or "imagined" by the soul. The same is true across sensory modalities at a given time. Physical objects are perceived only by sight and touch, but the identification of an object held in one's hand with an object currently being seen with one's eyes is the work of reason and not of perception. Such identifications require one to be able to assume a point of view which spans times and crosses sensory modalities. Rationality then has a reconstitutive role in aligning our perceptions with each other, so that they come to represent a world of temporally extended and modality-independent objects.[24]

The possibility of transtemporal and transmodal identification of objects is said by the Nyāya to be the best argument for the existence of the soul as distinct from the mind or the senses, and as the final refutation of the Buddhist analysis of the person as a mere continuum of discrete consciousnesses. For how is a *re*identification of an object possible by one who exists only for a moment? Only a single consciousness spanning time can "simultaneously" witness the same object at two different times, and recognize it as time same. Only a single consciousness spanning sense modalities can "simultaneously" witness a single object through two modalities, and recognize it as the same. The Buddhist asserts that a momentary consciousness can compare a *current* perception with a *current* memory (produced by the past perception of an earlier momentary consciousness), and so there is no need for there to be a single subject of the current and past perceptions. The Naiyāyika reply is that there is a *logical* difference between, on the one hand, judging that an object seen now is the same as an object seen some time ago, and, on the other, keeping track of an object over a period of time. It is perhaps like the difference between discovering that two different names refer to the same thing, and using a single name twice.[25]

The ability to turn fleeting modality-specific perceptions into thoughts about enduring physical objects is a concealed art of the soul. It is rational because it admits of a standard of correctness. Interperceptual identifications can be right or wrong – the degree to which one can make them accurately, and the extent which one can do so for perceptions more distant from one another in time or appearance, is the index of a rational capacity.

1.6 Rationality and Extrapolation

The discovery of identities among the contents of one's perceptions is a core function of reason. There is another. This is the capacity to extrapolate from what one has perceived to what one has not. That extrapolation is a key concept in the early history of Indian logic is clear from some of the examples Vātsyāyana gives under NS 1.1.5.[26] Seeing a rising cloud, one infers that it will rain. An interesting variant is: seeing the ants carrying their eggs, one infers that it will rain. Seeing a full and swiftly flowing river, one infers that it has been raining. Seeing a cloud of smoke, one infers the existence of an unseen fire. Hearing a cry, one infers that a peacock is nearby. Seeing the moon at one place at one time and at another place at another time, one infers that it is moving (even though one cannot *see* it move). The medical theorist Caraka[27] has some other examples: inferring impregnation from pregnancy; inferring the future appearance of fruit from the presence of seeds. In the ancient Buddhist logical text, *The Essence of Method*,[28] we also find: inferring from a child's special mark that this person is that child, now grown up; inferring from the salty taste of one drop of sea water that the whole sea is salty. The *Ts'ing-mu*[29] (a commentary on Nāgārjuna's *Middle Stanzas*) has a similar example: inferring that all the rice is cooked on tasting one grain. And the *Vaiśeṣikasūtra* mentions another sort of extrapolation – the inference of an entire cow from the perception only of its horns.[30]

Extrapolation from the seen to the unseen can take place in any of the three dimensions of time – past, present, and future. Our interest is in the Indian theory of rationality, and for this we want to look at answers given to the question: on what basis, if any, ought the extrapolation be made? For while dice-throwing, guesswork, and divination are ways of extrapolating, they are not rational ones. Extrapolation, like critical investigation, must be done "on the basis of reasons," and a theory of such "reasons" is a theory of that in virtue of which an extrapolation is warranted. So we can discover Indian theories of rationality in their explanations of why the extrapolations in the examples mentioned above are warranted. Rationality now is the search for extrapolative license.

While Vātsyāyana says only that there should be a *connection* between what is seen and what is inferred,[31] many of the early writers have a definite interest in prediction and scientific explanation, and assume that extrapolation is warranted when underwritten by a causal relation. On the other hand, it is clearly recognized too that not all warranted extrapolation is causal. The *Vaiśeṣikasūtra* lists, in addition, the relations of contact, inherence, coinherence in a third, and being contrary (VS 3.1.8, 9.18), while the early Sāṃkhya *ṣaṣṭitantra* has an overlapping list of seven.[32] Take the inference from a drop of salty sea water to the conclusion that the whole sea is salty. This is not an inference based on any causal relation between the drop of sea water and the sea as a whole; rather, the relation between them is mereological. One would say that it is an inference from sampling a "typical" member of a group. This is a very common and useful form of reasoning (witness the example of checking that all the rice is cooked by tasting a single grain). It is not formally valid, but it is a pervasive and powerful species of informal reasoning. We will see in the next section that it acquires particular significance in the context of a debate.

There is also an intriguing example from Vātsyāyana I have not yet mentioned. This is the inference of the "residual" by elimination.[33] Wondering whether sound is a substance, a quality, or an event, and finding reasons to deny that it is a substance or an event, one draws the conclusion that it is a quality. What is interesting is that the early writers are well aware that not all warranted inference can be reduced to the causal model. An adequate theory of inference has to find a description of the extrapolation-warranting relation at a level more general than that of the causal.

The difficulty in finding adequately general bases for extrapolative inference encouraged a skepticism about their existence. In one form, scepticism about the possibility of rational extrapolation is just the claim that there is no adequate extrapolative basis. It is the view allegedly of the Lokāyata "materialist," and most notably of the sceptic Jayarāśi (ca. AD 600). An early version of the skeptic's argument is recorded in the *Nyāyastūtra* (NS 2.1.37):

> [Objection:] Inference is not a means of knowing, because there may be errancy arising from embankment, damage and similarity.

Gautama is referring to the examples of the swollen river, the ants, and the peacock. His point is that the observed facts admit of different explanations: the swollen river might have been caused by a dam or embankment further downstream, the ants might be carrying their eggs because their nest has been damaged, and the peacock's cry might have been made by a human or animal impersonator. There are alternative causal explanations for each perceived event. This is a standard skeptical move. The sceptic introduces an alternative possible explanation (that our experiences are all dreams or produced by an evil genius, that the world was created five minutes ago with all its fossil records) and then claims that the existence of such an alternative explanation shows that one is not entitled to assume that the common-sense expanation is the correct one. Gautama's reply is interesting (NS 2.1.38):

> No. Because it is a different thing from a [mere] partial case, fear, and [mere] similarity.

The compact response is that there is an observable difference between a river which is swollen because of upstream rain and one which is swollen because of a downstream blockage, a difference between the orderly procession of ants when it is about to rain and their fearful scurrying when the nest is disturbed, and a difference between a genuine peacock's cry and that of an impersonator.

The implication of Gautama's reply for the rationality of extrapolation seems to be this. An extrapolation from the seen thing to the unseen thing is rational when there is a relation of some appropriate (as yet unspecified) sort between the two. The relation does not obtain between the unseen thing and something which merely resembles the seen thing. The rational extrapolator, therefore, must have the capacity to discriminate between the thing in question and other things which merely resemble it, but do not stand in the appropriate relation to the unseen thing. Only someone who can tell the difference between a flood river and a dammed river is entitled to infer from swelling to rain; only someone who can tell the difference between marching ants and frightened ants is entitled to infer from marching to rain; and only someone who can tell the difference between a peacock's cry and a human impersonator is entitled to draw the inference from cry to peacock.

The skeptic will reply, of course, that he can always find an alternative explanation for the occurrence of a perceived event, no matter how finely attuned the perceiver's discriminating powers. Even the best expert can be fooled by a good enough forgery. But the question is whether it is rational to concern oneself with such extreme skeptical possibilities. The Naiyāyika proposes a common-sense maxim for extrapolative reasoning: do not extrapolate beyond the level of your competence. The skeptic has a different maxim: do not extrapolate if there is any possibility of error. Since human beings have finite discriminatory capacities, there is always the possibility of error, and so the skeptic's maxim implies that it is never rational to extrapolate. (Jayarāśi[34] claims even that there is no rational extrapolation from the rising to the setting of the sun!) To reach the skeptical conclusion, however, the skeptic has further to prove that his maxim of extrapolation is the rational one to adopt, while the common-sense Nyāya maxim is not. And that is precisely what Gautama is here denying.

1.7 Rationality and Debate

H. N. Randle observed a long time ago that "the Naiyāyika was from first to last a *tārkika*, a disputant."[35] More recently, B. K. Matilal has called debate the "preferred form of rationality" in classical India.[36] There is a good deal of truth in these observations. A sophisticated theory of rationality evolved in the arenas of debate. Kauṭilya observed that rationality is about the best means to an end, and the end of the debater is to win. But what counts as winning a debate? If the debate is the victory-at-any-cost sort, and a debater wins when his opponent is lost for words or confused or hesitant, then the best and so most rational way to proceed would be to employ such tricks as play on the opponent's weaknesses: speaking very quickly or using convoluted examples or referring to doctrines of which one suspects one's opponent is ignorant. In the other sort of debate, the truth-directed sort, "winning" is a matter of persuading one's opponent, and also an impartial audience, that one's thesis is true, and the rational debater must find some other methods. Nothing is more persuasive than an argument backed up by well-chosen examples and illustrations. And so, when the Naiyāyikas came to codify the form of rational debating demonstration, the citation of examples was given at least as much prominence as the citation of reasons. When the Nyāya theory of inference was "rediscovered" by Henry Colebrooke (he broke the news at a meeting of the Royal Asiatic Society in London in 1824), the Indologists of the day in their excitement failed to pay due attention to this fact, and were led to some rather extraordinary speculations about the origins of syllogistic theory. The Sanskritist Görres apparently arrived at the view that Alexander, having been in conversation with the logicians of India during his campaigns, sent some of their treatises back home to his tutor who worked them up into a system! Equally remarkable was Niebuhr's claim that the Indians must have derived their theory from the Indianized Greeks of Bactria (it is a view Vidhyabhusana was to repeat much later on). If there is a lesson here, it is that a little comparative philosophy is a dangerous thing.

The debating room is a theater for the art of persuasion. It is a metaphor for any situation in which one wants to persuade others of the correctness of one's point of view. It will include by extension both the mundane situation of persuading one's companion that something is about to happen, and persuading a scientific or academic community of the truth of one's thesis. The model of rationality which comes out of the theory of debate is public, explicit, demonstrational. The norms of public reason are those of mutual agreement.

The proper way to formulate one's position is in accordance with a "five-limbed" schema: tentative statement of the thesis to be proved; citation of a reason; mention of an example; application of reason and example to the case in hand; final assertion of the thesis (NS 1.1.32). Suppose I want to persuade my walking companion that it is about to rain. I might reason as follows: "Look, it is going to rain. For see that large black cloud. Last time you saw a large black cloud like that one, what happened? Well, it's the same now. It is definitely going to rain." In order to be able to generalize the structure of such patterns of reasoning, the Naiyāyikas make an important simplifying assumption. They assume that the underlying pattern is one of property-substitution. The claim is that all such patterns exemplify the same canonical form: *Ta* because *Ra*. An objent (the *pakṣa* or "site" of the inference) is inferred to have a property (the *sādhya* or "target") on the grounds that it has some other property (the *hetu* or reason). The first simplification, then, is to think of reasoning as taking us from an object's having one property to that same object's having another.

The simplification scarcely seems justified. A cursory inspection of the cases mentioned at the beginning of the last section shows that only about half fit such a pattern. The cases of the swollen river, the ants, the peacock's cry, the fruit, and the salty sea do not seem to fit at all. Neither can we fit reasoning to the remainder by elimination. The canonical schema seems to fit the case of the moon, the pregnancy, and the child's special mark, but it is only at a stretch that one can force the case of smoke and fire into the pattern (an irony as this is a hackneyed example which all the logical texts quote). Bearing in mind the ways in which Indian logic was later to develop, one can be forgiven for feeling that this adoption of a property-substitution model at an early stage, while perhaps a helpful and necessary simplification for the sake of initial progress, also restricted the study of other patterns of inferential reasoning. Only the Jaina logicians explicitly tried to develop a theory of extrapolation free from this restriction.

What licences the inference from *Ra* to *Ta*? The *Nyāyasūtra* answer is given in five brief and controversial aphorisms (NS 1.1.34–8):

> A reason is that which proves what is to be proved by being like an example.
>
> Again, by being unalike.
>
> An example is an observed instance which, being like what is to be proved, possesses its property.
>
> Or else, being opposite, is opposite.
>
> The application is an assimilation to what is to be proved "this is thus" or "this is not thus" depending on the example.

Likeness and unlikeness are relative to properties. Something is "like" another thing if both possess a given property. They are unalike with respect to that property if they do not both share it. Now arguably the natural way to interpret these *sūtras* is as follows. Either the locus of the inference is like the example (in that both possess the reason property, *R*) and, since the example has the to-be-proved property, so does the locus. Or else the locus of the inference is unlike the example (it possesses the reason property, but the example does not), and since the example *does not* have the to-be-proved property, the locus *does* have it. If we let "*b*" stand for the example, then we seem to have:

a is like$_R$ b	a is unlike$_R$ b
Tb	$\sim Tb$
$\therefore Ta$	$\therefore Ta$

This formulation actually makes the inference a generalization of the inference from sampling. The example is a typical member of the class of things having the reason property. And it has this other property, the to-be-inferred target property. But the site of the inference is also a member of the class of things having the reason property. So it too has the target property (the negative formulation is similar). This is a powerful form of reasoning, one which we engage in all the time. It is not formally valid, but it is a pervasive type of informal reasoning. We employ it whenever we infer that an object has a property on the grounds that it belongs to a type, the typical members of which have that property. Compare: this grain of rice is typical of the whole pan of rice, and it is cooked. So any other grain will be cooked as well. This drop of water is typical of the entire sea, and it is salty. So this other drop must be salty as well.

We said that in the debating model, rationality is subject to public norms of correctness. In arguments of the kind being considered, public norms do indeed have a role to play, for they determine whether the object adduced by the debater as an "example" is adequate. For something to be capable of playing the role of example, it must be generally and uncontroversially accepted as a member of *R* and as a *T*. The debater must, when he chooses an example, be careful to select one that will fit public criteria of acceptability. Warranted extrapolation, clearly, is context dependent and occurs, in particular, only when there is a background of shared knowledge. For one grain of rice is an adequate exemplar of all only if it is commonly known that all the rice has been cooked in the same pan, at the same temperature, and with the same amount of water. It is for this reason that the pattern of reasoning here is neither formally valid nor reducible to an Aristotelian syllogism.[37]

There is a strong pressure, nevertheless, to fit such arguments into a deductive-nomological model. These arguments, the thought goes, rest on an underlying lawlike universal generalization – that all the members of kind *R* are *Ts*. The argument is then enthymematic for a deductively valid one: *Ra*, all *R* are $T \therefore Ta$. The role of the example, it is alleged, would be to provide empirical support for the universal rule, either by being something which is both *R* and *T*, or by being something which is neither *R* nor *T*. The pioneer indologist, Stanisław Schayer, had a different idea.[38] He read the step labeled "example" in the five-step proof as an application of a logical rule, the one we would now call "universal instantiation." This is the rule that permits one to infer from "$(\forall x)(Rx \rightarrow Tx)$" to "$(Ra \rightarrow Ta)$". And he read the step called "application" as the application of another logical rule, *modus ponens*. But he still sees the overall inference as a formally valid one whose validity is a consequence of the fact that there is a hidden premise "$(\forall x)(Rx \rightarrow Tx)$."

More light can be thrown on this point if we examine the early Nyāya account of a pair of debating moves called the "likeness-based" rejoinder and "unlikeness-based" rejoinder. A sophistical rejoinder (*jāti*) is a debating tactic in which the opponent tries unsuccessfully to produce a counter-argument, an argument designed to prove the opposite thesis. It is sophistical because the counter-argument is based on a false or superficial resemblance. *Nyāyasūtra* 5.1.2–3 state:

> When there is assimilation through likeness or unlikeness, the likeness-based and unlikeness-based rejoinders lead to the opposite property.
>
> [The reply is:] the proof [of the thesis] is just like the proof of a cow from cowhood.

One debater, debating properly, tries to prove that a certain object has a certain property by pointing out that it is like another object which does have that property. (The black cloud overhead now is like the cloud we saw yesterday – both are black. But that cloud caused it to rain, so this one will too.) The opponent now tries to counter by pointing out that the object is also like an object which does not have the property. (The black cloud overhead is like the white cloud we saw the day before yesterday – both are clouds. But that cloud did not cause rain, so this one won't either.)

a is like$_{R1}$ b	a is like$_{R2}$ c
Tb	$\sim Tc$
$\therefore Ta$	$\therefore \sim Ta$

As an argument, the rejoinder seems to follow the very same pattern as the original one, so why is it false? The existence of such rejoinders shows that mere likeness is not sufficient for good argument. The likeness has to be of the right type. When is the likeness of the right type? The *Nyāyasūtra*'s very cryptic comment is that the "right type" is the type displayed by the relationship between a cow and its genus cowhood. Vātsyāyana, the commentator, is unclear and confused on this point. He does, however, make one important observation:[39]

> If one proceeds to establish the required inferable property on the basis simply of likeness or unlikeness then there will be lack of regularity (*vyavasthā*). Irregularity does not arise with respect to some special property. For something is a cow because of its likeness with another cow, which likeness is actually cowhood, not the cow's having dewlap, etc. It is because of cowhood that a cow is unlike a horse, etc., not because of a difference of particular qualities. This has been explained in the section on the limbs of a demonstration. In a demonstration, each limb serves a single purpose because they are connected with the means of knowing. The irregularity rests only on a bogus reason.

If the likeness must be of the right type, then the reason property, as determiner of the likeness relation, must also be of the right type. The object under investigation must be like objects which belong to a group, the typical members of which have the target property. Vātsyāyana implies that if the property in question is a property shared by typical members of the class of cows, then the reason property must be the class-essence cowhood.

In the last section, we saw that rational inference is linked with warranted extrapolation, and we wondered what it was that made an extrapolation warranted. The problem we have here is similar. We are now asking for the conditions under which it is admissible to extrapolate a property from one object to another. It appears to be admissible to extrapolate the property "rain-maker" from one black cloud to another black cloud, but not from a black cloud to a white cloud. It appears to be admissible to extrapolate the property "has a dewlap" from one cow to. another cow, but not from one four-legged animal (a cow) to another (a horse). There seems to be an order in the world of objects, a structure which licences the extrapolation of properties in some directions, but not others. Objects are grouped together on the basis of their likenesses and unlikenesses to one another. The possibility of likeness-based and unlikeness-based rejoinders shows, however, there are many different ways of making these groupings, many different metrics of likeness. So the problem is this – given some arbitrary property we wish to extrapolate from one object to another, how do we decide which such metric determines a standard for proper and warranted extrapolation? For an extrapolation may be warranted under one likeness relation, but not another. So not every inference of the standard pattern is permissible:

a is like$_R$ b
Tb
$\therefore Ta$

The response given in the tradition to this problem is to impose further constraints on the relation of likeness. Relevant or extrapolation-warranting likeness consists in the sharing of a property at least as narrow in extension as the property to be extrapolated. The idea is clearly expressed and ably defended by Diṅnāga, and for that reason he is rightly thought of as one of India s finest logicians. I also think that the pre-Diṅnāga Naiyāyikas would not have developed the theory of inference in the way they did unless they had some such idea in their minds. But I do not believe we should be led by this to try to reinterpret what they said as an unequivocal expression of the idea. Matilal puts the matter well when he says that "the conception of a universal connection is being hinted at on the analogy of a universal property."[40] The *hint* was there, but it was for Diṅnāga to lend that hint articulation (and perhaps it is only at moments when a theory is being revised that a precise definition is needed). The important point is this need not be read as the introduction of a new *premise* into the inference pattern, but rathet as a condition on when an inference is admissible. The constraint is of the form: it is valid to infer Ta from Tb if a is like$_R$ b when b, the example, is relevantly like a (i.e. when the property it shares with a is narrower in extension than the property being extrapolated). An inference rule is not another premise in the inference, but rather that in virtue of which the inference is valid or invalid. And the treatment of the early Nyāya theory as a theory of inference from sampling shows how the rule that there be a "universal connection" (*vyāpti*) of this kind between the properties is not an enthymematic premise, but a genuine inference rule of an informal logic.

Five sorts of bogus reason (*hetvābhāsa*) are mentioned in *Nyāyasūtra* 1.2.4: the *wandering*, the *contradictory*, the *unproven*, the *counter-balanced, and* the *untimely*.[41] Of special importance here is the one called the "wandering" (for the unproven" and the "counter-balance," see section 1.9). This was interpreted by later Naiyāyikas as meaning that the reason property deviates from the target, and so as a case in which the criterion enunciated in the above paragraph is violated. If a faulty reason is one which is present somewhere the target property is not, then by contraposition, a proper reason is one which is not present somewhere the target property is not, and so is at least as narrow in extension. The *Nyāyasūtra* definition is, however, less than explicit, and Vātsyāyana's explication of this most important *sūtra* is all over the place:

> The wandering is that which does not remain at only one end. (NS 1.2.5)
>
> An example is: sound is eternal because it is intangible. A pot is tangible and is seen to be non-eternal. Sound is not tangible in the same way. What then? It is intangible. One might say, therefore, that because it is intangible, sound is eternal. However, in this example tangibility and non-eternality are not grasped as standing in a prover–proven relationship. For example, an atom is tangible and it is

> eternal. And when something like the soul is the example, then the reason, which is taken to be "because of being intangible" in accordance with the *sūtra* "a reason is that which proves what is to be proved by being like an example (1.1.34)," deviates from eternality. For a thought is intangible as well as non-eternal. So, as there is deviation in both sorts of case, there is no prover–proven relationship as the mark of a (proper) reason is absent. One end is eternality, one end non-eternality. So we understand "being at one end." Opposite to that which is at one end is that which does not remain at only one end, because it is a pervader (*vyāpaka*) of both ends.

Four inferences are compared. (1) A pot is non-eternal. Sound is unlike a pot – one is tangible, the other intangible. So sound is eternal. However, we also have this. (2) An atom is eternal. Sound is unlike an atom – one is tangible, the other intangible. So sound is non-eternal. Again, we have: (3) The soul is eternal. Sound is like the soul – both are intangible. So sound is eternal. But also: (4) A thought is non-eternal. Sound is like a thought – both are intangible. So sound is non-eternal. The implication is that what undermines the inference is the existence of examples which do not fit, i.e. counter-examples. Another maxim of extrapolation is in play: do not extrapolate if you know of any counter-examples (there is no implication that the extrapolator is obliged to look for counter-examples, however). A prover–proven relationship is one for which no counter-examples exist. What Vātsyāyana lacks, however, is a clear grasp of what makes something a counter-example. He does not see that only a thing which is intangible and non-eternal ought to be thought of as a counter-example to the inference from intangibility to eternality. Something which is tangible and eternal (an atom) is *not* a counter-example. For the existence of tangible eternal things is not inconsistent with the rule underpinning the inference, that whatever is intangible is eternal It is the gaining of a clearer grasp of the notion of a counter-example that leads one to an understanding of the proper form of the prover–proven relationship. Again, Diṅnāga is extremely precise on the nature of counter-examples, and can take a lot of the credit, even if the essential point had been appreciated before him.

My point has been that there are many ways to arrive rationally at belief, other than that of formal deduction. Informal argument schemes, such as the inference from sampling, are just as much ways of reaching beliefs that it is rational for someone to hold, and it is with this wider concept of rational belief that we make better sense of the early Nyāya philosophical enterprise.

1.8 Reason, Scripture, and Testimony

Is it rational to believe the testimony of others or the statements of the scriptures? Does the assumption that it is rational to believe what we hear or read require us to think of rationality in a new way? We have so far encountered two epistemic models of rationality: the perceptual model, according to which rationality provides norms for the temporal and cross-modal integration of perceptual experiences; and the extrapolative model, according to which rationality provides norms for the extrapolation from the perceived to the unperceived. The Naiyāyika thinks that belief in the testimony of others is indeed rational, but that neither the perceptual nor the extrapolative model of rationality can account for why this is so. Testimony is a *sui generis* source of rational belief (i.e. *a pramāṇa*).

The Nyāya theory of testimony is simple. Nyāyasūtra 1.1.7 states that testimony is the utterance of a "credible person" (*āpta*). On this *sūtra*, Vātsyāyana adds the following important comment:

> A credible person is a speaker who has knowledge of the object and is motivated by the desire to tell of the object as known. This definition of a credible person is equally applicable to the seer (*ṛṣi*). the noble (*ārya*), and the outsider (*mleccha*).[42]

The comment is important because it implies that the scriptures do not have any special claim to our assent, but are to be believed for precisely the same reasons as any other piece of testimony, namely because the transmitter is credible. A credible person is one who is knowledgeable about the subject matter, and who has a sincere desire to communicate that knowledge, and can come from any walk of life or branch of society.[43] Vātsyāyana elaborates the point while discussing the *Nyāyasūtra* argument (NS 2.1.68) that the authority of the Veda is just like that of a medical treatise, in that it rests on the credibility of the communicator. He comments:

> To what is this authoritativeness due? It is due to the direct knowledge of what is prescribed, compassion for fellow beings, and the desire to communicate rightly. Credible communicators, having direct knowledge of what they prescribe, show compassion for fellow beings, (advising) "this is to be avoided," "this is a cause of pain," or "this is to be attained" and "this is the means to its attainment." For creatures who cannot themselves understand, there is no other way of knowing all this . . . Thus a credible communicator is a source of knowledge.[44]

When a person speaks who is knowledgeable, well motivated, and caring, it is rational to believe what they say. The scriptures, as it happens, are transmitted to us by such persons, and so we are entitled to believe them and regard what they say as a valuable source of knowledge, especially about moral and soteriological matters we would not otherwise be informed of. It is rational to believe the scriptures in just the same way and to just the same extent as it is rational to believe a medical text about medical matters, or any other experts about their respective field of competence.

A dilemma threatens this account of testimonial rationality. Must we *know* that the speaker has the qualities of competence, sincerity, and compassion in order to be entitled to believe her, or not? It can hardly be right to say that we are entitled to believe any utterance we hear, and just hope that its author is competent and sincere. That would be an epistemic charter for the gullible.[45] But if we have first to establish that the speaker is competent and sincere, then it seems that our grounds for believing are inferential, and the rationality implicated in testimony is nothing but a variety of extrapolative rationality. We reason, in effect, that the present utterance is relevantly similar to past utterances of the same speaker, which have been seen to be true. Someone who accepts this (David Hume is a notable case) is led to conclude that it is indeed rational to believe the utterances of a sincere and competent speaker, but that no new model of rationality is involved.

What saves the Nyāya theory is the idea that one can "monitor" the competence and sincerity of the speaker without forming any *beliefs* about her competence or sincerity. One might simply have an internal "lie-detector" subconsciously monitoring for signs of blushing, fidgeting, and so on. The existence of such a mechanism makes the following counterfactual conditional true: if the speaker were lying, one would come to believe it. In the presence of a subdoxastic faculty of this sort, one need not attempt to acquire knowledge about the speaker's credentials. For one's readiness to assent to what is being said will be overridden if she were to lie. Assent is made rational in a negative way, by the absence of evidence that the speaker is deceitful, rather than by positive evidence that she is sincere. it is rational in the same way that it is rational for one to believe that one has not just trodden on a nail. One need have no positive reason for so believing (a visual inspection of the foot, for example) for one knows that, if one had just trodden on a nail, one would have come to know about it. The "reasoning" is *ab ignorantiam* and not inductive.[46]

While the worry about the reduction of testimony to inference is raised in the *Nyāyasūtra* (NS 2.1.49–51), this defence is not to be found there. It emerges in the later idea that a precondition for testimony is the "absence of knowledge of unfitness" and not the "knowledge of fitness," Vātsyāyana says only that testimony depends on the speaker's credibility and that "inference is not like this."[47]

1.9 Reason's Checks and Balances

I began this examination of rationality in the early Nyāya with a description of the disreputable "reasoners" mentioned and criticized in the epics. The ill-repute was on the grounds that their use of reason was unmotivated, groundless, unconstrained. The Naiyāyika is very careful to avoid this charge. The very term *nyāya*, which Vātsyāyana identified with reasoned inquiry itself, is contrasted with another, *nyāyābhāsa* – a pseudo-inquiry. A pseudo-inquiry is one which, although-otherwise in accord with the rules governing proper reasoning (setting out the demonstration in a five-limbed format and with a proper reason property), *contradicts observation and authority* (see section 1.2). The same point is made time and again. A properly conducted debate, one which is friendly and truth-directed, is one which proceeds with the help of the methods of knowledge-acquisition, employs the five-limbed format, and is not in contradiction with, any doctrinal base (NS 1.2.1). A reason property which proves a thesis contradictory to a doctrinal base is a mere bogus reason (NS 1.2.6). Reason in Nyāya has had its wings clipped. It can override neither observation nor authoritative doctrine!

Descartes observed that our perceptions can sometimes contradict one another, and that when they do it is the role of reason to adjudicate. A tower might look round from a distance, but square closer up. A star and a distant lamp both look like specks of light, but one is vastly larger than the other. It is reason (belief and inference) that tells us that the star is larger than the lamp, even though they both look the same size. It is reason that allows us to decide whether the tower is really square or round. How, then, can one deny that reason sometimes overrides perception? However, there *are* cases where perception overrides reason. Vātsyāyana tries to find a case where a reasoned argument meets all the criteria as laid down in the theory of inference, but whose conclusion has to be rejected because it goes against perception. His example is: fire is not hot, because it is a creation, like a pot. Fires and pots are alike in that they are both products of human effort (let us restrict the extension of "fire" to those produced by humans). A pot, however, is a thing made of clay and so is not hot (material things are composed out of the four material elements, earth, water, fire, and air, and only those containing elemental fire are hot). So fire too is not hot! The inference goes through even if we insist on a universal connection between reason and target. For it is indeed true that, among everything seen, created things are not hot. The point is that the inference extrapolates from the seen to the unseen, and fire's heat therefore belongs here with the unseen. The thermal properties of fire, as the matter under investigation, are, as it were, *sub judice*. Every created thing ever encountered (excluding fire) has been found to be cold. So, extrapolating fire too as a created thing must be cold. Uddyotakara says that the inference is *baffled* by a perception of fire.

The conflict here is between a prediction based on an inductive generalization and an actual observation. In general, one faces a choice whenever one has both an inference to the truth of some conclusion and strong evidence that the conclusion is false. One can either reject the evidence for the falsity of the conclusion, or else reject one of the premises in the inference. The examples of Descartes are cases where the first option is the correct one to choose. The evidence of the senses is defeated in one case by its own internal inconsistency and in the other by a generalization with enormous empirical support (that things look smaller when they are further away). But the example of Vātsyāyana is a case where the second option is the correct one. In the face of incontrovertible observation, one must reject the similarity metric on the basis of which the extrapolation was made.

When is it rational to reject the premise, when the conclusion? Is this not a question for reason itself to decide, and when it decides in favor of the conclusion (i.e. of perception) does it not therefore decide to override itself? It is to avoid the apparent absurdity of such a result that the Nyāya insist on there being two different models or faculties of reason: reason as the rational extrapolator, and reason as the rational integrator of mental contents (perceptual and inferential). Integrative reason strikes a balance between perception and extrapolation, preferring one or the other according to its own standards. What is true of the relation between perception and inference is true too of the relation between testimony and inference, and true also of the relation between perception and testimony. What is the norm on integration? What principle does it follow in deciding who to override? Maximizing consistency is the obvious answer, but there is scope for weighting. The Nyāya, it would seem, wants to weight testimony (and especially scriptural testimony) more heavily than anything else, and to weight observation more heavily than extrapolation. The pure reasoner of the epics would maximize the weight given to inference – no doctrine is unrevisable, no scripture sacred – or else, like the materialist, to observation. Such an anti-dogmatism may have led him to be banished from the company of the virtuous, but for us a question still remains. If there is a choice of weightings, which one is the rational choice? On what principle does one choose? The search for reasons goes on. Unfortunately there isn't sufficient space here to discuss how the later Naiyāyikas brought this search for reasons to a close.

Can reason really override itself? As we have seen (section 1.7), five sorts of bogus reason are mentioned in *Nyāyasūtra* 1.2.4. In two of them, the *unproven* and the *counter-balanced*, reason acts as its own regulator. These are important, for they are favourite weapons of the sceptic. The situation called "counter-balanced" is one in which, in order to resolve the point at issue, the debater adduces a reason which might equally well prove the point either way. The reason meets all the criteria for warranted extrapolation, and would have been entirely adequate in settling the matter, were it not for the possibility of an equally acceptable and adequate extrapolation to the opposite conclusion. Vātsyāyana's example is: sound is non-eternal because we do not apprehend in sound the properties of eternal things, just like the pot, etc. The objection to this otherwise admissible extrapolation is that it is reversible. For we can equally well argue as follows: sound is eternal because we do not apprehend in sound the properties of non-eternal things, just like the sky, etc. This too, on its own, would have been an admissible extrapolation. (A simpler, if not entirely suitable, example would be: sound is eternal because it is eternal; and: sound is non-eternal because it is non-eternal.) In the absence of any ground for preferring one of these over the other, the most reasonable thing to do is to accept neither. Behind this bogus reason is another maxim of extrapolation: when faced with equal, but opposite bases for extrapolation between which you cannot choose, *do not extrapolate*. When reasons are balanced against each other, one is driven instead towards the skeptic's *ataraxia*.

The other bogus reason of interest to us here is the one called "unproven," or more literally, "same as the thesis" (*sādhyasama*). The reason is one which has not itself been established, and in that sense is in the same state as the thesis to be proved. Vātsyāyana's intriguing example is: a shadow is a substance because it moves. We have again an otherwise admissible extrapolation, but one that would be a false move in a debate. The problem is that the movement of shadows is not itself an established fact: it is neither a shared doctrine nor an indisputable observation. For one needs to know whether shadows are seen to move like men, or whether what takes place is a succession of perceptions of dimly lit things produced by the obstruction of the light by a moving cover. Extrapolation proceeds from the seen to the unseen or more generally, from the proven to the unproven. The underlying maxim on extrapolation is therefore: only extrapolate from what you have already established. The fault of being "the same as the thesis" is a violation of this maxim.

The Mādhyamika sceptic Nāgārjuna uses this fault to devastating effect. He argues that any reason adduced to refute the skeptical thesis will suffer the fault of being the same as the thesis. For if the skeptical thesis is that nothing can be known, then to refute it is to prove that something can be known. But if it is not yet established that anything can be known, one can adduce no known or established fact to prove it. So any putative reason one adduces to prove that something can be known will be the "same as the thesis" in being as yet unproven. The two propositions, "A proves B only if A is proven in advance of B" and "B = something is proven" in combination entail that A has to be something which is proven in advance of anything being proven, and this entails that there is no such A. The skeptic's thesis is indefeasible!

Such is the account of reason as it was conceived in early India. The concept is a shifting, not to say shifty, one, an interplay of different themes. The collection of ideas presented here was supposed to describe the way people actually do reason and explain why they are justified in doing so. It is a common-sense theory of common sense. In the subsequent chapters [of *Philosophy in Classical India*, 2001, the source from which this chapter is extracted], I look at attacks on this account from several directions. The Mādhyamika skeptic's claim that reason is *self-defeating* has already been mentioned. It is self-defeating because, if true, it is provable that nothing is provable (chapter 2). The Jainas are diametrically opposed: reason, they say, is *over-complete*: everything is provable (chapter 5). And Diṅnāga, a founder-member of Yogācāra-Vijñānavāda Buddhism, is neither a skeptic nor a syncretist, but a *unificationist* about reason. What he rejects is the idea that there is a plurality in the concept of rationality (rationality *qua* integrator, *qua* extrapolator, and *qua* recipient of testimony). Such a unification of reason, it turns out, necessitates a radical departure from naiveté (chapter 4). At the end of the book, I return to Nyāya, and see how in the later period, responding to the many and varied assaults on the concept of rationality embedded in common sense, it revitalized its defense of the common-sense account.

Further Reading

Texts

Gautama ca. AD 150, *Nyayasūtra* (NS).
Vātsyāyana AD 450, *Nyāyabhāṣya* (NBh).

Rationality, philosophical method (1.1–3)

Arindam Chakrabarti, "Rationality in Indian Philosophy," in Eliot Deutsch and Ron Bontekoe, eds., *A Companion to World Philosophies* (Oxford: Blackwell Publishers, 1997), pp. 259–78.

Wilhelm Halbfass, "Darśana, Ānvīkṣikī, Philosophy," in his *India and Europe: An Essay in Understanding* (Albany: State University of New York Press, 1988), pp. 263–86.

Bimal Krishna Matilal, "On the Concept of Philosophy in India," in *Philosophy, Culture and Religion: Collected Essays* (Delhi: Oxford University Press, 2001).

Bimal Krishna Matilal, *Perception: An Essay on Classical Indian Theories of Knowledge* (Oxford: Clarendon Press, 1986), ch. 3.

C. Ram-Prasad, *Knowledge and the Highest Good: Liberation and Philosophical Inquiry in Classical Indian Thought* (Basingstoke: Macmillan, 2000).

Perception, mind (1.4–5)

Bimal Krishna Matilal, *Perception: An Essay on Classical Indian Theories of Knowledge* (Clarendon Press, Oxford, 1986), Chs. 6, 8.

Bimal Krishna Matilal, "A Realist View of Perception," in P. K. Sen and R. R. Verma, eds., *The Philosophy of P. F. Strawson* (New Delhi: Indian Council of Philosophical Research, 1995), pp. 305–26; repr. in his *Philosophy, Religion, Culture: Collected Essays* (Delhi: Oxford University Press, 2001).

Arindam Chakrabarti, "I Touch What I Saw," *Philosophy and Phenomenological Research* 52 (1992): 103–17.

Kishor Chakrabarti, *Indian Philosophy of Mind: The Nyāya Dualist Tradition* (Albany: State University of New York Press, 1999).

Extrapolation, informal logic, debate (1.6–7)

Esther Solomon, *Indian Dialectics* (Ahmedabad: B. J. Institute of Learning and Research, 1976), 2 vols.

Mrinalkanti Gangopadhyay, *Indian Logic In Its Sources* (Delhi: Munshiram Manoharlal, 1984).

Claudius Nenninger, "Analogical Reasoning in Early Nyāya-Vaiśeṣika," *Asiatische Studien* 48 (1994): 819–32.

Claus Oetke, "Ancient Indian Logic as a Theory of Non-Monotonic Reasoning," *Journal of Indian Philosophy* 24 (1996): 447–539.

Bimal Krishna Matilal, *The Character of Logic in India* (Albany: State University of New York Press, 1998).

Testimony, tradition (1.8–9)

Bimal Krishna Matilal and Arindam Chakrabarti, eds., *Knowing from Words* (Dordrecht: Kluwer, 1994).

J. N. Mohanty, *Reason and Tradition in Indian Thought* (Oxford: Clarendon Press, 1992), chs. 8, 9.

Jonardon Ganeri, "Testimony," in *Semantic Powers: Meaning and the Means of Knowing in Classical Indian Philosophy* (Oxford: Clarendon Press, 1999), pp. 72–81.

Notes

1 *Manusaṃhitā* 2.11.
2 J. W. McCrindle, *Ancient India as Described by Megasthenes and Arrian: Being a Translation of the Fragments of the Indika of Megasthenes and the Fist Part of the Indika of Arrian* (Calcutta, 1926); Allan Dahlquist, *Megasthenes and Indian Religion: A Study in Motives and Types* (Uppsala: Almquist & Wiksell, 1962).
3 Hermann J. Jacobi, "A Contribution Towards the Early History of Indian Philosophy," translated by V. A. Sukthankar, *The Indian Antiquary* XLVII (1918): 101–9.
4 Paul Hacker, "Ānvīkṣikī," *Wiener Zeitschrift für die Kunde Süd- und Ost-Asiens* 2 (1958): 54–83. For a detailed discussion: Wilhelm Halbfass, "Darśana, Ānvīkṣikī, Philosophy," in his *India and Europe: An Essay in Understanding* (Albany: State University of New York Press, 1988), ch. 15.
5 Franklin Edgerton, "The Meaning of *sāṃkhya* and *yoga*," *American Journal of Philology* 45 (1924): 1–47; Gerald James Larson, "Introduction to the Philosophy of Sāṃkhya," in Gerald James Larson and Ram Shankar Bhattacharya, eds., *Sāṃkhya: A Dualist Tradition in Indian Philosophy*, Encyclopedia of Indian Philosophies, vol. 4 (Delhi: Motilal Banarsidass, 1987), pp. 3–9, 114–16.
6 Bertrand Russell, *Human Society in Ethics and Politics* (London: Allen and Unwin, 1954), p. viii.
7 *Nyāyabhāṣya* 3, 11–14. All references are to page and line numbers in Thakur's critical edition: *Gautamīyanyāyadarśana with Bhaṣya of Vātsyāyana*, critically edited by Anantalal Thakur (Delhi: Indian Council of Philosophical Research, 1997)
8 *Nyāyabhāṣya* 3, 15–20.
9 *Nyāyabhāṣya* 1, 6–10.
10 *Nyāyabhāṣya* on 4.2.29.
11 Herbert Simon and Allen Newell, *Human Problem Solving* (Englewood Cliffs, NJ: Prentice-Hall, 1972), pp. 71–105. Robert Nozick, *The Nature of Rationality* (Princeton: Princeton University Press, 1993), pp. 163–74.
12 *Nyāyabhāṣya* 4, 14–18.
13 Uddyotakara. *Nyāyavārttika*, 24, 3.
14 Kalidas Bhattacharya, "An Idea of Comparative Indian Philosophy," *All India Oriental Conference* (Santiniketan, 1980), p. 80.
15 *Nyāyavārttika* 28, 19–29, 1.
16 Roderick Chisholm, *Theory of Knowledge* (Englewood Cliffs, NJ: Prentice-Hall, 1966), pp. 56–69.
17 Bimal Krishna Matilal, *Perception: An Essay on Classical Indian Theories of Knowledge* (Oxford: Clarendon Press, 1986), p. 314.
18 Diṅnāga, *Pramāṇasamuccaya* 1, 17; Uddyotakara, *Nyāyavārttika* 208, 12–237, 5 (under 2.1.33–6).
19 Vātsyāyana's comment under NS 1.1.4, and *Vaiśeṣikasūtra* 3.1.13.
20 *Nyāyavārttika* 36, 1–14 (under 1.1.4).
21 Compare Sartre's criticism of Freud's concept of a "censor" governing unconscious repression: "the censor in order to apply its activity with discernment must know what it is repressing . . . the censor must choose and in order to choose must be aware of choosing . . .". J.-P. Sartre, *Being and Nothingness: An Essay on Phenomenological Ontology*, trans. H. E. Barnes (London: Methuen & Co., 1966), p. 52.
22 *Nyāyabhāṣya* 19, 2–3 (above 1.1.16).

23 Joerg Tuske, "Being in Two Minds: The Divided Mind in the *Nyāyasūtra*," *Asian Philosophy* 9.3 (1999): 229–38. The "weak" division, in which rationality is attributed only to the whole person and not to any of its subsystems, is that of Davidson: Donald Davidson, "Paradoxes of Irrationality," in R. Wollheim and J. Hopkins, eds., *Philosophical Essays on Freud* (Cambridge: Cambridge University Press, 1982), pp. 289–305.

24 The classic exposition: Udayana, *Ātmatattvaviveka*, pp. 710–19, p. 752. See also Arindam Chakrabarti, "I Touch What I Saw," *Philosophy and Phenomenological Research* 52 (1992): 103–17.

25 For further analysis of the Nyāya anti-reductionist argument: Jonardon Ganeri, "Cross-modality and the Self," *Philosophy and Phenomenological Research* (Nov. 2000). There is interesting evidence from developmental psychology that an infant's acquisition of cross-modal capacities, specifically the ability to identify its own tactually perceived facial expressions with the visually perceived facial expressions of an imitating adult, is instrumental in its development of a sense of self; see Andrew Meltzoff, "Molyneux's Babies: Cross-Modal Perception, Imitation, and the Mind of the Preverbal Infant," in N. Eilan, R. McCarthy, and M. W. Brewer, eds., *Spatial Representation: Problems in Philosophy and Psychology* (Oxford: Blackwell, 1993).

26 *Nyāyabhāṣya* 12, 7–16 (below 1.1.5).

27 *Carakasaṃhitā*, sūtrasthāna 11.13–14.

28 *Upāyahṛdaya* or *Prayogasāra*. G. Tucci, *Pre-Diṅnāga Buddhist Texts on Logic from Chinese Sources* (Baroda: Oriental Institute, Gaekwad's Oriental Series 49, 1929), pp. xvii–xviii.

29 G. Tucci, *Pre-Diṅnāga Buddhist Texts on Logic from Chinese Sources*, p. xviii.

30 VS 2.1.8: "It has horns, a hump, a hairy tail at the extreme and a dewlap – such is the perceived mark of cowness."

31 *Nyāyabhāṣya* 12, 4 (below 1.1.5).

32 The relations of master to property, matter to its altered condition, cause to effect, efficient cause to caused, matter to form, concurrent occurrence, and hindering to hindered. Further discussion: E. Frauwallner, "Die Erkenntnislehre des Klassischen Sāṃkhya-Systems," *Wiener Zeitschrift für die Kunde Süd- und Ost-Asiens* 2 (1958): 84–139, esp. pp. 123, 126–7; Nancy Schuster, "Inference in the Vaiśeṣikasūtras," *Journal of Indian Philosophy* 1 (1972): 341–95; M. Nozawa, "Inferential Marks in the Vaiśeṣikasūtras," *Saṃbhāṣā: Nagoya Studies in Indian Culture and Buddhism* 12 (1991): 25–38; Claus Oetke, "Ancient Indian Logic as a Theory of Non-Monotonic Reasoning," *Journal of Indian Philosophy* 24 (1996): 447–539.

33 *Nyāyabhāṣya* 12, 16–19 (below 1.1.5).

34 Jayarāśi, *Tattvopaplavasiṃha* 74, 8–9.

35 H. N. Randle, *Indian Logic in the Early Schools* (Oxford: Oxford University Press, 1930), p. 148.

36 B. K. Matilal, *The Character of Logic in India* (Albany: State University of New York Press, 1998), p. 32.

37 For an anlysis of such reductive attempts in a wider context: Jonardon Ganeri, "Indian Logic and the Colonisation of Reason," in Jonardon Ganeri ed., *Indian Logic: A Reader* (London: Curzon Press, 2001).

38 Stanisław Schayer, "Über die Methode der Nyāya-Forschung," in O. Stein and W. Gambert, eds., *Festschrift für Moritz Winternitz* (Leipzig, 1933), pp. 247–57. Schayer's paper is translated into English by Joerg Tuske in Jonardon Ganeri, ed., *Indian Logic: A Reader* (London: Curzon Press, 2001).

39 *Nyāyabhāṣya* 285, 4–8 [below 5.1.3].
40 B. K. Matilal, *The Character of Logic in India* (Albany: State University of New York Press, 1998), p. 63.
41 For detailed analysis: Pradeep P. Gokhale, *Inference and Fallacies Discussed in Ancient Indian Logic* (Delhi: Sri Satguru Publications, 1992).
42 *Nyāyabhāṣya* 14, 4–5.
43 On the status of the *mleccha*: Aloka Parasher, *Mlecchas in Early India: A Study in Attitudes Towards Outsiders up to AD 600* (New Delhi: Munshiram Manoharlal, 1991).
44 *Nyāyabhāṣya* 96, 16–97, 7 (below 2.1.68).
45 Elizabeth Fricker, "Against Gullibility," in B. K. Matilal and A. Chakrabarti, eds., *Knowing from Words* (Dordrecht: Kluwer, 1994), pp. 125–61.
46 For a fuller development of this defense: Jonardon Ganeri, *Semantic Powers: Meaning and the Means of Knowing in Classical Indian Philosophy* (Oxford: Clarendon Press, 1999), chs. 1 and 2.
47 *Nyāyabhāṣya* 87, 11–12 (below 2.1.52).

CHAPTER 21

Restoring "Hindu Theology" as a Category in Indian Intellectual Discourse

Francis Clooney, SJ

Setting the Framework

The opening question: should there be such a thing as Hindu theology?

Two questions guide this chapter. First, can we identify a mode of discourse which can justly be called "Hindu theology"? Second, if we can, is it worthwhile to do so? In this introductory section I consider both questions.[1]

In general, theology, philosophy, religious literature, and a wider range of value-oriented cultural studies resist neat division from one another. Both the intersections and overlaps are of value, and usually one need not fuss over fixed separations. In particular, the relationships and differences between philosophy and theology are rich and important, and it is difficult to distinguish them without caricaturing one or the other as if to postulate a philosophy devoid of spiritual values, or a theology bereft of intellectual credibility. Both are theoretical discourses which edge into more practical and moral concerns, or indeed derive from such concerns. Both theology and philosophy prize the cultivation of insight and the achievement of wisdom through disciplined practice; in turn, both quests, once properly defined, can be broadened again in relation to a yet wider range of popular resources in mythology, narrative, poetry, ritual practice, imagery, etc., all of which can flourish in numerous forms which resist neat definition according to particular academic terminologies. When these rich possibilities are recognized, we are still left with the question: what merits the title "theology," or, indeed, which schools of Hindu thought are not "theological"?

The project of identifying theology as distinct from other religious or intellectual discourses involves challenges which for the most part are not peculiar to the Indian context. To understand the presuppositions of a search for "Hindu theology," it is helpful first of all to back up and recall some aspects of the religious and cultural situation in the West, where "theology" evolved as a useful term, and not always a term of approbation. In the pre-Christian Greek context theology was a lesser discourse, a reflective narrative about gods, and akin to mythological discourse. As such, it did not measure up to the newer, higher standards marked by "philosophy."

But thereafter the Christian tradition rehabilitated "theology" and used the term to mark a superior mode of human reasoning which, infused with divine light, was able to inquire deeply into the mystery of God and into matters of faith related to God. Rooted in gracious divine revelation, theology was nonetheless also careful reasoning aimed at apprehending the mysteries of God insofar as the mind was capable of such an apprehension. One of theology's goals was also to enunciate defensible truth claims in accord with the faith, and arguable in the wider public sphere. In the emerging Christian context, theology was considered foremost among modes of human knowing, and in the medieval West it was the "queen of the sciences."

More negative connotations resurfaced in Enlightenment Europe, where leading intellectual voices favored philosophical and scientific knowledge over a "theologizing" burdened with myths and constrained by narrow-minded faith, the pseudo-science of the Bible, and extrinsic ecclesiastical authorities.[2] Instead of philosophy being completed in theology, one now had to rise beyond theology to philosophy and true science. Today, though, the views of theology in relation to science and philosophy are more nuanced and less heated. Depending on one's discipline and intellectual position, one can formulate a variety of pro- or anti-theological stances or, often enough, simply ignore the category of "theology" altogether. Yet as we shall see below, theology persists in resurfacing as a serious intellectual discipline, and today it again commands more urgent attention. Here I will argue that it is also an appropriate and useful term in the context of the study of Indian thought.

However the debate worked out in the European context, there is no exact historical parallel in India, and so too there is also no identical requirement to differentiate the terms "philosophy" and "theology" (or any other candidates) in the same way. Nevertheless, when Western scholarship turned its attention to India, one of the carry-over battles pertained to whether Indian thought was respectable, like science and philosophy, or secondary, like theology.[3] Modern Indian scholars have often enough appropriated the European debate on European terms, found persuasive the Western scholarly skepticism about "theology," and therefore taken the very idea of "Hindu theology" to be a pejorative term aimed at relegating Indian thought to a level below philosophy. On this basis, twentieth-century Indian scholars have reasonably resisted the appellation "theology" for the works of major Indian thinkers, even those who were scriptural exegetes, temple priests, etc.[4]

But I suggest that denigrating or excluding "theology" is not a service to Indian thought. Rather, such a denigration reads a problem indigenous to European history into an Indian context where religious commitments have so often been deeply intertwined with the most rigorous reasoning; even a richer sense of philosophy seems inadequate to the spiritual and religious values at stake; differences aside, "theology" remains a most viable and useful term.

But such a claim in favor of theology is only a beginning, not a conclusion. If one decides to look for theology in India, the task involves reflection on Hindu intellectual discourses and an intelligent re-use of ideas rooted in Christian and Western intellectual sensitivities.[5] As we shall see below, theology marks a kind of reasoning located between attention to sacred texts (*śravaṇa*) and meditation (*nididhyāsana*); it is sufficiently respectful of religious sources and authorities so as to allow them to affect how one thinks; it is likewise open to logical and reasoned conclusions which are powerful enough to change how religious people think about their beliefs. When Hindu reasoning is studied by Hindus and others who are genuinely interested in learning religiously from Hindu thought, the recognition of "Hindu theology" seems a timely step toward making different faiths and different reasons mutually intelligible.[6]

Why bother identifying "Hindu theology"?

But why? We must ask a bit more closely whether it is really important to defend reference to "theology" in the Hindu context, and whether "theology" is more useful than "philosophy" in identifying key aspects of Hindu thought. To begin with, we can observe that numerous Hindu traditions were not oblivious to differences which support reference to the "theological." Reasoning carried forward without regard for authoritative religious sources needs to be distinguished from reasoning marked by attention to scripture and other religious authorities; the latter is theological reasoning. Some Hindu reasoning is only very indirectly connected with religious truth claims or religious practices; some Hindu piety is deeply religious, but relatively immune to critical examination. But much reasoning and piety express a faith received and reviewed in a critical fashion. The former reasoning and piety are close to what we mean by "philosophical reasoning" and "religious sentiment," while the latter is more properly "theological reasoning." These distinctions are important, since "theology" most accurately describes some of the major trajectories of Hindu thought. Since modern India has in fact been influenced by distinctions which originate in the West – everything ultimately will have some name in English – and since the designation "theology" need not be pejorative,[7] there is no *a priori* reason to avoid talking about "Hindu theology" in distinction from "Hindu philosophy" and "Hindu religiosity."

Rather, it is also profitable to use the category, "Hindu theology," even when as scholars our goal may first of all be simply to describe what we find in Indian texts, without making claims about the interconnections of faith and inquiry. If we work with a broad and nuanced notion of theology – along with a less idealized and less all-encompassing notion of philosophy – we will be able to see the virtue of reviving theology as a category for understanding Hindu thought. If we do so, we can more accurately understand which strands of Indian thought are most fruitfully aligned with which strands of Western thought. While Western philosophy can provide a viable conversation partner for some Hindu thought, the sharp divergence of much of contemporary Western philosophy from much of contemporary Western Christian theology suggests too that theology will probably be a better partner for illuminating comparisons with the majority of the great works of the premodern Hindu tradition.

We can also point to experiments in comparative theology which take theology seriously as a viable crosscultural category, and which illumine Indian thought successfully, and more fully than would simple religious or philosophical analyses. A clear example is the volume *Scholasticism in Cross-cultural and Comparative Perspective*. Jose Cabezon, the editor, and his fellow contributors (myself included), begin with the intuition that although the elaborate theological production and system of thought known as "scholasticism" is most easily rooted in the theology of medieval Europe, and in the works of authors such as Thomas Aquinas, it is possible and fruitful to use "scholasticism" to identify ways of reasoning and even areas of content in other religious traditions (although similarities will always be accompanied by differences in detail and in overall structure).[8] As "scholasticism" is useful cross-culturally, so too "theology."

Perhaps the most extensive recent evidence of the fruitfulness of theological comparison lies in the lifelong work of Gerhard Oberhammer, retired Director of the Indological Institute at the University of Vienna. For more than three decades Oberhammer has been committed to comparative study involving Asian and Western thought (primarily Hindu, Buddhist, and Christian) which operates at a sophisticated theological level. Throughout, he has presumed that these traditions share interestingly similar categories (such as "revelation," "transcendence," and "sacrament") which are not reducible to sociological or even philosophical concepts, and that through comparisons one can illumine the theological traditions involved. Volumes in his ongoing comparative theological project focus on the experience of transcendence, the manifestation of salvation, the transcendental hermeneutic, the notion of encounter as a religious category, and the sacramental dimension of religious traditions.[9] In his writings Oberhammer is clearly aware of the perils inherent in comparative study. He knows that terms like "epiphany," "transcendence," "encounter," and "sacrament" are rooted in technical Christian theology, and he admits that it would be facile to reduce the complexities of Indian thought to settled Christian equivalents. Arguing by analogy, though, he insists that if religious traditions such as the Vedic, Buddhist, and Hindu traditions of India claim to lead practitioners beyond the confines of this world, one can legitimately draw out the parallels with what the Christian theological tradition names as "sacrament," etc.[10] The purposes and goals of Hindu and Christian thinkers are sufficiently shared that "theology" is useful as an overarching term which renders plausible more specific and detailed theological comparisons. We can add that since this application helps us to reorganize more lucidly our understanding of Indian thought, it also aids us in reconsidering, now in a broader perspective, theology in the West and in the Christian traditions.

Other examples too can be adduced. Some Hindu scholars (in the West, thus far) are recognizing the value of theology as a category. For instance, in 1997 a group of scholars published *Meditation Revolution: A History and Theology of the Siddha Yoga Lineage*,[11] in which they explicitly turn to the language of theology to explain the Siddha Yoga tradition and to characterize themselves as theologians, believers, and practitioners who study their own tradition according to recognized scholarly standards. If it is indeed the first work in what must be a longer and richer tradition of religious reasoning about Siddha Yoga, *Meditation Revolution* promises rich theological results. Similarly, John Makransky and Roger Jackson recently edited *Buddhist Theology*,[12] which similarly brings together the work of scholars willing both to testify to their own identity as Buddhists and to characterize their scholarship on Buddhism as "theological."

Clues toward the Identification of "Hindu Theology(ies)"

In the first part of this chapter I simply proposed an initial case as to why it is possible and worthwhile to interpret some strands of Indian thought as "theology." I now wish to get more specific by identifying what can justly be called theological in the Hindu context. For this task, I now present a series of considerations – e.g., themes, modes of reasoning, styles, audience expectations, the judgment of theologians – by the measure of which we can determine whether a Hindu text or system of thought ought to be counted as theological. Each of the following clues has some merit on its own, but none is independently sufficient, and it will not be necessary to accept all of them to justify the acceptance of the category, "theology." Nevertheless, in significant combinations they can help us to make choices about texts (and systems of thought) that should be called theological.[13]

Theology as the study of God

The simplest way to demarcate *Hindu* theology is to stipulate that texts which are theological are those which have God as their primary object of intellectual inquiry. In much of what may be counted as Hindu theology the fact of a focus on a supreme, personal intelligent being who is the world source and guarantor of the significance of human life is an adequate working criterion. One can immediately raise the question of what is meant by "God" and "gods," and ask whether it is fair to appeal to terms like *īśvara*, *bhagavān*, *puruṣa*, etc.; much of the work of theology – Hindu or other – is devoted to specifying what we mean when we use "God" and accompanying words. Nonetheless an appeal to terms indicative of a highest and original source of reality – who can be referred to by words such as "intelligent," "spiritual," "person" – is a legitimate starting point in the project of identifying "theology."[14]

Some substantive issues which characterize Hindu theology

I now list seven themes which help to define Hindu theology. In question are topics of religious import which have a scriptural basis and practical import, which are not esoteric, and which can be argued even if rooted in faith. I suggest just seven topics which can usefully distinguish theological discourse: a) the nature of a sufficient world cause, world maker; b) whether God is one or many; c) divine embodiment; d) the problem of evil; e) the nature and time of liberation; f) the appeal to revelation; g) "ignorance" as a theological category.

a) The nature of a sufficient world cause, world-maker In general, the debate over the existence of God can be understood as a subdivision of a wider debate about whether the world itself does or can have a satisfactory explanation. While the wider topic can be termed scientific or philosophical, the narrower form, focused on the hypothesis that there is a person who is the source of the world, is a specifically theological topic. More particularly, the question is whether the world cause can be thought of as simply a material principle, or whether a spiritual and conscious principle is the most reasonable prospect.

A more particular form of the preceding initial question within the broader Indian arguments regarding religious matters and the reliable means of religious knowledge is whether there can be a convincing induction of the existence of a world-maker. Can one offer a satisfactory explanation of the world without positing that it has a maker? This question can be raised as an issue of epistemology or an example of induction, but eventually it became a question about God and a distinctively theological matter. In Vaiśeṣika empiricism, particularly in its earlier stages, the project of a complete description of material reality led to the question of whether that reality is explicable without reference to an external cause and measure of intelligibility, God. Eventually the Vaiśeṣika thinkers, and more prominently the Nyāya logicians who commented on the basic *Nyāya Sūtras* (from before the beginning of the Common Era), decided that reality could not be self-explanatory, and that accordingly some appeal to an exterior cause was required. The facts of ordinary reality raise questions which cannot be answered by appeals to other aspects of ordinary reality. A clay pot is relatively simple, but one must still explain how it got its particular shape, and perhaps too who fused its upper and lower parts into a whole. All the more, the complexity of the world requires the postulation of an intelligent maker. Even if this maker is not seen, "he" must be posited as the cause who synthesizes the things that are seen. This synthesizer is God.

Once the Logicians entered upon this debate and decided to link the postulation of the existence of God with the foundations of intelligibility, they pursued the argument with great vigor. There was significant support for this kind of reasoning about God's existence, but the Nyāya position was also criticized on logical grounds and with respect to its religious implications, not only by nontheists but also by some theists who were not eager to adhere to a "God" (merely) knowable by induction. The outcome was a widespread debate, which included a variety of Hindu, Buddhist, and Jain interlocutors, and it was a debate which made sense intellectually because "God" was accepted as a term worth arguing about.[15]

Many Hindu thinkers – in Nyāya and Vedānta, for instances – defended the idea that the world has a maker. While this argument can certainly be treated as philosophical, particularly regarding one's preliminary understanding of terms such as "cause" and "effect," "world" and "person," most of those willing to debate the issue agreed to make the question of the nature of the cause a question of the nature of God; and for many this was also a question of understanding God as known in scripture. In the Vedānta version, the point is argued repeatedly in key texts, such as *Uttara Mīmāṃsā Sūtras* 1.1, 2.1, and 2.2, often in opposition to Sāṃkhya thinkers who held that there were two principles, material and spiritual. By Sāṃkhya reasoning, the material principle itself simply evolves into complex forms, and there is no need to hold that some spiritual power governs the material principle or is its ultimate source. According to Vedānta, the Upaniṣads offer a more reasonable explanation: the world cause must be a unitary principle which evolves into both spiritual and material realities. Since "God" is one of the more familiar terms (in English) for this spiritual cause, and since terms such as "Brahman" do not shift the force of the arguments significantly, the debate in general seems most easily described as theological.

b) Whether God is one or many Even if it makes sense to argue about causality – divine or other – and about the possible existence of a divine world-maker, it requires a greater and more intense consensus to argue about further, more specific issues, such as whether more can be said about God. In some circles, though, the topic of more specific knowledge of God was considered arguable, not merely a matter of belief and personal preference but as a matter of sense and truth, and was debated vehemently, in a debate best described as theological.

To draw on just one sectarian example: Vedānta Deśika, the fourteenth-century theologian of the Viśiṣṭādvaita Vedānta school (in turn rooted in the theology of Rāmānuja [eleventh century]), argues that there is only one ultimate reality, who is the Lord Nārāyaṇa (Viṣṇu) eternally accompanied by the Goddess Śrī. At the same time Viṣṇu is also Brahman, the Reality described in the ancient Upaniṣads. In his *Śrīmad Rahasyatrayasāra*, after a consideration of God's perfections in relation to other components of reality, Deśika turns to the question of Nārāyaṇa's relation to other deities. He argues that there can only be one true God and it is possible and urgent to decide which deity is that true God. Since religious practice and salvation are ultimately dependent on a right relationship with the true God, it is possible and necessary to know this God correctly. Proper exegesis and clear reasoning will indicate that Nārāyaṇa alone is the lord of the universe, neither Śiva nor Brahmā.

In his *Nyāya Siddhāñjana* Deśika sets the argument on a firm philosophical ground, arguing that the notion of divine perfection requires that God be one, while the human experience of the divine, however limited, does not require that God be imagined in numerous forms rather than one form.[16] Although nondualist Vedānta thinkers did not see a personal God as a primary constituent in their system, they were willing to debate the oneness of God; a multiplicity of gods makes no sense in terms of ultimate reality, but only on the level of popular piety.[17] This kind of argument – one God, or several gods, or a Reality beyond gods – makes sense only within the frame of certain presuppositions which, I suggest, are "theological."

c) Divine embodiment A third, consequent theological topic has to do with whether it is meaningful to claim that God can be embodied. The Hindu (and Buddhist and Jaina) intellectuals who argued for and against the existence of God and about the divine nature also asked whether it makes sense to say that God can have and actually does have a body. On one level, this is a faith matter of great importance for the Śaiva and Vaiṣṇava communities; each in its own way celebrates divine embodiment. But in both cases, it is also an issue requiring extensive intellectual inquiry.

On the Śaiva side, for instance, Aruḷnanti's thirteenth-century *Civañānacittiyār* offers a rich positive exposition of Śiva's embodiment, developed forcefully and in considerable detail. In section I.2 of the constructive part (*Supakkam*) of *Civañānacittiyār* Aruḷnanti defends the idea that the Lord can have a body, for the simple reason that God is all-powerful and can do anything he chooses. Aruḷnanti firmly asserts the perfection and freedom of Śiva in his choice of forms simply as a matter of divine freedom. Śiva's mysterious play of forms, his complex and shifting use of forms, is a purposeful divine pedagogy, aimed at leading humans through the mystery of physical and spiritual forms of existence, from mere identification with material form to deeper and more spiritual understandings of the true meaning of "self" and "having a form."[18]

For Vaiṣṇava theologians too, the discussion of body as limitation aimed at ruling out notions of divine embodiment which would constrict the divine perfection. Yet in certain important features the Vaiṣṇava theology of the divine body differs from Śaiva theology. Both material and spiritual realities arise from a single source and need not be seen as contrary to one another. God relates to the world as that upon which the world depends entirely and that which gives it life, though without God's being dependent on the world; analogously, the soul inhabits, gives life to, and guides the material body, without itself suffering materiality. Accordingly, Vaiṣṇava theologians seem more open to the idea that God can assume specific bodies, either animal or human, and live over time within those specific forms.

Whether or not one agrees that it makes sense to claim that God can assume a physical body, I suggest that in the Hindu context this is an intelligible issue perceived of as worthy of argument. So too, it is best seen as a marker of a debate which is best understood as theological and not simply philosophical nor merely a sectarian protestation.

d) The problem of evil The problem of evil is discussed in India as in the West, despite important differences in the framing of the discussion, ranging from the factor of rebirth to the significance rendered to pain itself. But theodicy was still an issue: if there is a God (or transcendent world source) who is all-powerful, how are suffering and inequality to be accounted for? In *Uttara Mīmāṃsā Sūtras* 2.1.34–6 this question is addressed by both nondualist Vedānta thinkers (such as Śaṃkara) and theistic thinkers (such as Rāmānuja). To argue that the intelligent divine source who consciously arranged the world is cruel and unfair is also an argument that the Vedānta position in favor of a unitary material and spiritual cause is ultimately incoherent; to support their view of the origin of the world, the Vedānta thinkers must account for evil. This argument, for and against the idea that divine perfection is harmonious with the state of the world as humans experience it, is important and intelligible in a theological context where notions of God, divine power, moral standards of good and evil, responsibility and guilt, are accepted as arguable and intelligible. While the argument that there is an ultimate right order and justice in the world need not be theistic, they are most likely theological. The problem of theodicy can arise because there is some expectation of perfection or of an intelligible order, which leads to the mounting of a defense of the world as a coherent and intelligible whole. If there is no such perfection, the theology dissolves and the problem loses its urgency.[19]

e) The nature and time of liberation Another important question which serves to mark off theological ground is whether liberation is possible within a given lifetime (as *jīvanmukti*) or only after death. This too is a "boundary" question best considered theological, since it relies on the premise that it is intelligible to speak of "liberation," and that arguing between the alternatives of "liberation while alive" and "liberation after death" is important and makes sense, given intelligible positions about the world and the possibility and need for liberation. To be sure, arguing about *jīvanmukti* involves factors which can be examined nontheologically: for example, estimates of the human condition, whether that condition can be radically improved, the means by which one overcomes the ailments of life, why death might be considered not merely the end but also a transitional state, and how one might even know that a person is to be judged not merely holy or wise but actually liberated. The presuppositions are specific enough and involve sufficient religious values that one can rightly see discussions of liberation as most intelligible in a theological context.[20]

f) The appeal to revelation Our sixth example of a kind of discussion that is most properly termed "theological" has to do with the appeal to revelation, authoritative verbal testimony. We can begin by noting that Indian intellectuals were concerned to determine the proper modes of knowing which produce proper and reliable knowledge, and likewise uncover and dispel ignorance. The concern to understand properly the criteria for right knowledge is of course not a disposition unique to theology; but the disposition of some Hindu systems not only to defend the need for reliable verbal communication but also to highlight specific privileged (oral and written) texts does characterize theological discourse.

In arguments among themselves and also with Buddhist and Jaina interlocutors, Hindu thinkers analyzed the knowing process in a sophisticated fashion, arguing the viability of truth claims and proposing subtle distinctions and relations among the means of right knowing (*pramāṇa*), objects of right knowing (*prameya*), and right knowledge (*pramā*).[21] Ideally, perception is the sufficient reliable means of knowledge.

But since the argument that everything knowable can be known by simple perception is never persuasively argued, supplementary means of right knowing multiply. Intellectuals who are theologians are concerned with the truth of their faith positions, and are compelled to articulate and defend verbal authority, and ultimately a idea of a privileged verbal knowledge, revelation. It is properly and distinctively theological to ask whether there is something that can be called "revelation," a privileged body of verbal testimony which informs humans about aspects of reality which are not otherwise knowable.

It is within a theological context that one can argue about this. Indian intellectuals may be divided into those who accept this privileged verbal information and those who do not. In turn, those accepting revelation are further differentiated when one attempts to discern which words and texts, in which language(s), are revelatory. We see revelation defended in the Mīmāṃsā and Vedānta, for instance, particularly in argument with Buddhists and others skeptical about the authority of the Veda. Here one can distinguish thinkers inside and outside the Vedic tradition, and those adhering strictly to Sanskrit-language revelation from those willing to admit vernacular revelations.

g) "Ignorance" as a theological category If right knowledge becomes a theologically distinctive category, it follows too that ignorance too becomes an epistemological issue with theological and soteriological import. In the nondualist Vedānta tradition *avidyā* is treated as a problem but also afforded an explanatory role, since this Vedānta tradition has a vested interest in seeing ignorance as the cause of suffering and its removal as the appropriate response to suffering. The issue is both whether the incongruities between scriptural promises and realities on the one hand and the evident realities of ordinary life on the other have to be explained in terms of objective differences and contradictions, or rather by appeal to a concept of ignorance which reduces differences to temporary defects in the observer. Perhaps things are as they are because of an individual and even cosmic confusion which distorts reality and alienates humans from their world. "Ignorance" thus has considerable implications for the analysis of the human condition, the problem of bondage, and prospects for liberation. The study of ignorance too merits the title of a theological topic and, since it is not a topic which is restricted to one or another sectarian audience, it can be argued among a wider range of Hindu thinkers.

To conclude this section: the preceding considerations sketch a range of themes likely to be found in theological discussions and so too to distinguish those discussions. Someone can believe that there is one God who is maker of the world, takes on a body, is testified to in scripture, yet without also being willing to argue in defense of those beliefs. So too, there can be intellectuals who disagree with such beliefs, but who also think that it is possible and important to argue through one's objections to those beliefs. It is when we find a context in which these matters are subjected to intellectual scrutiny, for the sake of approval or disagreement, that we have a theological context.

Manana *as theological reasoning*

In the preceding sections I have linked theology not simply to religious beliefs, but also to religious truths and "public" positions liable to reasoned argumentation. Now I further develop this view, since key to theology is the convergence of belief and reason: certain strands of Hindu thought are theological also because in them we see operative a certain kind of reasoning that is focused – and constricted – by religious concerns. Often appeals to this kind of reasoning balance an insistence that such reasoning is entirely logical with an insistence that it is deeply indebted to sources ordinarily inaccessible to the hman mind. It is a reasoning "freely" constrained by boundaries set according to some recognized authority, most commonly (though not only) verbal authority as revelation and/or scripture.[22] The Vedānta commentators, for example, agree that reasoning leads to knowledge of Brahman, but also that Brahman can be known only by a reasoning which submits to revelation and draws its conclusions consequent upon revelation.

A key source for the influential Vedānta understanding of the ordering and organization of knowledge as theological is related to the injunction in the *Bṛhadāraṇyaka Upaniṣad*, 2.4.5: "One's self must be seen, must be heard, must be reasoned about, must be meditated on" – hearing properly (*śravaṇa*), reasoning properly (*manana*), meditating properly (*nididhyāsana*), together climax in vision (*darśana*). As attention to scripture, hearing (*śravaṇa*) is the necessary beginning of the project of learning; it must be followed by reasoning (*manana*) which inquires into the meaning and implications of what has been understood. But neither is reason theologically conclusive, since one must also go farther and engage in meditation, *nididhyāsana*.[23]

The intermediate stage, *manana*, is the reasoning which interests us here as properly theological reasoning. It opens in both directions – toward sacred word and toward meditation, constrained by scriptural boundaries and oriented to a completion in religious practice – yet it remains recognizably logical, aimed at understanding, assertive of truth claims which are to some extent generalizable, accessible to argument and critique. Other kinds of reasoning, such as might operate mainly in terms of an analysis of human experience or simply in terms of repetition of scriptural claims without analysis, can be accounted for by other terms, e.g., as philosophy or as confessional religious testimony.

In numerous contexts Hindu thinkers sought to defend the possibility of and need for rational reflection on faith issues, aiming at a delicate balance. Rationalists, including some philosophers, may argue that reasoning should proceed simply in terms of questions, problems, and doubts which can be resolved strictly on logical grounds, and that all other matters are less intellectual matters, of religious sentiment. Religious conservatives may insist that the Veda is totally clear, coherent, and need not be subjected to any critical examination. Against both positions, the theological mean represented by *manana* holds the view that faith can be reasonable, yet still faith; thinking can submit to scripture, yet still be thinking.

To illustrate how this reasoning was understood in the Hindu context I will draw on three texts, two classical and one modern, which indicate respectively how there is a reality, beyond texts, which can be known; how even the truth of scripture can be argued; how theological reasoning is submissive to revelation. I begin with several of the *vārtikas* of Sureśvara (ninth century) on Śaṇkara's commentary on the *Bṛhadāraṇyaka Upaniṣad* 2.4.5. Sureśvara explains how the four seeming injunctions – "it must be seen, it must be heard, it must be reasoned about, it must be meditated on" – form a single integral enjoined activity.[24] He says that while the "seeing" mentioned in the Upaniṣad ("it must be seen") cannot be enjoined, the means to that seeing – i.e., the "hearing" of the Upaniṣadic texts, and the intellectual consideration of those texts – can be enjoined as the necessary means. This appropriate, always subsequent "reasoning" focuses on the direct and implied meanings of scriptural texts and similar issues. Conformed to the words of the Veda, it aims at determining the relationship between verbal expressions and what is expressed by them. Revelation is the source of liberative vision, but (with a teacher's help) one must understand scripture first. Neither does reasoning conclude merely in understanding texts, since the primary claim, "one should see," also indicates a desire to know reality in its essence. Were the goal simply the experience of insight, without an objective referent, the requirement that one must reason about the meaning of scripture would have no point. Reasoning must therefore open into meditation.

Thus, to draw on another familiar Vedānta text as an example, the Vedānta student must inquire into the meaning of "that" (*tat*) and "thou" (*tvam*) in the *Chāndogya* phrase "that thou art" (*tat tvam asi*). The goal of this inquiry is to learn about the nondual nature of reality itself. This reasoning opens into that accomplishment of vision which "dawns" subsequently in meditation, like the rising sun. Based in revelation and open to a more experiential completion, this reasoning, supported by both the *Chāndogya* and *Bṛhadāraṇyaka* Upaniṣads, is a reasoning which we can call theological reasoning.

A second interpretation of *manana* is drawn from the introduction to the *Nyāyakusumāñjali* of Udayana (tenth century), specifically a section of Vardhamāna's *Prakāśa* commentary in which Vardhamāna explores the kind of inquiry that is possible and appropriate when God is the topic of inquiry. In agreement with other commentators on Udayana's text, Vardhamāna seeks to justify the kind of inquiry that Udayana undertakes in his treatise; he too is concerned to defend it against views which would make reasoning about God unviable: i.e., God is so well known that there is nothing to think about; everybody knows something about God, but nobody can speak with certainty, so it is all a matter of opinion; scripture is so perfectly informative that there is no need to think about God at all, since one already *knows*.

Vardhamāna discusses the *Bṛhadāraṇyaka* injunction to think – "one should reason on it" in light of its implications for reasoning that is submissive to the Upaniṣads, and specifically with regard to whether it is even possible to argue about "God." Following the intuition which underlies the *Nyāyakusumāñjali*, he wants to explain the inquiry into God as respecting scripture without treating it as inadequate, yet too without allowing it to snuff out thinking; respecting common opinions while critiquing them; and not projecting knowledge of God as merely the ever-receding horizon of inquiry.

Vardhamāna argues that the inquiry into the existence of God which is taken up in the *Nyāyakusumāñjali* is a real inquiry, not simply a review of positions already known by faith. While some observers might be tempted to reverse the sequence of "hearing" and "reasoning" and give preference to reasoning, such that scripture is to be consulted only for clarification, it is more plausible, given the sequence found in the *Bṛhadāraṇyaka* text – "it must be heard, it must be reasoned about" – that the study of the texts comes first, and that reflection is subsequent to that study. It is economical to see this reasoning as focused on textual interpretation and not more broadly on the wider variety of aspects of "God" that might come to mind. Were the objects of "it must be heard" and "it must be reasoned about" different, then no real progress could be made by combining the study of texts with reasoning. The implication is rather that real exegesis must lead to real reasoning.

It is true, Vardhamāna concedes, that religious people may not have doubts about God, since there is nothing to be learned about the lord which is not in scripture, and since what scripture says about the lord is reliable knowledge. *Manana* must therefore be respectful reasoning, which does not call into question the authority of the scriptures. Indeed, there would be no motive to think about scriptures were they not authoritative. But neither is this reasoning merely an explication of the texts which sorts out what is to be taken literally over against what is metaphorical. Rather, reasoning aims at grasping the texts' meanings more precisely, even while never doubting their truth. Moreover, doubts can arise. Even if one may not doubt God's existence, one can take seriously doubts about the inference of a world-maker. One cannot know God without attributing some characteristics to him, which can be sorted out only by comparing and contrasting them with one another, in a reasonable fashion.[25]

Our third reference which illuminates the nature of *manana* as theological reasoning draws on the theory of a twentieth-century pandit, Vasudeva Shastri Abhyankar. In his Sanskrit introduction to the *Sarvadarśanasaṃgraha* of Vidyāraṇya (fourteenth century), he distinguishes two kinds of *darśana* (ways of thinking, systems of thought): the "scripturalist" (*śāstriya*) *darśanas* and the "rationalist" (*tarka*) *darśanas*. In the former category he places Mīmāṃsā ritual theory, Vedānta Upaniṣadic interpretation and system, and Grammar (*Vyākaraṇa*), while in the latter he places Nyāya logic, Vaiśeṣika naturalism, and the Sāṃkhya/Yoga theory of the separate material and spiritual causes. The reason for the distinction of the *śāstriya darśana* and *tarka darśana* is not simply that the former rely on scripture while the latter rely only on reason; thinkers in both groups respect both sources of knowledge. But Abhyankar's concern is the "bottom line": if one is concerned with ascertaining the real truth about something, and if there is a conflict between scripture and reason, what is one's final resort? He says that Mīmāṃsā, Vedānta, and Grammar are all *śāstriya darśanas* which come down on the side of scripture, to which reason must conform itself. Conversely, Sāṃkhya, Yoga, and Nyāya are *tarka darśanas* because even if their theoreticians respect scripture, the fundamental resource is reason, not scripture. Arguments and authorities must make sense, and scripture must be interpreted in such a way that it conforms to reason. It seems evident, I suggest, that the *śāstriya darśanas* are "theological," and the *tarka darśanas* are "philosophical";[26] *manana* is theological, *tarka* philosophical.[27]

Throughout, however, it is important to retain a sense that even theological positions are arguable positions. This arguability is crucial, since where positions are asserted merely on the basis of authority – the text, a guru, a divine speaker – we have something less than a rational discourse, something which is not theology. When argument is possible, it characterizes important, complete systems of thought in which progress is possible even on matters important for religious believers and practitioners. Most Nyāya, Mīmāṃsā, and Vedānta texts, and some vernacular texts, e.g., in the Tamil Vaiṣṇava and Śaiva traditions, demonstrate this argumentative possibility, and thus are theological texts.

Language, commentary, and community

A final set of clues has to do with issues related to style, context, and community: like other intellectual discourses, theology communicates in a certain way, and meets certain expectations. Here I suggest just three ways of beginning to explore these more elusive, contextual factors.

Commentary Some religious texts stimulate commentary while others do not; some texts are commentaries, while others are not. I suggest that within the broader range of religious literature, the fact of commentary can be an important clue to the presence of theological discourse. While being-commented-on is not an obligatory feature of a theological text, texts with commentaries are better candidates for the title "theological" than those not commented on, since commentary indicates the recognition that the text's ideas are worthy of further reflection and expansion. Authors who comment on some older religious texts are marking those texts as possessed of important though often difficult or subtle theological import which needs to be brought to articulation. Some texts deserve and require commentary, because they contain truth which requires elucidation; and such texts, along with their commentaries, are theological. Sacred texts which are not commented on, or only in the simplest of word by word explications, may be considered religiously inspiring but not theologically weighty. Thus, the *Bhagavad Gītā* receives multiple serious commentaries, while most other portions of the *Mahābhārata* do not. In turn, we may attribute theological significance to secondary texts, some themselves commentaries, which have in fact generated further commentary, since further commentary too indicates the *intellectual* respect afforded to such relgiious texts.

Must Hindu theology be Sanskrit-language discourse? A still more elusive clue has to do with the importance of the Sanskrit language itself with respect to Indian intellectual systems. While one cannot endorse the assertion that Indian intellectual discourse is always Sanskrit language-discourse, one can say that much of it is precisely that, or at least composed in a context heavily indebted to Sanskrit. Of course, a pervasive reverence for sacred sound and sacred word accrues to writings in Sanskrit; it seems that almost anything written in Sanskrit can elicit religious reverence. But in addition we can more narrowly assert that "Sanskrit reasoning" distinguishes much of what in fact counts as integral Hindu theology. To think and write systematically in traditional Hindu India was to compose in Sanskrit or in a way deeply indebted to Sanskrit. On this basis, theology might be treated as a Sanskritic mode of discourse, while writings in vernacular languages are less likely to achieve the "religious intellectuality," systematic specificity, and arguability which characterize the theological.[28] I propose that Hindu theology is ordinarily Sanskrit-language discourse, either composed in the Sanskrit language or in languages deeply influenced by Sanskritic reasoning. While in theory this need not be the case, it seems in fact to be so.

There are vernacular texts which fit the description of theology offered here without being deeply influenced by Sanskrit language discourse, but they are rare. I think immediately of key Tamil Vaiṣṇava and Śaiva texts, works which are richly reflective and critical in their reasoning: e.g., in the Vaiṣṇava tradition, Tirumaḻicai Āḻvār's *Nāṉmukaṉ Tiruvantāti* and Śaṭakōpaṉ's *Tiruvāymoḻi* (ca. ninth century) and the long and rich tradition of commentary and treatise which the latter inspired,[29] and the Śaiva *Civañānapōtam*, works which it inspired such as Aruḷnanti's *Civañānacittiyār*, along with other Śaiva treaties such as Umāpati's *Tiruvaruṭpayaṉ* (fourteenth century).[30]

Theology within a community at home with theology Finally, it is worth observing that theology does not occur in isolation from the community of those who write it and those who read it. It is recognizable as it is received, according to certain audience and professional theological expectations. We have already seen that the reasoning here proposed as theological is a reasoning which opens itself for a completion in religious realization, e.g., in that meditation (*nididhyāsana*) which is subsequent upon a reasoned reflection (*manana*) on what one has learned from scripture (*śravaṇa*). Theological reasoning imposes particular expectations upon persons who read particular texts, texts revered within some community.

These expectations can be read in two directions. From one vantage point, a community may have specific expectations regarding particular authors who are, or aren't, to be called theologians. If a community expects an intellectual production to be merely informational or merely the explication of technical details for the sake of a specialized audience, that writing will probably not be theological. If a community expects a text to report encounters with God, to arouse deep inspiration, or offer instruction on moral and ritual practices, the likely author may be honored as a saint or prophet or teacher, but not as a theologian. Only if a community (or at least its elite) values the intellectual content of religious texts and the truth claims generated in relation to those texts will it interpret texts or commentaries as intelligently explicating the beliefs of the community, undergirding them with sufficient philosophical foundations, and defending them against competing philosophical and religious systems. Received in this way, texts may be properly recognized as "theological," and their authors as theologians.

From the author's vantage point, of course, the matter comes to much the same thing, since authors intend particular audiences. Communities expecting theology and authors seeking a theological audience find one another within larger religious communities. If an author aims at aiding a religious audience in thinking through the meaning and implications of its faith (in general, and particularly in its scriptural sources), or at least in defending the intelligibility and plausibility of faith, then that author's work is an intellectual production distinguished by theological intentions. But if the author intends no such communication with a practicing religious community, he or she is likely not to be a theologian.

Finally, a simpler way to state the preceding is to suggest that theology will be recognized by those who have theological commitments already. If one has theological sensitivities, one will be able to decide what is theological and what is not. It makes no sense to leave the judgment on this matter to those who have decided that theology is not a possible and useful category by which intellectual materials can be categorized. This circularity is surely not very different from the situation evident in other fields; it is no surprise that historical or literary studies depend on historians or critics for apt recognition of the categories of texts involved. Indologists recognize other Indologists, subaltern critics their own contrary peers, and theologians find their own kind too. I admit this circularity not to mark off theology as the exclusive preserve of theologians – it must remain intellectual, arguable, etc., and surely others can have negative as well as positive opinions – but rather to stress that judgments in this regard cannot be entirely bereft of theological sensitivity.

Of course, since theology has communal roots, it must be the theologians of the Hindu tradition who must take the lead in maintaining and fostering Hindu theology. Theologians from other traditions (such as this author) must make only tentative judgments about what seems to be theological and where Hindu theologizing might lead. In any case, it is opportune to admit here that if much of this chapter is dedicated to identifying "Hindu theology" in the great classical traditions, it will be up to intellectuals writing today, who are willing to be called "Hindu theologians," to chart the course of the future of Hindu theology.

Theology as complex discourse

Even if we decide that there is such a thing as Hindu theology and are willing to draw upon the preceding suggestions to build a case for identifying specific Hindu theological texts, the decision about what is theological will never be a matter of determining a text "theological," or not, in a simple, straightforward manner, as if theology can be only a simple discourse produced simply. A work that is justly called "theological" need not be uniformly theological in all its parts; theology can be divided into parts and subdisciplines, some of which are not theological. In the Catholic theological context, for example, in schools and seminaries where theology is taught, one finds it standard to differentiate theology into disciplines such as Biblical Studies, Church History, Dogmatic and Systematic Theology, Moral Theology (and/or Theological Ethics), Pastoral Theology, etc. In his *Method in Theology*, the twentieth-century Christian theologian Bernard Lonergan argued that theology is a necessarily complex activity which operates in harmony with the different levels of human cognition and includes eight disciplines which complement and confirm one another.[31] "Theology" is the umbrella term for all these disciplines in the Roman Catholic tradition, since they are all intended to contribute to an overall theological education which necessarily includes such subareas, and since all together contribute to the still larger task of understanding the faith, accomplishing knowledge of God insofar as this is humanly possible. Moreover, a line of reasoning or argument that at one point meets the criteria for theology may later on cease to be theological. Theology is complex and complicated, and it has a history.

There is no reason to assume that Hindu theology should be any more simple or uniform than Christian theology. It is necessary to differentiate Hindu theology according to its subsidiary disciplines, some of which may be particularly philological or philosophical, others more exegetical, and still others more practical. For instance, a very old model for the distinction among disciplines contributing to a single whole is found in the Vedic ritual field, where the Veda, as (oral) text and practice, is supported by six ancillary disciplines: recitation (*śīkṣā*), metrics (*chandas*), grammar (*vyākaraṇa*), etymology (*nirukta*), astrology (*jyotiṣa*), rubrics (*kalpa*). Taken in isolation, some of these disciplines are intellectually interesting discourses which can well be studied apart from any relationship to Vedic performance, but in light of the stipulation that they are ancillary to the Veda they are defined as contributing to the overall project of Vedic theory and practice.

Other models too are available. After 300 BCE the Mīmāṃsā ritual theorists formalized their division of the Veda into a series of interlocking subsidiary modes of discourse, for example, *mantras* (recited in rituals), *brāhmaṇas* (descriptive and prescriptive of ritual actions), and *arthavādas* (narratives and other literary formations supportive of performance). Underlying this division is the recognition that the fundamental Mīmāṃsā project, *dharma-jijñāsā* (the inquiry into the intelligibility of *dharma*) was rightly differentiated into subdisciplines, all of which together constituted the study of *dharma*.

Similarly, the Vedānta (Uttara Mīmāṃsā) system distinguished the fundamental inquiry into *brahman* (*brahma-jijñāsā*) by discerning more limited tasks, such as demonstrating that Brahman alone is the real topic of Vedānta (*Uttara Mīmāṃsā Sūtras* I), defending the reasonability of Vedānta exegesis against a variety of theological and nontheological opponents (II), harmonizing meditation texts with one another (III), and clarifying the cosmology of the post-mortem world and other objective referents important for the coherence of the Vedānta system (IV). None of these tasks is the same, and some may be conceived of as pretheological, yet together they form a unitary theological system.

Or, in Śaiva Āgama and Vaiṣṇava Pañcarātra texts, we find a standard distinction of four sections devoted respectively to knowledge, ritual practice, meditative practice, and proper behavior. This differentiation too makes sense. While the "knowledge section" and its discussion of God's existence and nature most smoothly fit the notion of a systematic theology, it would be pointless to limit theology to this kind of theory; the more practical considerations of ritual, meditation, and ethics are important too, as complementary discourses which fulfill a theological function and together combine to form a richer whole that is theological.[32]

Using the Clues: Some Theological and Nontheological Texts

We have thus far identified clues toward the identification of Hindu theology: content, mode of reasoning, "style," and (in an admittedly circular fashion) the expectations of communities valuing theology. In calling these factors "distinguishing features" or "clues," I readily concede that there is unlikely to be a sure and exclusive determination of what's theological and what's not. But let us conclude by applying what we have discovered, nominating some texts for the title "theology" and denying this appellation to others. The point of what follows is not to determine a conclusive list of major Hindu theologians and theological works, but rather to illustrate the nature of the judgments necessarily involved, by attention to some Nyāya, Vedānta, and Mīmāṃsā texts, and a few other instances of Hindu intellectual discourse. I assume from the start that our attention is focused only on plausible candidates for the title, and thus omit consideration of the wider range of intellectual production in the sciences and literary fields. I also exclude works which may be theology, but not Hindu theology, e.g., the entire corpus of Buddhist and Jaina writings in traditional India. Finally, I limit my consideration to premodern works, though one could easily extend the analysis to the theological credentials of more recent authors, ranging from Ram Mohan Roy and Keshab Chandra Sen to Sri Aurobindo and Ramana Maharshi, and to contemporary Hindu scholars writing both inside and outside of India.

Let us begin with Nyāya. The early commentators on the *Nyāya Sūtras* and authors like Jayanta Bhaṭṭa (ninth century) who wrote more systematic treatises developed increasingly sophisticated treatments of God's existence and the divine nature. Theological reflection – about God, using religious sources of knowledge – came to the fore in the midst of a broader concern for proper logic, rhetoric, epistemology, and ontology. Much in the commentarial texts and in Jayanta's *Nyāyamañjarī* is not solely or primarily theological, and could just as well be located in some other disciplines. By contrast, Udayana's *Nyāyakusumāñjali* is a substantive theological work entirely devoted to the topic of God's existence. Building on earlier resources in the Nyāya tradition, it brings great originality to its consideration of the question of God, and argues its claims about God within a broad framework capable of convening a conversation across numerous religious boundaries.

But some Nyāya treatments of God move from the realm of intentional theology to that of a more rarified logical analysis which simply retains older and more theological elements. Although "God" is considered in a way that may be theologically useful in such works, they need not be thought of as theological. For example, I suggest that the *Īśvaravāda* (Discourse on God) section of Gaṅgeśa's *Tattvacintāmaṇi* (thirteenth century) takes up the topic of God as an intellectually interesting one, but not as a living theological concern. Gaṅgeśa explores the arguments about God's existence in great detail, yet only within an exhaustive treatment of a wider range of epistemological concerns.[33] The *Īśvaravāda* is only the twenty-first part of the second book, itself devoted to an analysis of inference. The consideration of God is preceded by sections on the construction of a good inference, fallacies, and generalization. It is followed by sections on causal efficacy and liberation. The third book then turns to the topic of comparison (*upamāna*). "God" is one more topic to be sorted out and understood properly, one component within a much larger philosophical work; what had been a standard theological topic is taken up by Gaṅgeśa primarily for its epistemological value. Gaṅgeśa is a superb logician who can analyze theological topics with subtlety; but he is not a theologian even when discussing God.

If we can admit that a tradition need not be focused on God to be theological, we can recognize many writings in the Mīmāṃsā tradition of ritual analysis as theological, despite Mīmāṃsā's rejection of the notion of a God who is creator of the world or author of the Veda. Given the orientation of the earlier Mīmāṃsā texts to the proper understanding of ritual and text – the *dharma* in theory and practice – we can hypothesize that much of the writing of the eighth-century scholars Prabhākara and Kumārila is theological, even if sections of their lengthy commentaries are primarily grammatical or epistemological. Among later treatises, one notices texts like the *Mīmāṃsā Paribhāṣa* of Kṛṣṇa Yajvan (eighteenth century) which focus on the terms and distinctions essential to ritual analysis.[34] Others, such as the *Mānameyodaya*, a seventeenth-century Bhāṭṭa Mīmāṃsā work composed by Nārāyaṇabhaṭṭatiri and Nārāyaṇasudhī,[35] focus on epistemological issues and a standard list of the objects of proper knowledge, including God, the elements of the cosmos, and the self of the ritual agent. Both the *Mīmāṃsā Paribhāṣa* and the *Mānameyodaya* may be considered primarily theological works which however include major sections only propaedeutic to the specifically religious topics related to ritual performance. Finally, however, we can point to a nontheological Mīmāṃsā treatise, such as the thoroughly analytic *Nītitattvāvirbhāva* of Cidānanda (thirteenth century), which focuses on the nature of causality, sense perception, etymology, relation, the ultimate constituents of reality, truth and falsity, the nature of reality as nondual or dual (argued on logical grounds), and the nature of God, self, and words. Even if Cidānanda takes up issues of vital importance in theological contexts, his treatise is significantly enough removed from the concerns of ritual, dharma, theism and atheism, that his *tour de force* can be treated as a philosophical and not theological work.

Vedānta, in its various schools, is by most standards theological, the hesitations reported by DeSmet notwithstanding. Vedānta gives clear priority to scripture over all other means of right knowledge. In the nondualist Vedānta we see operative that theological reasoning (*manana*) which positions itself between scripture and religious practice; yet one also sees Vedānta works which stand at a slightly greater distance and contribute indirectly to Vedānta theology. These points can be exemplified with reference to two nondualist Vedānta texts, the *Vedānta Paribhāṣa* and the *Vivekacuḍāmaṇi.*

The *Vedānta Paribhāṣa* by Dharmarāja Adhvarīndra (seventeenth century) is a basic Nondualist Vedānta manual.[36] In its first six chapters it analyzes the means of right knowledge, including perception, induction, comparison, verbal knowledge, presumption, and non-apprehension. These chapters can be taken as philosophical clarifications of issues which must be worked out for the sake of a smoothly functioning theology, and in light of them Dharmarāja considers the specific scriptural subject matter and religious purposes of Vedānta in the *Paribhāṣa*'s seventh and eighth chapters respectively. While most of the *Vedānta Paribhāṣa* might be taken as philosophical and not theological, all the parts cohere and find integration in the final soteriological concern, so one can term the whole of it theological.

The *Vivekacuḍāmaṇi* (after 800 CE) is a work of 580 (mostly) two-line verses.[37] It is implicitly and sometimes explicitly structured according to the line of thinking evident in some key Upaniṣadic texts; it subtly weaves together the tasks of studying the texts, reflecting on their meaning, and drawing that meaning into meditation leading to realization. The *Vivekacuḍāmaṇi* is explicitly religious and critically reasonable all the way through, and likewise it subjects that religious reasoning to critical reflection. In a more integral fashion than is the case with the *Vedānta Paribhāṣa*, the *Vivekacuḍāmaṇi* is a coherent theological text from beginning to end. We must also note, however, that there seem to be few premodern commentaries on this work; perhaps it was not deemed weighty enough to deserve commentary?

By contrast, Vimuktātman's *Iṣṭasiddhi* is a formidable Advaita work which treats in great detail an entire range of epistemological and ontological matters, and even issues specific to the terminology of Vedānta on Brahman, self, liberation, etc. While there is no strong reason to exclude the *Iṣṭasiddhi* the title of a theological work, its strong interest in the logical and philosophical underpinnings of theological concerns suggests that it too, like the *Tattvacintāmaṇi*, might well be termed a philosophical treatise which addresses some theological topics.[38]

When we turn to a clearly theistic school of Vedānta such as Rāmānuja's and Vedānta Deśika's Viśiṣṭādvaita, it will be no surprise that many of its works can easily be counted as theological. Commentaries, such as Rāmānuja's *Śrībhāṣya* and *Gītābhāṣya* are richly theological, and so too treatises such as his *Vedārthasaṃgraha*, which expounds both right exegetical principles and right ontology in support of theistic Vedānta. But even in regarding theistic Vedānta it is illuminating to distinguish primary theological writings from those which are either accessory or devotional. Rāmānuja's three more devotional writings, collected in the *Gadya Traya*, are best taken as intelligent devotional masterpieces intended to inspire the community of believers. But I suggest that they are not theological works, even if the Śrīvaiṣṇava tradition has rightly found in them a wealth of theological meaning.

Vedānta Deśika presents us with an array of works, some of which may merit the title of "philosophy" or "philosophical theology," some "devotional compositions," and some "theology." For example, a work such as the *Paramatabhaṅga* aims at refuting the doctrines of other schools, as Deśika argues his views largely on the basis of correct reasoning; this might be counted as philosophical or apologetic theology.

More complicated is the case of the paired volumes, the *Nyāya Pariśuddhi* and the *Nyāya Siddhāñjana*. The *Nyāya Pariśuddhi* offers primarily philosophical analysis in support of theology; in it Deśika meticulously considers Nyāya positions and also corrects them wherever necessary. Throughout, his aim is to review and clarify problematic and unclear aspects of the system of logic set forth in the *Nyāya Sūtras* of Gautama. It seems clear that this is a corrective work which is preparatory for theology, and only indirectly theological itself. The corrective work of the *Nyāya Pariśuddhi* is complemented in the *Nyāya Siddhāñjana* which itself has a kind of philosophical focus in its concern for the objects of knowledge: inert material reality; the individual dependent self; the lord; the eternal abode of the lord; understanding, constitutive knowledge; qualities as real but not material elements. But here the emphasis is on the truth of the community's faith positions. If the *Nyāya Pariśuddhi* is preparatory to theology, the *Nyāya Siddhāñjana*, its deeply logical and philosophical nature notwithstanding, is more explicitly a reasoned defense of faith positions and accordingly more obviously theological.

For the sake of argument I have stated that texts such as the *Tattvacintāmaṇi*, *Nītitattvāvirbhāva*, *Iṣṭasiddhi*, and *Nyāya Pariśuddhi* are not theological, on the grounds that although important components of their subject matter are recognizably theological, they stress logic and epistemology over against theological issues. Other texts can be denied the title of theology because they are primarily religious, edifying, or inspirational texts in which religious reasoning is secondary. In this category we can place most ritual manuals and most mythology – not because such are devoid of intellectual content, but because that content has not been explicitated in an arguable form conducive to *manana*. So too, various hymns of praise – Vedic hymns and later praise hymns (*stotra*) – which laud a supreme God or Goddess may be religiously rich and even provocative of theological reflection, but in themselves they are primarily meant to inspire and deepen religious faith. Hindu India abounds in religious works which promote religious values in various ways but (unless one mentally transposes them into more theoretical and prose discourses) without providing a sufficient space for critical reflection on arguable themes.

There are religious works which have great religious and intellectual power but nonetheless are best counted as not theological because they do not systematize their intended meanings in ways that can be analyzed, debated, and argued. The *Rāmāyaṇa*, for example, is a persuasive and vastly influential religious narrative which manifests great religious intelligence, but in itself it does not give evidence of a critical distance which invites the believer to stand apart from the text and think *about* it. It may be that some *Rāmāyaṇa* commentaries are more theological than the epic itself. The *Mahābhārata* surely has sections of great theological import in it – most notably the *Bhagavad Gītā* – but it would be uselessly broad to claim that the whole of the epic is theological. The *Gītā* itself, though perhaps inherently rich in theological meaning, is established as properly theological only by its further specification through commentaries and synthetic summations such as Yāmuna's *Gītārthasaṃgraha* (eleventh century) and the commentaries of Śaṃkara and Rāmānuja.

If reasoned theistic texts may be judged more readily theological, we will want to scrutinize closely and possibly differently works about Goddesses which often expound comprehensive even if not entirely systematic Goddess theologies. Perhaps gender is yet another issue affecting how theology works out. Some Goddess treatises are poetic, and perhaps deliberately dissimilar to "standard" theological texts. For example, the Śrīvaiṣṇava *Guṇa Ratna Kośa* of Parāśara Bhaṭṭar (twelfth century) is a Sanskrit language text of 61 verses in honor of the Goddess Lakṣmī. Though florid in its descriptions and not easily read as a treatise in Goddess theology, commentators find in it all the theological depth one might hope for in terms of spelling out the relationship of Lakṣmī and Viṣṇu. If not formally theological, it is certainly a rich resource which encapsulates earlier reflection on Lakṣmī and prepares for later theological reflection.

In Tamil we find the *Apirāmī Antāti* (ca. eighteenth century), 100 verses in honor of the Goddess Abhirāmi who is both a consort of Śiva and a preeminent Deity by herself. The 100 verses are similar to those found in other Tamil devotional works, such as those of the āḻvārs and nāyaṉmārs, and thus easily fall into that category of poetic works which are deeply reflective on divinity. Whether they are profitably counted as theological is another matter; part of the answer has to do with how much emphasis one places on critical reasoning and systematic presentation, and how determined one is to dig deeper inside the deceptively simple verses. For this chapter, however, I leave it an open question as to whether the *Apirāmī Antāti* ought to be called theological.

The Tamil-language drama *Cilappatikāram* (ca. fifth century) is a striking work which can be appreciated for numerous insights of great theological interest. Though dramatic and poetic in form, it proposes an (ultimately Jaina) analysis of the individual, social, political, philosophical, and religious constituents of society, while offering a good deal of Goddess theology along the way. But here too, the form of the arguments does not invite further elaboration, and (to my knowledge) the drama has not received significant theological commentary.

Different problems are posed by a work such as Pāṇini's *Aṣṭādhyāyī* (fifth century BCE) the normative Sanskrit grammatical treatise. We know that Grammar is not merely a instrumental discipline, but one with great religious import. Earlier, we saw Abhyankar's comment that Grammar, like Mīmāṃsā and Vedānta, is a scriptural system of thought (*śāstriya darśana*), due to its commitment to the words of the Veda. But Abhyankar seems to have been thinking mainly of Bhartṛhari and other such grammarians who made explicit their "theologies of language," e.g., in relation to Brahman as sound (*śabda brahman*). Such commitments and understandings can be taken as signifying Grammar as "theological." But in terms of the actual content of Pāṇini's Grammar, though, we might also be inclined either to exclude the work or to relegate it to an important but ancillary role.

So too, even some systematic religious texts present religious truths in ways that are evidently deeply intellectual and reasoned with scriptural roots, but without presenting them as arguable conclusions open to the kind of argument that characterizes theology. For example, *The Laws of Manu* gives evidence of a kind of juridical theological intent, as it reorganizes earlier legal materials, schematizing them according to the idealization of society according to class and stage of life, and then imbedding the whole in an account of the origins of the world as a natural, social, and religious reality. *Manu* thus reorganizes earlier religious and legal debates in a way that could well be taken as theological yet, since it also presents its arguments in a way that appears final and intended to preclude further debate, perhaps it strives to be a post-theological text.

As noted above, though, decisions about which texts are theological or not are ultimately more than descriptive claims about past learning and writing; at an important level, such theological judgments must be made within a community of Hindu theologians willing to take up the task today.

Some Final Reflections

I do not suppose that all readers will be persuaded by the complex case made in favor of "Hindu theology" in the preceding pages, but I do hope that they will give a serious hearing to my case. Nor would one have to accept every argument or definition proposed in order to agree that "theology" is a viable and useful term in the Indian context. The acceptance even of various portions of my arguments should suffice: certain topics and themes are justly termed "theological"; *manana*, which reflects on verbal knowledge but has its finality in meditation, is justly termed "theological reasoning"; the presence of commentary and, in most cases, a Sanskrit language discourse, can confirm that a religious text is also a theological text; communities which accept the project of faith in tension with reasoning will value theology; and so on.

For now, my approach should at least alleviate some of the misapprehensions about theology which arose in the earlier history of Europe and which have influenced Indian thinking about theology. With the ground cleared, we should be able to consider with some objectivity the claim that better than any other term "theology" names in English what many important Hindu thinkers have done and are doing. In turn, the admission of this term opens more fruitful ways of understanding traditional Hindu thinking, and stimulates an exchange of ideas between India, still coming to terms with its own theological and non-theological heritage, and the contemporary scholarly world.

I close then with two observations. First, I claimed at the beginning of this chapter that it was not my task to explain the word "Hindu." This is of course an admittedly difficult task in light of the contemporary consensus that it may be misleading to apply "Hinduism" to how people believe, think, speak, and act religiously in India; historians, social scientists, and Indologists have all in their own way determined that "Hindu" and "Hinduism" refer to nothing substantial or particular, and they have often concluded that the words ought not be used at all. However, without disregarding the historical and religious factors which make caution imperative, I suggest that it may be from a newly rejuvenated appreciation of "theology" that "Hindu" can be reestablished – as a plausible, arguable, and useful theological category with which one can usefully begin to understand the predominate Indian religious ways of believing and practicing.

Second, as conceded above, I admit that since we are speaking of *Hindu* theology and not just *theology*, the final test must occur in a communal context, among thinkers who are willing to identify themselves as both "Hindus" and "theologians." If this chapter has been properly dedicated to a retrospective consideration of where "theology" may be appropriately found in the Hindu traditions, it will still matter, and matter more, to discern the present and future of Hindu theologizing by listening to those willing to think through the Hindu faith(s) in a way that is intelligible in the contemporary, global conversation of believers and scholars interested in religion.

Notes

1 It is not part of the task of this chapter to explain or defend usage of the word "Hindu," but see my comment at the conclusion of the chapter on the rehabilitation of "Hindu" as a theological term.

2 See *Dictionnaire de Théologie Catholique*, vol. 15.1, cols. 342–6.

3 See Wilhelm Halbfass, *India and Europe* (Albany: State University of New York Press, 1988), particularly "On the Exclusion of India from the History of Philosophy," pp. 145–9.

4 Over 40 years ago Richard DeSmet surveyed the Indian antipathy toward "theology." He showed how in the twentieth century it became commonplace to see "theological" as equivalent to "burdened with dogmatic commitments" or "deficient in rational excellence." Even religious thinkers like Śaṃkara were best defended by declaring, as did S. Radhakrishnan, that "the austere intellectualism of [Śaṃkara's] system, its remorseless logic, which marches on indifferent to the hopes and beliefs of man, make it a great example of a purely *philosophical* system" (Richard DeSmet, unpublished dissertation, "The Theological Method of Śaṃkara," Gregorian University, Rome, 1955, p. 8; my emphasis). DeSmet's thesis will be published in 2004 by the University of Notre Dame Press.

5 One also needs to be able to find one's way back and forth between the terminology of Sanskrit (and other Indian) languages and English (and other contemporary Western and global) languages. This is not an endeavor for those who think that no term in English can ever suitably represent a term from the Sanskrit language. While we concede from the start that no single term from an Indian language can translate "theology," we need not be limited to the strictures of literal or one-to-one translatability, and we need to resist the temptation to exclude all English-language terms as inappropriate to the interpretation of Sanskrit discourses. As a model for the kind of distinctions we need to make, we can recall Wilhelm Halbfass's useful sorting out of questions related to whether Hindu thought can be treated as "philosophy." His analysis combined philological interest in the uses of terms like *darśana* (perhaps: viewpoint, worldview), *mata* (opinion, school of thought), and *anvikṣikī* and *mīmāṃsā* (analysis, inquiry), with a sense of the larger comparative issues which come into play when one affirms or denies that certain strands of Indian thought should be acknowledged as philosophical. He rightly looks for exact correlates to "philosophy," but rightly too does not rule out the possibility of Indian philosophy

even after determining that no one term adequately translates "philosophy." See Halbfass, *India and Europe*, "Darśana, Anvikṣikī, Philosophy," pp. 263–86.

6 Here and throughout this chapter I draw examples from those several areas of Hindu thought which are most familiar to me. I do not attempt a broad survey of positions, but neither do I wish to suggest that theology is limited to the schools of thought highlighted in my examples.

7 Naming something "theological" will be no more insulting or problematic than other labels which one might apply to the intellectual systems found in cultures other than their own. Rather, it is useful to use the term "theology" and not just "religion," "philosophy," or "indology," when attempting to understand Hindu thought by correlating it with Western counterparts.

8 Albany: State University of New York Press, 1998. Cabezon highlights several important features which distinguish scholasticism, distinctions which can just as well apply to theology: a strong sense of *tradition*, which includes the handing down of the texts which define the community; *proliferativity*, "the tendency to textual and analytic inclusivity rather than exclusivity"; *rationalism*, "the commitment to reasoned argument and noncontradiction"; *completeness* along with *compactness* (nothing missing, nothing extraneous); *systematicity* (the endeavor to reproduce in writing "the basic orderliness found in the world"); and *self-reflexivity* ("the tendency to objectify and to critically analyze first order practices"). Since "scholasticism" has been closely aligned with "theology" in the West, the same features can apply in a theological context as well. Cabezon's comment on the comparative inquiry underlying *Scholasticism* could just as well be adapted to our inquiry into "Hindu theology" in this chapter: "Though I see no value in – or need for – an *a priori* definition of scholasticism preceding comparative work on the subject, I do recognize that as a result of such work there may emerge a series of traits that will be considered more characteristic of scholasticism than others. They will become so not by virtue of being part of the innate character of scholasticism – its essence – but because the traditions that have most benefited from being considered under the rubric of this category have these as *their* traits . . . a texture is given to the category by the fact that certain traits will be more prominent than others, and this as a result of the fact that certain traditions will be considered more prototypically scholastic than others. If scholasticism is a useful category . . . then, like other such categories (religion, myth, symbol, scripture, ritual), it will survive and evolve in this way over time" (p. 8).

9 *Transzendenzerfahrung, Vollzugshorizont des Heils* (Vienna: Publications of the De Nobili Research Library, vol. 5, 1978), *Epiphanie des Heils: zur Heilsgegenwart in Indischer und Christlicher Religion* (Vienna: Publications of the De Nobili Research Library, vol. 9, 1982), *Versuch einer transzendentalen Hermeneutik religiöser Traditionen* (Vienna: Publications of the De Nobili Research Library, Occasional Papers 3, 1987), and *"Begegnung" als Kategorie der Religionshermeneutik* (Vienna: Publications of the De Nobili Research Library, Occasional Papers 4, 1989), *Raum-zeitliche Vermittlung der Transzendenz: Zur "sakramentalen" Dimension religiöser Tradition* (Vienna: Verlag der Österreichischen Akademie der Wissenschaften, 1999).

10 See also my *Hindu God, Christian God: How Reason Helps Break Down the Boundaries among Religions* (New York: Oxford University Press, 2001) in which I show the common theological ground of mainstream Christian and Hindu theologies on the themes of God's existence, the true religion, divine embodiment, and the judgment of revelation upon religion.

11 Albany: State University of New York, 1997.

12 Richmond, UK: Curzon Press, 2000.

13 In what follows, I refer to Sanskrit-language and (to some limited extent) Tamil-language sources; of course, other language traditions of India can also be drawn upon in this regard.

14 While God or gods can be theology's central topic, this rule can bear exceptions. Too rigid and exclusive a link between "God" and "theology" might unnecessarily exclude schools of Hindu thought which on other grounds might seem to merit the title "theological," e.g., Mīmāṃsā ritual theory and nondualist Vedānta. One might still term a system theological if some other comprehensive explanatory referent is put forward, such as a transcendent Self (*ātman*), or a higher reality which is the source of the world as a whole and yet also the pervasive life-force within it (*brahman*), or an apprehension of the world in all its interconnected parts (*dharma*).

15 See Johannes Bronkhorst, "God's Arrival in the Vaiśeṣika System," *Journal of Indian Philosophy* 24 (1996): 281–394, and George Chemparathy, *An Indian Rational Theology: Introduction to Udayana's Nyāyakusumāñjali*, p. 78. On the development of the argument about God in the Buddhist context, see Roger Jackson, "Dharmakīrti's refutation of theism," *Philosophy East and West* 36.4 (1985): 315–48. Dharmakīrti's critique of the argument from effects to the existence of God is also described briefly in Gerhard Oberhammer, "Der Gottesbeweis in der Indische Philosophie," *Numen* XII.1 (1965): 1–34, esp. 10–22. On the general project of the Nyāya induction of God's existence, see also Kisor K. Chakrabarti, *Classical Indian Philosophy of Mind* (Albany: State University of New York, 1999), pp. 159–73; for reflection on the induction in a comparative context, see Francis X. Clooney, SJ, "The Interreligious Dimension of Reasoning about God's Existence," *International Journal of the Philosophy of Religion* 46.1 (1999): 1–16.

16 See "Vedānta Deśika's "Definition of the Lord" (*Īśvaraparicchedа*) and the Hindu Argument about Ultimate Reality," in *Ultimate Realities*, ed. Robert Neville (Albany: State University of New York Press, 2000), pp. 95–123.

17 Narasiṃhāśramin (sixteenth century) offers this critique in the third part of his *Advaita Dīpikā*. Against the view that it is appropriate to describe Brahman as possessed of certain qualities which enable one to identify who God is, Narasiṃhāśramin argues that sectarian symbolizations of the divine and indeed all positive language about Brahman can only be secondary. Sectarian views rely on misreadings of the Upaniṣads; even texts which attribute qualities such as omniscience to Brahman are simply corrective of misconceptions, and not positively informative about real qualities existing in Brahman. All texts which describe God with attributes must be interpreted in conformity with primary texts which deny that Brahman has qualities. Distinct gods are really just one, diversely understood; see *Advaitadīpikā* pp. 447–63.

18 I.2.38–9; see my exposition of this theme in ch. 4 of *Hindu God, Christian God*.

19 On theodicy, see Michael Stoeber, *Evil and the Mystics' God: Toward a Mystical Theodicy* (Toronto: University of Toronto, 1991), and Francis X. Clooney, "Evil, Divine Omnipotence and Human Freedom: Vedanta's Theology of Karma," *Journal of Religion* 69 (1989): 530–48.

20 See Andrew O. Fort, *Jīvanmukti in Transformation: Embodied Liberation in Advaita and Neo-Vedānta* (SUNY, 1998), and *Living Liberation in Hindu Thought*, eds. Andrew O. Fort and Patricia Y. Mumme (Albany: State University of New York Press, 1996).

21 On the complexities of brahmanical Hindu epistemology, see *Théorie de la Connaissance et Philosophie de la Parole* by Madeleine Biardeau (Paris: Mouton and Co., 1964), and *Śabdapramāṇa: Word and Knowledge* by Purusottama Bilimoria (Boston: Kluwer Academic Publishers, 1988) vol. 10.

22 The basic Vedānta position is spelled out in the commentaries on *Uttara Mīmāṃsā Sūtras* 1.1.2, even though this sūtra seemingly identifies the subject of the *Sūtras* in terms of an induction: "That from which there is the birth, [continuation, and dissolution of the world]."

23 One might also take up the term *jijñāsā*, which is important in the Mīmāṃsā and *Vedānta Sūtra* texts, marked respectively as *dharma-jijñāsā* and *brahma-jijñāsā*; but it is the objects which distinguish the systems as theological, not the acts of knowing *per se*.

24 Vārtikas 213–19, pp. 692–3 in the *Bhāṣyavārtikam of Sureśvara with the Śrutaprakāśikā of Ānandagiri* (Mahesh Research Institute, 1982), vol. 1 (Advaita Grantha Manjusha Ratna, vol. 237).

25 See the *Nyāya Kusumāñjali of Sri Udayanācārya with four commentaries* (Varanasi: Kashi Sanskrit Series 30, 1957). I have summarized Vardhamāna's position as stated on pp. 19–30 of his *Prakāśa* commentary, where he is expounding Udayana's *kārika* I.3.

26 Interestingly, though from an Advaita viewpoint and somewhat dubiously, Abhyankar includes Rāmānuja's Vedānta among the "concealed rationalist" *darśanas*, due to Rāmānuja's proclivity to reinterpret the nondualist *mahāvākyas* in order to make sense of them.

27 See also Cabezon's introduction to *Scholasticism*.

28 A good example of how language affects the formulation of issues is Edwin Gerow's grammatical derivation of the theoretical issues related to *karma* as deeds and rebirth. See Gerow, "What is *Karma* (*Kiṃ Karmeti*)? An Exercise in Philosophical Semantics," *Indologica Taurinensia* 10 (1982): 87–116. Gerow argues that the traditional Indian philosophical understanding of *karma* – as action, as deeds leading to rebirth – bears a significance largely inseparable from the semantics of the Sanskrit language; the conceptual issues related to human acting and the nature of agency are more simply understood if we interpret them in terms of how action is understood grammatically. Gerow certainly would not assert that belief in *karma* as rebirth is only a consequence of Sanskrit syntax, but the logic of the case for *karma*, and the very significance of *karma*, are explicable most directly in terms of the dynamics of the Sanskrit language.

29 To admit the real but somewhat rare possibility of a non-Sanskrit language Hindu theology, let us consider just *Tiruvāymoḻi*. This work of 1,102 verses can, from various perspectives, be considered diffuse and unsystematic, rich in myriad themes and images which are simply juxtaposed. Although it is tightly bound by the strategy of having each verse begin with the word or phrase which ended the previous verse (the strategy of *antāti*), it may still seem nothing but a canonical anthology. Yet as I have explained elsewhere (see Francis X. Clooney, *Seeing through Texts* [Albany: State University of New York Press, 1996), ch. 2]), Śaṭakōpaṉ has exploited the possibilities and strictures of the Tamil literary traditions, to highlight how God – Viṣṇu, Nārāyaṇa – can be talked about yet also encountered within the limits of particular literary and religious genres. Certainly, the south Indian Śrīvaiṣṇava tradition found enormous significance in *Tiruvāymoḻi*, commented on it very extensively, and made it the basis for just about all later Śrīvaiṣṇava theo-

logy. There are numerous weighty commentaries on the songs, and independent treatises explicating its meaning. Aḻakiya Maṇavāḷap Perumāḷ Nāyaṉār's *Ācārya Hṛdayam* (fifteenth century) is a systematic Tamil language analysis of *Tiruvāymoḻi*, entirely dedicated to showing the rich thematic import discoverable in the words of the songs themselves. Vedānta Deśika's *Dramiḍopaniṣat Tātparyaratnāvaḷi* is a succinct Sanskrit-language assessment of the theological import of each song in *Tiruvāymoḻi*, a theological commentary which recognizes and a theological primary text in a vernacular not dependent on Sanskrit, and which seeks to spell out its theological meaning.

30 Karen Pechilis-Prentiss's *The Embodiment of Bhakti* (New York: Oxford University Press, 1999) finely discusses the conscious development of Śaiva Siddhānta theology in the Tamil south Indian context. In particular, the appendices which include Umāpati Ācārya's *Tiruvaruṭpayaṉ* (perhaps, "Fruit of the Holy Grace") and a companion anthology, *Tēvāra Aruḷmuṟaittiraṭṭu* (perhaps, "Anthology of Verses on Grace from the *Tēvāram*") are fine examples of theological works.

31 Bernard J. F. Lonergan, SJ, *Method in Theology* (New York: Herder and Herder, 1972). He lists the eight specialties as follows: research, interpretation, history, dialectic, foundations, doctrines, systematics, and communications.

32 We can also think of texts aimed primarily at coherent ritual practice, such as some *pūjā* manuals, yogic texts such as the *Yoga Sūtras*, and guides to tantric practice such as the *Kulārṇava Tantra*. Such works may be highly reflective and intelligent, and rich in theological import, and in some cases attention to their commentaries may help make the case that these texts are theological.

33 See John Vattanky's *Gangeśa's Philosophy of God* (Madras: The Adyar Library and Research Centre, 1984).

34 Trans. Swami Madhavananda (Calcutta: Advaita Ashrama, 1987).

35 The *Mānameyodaya* has been edited and translated by C. Kunhan Raja and S. S. Suryanarayana Sastri (Madras: Theosophical Publishing House, 1933).

36 For the *Vedāntaparibhāṣa*, see the translation by Swami Madhavananda (Calcutta: Advaita Ashrama, 1983).

37 Trans. Swami Madhavananda; Calcutta: Advaita Ashrama, 1992.

38 The *Iṣṭasiddhi* has been translated by P. K. Sundaram (Madras: Swadharma Swaarajya Sangha, 1980).

References

Biardeau, M. 1964. *Théorie de la Connaissance et Philosophie de la Parole*. Paris: Mouton and Co.

Bilimoria, Purusottama. 1988. *Sabdapramana: Word and Knowledge*. Boston: Kluwer Academic Publishers.

Bronkhorst, Johannes. 1996. "God's Arrival in the Vaisesika System," *Journal of Indian Philosophy* 24: 281–394.

Cabezon, Jose. 1998. *Scholasticism in Cross-cultural and Comparative Perspective*. Albany: State University of New York Press.

Chakrabarti, Kisor K. 1999. *Classical Indian Philosophy of Mind*. Albany: State University of New York.

Chemparathy, George. 1972. *An Indian Rational Theology: Introduction to Udayana's Nyayakusumanjali*. Vienna: De Nobili Research Library.

Clooney, Francis X. 1989. "Evil, Divine Omnipotence and Human Freedom: Vedanta's Theology of Karma," *Journal of Religion* 69: 530–48.

——. 1996. *Seeing through Texts*: Albany: State University of New York Press.

——, SJ. 1999. "The Interreligious Dimension of Reasoning about God's Existence," *International Journal of the Philosophy of Religion* 46.1: 1–16.

——. 2001. *Hindu God, Christian God: How Reason Helps Break Down the Boundaries among Religions*. New York: Oxford University Press.

DeSmet, Richard. 1955. "The Theological Method of Samkara." Unpublished dissertation, Gregorian University, Rome.

Dictionnaire de Théologie Catholique. 1923–50. 15 vols.; vol. 15.1. Paris: Librarie Letouzey et ané.

Fort, Andrew O. 1996. *Jivanmukti in Transformation: Embodied Liberation in Advaita and Neo-Vedanta*. Albany: SUNY Press.

Gerow, Edwin. 1982. "What is Karma (Kim Karmeti)? An Exercise in Philosophical Semantics," *Indologica Taurinensia* 10: 87–116.

Halbfass, W. 1988. *India and Europe*. Albany: State University of New York Press.

Jackson, Roger 1985. "Dharmakirti's Refutation of Theism," *Philosophy East and West* 36.4: 315–48.

Kunhan Raja, C. and S. S. Suryanarayana Sastri, ed. and trans. 1933. *The Manameyodaya*. Madras: Theosophical Publishing House.

Lonergan, Bernard J. F. 1972. *Method in Theology*. New York: Herder and Herder.

Madhvananda, Swami, trans. 1983. *Vedantaparibhasa*. Calcutta: Advaita Ashrama.

——, trans. 1987. *Mimamsa Paribhasa*. Calcutta: Advaita Ashrama.

——, trans. 1992. *Vivekacudamani*. Calcutta: Advaita Ashrama.

Makransky, John and Roger Jackson, eds. 2000. *Buddhist Theology: Critical Reflections by Contemporary Buddhist Scholars*. Richmond: Curzon Press.

Muller-Ortega, P. et al., eds. 1997. *Meditation Revolution: A History and Theology of the Siddha Yoga Lineage*. Albany: State University of New York.

Mumme, P. Y. 1996. *Living Liberation in Hindu Thought*. Albany: State University of New York Press.

Neville, Robert, ed. 2000. *Ultimate Realities*. Albany: SUNY Press.

Oberhammer, G. 1965. "Der Gottesbeweis in der Indische Philosophie," *Numen* X11.1: 1–34.

——. 1978. *Transzendenzerfahrung, Vollzugshorizont des Heils*. Vienna: Publications of the De Nobili Research Library, vol. 5.

——. 1982. *Epiphanie des Heils: zur Heilsgegenwart in Indischer und Christlicher Religion*. Vienna: Publications of the De Nobili Research Library, vol. 9.

——. 1987. *Versuch einer transzendentalen Hermeneutik religioser Traditionen*. Vienna: Publications of the De Nobili Research Library, Occasional Papers 3.

——. 1989. *Begegnung als Kategorie der Religionshermeneutik*. Vienna: Publications of the De Nobili Research Library, Occasional Papers 4.

——. 1999. *Raum-zeitliche Vermittlung de Transzendenz: Zur "sakramentalen" Dimension religioser Tradition*. Vienna: Verlag der Osterreichischen Akademie der Wissenschaften.

Pechilis-Prentiss, Karen 1999. *The Embodiment of Bhakti*. New York: Oxford University Press.

Stoeber, Michael 1991. *Evil and the Mystics' God: Toward a Mystical Theodicy*. Toronto: University of Toronto.

Sundaram, P. K. 1980. *The Istasiddhi*. Madras: Swadharma Swaarajya Sangha.
Suresvara. 1982. *Bhasyavartikam of Suresvara with the Srutaprakasika of Anandagiri*. Vol. 1. Mahesh Research Institute. (Advaita Grantha Manjusha Ratna, vol. 237.)
Udayana. 1957. *Nyaya Kusumanjali of Sri Udayanacarya with Four Commentaries*. Varanasi: Kashi Sanskrit Series 30.
Vattanky, John. 1984. *Gangesa's Philosophy of God*. Madras: The Adyar Library and Research Centre.

CHAPTER 22

Mantra

André Padoux

Mantras are among the most characteristic features of Hinduism. They existed in Vedic times and are still widely used today. They permeate Hindu ritual. As the saying goes, *amantraka kriyā na syāt*, "no rites should be accomplished without mantras," and ritual was and still very largely is part of the daily life of all observant Hindus. The term mantra, however, having been in use for some three millennia all over south Asia, has not always and everywhere had the same meaning. Mantras were used in different ways, in different contexts, and for different purposes: the meaning of the term, like that of all words, is context-dependent. It is therefore necessary to examine separately the various meanings, uses, and values attached to it in the course of time in different Hindu religious traditions. Not only has the meaning of the term mantra varied according to time and place, but at any given time the word has been used to refer to different ritual, meditative, yogic, and spiritual practices as well as to different forms or kinds of phonetic and linguistic utterance. It is therefore impossible to translate it by a single word in English or any other modern language. Several such translations have been suggested; none is satisfactory. But we need not dwell on them, since the term mantra is now in common use. It is to be found in dictionaries and needs no translation.

As regards the term itself, the Sanskrit noun *mantra* derives from the verbal root *MAN*, which means to think, but in the sense of an intentional, active form of thought. To this root is added the suffix *tra*, which is used to form words denoting an instrument, a faculty, or a function. A mantra, therefore, is etymologically a means or an instrument of thought, this thought being intense, concentrated, efficient: all traits variously to be found, as we shall see, in every form and use of mantras, ancient or modern. Later, and especially in the Tantric theory of mantra, the *mantraśāstra*, the suffix *tra* was related to the verbal root *TRAI*, to save, mantras being therefore seen as a form of thought leading to salvation. Thus the Tantric philosopher Abhinavagupta (tenth to eleventh centuries) said that mantras are *mananatrāṇarūpa*, thought and salvation, that is, a liberating form of thought. We should perhaps add here that the language of mantras is normally Sanskrit. They are formed from Sanskrit words or syllables, which is logical enough since they are regarded as forms of the power of *vāc*, the primordial Word uttered in the sacred Sanskrit language. In Tantric practice, however, there are exceptions to this rule, especially in recent times.

Mantras in Vedism

In the Vedas, the noun mantra refers to the metrical texts collected in the Saṃhitas that are recited, muttered, or chanted during Vedic sacrifices, be they *ṛc*, *yajus*, or *sāman*, that is, hymns or poems, sacrificial formulas, or chants. All that is not *brāhmana* (rule or explanation) is mantra; and mantras, in Vedic religion, are the essential element of ritual performance, however complex in its procedure and *mise en scène* that performance may be. They are considered as instrumental in the accomplishment of sacrificial acts: they are what causes and effects the efficiency of the sacrifice.

The word mantra appears thus in Vedism as referring to something different, at least in its verbal form – poems, hymns, chants – from what it referred to later on, but even in those early times some permanent mantric traits were present. First, mantras constitute the essential and efficient element in all ritual. Moreover, brief ritual formulas such as *svāhā* (the exclamation used when making an oblation to the gods) were also regarded as mantras, and the three utterances called *vyāhṛti* (*bhūḥ*, *bhuvaḥ*, *svaḥ*) referring to the earth, the intermediate space, and the sky, chanted during Vedic ritual, were believed to be invested with the creative power of the primordial Word. Vedic chant also included meaningless syllables called *stobha*, such as *hā*, *bhu*, *phaṭ*, while in the Yajurveda other syllables of that sort (*hīm*, *hum*, *vet* . . .) were used, to one of which, *oṃ*, was attributed a particular and exalted position, which it has kept down to our days, as the very essence of all that exists. Vedism thus shows the origin of aspects of mantras which will be developed in the tantric *mantraśāstra*. The famous *gāyatrī*, the invocation of Savitar, the Sun, a particularly sacred formula which was later used as a mantra (sometimes with sectarian variants dedicated to other deities) is also originally Vedic, since it is verse 10 of hymn 3.62 of the Ṛgveda. In fact, as formulas or utterances imbued with power and believed to be of supernatural origin, mantras have inherited and carried down to the present the Vedic conception of *vāc*, the Word, seen as the supreme power, placed above everything else, identified with the *brahman*, the Absolute. But it is an absolute which is also the sacred formula: from earliest times, godhead has been seen both as power and as sacred word.

The Vedic solemn sacrificial rites have all but entirely disappeared in India. When they do endure, it is as a kind of archaeological reconstruction of the past, or as an artificial, domesticated form of return to some mythical origin. Certain ancient Vedic notions and rites, however, have survived as elements, sometimes very vital ones, of Purāṇic, then Tantric, and even modern Hinduism: and among these, in particular, are the Vedic notions and speculations on the divine nature and power of the Word, especially in its mantric aspect.[1] Mantras have never ceased to be regarded as of divine origin and nature, as endowed with supernatural powers, and as ritually effective for evoking deities or for putting their user in touch with a deity or even identifying him/her with the deity. Mantras may be generally described as sentences, words, or syllables of superhuman origin, eternal, used to evoke deities or supernatural powers and also to put in touch or identify their users with these deities or powers. They are thought of as able, when uttered according to certain precise rules, to realize the intentional thought they embody and/or to accomplish different tasks or actions. These characteristics are variously emphasized in different rituals and at different times. The function of praising a deity or beseeching it to accept or be pleased with the gifts or oblations offered is stressed in Vedism, whereas that of evocation or identification, or of accomplishing some religious or magic task, is more prominent in the Paurāṇic and still more in the Tantric context. Whatever the period, however, an essential trait of mantras is and has always been that their nature is that of the uttered, the spoken, or rather the speaking word (*vāc vadantī*), transmitted orally, not in writing.[2] Even when they are poems or hymns, they are not Scripture.

Descriptions of the yogic meditative uses of mantras, mysticolinguistic speculations on their nature, phonetic structure, symbolic values and powers are to be found in the older ("Vedic") Upaniṣads and in the Brāhmaṇas.[3] For instance, in the Jaiminīya Upaniṣad Brāhmaṇa, the god Prajāpati creates the sky, the intermediate space, and the earth by means of the three *vyāhṛtis, bhuḥ bhuvaḥ svaḥ*, the essence of his speech being *OṂ*. The Chāndogya Upaniṣad tells the same mythic tale and adds "the sound *OṂ* is the whole universe." "*OṂ* is *Brahman*," says the Taittirīya Upaniṣad. The divine nature and power of the mantra *OṂ* is extolled in other older Upaniṣads, too: this extolling of *OṂ* as condensing and encapsulating in one syllable the totality of the Vedas (i.e., knowledge) is interesting in that it shows that, from Vedic times, brief, condensed utterances have been given primacy over extended, discursive ones, a concept to be found later in the tantric *bījamantras*. Vedic sources also show the breaking up of *OṂ* into its constituent phonemes, *A, O, Ṃ*, which are then correlated with different triads: the three Vedas, three parts of the cosmos, three vital breaths, and so forth, a trait later to be found in the tantric *mantraśāstra*. Also worth mentioning here is the Maitrī Upaniṣad (one of the latest of the ancient Upaniṣads), which says that *OṂ* is the essence of everything in the human heart, that meditation on Brahman rests eternally upon it, and that when stirred up it rises to the throat as an atom of sound, then reaches the tip of the tongue, finally flowing out as speech. The person who sees all this, the Upaniṣad adds, sees only the Absolute and is freed from death and suffering: this mental and bodily process does not differ much from later tantric mantrayoga practices. The origin of such anthropocosmic concepts, as well as that of a number of other mantric notions and practices, can thus be traced back to Vedic times. The idea, too, that the whispered (*upāṃśu*) or inaudible utterance of a mantra is superior to, and more effective than, its audible one, the silent (*tuṣṇīm*) one being the highest of all, dates from the Vedic period. For the Śatapathabrāḥmaṇa, the silent or indistinct (*anirukta*) speech is the highest one of all, since it represents the unlimited. Ritual speech, says the same text, must be silent, "since seed (*retas*) is cast silently." Another theme which continued to be discussed in later times is the question of the meaning or meaninglessness (*ānarthakya*) of mantras. It was first taken up in the Nirukta, their meaninglessness being upheld by the grammarian Kautsa, according to whom mantras are uttered simply for the utterance's sake – *uccāraṇamātreṇa*; the question being less whether they themselves mean anything than whether they are uttered to express a meaning which they have, or, on the contrary, do not contain. The issue is still relevant, for while some mantras are evidently meaningless, they all have, as ever, a ritual function or a magical efficacy.

Mantras after the Vedas

The Vedic mantra needed to be considered first, not only because it came first historically, but also because in the Vedas the term mantra had the special, wider meaning of hymn or chant. Also because, as we have seen, some general and durable mantric characteristics appeared in those early times. The Vedic period, however, cannot be separated from the one that follows. There never was a discontinuity: Vedic mantras, as well as some Vedic rites, never ceased to be in use, since orthodox Hinduism has always regarded itself as "Vedic." While Vedic hymns and chants recited during solemn Vedic rites tended to fall into disuse, other mantras of Vedic origin went on being used in the worship of deities and in various public or private, daily, or calendrical rituals, and still more in the life-cycle rites, the *saṃskāras*, which consisted mainly in the utterance (and/or transmission) of mantras and which ranged from the rite performed to ensure conception to those carried out after death. Every morning all twice-born male Hindus went on (and are still supposed to go on) reciting the sacred *gāyatrī* (also called *savitrī*), from Ṛgveda 3.62 (*tat savitur vareṇyam bhargo devasya dhīmahi dhiyo yo naḥ pracodayāt*), preceded by OṂ and the three *vyāhṛtis, bhurahbhuvaḥ svaḥ*. Practically all the daily activities (as well as the exercise of bodily functions) of the pious Hindu (or at least of the observant brahmin) were to be accompanied, preceded, or followed by the utterance of mantras, mostly Vedic ones. However, as cults other than the Śrauta and Smārta Vedic cults[4] developed, other mantras appeared. In these new systems, which tended henceforth to replace the Vedic religion and which are called Paurāṇic since their textual theological and mythical basis was the vast literature of the Purāṇas, other mantras were added to or displaced the Vedic ones – even though some traditions, the Vaiṣṇava ones especially, went on using Śrauta mantras to enhance their claim to brahmanic orthodoxy. These paurāṇic mantras – "Vedic" in the sense that they were not Tantric – were used in the liturgy rather than to obtain supernatural rewards. They usually consisted in the name of the deity or of the supernatural entity being invoked or worshipped, in the dative case, preceded by *OṂ* and followed by the ancient liturgical formula *namaḥ*, meaning hail or obedience to, or by *svāhā*, the exclamation used in making oblations. For instance, Śiva's mantra is *OṂ ŚIVĀYA NAMAḤ*, or *OṂ NAMAḤ ŚIVĀYA*.

It is often said that deities are to be worshipped with their own special mantra, *tattatmantreṇa*. Whatever the cult, be it the thrice-daily invocation prayer, the *sandhya*, or the ritual devotional worship, the *pūjā*, the rite always consists in the utterance (*uccāra*) or repetition (*japa*) of mantras, each of which plays an effective, operative role in the ritual process, the outwardly visible actions of the officiant accompanying, confirming the action of the mantras rather than being themselves effective. The importance of the mantras even in the nontantric *pūjā*, is also underlined by the fact that the worship of a deity normally ends with a *japa*, the recitation of that deity's mantra. We may note here that the mantra of a deity is not the same thing as that deity's name. But since Vedic times lists of names of deities have existed, the recitation of which was prescribed and considered as ritually efficacious or as salvific. The Śatarudrīya, The Thousand [names] of Rudra, of the Yajurveda (4.5), is one of the oldest of these lists. Hinduism proposes a large number of *nāmastotra*, hymns of praise to the Name, or *sahasranāma*, Thousand Names of deities, and there are cases where the name or names of a deity is/are to be uttered like, and with the same expected effects as, a mantra.[5] The Śivapurāṇa, for instance, contains a list of a thousand names of Śiva and enumerates the benefits resulting from its recitation. It also prescribes the recitation of "multiple *nāmamantras*," one of which consists of eight names of Śiva preceded by *śrī*. For this Purāṇa, however, the supreme mantra is *OṂ*, from which, this text says, all the Vedas were born. The devotional use of such *stotra*, *stuti*, or *stava* (or nowadays of *kirtan* or *bhajan*, devotional singing of divine names) is and has certainly always been very widespread. This practice is not to be confused with the *japa* of mantras, though it too rests on the conviction that certain sacred words have a salvific power.

In theory, Vedic mantras cannot be used by, or for, others than male members of the three "twice-born" (*dvija*) classes, a very small minority of Hindus. Hence the importance of non-Vedic mantras, which are all the more important because they are the majority of those used in all sectarian cults – that is, Śaiva, Vaiṣṇava, and "Śākta," domestic or public (temple) cults; in other words, the rites performed, or attended by, almost the whole Hindu community for the last thousand years of Indian history. In the ritual performed in such temples (whose priests are normally brahmins, though the rites are either Tantric or tantricized), both Vedic and non-Vedic (often Tantric) mantras are used. Hindu-Tantric mantras did not follow Vedic-Brahmanic ones chronologically. Nor are they two entirely separate sets of ritual formulas: the two categories co-exist, and sometimes overlap.[6] Characteristic from this point of view are the sectarian forms of the Vedic *gāyatrī*, where the name of the Sun, Savitar, is replaced by that of another deity, and sometimes the wording (but not the meter[7]) is modified so as to fit the deity invoked or the aim pursued.

Regarding mantras in a non-Tantric context, we cannot overlook the Yogasūtras of Patañjali, (1.27, 28) which say "The [term] expressing Him (that is, Īśvara, the Lord) is the *praṇava*" (*tasya vācakaḥ praṇavaḥ*), and "[One should] repeat and meditate intensely its meaning" (*tajjapaḥ tadarthabhāvanam*). The Yogasūtras thus emphasize two essential aspects of mantra and mantric practice. On the one hand, that the mantra is the *vācaka*, i.e. that which "expresses" the deity, that which brings about its presence for the utterer. The deity being "to be expressed" (*vācya*) by the mantra tends therefore, in the context of the Indian conception of the power of the Word, to be considered as ontologically secondary to it – a notion which was to be expatiated upon in the Tantric *mantraśāstra*. Then, for the mantra to carry out its functions, it must be repeated and intensely meditated. The repetition (*japa*) of mantras and their intense meditation (*bhāvana*[8]) remain to this day two essential elements of mantric practice. The meditation of mantras is also designated by the more general term *dhyāna*, sometimes associated with *japa*, repetition, in the compound *japadhyānam*. In this case, it is the continuous flow of thought applied to the mantra being repeated that is emphasized rather than the intensity of concentration, as is normal in practices whose aim is devotional rather than magical. The Pāśupatas, who were pre-Tantric Śaivas, prescribed, too, a meditative muttering of mantras (*japa*), but mainly so as to purify the soul of the worshipper and fix his attention. Characteristically, the five *brahmamantras* (Aghora, Sadyojāta, etc.) used by the Pāśupata ascetics were called "the five purifiers" (*pañcapavitrāṇi*), a role of mantras also mentioned by Vyāsa in his commentary on the Yogasūtras. For the Pāśupatas, however, the essential function of mantras was to obtain union with the Lord (*īśvarasaṃyoga*).

But mantras were considered efficacious and necessary in all aspects, religious and secular, of life in post-Vedic times. The Mahābhārata alludes to their power. The images of deities were ritually established, that is, infused with the being of the deity, with mantras. Mantras were also recited when temples were built. The Arthaśāstra says that sowing is to be accompanied by the uttering of appropriate mantras. From ancient times, mantras were used for medical and magical purposes. The Āyurveda prescribes the use of amulets inscribed with mantras to protect children from illnesses caused by demons. Mantras were used also in veterinary medicine: the Hatyāyurveda, a treatise on illnesses of elephants, said that no remedy should be used unless it was consecrated with mantras. Mantras were also used in the administration of the state, not only to propitiate the deity that protects the kingdom but also to increase the wealth and power of the king, to support his armies in battle, and so forth. A minister, in Sanskrit, is called *mantrin*, not only as a counsellor (root *MANTR*) to the king, but also as being able to use mantras for political ends. Such uses are, in fact, more tantric than *śrauta* or *smārta*. But many examples of the uses of mantras in all walks of life in non-Tantric contexts could easily be quoted.

Tantric Mantras and the *Mantraśāstra*

However important the notion and uses of mantras may have been from early times, it was only with the development within Hinduism of Tantric notions and practices that mantras really pervaded all types of religious, ritual, and magical action. Speculations on the subject thrived, and innumerable treatises, digests, or ritual manuals were written, dealing with their nature and uses and extolling their power. Tantric and mantric practices and notions were so interwoven that *mantraśāstra*, the science or doctrine of mantras, was not only looked on as the most important portion of Tantric teaching, but it was also identified with it, the terms *mantraśāstra* and *tantraśāstra* often being taken as synonymous. An early form of Tantric Śaivism was named *mantramarga* and a traditional division of Śaiva tantras is between those of the *mantrapīṭha* and those of the *vidyāpīṭha* (*vidyās* being female mantras). All tantric texts deal either entirely or in part with mantras. The extent of this literature (noteworthy, though not always interesting and often repetitive) is enormous. It includes all the basic Hindu sectarian works: the tantras, āgamas, saṃhitās, philosophico-religious texts of all persuasions, hymns, eulogies (*stotra*), lists of divine names, and so forth, whether Śaiva or Vaiṣṇava – and this literature went on being added to down to our own days. Even texts of the *śruti* such as certain upaniṣads came also to include tantric mantras.[9] These were also to be found in a number of Purāṇas (the Agnipurāṇa, for instance, is a rich repertoire of *mantraśāstra*), and even in some *dharmaśāstra* texts. And so forth.

Tantric developments, however, did not obliterate earlier practices. Tantric texts and practices went on prescribing and using *śrauta* or *smārta* mantras. Formally, too, the Tantric mantras did not always differ very much from nontantric ones. Their most noteworthy development lay in the increased use of nonlinguistic elements, that is, syllables or groups of syllables devoid of meaning but deemed to be imbued with power and efficacy. Either one or several such syllables were added to the initial *OṂ* of the mantra, or before the final ritual exclamation, the *jāti*: *namaḥ*, *svāhā*, etc. (*OṂ HAUṂ ŚIVĀYA NAMAḤ*, for instance), or else the whole mantra was made up of one such meaningless syllable, or of several either enumerated separately or grouped together. Such, for instance, is the mantra *SAUḤ*[10] of Parā, the supreme goddess of the Trika, or the mantra of the goddess Tripurasundarī, consisting of 15 syllables: *HA SA KA LA HRĪṂ, HA SA KA HA LA HRĪṂ, SA KA LA HRĪṂ*, or the Navātmamantra *HSKṢMLRVYŪṂ*.

The use of such syllables or groups of syllables as elements of mantras or as mantras was justified by the fact that they are made up of Sanskrit phonemes and therefore of forms of the power of *vāc*, the Word originally spoken in the sacred Sanskrit language. A well-known Tantric saying runs: "All mantras are made up of phonemes, the nature of all phonemes being that of Śiva" (*mantrāḥ varṇātmakāḥ sarve, varṇāḥ sarve śivātmakāḥ*). As we have seen, the privilege of brief and esoteric utterances over discursive ones goes back to Vedic times. The idea was also sometimes expressed in this connection that inarticulate sounds or ungrammatrical Sanskrit (or Prākrit) forms, being farther from the norm of articulate rule-governed speech, were nearer to the Absolute. The notion that mantras are in essence made of *nāda*, the primeval subtle phonic vibration which is the substrate of verbal enunciations, was also founded on the idea of the particular power and nearness to the godhead of prelinguistic utterances. The *bindu* (the *anusvāra, ṃ*, the nasal phonetic element shown in writing as a dot) which ends most *bījas*, was also the subject of similar developments, being considered – because it is inarticulate and written as a mere dot – as a concentrated form of phonic energy both symbolizing the supreme level of the godhead and encapsulating the total power of *vāc*. Differently, but in the same spirit, *OṂ* was often considered as divisible into its constituent phonemes, *A, U, M*, followed by *bindu* whose subtle sound was conceived as prolonged by eight other ever-subtler forms of inaudible phonic vibration until it dissolved into the utter silence of the Absolute, a plane which is also that of the highest, "transmental" (*unmanā*), consciousness. Silence was always held in higher esteem than uttered word or audible sound. As we have seen, this also goes back to vedism, where mantras are often used silently. We have also seen that the distinction between three different ways of uttering mantras was Vedic. In the tantras these three ways are usually described as "voiced" (*vācika*), "made in secret" (*upāṃśu*), that is, pronounced so as not to be overheard, and "mental" (*mānasa*), each form being (as in Manu 2.85) higher, but also more effective than the preceding one. Though this distinction may seem in a way to invalidate the equally stringent rule prescribing the absolutely exact pronunciation of mantras, it remains valid to this day.

As has perhaps been apparent in the above, Hindus have always tended to mix up theological, mystico-metaphysical, yogic, and ritual speculation, hence the (for us) ambiguous and unclear nature of mantras. These hymns or formulas originally used for sacrificing to the gods not only came to be used in all sorts of rites or actions, but they were also given metaphysical characteristics and moreover were put to both ritual and meditative use by means of the somato-psychic practices of yoga. Tantric texts very often do not distinguish between different forms or aspects of mantras and mantric practice. In different texts, or in different places of the same text, mantras are viewed, defined, or made use of differently: as mere ritual (but powerful, efficacious) formulas, as esoteric forms of the divine Word, or as the essence of deities, as what brings them into being and/or makes them present in their icons, or even as being themselves deities. These varying conceptions of their nature and role were often used differently, but sometimes also without apparently distinguishing between them. This appears, for instance, in the opposing conceptions of mantras to be seen in, on the one hand, the dualist Śaiva āgamas, where mantras are often called *aṇu* (which means minute, atomic, and, in these texts, soul), and as such are considered as individualized powers, and are therefore made use of as discrete, quasi concrete, elements to be employed ritually (and/or yogically); and, on the other hand, in the nondualist Śaiva traditions (and especially in the Kashmirian Trika philosophical treatises), where mantras are considered as being, at least in essence, pure forms of the absolute power of *vāc* or of the supreme Consciousness, powers used ritually and yogically too, but also and more essentially so as to unite the consciousness of their user with the supreme divine Consciousness. When one looks, as we shall (very briefly) do, at the various mantric practices used from comparatively early times down to our days in Tantric or tantricized rites or cults, one finds stressed and made use of, according to circumstance, either the first or the second of these two concepts, but also sometimes both, as for instance when a mantra is conceived of as an aspect of the absolute divine Consciousness, or as a deity, yet is nevertheless used as a ritually manipulable entity, or is imagined and visualized by an adept as circulating in the subtle centers and canals of his body during a yogic mental-cum-bodily practice. The dual nature of mantras and of their functions is underscored for instance in the Spandakārikā, a Śaiva Kashmirian text of the ninth century, which says that though they are the very Absolute, mantras act like ordinary living beings, that is, they perform all sorts of actions, but they also liberate their user, whose mind is united with them and whom they eventually cause to fuse with the supreme godhead. We may note here, too, that mantras are also considered as constituting a particular category of supernatural entities. This is the case notably in Śaiva texts, which consider that there are seven forms or levels of consciousness, called *pramātṛ*, "knowers," the highest of which is Śiva, after whom come the "Great lords of mantras" (Mantramaheśvara), then the "Lords of mantras" (Mantreśvara), then the 70 million mantras, followed by three other levels down to ordinary human beings. This is worth mentioning since it places mantras (and their "Lords") in a hierarchy of individual entities, rather than on a particular level, or as particular forms, of the Word – though, of course, these different mantric entities are deemed to exist on the three different levels of *vāc* known to the philosophy of grammar – for *vāc* is the ever-present substrate of all that exists. We must also remember – nor did the Indians forget – that mantras, whatever their nature, must be spoken or somehow uttered when used, and that they therefore have also an empirical physical existence: mantras as audible or inaudible sounds articulated by the organs of phonation are sometimes distinguished from mantras as powers.

All deities, supernatural entities, and so forth, have a mantra which is their *vācaka*, "that which expresses" them, the deity or entity being "what is to be expressed" (*vācya*), a conception which (see above) definitely subordinates the deity as an entity to its mantra. All deities have a *mūlamantra* (or *mūlavidyā* if they are feminine), a basic or root mantra which, according to some sources, is the substrate of all the mantras of that deity, for there are mantras corresponding to the different forms, aspects, or constitutive elements of deities. Such are, for instance, the five *brahmamantras* of the five faces or mouths (*vaktra*) of Śiva, whence all Śaiva Scriptures are deemed to have issued, or the *aṅgamantras*, the ancillary mantras of the "limbs" of Śiva or of Viṣṇu. The "weapons" (*āyudha*) or attributes of the deities also have their mantras. All these mantras are used to invoke the deities or entities concerned and/or to install them ritually in the icon, yantra, or whatever support they are to be worshipped on or made use of for some purpose. (This empowerment of the icon by mantras is absolutely necessary: without it the icon would be void of any divine element and therefore useless.) Deities to be worshipped have also a *mūrtimantra* or *mūrtividyā* used to invoke or call forth their visible form (their *mūrti*). There are also *kalāmantras*, used to manifest the different parts (*kalā*) constitutive of the deity, which is thus conceived as made up of, ritually constructed with, mantras. The latter are therefore ontologically prior and superior to the former: in many respects tantric pantheons are systems or configurations of mantras rather than of deities. Since there are mantras for, or corresponding to, or included among the constitutive elements or divisions of the cosmos described in tantric texts – the *tattvas*, *kalās*, *aṇḍas*, *bhuvanas*, *adhvans*, and even mantras – and since mantras are used to evoke these entities, the very cosmos can be conceived of as basically made up of mantras. Indeed, in the cosmogony of the Ahirbudhnyasaṃhitā of the Pāñcarātra, the condition the god Viṣṇu assumes before creating the cosmos through a phonetic process is described as "mantric" (*mantramaya*). In this saṃhitā as well as in Śaiva texts, the manifestation of the cosmos results from the apparition in the supreme godhead of the 49/50 phonemes of the Sanskrit alphabet,[11] from *A* to *KṢA*: all these phonemes can be considered as so many mantras ("seed-mantras," *bījamantras*, rather, since they are made by adding to each individual letter the *bindu ṃ*, from *AṂ* to *KṢAṂ*). But the whole alphabet can also be considered as an alphabetic form of the god Bhairava: "Bhairava of the totality of sound," Śabdarāśibhairava, who is thus considered, and can be made use of, as a mantra of 50 syllables. Similarly, a different order of the alphabet (going from *Na* to *Pha*), called Mālinī, is both a goddess and a mantra. In such cases it is sometimes difficult to distinguish mantra from deity, for a deity may be considered as made up of, as *being*, a mantra, or as made up of letters of the alphabet – these are "mantra-deities" (*mantradevatā*), "alphabet-deities" (*varnadevatā*), or "letter-goddesses" (*lipidevī*) such as Sarasvatī in her form as Vāgīśī.[12] The three supreme goddesses of the Śaiva system of the Trika, Parā, Aparā, and Parāparā, are *mantradevatās*, being made up respectively of *SAUḤ*, of a mantra of 38 syllables, and of the three *bījas HRĪḤ HŪṂ PHAṬ*.

Like Hindu deities – only more so – mantras are innumerable. They are traditionally said to number 70 million – one of those large numbers in which India delights. But nobody has ever counted them, in spite of the many lists that exist. The fact that mantras are regarded as secret formulas, powerful spells that can be used for any purpose, good or bad, may explain the absence from all traditions of any complete catalog. Moreover, in the existing lists, and more generally in nearly all Tantric texts, mantras are usually not quoted in full. They are referred to instead by their names – Śrīvidyā, for instance, or Hṛdayabīja, for *SAUḤ*, Piṇḍanātha or Mātṛsadbhāva, for *KHPHREṂ*, etc. –, or by the name of their devatā, or by their own names if they are *mantradevatās*, like Navātman, or else by the number of their syllables, such as *pañcadaśākṣaramantra* for the Śrīvidyā of 15 syllables, etc.

The secret character of mantras, together with the fact that they embody the highest and most efficacious power of *vāc*, the spoken-speaking Word, a power called *mantravīrya*, is the reason why they may be transmitted and received only in secrecy and by word of mouth. They go, as is said, "from ear to ear" (*karṇāt karṇam*). A written mantra (and this is true not only in Tantric circles) or a mantra found in a book is lifeless, powerless,[13] since it lacks the spiritual element which only a qualified master can transmit. When their use is prescribed in a text, secrecy in transmission is upheld by employing conventional names for their constituent letters, or by quoting these letters in reverse order or in disorder, or else by using secret diagrams called *prastāra* or *gahvara* ("display" or "cavern"), which are ritually drawn and in which the letters of the Sanskrit alphabet from which those of the mantra are to be chosen are displayed in a particular order. These conventional ways of quoting mantras without actually revealing them are called their "extraction" (*mantroddhāra*). The secret esoteric transmission of mantras applies to those conferred during initiation and especially to those which are to be used for a specific religious or magical purpose. Such devices are not necessary for mantras used in the course of ordinary rituals, even if only selected (initiated) individuals are permitted to perform these rites.

Each Tantric tradition has its own system of mantras and usually considers the mantras of other traditions ineffective or dangerous. Such inadequate mantras, whether they belong to one's own or to another initianic lineage, are sometimes described as suffering from defects (*doṣa*), usually described as of a very human character (being hungry, asleep, poor, cross-eyed . . .). Rites called *mantrasaṃskāra*, "purification of mantras," aim at removing such defects. We have here cases where mantras seem to be regarded more as supernatural individual entities than as forms of *vāc* – even though the defects so concretely described consist mostly in the presence (or absence) of particular letters or combinations of letters. There are also mantras which are by nature faultless, or which can be used without restrictions as to their form or nature: *OṂ* is an example. Such mantras, or those which can be used for different purposes associated with other mantras, are said to be *sādharaṇa*, generally applicable. The distinction between two categories and uses of Tantric mantras is worth noting, for there appear to be, on the one hand, ritual formulas which *do* things when used by authorized persons at the proper time and according to prescribed rules, which are usually not secret, being found in all ritual manuals, though they may include *bījas* which are esoteric in character. On the other hand, in initiations and/or for particular rituals, in particular those that may be called magical, mantras are esoterically transmitted from a master, who is a *mantrin* in that he knows and masters mantras, to a qualified disciple. This is especially the case in the Tantric initiation (the *dīkṣā*) thanks to which the initiand will be admitted into a particular group and be permitted to perform certain rites. If the initiate does not seek merely liberation (*mokṣa*), if he is not what is called a *mumukṣu*, but intends to attain particular powers (*siddhis*), or enjoy particular mundane or supramundane rewards, an intent denoted by the Sanskrit root *SIDDH*, he is a *bhubukṣu*, a seeker of *bhukti*, and more specifically, if he receives the proper *dīkṣā*, a *sādhaka*. The mantra he has received (after its compatibility – its *aṃśa* – with him has been carefully checked) must then be mastered by means of a specific and often long and complex process of worship called *mantrasādhana* during which it will be treated as a deity to be honored and propitiated so that it will eventually bring this *sādhaka* all he desires. In the Śaiva kaula *dīkṣā*, too, there is a moment when the initiand is possessed by the mantras placed in a ritual diagram. These are cases where the distinction between mantra and deity tends to disappear. We cannot enter here into the difficult question of the nature of Tantric mantras, a subject on which traditions often disagree. We may, however, say that, depending on texts and circumstances, mantras are seen either as deities or powers, or as powerful formulas, formulas which exist empirically as linguistic or metalinguistic elements, but which are divine in essence, and this is why they are powerful. But they can also be seen and manipulated as both formula and deity – a deity that is a mantra. This ambiguity probably results from the fact that Tantric conceptions of mantras unsystematically combine notions of Vedic origin on the power of *vāc* with āgamic rites and theological beliefs. The former are more prominent in the tantras of Bhairava and still more in the often nondualist Śaiva metaphysical systems (and in the texts of the Pāñcarātra), while the latter prevail in the generally dualist and highly ritualistic Śaivāgamas.[14] In India today, apart from ritual, it is the magical use of mantras that is the most in evidence.

The scope of this chapter does not permit us to review, even briefly, the many and varied mantric practices described in Tantric texts; nor can we look at the beliefs which go with them, however interesting (and sometimes curious) they may be. The often very subtle philosophical disquisitions on the nature, effective power, and spiritual ways of access to the power to be found, for instance, in the work of such Śaiva Kashmirian masters as Abhinavagupta or Kṣemarāja (tenth to eleventh centuries) must also be left aside in spite of their interest. We shall therefore limit ourselves to a rapid survey of just two important aspects of the use of Tantric mantras, namely their ritual and their yogic applications.

As has already been pointed out, all Tantric rituals consist essentially in the utterance of mantras. A rite, even a ritual worship, a *pūjā*, can be performed without any icon or concrete object of any sort, but it cannot be carried out without mantras. In a *pūjā* the deity is invoked and made present in the icon or diagram; it is kept there and made to pay attention to the cult by mantras. It is bathed, it is offered flowers, incense, food, etc., with mantras which do not merely accompany these actions and offerings, but actually perform them. Indeed, a *pūjā* can be perfomed without any concrete substances, etc., being offered, but with only mantras being uttered. This goes on until the deity is "dismissed" by the appropriate mantra; after which there normally takes place a recitation (*japa*) of the deity's mantra, which is finally "offered" to it. Since there is a Tantric rule that "one who is not a god cannot worship god," the officiating person's body and mind must be deified before the worship begins. This preliminary ritual is performed by placing (by *nyāsa*) mantras on the performer's body, which they pervade with their power. Thus divinized, the officiant must then perform on himself as a divine being an "inner" mental worship which is carried out by means of mantras only. During the ritual "outer" (*bāhya*) worship that follows, the mantras are deemed to create the body of the deity, and to make up its throne (a *mantrāsana*, formed by all the levels of the cosmos, the *tattvas*, from the lowest to the highest, all represented by their mantras mentally piled on each other). Mantras, too, accomplish such ritual acts as transforming water into nectar (*amṛta*), infusing ritual implements or substances with divine power, protecting the ritual area, destroying obstacles, burning impurities, and so forth. Their utterance is often accompanied by ritual gestures (*mudrā*), usually considered as merely accompanying them, underlining their power, rather than as directly operative. The effectiveness of mantras is particularly stressed and valued in the so-called *kāmya*, "desiderative," rites performed so as to obtain some desired result. In all such practices one finds at work the dual nature of mantras: as words of power which effect what they say or symbolize, and as powerful supernatural entities.

Mantras are also used in meditation and/or yogic practices, where they are mentally perceived and meditated by the adept so that he may assimilate their power in mind and body, and thus attain either rewards or liberation. This is done either through meditation – *dhyāna* or *bhāvanā* – or as part of a cult, the Tantric *pūjā* often including yogic practices designed to foster the process of identification with the deity worshipped, a characteristic feature of the Tantric worship. These mantric practices sometimes consist in the intellectual and mystical realization of the "meaning," that is, the symbolic value, of the mantra. Such is the case, for instance, when the adept is to realize the inner creative movement of the supreme godhead as symbolized by the three letters of the mantra *SAUḤ*. The movement goes from pure absolute being (*sat* = *S*), to the coalescence of the three basic creative energies of Śiva (*AU*, because this syllable is called *trikoṇabīja*, triangular seed), energies which are eventually emitted (*Ḥ* since this letter is called *visarga*, which means emission) in the absolute divine consciousness.

The *bījamantra* (for such practices do not concern longer formulas) can also be uttered by associating its utterance (*uccāra*, a term connoting an upward movement) with the ascent of the *kuṇḍalinī*, the human and cosmic form of divine power. The adept feels the presence of the mantra in himself as an ascending subtle phonic vibration, the *nāda*, going from the lowest of his bodily *cakras* to a subtle center above his head. Being carried upward by this movement which he imagines but also experiences somehow in his body, he eventually unites with the Absolute on the ultimate plane of *vāc* as well as of consciousness. In some cases the mantra, after having reached this supreme level, is imagined as flowing down like a fluid substance, pervading the whole body of the yogin, who thus becomes perfect and immortal. This quasi-physical conception and perception of the mantra is very typically tantric.

We may add that mantras are abundantly used in any number of magic practices, often as amulets (*kavaca*), and so in written form, nowadays at least, not always in Sanskrit. In some amulets or yantras, they may even be written in

Arabic script. These are popular forms of mantra, but, like more sophisticated ones, they are signs of the Indian, nay universal, belief in the power or magical efficacy of the word.[15]

Notes

1 It is important to note that Vedic – *vaidika* in Sanskrit – is the term that has been used for centuries to denote orthodox Hindu beliefs and practices. But even such non-Vedic texts as the tantras often tell their adepts to follow orthodox "Vedic" rules of behavior in their social lives.

2 There are exceptions to this rule, as we shall see; however, they do not affect the general principle of the fundamentally oral/aural character of mantras. It may be interesting to note here that though forms of *vāc*, the Word, the Vedic hymns revealed to the ancient Vedic poet-seers, the *ṛṣis* were deemed to have been seen by them.

3 On these texts, see pp. 81–6.

4 Which were "Vedic" – *vaidika* – insofar as their rules and beliefs did not contradict the Veda.

5 The ritual and devotional reading and recitation of the Devīmāhātmya, where the utterance (*uccāra*) of this Purānic text is preceded and followed by that of hymns from the Ṛgveda, is another example of the religious use of the recitation of a sacred text. On this, see Coburn 1991.

6 We may perhaps quote here the French indologist Louis Renou, who once wrote: "It is as easy in India to notice continuities as it is difficult to point out breaks in continuity" (my translation).

7 A rule which underlines the priority of the form over the "meaning" of mantras.

8 *Bhāvanā*, from the verbal root *BHŪ*, to come into being, is an intense form of mental concentration which activates the mantra, makes it perceptible to the meditating person, and identifies him/her with it.

9 Such is in particular the case of the so-called Śaiva-, Śākta-, or Yoga-Upaniṣads of the canonical collection of the 108 Upaniṣads, a collection (as we know now) put together, and in some cases reworked, in the first half of the eighteenth century by one Upaniṣadbrahmayogin.

10 Contrary to what is often believed, monosyllabic mantras do not necessarily end with the *bindu ṃ*.

11 There are 49 phonemes (*varṇa* or *akṣara*) in Sanskrit, to which is traditionally added the group *K* + *S* = *KṢA*.

12 The well-known Tantric treatise Śāradātilaka describes a Lipitanu Vāgīśvarī, a "Goddess of the Word whose body is made of letters."

13 This is the general rule. But exceptions could easily be quoted. In India, there are as many stringent rules as there are exceptions to them.

14 But tāntrikas, whatever their persuasion, are "super-ritualists" – when ritual is rejected, it is only for those who have attained the highest esoteric plane.

15 For a very interesting study of modern mantric practices see Diehl 1956. The most thorough study of mantras to date is Alper 1989. It includes in particular a "Working Bibliography for the Study of Mantra," which is still the most complete one available.

Bibliography

Alper, Harvey B., ed. 1989. *Understanding Mantras.* Albany: SUNY Press.
Coburn, Thomas B. 1991. *Encountering the Goddess.* Albany: SUNY Press.
Diehl, Carl Gustav. 1956. *Instrument and Purpose: Studies on Rites and Ritual in South India.* Lund: Gleerups.
Padoux, A. 1990. *Vāc: The Concept of the Word in Selected Hindu Tantras.* Albany: SUNY Press.

PART IV

Society, Politics, and Nation

23 On the Relationship between Caste and Hinduism 495
Declan Quigley

24 Modernity, Reform, and Revival 509
Dermot Killingley

25 Contemporary Political Hinduism 526
C. Ram Prasad

26 The Goddess and the Nation: Subterfuges of Antiquity, the Cunning of Modernity 551
Sumathi Ramaswamy

27 Gender in a Devotional Universe 569
Vasudha Narayanan

CHAPTER 23

On the Relationship between Caste and Hinduism

Declan Quigley

Every serious work on Hinduism emphasizes the extraordinary diversity of that "religion" to the point where many ask whether it makes a great deal of sense to call Hinduism *a* religion at all in the sense of a relatively cohesive or core set of beliefs and ritual practices. On the other hand, every serious work on caste emphasizes the extraordinary uniformity of the beliefs and ritual practices associated with this institution (or set of institutions). It is a curious fact, then, that there is a near-unanimous consensus that caste and Hinduism are inextricably linked. A statement cited in the opening pages of Lipner's textbook on Hinduism might well have come from Weber or any of his intellectual descendants whose interpretations of caste have dominated intellectual discussion of the subject in the disciplines of sociology and social anthropology: "Caste is the Hindu form of social organization. No man can be a Hindu who is not in caste" (Farquhar 1913: 216, cited in Lipner 1994: 3). However, Lipner reminds us that there is a dissenting, minority view which states that one must be very careful in making this equation: "The caste system, though closely integrated into the [Hindu] religion, is not essential to it . . . Even the profession of belief in the authority of the Veda is not essential" (Brockington 1981: 4, see Lipner 1994: 3).

In this chapter I will support Brockington's decoupling of caste and Hinduism, though from a rather different perspective. Those who insist on the connection, it will be argued, invariably select only certain ideological features of caste as worthy of consideration while dismissing others as if they simply did not exist. This typically goes hand in hand with an obliviousness to certain historical and sociological features which characterize caste and which explain its distinctiveness from other forms of social organization, such as tribe or estate or class.[1]

What exactly do we mean by caste? What almost everyone can agree on is that wherever there is caste, certain features are found linked together in a systematic fashion. Perhaps most noticeable, particularly to Western, (relatively) liberal, egalitarian eyes, is an apparently constant preoccupation with maintaining differences between groups and expressing these differences through concepts of pollution and inauspiciousness. These groups are based on lineal kinship, and tightly regulated marriage alliances between households of different lineages. From one perspective, regulating marriage often appears to be a device on the part of wealthy households for inhibiting the dispersal of land ownership. But non-landowning lineages, whether wealthy merchants or impoverished groups, also regulate their marriages just as strictly as members of landowning lineages. The fundamental message being circulated by members of all "castes" (i.e. groups of intermarrying lineages) is invariably phrased in terms of an encouragement to prevent one's own "kind" from being contaminated, with the word for "kind" in most Indian languages being *jāti* (or some variant thereof), a concept which might also be translated as "species."

It is as if members of different groups were saying: "We are different from each other in the same way that different animal species are. Just as cats and dogs cannot interbreed, neither can we." Since some relativist thinkers are reluctant to say that people with other cultural ideas are "wrong," it needs perhaps to be stressed (if we are going to explain the ideology that different castes must not miscegenate) that there is, in fact, only one human species and its members are not prevented from interbreeding because of their different origins. The arbitrary, cultural nature of the prohibition on intermixing is shown more clearly still by the fact that it is not restricted to procreation. Members of different castes are generally convinced that they should not eat together except on special occasions (and then should not eat "normal," everyday food), and that they should abstain from performing certain rituals together.

It is not uncommon for a village to have 20 or more castes all claiming to abjure relations of any fundamental kind with each other. But why should there be such a proliferation of "kinds" wherever there is caste? A preliminary clue is that in caste-organized communities normally one kind predominates in every sense – politically, economically, numerically, and as the provider of the main patrons of rituals. Conventionally referred to as the "dominant" caste (following Srinivas 1959), they are more accurately entitled the "noble" or "kingly" caste, it being understood that nobility and kingship are refractions of each other, as will become clearer later. All of the other castes are groups of lineages which have an obligation to provide people who will perform specialized ritual duties for the noble caste. To default on these obligations always incurs some kind of sanction, which is frequently underpinned by the threat, if not the actual use of, violence. Generally, the only people who can escape from these ritual obligations are those merchants who are not dependent on landowners, or renouncers who live a mendicant life outside of the sedentary communities organized along caste lines.

While there is a great deal of variation among theorists regarding the alleged underlying mechanisms which generate this phenomenon whereby a multiplicity of groups all fastidiously distinguish themselves from each other, most people would agree that certain features stand out when caste is compared to other forms of social organization. Of these perhaps the most striking is the institution of untouchability whereby members of certain castes are so excluded that they appear on occasion to be beyond the pale of normal society. One very common, and perfectly acceptable, way to approach caste is thus by explaining untouchability.[2]

Crudely, though not inaccurately, there are two main explanations for untouchability, both of which present Untouchables as the "opposites" of Brāhmaṇas (spelled in various ways). Both of these approaches envisage caste organization as "hierarchical," in the commonly accepted sense of this term: a ladder-like system of statuses. In both approaches, Brāhmaṇas are at the "top" and Untouchables are at the "bottom." According to one approach this is so because Brāhmaṇas are priests and priests are pure, while Untouchables are polluted because they perform degrading tasks which deal with the inauspicious facets of life and death. According to the other approach, the superiority of Brāhmaṇas is fundamentally based on landed wealth and the power which derives from it, while the wretched condition of Untouchables results from the fact that they are typically landless and dispossessed. According to this latter theory, all talk of purity and pollution, whether by those who practice caste, or those who analyze it, simply obscures the underlying economic and political reality.

I will show shortly that neither of these theories is sustainable because the underlying assumption of a stratified, ladder-like series of caste statuses does not match certain crucial features of the known ethnography. Before elaborating on this, however, it is necessary to consider the most celebrated and influential (though also the most attacked) theorist of caste, Louis Dumont, who argues against the idea of caste-as-stratification but then confuses the issue by appearing to employ precisely this concept. Dumont (1980 [1966]) attempts to escape from the notion of caste-as-stratification by introducing us to a second meaning of "hierarchy," that of the encompassment of the part by the whole, which implies also the encompassment of something by its contrary. Thus, for example, in traditional societies the individual is encompassed by society and in caste society, argues Dumont, the pure encompasses the impure.

Dumont argues that Western theorists and those influenced by them tend to see caste through modern, individualistic spectacles and to apply a set of judgments which are not applicable in the "holistic" traditions of caste-organized communities where the individual is subordinated to, encompassed by, the moral claims of the collective. He is perfectly correct to state that caste ideology gives primacy to the whole community and has no place for the modern Western concept of individualism where people are free to make their own choices about whom they associate with. In connection with this, everyone will agree with Dumont that caste involves a "heavy" and pervasive use of ritual for structuring social relations which in many other societies are structured by centralized political and economic institutions.

In the Indian case, argues Dumont, this holism expresses itself with reference to two ideological features: the opposition of the pure and the impure, and what he calls the "disjunction between status and power." By the latter he means that those who are the most politically powerful defer to the representatives of religious values because the ultimate meaning of the society derives from those values. This is why, he claims, in everyday life the priest ranks higher than the king, and in the *varṇa* schema of the Vedic texts the Brāhmaṇa ranks higher than the Kṣatriya.

Dumont's theory has had pervasive and enduring appeal in spite of a torrent of criticism from every conceivable angle. The reason for this appeal is simple. Hindus themselves often claim that Brāhmaṇas are the "highest" caste and Untouchables the "lowest" and Dumont's approach appears to provide an explanation for this. But this common popular formulation of the order of castes runs into problems immediately. First, there are thousands of Brāhmaṇa castes whose members daily dispute each other's status.[3] Evidently, if one Brāhmaṇa caste claims superiority over another Brāhmaṇa caste, not all of them can be the "highest." And if some Brāhmaṇas are "higher" than others, then the criterion of being "higher" obviously must be by virtue of something other than simply being a Brāhmaṇa. But what? This is one of the trickiest, and most contested, questions in the explanation of caste.

The evidence needed to resolve this question, however, points overwhelmingly in one direction. The work of some "priests" (i.e. performers of ritual activities on behalf of others) is clearly regarded by everyone in caste-organized communities as defiling. This seems relatively uncontroversial in relation to the members of those castes who deal overtly with death or the disposal of liminal substances such as cut hair and nails, feces, menstrual blood, and afterbirth. Which society does not have to deal with these by setting them apart? But the work of a number of authors (see especially Heesterman 1985; Parry 1980; 1986 and Raheja 1988a) suggests a much more radical view of ritual activity, for it would appear that it is not merely dealing with the physical byproducts of human life and decay which is dangerous. It is not just castes such as Barbers and Tanners, Washermen and Sweepers, they argue, whose status is endangered by their ritual activities. So too is the status of Brāhmaṇa priests who are normally conceived of as the "highest" caste(s) because of their alleged distance from the polluting functions of Untouchable and other "lowly" specialist castes. *All* priestly activity is dangerous because it involves the acceptance of "gifts," commonly referred to as *dāṇa*, which act as vessels for the inauspicious qualities which the patron of the ritual is attempting to shed. The evidence for this is both ethnographic and textual and indicates clearly that members of Brāhmaṇa castes who function as priests are tainted, or compromised, by their ritual activities. Many members of Brāhmaṇa castes display their awareness of this problem by their reluctance to take on priestly duties. These nonpriestly Brāhmaṇas, we are told, "widely despise Brahman priests" (Fuller 1984: 50; see also Guneratne 2001: 539).

This is not to imply that all ritual tasks enjoy equal esteem or lack of it; manifestly this is not the case. As a rough rule of thumb one might say that those castes whose functions are most closely associated with death and decay have the lowest status, while those whose functions are more ethereal enjoy the highest status. However, the relative evaluation of caste statuses is far from being an easy matter since the paradigmatic ritual which connects members of noble castes to others is sacrifice, and this is, by its nature, simultaneously ethereal and implicated in violent death. Brāhmaṇas normally represent themselves as being removed from the violent aspect of sacrifice but this is always relative and, in the final analysis, something of an illusion (or delusion). This theme cannot be pursued here without a full-blown exploration of the nature of sacrifice. Suffice it to say that the ambiguity which is at the heart of this primal ritual of death and rebirth translates into caste relations, as we will see a little later.

One might object, however, that if it is the actual performance of ritual functions which is hazardous for one's status, it is curious that the status of other members of the caste is also compromised even when they do not themselves perform impure tasks. These people are affected because they either come from one's own lineage (i.e. they are related consanguineally), or they come from other lineages with whom members of one's own lineage conventionally marry (i.e. they are related affinally). Caste status cannot therefore be simply "interactional" as Marriott (1968) argued in a very influential article which contrasted with the "attributional" theory of Dumont. Kinship and marriage are also primary determinants of caste status.

Ethnographic reports often fail to make clear that all members of castes do not need to perform the ritual function from which they derive their status. What is crucial is that one or more members of the caste in question provide the necessary ritual functionary. Caste is often reported to be a matter of occupation. This is false: what is at issue is a periodic ritual contribution to the community. All of the members of one caste may be agricultural labourers yet only some among them may be required to perform a particular ritual function – say, to play music on the occasion of worshipping a particular deity. Another caste (i.e. a group with whom the former will not intermarry) may also be agricultural laborers and have a different ritual function – say, to be pall-bearers for noble castes. Discrimination of this kind can be endless – as with totemic groups (see Lévi-Strauss's interesting comparisons, 1963, 1966 [1962]). Even among groups where the link between caste and occupation appears more clear-cut, it is rarely the case that all members of the caste perform the job in question. Thus, to be a Barber is not to be a hair-cutter, but to be related to others whose ritual function involves the cutting of hair and other related tasks, such as nail-paring and midwifery, as elements of purificatory ceremonies. A Barber could, therefore, be a taxi-driver, while the man cutting hair in the barber's shop (i.e. as a profession rather than as part of a ritual function) could well be a member of another caste. Similarly, a Brāhmaṇa need not be a priest, a Farmer may be a rickshaw driver, and so on.

These three indisputable ethnographic realities – the fundamental nature of lineal affiliation in providing caste status; the fact that only some members of a caste perform the ritual function which gives all of the members of the caste their status; and the fact that members of a variety of castes perform ritual functions which are widely regarded as inherently dangerous – mean that there are four mistakes in the oft-repeated formula that "Brāhmaṇas are the highest caste because they are priests."[4]

1 Not all priests are Brāhmaṇas;
2 Many Brāhmaṇas are not priests. They are Brāhmaṇas because they are related to other Brāhmaṇas (who may or may not be priests themselves; if they are assumed to be related to priests at some point, this may be in the distant, or forgotten, past);
3 At least some priests are degraded by their ritual activities and, according to some authorities, *all* of them are;
4 If the performance of ritual functions is degrading or compromising, this implies that only the renouncer, who is by definition outside caste-organized society, can claim to be "pure." The concept of "most pure" cannot then be equated with "highest" since "highest" indicates "inside."

The most important conclusion one can draw from these observations is that the idea that "Brāhmaṇas are the highest caste" makes no sense (irrespective of the fact that it is very widely held by Hindus themselves and by commentators on Hinduism). There is no doubt that ritual activity is directed at the ridding of inauspicious qualities, but this does not indicate a capacity to rank groups as higher and lower. On the contrary, careful study of the ethnographic record shows that it is always impossible to rank castes unambiguously or without contestation: ambiguity and dispute are built in to the structure of caste relations. This is seen both in the relations between patrons of rituals and priests of various kinds, and among patron castes themselves.[5]

Once these points are admitted, much of Dumont's theory of caste quickly starts to unravel. For Dumont, the opposition of the pure and the impure depends on priests monopolizing ritual functions which were once the preserve of the king: "power in India became secular at a very early date" (Dumont 1980: 76). But in spite of the fact that his entire theory of caste hangs on this claim, Dumont provides no evidence to support it – bar his own assertions that Brāhmaṇas are now unambiguously the "highest" caste and Untouchables the "lowest." With much textual and ethnographic evidence suggesting otherwise, it is fortunate that there is an alternative way of approaching the problem which does not depend on concepts of highest and lowest.

The pollution concepts which are the hallmark of caste are conventionally said to be an expression of "Hinduism," even though we know perfectly well that this is not a monolithic set of beliefs. An alternative representation of caste values portrays them as an expression of institutions associated with kingship. This approach, which is often associated with the seminal work of Hocart (1950 [1938]), has certain advantages over any other explanation of caste. First, it offers an explanation of why caste organization is found in some parts of the Indian subcontinent but not others. Typically, caste originates in regions which are ecologically capable of sustaining kingdoms: relatively large populations in a relatively small area. Caste is associated with fertile agriculture, not with barren mountainous or desert regions. Secondly, it offers an explanation of why caste organization is found among non-Hindu communities in India, Nepal and Sri Lanka and why very similar forms of social organization are found in other monarchical and feudal societies which give ideological stress to what Geertz (1980) has aptly called "the exemplary center."

Caste ideology is an expression of the conflicting demands of two different principles of social organization. On the one hand, there is the hierarchical principle of monarchy, a form of centralization which, of itself, is always very tenuous because it is dependent on personal patronage.[6] On the other hand, there is the relatively egalitarian principle of lineage organization which simultaneously stresses kinship (sameness) and marriageability (difference, but bridgeable difference). To be a member of a lineage in a caste-organized society is to identify first with one's lineal kin in opposition to members of all other lineages, then to identify with that group of lineages inside of which one may seek spouses in opposition to those lineages which are not acceptable marriage partners.

Hocart brings together these principles of organization in caste society by arguing that castes are "families" which hereditarily transfer ritual functions in order to ensure that the king and nobles remain in a pure state (1950: 17, 20). In contrast to the idea that caste is orientated to a pure–impure axis with Brāhmaṇas and Untouchables at polar ends, Hocart argues that what is at stake is the integrity of kingship, the institution to which everyone is connected. By implication, it is a very fragile integrity which can only be maintained by the repeated performance of rituals (sacrifices). The integrity of kingship provides a model – an exemplary center – for others to emulate by replicating the king's rituals on a lesser scale.

Hocart's approach endorses Dumont's assertion that the separation of king and priest (as he put it, the "disjunction between status and power") is central to the theory of caste. But it shows that Dumont was quite wrong about the dynamic of relations between kings and priests and the underlying structure they depended on. Nobility and kingship are not a simple matter of material dominance, but are concerned with the ability to command rituals which bring the community together and expurgate the inauspiciousness which social life habitually generates. Priests are the instruments who perform this purging function and who therefore make possible kingship and nobility. Caste organization could thus be said to be a division of the community into noble and kingly families on the one hand and priests on the other, provided it is understood that the primary function of priests is to cleanse the society of anything which threatens it with death and evil.

In the modern, postcolonial period, the ostensible disappearance of kings from the political scene has not led to the disappearance of king*ship* as an organizing principle of ritual and social relations though this has often been obscured by modern political realities (see also Galey 1989). Even Raheja, whose brilliant ethnography exposed the faultlines of Dumont's theory more clearly than any other recent work, muddies the waters somewhat when considering the nature of caste in contemporary India. She writes that "[k]ingship no longer exists, but it has been, perhaps, replaced by the ritual centrality of the dominant caste" (Raheja 1988b: 517). The word "replaced" is unfortunate because it has *always* been the function of members of dominant castes to patronize ritual, replicating on a diminished scale the role of the king. Put differently, members of dominant castes continue to be mini-kings, not just materially, but in terms of their political/ritual function. They are "at the center of a complex ritual organization that permeates nearly every aspect of the everyday life of the village" (ibid.). This real-world fact of kingship/patronage sits uneasily with Dumont's insistence that the king's role has been secularized, and much more comfortably with Hocart's claim that the king/patron is the "principal" of the ritual (Hocart 1970 [1936]: 61).

A phrase which I have elided from the two quotes from Raheja in the previous paragraph further confuses understanding of both kingship, and relations between patrons of rituals and the priests who carry them out. In the village of her fieldwork, she says, "as in many of the textual traditions on kingship, the Brāhmaṇa is hierarchically superior, yet the dominant landholding caste stands at the center of a complex ritual organization ..." (ibid.). It is difficult to see what the foundation for this alleged superiority is, other than an engrained idea that Brāhmaṇas *must* be superior because that is what everyone else seems to believe these days. In practice, superiority seems to attach to members of the landholding caste in both ritual and nonritual domains. If the Brāhmaṇa is "hierarchically superior" in an ideological sense, it is a Brāhmaṇa who is so idealized that he cannot possibly belong to the world of caste relations where he would be tainted by the receipt of prestations for performing ritual services. It cannot be the Brāhmaṇa of the village who is necessarily immersed in caste (i.e. interdependent) relations, and who is therefore, like everyone else, caught up in the web of inauspiciousness which is the product of the dealings of normal social life. Interestingly, Dumont's theory predicts just this eventuality: "In theory, power is ultimately subordinate to priesthood, whereas in fact priesthood submits to power" (Dumont 1980: 71–2).

One of the problems with any understanding of caste is that the word "caste" itself has been used to translate two quite different Sanskrit concepts which are assumed, quite wrongly, to have an automatic connection. We have already encountered the concept of *jāti* and its sense of "kind" or "species." Another way of glossing this concept might be to say "the group that one was born into," the relativity of this gloss conveying the contextual nature of *jāti* ascriptions. When asked to name their *jāti*, people may name their patrilineage, the name of the group of lineages they conventionally marry into, or even the name of what would now be called an ethnic group. However, even though the concept is elastic, the idea of origin by birth is constant. There is no mystery about this. If a British person is asked: "where are you from?," he or she may give the name of a village, a county, a country, or even a continent depending on the interpretation given to what the questioner is seeking.

Scholars approaching caste through the study of Hinduism and comparative religion may be less acquainted with sociological and anthropological studies of caste on the ground and are more likely to be familiar with the Vedic concept of *varṇa* which is also used to translate the word "caste." The referent of this concept is rather different from that of *jāti* since the fundamental idea is less "belonging to a group by virtue of common birth" than "functions which must be performed if cosmic harmony and social harmony are to prevail" – it being understood that cosmic harmony and social harmony are dependent on each other. What the *varṇa* and *jāti* concepts share is an idea of "keeping apart" and it is this which allows them to become conflated in the concept of caste.

In fact the original idea of *varṇa* does seem to imply differences of origins between the "Vedic Indians, who called themselves "noble ones" (*āryas*), [and] the other peoples they encountered (chiefly the Harappans to begin with)" (Lipner 1994: 88). But the idea of separating conquerors from indigenes seems to quickly become subordinate to an idea of protecting nobility which is independent of any consideration of ethnic origins. It has been mentioned that rituals performed by priests on behalf of members of patron (noble, kingly) castes are paradigmatically sacrifices. It is no accident that the concept of *varṇa* is inextricably tied to a sacrificial theory of human society. The famous verse from Rgveda x, 90 speaks of four *varṇas*: Brāhmaṇa, *rājanya* (later conventionally referred to as the *kṣatriya*), *vaiśya*, and *śūdra*, each of which springs from a different part of the body of Puruṣa – the lord of beings – who is portrayed as having been sacrificed at the beginning of time.

Note that there is nothing here about lineage or pedigree, and neither is there in the later law book known as the Code of Manu (ca. 200 BCE to CE 200). In this text each *varṇa* is portrayed as having a quintessentially different function. These functions revolve around sacrifice: just as the world and the four *varṇas* were created through an initial sacrifice, repetitions of this primal act are necessary if order and harmony are to be maintained. To achieve this, each *varṇa* has a specific function:

> Manu lays down that the duty of the Brāhmaṇa is to study and to teach, to sacrifice, and to give and receive gifts; the kṣatriya must protect the people, sacrifice and study; the vaiśya also sacrifices and studies, but his chief function is to breed cattle, to till the earth, to pursue trade and to lend money; the śūdra's duty is only to serve the three higher classes . . . for each man there was a place in society and a function to fulfil, with its own duties and rights. (Basham 1971: 139)

Note again that there is no mention of any idea that a person performing any specific function must be born into a particular group. Yet there is a common idea that people who belong to a particular *jāti* must automatically have a corresponding *varṇa* or belong to the residual category of Untouchables who are not mentioned in the Vedic schema. Unfortunately reality is not so simple.

There is a great deal of dispute about which *varṇa* a particular *jāti* should be associated with because everyone wants to be linked with the most noble lineages possible, and to dissociate themselves from anyone who might threaten their status. Thus, from one perspective, someone may say: "All those people are landowners and come from the Rājput *jāti*; their *varṇa* is *kṣatriya*." Yet some of the people referred to may not go along with this. They may say: "it is true that other people consider those people over there as Rājputs like us, but in fact they come from different lineages and are not nobles like us. Our *varṇa* is *kṣatriya*, but theirs is *śūdra* and we would never marry them" (see especially Parry 1979). Similarly one group of priests may say that they are the priests of the former kings and nobility and that this is made clear by the name of their *jāti* (e.g. Rājopādhyāya in the Kathmandu Valley, Nepal). They might then claim that their *varṇa* is *brāhmaṇa* but distinguish themselves from other people in the community who call themselves Brāhmaṇas but who perform rituals for "low caste" households. They might insist that they would never marry with this other group of *soi-disant* Brāhmaṇas and might insist that the latter are "really" *śūdra*. Considering yet another group of people who also call themselves Brāhmaṇas, they might point out that the ritual role of this other group is restricted to the performance of funeral rites and that they, the "real" Brāhmaṇas, consider them to have a very low status, indeed to be "in fact" kinds of Untouchables.[7]

These kinds of invidious distinctions are part and parcel of how caste works. Contrary to the impression given by some earlier commentators that caste distinctions were rigid and universally agreed upon, others have always realized that there is a great deal of dispute about status:

> By organization and propaganda a caste can change its name and in the course of time get a new one accepted, and by altering its canons of behaviour in the matter of diet and marriage can increase the estimation in which it is held . . . [A number] who claimed to be some special sort of Kshatriya or Vaishya at the 1921 census claimed to be some peculiar kind of Brahman in 1931. (Hutton 1963 [1946]: 98, 113)

Both *varṇa* ascription and *jāti* ascription are subject to claim and counter-claim, though there is a kind of obvious upper limit in that the more kingly a lineage can present itself, the less will its claims to *kṣatriya* status be open to contest. Similarly, the more that a lineage can present itself as the domestic priests of kings and nobility, the less will its claims to *brāhmaṇa* status be disputed. One should not, however, assume that because certain people *claim* to be of *kṣatriya* or *brāhmaṇa* status, that other people accept this claim. And one should not assume that there is an automatic correspondence between *varṇa* and *jāti* any more that one should assume there is any inherent correspondence between English people called "Smith" and people who are smiths by occupation.

Readers of this book who wish to approach the problem of caste from the perspective of Hindu religious beliefs may be surprised that I have not referred to either of two indigenous Indian concepts: *karma* and *dharma*. Clearly this results from my comparative approach which seeks to explain the institution of caste in sociological terms rather than in terms of a regional ideology. Nevertheless, it *is* sometimes said that Hindus are fatalistic and accept their caste status because it is ordained by their *karma*, i.e. their destiny. No doubt this is sometimes true; but equally, Hindus rebel against their lot just as frequently as any other people. The idea that all Hindus meekly accept their caste position runs contrary to a mass of evidence. In modern times the attempts by millions of Untouchables to redefine themselves, whether as of Śūdra status, or as Christians or Buddhists (Isaacs 1964, Juergensmeyer 1982), provide perhaps the most striking instances of rebellion against the idea that one's fate is written in the stars.

But there are many other illustrations of refusing to accept the position one was born into which do not derive from modern conditions. The institution of hypergamy in north India, which is widespread among landowning castes, is a centuries-old competitive marriage strategy the purpose of which is to render one's caste status as noble as possible by allying oneself to the most aristocratic families who will accept one's overtures, and distancing oneself from those among one's kin and caste fellows who might compromise one's status. Other common examples of refusing to accept one's place include the employment of genealogists to "prove" that one's family has a glorious pedigree (Shah and Shroff 1958), name changing in order to make it appear that one "really" belongs to a higher caste (Rosser 1966), and moving to another locality in order to assume a new identity (Caplan 1975).

The question of *dharma* is more complicated. Many of the problems which Western interpretations of caste get into derive from a division between the spheres of religion and power which may be applicable to modern democratic societies, but which is meaningless in all of the complex, preindustrial, "traditional" societies where the arena of politics is always heavily ritualized. In caste-organized communities, to refer to the arena of kingship as "secular" in order to contrast it with the "religious" domain of priests is to introduce a division which cannot be sustained. If we translate *dharma* as "religion," it will be impossible to understand the character of any of the ritual mechanisms which are used to maintain caste divisions.

The word "morality" much better conveys the sense of *dharma*: the idea that all positions carry with them certain expectations. If, as I have argued, the king's exemplary centrality provides the key to the structure of caste relations, one might expect that the *dharma* of the king would be particularly onerous, and so it turns out to be:

> that brings us to the real nature of *rājadharma*, the teachers of which (all of them brahmans) regarded kingship as a practical *and* religious necessity, for they feared nothing more then chaos . . . *Rājadharma* is "the way a king should comport himself in order to be righteous." (Derrett 1976a: 606)

> The monarch is responsible for rainfall . . . The monarch is always pure lest his business be impeded. (Gonda 1966: 7, 16).

> The rāja looks after the spiritual needs of the kingdom by exercising his special priestly functions, without which fertility and security will be endangered. (Derrett 1976: 57)

> [F]ar from being simply a matter of secular power and force, the role of the king is ritually central to the life of the kingdom . . . Kings are enjoined, in the textual traditions, to give gifts if they wish to wish to enjoy sovereignty [here the work of Gonda 1965, 1966 is cited]; and to give is seen as an inherent part of the royal code-for-conduct, *rājadharma*. (Raheja 1988b: 514–15)

A second problem with conceiving of *dharma* as "religion" is that Hindus (like most other people) repeatedly contradict each other, and themselves, in relation to core values (see also Burghart 1978). There is a particular ambiguity surrounding the relations between patrons and priests because they are involved in an endless flow of inauspiciousness and this can be represented in contradictory ways. The widely reported uniformity in the structure of caste relations can hardly be said to derive from adherence to a set of values in relation to priestly purity when, as we have seen, many Hindus regard all priests as contaminated by their ritual duties.

The uniformity of caste structure derives rather from a common sociological predicament which is resolved through the institutions of kingship. This is why it is perfectly possible to call oneself a Hindu and reject caste practices, but it is generally only possible to do so when one is living outsides the confines of a monarchical system – whether as a renouncer in the "traditional" world, or as a member of a more fluid, modern society.

Notes

1 A much more detailed exposition of the argument that follows can be found in Quigley (1993).
2 Deliège (1999 [1995]) provides a comprehensive exploration of writings on untouchability.
3 Levy (1990) provides an encyclopedic survey of ritual practitioners in one of the most complex examples of caste organization on the Indian sub-continent. See Quigley (1997) for an extended review of this work.
4 "In theory, the Brahmins had the most exalted status and were set up as the unattainable model of society in many respects. This is because, by hereditary occupation, they presided over the most important form of available power: that of the sacrificial ritual which was the source of temporal and spiritual well-being" (Lipner 1994: 89).
5 For further references and a more detailed examination of this, see Quigley (1993, ch. 4).
6 Yalman (1989) is particularly insightful on the connection between caste and royalty.
7 For ethnographic illustrations of Brāhmaṇas making distinctions among each other in this way, see especially Levy (1990), Parry (1980), and Fuller (1984).

References

Basham, A. L. 1971. *The Wonder that was India*. London: Fontana/Collins.

Brockington, J. L. 1981. *The Sacred Thread: Hinduism in its Continuity and Diversity*. Edinburgh: Edinburgh University Press.

Burghart, R. 1978. "Hierarchical Models of the Hindu Social System," *Man* NS 13: 519–36.

Caplan, L. 1975. *Administration and Politics in a Nepalese Town*. Oxford: Oxford University Press.

Deliège, R. 1999 [1995]. *The Untouchables of India*, trans. from the French by Nora Scott. Oxford: Berg.

Derrett, D. M. 1976. *Essays in Classical and Modern Hindu Law*. Leiden: Brill.

Dumont, L. 1980 [1966]. *Homo Hierarchicus: The Caste System and its Implications*. Chicago: University of Chicago Press.

Farquhar, J. N. 1913. *The Crown of Hinduism*. Oxford: Oxford University Press.

Fuller, C. J. 1984. *Servants of the Goddess: The Priests of a South Indian Temple*. Cambridge: Cambridge University Press.

Galey, J.-C. 1989. "Reconsidering Kingship in India: An Ethnological Perspective," *History and Anthropology* 4: 123–87; repr. in J. C. Galey, ed., *Kingship and the Kings*, Chur (Switzerland): Harwood Academic Publishers, 1990.

Geertz, C. 1980. *Negara: The Theater State in Nineteenth-Century Bali*. Princeton, NJ: Princeton University Press.

Gonda, J. 1965. *Change and Continuity in Indian Religion*. The Hague: Mouton.

——. 1966. *Ancient Indian Kingship from the Religious Point of View*. Leiden: E. J. Brill.

Guneratne, A. 2001. "Shaping the Tourist's Gaze: representing ethnic differences in a Nepali Village," *Journal of the Anthropological Institute* 7(3): 527–43.

Heesterman, J. C. 1985 [1964]. "Brahmin, Ritual and Renouncer," in *The Inner Conflict of Tradition: Essays in Indian Ritual, Kingship, and Society*. Chicago: University of Chicago Press.

Hocart, A. M. 1950 [1938]. *Caste: A Comparative Study*. London: Methuen.

——. 1970 [1936]. *Kings and Councillors: An Essay in the Comparative Anatomy of Human Society*. Chicago: Chicago University Press.

Hutton, J. H. 1963 [1946]. *Caste in India: Its Nature, Function and Origins*. Bombay: Oxford University Press.

Isaacs, H. R. 1964. *India's Ex-Untouchables*. New York: Harper & Row.

Juergensmeyer, M. 1982. *Religion as Social Vision: The Movement against Untouchability in 20th Century Punjab*. Berkeley: University of California Press.

Lévi-Strauss, C. 1963. "The Bear and the Barber," *Journal of the Royal Anthropological Institute* 93: 1–11.

——. 1966 [1962]. "Totem and Caste," ch. 4 of *The Savage Mind*. London: Weidenfeld and Nicolson.

Levy, R. with the collaboration of K. R. Rajopadhyaya. 1990. *Mesocosm: Hinduism and the Organization of a Traditional Newar City in Nepal*. Berkeley: University of California Press.

Lipner, J. 1994. *Hindus: Their Religious Beliefs and Practices*. London: Routledge.

Marriott, M. 1968. "Caste Ranking and Food Transactions: A Matrix Analysis," in M. Singer and B. S. Cohn, eds., *Structure and Change in Indian Society*. Chicago: Aldine.

Parry, J. P. 1979. *Caste and Kinship in Kangra*. London: Routledge & Kegan Paul.

——. 1980. "Ghosts, Greed and Sin: The Occupational Identity of the Benares Funeral Priests," *Man* NS 15: 88–111.

——. 1986. "*The Gift*, the Indian Gift and the 'Indian Gift,'" *Man* NS 21: 453–73.

——. 1994. *Death in Banaras*. Cambridge: Cambridge University Press.

Quigley, D. 1993. *The Interpretation of Caste*. Oxford: Clarendon Press.

——. 1997. "Kingship and 'Contrapriests,'" *International Journal of Hindu Studies* 1(3): 565–80.

Raheja, G. G. 1988a. *The Poison in the Gift: Ritual, Prestation and the Dominant Caste in a North Indian Village*. Chicago: University of Chicago Press.

——. 1988b. "India: Caste, Kingship and Dominance Reconsidered," *Annual Review of Anthropology* 17: 497–522.

Rosser, C. 1966. "Social Mobility in the Newar Caste System," in C. von Fürer-Haimendorf, ed., *Caste and Kin in Nepal, India and Ceylon*. Bombay: Asia Publishing House.

Shah, A. M. and Shroff, R. G. 1958. "The Vahivancha Barots of Gujerat: A Caste of Genealogists and Mythographers," *Journal of American Folklore* 71: 248–78, repr. in M. Singer, ed., *Traditional India: Structure and Change*. Philadelphia: American Folklore Society, 1959.

Srinivas, M. N. 1959. "The Dominant Caste in Rampura," *American Anthropologist* 61: 1–16.

Yalman, N. 1989. "On Royalty, Caste and Temples in Sri Lanka and South India," *Social Analysis* 25: 142–9.

CHAPTER 24
Modernity, Reform, and Revival

Dermot Killingley

Introduction

In the nineteenth and twentieth centuries, Hindu traditions have been understood and followed in new ways. Change was prompted by the political and cultural situation brought about by the British presence in south Asia, and by new means of communication. Challenges and opportunities came through contact with cultures which had hitherto been inaccessible or unfamiliar. Foremost among these was British culture, which was embodied, in various limited ways, by officials, teachers, missionaries, journalists, businessmen, soldiers, and others on south Asian soil. Further, British culture in all its variety surrounded those Hindus who traveled to Britain in increasing numbers through the nineteenth and twentieth centuries. Hindus looked not only to Britain but to the United States, and to France, Germany, and other European countries, through books and periodicals, and sometimes through correspondence. In 1905 some were fascinated by the victory of Japan, another Asian country, over Russia; and from 1917, some were stirred by events in what became the Soviet Union.

At the same time new facilities for communication with the past led to a concern with the literary, cultural and religious heritage of South Asia, which will be discussed below. This was also the period in which Indians acquired a common identity. Hitherto they had identified themselves as Bengalis or Tamils, as Śaivas, Jains, Muslims, and so on. To the British they were all "Asiatics" or "Natives," as contrasted with "Englishmen" or "Europeans." With the consolidation of British India as a political entity in the first half of the nineteenth century, the term "Indian," which hitherto had often meant the British in India, came to mean the indigenous inhabitants. It thus becomes appropriate for us to use the term "Indian" rather than "south Asian" when referring to this period, remembering that in terms of present boundaries it covers not only India but also Pakistan and Bangladesh. In the same period the term "Hindu," which had been first a geographical and then an ethnic label, came to be used as a religious one, and a religion called Hinduism was discovered or invented (see Gavin Flood's Introduction to this volume).

The period referred to as "modern" in which these changes took place extends, very roughly, from the end of the eighteenth century through the twentieth. Some twentieth-century developments are considered in chapters in the present volume (Prasad, Ramaswamy, Viswanathan, Smith). For our present purposes, India becomes modern when communication is facilitated by means such as printing, translation, and education, both in Indian languages and in English, forming an arena in which public debate can take place. This arena, however, was a restricted one, to which most of the population had no access; it functioned mainly in large cities, and even there it was the preserve of an elite. It follows that in the modern period some parts of India, and some classes in Indian society, were more modern than others.

The Political Framework

Most of the religious thinkers we shall mention were involved in politics, and all were aware of the great political fact of foreign rule. Much has been written about colonialism as a factor in Western (or more precisely North Atlantic) understanding of India, and in Indian self-understanding (e.g. Kopf 1969; Inden 1990). However, the use of this term, suggesting a single relationship of power and exploitation, conceals the variety of relationships that existed at different times and places between different groups of Indians on the one hand, and different British groups on the other.

In the eighteenth century the East India Company, which embodied British power in India from its establishment in 1600 to its abolition in 1858, still regarded itself as a trading company, and as deriving its political and fiscal authority from the Mughal Emperor and other indigenous powers. However, successive renewals of the Company's charter, at twenty-year intervals from 1773 to 1853, brought it increasingly under the control of Parliament until the government of British India was placed directly under the Crown in 1858.

From the mid-eighteenth to the mid-nineteenth century the Company acquired power in different territories at different times, by different means, and with different intentions. Moreover, even from the 1850s, when the political map of India reached the form which it retained, with a few changes, until 1947, about a third of the area was not ruled directly by the British, but by indigenous princes bound by treaties requiring them to accept the advice of officials who were partly diplomats and partly colonial governors. Some enclaves, again, were colonies of European powers other than Britain: Denmark, France, the Netherlands, and Portugal.

The policies of the Company's directors in London were often at odds not only with those of the British government but with those of its employees in India, who themselves were not unanimous. Most notably, while the Company traditionally held that its position required it to refrain from interference in Indian society, some of its high officials thought that reform of society was a positive duty, without which its presence in India would be unjustified. Such officials included Lord Bentinck (1774–1839), Governor-General from 1828 to 1835, who came to India imbued with the utilitarianism of Jeremy Bentham, and Sir Charles Grant (1746–1832), a member of the evangelical Clapham Sect, who believed that society could only be reformed by conversion to Christianity.

Besides the Company's employees, the British in India included independent entrepreneurs, journalists, and missionaries, all of whom were regarded with hostility by the Company. Matters of public policy were debated by members of all these groups, and by an increasing number of Indians. Debate was carried on in print and in public meetings; and these, together with formal petitions, influenced the Governor-General and his subordinates to the extent to which they were willing, or considered themselves obliged, to listen. One of the recurrent questions was whether there was, or ever could be, a truly representative public opinion in India.

New Communications

The nineteenth century saw rapid increases in communications, spreading from the three seaports in which British power was based: Bombay (Mumbai), Madras (Chennai), and Calcutta (Kolkata), the capital of British India and seat of the Governor-General until 1911. The Grand Trunk Road linking Calcutta with the upper Ganges basin was developed from 1836 onwards. The first telegraph line was laid in 1852, from Calcutta to Diamond Harbour, and the first 200 miles of railway were built between 1853 and 1856, starting at Bombay; by 1880 the railways had reached 4,300 miles (Schwartzberg 1978: 61; Bayly 1988: 198). Besides facilitating the movement of goods and people, the railways provided men from the presidency towns with employment opportunities elsewhere, which facilitated the spread of ideas: for instance, many of the branches of the Brāhmo Samāj which opened in the second half of the nineteenth century were formed by Bengali railway officials from Calcutta (Damen 1983). Developments in international communications included the opening of the Suez Canal in 1869, and a telegraph link to Britain in 1870.

The transmission of ideas was revolutionized by printing – in English, the vernacular languages and Sanskrit. Though missionaries had pioneered printing in Indian languages, starting with Tamil in 1577, there was no printing in Calcutta, even in English, until 1777 (Nair 1987: 26). English-language newspapers soon followed, in Bombay and Madras as well as Calcutta. Vernacular newspapers began in Bengali in 1818, followed by Gujarati in 1822 and Marathi in 1832 (Schwartzberg 1978: 105).

Another important development was in communication with the past. The study of the ancient Sanskrit literature of India had been carried on for centuries by pandits for whom it was a family tradition, but the patronage on which they depended declined in the eighteenth century. The British presence brought new forms of patronage, and a new kind of scholar: the European Indologist, who drew on the work of pandits and depended on their assistance, but interpreted the tradition through Western forms of thought. At first there were no professional Indologists: the only establishment for them at the beginning of the nineteenth century was Fort William College, a training college for the East India Company's British recruits which lasted only from 1801 to 1854 (Das 1978). On the other hand, amateur Indology flourished, though it was rarely officially rewarded except for work on dharma, which was considered to have a direct application in the courts (Kejariwal 1988: 226f.). Pandits found new forms of employment at Fort William College, at missionary establishments, as teachers and translators to individuals, and in the law courts, where they were consulted on questions of Hindu dharma.

An unintended consequence of the introduction of a judicial system on the English model in 1773 was the appointment of Sir William Jones (1746–94) as a judge. He came to Calcutta in 1783, imbued with Enlightenment ideas about Indian culture, and eager to see it at first hand. He had drawn up a list of research topics during his voyage out (Mukherjee 1968: 74), and in January 1784, within four months of his arrival, he founded the Asiatic Society of Bengal, devoted to historical and literary research on India. The society had no Indian members till 1829 – not as a matter of policy, but because none applied (Kejariwal 1988: 152f.). However, the kind of research which it encouraged brought British amateur scholars into collaboration with Indian scholars. Similar collaboration was fostered by the employment of pandits in various educational institutions, and by missionaries.

For Hindus, such study led to a new view of the past. Ideas which had hitherto been the preserve of pandits trained in particular traditions of thought, could now be studied through printed editions, translations, and historical accounts. Most notably, Buddhism came to be part of the world of the Hindu intellectual: not as a system of errors to be refuted, as it appears in Sanskrit texts, but as a towering achievement of ancient Indian thought, and as a historical reality whose monuments still stood on Indian soil. Even if it was viewed as having been superseded by later developments such as Vedānta or bhakti, Buddhism was remembered as India's spiritual gift to Asia.

Challenges

These developments in communication opened Hindu practices and ideas to criticism from the outside. Such criticism had come before, of course, from Muslims; and we must not forget the bhakti traditions with their often trenchant critiques of particular social and ritual practices. But the new conceptualization of Hinduism meant that the hostile accounts of image-worship, the status of women, or Advaita Vedānta, for instance, which were frequent in the nineteenth century, were taken as attacks on Hinduism itself, which had to be defended against them either by justifying the beliefs and practices in question, or by repudiating them as aberrations from the true Hinduism, or as misrepresentations on the part of its opponents. Moreover, the dominance of Enlightenment ideas in the arena of public debate, together with widely held assumptions of Christian and British superiority, meant that the resulting body of Hindu apologetic was presented in terms of Western ideas of reason and morality which were assumed to be common to all civilized people.

Eighteenth-century Western writers – for whom, it should be remembered, there was no such word as "Hinduism" – had often believed that the Hindus possessed an ancient wisdom of immense value, even if its contemporary heirs did not fully understand it. Brahmins were idealized as wise law-givers who gave up all claim to political power: an ancient embodiment of the separation of the legislative and judicial departments of government from the executive. Hindu religious beliefs were upheld as supremely rational and moral; Sir William Jones, for instance, wrote in a letter of 1787:

> I am no Hindu but I hold the doctrine of the Hindus concerning the future state to be incomparably more rational, more pious and more likely to deter men from vice than the horrid opinions inculcated by the Christians on punishment without end. (Mukherjee 1968: 119)

This liberal view was opposed by an evangelical view which is expressed in an extreme form by the pioneer Scots Presbyterian missionary in India, Alexander Duff (1806–78):

> Of all the systems of false religion ever fabricated by the perverse ingenuity of fallen man, Hinduism is surely the most stupendous. (Majumdar 1965: 155)

Missionaries were banned from the East India Company's territories until 1813, when evangelical pressure in Parliament forced a change. However, the Baptist Missionary Society, founded in 1792, had a base in the Danish colony of Serampore, near Calcutta, from 1800, and other missionary societies soon followed. A view of Hinduism as evil helped to raise funds for the societies in Britain; it also followed from an extreme Protestant interpretation of the doctrine of the Fall, in which all religion outside the Christian revelation is a product of human endeavor, and therefore inherently sinful.

The evangelical view of Hindu degeneracy was partly matched by the utilitarian one. This found an influential advocate in one of the foremost Utilitarians, James Mill, whose *History of British India*, first published in 1817, included a condemnation of Hindu culture. But whereas evangelicals considered that Hindu society could only be reformed through conversion to Christianity, Utilitarians believed that it was the duty of governments to reform society through education and legislation. In practice the two groups, both of which had followers among the Company's officials (including Bentinck and Grant, already mentioned), often worked together. The missionaries put much of their effort into secular education, believing that the enlightened mind would naturally gravitate to Christianity (Laird 1972). They also supported campaigns for legislation in social matters. Most notably, the Baptist missionary William Carey was one of the foremost advocates of legislation banning *sahamaraṇa*, the burning of wives on the funeral pyres of their husbands, and his arguments, together with those of the Hindu pandit Mṛtyuñjay Vidyālaṃkār, the Hindu reformer Rammohun Roy, and numerous officials, led the utilitarian Governor-General Lord Bentinck to introduce such legislation in 1829. (The woman who so burns herself, in principle voluntarily, is not regarded as a widow in the terminology of dharma. By accompanying her husband into the other world, she becomes a *satī*, meaning a true or good woman. The term *satī*, often in the older spelling *suttee*, was applied in English to the practice as well as the person; the Sanskrit term is *sahamaraṇa* "death together.")

Thus groups which differed widely in their credal foundations could cooperate on issues of social reform. A practice such as *sahamaraṇa* could appear to an evangelical as evidence of the Hindus' need of the gospel, to a utilitarian as calling for punitive legislation, and to a pandit as calling for a more accurate interpretation of the Śāstras, while to Rammohun it showed the evil effects of idolatry. Social reform became a topic for debate throughout the nineteenth century; its targets ranged from the fate of wives on the death of their husbands, to the proper form of dress for women. The agenda of social reform was set by an interaction between the actual state of Hindu society and the various ideologies of the reformers. It therefore changed in the course of its history, as we shall see. The movements which are loosely called orthodox or conservative arose as conscious responses to particular reform movements: the first such movement, the Dharma Sabhā in Calcutta, was formed to oppose legislation prohibiting *sahamaraṇa*, while the Bhārat Dharm Mahā Maṇḍal ("great society for Indian dharma") was formed in the Panjab in 1887 to defend image-worship and the position of Brahmans against the Ārya Samāj (Jones 1976: 109–11). Orthodoxy or conservatism, like reform, was a construct formed in a historical context.

Early Nineteenth-century Calcutta

The new influences first took effect in Calcutta, the capital. The British presence had encouraged the growth of a class known as *bhadralok* (literally "good people"), who gained their wealth from new opportunities for employment and commerce, and came to dominate education and the professions. The ethnically diverse population of Calcutta included incomers from many parts of India and beyond, outnumbering and marginalizing its indigenous population (Sinha 1978; Killingley 1997); the *bhadralok*, who were equally incomers, were Bengali Hindus of high caste. Besides Brahmans, they comprised Vaidyas, traditionally physicians, who rank themselves next to Brahmans, and Kāyasthas, traditionally clerks, who claim Kṣatriya origin (Killingley 1991: 16). Being highly conscious of their caste status, and sensitive to accusations of having forfeited it by taking up new occupations and consorting with foreigners, many of the *bhadralok* were meticulous about ritual purity, and lavish over rituals and patronage of Brahmans. Many of them also eagerly took up the opportunities for communication represented by printing, the use of English, the growing education system, and a new fashion for forming societies.

One such society was formed by Rammohun Roy (1772?–1833; the name is sometimes spelled Ram Mohan Roy or Ray), the first notable Hindu to involve himself in the new forms of communication. He founded newspapers in Bengali and in Persian (which was a language of culture for Hindus as well as Muslims). He published books in Bengali and English which attracted favorable notice overseas and controversy at home, and he corresponded with writers in Britain and the United States.

Rammohun's interests covered political and legal matters, education, and religion. He believed that each religious tradition had a core of truth consisting of belief in God and a humanitarian morality, but that each tradition had overlaid this core with unnecessary or even pernicious doctrines and rules of practice. In Hinduism – he was probably the first Hindu to use the word, in 1816 – one of his targets was "idol-worship – the source of prejudice and superstition, and of the total destruction of moral principle" (Roy 1906: 21). Another was the elaboration of ritual, which he claimed was promoted by Brahmans for their own profit. He claimed, however, that the rational worship of one formless God, without the use of images or rituals, was authorized by the Upaniṣads. It was thus quite possible to reject image-worship and other rituals and yet remain a Hindu, because "the doctrines of the unity of God are real Hinduism, as that religion was practised by our ancestors, and as it is well known at the present day to many learned Brahmins" (Roy 1906: 90).

To promote this "real Hinduism," Rammohun published Bengali and English translations of some Upaniṣads, and the *Vedānta-Sūtra* or *Brahma-Sūtra* (see Part II in this volume), following Śaṅkara's commentaries in the main, but departing from them at crucial points (Killingley 1993: 95–9). He also published controversial tracts in which he supported his views with quotations not only from the Upaniṣads and *Vedānta-Sūtra* but from the Purāṇas, Tantras, and other Sanskrit texts. From 1815 to 1830, when he lived in Calcutta and wrote most of his publications, he led a society which was at first known as the Ātmīya Sabhā ("friendly society"); in 1828 it was given a more formal shape as the Brāhmo Sabhā or Brāhmo Samāj. *Brāhmo* is an English spelling of the Bengali word *brāhmya* or *brāhma* (these two spellings are pronounced alike), meaning literally "belonging to Brahman," this being Rammohun's preferred name for God. Members of the Samāj often translated *brāhma* as "theist," and called the Brāhmo Samāj the Theistic Society. From Rammohun's time the Brāhmos had links with the Unitarian movement in Christianity, which denies the doctrine of the Trinity (Lavan 1977; Kopf 1979). Rammohun's followers were also known as Vedāntīs or Vedāntists (Killingley 1993: 103), since he based his teachings on Advaita Vedānta, often called simply Vedānta.

Rammohun attacked not only Hindu beliefs and rituals but the moral evils that he believed resulted from them. Besides *sahamaraṇa*, these included polygyny, infanticide, the placing of the dying in the Ganges, and caste discrimination. Other societies had other aims. The Dharma Sabhā, already mentioned, was formed in 1830 to oppose legislation against *sahamaraṇa*, and any other interference with Hindu practice. One of its founders, Rādhākānta Deb (1783–1867), was at the same time active in promoting some of the same causes as Rammohun, particularly education, including the education of girls; another, its secretary Bhavāṇīcaraṇ Banerjee, had edited a Bengali newspaper founded by Rammohun. The Brāhmo Samāj and the Dharma Sabhā, like other societies in nineteenth-century India, cannot be understood in terms of a simple opposition of reform and reaction; each of them was negotiating a way of being Hindu in the modern situation.

Opposed to both was "Young Bengal," a name which embraces many societies of young men, some still in their teens, which met in the 1830s and 1840s to put Indian society to rights in the light of utilitarian and other rationalistic ideas. Some of these men openly renounced Hinduism, and flouted its rules of purity. Such attitudes flourished especially among the pupils of the young Eurasian teacher and poet Henry Derozio (1809–31), who was dismissed from the Hindu College, the leading English-medium school in Calcutta, on a charge of corrupting Hindu youth and teaching atheism. One such pupil, Krishna Mohan Banerjea, was converted by Alexander Duff into the Presbyterian church in 1832 but was later ordained as an Anglican priest. Others remained rebel Hindus, proclaiming their rebellion by eating beef and drinking alcohol.

The Brāhmo Samāj

In 1843 the Brāhmo Samāj was reorganized by Debendranāth Tagore (1817–1905) around a "Brāhmo Covenant" in which members undertook to worship one God and to renounce idolatry. Debendranāth's idea of God was influenced by his English education at the Hindu College, and he was sensitive to Western-inspired critiques of Hinduism. One such critique appeared in 1845 in the *Calcutta Review*, edited at that time by Duff, under the title "Vedāntism; – what is it," professing a utilitarian standpoint but clearly based on evangelical theology. It accuses Rammohun of whitewashing Vedānta (meaning Advaita Vedānta, as was usual at the time), and denounces it as a form of pantheism which lacks an idea of God's love, arrogantly identifies the self with God, denies the reality of the world, leaving no lasting value to moral action, and offers virtual annihilation as the final goal. This critique provoked debate within the Samāj, and eventually Debendranāth distanced himself from Vedānta and sought a theology grounded in the Vedas which was not liable to these accusations.

Here he found insuperable difficulties. In the modern situation Vedic texts were becoming accessible, even to non-Hindus, through printed editions, translations, or descriptions; and it was becoming apparent that they spoke of many gods and of elaborate rituals for their worship. Already in 1833 Krishna Mohan Banerjea had attacked Rammohun's Vedānta, albeit using very imperfect knowledge, partly on the grounds that it was incompatible with the actual Vedas (Banerjea 1833). In the 1840s Duff took up the same argument, driving a wedge between Debendranāth, who wanted to believe in the literal truth of the Vedas, and his rationalistic associate Akshoy Kumar Datta. In 1850 Debendranāth reluctantly abandoned the Vedas as his authority; he soon abandoned textual authority altogether, in favor of "the pure heart, filled with the light of intuitive knowledge" (Tagore 1916: 161; Rambachan 1994).

The Brāhmo Samāj took a new direction when Keshub Chunder Sen (1838–84) joined in 1858. Debendranāth was a Brahman, whose father Dwarkanath Tagore was one of the wealthiest of the *bhadralok*; Keshub was a Vaidya who earned his living in a bank. Nevertheless, Debendranāth became like a father to Keshub, and in 1862 made him an *ācārya* of the Samāj. *Ācārya*, a Sanskrit word meaning "teacher," was the term used for the Brahmans who expounded Sanskrit texts and led worship in the Samāj. The abandonment of Sanskrit texts as authorities, and the appointment of Keshub, a non-Brahman, changed the nature of the *acaryas*; they were referred to in English as "ministers," and Keshub wore a black gown like a British nonconformist minister. He also insisted that, whether Brahmans or not, they should not wear the sacred thread which was the mark of Brahman status.

The group of younger Brāhmos who gathered round Keshub wished to abolish caste distinctions; they promoted intercaste marriage, interdining and the abandonment of the sacred thread. They tended to identify reform with the adoption of Western ways of thinking and behavior; and while they saw Brāhmoism as a bulwark against Christianity, they emulated the missionaries' self-denying zeal for their faith, opening branches of the Samāj outside Calcutta, and refuges for young men and women who had broken with their families over religious practice. They also wished the Samāj to be directed by a representative body rather than an unelected leader. All these points separated Keshub from Debendranāth, who envisaged a movement rooted in Hindu tradition and fitting into *bhadralok* society rather than separating itself from it. In 1866, after an incident in which Debendranāth allowed Brahman *ācāryas* to wear the sacred thread, the Samāj split, and the majority joined Keshub in a new organization, the Brāhmo Samāj of India. Tagore's party, consisting mainly of his relatives and friends, became known as the Ādi ("original") Brāhmo Samāj.

Keshub went on lecture tours, demonstrating his commanding rhetoric, his devotional enthusiasm, and the power of steam travel and the English language to spread ideas throughout India and beyond; in 1870 he visited England. His message was that God was to be found not in "the dry wells of ancient traditions and outward symbols" but in "the deep fountain of divine revelation" (Scott 1979: 75); and revelation could only be apprehended by spiritually sensitive persons. He was such a person; so too were his hearers, if they would open themselves to God's inspiration as he exhorted them to do. This spiritual awakening would be the key to social reform. His success depended on his audiences' knowledge of English, and on other forms of knowledge which came with an English education, enabling them to recognize his references to the Bible, English literature, European history and contemporary philosophers. Keshub used ideas from Christian theology, including Jesus himself, for whom he expressed a fervent devotion. Jesus, he pointed out, was an Asiatic, and Asiatics were better able than Europeans to understand him (Scott 1979: 64). This argument, which exploited the English habit of referring to Indians as Asiatics, gratified nationalistic sentiment by taking Jesus out of the hands of the missionaries and placing him in those of Hindus.

Keshub's emphasis on individual intuition of God made him indifferent to religious traditions; it is impossible to identify him as a Hindu or a Christian, because he interpreted doctrines such as the atonement or *avatāra* in his own way. This opened him to the charge of arbitrariness, and some of his followers objected to his acceptance of doctrines and practices which Brāhmos had rejected as idolatrous; around 1875 he became an admirer of the uncouth sage Ramakṛṣṇa (1836–86), who despised Brāhmoism and social reform. As Keshub's interest in Hindu traditions increased, his zeal for social reform seemed to wane, and like Debendranāth he was judged autocratic.

The incident which brought these concerns together was the marriage of Keshub's daughter in 1878 to the crown prince of Cooch Behar, a state under indirect British rule. She was 13 and the prince 15 (Borthwick 1977: 180); the ritual included elements which Brāhmos condemned as idolatrous, and polygyny was traditional in the family. The intention of the British officials who arranged the marriage was to bring modernity into an underdeveloped state (Borthwick 1977: 174–8), and this was successful (Kopf 1979: 328f.); but to many Brāhmos it was a betrayal of their struggle against child marriage and idolatry, and showed an arrogant disregard of their views. Rejecting Keshub's leadership, they formed a more democratic organization, the Sādhāraṇ ("general") Brāhmo Samāj, in 1878. In 1881, Keshub formed his remaining followers into the Church of the New Dispensation, which was more interested in worship and spiritual experience than in social reform.

The example and missionary effort of the Brāhmo Samāj, particularly Keshub's tours, led to similar societies being formed elsewhere. The most influential was the Prārthanā Samāj ("prayer society") in Bombay. The situation in Bombay Presidency was very different from that in Bengal: British power was established later and more quickly, from 1800 to 1818, and followed a more concerted policy. High positions were given to Indians, most of whom were of the Chitpavan Brahman caste which had run the Maratha empire which the British had conquered. They and other Hindus took up English and Western learning eagerly, while continuing also to write in Marathi. The Prārthanā Samāj, avoiding the problems over tradition and authority which split the Brāhmo Samāj, showed its continuity with the past by using the Marathi poems of Tukārām and other bhakti saints in its worship.

Social Reform

One of the points which distinguished the Brāhmo Samāj of India from the Ādi Brāhmo Samāj, and in turn distinguished the Sādhāraṇ Brāhmo Samāj from the Church of the New Dispensation, was zeal for social reform. The main areas of concern were caste and the position of women; each of these involved several issues.

Discussion of caste in the twentieth century has centered on the privileges of higher castes, the oppression of lower castes, and the economic disparities between them. Many nineteenth-century discussions dwelt more on the divisions among the higher castes, and restrictions on their conduct. In the Brāhmo Samāj, the movements to discard the sacred thread, to allow intercaste marriage, and to encourage interdining were aimed not so much against caste privilege as against the division within the *bhadralok* between Brahmans, Vaidyas, and Kāyasthas. Caste also meant pressure to follow rules of purity which were especially irksome to those members of the higher castes who were most affected by modernity; relaxation of such rules provided a middle way between the ostentatious observance of purity by many of the new urban class, and the ostentatious rejection of it by Young Bengal.

Use of the word *caste* can give a misleading impression that we are talking about a single phenomenon, or even a system inherent in Hindu society. It is better to think of it as a cover term for a number of phenomena which may vary from region to region, and are constantly open to change. The situation in Bengal, where elite status is shared between brahmins, Vaidyas, and Kāyasthas, is different from that in Maharashtra or Tamil Nadu, where there is a clear division between brahmins and those below them, and another between Dalits (see Quigley in this volume) and those above them. The modern situation in some ways rigidified caste identity: the use of caste titles became more widespread in the early nineteenth century, while increasing contact between communities, and the British attempt to codify Hindu law, brought matters which had been the preserve of specialists into the arena of public debate (Bayly 1999: 94, 168). In the late nineteenth and early twentieth centuries, the methods and theories of physical anthropology with which the British reinforced the boundary between Indians and themselves, and classified Indians into hereditary types with different abilities, were also used by Hindu theorists to justify caste divisions. At the same time, the increasing accessibility of the Sanskrit tradition facilitated the discussion of caste issues in terms of dharma.

Dharma literature says far less about caste than it does about varṇa, the theoretical division of society into Brahman, Kṣatriya, Vaiśya, and Śūdra. The first of these categories can be identified, in any given region, with a particular group of castes, since in Hindu society the boundary between Brahman and non-Brahman is usually clear, though not always undisputed. It is harder to identify any of the other three divisions with a group of castes, since castes which claim to be Kṣatriya or Vaiśya may be regarded by others as Śūdra (see Quigley's chapter in this volume). When writers discuss caste in terms of dharma, therefore, they do so in theoretical terms which may not be easily related to the realities of caste in the region where they live.

In south India, the most fiercely contested intercaste issue was between the Dalits and the rest. The boundaries were clearly marked, socially, ritually, and spatially: members of Dalit castes had to keep a certain distance from others, and not walk on the same road. When economic advancement encouraged a low-caste group to transgress these boundaries, fighting broke out; another possible outcome was a mass religious movement. Such movements include the conversion to Christianity of many of the Nadar caste, first by Jesuits in 1680, and later by Anglicans from 1784 onwards (Jones 1989: 156–60). The traditional occupation of the Nadars is to tap juice from palmyra palms and ferment it into a liquor known as toddy; their economic dependence on this disreputable trade, and their personal dependence on toddy, justify their low status in the eyes of higher castes, while the Christian Nadars set great importance on abstinence. A caste of similar status and occupation, the Izhavas of Kerala, was transformed by a movement initiated by one of its members, Nārāyaṇa Guru (1854–1928). This too sought independence from toddy, but it was also a Sanskritizing movement, using Advaita Vedānta to show that caste is not essential to a person (Jones 1989: 179–82, 203–7; Samuel 1977).

The most radical attack on caste using arguments from the Sanskrit tradition was made by Dayānanda Sarasvatī (1825–83). Dayānanda was a Brahman from Kathiawar in Gujarat, but spent much of his life wandering as a saṃnyāsin over north India; the Ārya Samāj, which he founded in 1875, had its greatest success in the Panjab, a region where Brahman authority was weak. Though he learned from pandits, knew no English, and appealed to the Veda as his authority, he was influenced by modern ideas, especially after a visit to Calcutta in 1872 (Jordens 1978: 75–98). He denounced the worship of images and elaborate rituals, and taught the worship of one God through *homa*, the Vedic offering of ghi and plant products in a fire. He aimed to restore the practices of the ancient Āryans (hence the name of his society); people should therefore be divided not into hundreds of castes but into the four varṇas known in the Veda. Moreover, membership of the varṇas should not be hereditary, but should be decided by public examination at the age of 16 for girls and 25 for boys (Sarasvatī 1972: 87). On intermarriage and interdining, Dayānanda was conservative: they should be prohibited between the true, nonhereditary varṇas (Killingley 1991: 27f.). His proposals have never been put into practice, but the idea of four varṇas, based on merit and not birth, has become generally accepted in modern Hindu discourse (Killingley 1991: 30f.).

Reform of the position of women again involved several issues. After *sahamaraṇa* was made illegal, attention focused on the situation of widows. According to the dharma books widowers can remarry, but a woman can only be one man's wife; and since girls could be married at five or even younger, they could become widows at any age. A widow, being neither an actual nor a potential wife, was a person without status, an unwanted burden on her marital family. The voice which was heard most clearly on this subject was that of Īśvarcandra Vidyāsāgar

(1820–91), a paṇḍit who was a close associate of Debendranāth Tagore. Like Rammohun's against *sahamaraṇa*, his arguments were both textual and humanitarian; the outcome was the Widow Remarriage Act of 1856. Īśvarcandra was also among those who attacked polygyny, which was widely practiced by Brahmans in Bengal; but this attack did not lead to legislation.

Another issue was child marriage, in particular the early marriage of girls. This was common among upper castes in many parts of India, and was opposed by the Brāhmo Samāj, the Prārthanā Samāj, Dayānanda, Īśvarcandra, and others. In 1860 the first relevant legislation, affecting not marriage but consummation, set the age of consent for girls at ten. Renewed controversy, heightened by the death of a girl of eleven in Calcutta in 1890, led to the raising of the age to 12 in 1891. The law was controversial but ineffective, as was the Child Marriage Restraint Act of 1929, which set the ages of marriage at 14 for brides and 18 for bridegrooms (Forbes 1996: 83–90).

While the government was wary of prohibiting any Hindu custom, it was more ready to pass permissive laws if there was demand for them, as shown by the Widow Remarriage Act. Another example is the Marriage Act of 1872. This was passed in response to demands from the Brāhmo Samāj for a legally recognized form of marriage which disregarded caste, was monogamous and did not involve idolatry; the bride had to be at least 14 and the bridegroom 18. To avoid attempting to define Brāhmos as a community, the legislators required the participants to declare that they were not Hindus – nor Buddhists, Christians, Jains, Muslims, or Parsis (Kopf 1979: 103–5). This law was part of the background to the Cooch Behar marriage (p. 518 above): although the marriage did not contravene it, since the Act did not apply in a princely state, it betrayed the principles underlying it.

These movements to improve the condition of women were the work of men, and treated women as passive rather than active. They were partly prompted by the view of James Mill and others that ill-treatment of women indicated a low degree of civilization (Forbes 1996: 13). While the male reformers had genuine regard for women as persons, they also thought of them in terms of their procreative and nurturing roles: child marriage was condemned as pernicious to the health of (male) offspring. Women's education could be a way of furthering the concerns of men, whose efforts at reform were hampered by the conservatism of their wives and mothers. A Bengali wrote in 1848:

> An educated native who is even at the head of his family is connected with poojah [*pūjā*, worship of images] which he under the existing state of Society cannot remedy and thinks it expedient for preserving domestic happiness to perpetuate it so long as education is denied to our females. (Palit 1972: 67)

It was not until the end of the nineteenth century that women themselves became public champions of reform (Forbes 1996).

There was also a caste dimension to gender issues which the reformers tended to ignore. As the Bengali preacher Swāmi Vivekānanda (1863–1902) put it,

> All that you mean by your social reform is either widow remarriage, or female emancipation, or something of that sort . . . And again these are directed within the confines of a few of the castes only. (Vivekānanda 1972–8: 5, 333).

The issue of widow remarriage did not affect the lower castes, among whom widows traditionally remarried; while interdining and intercaste marriage, as well as female education, were mainly concerns of the *bhadralok*. Vivekānanda considered that effective social reform could only be built on a spiritual basis of Advaita Vedānta. The identity of the self and Brahman, he said (echoing Paul Deussen, the German interpreter of Advaita), was "the basic metaphysical truth underlying all ethical codes" (Vivekānanda 1972–8: 1, 385; cf. Hacker 1995: 292–8; Killingley 1998: 145–9). Hindus did not need alien moral norms.

Re-presenting the Past

We have seen how Rammohun and Īśvarcandra questioned prevailing customs by reference to ancient Sanskrit texts. In 1891, during the age of consent controversy, M. G. Ranade (1842–1901) and R. G. Bhandarkar (1837–1925), both members of the Prārthanā Samāj, opposed the early marriage of girls by showing how the age prescribed for a girl's marriage had been progressively lowered in the course of history (Ranade 1902: 26–52; Bhandarkar 1928: 538–83). We have also seen how Dayānanda used texts to argue that the ancient Āryans practiced nonhereditary varṇa. Those who opposed reform also appealed to the past; but as Ranade (1902: 170) put it, "When we are asked to revive our old institutions and customs, people seem to me to be very much at sea as to what it is they seek to revive." Ranade and others used a consciously selective approach to the past, guided by "the voice of God in us" (Ranade 1902: 174). Bhandarkar saw the past as a progressive revelation to which the Vedic sages, Buddhism, the Gītā, and the bhakti tradition had each contributed (Bhandarkar 1928: 615f.).

Another Chitpavan Brahman, B. G. Tilak, used textual study, astronomy, and geology to argue that the Vedas were composed in 4,000 or even 8,000 BCE (Wolpert 1962). His reading of history, like Dayānanda's, pointed to the Vedas as records of an ancient and divinely ordained culture. Unlike him, however, he presented the Brahmans as the heirs and guardians of that culture. Tilak also extolled the seventeenth-century Maratha king Śivājī as a Kṣatriya protector and patron of the Brahmans, and hinted that resistance to British rule was a duty which Hindus owed to his memory.

A very different history of Brahman and Kṣatriya was presented by Jotirao Phooley (or Phule, 1827–90), a member of the non-Brahman Maratha peasantry. In Phule's narrative the Brahmans had invaded India, seized the land from its rightful owners the kṣatriyas, and attempted to destroy them as recorded in the myth of Paraśurāma (see Matchett's chapter 6 above). They enslaved the survivors by inventing the caste system, classifying them as Śūdras. Śivājī was the champion of the indigenous non-Brahman against the alien Brahman, and his role as protector was now taken by the British. Phule thus combined a common mythical motif in which low castes claim to be descended from Kṣatriyas who were cheated of their status, with the Indologists' narrative of an Āryan invasion (O'Hanlon 1985: 141–51). The view of the Brahman as an alien oppressor was taken up and elaborated by the Tamil anti-Brahman movement in the twentieth century, which was able to point to a 2,000-year-old Tamil literature independent of Sanskrit.

Religious and Secular

In the course of the modern period, movements to reform Hindu society became more varied, and leaders emerged among oppressed groups as well as elites. Yet there was general agreement that Hindu society must have roots in the past, and it must have a religious basis. The emphasis on the past refuted both those who thought reform could only come from the West, and those who thought it was precluded by an unchanging dharma. The emphasis on religion was natural when so much criticism of Hindu society attributed its evils to religion, while most of the ancient literature which became accessible was religious, or used religious motifs. Keshub, Vivekānanda, Rādhākrishnan and others promoted the idea that Indian culture was essentially spiritual, in contrast to the materialism of the West (King 1985).

There are exceptions to this religious approach to reform. E. V. Ramaswamy Naicker (1879–1973), leader of the Tamil anti-Brahman movement, denounced belief in God along with Brahmans and their texts and rituals; however, others in the movement discarded these while retaining God. Apart from Ramaswamy and some extreme nineteenth-century Utilitarians, secular programs have come mainly from twentieth-century Marxists, and it is notable that many of these were Brahmans: M. N. Roy, D. D. Kosambi, E. M. S. Namboodiripad. The Marxists, like others, used the past as an arena for the ideological contest; one of their methods was to reclaim ancient Indian materialism, which they believed had been deliberately forgotten in favor of a false picture of Indian spirituality (e.g. Chattopadhyaya 1968). Another Brahman secularist was Jawaharlal Nehru, whose book *The Discovery of India* is a personal reflection on the past and what it can say to the future; he too extols ancient Indian materialism, but also the *Bhagavad-Gītā*, Buddhism, and even Śaṅkara. Revival is not opposed to reform; it is the idiom in which it speaks.

References

Ahmed, A. F. Salahuddin. 1976. *Social Ideas and Social Change in Bengal: 1818–1835*. 2nd ed. Calcutta: RDDHI (1st ed. Leiden: Brill, 1965).

Anon. 1845. "Vedāntism; – What Is It," *Calcutta Review* 4: 43–61.

Banerjea, Krishna Mohan. 1833. *A Review of the Moonduk Oopunishad, translated into English by Ram Mohun Roy; to which is prefixed an Essay on the important subject of religion by the Editor of the Enquirer.* Calcutta.

Bayly, C. A. 1988. *Indian Society and the Making of the British Empire.* New Cambridge History of India, II, 1. Cambridge: Cambridge University Press.

Bayly, Susan. 1999. *Caste, Society and Politics in India from the Eighteenth Century to the Modern Age.* New Cambridge History of India, IV, 3. Cambridge: Cambridge University Press.

Bhandarkar, R. G. 1928. *Collected Works of Sir R. G. Bhandarkar*, ed. N. B. Utgikar, vol. II. Poona: Bhandarkar Oriental Research Institute.

Borthwick, Meredith. 1977. *Keshub Chunder Sen: A Search for Cultural Synthesis.* Calcutta: Minerva.

Chattopadhyaya, Debiprasad. 1968. *Lokayata: Ancient Indian Materialism.* Delhi: People's Publishing House.

Damen, F. L. 1983. *Crisis and Renewal in the Brāhmo Samāj (1860–1884).* Leuven: Department Orientalistiek, Katholieke Universiteit Leuven.

Das, Sisir Kumar. 1978. *Sahibs and Munshis: An Account of the College of Fort William.* Calcutta: Orion Publications.

Forbes, Geraldine. 1996. *Women in Modern India.* New Cambridge History of India, IV, 2. Cambridge: Cambridge University Press.

Hacker, Paul. 1995. "Schopenhauer and Hindu Ethics," trans. Dermot Killingley. In *Philology and Confrontation: Paul Hacker on Traditional and Modern Vedānta.* Albany: State University of New York Press, pp. 273–318. (Original: "Schopenhauer und die Ethik des Hinduismus," *Saeculum* 4 (1961): 365–99; repr. in Paul Hacker, *Kleine Schriften*, Wiesbaden: Harrassowitz, 1978, pp. 531–64.)

Inden, Ronald. 1990. *Imagining India.* Oxford: Blackwell.

Jones, Kenneth W. 1976. *Arya Dharm: Hindu Consciousness in 19th-century Punjab.* Berkeley: University of California Press.

——. 1989. *Socio-religious Reform Movements in British India.* New Cambridge History of India, III, 1. Cambridge: Cambridge University Press.

Jordens, J. T. F. 1978. *Dayānanda Sarasvatī: His Life and Ideas.* Delhi: Oxford University Press.

Kejariwal, O. P. 1988. *The Asiatic Society of Bengal and the Discovery of India's Past: 1784–1838.* Delhi: Oxford University Press.

Killingley, Dermot. 1991. "Varṇa and Caste in Hindu Apologetic," in D. Killingley, ed., *Hindu Ritual and Society.* Newcastle upon Tyne: S. Y. Killingley, pp. 7–31.

——. 1993. *Rammohun Roy in Hindu and Christian Tradition.* Newcastle upon Tyne: Grevatt & Grevatt.

——. 1997. "Mlecchas, Yavanas and Heathens: Interacting Xenologies in Early Nineteenth-century Calcutta," in E. Franco and K. Preisendanz, eds., *Beyond Orientalism: The Work of Wilhelm Halbfass and its Impact on Indian and Cross-Cultural Studies.* Poznan Studies series. Amsterdam: Rodopi, pp. 123–40.

——. 1998. "Vivekānanda's Western Message from the East," in William Radice, ed., *Swami Vivekānanda and the Modernization of Hinduism.* Delhi: Oxford University Press, pp. 138–57.

King, Ursula. 1985. *Indian Spirituality and Western Materialism: An Image and its Function in the Reinterpretation of Modern Hinduism.* Delhi: Indian Social Institute.

Kopf, David. 1969. *British Orientalism and the Bengal Renaissance: The Dynamics of Indian Modernization 1773–1835.* Berkeley: University of California Press.

——. 1979. *The Brāhmo Samāj and the Shaping of the Modern Indian Mind.* Princeton: Princeton University Press.
Laird, M. A. 1972. *Missionaries and Education in Bengal 1793–1837.* Oxford: Clarendon Press.
Lavan, Spencer. 1977. *Unitarians and India: A Study in Encounter and Response.* Boston, MA: Beacon Press.
Majumdar, R. C., ed. 1965. *History and Culture of the Indian People*, vol. 10, pt. II. Bombay: Bharatiya Vidya Bhavan.
Mukherjee, S. N. 1968. *Sir William Jones and British Attitudes to India.* Cambridge South Asian Studies, 6. Cambridge: Cambridge University Press.
Nair, P. Thankappan. 1987. *A History of the Calcutta Press: The Beginnings.* Calcutta: Firma KLM.
O'Hanlon, Rosalind. 1985. *Caste, Conflict and Ideology: Mahatma Jotirao Phule and Low-caste Protest in Nineteenth-Century Western India.* Cambridge: Cambridge University Press.
Palit, Chittabrata. 1972. "The Young Bengal: A Self-Estimate," in R. C. Majumdar et al., eds., *Renascent Bengal (1817–1857).* The Asiatic Society Seminar Series, 1. Calcutta: The Asiatic Society.
Rambachan, Anantanand. 1994. "Redefining the Authority of Scripture: The Rejection of Vedic Authority by the Brāhmo Samāj," in Laurie L. Patton, ed., *Authority, Anxiety and Canon: Essays in Vedic Interpretation.* Albany, NY: State University of New York Press, pp. 253–79.
Ranade, Mahadeva Govind. 1902. *Religious and Social Reform: A Collection of Essays and Speeches*, ed. M. B. Kolasker. Bombay: Gopal Narayen.
Roy, Rammohun. 1906. *The English Works of Raja Rammohun Roy with an English Translation of "Tufatul Muwahhidin,"* eds. Jogendra Chunder Ghose and Eshan Chunder Bose. Allahabad: Panini Office. (Repr. New York: AMS Press, 1978.)
Samuel, V. Thomas. 1977. *One Caste One Religion One God: A Study of Sree Narayana Guru.* Delhi: Sterling.
Saraswatī, Dayānanda. 1972. *Satyarth Prakash* ["light of truth" or "light of the true meaning"]. Trans. Durga Prasad. 3rd ed. (1st ed. 1908). Delhi: Jan Gyan Prakashan.
Schwartzberg, Joseph E., ed. 1978. *A Historical Atlas of South Asia.* Chicago: University of Chicago Press.
Scott, David C. 1979. *Keshub Chunder Sen: A Selection Edited with Introduction.* Madras: Christian Literature Society.
Sinha, Pradip. 1978. *Calcutta in Urban History.* Calcutta, Firma KLM.
Tagore, Debendranāth. 1916. *The Autobiography of Maharshi Devendranath Tagore.* Trans. Satyendranath Tagore and Indira Devi. London: Macmillan.
Vivekānanda. 1972–8. *The Complete Works of Swami Vivekānanda*, 8 vols. Calcutta: Advaita Ashrama. Cited by volume and page number.
Wolpert, Stanley A. 1962. *Tilak and Gokhale: Revolution and Reform in the Making of Modern India.* Berkeley: University of California Press.

CHAPTER 25

Contemporary Political Hinduism

C. Ram-Prasad

The very idea of "political Hinduism" raises questions generally about the nature of religion and specifically about the nature of Hinduism. To say that Hinduism has had a political role in twentieth-century India is already to say a good deal about an elusive and diffuse phenomenon. This is because many of the developments through the twentieth century that ostensibly were motivated by concerns of religion are arguably products of more general concerns about identity, ideological historiography, political power, and economic share. Few issues covered in this chapter are obviously religious in content, if by "religious" we mean anything pertaining substantively to the attainment of transcendence, or even a socio-ethic founded on commitment to transcendence. But to the extent that this book attempts to deal with all that might be considered "Hindu," this chapter focuses on developments in twentieth-century and contemporary India where politics was or has been affected by appeal to a certain reading of Hinduism. (But only a certain reading: after all, Gandhi's thought and action are incomprehensible without a consideration of their religious dimensions, but by no means can be integrated into the present topic.)

This chapter is in three parts. The first part looks at the seminal formulations of the concept of an essential Hinduness and its political implications for the nation-state of India. The second part looks at the unsuccessful history of political parties and organizations associated with the ideology of an essential Hinduness in independent India and the eventual electoral rise of the premier Hindu nationalist party to (shared) power. The last part analyzes the experience of Hindu nationalism in power and suggests that such experience says something about both Hindu nationalism and the problems of power in a democratic India.

The Formulation of "Hinduness": Its Political and Cultural Consequences

While issues of religion and culture are deeply implicated in the sociopolitical thinking of nineteenth-century India (see Dermot Killingley's chapter in this volume), a particular crystallization of Hinduism-based ideology occurred on the margins of the Indian nationalist struggle. This ideology, in brief, attempted to provide criteria for membership of a nation-state, India, through appeal to membership of a historical tradition defined, through certain putatively essential features, as the religion of "Hinduism."

The first nationwide move towards injecting a specific "Hindu" dimension into the political sphere came with the setting up of the Hindu Mahasabha (The Great Hindu Association) in 1915, which drew on existing Hindu Sabhas (associations) in different regions of British India. Initially, it was an organization within the Indian National Congress. The Congress itself was a nonsectarian, pan-national political body, and the Mahasabha was founded to press, generally, for a greater orientation towards concerns identified as important to Hindus, and specifically, for a Hindu counterweight to Muslim demands for quotas for newly created administrative and electoral positions. This lobby group later became more explicitly involved in political activity directed towards the attainment of a "Hindu nation"; for that, it required a systematic ideology, which was provided by Vinayak Damodar Savarkar.

The formulation of Hindutva

It was Savarkar who, in 1923, gave substance to the neologism "Hindutva" or Hinduness, in his book, *Hindutva: Who is a Hindu?* Unlike what the title by itself might suggest to a student of religion, the book was not about the doctrinal essence of a religion called Hinduism; it was not a contribution to that literature, so standard in later twentieth-century academia, on the definition of a religious tradition. It was the articulation of a certain form of nationalism. Savarkar argued that geography, race, and culture reveal a commonality, which he identified as "Hindutva." But the geography is not strictly territorial, being instead the ancestral homeland of a people, historically descended from a "race" called the "Aryans." Nor is race a biogenetic category, for Savarkar is willing to accept both the original intermarriage of the Aryans with older native inhabitants and the continuing absorption, through marriage and cultural adoption, of different peoples into Hinduism. So, the ultimate category for Hindutva is culture. But this culture is not, strictly speaking, religious, if by "religion" is meant a commitment to certain doctrines of transcendence. Savarkar himself does not profess religious faith, and takes religion – in the form of "Hinduism" – to be only a part of the larger "Hindu" culture; a distinction is usually maintained between Hindu religion and the larger Hindu (or even Indic) culture. In all these matters,

Savarkar is keenly aware of irreducible diversity, be it in conceptions of sacred geography, racial intermingling, or religious beliefs and practices. That is why he attempts to identify an essence, a commonality. Everything, then, comes down to understanding the essence of Hindu culture. But unfortunately, when identifying what is distinctly Hindu, he goes back to a religious concept: to be Hindu is to take India as the holy land. This is what distinguishes the Hindu from the Christian or the Muslim (although, on other counts, the possibility of Christians and Muslims being "Hindus" is granted). This is difficult to follow through, since the concept of what is holy is itself a religious one, but the religion involved derives its identity from a culture – which culture, exactly, Savarkar is attempting to essentialize in the first place.

Regardless of the intellectual coherence of his position, Savarkar articulated the idea that the nation could be construed in terms of Hinduness. Since Hindus did, as a matter of fact, exist, an appeal to their identity as the foundation of nationalism was possible even if exactly how that identity was determined in the first place was not clear.

The political consequence of this formulation lay, however, not so much in what it tried to do for Hindus as in how it used Muslims (and Christians) for its ideological ends. Arguably, it was a certain perception of Muslims and (in the form of the British) Christians that motivated the enunciation of Hindutva. Savarkar's call to Hindus to regain an ancient glory is explicitly premised on that glory having been tarnished by an invasion of and the clash with Islam (and, later, the Christianity of Western imperialism). A renascent Hindu nation (since Savarkar is convinced that there was such an original nation) must solve the problem of heterogeneity and diversity. That is to say, in order to create a Hindu state, the problems brought about by the presence of Islam and Christianity (rendered possible according to Savarkar only by the oppression of Hindus) must be solved. Such a solution might require the removal of alienness from Hindu society, but must at least involve Muslim and Christian acceptance of Hindu public culture in a nation-state. The coherence of any strategy to render India Hindu, then, requires recognizing the threat of Muslim and Christian otherness and dealing with it in a variety of uncompromising ways.

Subsequently, Savarkar led the Mahasabha, and his skills in this regard seemed likely to lead it to greater prominence. But the Congress was moving decisively into ever-wider constituencies, and by 1937, the Mahasabha was excluded from it, especially on charges of being "communal," i.e., pursuing the concerns purely of a religious community, rather than of all India. Thereafter, it had no real political role to play in the last decade of the independence movement.

The RSS and Hindu culture

Hindutva, however, gained a very different sort of organized support than the original involvement within the Indian National Congress might have suggested. Savarkar deeply influenced Keshav Baliram Hedgewar, who had learned various terrorist techniques before joining the Congress. Hedgewar left the Congress convinced of the inefficacy of Gandhi's peaceful "noncooperation" methods against British rule, and in 1925 founded a nationalist organization called the Rashtriya Swayamsevak Sangh (RSS, the Association of National[ist] Volunteers). His organizational model was the militant and ascetic sects of medieval and early modern India. But while borrowing elements from them such as shared rituals, a paradoxically ascetic engagement with worldly affairs, and tight-knit patterns of sacred leaders and dedicated initiates, Hedgewar also borrowed Western principles of organization and representation. The RSS sought to emulate what were perceived to be highly successful British (and European) forms of discipline, drill, and corporate spirit. Hedgewar's organizational skills and contacts with like-minded men from his sort of background (Maharashtrian brahmins) built up the RSS, but its ideological development came with Hedgewar's successor, Madhav Sadashiv Golwalkar.

Golwalkar provided a systematic articulation of the RSS's ideological grounds and aims in his work of 1939, *We, or Our Nationhood Defined.* Golwalkar both captured Hedgewar's working vision of the RSS and went beyond it to present a distinctive ideology. He captured the most striking aspect of RSS ideology – its concern for a nation rather than a state. Of course, this was still concern for the culture of a Hindu nation. But where Savarkar had approached culture in relation to a Hindu polity, Golwalkar approached it in relation to Hindu society. The RSS's primary aim was to foster within society those aspects of thought and conduct that would integrate and unite Hindus. Issues of state may follow, but that was not the objective of the RSS.

Like Savarkar, Golwalkar did not articulate the idea of Hinduness in terms either of territorially specific (as opposed to ancestral and sacred) geographic boundaries or of racial purity. He too sought to present what was essentially Hindu as an organic culture, which had become weak and divided. But where Savarkar's aim had been to make explicit the underlying unity of Hindus in order to create a political entity, the Hindu state (*raj*), Golwalkar claimed that the RSS would work to realise a society true to the Hindu nation (*rashtra*). In the narrow sense of involvement in the public mobilization of opinion for the purposes of affecting and attaining institutional power in a polity, the RSS was not conceived as a "political" organization. It did not involve itself in electioneering and running for office. It represented and still represents itself as a "cultural" organization, working to bring back into the functioning of society those principles that, according to it, exemplify the attitudes and values of Hinduness. (But I am not being evasive in not saying exactly what those attitudes and values are: it precisely is the conceptual problem for Hindutva ideology that it cannot list in any specific way what makes Hindus – and only they – essentially Hindus. Instead, there is the circular appeal to the beliefs and practices of a preexisting, albeit unreformed and disunited Hindu nation precisely in order to define that very Hindu nation.)

Organizationally, the RSS was successful, although its success bred its own limitations and problems. In drawing on traditional forms of organizations focused on physicality, militancy, asceticism, and sectarian membership, the RSS provided its own version of the ritually mediated Indian gymnasium, the *akhara*. At these gatherings, organized under the aegis of a more Westernized unit of control, the local branch (*shakha*), groups of men could train themselves, physically and morally, to become exemplars of "Hindu manhood," under the guidance of teachers/preachers (*pracharaks*). (The gender dimension was not systematically thought through, but rather an outgrowth of an unthinking androcentricism. As the ideological appeal of inducting women into the movement became clearer, a women's wing [the Rashtra Sevika Samithi, the National Council of (Women) Workers] was formed without much justification regarding gender.) The RSS expressed a combination of martial and spiritual values that drew from the previous few centuries of experience amongst the brahmins and other upper-caste men of Maharashtra. This cultural appeal was compounded by sociopolitical factors. The growth of the Congress was due to mass mobilization; and the involvement of and articulation of demands by other sections of Hindu society was as much a cause of unease amongst potential RSS men as was Muslim political activity. Consequently, the model developed by the founders of the RSS was attractive and recognizable amongst many groups of brahmin and other upper-caste Hindu men in and around Maharashtra.

The problem for the RSS was that it was founded with the aim of eventually transforming the whole nation while its cadres seemed to be drawn from a narrow caste and regional background. So the drive began to extend its appeal. The cultural background of its early members, however, never ceased to be influential, and the growth of the RSS was not a product of any change in its ideological character. The model of the teacher and the idea of disciplined acculturation helped widen its appeal at least to other parts of North India where young upper caste men could identify with the RSS. Not only has the RSS never been able to have appeal across castes, but it has tended to be weak in South India, outside the areas of Karnataka state on the borders of Maharashtra. Where the RSS has drawn from traditionally disadvantaged backgrounds, it has done so because of the ambition of castes and individuals to improve their social status through the emulation of the upper castes known as "Sanskritization."

Meanwhile, in the 1930s, the Hindu Mahasabha, which still based itself on the narrow appeal of elite groups of royal families and upper-caste notables, could not mobilize itself as a political force of any electoral or strategic consequence. Specifically political concerns about the place of Hindus and Hindu culture in an independent Indian state were articulated much more influentially by the Hindu traditionalists within Congress. They attempted to reconcile their fundamental sympathy for a more Hindu-oriented political dispensation with Mahatma Gandhi's determination to preserve harmony and equality between religions. Whatever the inner tensions of Hindu traditionalism within Congress, it had the immense advantage of working institutionally within the electorally dominant Indian political force of that time, leaving the Mahasabha without scope for influence.

Hindu Nationalism and the Politics of Independent India

Partition and its aftermath

The political impact of the growth of the RSS in the 1940s was magnified by the events surrounding the birth of Independent India. The RSS, implicitly basing itself on the concept of a cultural "majority," took a very different view of Hindu–Muslim differences than did the leaders of the Muslim League. But ironically, both were opposed to the dominant Congress idea of an India for all religions. The leaders of the Muslim League held that it would be impossible to have a single nation-state for all religions, and campaigned for the creation of a separate "Islamic state" of Pakistan. Hindu nationalists, and in particular, the RSS, equally disagreed with the concept of a state neutral (or equally tolerant) towards all religions. But they did not hold the Partition of India to be the solution. They argued instead that India (by then defined by the borders of the British Raj, although in Hindutva theory it was a much larger and ideal entity, perhaps encompassing everything between Iran and Singapore) was already a Hindu nation and should never be divided. Instead, all Muslims had to agree to participate in a national life that, in some constitutive way, was Hindu. The renascence of the nation would not consist only in the transformation of the attitudes and values of those who already counted themselves as Hindus. It would also require the recognition by both other native Indian religionists – Buddhists, Jains – and religionists of the "alien" religions – Muslims, Christians – that they were, in a cultural sense, Hindus. For this reason, the RSS implacably opposed the Partition of India. Hindu nationalists could not reconcile themselves to Partition, when those from Congress who negotiated for Indian Independence – Gandhi, Nehru, Patel – finally and reluctantly consented to it because they recognized that the idea of a unified and religiously neutral state was unacceptable to the Muslim League and its supporters.

With Partition, the political leadership within Congress showed potentially divergent attitudes to the emerging situation, based on different readings of the role of Hinduism in the Indian polity. Jawaharlal Nehru and others held the secular position that (the now partitioned) India should be a country in which the state was neutral towards all religions and, if anything, supportive of the minorities so as to compensate for any natural domination that a majority Hindu population would have in the polity. Vallabhai Patel and others sympathetic to a Hindu traditionalist position argued in precisely the opposite direction: given a natural Hindu majority, the structures and processes of the state should reflect that fact, so that the treatment of minorities, while having to obey all the dictates of legal equality and fairness, had to be derived from a Hindu position. This division was based on competing interpretations of Gandhi's own balance between his Hindu beliefs and his acceptance of the equality of religions. After Partition, Gandhi refocused his expression of interreligious amity, from opposition to Partition to harmony between India and Pakistan and between the religious communities within India.

The RSS and the Hindu Mahasabha had some affinity with the Hindu traditionalists within Congress, and on occasion were invited into its fold. But the Hindu traditionalists were still utterly loyal to Gandhi, whereas his morally unflinching strategy of reaching out to Muslims after the death of his political dream of an undivided India profoundly alienated Hindu nationalists. (There were, however, some Hindu traditionalists who abandoned Congress to join the Hindu Mahasabha, because they thought the Congress insufficiently resolute in its opposition to Partition.) Hindu nationalists saw this as the ceding of the goal of a Hindu India, although there were differences of opinion in the RSS and the Mahasabha about how to treat the offer of rapprochement from Hindu traditionalists within Congress. The potential for any development in such a direction was severely damaged when a Mahasabha (and former RSS) member, Nathuram Godse, assassinated Mahatma Gandhi for his sympathetic attitude to Muslims. Nehru saw this against his reading of all forms of Hindu nationalism as essentially fascistic, and acted strongly by banning the RSS.

In the years after Independence, Hindu nationalism was in a strange state. On the one hand, it had not only not got its demand for an undivided, Hindu India, but it had been implicated in the death of Gandhi. On the other, it not only had affinities with one wing of the utterly dominant Congress Party (and therefore some scope for future political influence), but it seemed well placed to occupy that space in the political sphere open for sociocultural conservativism. During the crisis caused by the issue of the treatment of Hindus in Pakistan (especially Bengalis in East Pakistan), Hindu nationalists sought to take the high ground against what they saw as Nehru's soft and weak strategy. But he acted decisively against their attempts to manipulate the political issue and build bridges with Hindu traditionalists within Congress.

The Jana Sangh and the dominance of Nehruvian secularism

There was no real growth in Hindu nationalism over the following two decades. The single most important reason was extrinsic to the Hindu nationalist organizations: the determination of Jawaharlal Nehru, India's first Prime Minister, to fashion a polity and a politics that was not only secular in the formal Indian sense of state neutrality towards religions, but also "noncommunalist," that is, strictly without any appeal to or role for religion-based identity in the public life of the nation-state. The Indian constitution that came into force in 1950 was very much a secular document, since many of its framers had views akin to Nehru in this regard.

The constitutional framework of Indian politics therefore made it difficult for the Hindu Mahasabha to operate on its basic ideology of a Hindu nation. Any explicit electoral appeal to putative Hindu values seemed to run counter to the legal concept of a polity in which religion was not a legitimate source of political identity. This difficulty was compounded by the fact that the other major opposition groups, the Socialists and the Communists, were in total agreement on this framework with the Nehruvian Congress. In a more organizational context, too, the Mahasabha was at a disadvantage; its lack of mobilizational capacity, its dependence on certain elite groups, its lack of grassroots support, all told against it everywhere but in certain strongholds in central India.

Nehru was not only successful in constitutional terms, by making secularism the norm of political activity. He was also successful within the Congress in both limiting the influence of Hindu traditionalist leaders, who may have had goals similar to the Hindu Mahasabha, and in developing a party system tied to a machinery of state-derived power and patronage that dissuaded even those unsympathetic to his ideals from leaving Congress.

In sum, Hindu nationalism could not make any headway in the politics of newly independent India. But there was to be some hope for it in the formation of a new party, the Bharatiya Jana Sangh, although it came to very little in the first two decades of its existence. The history of the Jana Sangh and its relationship to the RSS is important for what it tells us about the nature of Hindu nationalism and the conditions that led to the eventual re-formation of the Jana Sangh as the Bharatiya Janata Party (BJP). It was the BJP that eventually gained a measure of success in using the appeal of religion to gain power in government.

S. P. Mookerjee, a Hindu traditionalist in Nehru's original cabinet, found himself so much in disagreement with government policy, especially with regard to (Islamic) Pakistan, that he began to liaise increasingly with Golwalkar and the RSS. Eventually, he left to start the Jana Sangh. From the beginning, the relationship between the explicitly party political Jana Sangh and the "cultural" RSS was complicated. On the one hand, there was the consideration that by giving ideological and – more directly – organizational support to a political party, the RSS could hope to transform society through the political process while itself remaining outside of it. On the other hand, there was the more austere concern to remain untouched by political considerations in the pursuit of the ideal of sociocultural transformation. Eventually, the continued marginalization of Hindu traditionalists within Congress seemed to Mookerjee to open up the possibility of a Hindu nationalist opposition to Congress, and Golwalkar softened his suspicion of involvement with a political party.

The formation of the Jana Sangh did not lead to any significant impact by Hindu nationalism on the Indian polity, because of the combination of Nehruvian strategies mentioned above and the sheer personal authority of Nehru in removing nonsecular alternatives from serious political influence. Mookerjee's straightforward political aim of developing an alternative to the Nehruvian conseus therefore did not succeed, and in any case was always seen at odds with RSS ideals. However, the search for immediate political impact was rejected by the Jana Sangh after 1954, under the leadership of Deedayal Upadhyaya. The Jana Sangh began to espouse, in effect, the RSS goal of an ultimate transformation of the Hindu nation. Political activity was to be confined to necessary and strategic engagement with specific issues and the occasional electoral success.

Upadhyaya developed his views on Hindu nationalism, and thereby codified the Jana Sangh mission, in two books, *The Two Plans* and, more resonantly, *Integral Humanism*. From the RSS (to which, as most of the subsequent Jana Sangh leadership, he belonged), he accepted the ultimate aim of a cultural transformation of the nation, based on the organic notion of an existent Hindu society with its own essential historical features and functions. But the explicit political aim, which was to be the Jana Sangh's specific raison d'être, was the realization of the Hindu nation within the state of India, through the transformation of all political institutions from village to central government. However, such transformation, which would seem to require electoral success, was in fact going to be achievable only through gaining more diffuse support in society as a whole. The process was an idealization: it was not that the Jana Sangh would gain power through electoral success and then bring about social change; rather there would first have to be social change before there could be electoral success. The Jana Sangh could only then set about attending to its specific tasks within the Hindutva movement, namely, the realization of Hindu principles within the institutions of the Indian state.

This strategy had a profound effect on the way party political Hindu nationalism developed. Adhering closely to the idea of (self-)disciplined organization espoused by the RSS, the Jana Sangh concentrated on the so-called sanghathanist strategy. *Sangathan* means "consolidation," and the strategy was meant to focus on building disciplined cadres and inculcating Hindu values at the grassroots. The contrast was with the conventional political model of electoral calculation, alliances, elite support, manifestos with explicit socioeconomic promises, etc. The consequence of the sangathanist strategy was a sustained closeness between the RSS and the Jana Sangh, and lack of electoral success (for which the sangathan strategy offered idealized justification).

Hindu nationalism through the 1950s and much of the 1960s found it difficult to explicate a political position that made relevant use of the cultural arguments of Hindutva. This was primarily because of Nehru's and, initially, Indira Gandhi's refusal to allow any relaxation of the secularist framework of discourse and political contestation. The Jana Sangh had, instead, to engage through other oppositional strategies, especially on the economy. Here, there seemed to be no direct and obvious answer to the question of what economic model followed from Hindutva ideology. One wing of Hindu nationalism, which had an affinity with the still existent Hindu traditionalist element in Congress, made the link between cultural conservatism and economic liberalism. It saw not only an instrumental reason to oppose Nehruvian socialist and dirigiste policies but also an ideological continuity between an organic conception of a society comprised of different groups and an economic ideal of free activity. The other wing took the cultural conception of an organic society to involve commitment to social issues of development, which was to a certain extent compatible with Nehruvian socialism. This tension has continued to beset Hindu nationalism.

However, even the anti-free marketeers could find some disagreement with Nehruvian socialism, because the latter concentrated on the essentially modernist enterprise of creating an industrial economy, whereas the RSS type of social development was focused (in a way oddly reminiscent of Gandhi) on the agrarian economy, with its ties to an ancient civilizational way of life.

The first taste of power: the Janata Party

The ideological tension within the Hindu nationalist fold gradually fed into a tension over political strategy as well. In the face of the dominance of the Nehruvian Congress, the Jana Sangh had, as mentioned, adhered to its RSS roots of cultivating a cultural strategy on the ground, without overt concern for electoral success. But divisions within Congress opened up between Indira Gandhi and her older colleagues in the late 1960s, and the Jana Sangh was confronted with a choice. It could retain its old strategy or it could move in a more populist direction to benefit from any possible re-alignment with Hindu traditionalists opposed to Indira Gandhi.

Populism brought its own difficulties, as was evident during the "cow protection agitation." The cow being considered sacred, Hindu nationalists had always asked for legal provision against cow slaughter. In a bid to further their agenda, Hindu nationalists attempted to mobilize Hindu public opinion in the mid-1960s against the government's refusal to allow for such provision. This included appeal to Hindu religious organizations and holy men. Such a form of populism drew on the ideological roots of sangathanist strategy, by mobilizing people on the basis of cultural appeal to Hindu values. However, as violence resulted from the confrontation between demonstrators and the government, the Jana Sangh realized that such populism hindered instrumental strategies aimed at forming a coherent opposition to Indira Gandhi's Congress, because her other opponents were at least uncomfortable and usually hostile to Hindu nationalist concerns like "cow protection." So the Jana Sangh in Parliament had to try and build bridges with anti-Indira Gandhi groups, and the agitation proved a failure.

Indira Gandhi's adroit use of Indian nationalist sentiment during and after the victorious war with Pakistan and the birth of Bangladesh in 1971 politically marginalized the Jana Sangh. However, her drift into authoritarian rule, ending in the declaration of an Emergency, in which political rights were suspended, led to a recrudescence of Hindu nationalism. As legitimate leaders of the political opposition were jailed, the extralegal activity of the RSS, now led by another Maharahstrian brahmin, Balasaheb Deoras, had a chance to flourish. He initially tried to cooperate with her but she had no immediate gain in doing so, and continued to target RSS workers as much as she did anyone else. The RSS then traded on its old image as an organization willing to be exposed to political danger and oppression. It became a focal point of resistance, organizing anti-governmental activity alongside socialists and others by drawing on a new membership that was thrown, by Indira Gandhi's actions, into underground opposition. When the Emergency ended and she boldly decided to go to the people on her record in the Emergency, a new political topography shaped up. The opposition to her had come from across the political spectrum and, indeed, had been the prime cause of her extreme and undemocratic reaction. Jaya Prakash Narayan, the Gandhian reformer, had sought before the Emergency to develop an idealistic oppositional front to Indira Gandhi. This value-based ideal was predictably transformed into a highly political strategy (although much to his acknowledged discomfort). When the post-Emergency election was declared, an extraordinary political creature was born: the Janata Party, consisting of the Socialists, the Congress (the breakaway party of the 1960s), more recent Congress dissidents, some others – and the Jana Sangh.

The Janata Party was to be the Jana Sangh's means of entry into legitimate political power, and as such, the latter accepted the terms of its participation in the government the Janata Party formed after Indira Gandhi's defeat.

The RSS equivocally supported the Jana Sangh's strategy of engaging in politics with secularist parties. Its grassroots mobilization was crucial, but it refused to formalize any amalgamation into the Janata Party, firmly asserting its self-conception as a cultural guide that stood "above" political activity. In any case, there were strong internal differences of opinion within the Janata Party about the RSS, as the Socialist wing took the RSS to be against everything it stood for. This suspicion of the RSS was a feature of the Janata Party during its brief and unstable period in power.

The point to note about Hindu nationalism's first taste of national power was the extent to which its engagement with the political process depended on uneasy alliances with non-Congress parties. The same parties that, from the late 1960s, had drawn Hindu nationalists into opposition to Indira Gandhi felt it more rational to oppose them when power became an actuality. A common enemy was insufficient, outside times of crises, to keep secularist parties allied to Hindu nationalists, despite the claims of pragmatists within the Jana Sangh – like Atal Behari Vajpayee, External Affairs Minister in the Janata government – that they had set aside their original ideological goals in favor of the social reform agenda of the Janata Party. By the time of the next election, Indira Gandhi's use of secularism as an ideological counter-strategy had made non-Jana Sangh groups within the Janata Party appear antisecular – appearing to subordinate them to Hindu nationalism. After electoral defeat, the break-up of the Janata Party was inevitable, for its internal contradictions were insuperable.

The BJP and the Sangh Parivar

In 1980, the Jana Sangh refounded itself as the Bharatiya Janata Party (BJP). This party was going to take a very different course through the Indian political landscape. The RSS under Deoras was emphatic that the Jana Sangh had failed in its strategy of integrating with other parties primarily because it had not kept its ideological purity, a purity that could take the party to political power only through a mobilization of Hindus for a religiocultural cause. From now on, political power would come only through unique Hindu nationalist strategies aimed at a fundamental transformation of the attitude of Hindus towards the nature of the Indian polity. The RSS would be involved in this process because grassroots activity and cultural transformation were going to possible only if the BJP acted in accordance with the ideas behind its conception. This eventually led to the radical strategies of the late 1980s and early 1990s; and they were radical because Hindu nationalism combined, in that period, grassroots organization in the traditional RSS manner with mass mobilization through the politicization of Hindu cultural identity. But this was not before the new BJP had attempted to maintain some continuity with its predecessor.

In the early 1980s, Indira Gandhi appropriated Hindu sentiments in her increasingly extreme attempts to outflank all opposition. This included her dangerously confrontational treatment of the demand for a Sikh state in the Punjab, which ultimately led to her assassination. But Rajiv Gandhi, succeeding her on a wave of sympathy that brought Congress an unprecedented domination in Parliament, also found it expedient to invoke Hindu imagery in his attempt to secure support from sections of the Hindu population. The BJP's "liberal" strategy of fighting on social and economic issues, therefore, was quite unsuccessful, for it had abandoned its natural constituency and then found it taken over by the Congress. (Indeed, in this period, the RSS occasionally preferred Congress to the BJP in local disputes, as when it was challenged by the electorally successful Communists in Kerala. There, Congress alone provided opposition and partially used communalization to secure upper-class Hindu votes against the Communists.)

Partially because of the lack of political success, the RSS revivified a different organization, the Vishwa Hindu Parishad (VHP, the World Hindu Assembly). This had been founded in the 1960s with the support of religious leaders like Swami Chinmayananda, but had focused primarily on the teaching of Hindu religious beliefs. In the 1980s, it started developing as the activist arm of Hindu nationalism, working with the RSS but expressing its Hindutva convictions in overtly political areas and in a political manner. Its strategy was exemplified in demonstrations and marches meant to articulate the idea of a united Hindu India, covering places sacred in Hinduism and systematically conflating Hindu sacred geography with Indian political unity.

Then, for a variety of reasons (and when a late and unconvincing lurch towards getting back Muslim votes led to his loss of Hindu votes as well), Rajiv Gandhi's Congress lost power to the new left-wing party, the Janata Dal. The BJP almost recreated the situation of ten years previously, going into an anti-Congress coalition; but only almost, for it did not join the government. To understand what the BJP then did, we must see what was happening with Hindu nationalism in the 1980s.

Through the decade, Hindu nationalist mobilization had proceeded almost against or independently of the BJP's cautious and noncommunal parliamentary strategy. Hindu nationalism in this period became more focused and organized than it had previously been. In 1981, the conversion of low-caste Hindus to Islam in the Tamil village of Meenakshipuram has acted as a lightning rod for the alarmist tendencies of Hindu nationalism. Events like that could be presented as an attack on Hinduism and therefore a threat to the very fabric of India. Another rich source of threat perception was the illegal immigration of Muslims from Bangladesh. Although the bulk of them went to the contiguous states of West Bengal and Assam (where they interacted with other ethnic problems), the political consequence was most felt in Bombay. There, the right-wing Shiv Sena (the Army of Shiva), which had originally sprung up as a chauvinist Maharashtrian party targeting internal immigrants from south India, repositioned itself as a Hindu nationalist party targeting Muslims. As with conversion, so with illegal immigration, the threat of an Islamic invasion of a Hindu land was used as a cultural gloss on prevailing economic insecurities and tensions.

The non-BJP organizations in the Hindutva family of organizations (the Sangh Parivar), then, were busy developing a mobilizatory rhetoric. The fundamental strategy was to interpret economic tensions in cultural terms, and conflate the identities of culture and the nation-state. Muslims, it was argued, were unfairly pampered by the secular nation-state, which was blind to the threat posed by them to its very existence. The ideal way to safeguard the nation-state was to remove the threat, but that could be done only by those whose loyalty was only to it; and they were the Hindus, whose nation, after all, India was. If, in that process, the resources of the state were redirected to Hindus, that was only fair and proper. Indira and Rajiv Gandhi recognized that targeting economic resources (jobs, places in educational institutions, other forms of preferential treatment) was an effective means of mobilizing key constituencies; hence their concern to express a Hindu identity. But whereas, in this period, the BJP's parliamentary caution allowed it to be outflanked, the other Hindu nationalist organizations persisted with their strategy, hindered though they were by Congress's actual control of economic resources. These organizations were working for the longer term. Also, when Rajiv Gandhi recognized the need to woo back Muslim voters after his flirtation with Hindu symbolism, the Hindu nationalists were ready to welcome disaffected Hindus.

Electoral Success and the Problems of Power

In the late 1980s, the BJP faced a delicate task. Its strength would come electorally only through the grassroots mobilization undertaken by the rest of the Sangh Parivar; and it was that very strength that would make it a worthwhile ally in any anti-Congress alliance. But that alliance was to be with the Janata Dal, which was extremely hostile to Hindu nationalism; indeed, more so than the old Janata Party, which had at least had old-style Hindu traditionalists at its core.

In the elections of 1989, the BJP went into an agreement with the Janata Dal, but did not join the government formed after the defeat of Congress, merely offering parliamentary support from outside. Calculations over parliamentary majority alone kept the Janata Dal in its relationship with the BJP, and the BJP bided its time as part of an anti-Congress front without worrying its fellow organizations in the Sangh Parivar.

The Hindu nationalism of the rest of the Sangh Parivar, which the BJP was now acknowledging as successful in the mobilization of the Hindu vote, was able to reinterpret basic socioeconomic concerns amongst a large section of the population as a cultural issue, wherein lay its success. A small, but influential urban elite was concerned to increase its wealth and power through access to the instruments of state, in a way directly opposed by the Left parties (including the Janata Dal) and indirectly by the promiscuous and erratic populism of Congress. The Hindu nationalists, by claiming that they would recast the state as a traditional (if unspecified) Hindu organism, promised these aspirational elites a dispensation in which they were likely to gain influence commensurate with their perceived standing in traditional (caste) society. The larger group to appeal to, however, was the middle-class (and middle-caste) semi-urban groups caught in the uncertainties of economic modernization – scarce public sector jobs, a competitive educational market, erosion of agricultural certainties. This group had a perception of loss of access to economic wherewithal. Hindu nationalists explained this as being caused by the unfair and threatening discrimination by the state in favor of Muslims – the very people who, by virtue of history and transnational loyalties, were alleged to be least "deserving" of statal support. To both these groups, Hindu nationalist offered a Hindu state, in which natural, organic privileges would come to those who "belonged."

The crucial political achievement, however, lay not in this targeting, but in the symbolization of Hindu identity for a Hindu state. Clearly, in order to draw upon the support of Hindus as Hindus, a definable conception of Hinduism as the cultural essence of India had to be given; and this, as we will remember, was the concern of both Savarkar and Golwalkar. The success of Hindu nationalism in the late 1980s and early 1990s lay in presenting identifiable symbols of such an essence. The most potent symbol the Hindu deity, Rama, and his supposed birthplace, Ayodhya, in the northern Indian state of Uttar Pradesh.

Ayodhya and the consequences of mobilization

Rama has a long and complex history in Hinduism; but suffice it to say that, warrior though he is from the beginning, his divinization by the tradition depends heavily on seeing him as the exemplar of compassion, forgiveness, and gentleness in the most extreme circumstances of war, conflict, and misfortune. In contrast, Hindu nationalism selectively reread him as a martial hero, a lopsided guardian of cultural honor. They also took the Gandhian idea of a Utopian "rule of Rama" (*ram rajya*) as an age of balance, harmony, and peace, and refashioned it as the exemplification of a culturally pristine Hindu nation. Thus reread, the popular worship of Rama (mostly in north India) could become an already existent manifestation of Hindu nationalism. This process was helped, indirectly and largely unwittingly, by the simplistically refashioned but enormously successful television serialization of the *Ramayana* by the state broadcasting corporation.

This process of creating a political focus on a religious symbol would not have worked without a specific means of relating the ideal of a Hindu nation to the threatening reality of Islam; for the stigmatizing of Muslims was, as we have seen, the obverse of the Hindu nationalist conception of a Hindu polity. To a certain extent, the present was potent enough – as the agitation over Muslim immigrants from Bangladesh showed. But, despite militancy amongst some Muslim groups, especially those ideologically (and sometimes financially) linked to transnational Islamic fundamentalism, the inescapable reality was of a largely depressed community usually socially integrated into Indian society. So, the revivification of Hindu India had to come from history.

Turning to an old concern going back to the 1940s, Hindu nationalists began agitating for the reclamation of Hindu holy sites taken over by Islam in the past. Undoubtedly, it was the practice of some Muslim rulers to build mosques on the site of destroyed Hindu temples; in Benares and elsewhere, this was the case. There was, in any case, the fundamental question of what significance to attach to these historical events in today's multireligious and secular polity; but the Hindu nationalists chose as their main target a more problematic site, a mosque in a small and nondescript village that bore the same name as Rama's traditional capital, Ayodhya. That there had been a temple at all there was uncertain; that there was any local tradition associating the village with a traditional sacred site was uncertain; that Hinduism reads literal meaning into sacred geography is questionable. But the connection between a mosque, a place-name resonant with meaning to many Hindus, and a divinity with pan-Hindu appeal was irresistible. The start of the re-creation of a Hindu nation, then, was the liberation of Hindu holy places, and the first place, the most important, because common to all Hindus, was to be Ayodhya. For this, the mosque had to be destroyed and a temple (re)built in its place.

By 1990, an unsustainable division was emerging between the Janata Dal, led by Vishwanath Pratap Singh, and the BJP. The Janata Dal's own populism was targeted, in conventional Leftist fashion, at the economically weak sections of society – in India, those castes specified by the Constitution as either "Backward" or "Scheduled." The proposal was to increase massively the reservation of educational seats for these castes. While the BJP was concerned not to antagonize potential voters amongst them, its own targeting was of different sections of society, as we have seen. As agitation and counter-agitation over the proposed reservation policy spread across India, the BJP decisively swung towards the Hindu nationalism propagated by the rest of the Parivar. The President of the BJP, Lal Krishna Advani, who had been trained in the RSS, threw himself into a plan of mobilization. He began a "pilgrimage of the chariot" (*rath yathra*) across the country. Ayodhya became the focus of Hindu nationalist mobilization. To destroy the mosque was to destroy the deleterious consequence of alien rule over a native Hindu land, to (re)build a temple on the site was to reclaim history itself for Hinduism.

This campaign was calibrated in its rhetoric. It built up a series of appeals, through public meetings, repeated use of messages, the playing of tapes in public places, and the association of sacred symbols and places with the Hindutva conception of the nation. All this was meant to create and sustain an identity through psychoses. It cannot be said that the strategy was thought out in abstract terms. Rather, a direct and unquestioning connection was made between targeting Muslims and creating support amongst Hindus who were potentially or already hostile to Muslims. But the actual process was, in its way, sophisticated. By heightening a sense of the alienness of an identifiable (minority) group, the campaign would bring together those who shared that sense. From the negative identification of otherness would emerge a positive common identity, multiplied through the psychology of crowd agglomeration. This would, if sustained, convert into a longer-lasting support for the leaders of the mobilization. Such support could translate into electoral strength. But that sense of the alienness of Muslims, to be sustained for such ends, would inevitably require a mass emotionalism, which would seek immediate and cathartic expression: in violence. In short, violence appeared to be intrinsic to this method of mobilization. Even aside from the trauma of Partition, there has been communal clashes between Muslims and Hindus in India in the past, some extremely serious; but this time its occurrence was a result of a political strategy, not due to a random collection of pressures.

The mobilization proved successful on its own terms because it represented a concrete outcome as the first step of an abstract political process. It linked the vast ideological goal of a Hindu polity with a tangible act meant as historical redress. Every expression of resentment over the Muslim role in India's past and present could be articulated in the campaign to tear down a mosque and build a temple in its place. The formal sentiment of Hindu pride was given substance through a more diffuse exaltation of Hindu sacrality – the ahistoric importance of Ayodhya had impressed itself on the minds of many Hindus. Some Hindus considered holy, either leaders or followers of various religious orders, undertook to support the movement.

The demolition on December 6, 1992, was driven by a mixed body of militants (especially those of the Bajrang Dal, the militant [but autonomous] youth wing of the VHP), most of them completely out of the control of the politicians and other leaders who had led the movement and sought to gain political advantage from it. The ruling Congress dithered in its response, both to the movement and to the actual demolition, vacillating between acting strongly against Hindu nationalist leaders (but alienating a potentially huge Hindu vote) and being conciliatory (and alienating both Muslims and the evident majority of Hindus opposed to the entire strategy). Some leaders were charged, some of the local police were implicated in the destruction, there was an angry response from Muslims, the violence escalated, and in Bombay, where the Shiv Sena was ready to exploit its communalist muscle, there were serious riots. Apart from the actual violence and death, however, a more abstract if extremely grave issue was at stake: the status of the Indian polity as one in which religions were treated with equal respect and religion itself was not a legitimate concern of the political process.

In the event, the issue has proved irresolvable. On the one hand, the immediate political fallout revealed a striking resistance amongst Hindus to the process of communalization, i.e., the process of recasting politics as a struggle over religious identity and between religious communities. Geographically, there was a strong rejection of the strategy in most of south India, removed from the events in Ayodhya and with a different history of intercommunal relations. Demographically, there was an immediate ebbing away of support for the BJP from the urban elite groups, who saw in the destruction of the mosque nothing but a loss of political credibility. On the other hand, the question still remained as to whether a suitably modulated version of this strategy could, in future, remobilize sufficient numbers of Hindus. This was because the very possibility of large-scale and violent communalization had now become conceivable within the political system.

Hindu nationalism's options

The subsequent history of Hindu nationalism over the decade revealed the fundamental differences of conception, goal and strategy that had long existed in India, but which emerged starkly after Ayodhya. Two factors made the choices facing Hindu nationalists ever clearer after Ayodhya. Firstly, the destruction of the mosque itself was such an extreme event in the context of India that, even if any ambivalence about its value and effect remained, it could not form the basis of a unified and sustained Sangh Parivar strategy such as had characterized the brief period between 1989 and 1992. Differences in the assessment of the value and effect of the destruction became a matter of sharp debate within the Parivar. Secondly, the BJP itself moved ever closer to national power (after having gained some power at the state level), and the electoral calculation did not add up to a simple endorsement of the mobilizatory strategy that had led to Ayodhya. There was a Hindu vote-bank, and that had helped the BJP in state elections, especially in Uttar Pradesh itself; but that vote-bank did not extend in any simply manner either to Uttar Pradesh or to the country as a whole.

These two considerations, one conceptual (and, perhaps, ethical), the other instrumental, led to the same outcome, which was a diversification of Hindutva strategy directed at different points of an ideological continuum. At one end of the Hindu nationalist continuum were those who thought that the realization of a Hindu nation – in which there was either no other religion or only suitably subordinated religions – was only just beginning, and its achievement through continued mobilization would come regardless of political cost and lack of democratically accredited power. At the end were those who thought that the most and the best achievement possible was a political manifesto that included some specifically Hindu conceptual categories regarding the Indian state, a manifesto that permitted conventional political calculations for the attainment of democratically accredited power. In short, the issue was what Hinduism could possibly mean in politics. The strongest and most ideological response was that Hinduism was the source of a collective transformation that could also transform the very nature of the Indian polity. In contrast, more instrumentalist politicians tended to represent Hindutva, in contrast, as (merely) the source of cultural ideas with which to interpret (and justify) actions within the existing polity.

The idea that Hindutva implied a transformation of the Indian polity appealed to those who were willing to challenge the current constitutional and procedural arrangments. That willingness manifested itself in hostility towards Muslims and Christians, along with conservative resistance to the perceived influence of the West on Indian social and economic life. Agitation for the removal of mosques from other favored Hindu sites continued, despite the wrangles and wider concerns following the destruction of the mosque at Ayodhya. The standard demands for a "uniform civil code" (the removal of special protection for Muslim personal law from legal generality), and the ending of special laws on property pertaining to the Muslim-majority state of Kashmir, continued to be made. Some attention also began to be directed at (especially Western-funded missionary activity directed at) conversion to Christianity represented yet again as a threat to Hindu culture. (This was an issue that was to be become much more critical by the end of the decade.) Against the backdrop of a wider nativist rejection of the economic liberalization that was occurring under a reformist Congress regime, Hindu nationalist organizations targeted, in particular, (mostly Western) multinational corporations entering the long-protected Indian consumer industry. All these were presented as struggles over the Hindu soul of India, threatened as it was held to be from within through the religious minorities and from without through Western materialist culture.

In the mid-1990s, the BJP attempted to retain the support of those who had been mobilized through appeal to the "hard" Hindu nationalism of the rest of the Sangh Parivar, even while it sought to appeal to those segments of the electorate more concerned with issues of efficiency (anticorruption, administrative competence, economic liberalization) than with religious identity. In pursuit of the latter, there was a projection of the BJP – especially in the form of Atal Bihari Vajpayee – as the party of good governance. After Congress under Narasimha Rao lost power, the BJP sought to position itself as the only alternative. But even its diversified strategy failed to bring it sufficient direct electoral support. At the same time, other parties, national and regional (with the exception, of course, of the Hindu nationalist Shiv Sena in Maharashtra), adhered to the "secularist" conception of politics, and refused to contemplate electoral alliances with the BJP. When given a chance, the BJP lasted less than a fortnight in government for lack of partners to form a coalition.

This experience was sufficient for the BJP to persuade itself that its best chance of success lay in pursuing the "soft" strategy of focusing on issues of governance rather than ideology. The Hindu vote bank mobilized through violence-based confrontational ideology, as on Ayodhya, would have nowhere else to go, while the chance of increasing votes in a wider constituency would only come through pursuing issues of governance. But beyond the votes themselves (which, even when maximized, might still not be enough) any hope of power lay with alliances, and alliance partners would be tempted only by a less ideologically motivated BJP.

As the "Third Front" of parties that came to power in 1996 found themselves unable to provide stability over a full term of Parliament, elections had to be called again. The failure of an alliance without the BJP made it look necessary – and the "soft" strategy of the BJP made it look possible – for many parties to think of dealing with it. The BJP's share of the vote in the next General Election went up slightly, although it still got less that 30 percent of the popular vote. It won the largest number of seats; but well short of a majority, so that it needed to put together a precarious coalition in order to form a government.

Democratic power and its constraints

By 1998, "Hindu nationalists" were in power in India. But what did that mean? Clearly, the Indian polity was not going to be transformed constitutionally or even culturally. The electoral arithmetic saw to that. There were too many political forces to constrain the core impulses of Hindutva, besides the divergences within Hindutva itself. This was most evident in economic policy: Jaswant Singh, a long-standing member of the BJP in the Rajya Sabha (Upper House) in the past, was perceived by the RSS and others to be too unideological and reform-minded to be allowed to hold the key post of Finance Minister. (He became [an influential] External Affairs Minister instead.) But the economic imperatives had to be met and the BJP-led coalition had perforce to continue the same inconsistent but liberalizing policies of the two previous regimes. This set the BJP-in-government against other organizations within the Parivar, whose instinctive nativism made them protectionist and antireformist. On other issues too, the strength of unsympathetic allies compelled the BJP to give up formally (in the government agenda) its traditional Hindutva demands. Ironically, when Hindu nationalists attained power, it could only be on terms that allowed little space for Hindu nationalism.

The decision to conduct nuclear tests in 1998 seemed on the face of it to be at least one unqualifiedly Hindu nationalist decision. Certainly, both supporters and opponents of the BJP often saw it as driven by the desire to express the strength of a Hindu nation. But the reality was more complex. Previous governments had come close to conducting the tests, and the defense establishment had consistently argued for tests and been heard sympathetically by previous Prime Ministers. Of course, it was seen as being of immediate domestic advantage to conduct the tests and ride a (rapidly diminishing) wave of nationalism. But what kind of nationalism – Hindu or Indian? Traditionalists in the BJP party hierarchy, and in the RSS and VHP, read the tests as expressing Hindu greatness, made possible through the decision of Hindus. This was clear in their portrayal of the tests in religious-ideological terms, characteristically anti-Islamic. The Hindu bomb would forever show the strength of India against Pakistan. Many of them seemed genuinely surprised when (as everyone else had expected) Pakistan, with massive Chinese assistance, managed a symbolic response through its own tests. The BJP-in-government was not unhappy about this response. It helped for the moment to heal divisions within the Parivar, brought about through unhappiness over the BJP's economic and social pragmatism. But it was not entirely happy either, wishing to use the tests to play more widely to Indian nationalism. The Defense Minister, from an allied party with a strong secularist base, claimed that the tests were meant to signal Indian preparedness against China. While this articulation was diplomatically unwise, it was part of the larger concern to present the tests as simply part of an Indian coming-of-age on the international scene, not a narrow anti-Islamic reflex. Gradually, opposition within India to the weaponization of nuclear capability also turned from rhetoric about Hindutva to substantive concerns about India's geostrategy. Shifts in the international response, from diplomatic condemnation to a tacitly acquiescent refocus on economic cooperation, strengthened this trend. The Hindutva dimension of the tests faded away into issues about India's place in the world and the proper means of attaining it.

By the end of the decade in which the BJP's drive to power had been impelled by grassroots appeal to an exclusivist Hindu identity, Hindu nationalism found itself at a crossroad. The use of real political power seemed to require instrumentalist alliances and economic governance, which meant the effective repudiation of an ideology to transform the Indian polity into a Hindu one. Against this, it had become possible to even think of political power in the first place only because of mobilization through appeal to Hindu identity. In power, the old tension between ideological purity and political realism remained. And so long as it remained, Hindu nationalism seemed doomed to attaining political power only by denying itself.

In the next election, brought about prematurely because of the loss of support from one regional party, an accident of personalities decided the strategy of the Sangh Parivar. The Prime Minister, Vajpayee, had the impeccable credentials of an RSS man who had been in the Jana Sangh throughout its existence and in the BJP since its inception. Yet he had chosen to represent himself as the leader of a national alliance of parties and views that subsumed the BJP and denied any role for Hindutva in its manifesto. And he alone was likely to deliver any political power to the Parivar, because of his personal standing with the national electorate. Reluctantly, they went into an election supporting leaders (not only Vajpayee but almost the entire front-rank of cabinet ministers) who had already declared that they would not permit core Hindutva demands to form any part of a new government's policies. The alternative was loss of all access to political power. In the previous election, the BJP leadership had hedged its bets and tacitly condoned inflammatory rhetoric and spasm of violence while officially following a much less ideologically loaded strategy. This time, it put all its eggs in one basket and concentrated on an ostensibly Vajpayee-led reasonableness and a noncommunal plan of action.

The second success of the BJP, this time as part of a stable coalition, appeared to confirm the view that Hindu nationalism could not hope to change the Indian polity, because of the nature of Indian politics. Indian political exigencies would broadly remain the same regardless of specific ideological agenda. The constraints of economic liberalization – to respond to globalization through deregulation, open markets, hard negotiation in bi- and multi-lateral forums – seemed, by the turn of the century, to be inescapable.

Geopolitical constraints too seemed to make a mockery of ideology. The tense relationship with Pakistan over Kashmir focused attention on this matter. From Independence, Kashmir had been a contested area. A state under British rule, its Hindu ruler had acceded to India despite its Muslim majority. Although the newly formed Pakistan failed in its attempt to annex Kashmir, a part of Kashmir stayed under Pakistan after a cease-fire. A plebiscite was supposed to have been held but never was. The situation by the late 1980s was roughly this: India maintained that Kashmir – including, nominally, that part in Pakistan – was an integral part of the secular Indian Union, the special constitutional provisions made for it being held adequate to its special status. Pakistan claimed that as a Muslim-majority state, Kashmir would more naturally be part of Islamic Pakistan, and that any plebiscite held would lead to this end. Meanwhile, Pakistan would be morally committed to any attempt by Kashmiri Muslims to break away from India. As Indian mismanagement of Kashmir led to the alienation of a large section of the population, the spread of Islamic fundamentalist ideology, and training, especially through Afghanistan, reached Kashmir via Pakistan. As various militant groups took to fighting the Indian army, the political situation settled into this dead-end equation: India would not talk about any change to Kashmir without the cessation of civil unrest, sustained, it seemed from the evidence, through Pakistani support for Kashmiri Islamic militancy. Pakistan refused to acknowledge that it overtly supported the militants but argued that India had to face the reality of a natural Islamic coincidence of interest between Kashmir and Pakistan. As for the militants, most followed Pakistan's line while claiming still to be fighting for outright independence (the end seemingly supported by a substantial portion of Kashmiri Muslims).

In this context, Hindu nationalists always argued for complete Indian control over Kashmir and an utter refusal to concede anything to either Pakistan or the militants. In government, the BJP found itself acting somewhat differently. First, Vajpayee initiated a confidence-building process with the Prime Minister of Pakistan; but this came to nothing. Worse, for mysterious reasons, Pakistan undertook a risky incursion into India, in cooperation with Kashmiri militants. The BJP-led government braved domestic anger with a highly restrained and defensive military policy that ruled out counter-incursion and incurred higher Indian casualties than a more aggressive tactic might have permitted. Immediate international support for Indian policy resulted and the mini-war came to an end without clear result but with Pakistan compromised on the international scene. This striking repudiation of Hindu nationalist ideology was followed by a series of other examples: in negotiations with militant hijackers of an Indian plane, in making contact with a range of militant groups, in declaring and maintaining cease-fires in the guerrilla war with the militants.

As the BJP-led government presided over an uncertain but discernible increase in Indian engagement in world affairs, politically and economically, Western and Islamic countries began to deal with India on purely geopolitical terms, seeming to regard the ideological considerations of Hindutva as irrelevant to geopolitics.

The question in the early years of the twenty-first century concerns the role of Hindu nationalism, not in world affairs but in the transmutation of domestic politics. Electorally, Indian politics seems set to remain what it became in the 1990s, an uneasy mix of national and regional parties, able to secure majority only through coalitions. This fragmentation has occurred through the emergence of a range of political organizations speaking for specific regional and caste-based interests. In this landscape, compromise and balance are essential, and that does not make for the success of ideology. There will continue to be internal institutional differences over exact tactics within the BJP and between it and other groups in the Sangh Parivar. Arguably, when the BJP was most effective in keeping its non-Hindu nationalist allies in government happy, the strongest opposition to it came from other members of the Parivar. In some instances, there has been a congruence of interests against the BJP, as when its (admittedly erratic) pursuit of economic liberalization threatens the protectionist instincts of both the Farmers Wing of the Parivar and various agricultural lobbies in other parties.

In short, once the BJP came to power (in a coalition), it was at odds with the very movement that brought it to power. We have already looked at the political exigencies of this uneasy relationship, and will shortly look at the fundamental divide between cultural and political imperatives. But before that, another issue has to be addressed, namely, the challenge of governance. Without doubt, mobilization and the pursuit of Hindu nationalist ends have demanded a variety of extra-legal tactics, mostly involving or resulting in violence. The BJP recognized the self-denying nature of its relationship with such mobilization, which both brought it hard-core support and alienated everyone else. Indeed, by the election of 1998, the BJP has assimilated with some success the contradictions of Hindu nationalist strategies. It presented itself as the only possible means of controlling unbridled Hindu nationalism, because it could control rather than merely oppose it. But this assimilation could not work well once it took on the burden of governance and actually had to assert that control. Civil disorder is not an effective mechanism for political engineering; and this is simply because a mechanism needs to be subject to order. A government (especially a democratic one, most especially a coalition) can least afford to use disorder – communal violence – to maintain sociopolitical stability. (Indira Gandhi had tried to use communal unrest to maintain her power, and even where she temporarily succeeded, she did not maintain stability.) So the BJP found itself having to act against the very forces unleashed – uncontrollably – by mobilization, forces for which the attainment of democratic power was irrelevant. Missionaries killed or nuns raped in the "defense of Hinduism" were law and order problems for the government – even or especially when that government was led by the BJP. Even far less extreme acts, like the Parivar's condemnation of the BJP's attempts to woo Muslims into its fold (not entirely unsuccessful), were problematic to a party engaged in procedural politicking. From representing itself as the only party capable of controlling Hindu nationalism, the BJP became the party most directly attacked by Hindu nationalists.

Culture vs. politics

What had happened was that a chasm had opened up between religiocultural goals and politics ends. Any tectonic shift in the Indian polity, if it comes, is therefore not likely to happen in the political landscape, but under a vaster, less clearly contoured cultural terrain.

In a sense, we can see the battle over the future of Hindutva as one between the visions of Savarkar and Golwalkar. The experience of Hindu nationalists in democratic power suggests that Savarkar's vision of a directly political transformation of India into a Hindu state is not, as far as we can see in 2002, likely to be realized. Hindutva ideologues came to understand this over the course of the years the BJP first came to national power. Despite the occasional polemical twitch (reviving the plan to reclaim Hindu "sacred sites" from mosques) and the institutional jerk (replacing Congress appointees on national academic bodies with those more sympathetic to Hindutva readings of history and culture), the inertia of coalition politics and the dictates of a fractious yet astute Indian electorate appeared to keep the BJP from becoming an effective vehicle for the recasting of the Indian polity. Ironically, where the BJP-led government had any success, it was in matters of economic governance and international relations, where Hindutva ideology played no role. This scarcely led to any a congruence of interest between the BJP high command and the rest of the Parivar.

The longer the BJP stayed in limited power, the more Hindu nationalism seemed to take on a religiocultural manifestation. The VHP began to organize the engagement of Hindu religious figures and organization in debates about the nature of India. The RSS ideal of a change in Hindu culture as the prerequisite for the creation of the Hindu nation seemed more and more the sustainable goal of Hindutva activity. During the great festival of the Maha Kumb Mela in Allahabad in 2001, for example, the VHP succeeded in organizing a "Hindu Sansad" or Convocation of religious figures, bringing under one roof what nearly amounted to a collective Hindu papacy, demonstrating the strength of the idea that there could be one unified "Hinduism." Although – and perhaps precisely because – many religious figures, orders, and organizations warned against such a gathering becoming used for "political" ends by the VHP, the general principle of pan-Hindu meetings and agreement seem to have been presupposed. To the extent that the growth of a sense of a common Hindu identity was long the aim of the RSS, the very organizational fact of such a Hindu gathering under the aegis of the Parivar suggested that there was some confluence between Parivar ideology and a shift in the nature of contemporary Hindu self-conceptions.

Contemporary political Hinduism, then, is a complex phenomenon. On the one hand, the actual experience of political power demonstrates the limits of religion-derived ideology in the governance of the Indian polity, democratic, pluralist, economically emergent, and geopolitically promising as it is at the beginning of the twenty-first century. On the other hand, as Hindu culture becomes implicated in the affirmation of identity in the face of global erosion of difference – as Hindus construct identities through creative interpretations of history and community – organizations mediating cultural politics can seem to offer ways and means for such construction. It is here that the VHP in particular seems able to exploit the need of some Hindus in their search for self-definition. By providing organizational wherewithal, apparently useful educational resources, and scope for relentless self-affirmation, the VHP can seem to offer a way for Hindu self-definition. If there is sufficient support for such activity, then the cultural route to making India a Hindu nation might still seem open. But this does not seem a straightforward or open route. The very plurality of the Indian people – especially the "Hindus" – that seemed to have made a direct political transformation of India virtually impossible, now stands in the way of any easy prognosis about the future of Hindu nationalism.

Annotated Bibliography

Basu, A. 1996. "Mass Movement or Elite Conspiracy? The Puzzle of Hindu Nationalism," in D. Ludden, ed., *Making India Hindu*. Delhi: Oxford University Press, pp. 55–80. Hindutva and the wider social context of India.

Bidwai, P and A. Vanaik. 2000. *South Asia on a Short Fuse*. Delhi: Oxford University Press. Highly critical polemic against India's nuclear policy.

Crossman, B. and R. Kapur. 1999. *Secularism's Last Sigh? Hindutva and the (Mis)Rule of Law*. Delhi: Oxford University Press. Critical review of the legal issues.

Fox, R. 1996. "Communalism and Modernity," in D. Ludden, ed., *Making India Hindu*. Delhi: Oxford University Press, pp. 235–49. The role of Western ideologies in Indian politics.

Gold, D. 1991. "Organized Hinduism: from Vedic Truth to Hindu Nation," in M. E. Marty and R. S. Appleby, eds., *Fundamentalisms Observed*. Chicago: Chicago University Press. Classic and seminal paper on Hindutva.

Gopal, S., ed. 1993. *Anatomy of a Confrontation: Ayodhya and the Rise of Communal Politics in India*. London: Zed Books.

Graham, B. 1990. *Hindu Nationalism and Indian Politics: The Origins and Development of the Bharatiya Jana Sangh*. Cambridge: Cambridge University Press.

Hansen, T. B. 1999. *The Saffron Wave: Democracy and Hindu Nationalism in Modern India*. Princeton: Princeton University Press. Wide-ranging historical and critical study; strongly negative conclusions on the role of populism in the rise of Hindutva.

Hasan, M. 1993. "Competing Symbols and Shared Codes: Inter-community Relations in Modern India," in S. Gopal, ed., *Anatomy of a Confrontation: Ayodhya and the Rise of Communal Politics in India.* London: Zed Books. Sympathetic exploration of the amicable dimension of Hindu–Muslim relations.

Jaffrelot, C. 1996. *Hindu Nationalist Movement in India.* New York: Columbia University Press. Authoritative and comprehensive study.

Ludden, D., ed. 1996. *Making India Hindu: Religion, Community, and the Politics of Democracy in India.* Delhi: Oxford University Press. Wide-ranging collection of essays on a range of relevant topics.

Madan, T. N. 1997. *Modern Myths, Locked Minds: Secularism and Fundamentalism in India.* Delhi: Oxford University Press. Thoughtful challenge to India's constitutional structure.

Nandy, A. et al. 1995. *Creating a Nationality – The Ramjanmabhumi Movement and Fear of the Self.* Delhi: Oxford University Press. Nuanced account of the psychological crisis of identity in relation to the Ayodhya issue.

Pandey, G., ed. 1993. *Hindu and Others: The Question of Identity in India Today.* New Delhi: Viking.

Ram Prasad, C. 1993. "Hindutva Ideology: Extracting the Fundamentals," *Contemporary South Asia* 2 (3): 285–309. Theoretical analysis of pluralism and Hindutva.

——. 2000. "Hindu Nationalism and the International Relations of India," in K. Dark, ed., *Religion and International Relations.* Basingstoke: Macmillan.

Richman, P., ed. 1991. *Many Ramayanas: The Diversity of a Narrative Tradition in South Asia.* Berkeley: University of California Press.

van der Veer, P. 1996. "Writing Violence," in D. Ludden, ed., *Making India Hindu.* Delhi: Oxford University Press, pp. 250–69. Eloquent and provocative study of the irreducible inexplicability of communal violence.

Vanaik, A. 1997. *The Furies of Communalism: Religion, Modernity and Secularisation.* London: Verso. Historical and theoretical critique of a variety of Hindu-based ideas and movements, from a strong left-wing perspective.

Useful Websites

www.bjp.org: Official site of the Bharatiya Janata Party.

www.india-today.com: Sophisticated interactive version of the premier Indian news magazine.

www.rss.org: Site of the RSS, contains writings of Hindutva ideologues, especially Golwalkar.

www.the-hindu.com: The respected and widely read Indian newspaper, *The Hindu.*

CHAPTER 26

The Goddess and the Nation: Subterfuges of Antiquity, the Cunning of Modernity

Sumathi Ramaswamy

The "fragile social achievement" (Appadurai 1996: 179) that is the modern nation has needed many symbolic fictions – some enduring, others more ephemeral – to sustain itself over time. Among the most intriguing of these fictions is the imagination of the modern nation as an ancient goddess who, as the embodiment of timeless values and cherished ideals, arouses adoration and commands reverence among her citizen-devotees. We see this fiction at work in many different parts of the modern world – the Americas, Britain, western Europe – but it is perhaps in colonial and postcolonial India, on the putative margins of the metropolitan West where it first started, that the contradictions of thinking the nation simultaneously as ancient and modern become most apparent. In this chapter, by focusing on two such goddesses who put in an appearance in late colonial India – Tami̱ttāy (Mother Tamil), and Bhārat Mātā (Mother India) – I reflect on some of these contradictions, inspired by Sudipta Kaviraj's observation that "the nation, in India . . . is a thing without a past":

> It is radically modern. It can only look for subterfuges of antiquity. It fears to face and admit its own terrible modernity, because to admit modernity is to make itself vulnerable. As a proposal for modern living . . . in a society still knowing only one legitimizing criterion – tradition – it must seek to find past disguises for these wholly modern proposals. (Kaviraj 1993: 13)

I will argue that although both Tami̱ttāy and Bhārat Mātā cloak themselves in the mantle of great antiquity, strategically borrowing for their "disguise" from a vast repository of symbolic practices and beliefs that I gloss here as "Hindu," they are products of a modern imagination, and telltale signs of their modernity set them apart from the pantheon of older Hindu goddesses on whom they are quietly parasitic. In making this argument, I want to obviously resist the notion, shared by both their devotees and some scholars, that these mother-goddesses are but natural expressions of the devotion to the mother-figure that has been deemed a timeless and universal ingredient of Hindu culture and society. Instead, I propose that the imagination of these goddesses has been possible because of a new, even "secular," ideology of motherhood that has accompanied the consolidation of modernity everywhere, India included. All the same, the passions that these goddesses have managed to arouse in the subcontinent, and the structures of sentiments in which they have come to be embedded, are distinctive enough that Tamiḻttāy and Bhārat Mātā are not mere rehearsals of similar symbolic fictions elsewhere, nor indeed are the nationalisms whose fertile imaginations have generated them.

Introducing Tamiḻttāy: Language Devotion in Tamil India

I begin my reflections on such matters with the figure of Tamiḻttāy (figure 26.1), who is the lesser-known and more local of the two, confined as she has been to the Tamil-speaking parts of India, in contrast to the pan-Indic Bhārat Mātā.[1] As the apotheosis of the Tamil language, and the founding mother and guardian deity of the Tamil-speaking community, the moment of her birth can be traced to an 1891 hymn in Tamil by the litterateur P. Sundaram Pillai (1855–97). In this hymn (which since June 1970 has served as the state of Tamil Nadu's official "prayer song"), the earth is imagined as a woman whose beautiful face is *paratak kaṇṭam* (" Bhārat," "India") and whose radiant brow is the southern peninsula. The southern *tirāviṭa nāṭu* ("Dravidian land") adorns that brow as an auspicious *tilakam* (sacred mark). The hymn then declares:

> O great goddess Tamil!
> Like the fragrance of that tilakam, your fame spreads in all directions, and delights the whole world.
> Spellbound in admiration of your splendid youth and power, we offer you our homage.
>
> (quoted in Ramaswamy 1997: 17)

Although there are occasional examples from before the 1890s of the glorification and feminization of the language (Ramaswamy 1998a), I have argued at length elsewhere that it is from the closing years of the nineteenth century that Tamiḻttāy emerges systematically as a figure of speech, worship, and identity in the context of the development of what I have characterized as "Tamil devotion" (*tamiḻpparru*) (Ramaswamy 1997). A loosely-connected network of praise, passion, and practices centered on the adoration of Tamil, Tamil devotion has underwritten many different projects over the course of the twentieth century, beginning with a religious revitalization movement which aimed to identify the authentic Tamil speaker as a follower of the lord Shiva whose worship was most efficacious when conducted through the medium of "divine"

Figure 26.1: Tamiḻttāy (Mother Tamil). Color poster, ca. 1941.
Source: Courtesy Kamban Kazhagam, Karaikkudi, Tamil Nadu.

Tamil (*teyvattamiḻ*). In tandem with this movement (and occasionally at cross purposes with it) were concerted efforts to establish the "classicality" of Tamil in order to prove that Tamil speakers were among the most "civilized" peoples of the world, if not the most. Both projects were largely spearheaded by literary and religious elites in whose musings Tamiḻttāy appears as a deity (*teyvam*) or a queen (*araci*), to be honored and worshipped very much in the manner that divinities and sovereigns are in this culture.

From the 1930s, under the growing influence of what has been characterized as "the Dravidian movement," the Tamil-speaking community also came to be imagined as an autonomous, sovereign nation (Dravida Nadu or Tamil Nadu) in clear opposition to the emergent idea of "India." Through the writings of the poets and publicists of the Dravidian movement, Tami̱lttāy moved out of the elite confines of learned religious and literary treatises and academies which had hitherto been her habitat, and was more widely disseminated through newspapers, street songs, political speeches, and even cinema. In this process, the figure of Tami̱lttāy, as indeed the language she embodied, underwent a fundamental transformation, from autonomous deity and sovereign queen, to a frail and endangered mother totally dependent on her "children," the loyal speakers of Tamil. As the figure of the mother emerged as a sign of the authentic, pure community, and as a metonym for "the people," and as their language – imagined as "mother tongue" – was configured as the bearer of the true soul, spirit, and genius of its speakers, the motherhood of Tamil was fashioned into an instrument with which to contest both British colonialism *and* Indian nationalism. So, Tamil speakers were told:

> There is no distinction at all between our mother who bore us for ten months, gave birth to us, watched over us, sang lullabies to us, and fed us milk and guarded us, and our Tamil language which taught us about good conduct and tradition, and granted us good values and knowledge, and which is the very reason that we live well and in prosperity. We have the same attachment to our language as we have for our mother; we have the same devotion to our language as we have for our mother; we have the same love for our language as we have for our mother. He who disregards his language . . . is like he who disregards his mother and forsakes her . . . (quoted in Ramaswamy 1997: 72)

This assertion that disregarding their language was like disregarding their mothers, even matricide, was frequently used to arouse a "sleeping" populace to come to the rescue of their endangered mother language. This was especially so in the middle decades of the past century when the Indian National Congress party vigorously promoted Hindi as the future national language of India, a cause that was taken up as well with even greater enthusiasm by the independent Indian state after 1947. In the writings of numerous devotees of Tamil, Hindi (caricatured as a bloodsucking demoness, a sultry temptress, an upstart maid, and a false mother) as well as its chief patron, the Indian state, were targeted as the principal enemies of Tamil and Tami̱lttāy, and hence of the incipient Tamil nation (Ramaswamy 1999). Between the late 1930s and mid-1960s, a series of vigorous, sometimes violent, anti-Hindi protests provided the context for the widespread deployment of Tami̱lttāy's body in various stages of distress and disarray. Anti-Hindi poetry as well as populist speeches from these decades abound with provocative images of Tamiḻttāy shackled in chains, or confined to a dungeon. Her "children" were told that their mother's body was riddled with scars and wounds; that her golden figure which was once adorned with magnificent jewels was now trapped in iron manacles; and that she was constantly in tears (Ramaswamy 1998b, 1999).

In her guise as a frail and endangered mother, the Dravidian and Tamil nationalists' Tamiḻttāy closely resembled another "nationalist" manifestation of the goddess in the imagination of those of her devotees who saw themselves simultaneously as "Tamil" and "Indian." For these Tamil "Indianists," Tamil is one among a larger "family" of "mother tongues," harmoniously flourishing within the framework of the Indian nation, rather than outside it. In turn, Tamiḻttāy is a companion to Bhārat Mātā, rather than her victim. Indeed, in their poetic musings, Tamiḻttāy and Bhārat Mātā are imagined in very similar terms. They are both virginal mothers. They are the most ancient of women, compassionate and nourishing. And they are *both* owed allegiance by the Tamil speaker who is simultaneously "Tamil" and "Indian." This is in stark contrast to the radical Dravidianist for whom Bhārat Mātā was a "false mother," and Tamiḻttāy is the only one who deserves the total and unconditional surrender of every loyal Tamil speaker.

In my longer work on the goddess, I have also argued that not only is Tamiḻttāy variously imagined thus by her devotees, as the language that she embodies is variously configured, but that devotion towards her is multiply manifested, as religious, filial, and erotic. Indeed, this is how Tamil devotion, fundamentally a network of patriarchal discourses and practices conducted largely by men, solves the problem of having a female figure enshrined at the very heart of its enterprise. She is first isolated and abstracted from the real world in which Tamil-speaking women of all shades have been disempowered through much of this century; she is then endowed with a plenitude of powers and possibilities which transform her into a strikingly exceptional Woman, not readily confused with the flesh-and-blood women on whom she is also obviously modeled. Though she may be thus empowered, her potential to exceed the control of her (male) creators is contained through her fragmentation. The plethora of multiple personae that she is endowed with works to prevent her consolidation as a threatening all-powerful being, even as it simultaneously opens up the possibility that her various selves may be deployed in contradictory ways for the different projects of her devotees. Tamiḻttāy is thus yet another classic example of the objectification of woman as a thing "to be appropriated, possessed, and exchanged in the social relations of cooperation and competition among men" (Uberoi 1990: 41). Although some Tamil-speaking women have appropriated her to stake out independent claims of their own (Ramaswamy 1992), Tamiḻttāy, like other exemplary female icons, is far from cutting a feminist figure in her guise as tame goddess, benevolent mother, and unsullied virgin. Visible and valorized she may be, but she is very much a figment of the patriarchal imaginations at work in colonial and postcolonial Tamil India (Ramaswamy 1997).

Revisiting Bhārat Mātā: Geopiety in Colonial and Postcolonial India

If Tamilttāy flourishes as an object of "language devotion," the more well-known figure of Bhārat Mātā circulates as an expression of what I have elsewhere characterized as "geopiety," passionate longing for and attachment to a territory named "India, that is Bhārat" (Ramaswamy 2002). As opposed to Tamilttāy who, prior to my own work on her, was quite under-studied by to the scholarly community (for passing reference see Kailasapathy 1970: 64–119; Lakshmi 1990; Pandian 1987; Thaninayagam 1963), Bhārat Mātā has received academic attention from various quarters. This may be partly because, in contrast to Tamilttāy, she was the subject of a fairly extensive official archive that was the product of the British colonial state's interest in her (for colonial interest in the goddess, see Chirol 1910; Ker 1973; McCully 1940: 264–9). Convinced about the centrality of this goddess to the popular mobilizations of Hindu religious revivalists and "revolutionary" nationalists alike, British officials – who were already quite ambivalent about the mother-goddess Kālī on whom she was partly modeled – censored poetry and visuals featuring Bhārat Mātā from the early years of the twentieth century well into the 1940s (Barrier 1974; Shaw 1985). Although this rich archive has yet to be sufficiently analyzed, what is clear is that soon after her initial emergence in the writings of Bengali devotees from the late 1860s, Bhārat Mātā became an all-India personage, appearing in the patriotic poetry of every major linguistic region of the emergent nation from the early years of the twentieth century. It is also clear that it was not just the obviously religiously-inclined nationalist like Aurobindo Ghose (1872–1950) or Subramania Bhārati (1882–1921) who sought her blessings and offered her their allegiance, but even the more "secular" of modernists like Rabindranath Tagore (1861–1941) or Jawaharlal Nehru (1889–1964) who invoked her, if only ambivalently.

Scholarly interest in Bhārat Mātā has also been provoked in recent years by her proliferation in the discourses and symbolic activities of various Hindu nationalist parties whose members have written poems about her, built temples and shrines in her honor, conducted all-India "pilgrimage" processions centered around her, sought to introduce her into their schools, and circulated her visually and materially through postcards and greeting cards, wall posters, and video film (see e.g. Bacchetta 1996; Brosius 1999; McKean 1996; Sarkar 1995; van der Veer 1994). The Bhārat Mātā of today's Hindu nationalists is much more divisive than her previous incarnations and, as Patricia Uberoi rightly notes, less inclined to participate in a "secular" union to which all Indians regardless of their religious affiliation are welcome. "In those days, her flag was invariably the Indian tricolour, not the monochromatic pennant of an imagined Hindu kingdom" (Uberoi 1999–2000: 34). Although Bhārat Mātā today stands as a symbol of militant "Hindu," rather than a composite "Indian," nationalism, I would nonetheless insist that part of the reason for her popularity among her present-day devotees is the hard work that has been done through the course of the previous decades to make her a part of political landscape of the subcontinent in the name of a "secular" India.

It is surprising, therefore, given her ubiquity in twentieth-century India, that Bhārat Mātā has not been subjected to the kind of critical scholarly scrutiny that a comparable figure like Marianne of France has received from Maurice Agulhon (1980) and others (see e.g. Hunt 1984; Mosse 1985). For instance, Bhārat Mātā's remarkable presence in the nationalist aspirations of diasporic Indians in the early decades of the twentieth century, such as the members of the San Francisco-based Ghadar Party, has barely been noticed, nor indeed has the poetry produced on her by Muslim and Sikh devotees (Bose 1997: 63–4; Puri 1993: 140–4), and by even the occasional white Christian votary like C. F. Andrews (Andrews 1914). There is some scholarly work on her place in the patriotic imaginations of her Tamil and Hindi devotees, although we know little yet about the differences that might set apart these regional manifestations from each other (Baskaran 1981; Goswami 1998: 332–45; Ramaswamy 1997).[2] Most of the existing scholarship on the goddess is narrowly focused on Bhārat Mātā in her Bengali guise (writ large as "Indian"), and largely limited to her place in the imagination of Bankim Chandra Chatterjee (1838–94) (see Bose 1997). Although Bankim's well-known musings from the 1870s and 1880s have been undoubtedly crucial to the popularization of the idea of the nation as a goddess and a mother, recent scholarship suggests that the ground had already been cleared for such an imagination to surface through the work of others. As Indira Chowdhury's work shows, Bhārat Mātā had already put in an appearance in the poetry and plays of various Bengali patriots associated with the "Hindu mela" (Hindu fair) in the late 1860s and early 1870s (Chowdhury 1998: 95–119). The notion of India as the female deity "Adibhārati," had also appeared by 1866 in the imagination of Bankim's contemporary, Bhudev Mukhopadhyay (1827–94), who turned for patriotic inspiration to an ancient Puranic legend in which the body of the goddess Satī was dismembered and scattered across the subcontinent in 52 different places which became pilgrimage spots in Hindu sacred geography (Raychaudhuri 1988: 39–41; 63–5). As Tapan Raychaudhuri writes, "Bhudev read into this myth a new meaning":

> When I was a student of Hindu College, a European teacher told [us] that patriotism was unknown to the Hindus, for no Indian language had any word to express the idea. I believed his word and was deeply distressed by the thought. I knew then . . . the mythical account of . . . Sati's death, but that knowledge did not help me refute the teacher's statement or console myself. Now I know that to the descendant of the Aryans the entire motherland with its fifty-two places of pilgrimage is in truth the person of Deity. (quoted in Raychaudhuri 1988: 39)

Bhudev's somaticization of the motherland, thus enabling the transformation of its inhabitants into each other's siblings by virtue of being born of her womb and raised on her milk, clearly anticipates the prolific use of similar somatic imagery in numerous poems on Bhārat Mātā which came to be composed and circulated over the course of the next century and more (Ramaswamy 1998b).

It is in this context of an emergent geopiety that Bankim Chandra's famed hymn "Bande Mātaram," "Homage to [the] Mother," was first published in 1875 in his journal *Bangādarshan.*[3] Incorporated later into his 1882 novel *Ānandamath* [Abbey of Bliss], and set to music by Rabindranath Tagore and sung publicly in 1896 at the Indian National Congress Party's Calcutta session, the hymn celebrated an unnamed "mother" in the following terms:

> I bow to you, Mother,
> well-watered, well-fruited,
> breeze cool, crop green,
> the Mother!
> Nights quivering with white moonlight,
> draped in lovely flowering trees,
> sweet of smile, honeyed speech,
> giver of bliss and boons, the Mother!
> Seven crore[4] voices in your clamorous chant,
> twice seven crore hands holding aloft mighty scimitars,
> Who says, Mother, you are weak?
> Repository of many strengths,
> scourge of the enemy's army, the Mother!
> (quoted in Bose 1997: 53)

Although the hymn is not explicitly or even implicitly territorial, nor does it unambiguously identify "the Mother" it celebrates, nevertheless it soon became the rallying cry for an emergent patriotic cult of Bhārat Mātā from the early years of the twentieth century in the context of the "Swadeshi" movement that swept across Bengal, Madras, the United Provinces, and other parts of British India (Bagchi 1990; Goswami 1998: 431–43; Sarkar 1973, 1987). From the mid-1880s, but especially from 1905 with Abanindranath Tagore's well-known painting featuring her, Bhārat Mātā also becomes an object of "visual piety" (Morgan 1997), as artists sought to convert poetic musing into pictorial reality (see, for example, figure 26.2). In doing so, they invariably turned, as many scholars have noted, to the emergent practices of picturing Hinduism's numerous deities in "god-posters" and "calendar art" (Guha-Thakurtha 1991; Larson, Pal and Smith 1997; Mitter 1994). Pictorial practice thus reaffirmed Bhārat Mātā's status as an ancient "Hindu" goddess that poetic imagination had already conferred on her.

In the course of the past century, her numerous devotees have invariably insisted that Bhārat Mātā is a manifestation of Devī or Durgā, of the female principle embodied in the paradigmatic female divinity, Śakti. So, Bankim's *Bande Mātaram* concludes by addressing the Motherland thus:

> You are Durgā bearing ten weapons of war,
> Kamala at play in the lotuses,
> Goddess of Learning, giver of knowledge,
> I bow to you
> (quoted in Bose 1997: 62)

Figure 26.2: Bhārat Mātā (Mother India). Frontispiece to V. Lakshmanan, *Putiya Arampakalvi Tamil (Mūnrām Puttakam)* (Mannargudi: Shri Shanmugha Publishing House, 1958)

Source: Courtesy Tamil Nadu Archives, Chennai.

Similarly, Bipin Chandra Pal, one of her most passionate of votaries, observed in an essay entitled "India: The Mother," that "[t]he outsider knows her as India":

> The outsider sees only her outer and lifeless physical frame. The outsider sees her as a mere bit of earth, and looks upon her as only a geographical expression and entity. But we, her children, know her even today as our fathers and their fathers had done before, countless generations, as a Being, as a Manifestation of [Śakti] . . . And we have always, and do still worship her as such. (Pal 1923: 106)

While her devotees may think and present her thus, I believe it would be a mistake to assume, as some scholars have indeed, a seamless and transparent connection between Bhārat Mātā and other female goddesses such as Durgā or the goddess of earth, Pṛithvī. So, Vidya Dehejia notes in passing that "[s]ince the land itself is spoken of in Sanskrit as Pṛithvī or goddess earth, it is perhaps not surprising that kingdoms, cities, districts, and boroughs are gendered feminine. India is 'Bhārat Mātā' or 'Mother India' . . . " (Dehejia 1997: 14–15). Diana Eck argues more insistently that since "Bhāratavarsha" or "India" is imagined in Puranic Hinduism as "the dismembered body of the Goddess," it would be erroneous for scholars to link the imagination of Bhārat Mātā to modernity alone, for "such a view of its history lacks a longer historical perspective."

> It is clear that the identification of devis [goddesses] with the land has much older roots in the symbolisation of the body-cosmos as inscribed in the land through its system of devi shrines. A considerable history of pilgrimage to the multitude of India's hilltop, cave, and cliff-side devis preceded the use of the rhetoric of the mother-land in 20th-century Hindu nationalism. (Eck 1999: 34)

I agree with Eck that there indeed is a long tradition within Puranic Hinduism of identifying the earth as female and as the goddess Pṛithvī, and of perceiving the land that we today know of as "India" as sacred (see also Kinsley 1987: 178–96). All the same, I would also insist that an entirely novel way of relating to national territory marks the modern moment in India, as it does elsewhere, and that this novelty manifests itself in the manner in which Bhārat Mātā has been imagined by her patriotic devotees as the presiding goddess of a modern geopolity. But before I detail this, I want to address the various "subterfuges of antiquity" through which "modern" goddesses like Bhārat Mātā (and Tami̱ttāy) have managed to persuade even the learned scholar to forget their modernity.

Subterfuges of Antiquity

Quite simply, the principal reason one can be lulled into believing that Tami̱ttāy and Bhārat Mātā are timeless ancient goddesses is because their devotees unambiguously assert so, and consciously endow them with personalities and powers that are associated with the "eternal" goddesses of the Hindu pantheon, especially Devī, the paradigmatic mother-goddess. So, in his poetry, her ardent devotee places Tamiḻttāy at the very beginning of time itself and in the company of the gods, and deems her to be "everlasting" and "boundless." She is the source of everything in the world – of knowledge and happiness, of wealth and prosperity, of bliss and light, indeed of life itself. In poem after poem composed on and about her since the 1890s, she is declared to be the destroyer of darkness and of false illusions. She cures her followers of anger and jealousy, and grants them true vision. She rids them of afflictions and weeds out their troubles. At her feet, even the worst sinners find salvation. By her very presence, she destroys the sins of her devotees. She is indeed their ultimate refuge (Ramaswamy 1997: 85–97). Listen to one such devotee, the poet Mudiyarasan (b. 1920), who addresses Tamiḻttāy thus:

> Residing in my heart that is your temple, offer me grace;
> Adorned in your garland of poetry, offer me protection; Resting on my tongue, grant me good sense;
> [so that] In verse and word, I will be strong.
> . . .
> I worship you every day and talk about your fame everywhere . . .
> (quoted in Ramaswamy 1997: 85)

And compare this to a random verse from the *Devī Māhātmya*, the paradigmatic text which marks the enshrinement of the idea of the Goddess in Puranic Hinduism:

> O Devi, we bow before you, who are yourself good fortune in the dwellings of the virtuous . . . intelligence in the hearts of the learned, faith in the hearts of the good, and modesty in the hearts of the high-born. May you protect the universe! (quoted in Jagadiswarananda n.d.: 53)

So, by praising her in terms that have been used over the centuries to praise goddesses in this society, Tamiḻttāy, although she is a product of a late colonial imagination, is eternalized and transformed into a timeless divinity. Further, she is not only praised in a manner befitting goddesses, but some well-known genres of praise used over the centuries to praise deities – genres such as the *tirupaḷḷiyeḻucci*, the *tirutacāṅkam*, the *piḷḷaittamiḻ*, the *tūtu*, and so on – are now deployed in praise poetry around Tamiḻttāy. Through the deployment of such poetic genres and praise strategies, her devotees have endowed their language with the powers and charisma that have gathered around deities over the century in this society. In turn, Tamil speakers are encouraged to relate to Tamiḻttāy as they interact with their gods – with a mixture of adulation, reverence, and deep love.

Much the same can be said of Bhārat Mātā who, from early on, was not just consciously modeled on the goddesses Kālī, and Durgā, but even imagined as their incarnations, as I noted earlier. So, soon after Bhudev consciously recast the Puranic Satī as his motherland, another of his contemporaries, Akshaya

Chandra Sarkar, appropriated a Tantric text called *Daśamahāvidyā*, and rewrote it in 1873 with a new protagonist, Bhārat Mātā, imagined variously as the Hindu goddesses Kālī, Bhuvanesvarī, Bhairavī, and so on (Chowdhury 1998: 96–7). Similarly, in Bankim Chandra Chatterjee's *Ānandamath*, a novel that is foundational to the patriotic cult of Bhārat Mātā that soon swamped the subcontinent, "the Motherland" (which shortly afterwards would come to be identified as Bhārat Mātā) is explicitly visualized as an icon housed in a temple, much in the manner that other Hindu goddesses would be enshrined. She manifests herself in three different forms, two of which are unambiguously named Jagaddhātri and Kālī, and the third, the "motherland" of the future, is quite clearly modeled on Durgā, the patron-goddess of all devout Bengalis. Note the similarity between "the motherland" of the future and Durgā in the following statement:

> This is what our Mother will become. Ten arms are spread in ten directions; in each a different weapon, a symbol of a different power, her enemy sprawled defeated at her feet, the lion she rides on mauling her adversary . . . (quoted in Kaviraj 1995: 139)

Such verbal attempts to constitute her as a divine figure through prose and especially verse, were also supplemented by visual productions in which Bhārat Mātā was unambiguously presented to her patriot-devotee as a goddess-like figure. So, beginning with the 1905 painting by Abanindranath Tagore through today's Hindu nationalist visualizations, Bhārat Mātā is invariably endowed with four arms – a somatic feature generally only reserved for deities in Hindu society – with one of her hands held up in a gesture of blessing her "children," in much the same way that Hindu icons are conventionally depicted. Frequently, especially in the pictorial imagination of her more militant devotees, be they her Punjabi-speaking Sikh followers attached to the expatriate Ghadar Party, or her Hindu nationalist devotees of recent years, she stands in the company of the lion, the animal most commonly associated with the goddess Durgā. She is also invariably shown carrying archaic weapons such as tridents and spears (rather than a modern gun), and the ornaments that adorn her body are archaic, as is her clothing.[5]

Many of Tamilttāy's visual representations as well bestow upon her an air of hoary antiquity, even though under the influence of the secular Dravidian movement (some of whose radical followers have even professed atheism), there are attempts made to present her as an everyday Tamil woman, clothed in a modern saree, shorn of any divine attributes. Although the official government of Tamil Nadu statue of the goddess shows her with two arms, the prototype on which it is based – which is currently housed in a "temple" to the goddess in the south Indian town of Karaikkudi – was cast with four arms, one of which is held in a gesture of blessing her subjects. Befitting her status as an ancient goddess of learning and culture, Tamilttāy is frequently shown carrying cadjan leaves (but rarely a printed book, although print capitalism has been critical to the dissemination of her cult).[6] Instead of choosing from a wide array of modern musical instruments that are in use in today's Tamil lifeworld, her devotees have preferred to show their goddess playing the archaic "yāḷ," a lute-like instrument whose great antiquity they laud. The items of jewelry that abundantly adorn her body are declared to be the great works of ancient (but never modern) Tamil literature: so the *Cilapatikāram* [the Lay of the Anklet] jingles on her feet as anklets, the *Maṇimēkalai* [the Jeweled Belt] encircles her waist, and so on. As with Bhārat Mātā, her jewelry and her clothing confer upon her an iconographic persona that consciously remove her in most cases from the everyday Tamil modern (again see figure 26.1).

The Cunning of Modernity

Yet, I insist that in spite of the best efforts of their devotees to pass Bhārat Mātā or Tamiḻttāy off as timeless ancient goddesses, signs of their novelty and modernity are quite apparent to the discerning eye. I do so insist not just because my historicist training allows me to trace their emergence to texts and practices datable to the latter half of the nineteenth century – and not any earlier. My insistence also does not just follow from the conclusions of feminist scholarship that such female figures emerge as iconic in the context of a late colonial world in which motherhood came to be newly privileged, both as the *sine qua non* of women's identity, and also as the foundational site on which pure and true subjectivities and communities could be imagined and reproduced. And lastly, my argument does not just rest on the new ways of visually presenting these goddesses to their devout public (through media such as calendar art, "god posters," cinema, and video) in poses and appearances that can be persuasively described as "modern."

Persuasive enough as these reasons might all be, I rest my case for the modernity of these goddesses on the entirely novel manner in which the entities that they embody – be it the territory of "India" or the Tamil language – come to be reconfigured in late colonial India. In the case of Tamiḻttāy, I have argued elsewhere that it was not until the latter half of the nineteenth century that Tamil emerged as an object of praise in and of itself, deserving adulation for its ability to ensure communication between its speakers, their schooling, and their governance, rather than for commanding the attention of the gods or being the language that they favor. We get a glimpse of this new people-centered ideology that emerges around Tamil in the following declaration from 1879:

> Tamil gave birth to us; Tamil raised us; Tamil sang lullabies to us and put us to sleep; Tamil taught us our first words with which we brought joy to our mothers and fathers; Tamil is the first language we spoke when we were infants; Tamil is the language which our mothers and fathers fed us along with milk; Tamil is the language that our mother, father, and preceptor taught us . . . [T]he language of our home is Tamil; the language of our land is Tamil. (quoted in Ramaswamy 1997: 11)

Such a declaration reflects a new sentiment in which the language comes to be imagined, for the first time, as the personal property of their speakers as a collective. The myriad practices of Tamil devotion place the people who speak Tamil at the very center of the project, as an imagined community of "Tamilians" (*tamiḻar*). This people-centered ideology of modernity inaugurates a patrimonial imagination in which language is constituted as a tangible, material possession that is transmitted from one generation of its speakers to another who relate to it as a property-owning "collective individual." It is such a new imagination which enables, indeed needs, the figure of Tamiḻttāy as the "mother" of all Tamil speakers who are converted into each other's siblings by virtue of the fact that they have been borne by her "womb" and nurtured on her "milk," and who in turn reproduce other future speakers.

The geopiety that produces the imagination of India as Bhārat Mātā is similarly new because the national territory that she embodies is configured in a novel way – as a clearly delineated piece of Earth that is imagined as the exclusive, sovereign, and collective property of its inhabitants, the nation's citizens. The proprietary relationship between the nation's citizens and the territory they inhabit comes to be best signified by maps of the nation that proliferate in the age of nationalism across the modern world, India included. Not surprisingly, visual representations of Bhārat Mātā, the "mother" of the nation, show her in the company of maps and globes (on which "India" is delineated) from the early years of the twentieth century. In some cases, she occupies the entire map of India, in other cases, she appears to rise from it, in still others she replaces the cartographic outline of India with her own body (Ramaswamy 2001; 2002). It is the territorialization of the goddess thus, through her association with a specifically delineated "geo-body" (Thongchai 1994) that colonial and post-colonial geographical identify as "India," which arguably sets apart Bhārat Mātā from Pṛithvī, the older goddess of Earth. The incorporation of the modern map (as indeed the Indian tricolor flag which she frequently holds) into the iconography of Bhārat Mātā signifies a novel way of relating to territory – as a geobody that is rendered visible to the citizen-devotee's eye through cartographic practices.

In both Tamil devotion and Indian geopiety, the objects of their adulation – the Tamil language and the Indian territory – are transformed from rarified abstractions into embodied entities that can be seen and touched. They are, in other words, framed as "pictures." In a provocative essay that has been the subject of much critical discussion, Martin Heidegger has observed that "the fundamental event of the modern age is the conquest of the world as picture." In making this observation, he was in essence underscoring the emergence of the modern subject who stands abstracted from a world that he could observe as "a whole," and in turn, manipulate and have at his "disposal." "There begins that way of being human that means the realm of human quality as a domain given over to measuring and executing, for the purpose of gaining mastery over that which is as a whole" (Heidegger 1977: 132–5). In the last analysis, it is because Tamiḻttāy and Bhārat Mātā are such "pictures," allowing their devotees to see as "a whole" the entities that they embody, that I characterize the imaginations that gave birth to them as "modern." As pictures, they place the language and the terrritory that they represent at the "disposal" of their speakers and inhabitants repectively, sealing the new proprietary attitudes towards "Tamil" and "India" that have been ushered in by modernity. The subterfuges of antiquity to which their votaries resort notwithstanding, it is the cunning of modernity that enables the very imagination of Tamilttāy and Bhārat Mātā as icons of new collective identites.

Notes

1 For brief discussions of Tamilttāy's presence in Sri Lankan Tamil culture, see Daniel 1989: 35–6 and Suseendirarajah 1980.
2 For example, in all the poetry in Tamil on Bhārat Mātā that I have read from the twentieth century, she is never imagined as a widow, whereas Indira Chowdhury notes that she does so appear in the imagination of Bengali patriots of the 1860s and 1870s. It is possible that this in itself reflects the preoccupation with the plight of widowhood among Bengali social reformers in the later half of the nineteenth century (Chowdhury 1998: 96–7). Similarly, see Joseph Alter's thoughtful comments on how the understanding of Bhārat Mata in the wrestling communities of northern India is significantly different from the "xenophobic chauvinism" that marks the Hindu nationalists (Alter 1996: 126–9).
3 There are numerous works on the hymn and its subsequent history, much of it fairly hagiographic and patriotic in content. For some useful observations, see Bose 1974 and Das 1984.
4 A crore is a unit of measure which is equivalent to ten million. This figure betrays the fact that Bankim's "Mother" was really Banga Mātā (Mother Bengal) rather than Bhārat Mātā (Bose 1997: 53).
5 It has to be noted that quite frequently, Bhārat Mātā appears wearing a saree and blouse in a style that became popular only from the later half of the nineteenth century – yet another telltale sign of her modernity. For a perceptive essay that considers the politics of "clothing' the goddess figure more generally in the pictorial practices of colonial and postcolonial India, see Guha-Thakurtha 1999.
6 Even when she occasionally appears holding a printed book – invariably the *Tirukkural* or the *Tolkāppiyam* – rather than cadjan leaves, this is carefully selected from Tamil's corpus of ancient rather than modern works.

References

Agulhon, Maurice. 1980. *Marianne into Battle: Republican Imagery and Symbolism in France, 1789–1880.* Trans. Janet Lloyd. Cambridge: Cambridge University Press.
Alter, Joseph S. 1996. "The Celibate Wrestler: Sexual Chaos, Embodied Balance, and Competitive Politics in North India," in *Social Reform, Sexuality and the State*, ed. P. Uberoi. New Delhi: Sage.
Andrews, C. F. 1914. "Bhārat-Mātā," *Modern Review* 15: 81.

Appadurai, Arjun. 1996. *Modernity at Large.* Minneapolis: University of Minnesota Press.

Bacchetta, Paola. 1996. "Hindu Nationalist Women as Ideologues: The 'Sangh,' the 'Samiti' and their Differential Concepts of the Hindu Nation," in *Embodied Violence: Communalising Women's Sexuality in Souih Asia*, eds. K. Jayawardene and M. d. Alwis. New Delhi: Kali for Women.

Bagchi, Jasodhara. 1990. "Representing Nationalism: Ideology of Motherhood in Colonial Bengal," *Economic and Political Weekly (Review of Women's Studies)* 24 (42/3): WS 65–71.

Barrier, N. Gerald. 1974. *Banned: Controversial Literature and Political Control in British India, 1907–1947.* Columbia, MO: University of Missouri Press.

Baskaran, S. Theodore. 1981. *The Message Bearers: The Nationalist Politics and the Entertainment Media in South India, 1880–1945.* Madras: Cre-A.

Bose, S. K. 1974. "The Mantra and the Monastery," in *Bankim Chandra Chatterji.* New Delhi: Publications Division, Government of India.

Bose, Sugata. 1997. "Nation as Mother: Representations and Contestations of 'India' in Bengali Literature and Culture," in *Nationalism, Democracy and Development: State and Politics in India*, eds. S. Bose and A. Jalal. Delhi: Oxford University Press.

Brosius, Christiane. 1999. "Empowering Visions: A Study on Videos and the Politics of Cultural Nationalism in India (1989–1998)." Ph. D., Anthropology, Europa University Viadrina, Frankfurt.

Chirol, Valentine. 1910. *The Indian Unrest.* London: Macmillan.

Chowdhury, Indira. 1998. *The Frail Hero and Virile History: Gender and the Politics of Culture in Colonial Bengal.* Delhi: Oxford University Press.

Daniel, E. Valentine. 1989. "Three Dispositions towards the Past: One Sinhala, Two Tamil," *Social Analysis* 25: 22–42.

Das, Sisir Kumar. 1984. "The Story of a Song," in *The Artist in Chains: The Life of Bankimchandra Chatterji.* New Delhi: New Statesman.

Dehejia, Vidya. 1997. "Issues of Spectatorship and Representation," in *Representing the Body: Gender Issues in Indian Art*, ed. V. Dehejia. New Delhi: Kali for Women in association with The Book Review Literary Trust.

Eck, Diana L. 1999. "The Imagined Landscape: Patterns in the Construction of Hindu Sacred Geography," in *Tradition, Pluralism, and Identity: In Honour of T N. Madan*, eds. V. Das, D. Gupta, and P. Uberoi. New Delhi: Sage.

Goswami, Manu. 1998. "The Production of India: Colonialism, Nationalism, and Territorial Nativism." Ph.D. dissertation, University of Chicago, Chicago.

Guha-Thakurta, Tapati. 1991. "Women as 'Calendar Art' Icons: Emergence of Pictorial Stereotype in Colonial India," *Economic and Political Weekly (Review of Women's Studies)* 26(43): 91–9.

——. 1999. "Clothing the Goddess: The Modern Contest over Representations of Devi," in *Devi, The Great Goddess: Female Divinity in South Asian Art*, ed. V. Dehejia. Washington, DC: Smithsonian Institution.

Heidegger, Martin. 1977. "The Age of the World Picture," in *The Question Concerning Technology and Other Essays.* New York: Garland.

Hunt, Lynn. 1984. *Politics, Culture, and Class in the French Revolution.* Berkeley: University of California Press.

Jagadiswarananda. n.d. *Devi Mahatmyam* (Glory of the Divine Mother). Madras: Sri Ramakrishna Math.

Kailasapathy, K. 1970. *Aṭiyum Muṭiyum* (Essays on Tamil Literature). Madras: New Century Book House.

Kaviraj, Sudipta. 1993. "The Imaginary Institution of India," in *Subaltern Studies VII: Writings on South Asian History and Society*, eds. P. Chatterjee and R. Guha. Delhi: Oxford University Press.

——. 1995. *The Unhappy Consciousness: Bankimchandra Chattopadhyay and the Formation of Nationalist Discourse in India*. Delhi: Oxford University Press.

Ker, James C. 1973 (1917). *Political Trouble in India (1907–1917)*, repr. ed. Delhi: Oriental Publishers.

Kinsley, David. 1987. *Hindu Goddesses: Visions of the Divine Feminine in the Hindu Religious Tradition*. Delhi: Motilal Banarsidass.

Lakshmi, C. S. 1990. "Mother, Mother-community and Mother Politics in Tamil Nadu," *Economic and Political Weekly (Review of Women's Studies)* 25(42/3): 72–83.

Larson, Gerald James, Pratapaditya Pal, and H. Daniel Smith, eds. 1997. *Changing Myths and Images: Twentieth-century Popular Art in India*. Bloomington: University Art Museum, University of Indiana.

McCully, Bruce. 1940. *English Education and Origins of Indian Nationalism*. New York: Columbia University Press.

McKean, Lise. 1996. *Divine Enterprise: Gurus and the Hindu Nationalist Movement*. Chicago: University of Chicago Press.

Mitter, Partha. 1994. *Art and Nationalism in Colonial India, 1850–1922: Occidental Orientations*. Cambridge: Cambridge University Press.

Morgan, David. 1997. *Visual Piety: A History and Theory of Popular Religious Images*. Berkeley: University of California Press.

Mosse, George L. 1985. *Nationalism and Sexuality*. Madison: University of Wisconsin Press.

Pal, Bipin Chandra. 1923. "India: The Mother," in *The Soul of India: A Constructive Study on Indian Thought and Ideas*. Madras: Tagore.

Pandian, Jacob. 1987. *Caste, Nationalism, and Ethnicity: An Interpretation of Tamil Cultural History and Social Order*. Bombay: Popular Prakashan.

Puri, Harish K. 1993. *Ghadar Movement: Ideology, Organisation and Strategy*, 2nd ed. Amritsar: Guru Nanak Dev University.

Ramaswamy, Sumathi. 1992. "Daughters of Tamil: Language and the Poetics of Womanhood in Tamilnadu, 1938–1940," *South Asia Research* 12(1): 38–59.

——. 1997. *Passions of the Tongue: Language Devotion in Tamil India, 1891–1970*. Berkeley: University of California Press.

——. 1998a. "The Language of the People in the World of Gods: Ideologies of Tamil before the Nation," *Journal of Asian Studies* 57(1): 66–92.

——. 1998b. "Body Language: The Somatics of Nationalism in Tamil India," *Gender and History* 10(1): 78–109.

——. 1999. "The Demoness, the Maid, the Whore, and the Good Mother: Contesting the National Language in India," *International Journal of the Sociology of Language* 140: 1–28.

——. 2001. "Maps and Mother Goddesses in Modern India," *Imago Mundi* 53: 97–114.

——. 2002. "Visualising India's Geo-body: Globes, Maps, Bodyscapes," *Contributions to Indian Sociology* 36(1&2): 157–95.

Raychaudhuri, Tapan. 1988. *Europe Reconsidered: Perceptions of the West in Nineteenth Century Bengal*. Delhi: Oxford University Press.

Sarkar, Sumit. 1973. *The Swadeshi Movement in Bengal, 1903–1908*. New Delhi: People's Publishing House.

Sarkar, Tanika. 1987. "Nationalist Iconography: Image of Women in 19th-Century Bengali Literature," *Economic and Political Weekly* 22(47): 2011–15.

——. 1995. "Heroic Women, Mother Goddesses: Family and Organisation in Hindutva Politics," in *Women and the Hindu Right*, eds. T. Sarkar and U. Butalia. New Delhi: Kali for Women.

Shaw, Graham, and Mary Lloyd, eds. 1985. *Publications Proscribed by the Government of India: A Catalogue of the Collections in the India Office Library and Records and the Department of Oriental Manuscripts and Printed Books, British Library Reference Division.* London: The British Library.

Suseendirarajah, S. 1980. "Religion and Language in Jaffna Society," *Anthropological Linguistics* 22(8): 345–62.

Thaninayagam, Xavier S. 1963. "Regional Nationalism in Twentieth-Century Tamil Literature," *Tamil Culture* 10(l): 1–23.

Uberoi, Patricia. 1990. "Feminine Identity and National Ethos in Indian Calendar Art," *Economic and Political Weekly (Review of Women's Studies)* 25(17): WS 41–8.

——. 1999–2000. "Times Past: Gender and the Nation in 'Calendar Art,'" *Indian Horizons* 46–7: 24–39.

van der Veer, Peter. 1994. *Religious Nationalism: Hindus and Muslims in India.* Berkeley: University of California Press.

Winichakul, Thongchai. 1994. *Siam Mapped: A History of the Geo-Body of a Nation.* Honolulu: University of Hawaii Press.

CHAPTER 27

Gender in a Devotional Universse

Vasudha Narayanan

Gender is understood and acted out in different ways in the many Hindu *sampradāyas* or traditions. The gender of the human being, the soul, and the deity are articulated, commented upon, debated, contested, performed through song and dance, poetry and theology. The discourses range from equating gender with biological sex, essentializing the "womanly" and "manly" characteristics, to changing behavior patterns which point to fluid gender identifications, to the rejection and transcendence of gender polarities. The resources for such discussions can be sought in brahminical Sanskrit literature which is frequently patriarchal in tone, vernacular poems, songs, narratives, rituals, icons, arrangement of temple spaces, folklore, and performing arts. The materials are plenty – we are looking at over 3,000 years of literature and over 4,000 years of material culture. One can move through the labyrinths of Śiva or Viṣṇu worship, or seek reinforcements for gender theories through literature and rituals relating to the Goddess. We find many socially celebrated narratives and rituals of deities and devotees taking on roles and raiments associated with the "other sex." One may spend the entire chapter deconstructing the many dimensions of Viṣṇu's incarnation as the enchanting woman, Mohinī, and its commemoration in annual temple rituals. We could explore the portrayal of deities in iconography and popular calendar art to see how and why they are depicted as simultaneously having what may be "commonly" perceived as "male" *and* "female" attributes. Alternatively, one may look at social constructions of gender by just looking at what is called India's "third sex" – the transgendered *hijra* community. On the other hand, philosophical discourses push us away from gender dichotomies to spaces which transcend the traditional polarities. The Hindu traditions have a wealth of materials which can inform us on how some human beings have understood gender in many ways over four millennia; narratives and arts which can contribute to the current academic discourses on gender.

In this chapter, I will discuss issues relating to gender in a modest fashion by using the Śrīvaiṣṇava tradition – one of the well known communities in south India and one which has a dominant influence in temple rituals in North America – as a thread to lead us through literature and rituals, songs and dance. Although the gender of the human being, soul, and the deity are all important, I will spend more time talking about devotees and the soul. There will only be a brief discussion on the all-important topic of gender and God in Hinduism, a topic which is worthy of a monograph on its own; and regretfully, no discussion at all of India's "third sex."[1] Since the Hindu traditions have transmitted their lore over centuries through the performing arts, I will allude to them several times. Even though it will not be possible to cover many areas in this chapter, using one tradition as a "base camp," I hope, will give us a vista point to look at the expansive landscape.

The Gender of the Devotee

The mother says of her "daughter":

> Night and day, her eyes know no sleep.
> She splashes her tears with her hands.
> *O conch, O wheel,* she cries and folds her hand;
> *O Lotus eyes* she cries and grows faint.
> *How can I survive without you?*
> she asks, and searches the earth, groping with her hands.
> O Lord of Tiruvarankam, where red *kayal* fish dart in the
> waters, what are you doing with her?
> (Tiruvāymoli, 7.2.1)

So sang the poet Nammāḻvār in the ninth century CE. This song, which is part of a set of 11 verses, embedded in longer poem of 1,102 verses, is recited in some Viṣṇu temples in south India every day and acted out in a ritual once a year. His poem, the Tiruvāymoli ("Sacred Utterance") is addressed to Viṣṇu, whom he addresses as a mother, father, support of all being, child, and lover. Although Nammāḻvār was a male, like many other devotional poets, he frequently spoke in the voice of a woman in his poems. His image, thought to be charged with his presence, is enshrined in many temples including the sacred temple town of Śrīraṅgam. During the ritual in which this particular verse is enacted, he is dressed as a beautiful woman. Exquisitely clad in silk clothes, with an artificial braid flowing from "his" head, and bejeweled, he is taken to meet "her" lover – the Lord Viṣṇu. In song and ritual, Nammāḻvār, the male poet, is portrayed as woman longing for "her" beloved.

Nammāḻvār's stance as a woman in this poem and in the ritual, waiting for the male God, is a trope that runs through the many Hindu *sampradāyas* or traditions. It comes up in literature, song and dance, and rituals, and we will use it to lead us into the issue of gender in the Hindu traditions. Nammālvār wrote four poems and in all of these he seeks to be united with Lord Viṣṇu. He is one of 12 poet-saints considered as paradigmatic devotees by a community called ŚrīVaiṣṇava. This community worships the Goddess Śrī (Lakṣmī) and Viṣṇu and considers the words of these 12 poet-saints to be a revelation, a Tamil Veda, paralleling the Sanskrit Vedas. In the eleventh century CE the ŚrīVaiṣṇava community introduced the Tiruvāymoli into the temple and home liturgies and began to comment on it – initially, orally and through the performing arts, and then later in writing. Selections from the Tiruvāymoli are recited daily at Śrīvaiṣṇava homes and temples. A full recitation with verbal and performative commentaries is also held during the Adhyayana Utsava, the annual Festival of Recitation. The program for 21 days starting with the new moon includes (a) the recitation of poems; (b) processions of the festival image through the streets; (c) the dressing up of the festival image of Viṣṇu and the poets in various costumes; (d) enactment of particular episodes from the saints' poetry or the epics by special cantor/actors called *araiyars* in Śrīraṅgam, Śrīvillpuṭṭur, and Ālvār Tirunāgari, all temple towns in the state of Tamilnadu, India. Of the many activities that take place during these celebrations, we will, in the course of this chapter, just look at two: the songs of Nammālvār (and other poets) composed from the voice of a woman, and particularly, the dressing up of Nammālvār as a young girl, and second, the portrayal of the male God, Viṣṇu, as an "enchanting woman" (Sanskrit: *mohinī*), to see how gender can function in some Hindu traditions. Specifically we will explore how the human being, the soul, and the Supreme Being are gendered in literature and the performing arts.

The Poet as a Woman: Nammālvār's Words for "Her" Beloved

About a quarter of the Tiruvāymoli is written from the voice of a woman. Nammālvār speaks through the voices of "women" characters whose literary roles were well known in Tamil poetry written in the first few years of the common era. In the love poems written around the first and second centuries CE (Ramanujan, Hart, Narayanan) we meet young women and men in love. The poet – frequently male – speaks in the voices of a young girl in love, or her mother or friend who seem concerned about her welfare. None of the men nor the women alluded to in these poems were named; the poems were supposed to be "universal" and naming them would limit them. Nammālvār adopts these voices; however, in this case, both the lovers are named. The "young woman" is Nammālvār, and the "young man" is Lord Viṣṇu. The later Śrīvaiṣṇava tradition even gave a name for Nammālvār's guise as a woman: they call "her" personality Parankusa Nāyaki or the Lady Parankusa. Tirumankai ālvār, another male poet who wrote such poetry is called the Lady Parakala by the community.

In the temple town of Śrīraṅgam, when the works of these poets (along with those of ten others) are recited annually during the Festival of Recitation, some episodes are acted out in rituals over a 21-day period in front of the icon of Viṣṇu. These are attended by thousands of people, with about 400,000 pilgrims coming in on important days. Viṣṇu, in Śrīraṅgam, is called Raṅganātha, the "lord of the stage" or the "lord of the island." Although the main icon within the inner shrine depicts him as reclining on the coils of the serpent called Ananta ("without end," "infinity"), the smaller festival icon of him standing upright is used in procession and celebrations such as the Festival of Recitation. On the tenth day of the recitation, this icon of Viṣṇu is dressed as a woman. This is considered to be a very special annual event and the ritual is called "Mohinī alankaram" ("the adornment as an entrancing woman.") The crowds are the thickest on this day and the next, the eleventh day after new moon (ekadaś) in the month of Margasirsa (December 15 to January 14). Viṣṇu, clad in white and red silks, with beautiful jewelry sparkles as a woman. "She" is taken in a procession around the temple as the throngs worship "her." This attire and dressing of Viṣṇu is a special favorite with the pilgrims; "truly," they say every year, "tonight, the Lord is more beautiful than the Goddess (Lakṣmī) herself."

The recitation of the Tiruvāymoli begins the next day; the eleventh day of the festival. On the seventeenth day of the festival (that is seventh day of the Tiruvāymoli recitation), the section in which Nammāḻvār, in the voice of a woman addresses, the lord at Śrīraṅgam (the poem given in the beginning of this chapter) is acted out. Just before the celebrations that day, the image of Nammāḻvār is dressed as a woman in beautiful silk garments, with a hairpiece and artificial limbs. The Lady Parankusa, as "she" is known, is carried in a palanquin to the Hall of a Thousand Pillars and the *araiyars* by "her" side recite poems with emotion. As they finish the moving verses, depicting "her" intense longing for union with the Lord of Śrīraṅgam, the priests who are standing by Viṣṇu's icon, lift him from his palanquin into their arms and walk towards Nammāḻvār. This festival icon of Viṣṇu, known popularly as "the Handsome Bridegroom," seems to be almost walking towards the devotee to be with "her" for a rapturous union, and the crowds applaud. The following day, Nammāḻvār is back in the Hall, back again in his usual clothes.

Sometimes, Nammāḻvār, Tirumankai Āḻvār, and other poets, step outside the Tamil literary conventions and see themselves as participants in an episode from the epics, the Rāmayana or the Mahābhārata, or one of the stories of Kṛṣṇa (an incarnation of Viṣṇu) given in the Purāṇas, devotional texts composed in the first millennium CE. Nammāḻvār, and especially Tirumankai, see themselves as women connected with Kṛṣṇa and speak in the voices of Yaśodā, Kṛṣṇa's foster mother, or one of the cowherd girls. The following verse by Nammāḻvār is typical of the genre:

> You were gone the whole day,
> grazing cows Kanna!
> Your soothing words burn my soul.
> Evening tramples like a rogue elephant
> and the fragrance of jasmine buds,

loosening my bonds, blows upon me.
Embrace my beautiful breasts
with the fragrance of the wild jasmine
upon your radiant chest.
Give me the nectar of your mouth,
and with your jeweled lotus hands.
adorn my lowly head.

The poet's identifying himself as a "gopi," one of the many cowherd girls who is in love with Kṛṣṇa, is a motif that we find in literature all over India. Although this is one of the earlier examples, in time, the love of the gopis, especially that of Rādhā, the girlfriend and consort of Kṛṣṇa, is seen as exemplary. Some poets approach Kṛṣṇa and speak as though they were the cowherd girl (Hardy, Hawley); others, in later centuries speak in the voices of Rādhā's girlfriends. Men and women poets adopt the voices of girls speaking directly to Viṣṇu or Kṛṣṇa; though as Hawley has shown, at least in the north Indian sixteenth-century literature, there *is* a discernible difference in the voice of the woman poet Mīrā and the voice of the male poet Sur who adopts a woman's voice (Hawley 1986).

The human being addressing the deity as a male lover is pronounced in some of the performing arts in the Hindu culture, especially classical dance. One has to note three elements in this scenario: first, that the intensity of the passion articulated in the song – whether it is distress or wrath at the lover not coming – is palpable and it is not *simply* or *just* a metaphor for or an allegorical description of the separation (*viraha*) between the human soul and the Supreme Being. To explain it away as only spiritual separation is to take away from the integrity of the poet's experience and his/her stark emotion. One cannot interpret away the intensity of the poet's bodily longing as an allegory; one cannot speak simply in terms of the soul's quest for god. That is to lose sight of the drama of the poet's longing and love. Second, the devotional theme and the spiritual longing are *also* integral themes undergirding or sometimes overt in the songs and dances; we cannot by any measure think of these songs as *just* romantic fictions or conceits. Finally, one cannot simply speak about the "lover" poems ("*nāyaki bhāva*," "mode of the heroine") and songs as a monolithic genre. There are many varieties of such "lover" poems with different portrayals of women; different notions of "femininities." It is this last point that I will be nuancing, to show that one cannot automatically stereotype the woman's voice as the helpless, pining lover.

One of the many ways in which the separation between God and the human being is portrayed is by speaking of the agony that prevails when one is separated from one's beloved. Frequently, one is suspicious of one's lover; a suspicion that transforms itself into wrath or distress. In many songs that are choreographed and performed in the Bhārata Natyam style, Viṣṇu, Śiva, or Murgaṉ, all revered Gods in the Hindu tradition, are seen as the absent or errant male. While, in general, the mood in the early Tamil poems (as in the Tiruvāymoli) we see more verses where a poet speaks in a distressed, "pining" tone than in an angry one, this is by no means the only sentiment expressed in the "woman's" voice.

Some women poets like Āṇḍāl (eighth century) tease Kṛṣṇa as "a prankster who knows no dharma" (*Nacciyar Tirumoli* 14: 4) and Nammāḻvār, in anger, speaks of Viṣṇu as the "cruel, wicked one" (Tiruvāymoli 5.3.5). Nammāḻvār, in the voice of a woman, also threatens to "ride the 'palmyrah horse' " (Tamil: *matal*) to show the extremity of "her" passion for Viṣṇu:

> Lifting my modesty, stealing my heart
> the Lord of the divine ones reaches the high heavens.
> My friend, this I swear:
> I shall shock all the earth,
> I shall do weird deeds
> and like a *wild woman*
> ride the palmyra stem like a horse.
> With no sense of shame, I shall ride
> the palmyra stem through every street in town
> and women from all the lands will cheer me on
> And I shall demand from the Lord
> a cool blossom from the tulai plant
> and adorn my head with it.
> (Tiruvāymoli 5.3.9–10)

This is an allusion to a ritual in which a *man* publicly proclaimed his love for a woman by making an artificial horse using sharp palmyra leaves and "riding it" through the village. The ritual is described in Tamil literature in the first two centuries of the common era. The lover, the hero, was now willing to throw all circumspection to the winds and publicly announce his love for a young girl. The heroine, the village leaders, and families of the young man and woman, would all be convinced of his passion, and hastily facilitated his union with his beloved. This ritual threatened to hurt the man physically and was considered to be an extreme step; the villagers, witnessing it, would be convinced that he had to get married to his love immediately and arrange for the wedding. "Riding a palmyra horse" was supposed to have been practiced *only by men*; Tamil texts describing love proscribed it for women. The act, even for men, was considered to be "scandalous." In Nammāḻvār's poem, we have a "double" crossing over – Nammāḻvār, a male, speaking as a woman, who wants to act like a male. The "essentializing" of women that may be perceived in the figure of a love sick girl of Tamil poetry is teased into other modes of behavior. We see a different twist in this scenario in a poem by Tirumankai Āḻvār, also around the ninth century CE. Tirumankai, also in the voice of a "girl," wants to ride the palmyra horse, but acknowledges that a woman resorting to this act is against the rules of love, at least according to Tamil conventions. He says:

> It is true we have heard and understand that in southern texts that it is not fit for young girls, girls with glances soft as a fawn, girls with the gait of a swan, to discard their shame and modesty and ride the *matal* for their men. But we do not accept it. We hold up the path shown in the north. (Periya tiru matal 21)

Note that Tirumankai Āḻvār says clearly that he knows the grammar of Tamil and the grammar of love in Tamil lands do not countenance women doing the *matal*. However, he says, he accepts the "northern" path. Women in the north, he says, ride the *matal* to show their unbridled passion for men. In his poems, he lists some of these women.

It is obvious that the concept and ritual of *matal* is completely south Indian. Yet, when Tirumankai lists his examples of women who recklessly proclaimed their love in northern India, he rounds up the usual suspects and then some. His lists include Umā, Ulupi, Uṣa (daughter of Banasura), Vegāvatī and Vāsavadatta, all women whose passion for their lovers has been celebrated in written and oral traditions. He also includes Sītā, who though known for the love she had for Rāma, is hardly the hotheaded exemplar of a *matal* riding lover. What Tirumankai is saying is that these women articulated their love in public and were prepared to die if it was not reciprocated. Understandably, some of this is exaggeration, but one gets the point. Umā is Pārvati and as Sātī had burnt herself to display the pride of her love for Śiva. Ulupi married Arjuna, Vāsavadatta, and Vegāvatī figure in stories in the Kathasarita sāgara. Ulupi, a woman, actually kidnapped Arjuna and took him to her land; Uṣa had a young man called Aniruddha (Kṛṣṇa's grandson) abducted and brought to her chambers. Umā/Sātī killed herself. By stating this, Tirumankai says that it is acceptable for women to go public with their passion because it is done in northern India, even though he is aware it is not inadmissible in the Tamil country. *What we have in this traditional literature is the painting of north and south Indian cultures and womanhood according to south Indian texts in broad strokes; what we have is a kind of "essentializing" of cultures and gender, and a ninth-century "protest" against the essentializing of gender.* And so, while Tirumankai, a man, has adopted the stance of a woman in love, he feels that desperate times call for desperate deeds and he is willing to take the initiative and declare his love publicly.

In any event, the love-sick woman is only *one* of the many kinds of women portrayed in literature. Speaking just about women in love, there are many discernible in texts and drama. This figure of the "heroine" or the primary character/dancer is developed in the *Natya Śāstra* or "Treatise on Dance," attributed to the sage Bhārata. This text, possibly compiled around the first two centuries of the Common Era, outlines the principal features of classical dance in its religious context. The *Natya Śāstra* becomes the reference for almost all classical dance forms of India in later centuries. In this text, Bhārata speaks about eight different kinds of "heroines." These are women in different kinds of romantic situations whom the dancer can portray in her performance. The "heroines" in these dramatic situations are: one who adorns herself expecting union with her lover; one who controls her husband by her love; one who is separated from her lover because of a quarrel; one distressed by separation from her lover; one who is enraged with her lover; one who is deceived by her lover; one whose husband is away on work; and one who boldly proceeds to meet her lover. Obviously, some of these are not quiet, resigned and patient women; they are dramatic, passionate, and subjects of the story, not characters who have been objectified. In text and performance, these "heroines" are the intense women in love; in religious commentary and interpretation, they represent the human soul and the "lover" is the "male" deity. He has either not come to see his girlfriend (portrayed by the dancer), or is involved with another girl. Depending on the scene that is depicted in the song, the dancer (*nāyikā* or the "heroine") exudes grief, anger, or rage at his tardiness or imagined behavior. The stances for such a behavior are prescribed by formulaic convention; thus there are a range of moods expressed when the deity, here envisaged as the male lover, is just absent, or when he is known to have spent time with another woman. The Bhārata Natyam dance recitals are replete with dozens of such songs.

In literature and performing arts, the romance and the passion between the soul and God is sometimes seen to be similar to that between Sītā and Rāma, the woman poet Mīrā and Kṛṣṇa, or Rādhā and Kṛṣṇa. Sītā was married to Rāma and they belonged to each other (*svakīyā*); but Mīrā, and in some versions of the story, Rādhā, were married to other men (*parakīya*), yet longed for Kṛṣṇa. In some cases, a woman may be seen as belonging to "all" and only going to *one* man for a price (*samanya*). These three situations become paradigms for the human–divine relationship in poetry, song, theology, literary and performative commentaries. Consider the following "padam," a genre of classical Karnatik music in south India, which is sung by musicians and choreographed by dancers. It belongs to the second category; that is, a woman who is married to one man, yet longs for another:

> My dear, handsome, good natured Venugopala!
> I was married when I was very young.
> Now, my husband beckons – and I have to take leave.
> But do not forget the love I have for you.
> The lotus and sun are distant from each other – but the distance is insignificant[2]
> And so too, wherever I am, my heart will be at your feet.
> I shall always regard only you as my Lord
> And that gives me the courage to bear all that comes my way in life.
> (Attributed to Kṣetrayya, seventeenth century; *Sahana raga*[3])

The voice of the woman in this and later padams is not that of a helpless woman who simply waits for her "man" to come. Here is a married woman who is addressing her lover, in violation of the norms. Songs such as these and those of the woman poet Mīrā remind us that chastity and marital fidelity, which are crucial concepts in understanding of women in the normative texts on dharma, are bypassed when a woman is enthralled with her "man." The environment is even more different in some other padams which speak of the *samanīyā* heroine; the one who will go to the highest bidder. The speaker is the male lyricist, Kṣetrayya, speaking in the voice of a sophisticated courtesan:

> *Pour gold as high as I stand,* I still won't sleep with you.
> Why be stubborn, Muvva Gopala? Why all these tricks?
> You set women afloat on your words,

break into their secret places,
deceive them with affectionate lies,
excite them in love play,
get together the whole crowd one day,
and then you steal away like a spinach thief . . .
You opportunist,
you excite them from moment to moment,
make mouths water,
show them love to make them surrender,
drown them in a sea of passion,
and by the time the morning star appears –
you get up and vanish.
Pour gold as high as I stand.
(Ramanujan et al. 1994: 98–9)

The protagonist is a worldly, educated woman, a courtesan from urban surroundings. We have sensual, sophisticated poems from a streetsmart woman, one who appeared in public like the men in the seventeenth century. It has been observed of this courtesan: "We thus achieve an image of autonomous, even brazen, womanhood, a far cry from the rather helpless female victim of the absent god in Tamil bhakti . . . in contrast to the torn female personality of Tamil bhakti, the courtesan in these poems is remarkably self-possessed" (Ramanujan et al. 1994: 38).

Thus, the love between the human being and the deity is articulated as the relationship between a woman and a man against the backdrop of early Tamil poetry and Sanskrit "heroines" in Bhārata's *Treatise on Dance*. The male or female poet, speaking in the *many* voices of a woman-lover, languishes, laments, cajoles, chides, threatens, and teases. The passion is striking, the drama, as a good drama should be, is engrossing.

But the lover is not the only kind of woman's voice that the male poet speaks in. Sometimes, he is Yaśodā, the foster mother of the toddler Kṛṣṇa, wanting to bathe him, comb his hair, drink his milk, and so on. Sometimes the poet is one of the cowherd girls who is complaining about Kṛṣṇa to Yaśodā about his apparent childish mischief that is tinged with erotic sentiments:

O mother Yaśodā:
At twilight, the other day, he came, as though one familiar with me!
He showed many tricks, he played with me.
Holding and pulling my garment, he demanded a ball of butter,
and so he warred with me, not letting go . . .
"Thaaye Yaśodā" in the raga Thodi by Oothukadu Venkata Subbaiyaiyar[4]

The twilight time is the hour for clandestine meeting between lovers. Yet here we see a child Kṛṣṇa who gets into trouble and who teases the cowherd girl. Whether it is Kulasekara Āḻvār in the eighth century, Oothukadu Venkata Subba Iyer in the eighteenth century, or Ambujam Kṛṣṇa, the sensitive woman lyricist in the twentieth century, the *rasa* or "flavor" created by the voice of a cowherd girl taunting Yaśodā about the toddler Kṛṣṇa's mischief, has been one that Hindu devotees have enjoyed in song and in dance. In other verses, the male poet in the voice of the mother or friend spank and scold Kṛṣṇa for his alleged mischief. The voices are many; the masks, numerous; the moods, ranging from distress to delight.

In what ways does this role-playing inform us about gender? Some may argue that in the laments of the lovesick woman as well as in the ritual with Nammāḻvār, the portrayal projects a social, "patriarchal" relationship on to and replicates the male–female social power structure in the human–divine relationship. This, indeed, is true in many instances, where the deity is seen as the supreme "Man" (*Puruṣottama*) and the woman's "lowliness" is exalted. In some cases, it is not just a "lowering" of a male to assume the role of a female, but that of a low-caste cowherd girl as well (Hawley 1986). Should we then look at gender like caste assume that since a woman seems obviously lower than men in Hindu society the male poets assume the female role?

Such a concept of gender would be correct, but only *partially* correct. As we just saw, the "helpless" woman is just *one* of the voices the male poet takes; he also takes those of a mother in command of her child; an excited cowherd girl; a lover who wants to proclaim "her" love to the whole village; a sophisticated, worldly-wise courtesan; and a wrathful lover, among other roles. In some rare cases, the male poet also takes on the voice of a father. In the following poem, Kulacekara Āḻvār (ca. eighth century CE) speaks in the voice of Rāma's father, who, as we see in the poem is separated from his son:

> **The words of Rāma's father Daśaratha:**
> Without hearing him call me "Father" with pride and with love,
> Without clasping his chest adorned with gems to mine,
> Without embracing him, without smoothing his forehead,
> Without seeing his graceful gait, majestic like the elephant,
> Without seeing his face (glowing) like the lotus,
> I, wretched one,
> having lost my son, my lord,
> still live.
> (Kulacekara Āḻvār, *Perumal Tirumoli* 9.6)

In this and other poems, it is the ache of the separation that comes through; the role is one which depicts the vehemence of this distress. In some ardent poems, the poet assumes the role of a woman who is "possessed" by a male deity whom she loves; thus the cries are both plaintive and powerful. Nammāḻvār, the same poet who spoke so achingly about "her" lover's absence, says in the voice of the "heroine's" mother:

> "It is I who created the earth and the sea,
> It is I who am the earth and the sea . . .
> It is I who ate the world and the sea

Is my daughter possessed by
the Lord of the earth and the sea?
What can I tell my daughter,
who claims to know the earth and the sea?"
(Tiruvāymoli, 5.6.1)

In this poem the "mother" of the heroine speaks in wonderment about her daughter who exults in her "union" with her lover. Nammāḻvār, the male, is speaking as a "mother" of her "girl" who is acting like the male deity. This double switch (male acting like a female who is "possessed" by a male") is not very common, but shows the fluidity of gender. "She" seems possessed by him; empowered and hardly distressed.

A dominant paradigm in Hindu literature, as we saw, is to depict the soul's separation from the deity by having the male take on the voice and role of the female. The overarching archetypes are the cowherd girls separation from Kṛṣṇa and the separation between the "hero" and "heroine" in Tamil poetry. Both these work themselves out in texts, arts, and rituals all over India. Although this assumption of a female role is common, we must note that such an assumption in not necessarily always one sided. We just saw a male assuming the role of other males who have experienced the "separation" situations.[5] In some rituals, a woman saint may take on the role of a male; thus in rituals in ŚrīVilliputtur in the state of Tamilnadu, Āṇḍāl, the eighth-century woman poet sometimes wears the dress of the male deity, Kṛṣṇa.

Whether it is a male or a female then, what is stressed is the intensity of the passion which can be depicted in many voices. The hierarchies seem to shift but it is not based only on gender – the *mother, courtesan, or friend does not cringe in front of the lover.* Here and elsewhere (Narayanan 1999) we see that gender is only one of the terms in Hindu hierarchies: there is caste, class, stage of life, age, and relationship among other factors which contribute to hierarchies. Gender here seems functional; when the mood warrants it, various roles are taken and there is no unilateral hierarchy in the literature. The many voices are important in the poet's articulation of love and no hierarchy (at least the south Indian examples) is seen in between the various kinds of love. The voices of women and men in certain kinds of relationships are valued and privileged in this discourse and in the changing roles, hierarchies are done, redone, affirmed, and subverted.

The Gender of the Soul: Three Encounters between Exemplary Men and Women

The poet, the human being assumes and moves between various gender roles. It is clear that in text and ritual, the human being assumes various genders. But, does the soul have a gender? We saw in the ritual of Nammāḻvār in Śrīraṅgam and in the songs of many male poets that they think of themselves as a woman.

Let us come back to this question after considering three short narratives, all well known in local regions of India.

There is only one male in Brindavan A popular story about the woman saint Mīrā (fifteenth century) narrates her meeting with Jīv Goswāmi, a holy man and a theologian. Jīv Goswāmi refuses to have anything to do with her – or any woman – even though she is filled with love for Lord Kṛṣṇa. She gently chides him and reminds him that there is only one "Male" in all of Brindavan (the land where Kṛṣṇa played with the "gopis") and, indeed, the universe – Kṛṣṇa. All other beings are "female" in relationship to him (Hawley, 1988: 126 and 203).[6] Goswāmi saw the point and saw her.

Tresses, not dresses Mahadeviakka, a woman poet of the eleventh century, in the Karnataka region, walks out on her husband, a king. She goes in search of her lover, Lord Śiva, and his devotees. In time, she is so focused on Śiva that she loses all sense of her own appearance; "she appears to have thrown away even modesty and clothing, those last concessions to the male world, in a gesture of ultimate social defiance, and wandered about covered in her tresses" (Ramanujan 1967: 112). She goes to Kalyana where the saints Allama and Basava have a congregation of devotees and run a school for them. Ramanujan calls the dialog between Allama and Mahadeviakka as one between "sceptic and love child which turned into a catechism between guru and disciple" (112). When Allama asked Mahadeviakka who her husband was, she said she was married forever to Śiva-Chennamallikarjuna ("Śiva who is white as jasmine"). Allama then asked her why she had taken off her clothes as though by that act she had peeled off her illusions; and yet, she was covered with her hair. He asks: if she was so free and pure in heart, why did she have to replace her sari with a covering of tresses? Mahadeviakka replies that "Till the fruit is ripe inside the skin will not fall off" and goes on to say dryly that if she were to display her body, it would hurt him! (Ramanujan 112–13). She is accepted into the company of saints; but restless, she leaves them in search of her divine lover. While Mahadeviakka is apparently not self-conscious about her own body and female nakedness she recognizes that others do not have the same perception – but when they do, she implies, her femaleness and her body should not matter.

No admission, without permission A story in the epic Mahābhārata (XII.321) speaks about Sulabhā, a woman with great religious knowledge, who apparently wants to see if King Janaka is truly enlightened. At her request, Janaka expands on his spiritual attainment and affirms that he is enlightened. He concludes by saying that his soul is free of all attachment, is fixed on the supreme truth, and that he treats all creatures equally. Sulabhā wants to see if this is true and through her own yogic powers enters his mind. Janaka accuses her of trying to seduce him, a righteous man. He tells her that she has no right to pollute him with her touch. Sulabhā is not affected by his decrying her; she says that he has confused the soul and the body, for she has not touched him at all.

> True, our bodies should not touch, but I have not touched you with any part of my body. I rest in you like a drop of water on a lotus leaf, without permeating it in the least. How can you distinguish between souls which are in essence the same? How can you call the contact of two enlightened beings unlawful? (Leslie 1983: 89)

Sulabhā concludes that anyone so obsessed with the external fact that she is a woman cannot be enlightened (Leslie 1983: 99).

All three stories, all encounters between a male and a female, address the notion of gender directly. In all of them, the male figure is the learned, wise patriarch, the acknowledged "saint." The first two stories reverse many hierarchies traditionally accepted in many Hindu communities – male gender, meditative focus, priestly functions, learning are all questioned by a woman who is obsessed with devotion to God. They, of course, highlight the importance of devotion over ritual practice and male learning. If it were not for the last story (and many others in the Hindu tradition) we would almost be tempted to think of traditional learning as male and devotion as female. But it is not so simple.

The first story flows with the some of the moods in the devotional poetry we saw earlier – the deity is the male, and all, including Jīv Goswāmi, are female in relation to the divine. And yet, here and in many stories, the learned or the high-caste male forgets it (Venkatachari), and the female devotee has to nudge him, "awaken" him. In the second story, Mahadeviakka knows only Śiva as a bridegroom. She is gendered as a devotee, but she is oblivious to her body. The outer signs of her biological womanhood do not matter to her as a person, yet she is aware that the male saint is aware of it. Her answer is ambiguous; but Ramanujan and others have interpreted her as saying that while she is indifferent to her body (and its sexuality), this nominal covering with her hair is her concession to the male company around her. Eventually, though, she implies, it will not, should not matter; that is just the shell.

Which brings us to the last story. Sulabhā is clearly a woman and Janaka a man. They meet as peers, as philosophers and aspirants in search of enlightenment. Both are knowledgeable, both engaged in the practice of religious exercises. Janaka thinks of himself as enlightened but is conscious, indeed, outraged over his suspicion that Sulabhā's femaleness will somehow compromise his enlightenment. Sulabhā's answer is very different than Mīrā's query to Jīv Goswāmi. It is not the case that *all* beings are female; it is that *none* are female – or for that matter, male. It is this last position, exemplified in the Sulabhā story, that many contemporary women gurus have taken. Ma Ānandamāyī's disciples thought she was beyond gender. Ma Jaya Sati Bhagavati, a guru originally from New York and who works extensively with AIDS patients, also says "there is no male or female."[7]

The notion that the soul is beyond gender would be consistent in philosophical discourses within the Hindu traditions. The Bhagavad Gītā, one of the important texts of the philosophical traditions, has many detailed discussions on the soul (translated as "self" in many editions).

> It cannot be cut, it cannot be burnt, cannot be made wet, cannot be dried. It is eternal, present everywhere, fixed, free from movement, and perennial. (Bhagavad Gītā 2–24)

In these and many other verses in the second chapter, the status of the soul is discussed. It is interesting that while in this translation and some others translated by Indians (Radhakrishnan is a major exception) the soul is translated as "it," most western translators automatically refer to the soul in the masculine pronoun. The point made in the Bhagavad Gītā is that the body is transient and the soul is definitely beyond the reach of material change and modification.

> Just as there are for the embodied soul childhood, youth and senility in the body, similarly there is also the attainment of another body (after death). (Bhagavad Gītā 2:13)

Here, the various changes one associates with the body are projected onto the many bodies the soul takes in the course of its reincarnations. The soul itself is not affected by these changes. This notion is picked up by many theologians, including Rāmānuja in the eleventh century. Commenting on the verse quoted above, he says, "The eternal souls, on account of their being subject to beginningless karma, become endowed with bodies suitable to their respective karmas" (Sampatkumaran 1969: 26). Passing over the notion of "beginningless" karma, what is of interest to us here is the concept that the souls simply take on bodies which are most suitable to them at that point. Gender certainly seems to figure in this list that is here today, gone tomorrow, in the next life. Rāmānuja elucidates on the fact that the soul is different from all material influences, like that of the body. Commenting on Bhagavad Gītā 2:20 and 25, Rāmānuja says of the soul:

> It is (now) pointed out that, as the self is eternal for the reasons mentioned, and hence free from evolutionary changes, all the attributes of the insentient (body) like birth, death, etc., do not exist (for it) . . . [B]irth and death which are being experienced by all in all bodies do not ever touch the soul.
>
> As it is different in kind from all material objects, it cannot be thought of as possessing the essential quality of any of them. Hence it is immodifiable, absolutely incapable of modifications. (Rāmānuja's comment on Bhagavad Gītā 2:20 and 24; Sampatkumaran 1969, 34 and 37)

The philosophical traditions preserve the soul's existence in a place beyond the issues of all physical constructs including gender. So, while the devotional milieux of Brindavan or Śrīraṅgam may demand that the human devotee is a female, the soul is simultaneously beyond it. This is not to imply that the realization that the soul is beyond gender is in any way "higher" to the other; as in many spaces in Hinduism, here too we have multiple engagements, multiple visions of gender and the human being and gender and the soul.

The Gender of Viṣṇu

Many of the "love poems" we saw explicitly addressed the deity as a male "God." This is obviously true for many Hindus at many times, but as anyone with even a cursory understanding of Hinduism can tell us, the supreme being is worshiped in many ways and many forms. The gender of the deity varies in the different traditions of Hinduism and in the philosophical texts. Let us simply consider the gender of the God Viṣṇu, who is clearly held to be a man. Many of the Vaiṣṇava texts tell us quite explicitly that the supreme being is the "highest of men" (*puruṣottama*). One of the most enduring hymns from the Vedas, recited regularly still, has been the "Hymn to the Cosmic Man" (*Puruṣa Sūkta*). "The Thousand Names of Viṣṇu" (*Viṣṇu Sahasranāma*), a popular devotional piece considered generally to be a part of the Mahābhārata and which is recited regularly in homes and temples, addresses Viṣṇu several times as the "highest of men"; an epithet that is commented upon by theologians. But even in the ŚrīVaiṣṇava tradition, Nammāḻvār, whose feminine voice we just heard, speaks of the supreme being as one who has *both* genders and as having *no* gender.

> Being my father,
> my friend, and the mother
> who gave birth to me . . .
> (Tiruvāymoli 6.3.9)

In several poems, he calls Viṣṇu "mother;" later Śrīvaiṣṇava theologians, commenting on the "auspicious qualities" of Viṣṇu stress the notion of *vatsalya*, that is, the maternal love that a mother cow has for its calf. Viṣṇu (as well as Rāma, Kṛṣṇa, et al.) is said to have this quality of maternal love towards his devotees (*asrita vatsalya*). So, the male deity incorporates in himself the quality that mother cows are said to have – the undiluted, "essential" maternal love which seems almost biological in texture.

Viṣṇu is not just the "mother," he is also the archetypal enchantress. One of his lesser known incarnations, which does not figure in the traditional list of 10 but which is included in the longer, unedited list of 24 that comes in the Bhāgavata Purāṇa, is as a beautiful woman, Mohinī ("enchantress," "the one who ravishes.") Although commentators and theologians emphasize the notion that Viṣṇu is the supreme male, poetry, narrative, and ritual feature the sparkling beauty of Mohinī. On the day before the Tiruvāymoli recitation and acting begins in Śrīraṅgam, and in many south Indian Viṣṇu temples across India and the world (Atlanta, Pittsburgh, Chicago, Malibu, etc.), the "festival" icon of Viṣṇu is dressed as Mohinī. This is on the eve of one of the holiest days in the Hindu calendar – the day called Vaikuṇṭha Ekadaśi. This day is the eleventh day (*ekadaśi*) after the new moon in the month of Margasirsa.

While there are many narratives of Viṣṇu's incarnation as a woman, the story of the churning of the ocean of milk is the most popular in performing arts and in sculpture. The grandest *bas relief* – one of the largest in the world – is on this theme at Angkor Wat, Cambodia, and the story is performed over and over again in Bhārata Natyam and Kuchipudi. When the Asuras ("demons") and the Devas ("divine ones") fight over the nectar of immortality, Viṣṇu appears in the form of a Mohinī, an enchanting woman. The Asuras, enraptured by her appearance, agree to let her mediate and distribute the nectar, and she gives it all (with a couple of minor exceptions) to the Devas. While there are many layers to this story, at least on one level it deals with the enchanting, seductive form of Viṣṇu which gives the divine beings a shot at immortality. In a sequel to this story, Lord Śiva requests Viṣṇu to take the form of Mohinī. Upon beholding "her," he falls in love with her. The deity Ayyappa is considered to be an offspring of Śiva and Mohinī. He is called "Hari Hara Putra" or the "son of Viṣṇu and Śiva." His temple is in Sabarimalai, Kerala, and it is one of the most popular places for male pilgrimage in India. About two million devotees gather there for the peak days in January.

The importance of the incarnation as Mohinī survives today only primarily in rituals where the male god is dressed as female. Devotees retain the ambiguity in their understanding of this ritual. One the one hand, Viṣṇu can take any form and he is father and mother; on the other hand, he can appear as the charming seductress if that is how the devotees envisage him. This trope – the male God as the entrancing woman and the devas (or human devotees) cast in the role of those who are enamored of "her" – has not become popular in later Vaiṣṇavism, as did the image of a male devotee who adopts a female role. It is possible that it reflects a time when notions of gender were more fluid than the centuries when such delineations based on sexual difference were prevalent.

Men wearing female garb are seen in the Mahābhārata as well as in other traditions of the Hindu culture. During a year in exile, Arjuna becomes a "female"dance teacher, in the palace at Virata. The male devotees of the Goddess Gaṅgāmma in Tirupati dress as females, emulating and being possessed by the Goddess during her festivals (Flueckiger, forthcoming).

It is possible that the appearance of Viṣṇu as Mohinī is not emphasized more in the Śrīvaiṣṇava tradition because of the Śrī/Lakṣmī's increasing importance after the ninth century. The Goddess Lakṣmī has a central role in Śrīvaiṣṇava theology and is worshiped at home and in temples. She is portrayed as being inseparable from Viṣṇu, residing on his chest, and we see this in all icons of Viṣṇu. This inseparability from Viṣṇu is seen in everyday life in the forehead marks that Śrīvaiṣṇava men and women wear. The white, U shaped mark is said to depict Viṣṇu's feet and the red line in the middle is Lakṣmī. The inseparability of the couple who are the divine supreme deities is even more dramatically seen in the figure of the Ardhanarīśvara ("the God who is half female") worshiped by the followers of the god Śiva. In this image, popular in icons and in calendar art, the right half of the figure is the male god Śiva and the left half is Pārvatī.

Viṣṇu is seen to be "the highest man" as incarnate as a woman. He is called "mother," but in later centuries he is better known as inseparable from the Goddess Lakśmī. But the same being is also *beyond gender*; listen to Nammāḻvār:

> Neither male nor female, nor is he neuter.
> He cannot be seen, he's not one who is,
> nor one who's not.
> When you desire him, he takes the form
> of your desire,
> but he's not that either:
> it's very hard indeed to speak about my Lord.
> (Tiruvāymoli 2.5.10)

Although later commentators stress the pronoun "he" in this verse and say it refers to the "highest of men," the verse itself pushes the limits of our understanding of gender and clearly says that the supreme being is neither male nor female. In saying so, Nammāḻvār is following that strand of the Upaniṣads which speaks of the ineffable nature of the supreme Brahman: "before it is reached, words turn back, along with the mind" (Taittirīya Upaniṣad, 2.9.1). The soul and the supreme being, then, are in the devotional universe; gendered, but in philosophical discourses, beyond gender.

Reflections

Are the rituals, the dances, the songs, constructed and performed by men and women in the Hindu tradition important in our understanding of gender? Ann Gold (2000) distinguishes between two approaches in the study of gender configurations in south Asia and the closely related subject of women's roles in south Asian society. There are scholars, she says, who highlight the endemic and systemic devaluation and consequent disempowerment of women at every level, from social and economic to cosmological and psychological. These scholars do not take the words of the women or their rituals as empowering them in any way, and conclude that "any moves women do make against their gender-determined fates are fairly futile and ultimately insignificant, given the overweening structural circumstances by which women's lives are circumscribed" (Gold 2000: 204). The second group tend to write from situated experiences and portray the different ways in which women live, negotiate, and imagine their gender identities. This group recognizes and acknowledges women's numerous disadvantages but also takes their speech and rituals as "possessing the actual acute potency in particular situations, and further potentiality to alter existing power structures" (ibid.: 204–5). The study of gender in this chapter has accepted the second model but also recognized that some of these women's roles are also available to male devotees under certain circumstances. In the devotional milieux, the female role of the Tamil "heroine" or Yaśodā, or a cowherd girl, is empowering to the male and female devotees and dancers because of its relational proximity to a male god. Narratives, song, and dance enhance this fluidity of gender roles and cannot be seen as just a helpless performances in a patriarchal universe.

In recent scholarship, the relationship between gender and sex is understood in at least three ways. One way is to see gender and sex as homologous: they are the same. According to this view the differences between "men" and "women" are natural and essential; one's gender is an inevitable result of the physiological differences. A second way is to see the relationship as analogous. Gender consciousness is understood to be based on socialization and lived experience; thus gender symbolizes sex. Thus, some feminist thinkers and social scientists perceive sex to be "natural while gender is cultural, subject to human variation and construction" (Warne 1999: 142). This model accepts, to some extent, the notion of a "normative heterosexuality grounded in biological nature, although it allows for particular cultural constructions which transgress a strict linkage of sex and gender" (ibid.). The third model sees sex and gender as heterogenous. Sex and gender are both not natural and innate; in fact, gender may construct sex. According to one position – in a range of positions that construct this model – "sexual dimorphism is not absolute; 'nature' produces humans with a range of combinations of hormones, chromosomes and sexual apparatuses" (ibid.). The choice involving a male/female continuum is a human choice and a conceptual construct. Power is central to the understanding of distinctions; divisions and hierarchy are inherent in the act of "gendering."

It is possible to discern, in the songs and rituals of the Hindu traditions, concepts which seem to allow for all of these ways of thinking; though the second way of interpreting the relationship between sex and gender may be more easily discernible. It is when one moves into philosophical and theological essays that one is urged to go beyond all dichotomies, including gender for the soul and for the deity. At the human level, however, the devotees happily distinguish between various gender roles but keep the boundaries permeable and fluid. There are many kinds of femininities as there are many kinds of women, as we saw earlier. Role-playing as a woman is not simply to feel weak in front of a patriarchal deity, but to enjoy the many nuances of love in the situations framed by the conceit of Tamil poems or Puranic/epic narratives.

Notes

1 There is a considerable body of literature on the *hijra* community of India. See, for instance, the works of Serena Nanda and Gayatri Reddy.

2 That is, the lotus blossoms when it sees the sun.

3 Translated by Vinod Menon of Chicago; personal communication.
4 "Thaaye Yaśodā" is a very popular song which is performed in many classical Bhārata Natyam recitals.
5 In his poem "Tiruviruttam," Nammāḻvār speaks in the voice of the (male) "hero" of classical Tamil poems.
6 Hawley, in a personal communication, writes that the saint is identified either as "Jīva or as Rupa Goswāmin, depending on the version. The earliest source for this story is the Bhaktirasabodhini commentary of Priyadas (1712 CE) on the Bhaktamal of Nabhaji. It is tika kavitta 514, which appears on p. 721 of the frequently consulted edition entitled "Sribhaktamal," for which there is a commentary by Sītāramsaran Bhagavanprasad Rupkala (Lucknow: Tejkumar Press, 1969: apparently first published by Naval Kishore Press, 1914).
7 Personal Interview with Ma Jaya Sati Bhagavati in Oct. 1998; interview with Professors Yudit Greenberg, Kathleen Erndl, and myself.

References

Gold, Ann Grodzins. 2000. "From Demon Aunt to Gorgeous Bride," in *Invented Identities: The Interplay of Gender, Religion, and Politics in India*, eds. Julia Leslie and Mary McGee. New York: Oxford University Press, pp. 203–30.

Hardy, Friedhelm. 1983. *Viraha Bhakti*. New Delhi: Oxford University Press.

Hart, George L. 1979. *Poets of the Tamil Anthologies: Ancient Poems of Love and War*. Princeton: Princeton University Press.

Hawley, John Stratton. 1986. "Images of Gender in the Poetry of Krishna," in *Gender and Religion: On the Complexity of Symbols*, eds. Caroline Walker Bynum, Stevan Harrell, and Paula Richman. Boston: Beacon Press.

——. 1988. *Songs of the Saints of India*. New York: Oxford University Press.

Kishwar, Madhu. 1990. "Why I do not call myself a Feminist," *Manushi* 61 (Nov.–Dec.).

Leslie, Julia. 1983. "Essence and Existence: Women and Religion in Ancient Indian Texts," in *Women's Religious Experience*, ed. Pat Holden. London: Croom Helm, pp. 89–112.

Nanda, Serena. 2000. *Gender Diversity: Crosscultural Variations*. Prospect Heights, IL: Waveland Press.

Peskowitz, Miriam and Laura Leavitt, eds. 1997. *Judaism Since Gender*. New York and London: Routledge.

Ramanujan, A. K. 1967. *The Interior Landscape: Love Poems from a Classical Tamil Anthology*. Bloomington: Indiana University Press.

——, V. Narayana Rao, and David Shulman. 1994. *When God is a Customer: Telugu Courtesan Songs by Ksetrayya and Others*. Berkeley: University of California Press.

Sampatkumaran, M. R. 1969. *The Gitabhashya of Rāmānuja*. Madras: Professor M. Rangacharya Memorial Trust.

Venkatachari, K. K. A. 1978. *The Manipravala of Śrīvaiṣṇava Acaryas*. Bombay: Ananthacharya Research Institute.

Warne, Randi R. 1999. "Gender," in *Guide to the Study of Religion*, eds. Willi Braun and Russell McCutcheon. New York: Cassell Academic.

Index

Abhinavagupta, 16, 202, 203, 220, 221, 222–3, 224, 478, 489
adharma, 102, 104
Āditya, 72, 78
Advaita Vedānta, 122, 246, 282, 467, 513, 516, 520, 522
Advani, Lal Krishna, 540
Afghanistan, 546
Africa, 33
agency, 31
Aghoraśiva, 210
Agni, 72, 73, 75, 80, 89, 118, 122, 137, 281, 353, 362
agnicayana, 80, 81, 232, 363
agnihotra, 80
agriculture, 103
ahiṃsā, 85, 125, 234, 255, 274
Ājīvikas, 274
akam poetry, 146, 149, 150, 160
Akbar, 127, 260
Al-Bīrūnī, 133
algebra, 357, 369, 378
Allahabad, 548
Allama, 580
Āḻvārs, 122, 148, 162, 163, 185, 186, 237–8, 247, 461
Ambedkar, B. R., 31
āmnaya, 202, 256
Āṇḍāl, 574, 579
Andhra Pradesh, 69, 189, 250
Anglicanism, 25
Anthropology, 13, 495
Anugītā, 125
ānvīkṣikī (critical inquiry), 412
Appar, 151
Aquinas, Thomas, 450
Arabic, 112
Āraṇyakas, 82
Archaeology, 2, 13
Ardhanarīśvara, 585
Aristotle, 50, 357
Arjuna, 117, 118, 119, 120, 121, 123, 124, 127, 184, 276, 284, 575, 584
Arnold, Edwin, 28
Art, popular, 569
Art History, 13
artha, 192, 416
ārya, 73
Ārya Samāj, 17, 36, 265, 514
Āryabhaṭṭa, 287, 366–8, 371, 373, 383, 388, 391
Aryaman, 71, 72
Aryans, 9, 54, 273, 290, 527
Asad, Talal, 28
Asiatic Society of Bengal, 512
ascetic warriors, 258
asceticism, 140, 209, 266, 273, 279
ascetics, 118, 119, 207, 209, 212, 221, 243, 247, 251, 252, 258, 262, 302, 529
Assam, 264, 538
āśrama, 5, 103, 274, 294, 302
āśrama system, 277–80, 281, 283, 292

astrology, 16, 102, 365, 378–80, 383, 464
astronomy (*jyotiḥśāstra*), 5, 16, 102, 365, 371, 376–91; mathematical, 388–91
Asura, 73, 584
aśvamedha, *see* horse sacrifice
Aśvins, 72, 80
Atharvaveda, 68, 69, 75, 76, 104, 379, 382, 394
ātman, 120, 242, 425
Aurangzeb, 263
Aurobindo, Sri, 465, 556
auspiciousness, 339
avatāra, 8, 116, 123, 124, 139, 167, 184, 242, 260; list, 139, 242
Ayyappa, 584
Ayodhyā, 117, 122, 126, 540, 541, 542
Āyurveda, 216, 394, 396, 397, 398, 399, 403, 404, 406–7, 483; Greek influence on, 395

Babri Mosque, 9, 540–1
Bakhtin, M., 4
Balarama, 121
Bali, 210
Balinese, 357
Bangladesh, 510, 538, 540
Basava, 255, 302
Beames, J., 49–50
Benares/Banaras/Varanasi, 15, 69, 182, 187, 191, 192, 207, 212, 284, 328, 329, 330, 331, 335, 336, 540
Bengal, 112, 113, 191, 261, 538, 558
Bengali, 262, 511, 515
Bentham, J., 511
Bentinck, Lord, 511, 514
Besnagar inscription, 231
Bhaga, 71, 72
Bhagavadgītā, 85, 86, 109, 120–1, 123, 124, 125, 134, 139, 170, 184, 205, 231, 242, 248, 251, 284, 285, 448, 461, 523, 582
Bhāgavata tradition, 124, 230, 232, 238–9, 266
Bhāgavatism, 230–3
Bhairava, 207, 212, 224, 487, 489
bhakti, 4, 8, 120, 121, 122, 125, 131, 137, 138, 140, 141, 149, 162, 164, 169–70, 177, 183, 184, 185, 210, 219, 234, 284, 285, 512
Bhandarkar, R. G., 522
Bhartṛhari, 469
Bhārat Mātā, 17, 551, 552, 555, 556–60, 562, 563, 564, 565
Bharata, 102, 140, 411, 575, 581
bhedābheda philosophy, 248
Bhikṣātana, 207
Bhīṣma, 117, 124, 125, 411
Bhojadeva, 210, 223
Bhṛgu, 90
Bible, the, 448
Bihar, 68, 85, 271, 337
BJP, 9, 127, 536–8, 539, 540, 542, 543, 544, 545, 548
Bloomfield, L., 357
body, 16, 83, 168, 183, 186, 190, 191, 209, 210, 211, 220, 222, 235, 244, 245, 248, 250, 282, 314, 329, 489, 490, 581; geo-body, 564; of God, 454, 457; medical, 397–401; purification of, 220, 245; of Satī, 557, 560; Tamilttay, 554, 555
Bopp, Franz, 357
bow songs, 154, 156, 157
Brahmā, 119, 122, 123, 124, 137, 139, 140, 207, 235, 253, 454
brahmacārin, 103, 105, 243
brahman, 85, 96, 119, 121, 126, 236, 248, 252, 253, 453, 457, 464, 467, 469, 479, 480, 585; *bráhman*, 70, 71
Brāhmaṇa texts, 5, 69, 81–2, 83, 84, 89, 104, 250, 362, 394, 480
Brahmans/Brāhmaṇas, 7, 8, 31, 47, 53, 57, 75, 79, 103, 161, 167, 168, 170, 174, 175, 176, 177, 207, 211, 247, 275, 278, 282, 289, 293, 294, 297, 298, 301, 319, 320, 322, 464, 497, 498, 500, 502, 503, 504, 514, 515, 517, 518, 519, 520, 521, 522, 523; of Kashmir, 296
Brahmo Samāj, 16, 34, 265, 511, 515–19, 521
Bṛhaspati, 348
Britain, 55
British Empire, 51–2
Buddha, 45, 54, 68, 85, 90, 139, 275, 279, 280, 365, 393, 396, 397
Buddhism/Buddhists, 31, 39, 107, 155, 159, 185, 210, 219, 255, 274, 275, 279, 283, 396–7, 425, 428, 442, 505, 512, 521, 531
Bühler, G., 48, 105, 106, 107

Caitanya, 191, 259, 260, 261–3, 264, 265, 302
cakra, 397–8
Calcutta, 514–16, 558
calendar, 376–8, 379, 385–8, 584
Cambodia, 46, 50, 240, 584
camphor, 24
Cāmuṇḍī, 319
caṅkam poetry/tradition, 145, 147, 148, 155, 160, 161, 164, 370
Caraka, 381, 393, 394, 398, 401, 402, 403, 404, 406, 407, 429
Carey, W., 514
Caribbean, 33
caste, 2, 16, 30, 53, 54, 55, 103, 161, 164, 168, 170, 172, 175, 176, 186, 187, 200, 209, 218, 243, 256, 257, 289, 296, 301, 309, 311, 312, 320, 323, 495–505, 519, 540, 578; system, 522
Caste Disabilities Act, 38
Catholicism, 35
celibacy, 207, 278; *see also brahmacārin*
Chatterji, Bankim Chandra, 557, 558, 562
Chatterji, Partha, 32, 38
Chaudhuri, Nirad C., 51, 52
China, 15, 126, 545
Chomsky, N., 356
Christianity/Christians, 2, 3, 25, 26, 30, 32, 33, 34, 35, 36, 38, 39, 49, 151, 155, 201, 505, 514, 515, 521, 528, 531, 543
Cidambaram, 7, 217, 218, 247
civilization, 25, 36, 37, 161
Clooney, F., 10, 16
Colas, G., 10, 11, 14, 17
Colebrooke, Henry, 25, 36, 39, 111, 432
colonialism, 26, 28, 29, 31, 33, 34, 36, 45, 51, 54, 161
colonization, 10
commentary, 6, 114, 460–1
compassion, 24
Congress, 9, 230, 527, 528, 529, 531, 533, 534, 536, 537, 538, 541, 543, 554, 558
Conrad, J., 45
consciousness, 16, 213, 214, 220, 224, 254, 425, 426, 428; political, 24
conversion, 30, 33, 36, 39
Coppola, F. F., 46–7, 50
cosmos, 16, 102, 142, 204, 213, 224, 480, 487
cow, veneration of, 125
critical emendation, 10
culture, 11, 25, 145, 200, 527, 528, 543, 548, 562, 573; courtesan, 168, 174; regional, 159

Dādū, 183, 188, 257, 258
Dādū Panth, 188, 258
dakṣiṇā, 79
Dalit movement, 9
Dalits, 31, 289, 310, 519, 520
dance, 307, 308, 575, 577
darśana (vision), 5, 7
darśana (philosophy), 460
Daśanāmi ascetics, 258
Dattātreya, 256
death, 8, 74, 83, 84, 88, 103, 120, 125, 154, 161, 187, 209, 210, 211, 243, 277, 282, 480, 501, 542; signs of, 402
debts, doctrine of, 78, 275, 278, 292
deconstruction, 31, 61
deity (*deva*), 7, 27, 36, 73, 78, 308
democracy, 31
Denmark, 510
Descartes, R., 440
detachment, 120
Deussen, Paul, 49, 53
Devī, 138, 184, 191, 202, 219, 558, 561
dharma, 8, 9, 70, 85, 89, 102–4, 106, 108, 111, 114, 115, 117, 121, 126, 131, 141, 211, 279, 283, 291, 293, 294, 299, 300, 339, 411, 464, 466, 504, 505, 506, 512, 514, 519, 523; *rājadharma*, 126
Dharmaśāstra, 5, 14, 102, 107–15, 207, 236, 281, 282, 283, 285, 301
Dharmasūtras, *see sūtras*
Dharmakīrtī, 424
Dhṛtarāṣṭra, 117
diagnosis, 401–2
Diṅnāga, 436, 437
discourse, 5–6, 28, 46, 56, 152, 447, 460, 461–2, 463, 470
disease etiology, 403–4
Divālī, 330, 331, 337
drama, 102, 152, 156, 170, 172, 195, 212, 238, 262, 272, 340
Draupadī, 8, 117, 119, 153, 154, 155
Dravidian culture/language, 160, 164
Duff, A., 513, 516, 517
Dumont, Louis, 283, 295, 497–500, 500, 501

Durgā, 90, 191, 220, 239, 558, 560, 561, 562
dvaita, 246, 251–3
dvaitādvaita, 246, 253
Dvārakā/Dvarka, 121, 328, 339
Dyaus, 73

Earth Goddess, 109, 560; *see also* Prthivi
East India Company, 112, 510–11, 512, 513–14
Eclipse Demon, 381–2, 383
Eknāth, 186, 256
Eliot, Sir Charles, 57–8
Empiricism, 452
Enlightenment, The, 3, 35, 51, 448
Epics, 7, 8, 14, 89, 116–28, 149, 160, 169, 170, 172, 176, 285, 290, 412
epigraphy, 229, 240
eschatology, 85
essentialism, political, 8–9
Europe, 46, 52, 55, 58
evil eye, 297
exegesis, 4, 6, 10
exorcism/exorcists, 147, 163, 164–5, 209, 216, 217
experience, 24

family, 15, 288–9, 295, 297, 517
feminism, 13, 30
festivals, 23, 24, 90, 152–5, 173, 175, 242, 246, 311, 313, 318, 324, 330, 571, 572
fieldwork, 10, 13
Filliozat, J., 48
food, 7, 78, 79
Forster, E. M., 23, 24
Foucault, M., 30, 46
France, 55, 509, 510
Freeman, R., 7, 13, 15
Freud, S., 47
fundamentalism, 540
funerals, 88, 209

Gandharvas, 72
Gandhi, Indira, 535, 537, 538
Gandhi, M. K., 28, 526, 529, 531, 532
Gandhi, Rajiv, 537, 538
Gaṇeśa, 219, 239
Ganges, river, 192, 328, 329, 330, 331, 334, 339, 516
Garbe, R., 49–50
Gargī, 37, 85, 88
Gārhasthya (householder stage), 290–5, 299
Garuḍa, 192
Garuḍa Pillar, *see* Besnagar inscription
Gaudiya Vaiṣṇavas, 191, 262
Gautama Akṣapāda, 414–19, 430, 467
gender, 16, 17, 186, 569–86
gender studies, 31
geometry, 362
Germany, 55, 509
Ghadar Party, 562
gift, 6, 7, 16, 79, 498
goals of life, 16, 419–20
Goddess, *see* Devī
Goddess theology, 468–9
Godse, Nathuram, 532
Gokul Ashtami Festival, 23
Golwalkar, M. S., 529, 539, 549
good and evil, 85
gopīs, 121, 190, 193, 333, 337, 339, 580
Goraknāth, 185, 258
Gosvāmis/Goswamis, 191, 259, 262, 580, 581
Govind Singh, 188
grace, 121, 211, 260
grammar, 10, 11, 12, 56, 145, 146, 160, 347, 353, 401, 405, 464, 469
Grammar, philosophy of, 460, 486
Grant, Sir Charles, 511, 514
Greek, 47, 69, 384
gṛhastha, 89, 103, 105
Gujarat, 261, 328
Gujarati, 28
guṇas, 120, 138, 235, 257
gurus, 4, 29, 170, 184, 193, 202, 203, 209, 222, 255, 264, 266, 315, 460, 581; Sikh, 302

Hacker, P., 413
Halhed, N. B., 25, 36, 39, 111
Hanumān, 117
Hardās, 188
haoma, 74
Hardy, F., 132, 133
Harivaṃśa, 120, 121, 122, 133, 231
Hastings, Warren, 39, 49, 56, 112
heaven (*svarga*), 79, 90, 118, 119, 231
Hedgewar, K. B., 528–9
Heesterman, J., 4, 77, 291, 295
Hegel, G., 35, 48, 55, 58

hegemony, 28, 33, 59
Heidegger, M., 564
hijra community, 569
Hiltebeitel, A., 153
Hindi, 14, 183, 554
Hindu, as a term, 3, 9, 145, 289
Hindu Mahasabha, 9, 527, 528, 532, 533
Hinduism, as a term, 8, 26–7, 527
hindutva, 9, 17, 527, 528, 529, 534, 537, 538, 543, 544, 545, 548
history, 2, 8, 14, 28, 29, 30, 32, 139, 145, 159, 177, 200, 201, 224, 448
historiography, 30
Hocart, A. M., 500, 501
horse sacrifice, 74, 80, 81, 83
house/home, 295, 296–7
householder, 15, 212, 243, 277
householder tradition, 288–302

identity, 9, 28, 33, 159, 323, 533, 539, 541, 543, 549, 552
ideology, 9, 17, 32, 131, 209, 216, 217, 234, 291, 292, 298, 309, 496, 505, 526, 527, 532, 534, 543, 552, 563; of caste, 501; of householder, 300, 301; of love, 299
imagination, 3, 57, 58, 60, 200, 220, 511, 552, 558
imperialism, 45, 52, 56
Inden, R., 13, 27, 47–8, 49, 52, 57–8, 59, 60, 330
India, 2, 5, 15, 17, 23, 24 *passim*
Indology, 49, 52, 295, 301
Indonesia, 210
Indra, 68, 72, 75, 118, 121, 122, 146, 348, 353, 360, 361, 411
Indus Valley/Harrapan civilization, 3, 90–1, 204, 273; script, 379
initiation (*dīkṣā*) 87, 203, 208, 210, 220, 243–4, 260, 266, 277, 488; *nirvana diksa*, 211; *samaya diksa*, 211
installation (*pratiṣtha*), 246
invocation (*āvāhana*), 315
Īśānaśivagurudeva, 211, 216
ISCON, 141, 265
Islam, 2, 26, 30, 33, 34, 35, 36, 39, 155, 185, 201, 255, 256, 257, 538, 540
Iśvara, 126
itihāsa-purāṇa, 151, 152

Jagannāth, Lord, 7, 138, 261
Jainism, 39, 107, 151, 155, 159, 219, 274, 275, 283
Jana Sangh, 532, 533, 534, 535
Janata Party, 535–6, 538
japa, 125, 482, 483, 489
Japan, 126, 357, 509
Japanese, 69, 357
Jaspers, K., 85
jāti (caste, species), 297, 496, 502–4
Java, 50, 126, 210
Jesus Christ, 38, 518
jīva, 235, 249, 252, 262
jīvanmukti, 245, 455
jñāna (gnosis), 242
Jñāneśvara, 38, 186, 256
Jones, W., 25, 36, 39, 46, 107, 113, 512, 513
Judaism, 39
jyotiḥśāstra, 16, 102; *see also* astronomy

Kabīr, 14, 182, 183, 185, 186–7, 193, 195, 285
Kabīrpanth, 188
Kālāmukhas, 207, 208, 219
Kālī/Kāḷi, 173, 191, 203, 213, 265, 556, 561, 562
Kālidāsa, 175
kaliyuga, 108, 112
Kalki/Kalkin, 123, 139
Kalpsūtras, 104
kāma, 102
Kāma Sūtras, *see* Vātsyāyana
Kampaṉ, 122, 152
Kanchipuram, 248, 249
Kāpālikas, 206, 212, 215
karma/karman, 79, 83, 84, 125, 141, 210, 282, 303, 403, 419, 420, 427, 504, 582
Karoshti, 357, 366
Karnataka, 184, 208, 219, 241, 248, 250, 252, 302, 309, 530
Kārtik, 15, 328–40
Kashmir, 3, 191, 209, 210, 213, 214, 217, 223, 248, 301, 543, 546
Kathakaḷi, 173
Kaula tradition, 212
Kauravas, 117, 120
Kauṭilya, 102, 110, 163, 365, 377, 412–14, 431

Kerala, 4, 6, 7, 14, 15, 69, 159, 160, 161, 162, 167, 168, 170, 171, 172, 173–4, 175, 176, 177, 215, 216, 219, 252, 307, 308, 309, 310, 313, 322, 323, 324, 373, 391, 520, 584
Keśin, 89
Khmer, 357
Khotanese, 357
Killingley, D., 3, 16
King, R., 26–7
kings, 8, 60, 85, 126, 140, 146, 152, 156, 161, 167, 176, 209, 217, 229, 319, 412, 501
kingship, 200, 292, 339
kinship, 288, 499, 501
Kirfel, W., 135, 136
Korea, 357
Koṟṟavai, 146
Kōvai poetry, 150
Krama tradition, 212, 213, 214, 215
Kṛṣṇa/Krishna, 15, 24, 117, 119, 120–1, 122, 123, 124, 126, 127, 138, 139, 150, 172, 183, 184, 185, 186, 189, 190, 191, 192, 195, 229, 230, 234, 235, 238, 251, 252, 254, 255, 256, 259, 260, 261, 262, 263, 264, 276, 284, 302, 327, 328, 332, 333, 334, 335, 336, 337, 338, 339, 572, 573, 574, 575, 576, 577, 578, 580, 583
Kṛṣṇa-Vāsudeva, 235
Kṣatriya, 79, 83, 85, 88, 103, 242, 295, 515, 519, 523
Kṣemarāja, 11, 221, 223, 224, 489
Kumb Mela, 548
Kuṇḍalinī, 222, 490

Lakṣmī, 249, 330–1, 332, 469, 584
Lalla, 191
language/s, 5, 6, 15, 16, 90, 145, 159, 170, 177, 183, 224, 351, 353, 355, 357, 460, 461, 469, 564; devotion to, 552, 556; science of, 348–58
Latin, 47
law, 14, 17, 24, 26, 31, 38–41, 89, 102, 107, 108, 109, 112, 113, 114, 519
liberalism, 534
liberation, 2, 16, 219, 221, 274, 284, 419, 455, 457, 488
life-cycle rites, 74, 76, 87, 289, 298, 331
līlā, 332, 333, 339
Linguistics, 15, 348, 357
Lipner, J., 9, 137
Literary Studies/Criticism, 2, 51
literature, 145, 146, 160, 162, 167, 174, 177, 229, 230, 281
logic, 348, 357, 429
lokāyata, 412, 413, 430
love, 161, 183, 217, 296, 298–9, 575, 579

Ma Ānandamāyī, 581
Madan, T. N., 5, 15
Mādhava, 259
Mādhava (mathematician), 373
Madhva, 5, 251–3, 259, 266
Madhya Pradesh, 230
magic/sorcery, 76, 90, 165
Mahābhārata, 8, 75, 86, 89, 107, 110, 116, 118, 119–21, 122, 123, 124, 125, 126, 130, 131, 132, 133, 139, 151, 154, 155, 156, 205, 206, 231, 251, 272, 279, 280, 281, 294, 365, 382, 411, 461, 468, 483, 580, 584
Mahādeviakka, 580, 581
Mahānubhāvas, 255, 256
Maharashtra, 230, 256, 519, 530, 543
Mahavīra, 90, 275
Maitreyī, 37, 85, 88
Malamoud, C., 358
Malayalam, 159–78, 308, 315
Malayans, 164–5, 173
manana (theological reasoning), 457–60, 462, 470
Mani, Lata, 39–40
Māṇikkavācakar, 150, 218
Maṇipravāḷam, 166–71, 172, 173, 175, 177, 249
maṇḍala, 69, 222
mantra, 16, 75, 76, 77, 81, 87, 203, 210, 216, 221, 222, 231, 236, 239, 248, 262, 263, 335, 336, 348, 349, 353, 357, 361, 464, 478–91; path of, 206, 209, 210, 212–14, 484
mantraśāstra, 478, 479, 480, 484
mantravāda, 322–3
Manu, 68, 78, 107, 108, 123, 282, 412, 469, 503
Marathi, 38, 357, 511
marriage, 40, 74, 87, 88, 297, 300, 499
Maruts, 72
mathematics, 15, 16, 348, 360–73

Mathurā, 121
Matilal, Bimal, 424, 431, 436
māyā (illusion, material substrate), 210, 224, 254
Māyōṉ, 146, 238
medicine, 5, 16; science of, 393–407
Mill, James, 34, 35, 48, 49, 50, 58, 513, 521
Mīmāṃsā, 5, 223, 358, 460, 465, 466, 469
Mīmāṃsāsūtra, 112
mind (*manas*), 425–8
Mīrābai, 183, 191, 192–4, 195, 573, 581
Mitra, 68, 71
modernity, 6, 16, 25, 30, 35, 36, 175, 176, 177, 201, 324, 552, 563–5
Mohammedan Hindus, 32
Mohinī, 569, 572, 583–4
mokṣa, 1, 118, 140, 141, 274, 299, 330, 406, 488
morality, 40, 298
morphology, 353, 356
Mother India, *see* Bharat Mata
Müller, Max, 10, 114
Murukaṉ, 146, 147, 151, 573
mūrti, 4, 7, 334, 335
music, 102, 153, 576
Muslim League, 9, 531
Muslims, 3, 26, 32, 33, 38, 39, 56, 151, 183, 187, 258, 301, 521, 528, 531, 532, 538, 539, 540, 541, 543, 548
myth, 7, 8, 152, 155, 170, 184
mythology, 31, 59, 74, 152

Nāga, 72, 90
Nāgārjuna, 442
Nambūtiris, 322–3
Nāmdev, 38, 183, 188, 256
Nammāḻvār, 570–1, 572, 573, 578, 579, 583, 585
Nānak, 183, 188, 195
Nandy, Ashish, 32, 33
Nārada, 107, 108, 109, 110, 123, 128, 365
Nārāyaṇa, 90, 123, 124, 141, 230, 233, 234, 235, 236, 242, 453, 454
Nārāyaṇa Guru, 520
Narayanan, V., 13, 17
Nārāyaṇīya, 123, 124, 125
narrative, 5, 7–8, 118
Nāth tradition, 185, 186, 201
Nāthamuni, 247, 249
nation, 16, 527, 529, 531, 533, 542, 544, 551, 564
nation state, 29, 30, 31, 528, 532
nationalism, 17, 32, 127; Hindu, 30, 526, 531, 532, 533, 534, 537, 538, 539, 540, 543, 548, 549
nationalists, 27, 539, 544, 555, 556
Nāyaṉmār, 148, 150, 162, 210, 217
Nehru, J., 523, 531, 532, 533, 556
Nehruvian Socialism, 534–5
Nepal, 2, 75, 501
Nepali, 357
Netherlands, 510
Nietzsche, F., 53
Nimbārka, 253–4, 266
Nimbārka tradition, 259
Nirṛti, 72, 84
Nyāya, 5, 406, 414, 417, 420–4, 434, 436, 437, 439, 440, 441, 452–3, 460, 465
nyāya (logic), 112

Olivelle, P., 5, 10, 15, 291–2, 293
oriental despotism, 50
Orientalism, 25, 29, 36, 46–7, 49, 50, 54
Orissa, 69, 232, 264
orthopraxy, 11, 86

Pabuji, epic of, 11
padapāṭha (word-for-word analysis), 349–51
Padoux, A., 16
Pakistan, 531, 532, 545, 546
Pali, 159
Pali Canon, 85, 89
Pāñcarātra Saṃhitās, 229, 235, 241, 264
Pāñcarātra tradition, 14, 233–5, 238, 239–41, 243, 244, 248, 250, 252, 464, 487, 489
pandits, 26, 31, 512
Pandits of Kashmir, 296, 297, 299, 300
Panjab, 68, 72, 81, 257, 302
Paṇḍu, 117
Pāṇḍavas, 117, 118, 120
Pāṇini, 68, 87, 104, 205, 281, 348, 349, 351, 352–6, 357, 393, 469
Parsis, 521
partition, 531–2, 541
Pārvatī, 575
Pāśupata tradition, 123, 124, 206, 208, 209, 212, 483

Patañjali (the grammarian), 68, 90, 205, 236, 351, 354, 356
Patañjali (author of the *Yogasūtras*), 483
Patel, Vallabhai, 531
penance, 282–3; *see also prayascitta*
perception, 420–5
performance, 171, 172
Persian, 112, 113, 357
Philology, 2, 10–11, 12, 13, 55
Philosophy, 15, 16, 26, 68, 104, 175, 411, 420, 432, 447, 448, 449; six systems of, 5
phonological rules, 353, 354–6
pilgrimage, 4, 23, 118, 258, 261, 540, 556
Pillai Lokacarya, 248–9
piṇḍa offerings, 294
pitṛs (ancestors), 72, 87
planets, 376, 377, 380–4, 390–1
Plato, 48, 414
poetics, 102, 145, 160, 262
poetry, 14, 68, 147, 148, 149, 150, 151, 160, 162, 208, 217, 218, 272, 554, 556, 561, 571, 579; vedic, 70–1
politics, 1, 2, 3, 16, 30, 102, 526–49; of translation, 10
polity, 163, 529, 531, 532, 533, 537, 541, 543, 544, 548
pollution, 82, 243, 496, 500
Poona, 69
Portugal, 510
possession, 176, 209, 215, 216, 217, 307, 308–9, 312, 323, 403; rites of, 313–18
postcolonialism/postcolonial discourse, 3, 10, 13, 51, 551
post-structuralism, 30
poverty, 23
power, 3, 7, 9, 13, 28, 29, 31, 50, 53, 222, 245, 313, 526, 533, 534, 536, 542, 543; magical, 211–12
Prabhupada, B. S., 141
Prajāpati, 3, 119, 361, 480
Prakrit, 159, 231, 485
pramāṇa (means of knowledge), 416, 456
prapatti (surrender), 249, 253
Pratyabjijñā, 223, 224, 225
pralaya (cosmic destruction), 109
prayaścitta (penance), 107, 108, 246, 283
Pṛthivī, 73, 560, 564
Ptolemy, 389, 391
pūjā, 6, 7, 90, 141, 205, 233, 296, 313, 482, 489, 490
Purāṇas, 8, 14, 89, 107, 110, 122, 126, 127, 129–42, 149, 152, 160, 162, 169, 170, 176, 205, 206, 209, 260, 290, 481, 482, 484, 515, 572; *Agni*, 137, 484; *Bhāgavata*, 121, 130, 132, 136, 137, 138, 140, 172, 184, 190, 251, 254, 259, 264, 583; *Bhaviṣya*, 137; *Brahmāṇḍa*, 137; *Brahmavaivarta*, 137; *Devībhāgavata*, 333; *Garuḍa*, 137, 139; *Kūrma*, 132, 137, 206; *Liṅga*, 137, 205; *Mārkaṇḍeya*, 131, 137, 138; *Matsya*, 130, 133, 135, 137, 138; *Nārada*, 137; *Padma*, 131, 135, 137, 329; *Śiva*, 131, 133, 137, 138, 141, 205, 482; *Skanda*, 131, 133, 137, 329; *Vāmana*, 137; *Vayu*, 130, 133; *Viṣṇu*, 121, 131, 133, 134, 135, 138
puṟam poetry, 146, 160
Puri, 261
purity, 184, 319, 497, 498
puruṣa, 71, 123
puruṣamedha (human sacrifice), 233, 362
puruṣārtha, 141, 299, 300; *see also* goals of life
Puṣṭimārga, 260, 261, 302
Pythagorean theorem, 362, 363, 370

race, 52–5
Rādhā, 190, 191, 254, 255, 259, 262, 263, 264, 302, 328, 334, 338, 339, 573, 576
Rādhāvallabhīs, 263
Raidās, 183, 186, 188, 193, 195, 258
Rajasthan, 18
rājasūya (king's consecration), 81
Rājputs, 504
Rām, 191, 192, 328
Ram-Prasad, C., 9, 13, 17
Rāma, 9, 117, 118, 119, 121, 123, 126, 127, 128, 166, 173, 183, 184, 195, 255, 264, 411, 539, 576, 578
Ramabai, Pandita, 34, 36
Rāmakaṇṭha, 12, 210, 223, 224
Ramana Maharshi, 465
Rāmānanda, 188, 257
Rāmānandis, 196
Rāmānuja, 186, 206, 239, 241, 248, 249, 250, 253, 257, 266, 453, 455, 467, 468, 582
Ramaswamy, S., 9, 13, 17

Rāmāyaṇa, 8, 107, 110, 116, 118, 119, 121–2, 123, 127, 134, 151, 152, 163, 165–6, 174, 184, 192, 272, 382, 411, 468, 540
Rāmlīlā festival, 122, 127, 192
Rammohun Roy, 3, 16, 465, 514, 515, 516, 521, 522
Ramprasad Sen, 191
Ranade, M. G., 522
Rao, V. N., 136
rasa (aesthetic emotion), 262, 263, 578
rationality, 15, 16, 57, 413, 419, 420, 423, 428, 429, 431, 437–9, 442; rational inquiry, 411–42
Rāvaṇa, 117, 118, 119, 122, 128, 184
reason, 3, 16, 35, 411–12, 437, 439, 442, 460
reasoning, 432, 433, 449, 458
recitation, 349
reform, 33, 34, 37
reincarnation, 2
religion, 1, 9, 10, 13, 24, 25, 27–8, 29, 31, 32, 34, 35, 36, 37, 39, 51, 102, 113, 145, 161, 184, 201, 495, 506, 526, 527, 531; rational, 30; world renouncing, 271, 275
Renou, L., 47–8, 49, 358
renouncer, 8, 86, 186, 248, 250, 256, 282, 283, 300, 301, 302; distinct from anchorite, 271–2; tradition of, 271–85
renunciation (*saṃnyāsa*), 15, 118, 120, 274, 275, 278, 279, 281–5, 292, 330
Ṛgveda, 68, 69–75, 76, 104, 204, 205, 281, 292, 360, 361, 376, 382, 479–81
rites of passage, *see* life-cycle rites
ritual, 5, 6–7, 11, 14, 15, 16, 23, 31, 36, 47, 69, 102, 118, 155, 163, 164, 167, 184, 210, 211, 216, 217, 276, 278, 379, 405, 464, 478, 501; mantras in, 479, 481, 488–91; possession in, 313–18; Śaiva, 201; science of, 348, 362–4; Śrauta, 74, 75, 77–81, 82; Vedic, 72, 73–5, 231, 234, 376
Rocher, L., 14, 129, 132, 134, 141
Rocher, R., 36
ṛṣi, 4, 68, 72, 78, 104
RSS, 528–30, 532, 533, 535, 536, 537, 544, 549
ṛta, 70, 71, 72, 79
Rudra, 73, 90, 204–5, 207, 482
Russia, 55, 509

sacrifice, 5, 8, 77, 120, 140, 161, 169, 176, 291–2, 293, 314–15, 479, 499, 501
Sadāśiva, 209, 210, 211, 213
sādhaka, 207, 211, 214, 220, 489
sādhana, 208, 213, 262
Sadyojoti, 210, 223
Sahajiyās, 262, 263
Said, E., 13, 46–7, 60
Śaiva Siddhānta, 11, 208, 209, 210–12, 213, 215, 217–19, 220, 223, 224
Śaiva Vedānta, 201
Śaivism/Śaiva traditions, 14, 15, 148, 151, 155, 162, 200–25, 460, 461, 484, 485, 488, 489; theology, 205
śākhā (vedic branch), 69, 83, 104, 236, 243, 341, 351
Śākta traditions, 200, 203
śakti (power), 200, 203, 209, 214, 217, 222, 245, 313, 317, 558
samādhi, 245
Sāmaveda, 69, 76, 104
Saṃhitā, 69, 75, 76, 81, 83, 90, 104, 350, 351, 376, 395, 479, 484, 487
saṃhitāpāṭha (continuous recitation), 349, 350
Sāṃkhya, 5, 124–6, 137, 234, 406, 412, 413, 429, 453, 460
sampradāya (tradition), 257, 569, 570
samsāra, 2, 85, 118, 140, 274
samskāra, 6, 87, 88, 109, 243, 298, 300, 481; *see also* life-cyle rites
sanātanadharma, 105
Sanderson, A., 204, 206, 209, 212, 301
Śaṅkara, 5, 11, 205, 206, 240, 246, 264, 373, 455, 458, 468, 523
sannyāsin, 82, 84, 103, 118; *see also* renouncer
Sanskrit, 3, 5, 6, 10, 11, 14, 26, 28, 46, 48, 50, 52, 68, 102, 112, 151, 159, 166, 167, 170, 171, 172, 175, 177, 184, 192, 224, 231, 247, 249, 254, 257, 261, 266, 348, 351, 352, 355, 356, 371, 372, 393, 405, 461, 484, 485, 490, 511, 523, 560
Sanskritization, 83, 90, 162, 317, 388, 530; of Vaisnava traditions, 259–64
Sants/Sant tradition, 4, 185, 257

Sarasvatī, 487
Sarasvatī, Dayānanda, 520, 522
śāstra, 102, 260
satī (widow burning), 31, 37, 39, 88
Satī, 557, 561, 575
Sāttvata tradition, 238–9
Saussure, F. de, 351, 357, 395
Savarkar, V. D., 9, 527–8, 529, 539, 548
Savitrī, 37
Scripture, 16, 31, 32, 40, 437, 438, 457, 460, 462, 466, 480, 486
self, 200, 223–4, 252, 412
semantics, 350, 353
Sen Keshab Chunder, 34, 517, 518, 523
sexual politics, 168
sexuality, 172, 216, 581, 586; withdrawal from, 272
Shiv Sena, 538, 541, 543
Shri Rangam/Śrīraṅgam Temple, 238, 247, 248, 570, 571, 572, 579, 582, 583
Siddha yoga/tradition, 201, 451
Sikhism, 39
silence, 485
Sinhalese, 357
Sītā, 117, 118, 122, 184, 192, 575, 576
Śiva, 4, 7, 8, 11, 12, 59, 73, 118, 119, 131, 137, 138, 139, 147, 150, 151, 152, 154, 155, 164, 170, 184, 185, 186, 192, 200, 201, 202, 204, 206–7, 209, 210, 211, 212, 213, 217, 218, 219, 221, 222, 223, 224, 239, 252, 319, 328, 334, 454, 482, 486, 490, 552, 569, 573, 580, 584
Śiva *liṅga*, 205, 210, 217, 219, 220
Śivaji, 127, 257, 522
Śivapaśupati, 91, 204
Skanda, 146, 329
Smārta Brahmans, 8, 204, 212, 218, 230, 239, 252
smṛti, 8, 68, 69, 87, 104, 105, 107, 112, 113, 114
society, 7, 8, 15, 16, 17, 37, 39, 40, 54, 55, 114, 120, 161, 172, 184, 200, 207, 209, 276, 278, 288, 289, 291, 295, 301, 365, 506, 523, 530, 540, 578, 585; caste and, 497–8; withdrawal from, 272, 290
sociology, 295, 301, 396, 495
Soma, 72, 73, 74, 80
Somaśambhu, 29, 211
soteriology, 419
soul, 83, 211, 249, 262, 426, 428, 569, 570, 576; gender of, 579–83; *see also atman* and *jiva*
śrāddha (rite for the dead), 87, 103, 105, 109, 113, 298
Śrī, 90, 247, 453, 571
Sri Lanka, 501
Śrīvaiṣṇava tradition, 17, 167, 246, 247, 250–1, 266, 330, 570, 583, 584
Śrīvidyā, 487
śruti (revelation), 4, 68, 104, 105, 484
Staal, Frits, 5, 15, 77, 405
Stietencron, H. von, 27, 29
subaltern studies, 31
subjectivity, 40, 206
Śūdra/s, 73, 79, 103, 167, 174, 192, 242, 244, 250, 253, 308, 309, 519, 522
Sufis, 185, 255
superstition, 26, 35
Sūrdās, 183, 189, 190, 191, 193
Sureśvara, 458
surgery, 404–5
Sūrya, 73, 239, 334
Suśruta, 399, 400, 401, 404, 405
Sūtras/sūtra literature, 14, 68, 69, 77, 104–7, 110, 111, 113, 115, 241, 348, 349; *Dharma-*, 89, 104, 106, 107, 110–11, 114, 277, 281, 293; *Gṛhya-*, 87–9, 104, 384; *Smārta-*, 236, 245; *Śrauta-*, 77, 86–7, 236, 245, 348; *Śulba-*, 362–5
suttee, 514; *see satī*
Svacchandabhairava, 214–15
Svāminārāyaṇa/Swaminarayan, 265
Syria, 68

Tagore, Debendranath, 516, 517, 521
Tagore, Rabindranath, 556, 558
Tamil, 8, 9, 14, 17, 145, 159, 160, 162, 164, 167, 169, 208, 218, 249, 357, 511, 552, 554, 555, 563, 574, 575
Tamil culture, 146
Tamil Veda, 148, 167
Tamiḻttāy, 17, 551, 552–5, 556, 560, 561, 562, 563, 564, 565
Tantras, 4, 5, 11, 12, 14, 16, 204, 206, 208–10, 212, 221, 225, 398, 484, 519
Tantrism, 177, 219
tapas (asceticism), 125
Telegu, 255

temple, 4, 6, 7, 149, 152, 155, 156, 164, 167, 168, 175, 208, 210, 216, 217, 239, 295, 322, 380, 583; culture of, 164; ritual in, 219–21, 482; Vaikhanasa ritual in, 241–6
text, 2, 4, 10–13, 14, 37, 38, 48, 59, 76, 77, 81–9, 113, 114, 126, 152, 156–7, 216, 217, 280–1, 368, 378, 461, 465; as mirrors, 396; study of, 235
teyyam/teyyam tradition, 4, 7, 15, 307–25
Thai, 357
Thailand, 126, 271
Theology, 2, 4, 15, 16, 210, 213, 217, 218, 223–4, 275, 447–71
Tibet, 216, 357
Tibetan, 208, 357
Tilak, Narayan Viman, 34, 38
time, 16, 74, 125, 426, 429, 452, 455
tīrtha, 118, 319
Tirumāl, 147
tolerance, 6, 32
Tolkāppiyam, 146
tradition, 1, 4, 6, 13, 14, 28, 29, 40, 200–2, 203, 204, 229, 230, 289; invention of, 30, 31; Sanskritic, 7; de- and re-traditionalization and, 6
transcendence, 8, 450, 526, 527
Tribals, 59
trigonometry, 369, 389
Trika tradition, 212, 213, 214, 215, 484, 487
trimūrti, 139
Tukārām, 38, 186, 256
Tulsīdās, 122, 183, 191, 192
Twice-born, 103, 233, 292, 482

Udayana, 459
Umāpati, 217, 461
untouchability, 31
Untouchables, 497, 503, 505; *see* Dalits
Upaniṣads, 5, 14, 37, 68, 69, 81, 82, 83–6, 88, 120, 125, 271, 276, 281, 285, 296, 394, 453, 458, 459, 480, 484, 515, 585
urbanization, 86, 273
USA, 509
Uṣas, 72, 575
Utpalācārya, 203
Uttar Pradesh, 261, 340

vāc (speech), 70, 79, 479, 484, 485, 486, 488, 489
Vācaspatimiśra, 135
vaidika, 14, 15
Vaikhānasa tradition, 14, 230, 233, 235–7, 238, 239, 240, 241–6, 248, 250
Vaiśeṣika, 5, 406
Vaiṣṇava traditions/Vaiṣṇavism, 14, 15, 123, 147, 148, 151, 155, 162, 164, 167, 229–66, 329, 460, 461, 584
Vaiśya, 79, 103, 104, 519
Vajpayee, Atal Bihari, 543, 545
Vallabhācārya/Vallabha, 189, 191, 195, 254, 259, 260, 264, 302
Vālmīki, 117, 122, 127, 128, 152, 173, 192
vānapratha, 82, 103, 118
Varāhamihira, 366, 368, 383, 388
Vārkarīs, 186, 256
varṇa (class), 103, 256, 292, 293, 295, 309, 503–4, 520
varṇāśrama-dharma, 131, 141, 205, 207, 219, 293
Varuṇa, 68, 71, 72, 73, 85, 89, 118
Varuṇaṉ, 146
Vasiṣṭha, 70, 89, 110
Vāsudeva, 123, 124, 231, 234, 235
Vasugupta, 202
Vātsyāyana, 104
Vātsyāyana Pakṣilasvāmin, 414–19, 427, 429, 430, 435, 436, 437, 438, 439, 440, 351
Veda, 4, 5, 6, 7, 8, 11, 14, 16, 37, 48, 68–77, 79, 104, 105, 127, 130, 131, 141, 148, 169, 206, 223, 234, 242, 247, 252, 260, 275, 281, 293, 348, 350, 351, 356, 360, 377, 396, 411, 412, 456, 458, 463, 464, 469, 479, 480, 481, 482, 571; Vedism, 4, 479, 480, 517, 520
Vedāṅga, 376
Vedānta, 5, 36, 83, 176, 230, 453, 455, 456, 457, 460, 464, 465, 466, 467, 469, 512, 516, 517; neo-, 28; Vaisnava schools of, 246–54, 255, 260
Vedāntadeśika, 247, 248, 249, 453–4, 467
vegetarianism, 125, 255, 274
Veḷḷāḻas, 242, 250
Vēntaṉ, 146
VHP, 537, 541, 544, 549
Vietnam, 46, 50
Vijayanagara, 209
village, 14, 276, 540

violence, 9, 33, 82, 162, 541, 542
Vīraśaivas/Liṅgayats, 184, 219, 302
Viśiṣṭādvaita, 237, 239, 241, 245, 247–51, 453, 467
Viṣṇu, 4, 7, 8, 14, 73, 90, 116, 118, 119, 121, 122, 123, 130, 138, 139, 146, 147, 152, 155, 163, 164, 167, 170, 184, 186, 192, 219, 220, 229, 230, 232, 233, 234, 236, 237, 239, 242, 243, 244, 245, 247, 249, 252, 253, 254, 255, 257, 284, 328, 331–2, 334, 337, 361, 453, 469, 486, 487, 569, 570, 571, 572, 573, 574, 584, 585; gender of, 583–5
Viṣṇusvāmin, 246, 247, 254, 260, 266
Viśvāmitra, 70
Viṭṭal, 186
Vivekānanda, Swami, 521, 523
vrata (vow), 170, 207, 283, 329
Vrātyas, 72, 88, 90
Vyāsa, 109, 130, 132, 251
vyūhas (emanations), 124, 235, 240

war/warfare, 8, 160, 161, 163, 169, 539
Wilkins, Charles, 36, 357
Wilson, H. H., 134, 135, 136
wisdom, 411
Witzel, M., 4, 5, 10, 11, 14
women, 83, 85, 88, 103, 168, 176, 184, 207, 216, 256, 257, 258, 274, 293, 300, 328, 335, 336, 340, 403, 513, 520, 521, 573, 575, 585; in RSS, 530

Yādava Prakāśa, 283
Yādavas, 117
yajamāna, 79, 88, 242, 244, 362
yajña, 76; *see also* sacrifice
Yajñavalkya, 84, 85, 90, 107, 108, 109, 110, 192, 283
Yajurveda, 69, 75, 76, 77, 87, 104, 105, 106, 109, 376, 482
Yama, 118
Yāmuna, 206, 239, 247, 250, 468
Yamuna River, 328
Yāska, 393
Yoga, 5, 120, 124–6, 211, 219, 221, 234, 235, 236–7, 245, 274, 398, 406, 412, 413, 460
Yudhiṣṭhira, 117, 124, 365, 411
yuga (period of time), 139–40, 390

zodiac, 16
Zoroaster, 89
Zoroastrianism, 39, 85